MW00397752

Deaf Cognition

Deaf Cognition

Foundations and Outcomes

Edited by Marc Marschark and Peter C. Hauser

OXFORD
UNIVERSITY PRESS
2008

OXFORD
UNIVERSITY PRESS

Oxford University Press, Inc., publishes works that further
Oxford University's objective of excellence
in research, scholarship, and education.

Oxford New York
Auckland   Cape Town   Dar es Salaam   Hong Kong   Karachi
Kuala Lumpur   Madrid   Melbourne   Mexico City   Nairobi
New Delhi   Shanghai   Taipei   Toronto

With offices in
Argentina   Austria   Brazil   Chile   Czech Republic   France   Greece
Guatemala   Hungary   Italy   Japan Poland   Portugal   Singapore
South Korea   Switzerland   Thailand   Turkey   Ukraine   Vietnam

Published by Oxford University Press, Inc.
198 Madison Avenue, New York, New York 10016

www.oup.com

Oxford is a registered trademark of Oxford University Press

Library of Congress Cataloging-in-Publication Data
Deaf cognition : foundations and outcomes / edited by Marc Marschark and Peter C. Hauser.
p. cm.—(Perspectives on deafness; v. 6)
Includes bibliographical references and index.
ISBN 978-0-19-536867-3
1. Deaf—Education. 2. Deaf children—Education. 3. Hearing impaired
children—Education. 4. Cognitive learning. 5. Deaf—Means of communication.
I. Marschark, Marc. II. Hauser, Peter C.
HV2430.D412 2008
371.91´2—dc22   2007049330

9 8 7 6 5 4 3

Printed in the United States of America

on acid-free paper

Preface

The 2003 International Mathematics and Science Survey (TIMSS) provided evidence for something that we already knew: the United States is falling behind other countries in preparing future generations of scientists, engineers, and other professionals in science, technology, engineering, and mathematics or STEM (Federal Interagency Forum on Child and Family Statistics, 2005). Ultimately, increasing the number of students successfully majoring in science will increase the number of individuals employed in and making contributions in related fields. "Success" in STEM education is elusive for many students, however, particularly those with learning challenges and those who simply learn differently from most of their classmates.

Despite a long history of deaf and hard-of-hearing (DHH) individuals making contributions to science and technology (Lang, 1994; Lang & Meath-Lang, 1995), relatively few DHH individuals hold high-visibility science positions today, either in academia or the corporate world. We can cite a handful of contemporary deaf individuals, in the United States at least, who are prominent in the world of technology (particularly in telecommunications), but most of these have made their mark on the commercial side rather than the science/development side of their fields. One might argue that the situation is the result of "the bar having been raised," that the level of education needed for success in such domains is greater than ever before. But that is only a matter of perspective, and there is little reason to believe that the current demands are any greater than those faced by Guillaume Amontons (1663–1705) or John Goodricke (1764–1786) in their times (Lang, 1994).

As we initially considered whether there might be particular barriers to the participation of DHH individuals in STEM fields, it became evident that most of the likely explanations for the paucity of these individuals' participation in those fields were far more general. For example, with the "information explosion" of the late twentieth century, the level of reading and writing abilities necessary for an individual to be considered "functionally literate" appeared to increase significantly, leading investigators such as Waters and Doehring (1990) to suggest that an eleventh-grade level of functioning was more appropriate than the fourth-grade level traditionally designated in the United States. Yet, DHH students continue to confront challenges with regard to print literacy, with 50% of 18-year-olds in the United States reading at or below a fourth-grade level (Traxler, 2000).

The many multimedia technologies spawned by scientific progress also may have created barriers to engagement of DHH individuals in STEM fields, as the proliferation of multiple visual displays in STEM classrooms require students with significant hearing losses to process multiple information inputs, such as a sign language interpreter, an LCD projector, and a computer screen, "simultaneously," whereas hearing classmates can listen to a lecture while looking at visual materials or taking notes (Marschark, Lang, & Albertini, 2002, Chapter 9; Pelz, Marschark, & Convertino, this volume). These potential barriers are not specific to STEM fields but fundamental characteristics of essentially all classrooms today as more DHH students find themselves in mainstream programs. These are challenges that will have to be dealt with and overcome.

Although the issues mentioned thus far might be laid at the feet of educational programs insensitive to the diverse needs of today's learners, recent research in our laboratories and others' has suggested that potential barriers may have less to do with hearing loss or communication than would be expected. A variety of recent investigations suggest that the educational challenges appear to lie more in differences in the cognitive foundations of learning by DHH students (see Marschark, Convertino, & LaRock, 2006; Moores & Martin, 2006; Power & Leigh, 2005, for reviews). This possibility might explain why researchers and educators have made relatively little progress in improving DHH students' academic achievement (Allen, 1986; Traxler, 2000; Qi & Mitchell, 2007). Detterman and Thompson (1997) mounted an argument of this sort in regard to special education, claiming that educational interventions could never be fully effective if we did not understand the underpinnings of learning in students from special populations. Yet, despite widespread recognition that deaf children have early environments and experiences very different from their hearing peers (regardless of their preferred mode of communication), we frequently teach deaf children as though they are hearing children who cannot hear—as though all we have to do is to remove the language/communication barrier in the classroom and all will be right. All one has to do is to look at the available data concerning academic achievement for deaf students in K–12 programs and the graduation rates for those in postsecondary programs to realize that, despite the availability of communication–related and other support services, all is not right. What we need, as Detterman and Thompson so aptly recognized, is a better understanding of the cognitive foundations of learning by DHH students and the educational interventions provided to those students.

In an initial effort to better understand the cognitive foundations and potential barriers to DHH students' success in STEM fields, we sought to foster discussion among individuals working on what seemed to be two sides of an educational fence—a fence forming a long-time barrier. On one side were a number of investigators conducting basic research into cognition among deaf individuals, including memory, perception, and problem solving, but with little involvement in educating deaf students. On the other were a number of educators, some conducting applied research, who were very familiar with the characteristics of deaf learners, and who both provided models of "successful" teachers and portraits of frustrated ones. The solution, of course, was to bring them together.

With the support of the National Science Foundation (NSF), the National Technical Institute for the Deaf (NTID) at Rochester Institute of Technology, and the *Journal of Deaf Studies and Deaf Education* (Oxford University Press), NTID's Center for Education Research Partnership hosted an international conference in June 2007. An interdisciplinary assembly of scholars who have conducted research involving deaf individuals discussed how their work helped to elucidate the cognitive underpinnings of learning among DHH students. Educators and educational administrators with long service in deaf education served as discussants, and the audience was composed of teachers, researchers, service providers, parents, and deaf students. The audience, presenters, and discussants tried to obtain a better understanding of how deaf individuals learn by bridging research with practice. Unknown to most people attending the conference, the presenters had already written the first drafts of the chapters found in this volume. Following discussions, both with the larger audience and only among themselves and the discussants, the contributors refined their arguments, revised their chapters, attempted to integrate their research with that of the other presenters and endeavored to identify potential implications of their research for educating deaf students. This volume thus is not a "proceedings" of that conference, but an integrated description of the state-of-the-art at the intersection of cognitive science and deaf education, sharpened by having the individual contributors present their ideas in a public forum.

Keeping DHH students' learning in science, technology, engineering, and mathematics as the ultimate target, the authors of the chapters in this volume provide exciting new insights into the foundations of learning by deaf individuals at various ages and educational levels. Together with evidence concerning academic outcomes, and how the two influence each other, the result is a new perspective on the teaching–learning process and ways in which it can be improved. More importantly, this volume charts directions for further investigation and opens the gate for greater collaboration between research and practice.

Far too many people were involved in this effort to be able to thank them all here. Special appreciation is due our discussants, who both provided valuable input during the conference and offered individual contributors comments on their chapters:

- Lou Abbate – Executive Director of the Willie Ross School for the Deaf and its Dual–Campus Partnership in Springfield, Massachusetts
- John Albertini – Chairperson of the NTID Department of Research and Teacher Education
- Stephen Aldersley – Chairperson of the NTID Department of English
- Laurie Brewer – Assistant Dean for Academic affairs at NTID
- Peter Bryant – Professor Emeritus of Wolfson College, University of Oxford, Visiting Professor at Oxford Brookes University, and a member of the Department of Education at the University of Oxford
- Vince Daniele – Chairperson of the NTID Department of Science and Mathematics
- Harry Lang – Professor in the NTID Department of Research and Teacher Education.

We also wish to thank John Cherniavsky, our Program Officer at NSF, Alan Hurwitz, Dean and Vice President for NTID, and members of the NTID Center for Education Research Partnerships at NTID for their support. Finally, our thanks to Catherine Carlin and Oxford University Press, our obliging (if harried) contributors, and Rosemarie Seewagen, for helping us to "fast track" this book, so that it quickly could be in the hands of the people who need it.

Preparation of this volume and the "Cognitive Underpinnings" conference were supported by grant REC-0635447 from the National Science Foundation. Hauser's time was partially supported by NSF grant SBE-0541953 for Gallaudet University's Science of Learning Center on Visual Language and Visual Learning. Any opinions, findings and conclusions, or recommendations expressed in this material are those of the authors and do not necessarily reflect the views of NSF or NTID.

References

Allen, T. E. (1986). Patterns of academic achievement among hearing impaired students: 1974–1983. In A. N. Shildroth & M. A. Karchmer (Eds.), *Deaf children in America* (pp. 161–206). San Diego, CA: College-Hill Press.

Detterman, D. K., & Thompson, L. A. (1997). What is so special about special education? *American Psychologist, 52*, 1082–1090.

Federal Interagency Forum on Child and Family Statistics. (2005). *America's children: Key national indicators of well being.* Washington, DC: U. S. Government Printing Office.

Lang, H. G. (1994). *Silence of the spheres: The deaf experience in the history of science.* Westport, CT: Bergin & Garvey.

Lang, H. G., & Meath-Lang, B. (1995). *Deaf persons in the arts and sciences: A biographical dictionary.* Westport, CT: Greenwood Press.

Marschark, M., Convertino, C., & LaRock, D. (2006). Optimizing academic performance of deaf students: Access, opportunities, and outcomes. In D. F. Moores & D. S. Martin (Eds.), *Deaf learners: New developments in curriculum and instruction* (pp. 179–200). Washington, DC: Gallaudet University Press.

Marschark, M., Lang, H. G., & Albertini, J. A. (2002). *Educating deaf students: From research to practice.* New York: Oxford University Press.

Moores, D. F., & Martin, D. S. (Eds.). (2006) *Deaf learners: New developments in curriculum and instruction.* Washington, DC: Gallaudet University Press.

Power, D., & Leigh, G. (Eds.). (2005). *Educating deaf students: Global perspectives.* Washington, DC: Gallaudet University Press.

Qi, S., & Mitchell, R. E. (2007, April). *Large-scaled academic achievement testing of deaf and hard-of-hearing students: Past, present, and future.* Paper presented at the Annual Meeting of the American Educational Association, Research on the Education of Deaf Persons Special Interest Group Meeting, Chicago, Illinois.

Traxler, C. B. (2000). The Stanford Achievement Test, 9th Edition: National norming and performance standards for deaf and hard-of-hearing students. *Journal of Deaf Studies and Deaf Education, 5*(4), 337–348.

Waters, G., & Doehring, P. G. (1990). Reading acquisition in congenitally deaf children who communicate orally. In T. Carr & B. Levy (Eds.), *Reading and its development: Component skills approaches* (pp. 323–373). London: Academic Press.

Contents

Contributors

C. Tane Akamatsu
Toronto District School Board
Student Services—Psychology
Toronto, Ontario, Canada

Daphne Bavelier
Department of Brain and Cognitive Sciences
University of Rochester
Rochester, New York, USA

Daniel Bell
Department of Education
University of Oxford
Oxford, United Kingdom

Peter Bryant
Department of Education
University of Oxford
Oxford, United Kingdom

Rebecca Bull
School of Psychology
University of Aberdeen
Aberdeen, Scotland, United Kingdom

Diana Burman
Department of Education
University of Oxford
Oxford, United Kingdom

CAROL CONVERTINO
Center for Education Research Partnerships
National Technical Institute for the Deaf
Rochester Institute of Technology
Rochester, New York, USA

CHRISTOPHER M. CONWAY
Speech Research Laboratory
Department of Psychological and Brain Sciences
Indiana University
Bloomington, Indiana, USA

DENIS CORROYER
Laboratoire de Psychologie Environnementale
Université Paris Descartes
Boulogne-Billancourt, France

CYRIL COURTIN
Groupe d'Imagerie Neurofonctionnelle
Université Paris Descartes—Sorbonne
Paris, France

MATTHEW W. G. DYE
Department of Brain and Cognitive Sciences
University of Rochester
Rochester, New York, USA

DEBORAH EVANS
Department of Education
University of Oxford
Oxford, United Kingdom

SCOTT V. FRANKLIN
Department of Physics
Rochester Institute of Technology
Rochester, New York, USA

DARCY HALLETT
Department of Education
University of Oxford
Oxford, United Kingdom

STEVEN HARDY-BRAZ
US Department of Defense—Fort Bragg
Fort Bragg Schools—Psychology Department
Fort Bragg, North Carolina, USA

PETER C. HAUSER
Department of Research and Teacher Education
National Technical Institute for the Deaf
Rochester Institute of Technology
Rochester, New York, USA

SHIRLEY HENNING
Department of Otolaryngology,
Head and Neck Surgery
DeVault Otologic Research Laboratory
Indiana University School of Medicine
Indianapolis, Indiana, USA

LISA M. HERMSEN
Department of English
Rochester Institute of Technology
Rochester, New York, USA

TARA HILLMAN
Department of Research and Teacher Education
National Technical Institute for the Deaf
Rochester Institute of Technology
Rochester, New York, USA

DAVID L. HORN
Department of Otolaryngology,
Head and Neck Surgery
DeVault Otologic Research Laboratory
Indiana University School of Medicine
Indianapolis, Indiana, USA

JENNIFER KARPICKE
Speech Research Laboratory
Department of Psychological and Brain Sciences
Indiana University
Bloomington, Indiana, USA

RONALD R. KELLY
Department of Research and Teacher Education
National Technical Institute for the Deaf
Rochester Institute of Technology
Rochester, New York, USA

WILLIAM KRONENBERGER
Department of Psychiatry
Child and Adolescent Psychiatry Services
Indiana University School of Medicine
Indianapolis, Indiana, USA

GREG LEIGH
RIDBC Renwick Centre
Royal Institute for Deaf and Blind Children
North Rocks, New South Wales, Australia

JENNIFER LUKOMSKI
Department of School Psychology
Rochester Institute of Technology
Rochester, New York, USA

MARC MARSCHARK
Center for Education Research Partnerships
National Technical Institute for the Deaf
Rochester, New York, USA
Moray House School of Education
University of Edinburgh
Edinburgh, United Kingdom

CONNIE MAYER
Faculty of Education
York University
Toronto, Ontario, Canada

ANNE-MARIE MELOT
Groupe d'Imagerie Neurofonctionnelle
Université Paris Descartes—Sorbonne
Paris, France

LAURA MONTGOMERY
William Westley Primary School
Whittlesford, Cambridge, United Kingdom

TEREZINHA NUNES
Department of Education
University of Oxford
Oxford, United Kingdom

JEFF B. PELZ
Chester Carlson Center for Imaging Science
Rochester Institute of Technology
Rochester, New York, USA

DAVID PISONI
Speech Research Laboratory
Department of Psychological and Brain Sciences
Indiana University, Bloomington and
Department of Otolaryngology,
Head and Neck Surgery
DeVault Otologic Research Laboratory
Indiana University School of Medicine
Indianapolis, Indiana, USA

JOHN T. E. RICHARDSON
Institute of Educational Technology
The Open University
Milton Keynes, United Kingdom

BRENDA SCHICK
Department of Speech, Language, and Hearing Science
University of Colorado
Boulder, Colorado, USA

LOES WAUTERS
Institute of Signs, Language, and Deaf Studies
University of Applied Sciences, Utrecht, the Netherlands
PonTeM/Viataal
Nijmegen, The Netherlands

Chapter 1

Cognitive Underpinnings of Learning by Deaf and Hard-of-Hearing Students

Differences, Diversity, and Directions

Marc Marschark and Peter C. Hauser

In recent years, the intersection of cognitive psychology, developmental psychology, and special populations has received increasing attention from a variety of academic and educational audiences (e.g., Baron-Cohen, Tager-Flusberg, & Cohen, 2000; Florian, 2007; Marschark & Spencer, 2003). Both research and pedagogy associated with this nexus have been motivated by the awareness of large individual differences as well as international differences in educational attainment. Among the latter (presumably cultural) differences, the latest Trends in International Mathematics and Science Survey (TIMSS, 2003), indicated (a) wide variability in mathematics and science performance, (b) student performance in the United States rated as "below proficient" on a variety of standardized assessments (Federal Interagency Forum on Child and Family Statistics, 2005), and (c) an Office for Standards in Education report (OFSTED, 2005) in the United Kingdom surmised that children with below-average abilities in particular were not receiving sufficient support to be able to overcome academic challenges.

In efforts to improve academic opportunities and attainment of children with special needs, legislation in several countries and international efforts by the United Nations and other agencies have sought to proscribe requirements for their inclusion in various educational settings. In the United States, such efforts began with Section 504 of the Rehabilitation Act of 1973 (PL 93–112) and the 1975 Education for All Handicapped Children Act (PL 94–142). These laws combined to assure free and appropriate public education for children with disabilities, including children with significant hearing losses. PL 94–142 was amended by the Education of the Handicapped Amendments of 1986 (PL 99–457) and the 1990 Individuals with Disabilities Education Act (IDEA; PL 101–476). The IDEA was reauthorized in 2004 (PL 108–406). Among other things, these laws were aimed at assuring early identification of children with disabilities, so that such children would have access to education alternatives and personnel would be trained specifically to educate them.

To those in the field of special education, many of the specific legislative and community efforts to improve special education appear to have been motivated and guided by emotion, opinion, and politics rather than science and fact. Perhaps as a result, educational interventions intended for children with special needs (and strengths) have yielded only limited gains. Those aimed at children who are deaf or hard-of-hearing (DHH) are especially noteworthy for their lack of progress in the areas of greatest challenge—or at least in those that have been best documented—reading, writing, and mathematics (Qi & Mitchell, 2007; Stinson & Kluwin, 2003; Traxler, 2000). Fortunately, the *zeitgeist* in education is changing and, coupled with research in child development, cognitive psychology, and neuroscience, investigators are now seeking to improve special education by understanding its cognitive foundations. This view was perhaps best summarized by Detterman and Thompson (1997, p. 1083), who argued that "lack of understanding of the cognitive skills underlying educational interventions is the fundamental problem in the development of special education. Without understanding the full complexity of cognitive abilities, special educational methods can never be special." Detterman and Thompson cited deaf education—and, in particular, the move to educating deaf children through sign language—as a positive indication of change. These cognitive foundations of learning by DHH students are the focus here, because we believe that change is not coming rapidly enough.

Language, Cognition, and Learning

The link between cognitive functioning and language has long been of interest to investigators, with DHH individuals frequently being seen as the ultimate example of how the two are necessarily intertwined—or not—depending on the theoretical orientation of the observer. Investigations concerning this convergence over the past hundred years typically compared DHH children's performance to that of hearing children. Deaf children sometimes were studied in order to test ideas from theory and research on hearing children, such as links between language and learning, and thus to add to the general knowledge base concerning language and language development (e.g., Furth, 1966; Mayberry & Locke, 2003). Other studies involving deaf children were intended to identify aspects of language development that were robust enough to emerge independently of the modality of language (Courtin, 2000; Siple, 1978). More recently, investigations have explicitly focused on understanding the cognitive functioning of deaf adults and children and ways in which growing up with a sign language rather than a spoken language might affect cognitive and neuropsychological growth (e.g., Dye, Hauser, & Bavelier, this volume; Hauser, Lukomski, & Hillman, this volume).

Language As a Foundation of Learning

Research at the intersection of cognitive and brain science, behavioral development, and deaf education is beginning to offer a unique, integrated understanding of language, cognition, and learning. Interest in such interactions is not new (Bartlett, 1850; Fay, 1869), but fresh perspectives and ideas are certainly emerging. Most notably, perhaps, recent research indicates that findings previously viewed as reflecting cognitive, linguistic, or social-emotional deficiencies in deaf children now are more accurately seen as differences that are the product of early experience (Marschark, 2007). In large measure, such changes began with recognition that signed languages were true languages (Stokoe, 1960/2005), but the "cognitive revolution" of the 1970s and the emergence of cognitive neuroscience in the 1990s have driven efforts to understand the underlying determinants of learning, language, and cognition (e.g., Emmorey, 2002; Liben, 1978; Marschark, Siple, Lillo-Martin, Campbell, & Everhart, 1997; Siple, 1978). One product of such initiatives is recognition of the need to understand deaf children's early environments. Whether with reference to having a profound hearing loss or being hard of hearing, being a native user of a sign language versus a spoken language, or the quality of mother–child bonds, such differences can have subtle or not-so-subtle effects on subsequent development. Investigators thus have come to recognize the need to understand both the large individual differences within the deaf population as well as differences between deaf and hearing individuals of similar ages or language experience (Bebko, Calderon, & Treder, 2003).

The issue of language clearly is one that is woven throughout our understanding of cognition, learning, and the development of deaf children. The importance of language is made explicit in PL 108–406 with the requirement that individualized education program (IEP) teams:

> (iv) consider the communication needs of the child, and in the case of a child who is deaf or hard of hearing, consider the child's language and communication needs, opportunities for direct communications with peers and professional personnel in the child's language and communication mode, academic

> level, and full range of needs, including opportunities for direct instruction in
> the child's language and communication mode . . .

More implicit is the assumption underlying efforts to promote integrated education for deaf students that, once communication barriers in the classroom have been removed, teaching and learning processes for DHH and hearing students should be much the same. Similar assumptions are made with regard to the education of students learning English as a second language. In the case of deaf students, sign language interpreting and, more recently, real-time text have been assumed to provide them with access to classroom communication comparable to that of hearing peers. If this assumption is correct, the result should be comparable academic success for deaf and hearing students. Yet, the performance of DHH students on the Stanford Achievement Test throughout the school years shows them to score consistently at "below basic" levels relative to both hearing peers and criterion standards (Qi & Mitchell, 2007; Traxler, 2000). Of the more than 30,000 deaf students enrolled in postsecondary education programs in the United States, only about one in four will graduate.

A second assumption underlying mainstream placements for DHH students is that we are able to educate them and others with special needs in that environment as well as or better than we can in special settings (cf. Detterman & Thompson, 1997; Florian, 2007). In 1966, over 80% of American deaf children were educated in separate programs, with the remaining 20% of students educated in their local public schools or mainstream programs. By 2006, those proportions were reversed. Success for DHH students in mainstream classrooms, however, requires that the information communicated by a hearing teacher for a hearing class is consistent with the knowledge and learning styles of DHH students—that is, that the material is readily learnable (Brown, Bransford, Ferrara, & Campione, 1983; Marschark, Convertino, Macias, et al., 2007).

Until recently, there has been little question about the viability of mainstream educational placements in this regard, and educators and investigators frequently ascribe deaf students' academic challenges to impoverished literacy skills. As chapters in this volume reveal, recent findings from research on cognition and learning by deaf individuals have indicated the need to revisit that conclusion. A variety of studies over the past decade have demonstrated that DHH students often evidence knowledge, conceptual organization, and cognitive/perceptual strategies different from their hearing peers, differences that may put them at an academic disadvantage in mainstream classrooms, compared to settings designed to accommodate that variability. Even in separate settings, the assumption is that we have identified such differences and appropriately adjusted our interventions and instructional methods, an issue in need of empirical investigation (Detterman & Thompson, 1997; Florian, 2007).

What most DHH students have in common is their diversity: They tend to come to the classroom with experiences that vary more widely than their hearing peers and, partly as a consequence of those experiences, they have developed different problem-solving and learning strategies (Ansell & Pagliaro, 2006; Courtin, 2000; Hauser et al., this volume; Schick, deVilliers, deVilliers, & Hoffmeister, 2007; Strassman, 1997). While such findings raise concerns about potential academic achievement for DHH students in mainstream educational settings, the wealth of recent evidence elucidating how deaf students learn also portends well for changes in the future. To take us across the threshold, however, the historically diverse research in this field needs to be brought together, and a coherent research agenda articulated.

All Learning Is Not Created Equal: STEM Education

One of the more interesting implications of potential differences between deaf and hearing learners and among DHH students is the possibility of interactions among individual characteristics, content, and settings. Recent evidence, for example, suggests that, to provide educational equity for DHH students in integrated classrooms, communication of information of the sort used in science, technology, engineering, and mathematics (STEM) may need to differ qualitatively and quantitatively from that in nontechnical areas (McIntosh, Sulzen, Reeder, & Kidd, 1994; Pagliaro, 1998; Redden, Davis, & Brown, 1978; Roald & Mikalsen, 2000). Current instructional methods, for example, overlook DHH students' lack of prior scientific content knowledge relative to hearing peers (or the failure to apply it; see Kelly, this volume; Marschark & Wauters, this volume). They also fail to recognize that the need to divide visual attention during the reception of spoken language, sign language, or real-time text creates its own problems. Science education, in particular, carries challenges for students with hearing loss related to vocabulary, modes of presentation, and problem-solving styles (Ansell & Pagliaro, 2006; Lang, 2005; Redden et al., 1978). Deaf and hard-of-hearing students have been found, for example, to have more difficulty than hearing peers in integrating STEM information gained from classes, textbooks, and other study materials (Richardson, McLeod-Gallinger, McKee, &Long, 2000), leading to higher-level misconceptions about the nature of learning even greater than those observed in hearing students (Hammer, 1996; Redish, Saul, & Steinberg, 1998).

Although the centuries old "oral–manual debate" is not at issue here, the language used in educational settings is. Regardless of whether DHH students are raised with primary exposure to spoken language or sign language, most of those with greater hearing losses will eventually acquire sign language and will utilize it for some portion of their secondary and/or postsecondary educations (Seal, 2004). Yet little is known about teaching and learning outcomes for such students (Kluwin & Stewart, 2001; Massaro, 2006). This issue has been made more complex by the increasing number of students with cochlear implants (CIs) who use spoken language, sign language, or both (e.g., Burkholder & Pisoni, 2006; Pisoni et al., this volume; Spencer, Gantz, & Knutson, 2004). With regard to science education, in particular, Redden et al. (1978, p. 37) urged development of "sign language for scientific terms and [training of sign language] interpreters in techniques for interpreting technical scientific lectures and laboratory demonstrations." Harrington (2000), Lang (2002), and McIntosh et al. (1994) made similar arguments based on academic achievement data, but little has been done to address those issues. Meanwhile, the use of real-time text has become a common alternative to interpreting, although apparently only two studies have examined its effectiveness for learning (Marschark, Leigh, et al., 2006; Stinson, Elliot, Kelly, and Liu, in press). Despite its increasing popularity, it is unclear how deaf students can be expected to acquire course content from real-time text when 50% of DHH high school graduates read below the fourth-grade level (Traxler, 2000). Nonetheless, it is frequently seen as an alternative to educational interpreting, particularly for courses involving STEM content likely to be beyond the educational backgrounds of most interpreters (Lang, 2002).

Why Do DHH Students Learn Less Than Hearing Peers in Science Classrooms?

One way to account for the finding that DHH students learn less than hearing peers in science classes involves the fact that most deaf students are now educated via "mediated instruction." Mediated instruction through technology has been of interest for a number of years for both hearing and DHH students (see Bernard et al., 2004). The literature on DHH students' mediated instruction/learning through sign language interpreting, in contrast, has given little attention to educational outcomes. Instead, it has focused almost entirely on "best practices" for interpreters (e.g., Seal, 2004; Winston, 2005). Several recent studies have examined the linguistic and pragmatic characteristics of interpreted instruction (Marschark, Sapere, Convertino, & Seewagen, 2005; Napier & Barker, 2004), but factors considered important (or not) by interpreters for DHH students in today's classrooms have been based almost exclusively on intuition and tradition (Cokely, 2005). Similarly, the use of real-time text in mainstream classrooms containing DHH students largely has been based on student and teacher ratings of educational benefit, not actual outcomes (e.g., Stinson & Ng, 1983). Marschark, Leigh, et al. (2006), however, demonstrated that real-time text offered no significant benefits over sign language for the science learning of college or high school students. This result contrasts with findings of Stinson et al. (in press), which indicated that real-time text led to significantly better learning of sociology by DHH high school students but not college students, although the college students reported that they understood 90% of the real-time text.

A second possible explanation/contributor to recent findings in science classrooms concerns the necessity for attentional multitasking by DHH students. Studies by Emmorey, Bavelier, Corina, and others have demonstrated that deaf individuals have a variety of visuospatial advantages over hearing individuals, although some of those differences are a function of sign language fluency rather than auditory deprivation per se (Corina, Kritchevsky, & Bellugi, 1992; Emmorey, Klima, & Hickok, 1998; Emmorey, Kosslyn, & Bellugi, 1993; Proksch & Bavelier, 2002; see Dye et al., this volume). Investigations concerning ways in which those advantages might affect learning have just begun (see Pelz et al., this volume). At present, it thus remains unclear whether and how deaf–hearing differences demonstrated in simple, carefully controlled laboratory tasks might pertain to complex real-world environments. Evidence from cognitive psychology, however, suggests that the link between laboratory and classroom might not be a simple one.

The need for deaf students to attend to two visual information sources in the classroom represents a significant challenge, both practically and theoretically. Paivio's (1971) dual-coding theory, developed in the context of memory research, has been applied to learning in science and technology classrooms (e.g., Hegarty & Just, 1989; Tiene, 2000) and to learning via multimedia technologies (e.g., Iding, 2000; Presno, 1997). Iding (2000, p. 405) argued that the use of dynamic visual displays to accompany instructors' verbal descriptions are especially helpful for learning about "scientific principles or processes . . . that must be visualized in order to be understood." More generally, studies involving hearing students have shown that simultaneous presentation of verbal and nonverbal materials facilitates information integration, resulting in faster learning, better retention, and a greater likelihood of application (Presno, 1997). Students who have less content knowledge relating to a lecture—the situation of most deaf students—will particularly benefit from combined materials (Gellevij et al., 2002; Mayer & Morena, 1998). This opportunity is not available to DHH learners, however, because of their dependence on visual reception of language through sign language, real-time text, or speechreading; see Johnson, 1991). Thus, while there is evidence that concurrent, multimodal information processing is advantageous for learning, multimedia classrooms functionally require consecutive processing by deaf students, alternating their attention between instructor/interpreters and visual materials, a situation known to impede learning.

Another likely contributor to findings of deaf students' learning less from STEM instruction than their hearing peers is their academic preparation, in terms of both knowledge and their comprehension and/or learning strategies. One result of the heterogeneity found among DHH students is considerable variability in their conceptual and content knowledge, educational histories, and approaches to learning (*epistemological attitudes,* Hammer, 1996). McIntosh et al. (1994) argued that deaf students' learning of science, in particular, would be affected by (a) the fact that, as children, they would have had fewer opportunities for the unstructured play in which incidental learning occurs; (b) their tendency toward an external locus of control; and (c) their instrumental dependence. As a result, McIntosh et al. argued that DHH students may be less likely to engage in "discovery learning," less likely to engage spontaneously in mental or empirical experimentation, and more likely to treat scientific facts as unrelated pieces of information, rather than seeking commonality (Marschark, Convertino, & LaRock, 2006; Ottem, 1980). In the domain of mathematics, Pagliaro, Bull, and Nunes all recently have obtained results consistent with this suggestion (see Blatto-Vallee et al., 2007; Bull, this volume; Kelly, this volume; Nunes et al., this volume; Zarfaty, Nunes, & Bryant, 2004). In a study of mathematics problem-solving by deaf students, for example, Ansell and Pagliaro (2006) found a consistent failure by DHH students to relate problems to the real-world situations they depicted, even when those situations were explicitly described (Akamatsu, Mayer, & Hardy-Braz, this volume).

More generally, a variety of studies have demonstrated that DHH students are less likely than hearing students to make connecting inferences while reading or problem solving and less likely to automatically process relations among concepts or multiple stimulus dimensions (Marschark & Wauters, this volume; Ottem, 1980). As a result, DHH students' conceptual knowledge often appears to be less strongly and richly interconnected than that of hearing peers (McEvoy, Marschark, & Nelson, 1999). Lack of automatic integrative processing among concepts during learning also likely contributes to recent findings indicating deaf students' difficulty in linking classroom lectures and reading materials (Richardson et al., 2000) and their being relatively unaware of that fact (Marschark et al., 2005). It is unclear how much of their overestimation of comprehension is related to language fluency, having lesser content knowledge, or the product of some other factor (see Courtin, 2000; Strassman, 1997), and all may be involved. Rawson and Kintsch (2002) demonstrated that the role of background information on memory for text (by hearing students) lies in its facilitating the organization of new information through existing semantic links. Similarly, Brown et al. (1983) and others have shown that successful learners are those who use learning strategies appropriate to the materials, the task, and their own goals.

Even when DHH students have relevant knowledge, it often is not effectively applied in intentional memory tasks (Liben, 1979), reading

(Krinsky, 1990), or the comprehension of captioning (Jelinek Lewis, & Jackson, 2001; Marschark, Leigh, et al. 2006). Because DHH students frequently do not recognize contradictions in incoming information (Kelly, Albertini, & Shannon, 2001), they often have misunderstandings or gaps in their knowledge that do not become apparent until much later. Roald and Mikalsen (2000), for example, showed that younger deaf children have conceptions of scientific facts similar to those of their hearing peers, but that the scientific knowledge of deaf high school students tends to deviate significantly from hearing students. Those differences follow, at least in part, from DHH students' lack of experience with scientific reasoning and the mental models necessary for understanding and integrating new scientific facts (Hammer, 1996). Although one might expect that instructors and sign language interpreters could help to fill gaps in deaf students' knowledge and encourage the use of appropriate information processing strategies in classroom settings, interpreter training programs do not teach their students about the developmental or academic characteristics of deaf learners, and most mainstream teachers are unaware of either the needs or the strengths of their deaf students (Ramsey, 1997). If academic difficulties faced by DHH students are thus more a matter of a "mismatch" of their skills with the nature of their instruction, where do we look for solutions?

Foundations of Learning

The desire to optimize the education of deaf students has been of interest to philosophers and scientists for centuries. Although progress certainly has been made in teaching and learning since Renaissance scholars speculated on the language, thought, and learning of deaf children (see Lang, 2003), the relative lack of academic improvement over the last several decades suggests that there is still a long way to go (Qi & Mitchell, 2007; Traxler, 2000). A variety of investigators and commentators have hypothesized specific loci of the continued educational challenges faced by most deaf learners, but relatively few have provided empirical evidence for their positions. Those who have offered either research or logical arguments in support of their theories often have proposed "one-size-fits-all" solutions and/or largely ignored contradictory evidence and the large individual differences among deaf students. This criticism can be leveled at those who claim that education through spoken language is superior to that through sign language, those who claim that education through sign language is superior to that through spoken language, and those who claim that either integrated or separate educational programming for deaf and hearing students is academically preferable. This is not to say that such positions might not be valid; indeed, each of them certainly is for some subset of students. However, if particular educational methods are to be effective, students must have language and cognitive skills that make those methods pedagogically and psychologically accessible. The problem is that many of the relevant arguments are made without recourse to data or on the basis of misunderstanding or misinterpretation of previous research. As a result, limited results frequently are overgeneralized.

Early Intervention

Among all of the issues associated with raising and educating deaf children, the importance of early intervention is easily the least controversial. Universal newborn hearing screening (UNHS), or early hearing detection and intervention (EHDI), involve programming intended to support language development, parent–child communication, social skills, and appropriate amplification for residual hearing. Calderon and Greenberg (1997) reviewed the existing literature on early-intervention programming for deaf children and showed it to be generally facilitative for academic achievement as well as language and social development, particularly when sign language was part of the intervention. More recent studies by several investigators have indicated the importance of such support for social–emotional development and family functioning (Brown & Nott, 2006; Sass-Lehrer & Bodner-Johnson, 2003) and for spoken language development (e.g., Yoshinaga-Itano & Sedey, 2000). Still lacking, however, is research concerning what it is in those programs that facilitates particular domains of growth, including any aspects of cognitive development (e.g., problem solving, executive functions, attention). Yet, a large literature in early childhood education concerns the utility of alternative intervention and preschool methodologies for hearing children that might be particularly beneficial for deaf children. Parallel work involving deaf children would help to inform us about preschool programming that should follow early intervention as well as to better tailor early-intervention programming to the needs of particular children.

Montessori programs, for example, promote children's active learning and the integration of motor activity, cognitive processing, and social collaboration in educational activities (Lillard, 2007). These are precisely the characteristics that have been advocated by educators such as Lang and Albertini (2001) for use in deaf education. The utility of Montessori programming for deaf children apparently has not been evaluated, however, and investigators who have advocated for such methods for young deaf children largely have based their arguments on intuition and anecdote rather than empirical evidence. Early play, meanwhile, has been shown to represent an essential foundation for cognitive development (Spencer & Hafer, 1998), and it would be useful to determine how

alternative early interventions promote different kinds of play and educational growth.

Piagetian- and Vygotskian-oriented preschool programs also appear
particularly suited to the needs of young DHH students. Emphasizing
learning via interaction with the environment, hypothesis testing, and the
understanding and internalization of regularities in the behavior of others, such methods would facilitate the incidental learning and integration
of information frequently suggested to be lacking in the development of
deaf children (Greenberg & Kusché, 1998; also see Hauser et al., this volume). Piaget (1952), in particular, emphasized that much of what children
know about things in the world comes from encountering new information, assimilating it with what is already known, considering it, and playing with it. Not all of this activity is active or conscious, but rather follows
from dynamic interactions with accessible environments, even when the
learning component is relatively passive. In learning about number, for
example, Piaget suggested that numbers "talk back to" children as they go
about playing with objects and noticing that their number remains constant regardless of the configuration in which they are placed (see Bull,
this volume; Nunes et al., this volume). He referred to this process in cognitive development as *logico-mathematical reasoning*. Marschark (2000)
suggested that a similar process, which he referred to as *psycho-linguistic
reasoning*, operates in language learning, as children interact and play
with language in different ways as it is encountered incidentally at different ages. Central to this activity is recognition that, as noted earlier, DHH
children may have different knowledge and different learning strategies
that can affect learning in a variety of ways. There appears to be abundant
evidence to support this view (see also Bebko & Metcalfe-Haggert, 1997;
Siple, 1997), but the possibilities for supporting the early development
of deaf children through targeted preschool educational programming has
not been explored.

One issue that should be of particular concern in preschool programming is the large individual differences found among young deaf children
(see Leigh, this volume). It is not clear whether the differences observed
among school-aged DHH students are somehow fundamental to the variability in the etiologies and ages of their hearing losses, the result of the diversity in their language experience and fluencies, or linked to differences
in their family in educational backgrounds. It is apparent, however, that
the cumulative and interactive nature of development is such that early
differences (at preschool age and before) are likely to grow larger "in the
wild" unless efforts are made to attenuate them. This is not to argue that
deaf children are in need of any homogenization. Hearing children, however, have early formal and informal education experiences that allow them
to succeed within the necessarily standardized public education system.
Similarly, we can recognize that, while deaf children are all individuals,

there is still a need to prepare them for schooling which is, of necessity, unable to adjust itself uniquely for each child.

School Placement

As the popularity of educational placements for deaf children has shifted from schools for the deaf to regular education classrooms, there has been an assumption that such placements are academically and socially beneficial. In fact, the evidence for positive outcomes from mainstream education for deaf children is rather limited. What evidence is available in the social domain indicates that deaf students, on average, are not as socially or emotionally comfortable in mainstream settings as they are in classrooms with other students who are like them (e.g., Antia & Kriemeyer, 2003; Stinson & Kluwin, 2003). Deaf students with better English skills and more residual hearing tend to fare better socially in integrated academic settings, but they are rather different from students who do not acquire such skills, either because of their hearing losses or other factors. In any case, to the extent that interacting with, collaborating with, and learning from one's peers is an essential part of the educational process, such findings suggest that, on social grounds alone, mainstream education may not be optimal for many deaf students. On the other hand, no empirical evidence appears to indicate that deaf children in separate academic settings generally demonstrate any long-term advantages in academic achievement or social cognition relative to their mainstreamed peers when other factors are controlled (Stinson & Kluwin, 2003).

Bilingual programs—those that offer instruction in both a natural sign language (e.g., American Sign Language) and the vernacular (e.g., English) and are often described as *bilingual-bicultural* programs—are claimed to produce superior language, academic, and social growth in deaf children. Thus far, however, proponents have failed to provide any empirical evidence that students in such programs gain fluency in their two languages, are comfortable in two cultures, or evidence long-term academic benefits (e.g., Nover, 2006). Similarly, educators and parents who advocate for the option of a separate school for the deaf often point out that the presence of deaf adults who are well educated and fluent in sign language should have a significant, long-term impact on young deaf children's educational, social, and personal well-being. However, evidence of a specific link between the academic success of deaf students and deaf role models or deaf teachers—as opposed to skill in teaching deaf students—is lacking.

More generally, the evidence concerning the cognitive and academic impact of alternative school placements is far less robust than is argued by proponents of one model or another. Stinson and Kluwin's (2003) review of the relevant literature indicated that "placement per se accounts for less than 5% of the difference in achievement" (p. 57), whereas variability in student characteristics accounts for at least 25%. With approximately 70% of the variance unexplained across studies, perhaps educators and investigators have been looking in the wrong place for the keys to predicting and improving educational success for deaf students. Clearly, different kinds of academic programming are likely to be more or less beneficial for children with different needs, and a greater heterogeneity among deaf children than hearing children makes it unlikely that either the sources of those needs or the possible solutions will be simple.

Adding to arguments about the appropriateness of placement in schools for the deaf versus local public schools are conflicting claims supporting each as leading to better educational outcomes for deaf children. Unfortunately, while most (hearing) mainstream teachers have no background in deaf education or the development of deaf children, most teachers of deaf students in separate settings do not have educational backgrounds in what they teach (Kelly, Lang, & Pagliaro, 2003). A variety of reports through the years have called for more deaf teachers and more hearing teachers who are fluent signers at schools for the deaf (Bowe, 1991), as well as for more teachers who are certified in the content areas they teach (see Marschark, Lang, & Albertini, 2002). Considerable evidence points to a lack of access to classroom information in academic settings encountered by deaf students who rely on sign language (e.g., Jones, 2005; Ramsey, 1997), although explicit assessments of learning are rare. Even when public schools offer interpreting services, interpreters are in short supply and often underqualified (Antia, 2007; Sapere, LaRock, Convertino, Gallimore, & Lessard, 2005; Schick, Williams, & Bolster, 1999).

Research apparently has not addressed the question of access to classroom information by deaf children who rely on spoken language (i.e., in naturalistic, noisy environments). The extent to which "oral" deaf students understand ongoing discussions in the classroom—with or without the support of an oral or sign language interpreter—thus remains unclear. Anecdotally, it is suggested that deaf students help each other in classes by providing clarification of ongoing communication. However, there is no evidence concerning the extent of such assistance, whether or not it is really helpful, and the extent to which the "helping" students, themselves, are understanding correctly.

Summary and Implications

To a greater or lesser degree, deaf children grow up in somewhat environments somewhat different from hearing children. They generally have different language and social experiences, different opportunities for learning incidentally and through reading, and qualitatively different educational histories. Deaf and hearing children also display differences in language fluencies, memory, problem solving, and academic achievement. The simple hypothesis articulated in this chapter is that these empirically documented facts are not independent. Unfortunately, consistent with the history of psychological research in North America, the development and education of deaf children traditionally have been treated in a piecemeal fashion. Perhaps because of the all-pervasive debates concerning language orientation and school placement, now compounded by variability introduced by early intervention and CIs, research concerning cognitive development, social development, and academic achievement have remained largely independent. Investigations concerning language, in contrast, frequently have been conducted with an eye toward understanding its role as both a foundation and an outcome of growth in these domains, even if they typically have involved only pairwise studies.

Within the domain of educational studies, and special education in particular, it is not entirely novel to suggest that we need to understand the cognitive underpinnings of learning and the tools that students bring to the classroom if we are to optimize academic achievement. For individuals who learn differently from the majority of their peers—by definition, those who are the target of special education—an even greater need exists to adopt a holistic approach to learning. Regardless of the source of their differences, such individuals are likely to evidence greater diversity than the majority who reside near the center of myriad normal distributions. Providing such students with full access to information in the classroom and ensuring that learning experiences designed for the majority are also appropriate for the minority present particular challenges for instructors at all educational levels.

Perhaps nowhere is the confluence of these issues more apparent than in the education of students with significant hearing losses. In some ways similar to second-language learners who struggle with the language of the classroom (and may evidence cultural differences), in some ways similar to gifted students who require particular instructional methods to match their unique knowledge sets, and in some ways similar to students with attention deficit/hyperactivity disorder (ADHD) who are easily distracted and have difficulty maintaining time on task, DHH students represent a unique population. Coupled with the fact that they are so heterogeneous, relative to hearing age-mates, educating DHH students in mainstream classrooms can be challenging indeed. Teachers who do not have experience with DHH students or have experience with only one or two will be at a definite disadvantage. Without a feel for what deaf students know or how to structure information and tasks in a way that will match students' cognitive organizations and learning styles, opportunities for formal and informal teaching-learning are easily missed.

Research has demonstrated cognitive differences between deaf and hearing students at a variety of levels, from visual perception to memory to problem solving (Dye et al., this volume; Hauser et al., this volume; Marschark, Convertino, et al., 2006). At the same time, studies have indicated them to be more similar than they are different. These are not mutually exclusive findings, but simply indicative of the fact that relatively small differences in knowledge or approaches to learning can have significant effects that may be cumulative over time. This means that investigations involving small, homogeneous groups of DHH students, although methodologically and theoretically attractive, are of lesser utility when it comes to practice. At the same time, investigations involving relatively large, heterogeneous groups of DHH students may yield mean results that obscure individual differences and also are of limited use to teachers and other practitioners.

Beyond the theoretical and pragmatic challenges of research and practice involving DHH students is the difficulty in bridging the two. One wonders whether the relatively slow pace of improvement in academic achievement by DHH students is more a function of our only recently gaining insights into the cognitive underpinnings of their language and learning, the "language wars," or the historical divide between those who teach deaf students and those who conduct research. All too often, investigators have insinuated themselves into homes and classrooms in order to conduct research, only to leave students, parents, and teachers without any information concerning their findings or their implications. In part, this situation arises from the length of time required to conduct well-controlled empirical research, but it also reflects the fact that research is rarely published in a language and location accessible to lay audiences. The result, in any case, is a common skepticism among educators about the utility of research for day-to-day classroom activities and little concern about possible, abstruse long-term implications. As one colleague noted in a discussion of research described in this volume, philosophically revolutionary changes in the education enterprise will gain a teacher's attention, but the results of an experiment published in an obscure scholarly journal are unlikely to change anyone's behavior.

It is time to look to the future, not the past. With recent progress in cognitive, educational, and behavioral research, and with the increasing needs of a population living in a technologically complex and interconnected global community, we are at a threshold. Although challenges remain, they are more than matched by opportunities that make this the best time ever to be a deaf student, or the parent or teacher of one. The bridging of research and practice related to deaf cognition and deaf education offers exciting possibilities for both researchers and educators, with DHH students as the primary beneficiaries. The Chinese proverb tells us that a journey of 1000 miles begins with a single step. We are ready.

References

Ansell, E., & Pagliaro, C. M. (2006). The relative difficulty of signed arithmetic story problems for primary level deaf and hard-of-hearing students. *Journal of Deaf Studies and Deaf Education, 11,* 153–170.

Antia, S. (2007). Can deaf and hard of hearing students be successful in general education classrooms? *TCRecord.* Retrieved May 17, 2007, from www.tcrecord.org/PrintContent.asp?ContentID=13461

Antia, S. D., & Kreimeyer, K. (2003). Peer interactions of deaf and hard of hearing children. In M. Marschark & P. E. Spencer (Eds.), *Oxford handbook of deaf studies, language, and education* (pp. 164–176). New York: Oxford University Press.

Baron-Cohen, S., Tager-Flusberg, H., & Cohen, D. J., (Eds.). (2000). *Understanding other minds.* New York: Oxford University Press.

Bartlett, D. E. (1850). The acquisition of language. *American Annals of the Deaf and Dumb, 3*(1), 83–92.

Bebko, J. M., Calderon, R., & Treder, R. (2003). The Language Proficiency Profile-2: Assessment of the global communication skills of deaf children across languages and modalities of expression. *Journal of Deaf Studies and Deaf Education, 8,* 438–451.

Bebko, J. M., & Metcalfe-Haggert, A. (1997). Deafness, language skills and memory: A model for the development of spontaneous rehearsal use. *Journal of Deaf Studies and Deaf Education, 2,* 131–139.

Bernard, R. M., Abram, P. C., Lou, Y., Borokhovski, A. W., Wozney, L., Wallet, P. A., Fiset, M., & Huang, B. (2004). How does distance education compare with classroom instruction? A meta-analysis of the empirical literature. *Review of Educational Research, 74,* 255–316.

Blatto-Vallee, G., Kelly, R. R., Gaustad, M. G., Porter, J., & Fonzi, J. (2007). Visual-spatial representation in mathematical problem solving by deaf and hearing students. *Journal of Deaf Studies and Deaf Education, 12,* 432–438.

Bowe, F. (1991). *Approaching equality: Education of the deaf.* Silver Spring, MD: T. J. Publishers.

Brown, A. L., Bransford, J. D., Ferrara, R., & Campione, J. C. (1983). Learning, remembering, and understanding. In J. N. Flavell and E. M. Markham (Eds.), *Carmichael's manual of child psychology, Volume 1.* New York: Wiley.

Brown, P. M., & Nott, P. (2006). Family-centered practice in early intervention for oral language development: Philosophy, methods, and results. In P. E. Spencer & M. Marschark (Eds.), *Advances in the spoken language development of deaf and hard-of-hearing children* (pp. 136–165). New York: Oxford University Press.

Burkholder, R. A., & Pisoni, D. B. (2006). Working memory capacity, verbal rehearsal speed, and scanning in deaf children with cochlear implants.

In P. E. Spencer & M. Marschark (Eds.), *Advances in the spoken language development of deaf and hard-of-hearing children* (pp. 328–357). New York: Oxford University Press.

Calderon, R. & Greenberg, M. (1997). The effectiveness of early intervention for deaf children and children with hearing loss. In M. J. Guralnik (Ed.), *The effectiveness of early intervention* (pp. 455–482). Baltimore: Paul H. Brookes.

Cokely, D. (2005). Shifting positionality: A critical examination of the turning point in the relationship of interpreters and the deaf community. In M. Marschark, R. Peterson, & E. A. Winston (Eds.), *Sign language interpreting and interpreter education: Directions for research and practice* (pp. 3–28). New York: Oxford University Press.

Corina, D. P., Kritchevsky, M., & Bellugi, U. (1992). Linguistic permeability of unilateral neglect: Evidence from American Sign Language. In *Proceedings of the Cognitive Science Conference* (pp. 384–389). Hillsdale, NY: Lawrence Erlbaum.

Courtin, C. (2000). The impact of sign language on the cognitive development of deaf children: The case of theories of mind. *Journal of Deaf Studies and Deaf Education, 5*, 266–276.

Detterman, D. K., & Thompson, L. A. (1997). What is so special about special education? *American Psychologist, 52*, 1082–1090.

Emmorey, K. (2002). *Language, cognition, and the brain*. Mahwah, NJ: Erlbaum.

Emmorey, K., Klima, E. S., & Hickok, G. (1998). Mental rotation within linguistic and nonlinguistic domains in users of American Sign Language. *Cognition, 68*, 221–226.

Emmorey, K., Kosslyn, S., & Bellugi, U. (1993). Visual imagery and visual-spatial language: Enhanced imagery abilities in deaf and hearing ASL signers. *Cognition, 46*, 139–181.

Fay, E. A. (1869). The acquisition of language by deaf mutes. *American Annals of the Deaf and Dumb, 14*(4), 13.

Federal Interagency Forum on Child and Family Statistics. (2005). *America's children: key national indicators of well being, 2005*. Washington, DC: U.S. Government Printing Office.

Florian, L. (Ed.). (2007). *Handbook of special education*. London: Sage Publications.

Furth, H. G. (1966). A comparison of reading test norms of deaf and hearing children. *American Annals of the Deaf, 111*, 461–462.

Gellevij, M., van der Meij, H., Jong, T. D., & Pieters, J. (2002). Multimodal versus unimodal instruction in a complex learning context. *Journal of Experimental Education, 70*, 215–239.

Greenberg, M. T., & Kusché, C. A. (1998). Preventive intervention for school-age deaf children: The PATHS curriculum. *Journal of Deaf Studies and Deaf Education, 3*, 49–63.

Hammer, D. (1996). More than misconceptions: Multiple perspectives on student knowledge and reasoning, and an appropriate role for education research. *American Journal of Physics, 64*, 1316–1325.

Harrington, F. (2000). Sign language interpreters and access for deaf students to university curricula: The ideal and the reality. In R. P. Roberts, S. E. Carr, D. Abraham, & A. Dufour (Eds.), *The critical link 2: Interpreters in the community*. Amsterdam: John Benjamins.

Hegarty, M., & Just, M. A. (1989). Understanding machines from text and diagrams. In H. Mandl & J. R. Stevens (Eds.), *Knowledge acquisition from text and pictures* (pp. 171–195). North Holland: Elsevier.

Iding, M. K. (2000). Is seeing believing? Features of effective multimedia for learning science. *International Journal of Instructional Media, 27,* 403–415.

Jelinek Lewis, M. S., & Jackson, D.W. (2001). Television literacy: Comprehension of program content using closed-captions for the deaf. *Journal of Deaf Studies and Deaf Education, 6,* 43–53.

Johnson, K. (1991). Miscommunication in interpreted classroom interaction. *Sign Language Studies, 70,* 1–34.

Jones, B. E. (2005). Competencies of K-12 educational interpreters: What we need versus what we have. In E. A. Winston (Ed.), *Educational interpreting: How can it succeed?* Washington, DC: Gallaudet University Press.

Kelly, R. R., Albertini, J. A., & Shannon, N. B. (2001). Deaf college students' reading comprehension and strategy use. *American Annals of the Deaf, 146,* 385–400.

Kelly, R: R., Lang, H. G., & Pagliaro, C. M. (2003). Mathematics word problem solving for deaf students: A survey of practices in grades 6–12. *Journal of Deaf Studies and Deaf Education, 8,* 104–119.

Kluwin, T. N., & Stewart, D. A. (2001, winter/spring). Interpreting in schools: A look at research. *Odyssey* (pp. 15–17). Washington DC: Gallaudet University.

Krinsky, S. G. (1990). The feeling of knowing in deaf adolescents. *American Annals of the Deaf, 135,* 389–395.

Lang, H. G. (2002). Higher education for deaf students: Research priorities in the new millennium. *Journal of Deaf Studies and Deaf Education, 7,* 267–280.

Lang, H. G. (2003). Perspectives on the history of deaf education. In M. Marschark & P. E. Spencer (Eds.), *Oxford handbook of deaf studies, language, and education* (pp. 9–20). New York: Oxford University Press.

Lang, H. G. (2005). Best practices: Science education for deaf students. Retrieved August 10, 2007, from http://www.rit.edu/~comets/pages/lang/langsciencelitreview5.pdf

Lang, H. G., & Albertini, J. A. (2001). Construction of meaning in the authentic science writing of deaf students. *Journal of Deaf Studies and Deaf Education, 6,* 258–284.

Liben, L. S. (Ed.). (1978). *Deaf children: Developmental perspectives.* New York: Academic Press.

Liben, L. S. (1979). Free recall by deaf and hearing children: Semantic clustering and recall in trained and untrained groups. *Journal of Experimental Child Psychology, 27,* 105–119.

Lillard, A. S. (2007). *Montessori: The science behind the genius.* New York: Oxford University Press.

Marschark, M. (2000). Education and development of deaf children—or is it development and education? In P. Spencer, C. Erting & M. Marschark (Eds.), *Development in context: The deaf children in the family and at school* (pp. 275–292). Mahwah, NJ: LEA.

Marschark, M. (2007). *Raising and educating a deaf child* (2nd ed.). New York: Oxford University Press.

Marschark, M., Convertino, C., & LaRock, D. (2006). Optimizing academic performance of deaf students: Access, opportunities, and outcomes. In D. F. Moores & D. S. Martin (Eds.), *Deaf learners: New developments in curriculum and instruction* (pp. 179–200). Washington, DC: Gallaudet University Press.

Marschark, M., Convertino, C. M., Macias, G., Monikowski, C. M., Sapere, P. M., & Seewagen, R. (2007). Understanding communication among deaf students who sign and speak: A trivial pursuit? *American Annals of the Deaf, 152*, 415–424.

Marschark, M., Lang, H. G., & Albertini, J. A. (2002). *Educating deaf students: From research to practice.* New York: Oxford University Press.

Marschark, M., Leigh, G., Sapere, P., Burnham, D., Convertino, C., Stinson, M., Knoors, H., Vervloed, M.P.J., & Noble, W. (2006). Benefits of sign language interpreting and text alternatives to classroom learning by deaf students. *Journal of Deaf Studies and Deaf Education, 11*, 421–437.

Marschark, M., Sapere, P., Convertino, C., & Seewagen, R. (2005). Educational interpreting: Access and outcomes. In M. Marschark, R. Peterson, & E. A. Winston (Eds.), *Interpreting and interpreter education: Directions for research and practice.* New York: Oxford University Press.

Marschark, M., Siple, P., Lillo-Martin, D., Campbell, R., & Everhart, V. (1997). *Relations of language and thought: The view from sign language and deaf children.* New York: Oxford University Press.

Marschark, M., & Spencer, P. E. (Eds.). (2003). *Oxford handbook of deaf studies, language, and education.* New York: Oxford University Press.

Massaro, D. (2006). A computer-animated tutor for language learning: Research and applications. In P. E. Spencer & M. Marschark (Eds.), *Advances in the spoken language development of deaf and hard-of-hearing children* (pp. 212–233). New York: Oxford University Press.

Mayberry, R. I., & Locke, E. (2003). Age constraints on first versus second language acquisition: Evidence for linguistic plasticity and epigenesis. *Brain and Language, 87*, 369–384.

Mayer, R. E., & Morena, R. (1998). A split-attention effect in multimedia learning: Evidence for dual processing systems in working memory. *Journal of Educational Psychology, 90*, 312–320.

McEvoy, C., Marschark, M., & Nelson, D. L. (1999). Comparing the mental lexicons of deaf and hearing individuals. *Journal of Educational Psychology, 91*, 1–9.

McIntosh, R. A., Sulzen, L., Reeder, K., & Kidd, D. (1994). Making science accessible to deaf students: The need for science literacy and conceptual teaching. *American Annals of the Deaf, 139*, 480–484.

Napier, J., & Barker, R. (2004). Access to university interpreting: Expectations and preferences of deaf students. *Journal of Deaf Studies and Deaf Education.*

Nover, S. (2006, March). Language planning in deaf education and a model of ASL-English bilingual professional development. Presentation at Language and Deaf Education: Into the 21st Century Conference. Dunblane, Scotland.

Office for Standards in Education (OFSTED). (2005). *Primary National Strategy: An evaluation of its impact in primary schools 2004/05.* HMI No. 2612.

Ottem, E. (1980). An analysis of cognitive studies with deaf subjects. *American Annals of the Deaf, 125,* 564–575.

Pagliaro, C. M. (1998). Mathematics preparation and professional development of deaf education teachers. *American Annals of the Deaf, 143,* 373–379.

Paivio, A. (1971). *Imagery and verbal processes.* New York: Holt, Rinehart, Winston.

Piaget, J. (1952). *The origins of intelligence in children.* New York: Basic Books.

Presno, C. (1997). Bruner's three forms of representation revisited: Action, pictures, and words for effective computer instruction. *Journal of Instructional Psychology, 24,* 112–118.

Proksch, J., & Bavelier, D. (2002). Changes in the spatial distribution of visual attention after early deafness. *Journal of Cognitive Neuroscience, 14* (5), 687–701.

Qi, S., & Mitchell, R. E. (2007, April). *Large-scaled academic achievement testing of deaf and hard-of-hearing students: Past, present, and future.* Paper presented at the annual meeting of the Research on the Education of Deaf Persons SIG of the American Education Research Association, Chicago.

Ramsey, C. (1997). *Deaf children in public schools.* Washington, DC: Gallaudet University Press.

Rawson, K. A., & Kintsch, W. (2002). How does background information improve memory for text? *Memory and Cognition, 30,* 768–778.

Redden, M. R., Davis, C. A., and Brown, J. W. (1978). *Science for handicapped students in higher education: Barriers, solutions, and recommendations.* Washington, DC: American Association for the Advancement of Science.

Redish, E. F., Saul, J. M., & Steinberg, R. N. (1998). Student expectations in introductory physics. *American Journal of Physics, 66,* 212–224.

Richardson, J.T.E., MacLeod-Gallinger, J., McKee, B. G., & Long, G. L. (2000). Approaches to studying in deaf and hearing students in higher education. *Journal of Deaf Studies and Deaf Education, 5,* 156–173.

Roald, I., & Mikalsen, Ø. (2000). What are the earth and heavenly bodies like? A study of objectual conceptions among Norwegian deaf and hearing pupils. *International Journal of Science Education, 22,* 337–355.

Sapere, P., LaRock, D, Convertino, C., Gallimore, L. & Lessard, P. (2005). Interpreting and interpreter education—Adventures in Wonderland? In M. Marschark, R. Peterson, & E. Winston (Eds.), *Interpreting and Interpreter Education: Directions for Research and Practice* (pp. 283–297). New York: Oxford University Press.

Sass-Lehrer, M. & Bodner-Johnson, B. (2003). Early intervention: Current approaches to family-centered programming. In M. Marschark & P. E. Spencer (Eds.), *Oxford handbook of deaf studies, language, and education* (pp. 65–81). New York: Oxford University Press.

Schick, B., de Villiers, P., de Villiers, J., & Hoffmeister, R. (2007). Language and theory of mind: A study of deal children. *Child Development, 78,* 376–396.

Schick, B., Williams, K., & Bolster, L. (1999). Skill levels of educational interpreters working in public schools. *Journal of Deaf Studies and Deaf Education, 4,* 144–155.

Seal, B. C. (2004). *Best practices in educational interpreting* (2nd ed.). Boston: Allyn and Bacon.

Siple, P. (Ed.). (1978). *Understanding language through sign language research.* New York: Academic Press.

Siple, P. (1997). Universals, generalizability and the acquisition of signed language. In M. Marschark, P. Siple, D. Lillo-Martin, R. Campbell, & V. S. Everhart, *Relations of language and thought: The view from sign language and deaf children* (pp. 24–61). New York: Oxford University Press.

Spencer, L. J., Gantz, B. J. & Knutson, J. F. (2004). Outcomes and achievement of students who grew up with access to cochlear implants. *Laryngoscope 114*, 1576–1581.

Spencer, P. E., & Hafer, J. C. (1998). Play as "window" and "room": Assessing and supporting the cognitive and linguistic development of deaf infants and young children. In M. Marschark & M. D. Clark (Eds.), *Psychological perspectives on deafness, Volume 2* (pp. 131–152). Mahwah, NJ: LEA.

Stinson, M. S., Elliot, L., Kelly, R., & Liu, Y. (in press). Deaf and hard-of-hearing students' memory of lectures with speech-to-text and interpreting/notetaking services. *Special Education*.

Stinson, M. S., & Kluwin, T. (2003). Educational consequences of alternative school placements. In M. Marschark & P. E. Spencer, *Oxford handbook of deaf studies, language, and education* (pp. 52–64). New York: Oxford University Press.

Stinson, M. S., & Ng, P. (1983, April). *Relations between communication skills and comprehension of an interpreted lecture by hearing-impaired college students*. Paper presented at the annual meetings of the American Educational Research Association, Montreal.

Stokoe, W. C. (1960/2005). *Sign language structure: An outline of the visual communication system of the American deaf.* Studies in Linguistics, Occasional Papers 8. Buffalo, NY: Department of Anthropology and Linguistics, University of Buffalo. Reprinted in *Journal of Deaf Studies and Deaf Education, 10,* 3–37.

Strassman, B. (1997). Metacognition and reading in children who are deaf: A review of the research. *Journal of Deaf Studies and Deaf Education, 2,* 140–149.

Tiene, D. (2000). Sensory mode and information load: Examining the effects of timing on multisensory processing. *International Journal of Instructional Media, 27,* 183–198.

Traxler, C. B. (2000). Measuring up to performance standards in reading and mathematics: Achievement of selected deaf and hard-of-hearing students in the national norming of the 9th Edition Stanford Achievement Test. *Journal of Deaf Studies and Deaf Education, 5,* 337–348.

Trends in International Mathematics and Science Survey (2003). National Center for Education Statistics. Retrieved August 18, 2007, from http://nces.ed.gov/timss/results03.asp

Winston, E. A. (2005). Interpretability and accessibility of mainstream classroom. In E. A. Winston (Ed.), *Educational interpreting: How it can succeed.* Washington, DC: Gallaudet University Press.

Yoshinaga-Itano, C., & Sedey, A. (2000). Speech development of deaf and hard-of-hearing children in early childhood: Interrelationships with language and hearing. *Volta Review, 100,* 181–212.

Zarfaty, Y., Nunes, T., & Bryant, P. (2004). The performance of young deaf children in spatial and temporal number tasks. *Journal of Deaf Studies and Deaf Education, 9,* 315–326.

Chapter 2

Changing Parameters in Deafness and Deaf Education

Greater Opportunity but Continuing Diversity

Greg Leigh

Developments in a number of related fields are providing greater opportunities for deaf children to access spoken language than at any time in
history. Most notable among these developments have been the advent of
universal newborn hearing screening (UNHS) and the increasing accessibility of cochlear implantation. In addition, an increasing emphasis on
inclusive education and continuing advances in understanding the foundations of learning by deaf children have served to dramatically alter expectations about both linguistic and educational outcomes for deaf children.
Nevertheless, the outcomes of therapeutic and educational interventions
with deaf and hard-of-hearing (DHH) children continue to be characterized
by considerable variability. Indeed, rather than serving to homogenize the
educational needs of this population of learners, new developments ensure
that those needs become ever more diverse and complex. Such diversity
raises particular issues for educators and places new demands upon service delivery systems, pedagogy, and research.

Increasing Diversity

Deaf and hard-of-hearing children are not, and never have been, a homogenous group. Diversity among deaf children is not simply a function
of degree of hearing loss or auditory capacity. Cultural and linguistic back-

ground, the existence of concomitant disabling conditions, as well as linguistic, social, personality, and cognitive developmental issues are all influencers of diversity within this population. From an educational perspective, it is clear that the profile of the population of DHH children has been undergoing a transformation for some time. Some of these changes have been largely independent of the more intrinsic influences just identified. In the Western world, at least, legislative developments such as the Education for All Handicapped Children Act (U.S. Public Law 94–142) and its successors, and the Australian Disability Discrimination Act (2002) and the regulations that succeeded it, have served to dramatically reshape the pattern of enrollment and delivery of educational services to DHH children. These changes have been evident at all levels from early intervention programs to high school. In 2001, more than two-thirds of all DHH students included in the *U.S. Annual Survey of Deaf and Hard of Hearing Children and Youth* were reported to be receiving all or part of their education in environments in which they were integrated with hearing peers (Karchmer & Mitchell, 2003). This contrasts dramatically with the corresponding survey in 1975–1976 (around the time of PL 94–142) that indicated that only 49% of DHH children were enrolled in special schools or similar centers (Karchmer & Trybus, 1977). This transition in Australia has been even more pronounced. Currently, in the state of New South Wales, more than 85% of children in school education programs are in regular class situations for part or all of their school education.

As profound as the impacts of legislative imperatives have been, a "chicken-and-egg" issue is at play here. Without question, the educational arrangements for DHH children were already changing prior to those developments. For the latter half of the twentieth century, multiple influences led to a greater definition of subgroups of DHH children and a dramatic increase in the diversity of associated educational responses to accommodate their differences.

Not least among the drivers of change were advances in hearing aid technology and, ultimately, the development of cochlear implants (CIs)—most notably the development of the multichannel programmable implant that is the established standard today. Collectively, such advances accounted for an ever-increasing proportion of DHH children who were able to access useable hearing for the purposes of acquiring spoken language as a first language. Use of spoken language and ability to access spoken communication in regular classrooms accounted for a significant drive toward integrated education well before legislative impacts were realized.

A second major influence for change in deaf education came from the dramatic expansion during this period in the understanding of deafness from a sociolinguistic perspective. The seminal work of Stokoe (1960/2005) and his successors in the field of sign language research placed sign languages and the sociolinguistic status of deaf people at the center of a new conceptualization of education for many DHH learners. The use of sign language at all levels of education during the latter part of the last century accounted for yet another set of differentiating dimensions within the broader population of deaf children and a corresponding expansion of developmental and educational issues to be addressed for subsets of that population.

Regardless of the reasons for change, the diversity of educational placements, experiences, and supports for deaf children has clearly been associated with an equally diverse range of linguistic, educational, and social-emotional challenges (for parents as well as for children). Each of these challenges raises questions about the nature of the educational interventions and supports that are put in place. Specifically, questions remain about the extent to which the needs of *all* DHH learners are being adequately addressed by the current array of responses, particularly in the very early stages of children's development.

For the most part, this chapter focuses on just two developments that are set to account for even faster rates of change in the population profile of DHH children: Early identification through UNHS and early cochlear implantation. In the post-newborn hearing screening world of early cochlear implantation, there will be children with severe and profound levels of hearing loss for whom the assumption of auditory access to spoken language is going to be more valid than it has been at any point in history. However, there will remain children for whom that access cannot be validly assumed. There will continue to be children for whom exclusively auditory–oral approaches will not produce outcomes commensurate with the expectations that early identification and early implantation may predict. Specifically, there will continue to be children—with and without implants—whose only viable access to social, cognitive, and language development will be via sign language, or at least through some form of manual supplement to their use of spoken language. The continuing diversity of experiences, communication needs, and educational management options among DHH children presents particular challenges for teachers, teacher education, and educational research in the framing of educational placements and programs.

Newborn Hearing Screening

According to the work of researchers such as Yoshinaga-Itano, Sedey, Coulter, and Mehl (1998) and Yoshinaga-Itano, Coulter, and Thomson (2000), children with early-identified hearing loss demonstrate language development within the low average range of development for all children in the first 4–5 years of life. The benefits are most evident, however, when outcomes for early-identified children are compared with those of children who were not identified early. In a study of 150 DHH children using the Minnesota Child Development Inventory (MCDI), Yoshinaga-Itano et al. (1998) showed that the language development of the 72 children whose hearing loss was identified before 6 months of age was significantly better than for the children whose hearing loss was identified at any time after the age of 6 months.

Yoshinaga-Itano (2004) summarized the results of a series of developmental studies in which an early-identified group was matched closely to a group of later-identified DHH children. The studies investigated the language, speech, and social-emotional development of the two groups. Advantages in favor of earlier identification were reported for children of both genders, of all socio-economic levels, and with all degrees of hearing loss from mild to profound. Yoshinaga-Itano concluded that a significantly higher proportion of early-identified than late-identified children developed age-appropriate language skills—notably, in both oral and signed language communication situations. Further, the advantages of early identification were shown to extend to development across a range of areas. Yoshinaga-Itano et al. (2000) found that children whose hearing loss was diagnosed early had significantly better general language development and vocabulary knowledge than those whose hearing loss was diagnosed after the age of 6 months. Similarly, Apuzzo and Yoshinaga-Itano (1995) and Yoshinaga-Itano et al. (2000) found that early-identified children had superior speech intelligibility. Pressman, Pipp-Siegel, Yoshinaga-Itano, and Deas (1999) and Pressman, Pipp-Siegel, Yoshinaga-Itano, Kubicek, and Emde (2000) also found that earlier identified children had more positive outcomes in regard to development of emotional availability and parental attachment associated with a diagnosis of early-childhood hearing loss.

Cochlear Implantation

The collective literature on the impact of cochlear implantation in children reveals a picture of increasingly positive outcomes. Successive studies provide compelling evidence of an improved rate and level of spoken language development for most children with severe to profound sensory-neural deafness who receive a cochlear implant, provided that they receive consistent input in spoken language (Blamey & Sarant, 2000; Geers, Nicholas, & Sedey, 2003; Svirsky, Robbins, Iler-Kirk, Pisoni, & Miyamoto, 2000; Tomblin, Spencer, Flock, Tyler, & Gantz, 1999). In some research, children with CIs have been shown to have a rate—if not necessarily a level—of language development approaching that of hearing children (Svirsky et al., 2000).

Although considerably less well researched, some limited evidence also suggests a possible cognitive advantage associated with cochlear implantation. Khan, Edwards, and Langdon (2005) compared the nonverbal intelligence test scores of a group of hearing children with groups of age-matched deaf children with and without CIs. They found that, unlike the nonimplanted group, the children with CIs performed at levels that were not significantly different from the hearing children (see Pisoni et al., this volume). The researchers acknowledged that higher-level language skills, spoken or signed, have previously been shown to be associated with higher levels of both verbal and nonverbal cognitive functioning in deaf children (Conrad & Weiskrantz, 1981). However, they did not assess or match the linguistic abilities of the children in the samples, leaving open the possibility that the observed differences were a function of linguistic ability or other factors, such as the nature and extent of intervention or parental engagement.

Notwithstanding these positive findings in a number of areas, it remains the case that considerable diversity continues among the outcomes experienced by children who receive CIs (Geers, 2002; Geers, Brenner, & Davidson, 2003; Geers, Brenner, Nicholas, Uchanski, Tye-Murray, & Tobey, 2002; Pisoni et al., this volume; Spencer & Marschark, 2003). A number of factors have been identified as being associated with both the range and magnitude of the benefits associated with implantation. These factors include, among others: (a) age of implantation and length of experience with the implant (Connor, Hieber, Arts, & Zwolan, 2000; Dettman, Pinder, Briggs, Dowell, & Leigh, 2007; Geers et al., 2003; Tomblin, Baker, Spencer, Zhang, & Gantz, 2005), (b) the type of early intervention/rehabilitation received (Geers et al., 2003), (c) the device technology (Tobey, Geers, Brenner, Altuna, & Gabbert, 2003), (d) the presence of associated disabilities (Holt & Kirk, 2005), and (e) the nature of the educational setting and communication mode employed with the child (Geers, Brenner et al., 2002; Geers et al., 2003; Kirk et al., 2002).

It is perhaps important to note at this stage that the focus of much of the research considered here has been on the language and communication outcomes associated with cochlear implantation—often very narrowly defined. In the context of a volume dedicated to cognition and deafness, it is appropriate to note that the area of cognitive outcomes associated with cochlear implantation requires significantly greater attention. As Pisoni et al. (this volume; Pisoni, 2000) indicate very clearly, there is much about the cognitive consequences and correlates of implantation that remains unknown. The outcomes associated with receiving a CI cannot just be considered in terms of improvements in speech perception, or even in regard to improvements in linguistic performance. There is much that remains to be known about how the signal received through a CI relates to a range of processes at the cortical level. As Pisoni and his colleagues argue in this volume, the effects of implantation likely impact on, or at least interact with, a range of functions including basic information processing skills and, subsequently therefore, on areas such as memory—particularly the ability to encode, store, and retain words and associated concepts—and other higher-order processes such as metacognition and problem solving. Pisoni and his colleagues have suggested that it may indeed be the impact of differences in certain cognitive processing abilities that are able, at least in part, to explain some of the considerable variability in outcomes associated with children using CIs.

Variability in outcomes among children who receive CIs, whatever the reasonable cause, is a universally recognized phenomenon in the literature and in practice. Without seeking to underplay the issues relating to cognition and cognitive development, the literature that has already been considered here does suggest one factor that accounts for a significant proportion of the variance in outcomes for children who receive a cochlear implant—age of implantation. In the context of a new era of earlier identified hearing loss, this factor warrants particular attention.

In several early studies examining the issue of age of implantation, children implanted before the age of 5 years were shown to have significantly better outcomes than those implanted later, using a range of measures including (a) expressive and receptive vocabulary (Connor et al., 2000), (b) verbal reasoning (Geers et al., 2003), and (c) reading skills (Geers, 2003). Taken together, these studies were indicative of the potential benefit of earlier implantation. Clearly, however, 5 years of age may not be considered to be all that early in the context of any optimal period for language acquisition.

Considerable theoretical and evidence-based support exists for the concept of an optimal (but not finite) period for development of speech perception abilities in early infancy (Mayberry & Locke, 2003; Mayberry, Locke, & Kazmi, 2002; Werker & Tees, 2005). Indeed there is evidence that the processes of speech perception and associated development commence even before birth. Several studies have revealed neonatal preferences for speech that are clearly experience-based, such as attraction to the mother's voice (DeCasper & Fifer, 1980) and to the native language (Mehler, Bertoncini, & Barriere, 1978; Moon, Cooper, & Fifer, 1993). Ruben (1997) suggested that a sensitive period for the development of phonologic perception and discrimination skills appears to commence by the sixth month of gestation and continues until around 12 months of age. This view is consistent with theories proposing that a sensitive period for neural plasticity exists and hence for the development of the central auditory system (Kral & Tillein, 2005; Sharma, Dorman, & Spahr, 2002). Collectively, such perspectives suggest that early implantation, within the first 24 months of life, is most likely to provide maximal benefit by ensuring the best possible conditions for the postnatal neural development and organization of the auditory system.

An increasing number of researchers have considered the issue of such early implantation. Hammes, Novak, Rotz, Willis, Edmondson, and Thomas (2002) conducted a retrospective study of 47 children who received implants between the ages of 9 and 48 months. The highest-level outcomes for speech perception and spoken language abilities were for the 10 children who received their implant before 18 months of age. Of that group, four children demonstrated spoken language skills comparable to hearing children within 6 months of their chronological age. Tomblin et al. (2005) examined the growth of expressive language skills of 29 children who received their CIs between the between ages of 10 and 40 months. They used repeated language measures to undertake growth curve analyses to assess the relationship between expressive language outcomes, age of implantation, and length of experience with the implant. Overall, age at implantation accounted for 14.6% of the variance in the children's expressive language abilities. Their analysis showed a significant beneficial effect of earlier implantation, with language growth being more rapid in children implanted as infants than in those implanted later.

Svirsky, Teoh, and Neuberger (2004) compared the receptive and expressive language abilities and the speech perception abilities of three groups of children who received CIs at various ages: 12 between 16 and 24 months of age; 34 between 25 and 36 months; and 29 between 37 and 48 months. They used a developmental trajectory analysis to compare the relative effects of age of implantation independent of length of experience with the device. Their analysis demonstrated significantly better speech perception and language development outcomes for the earlier implanted groups. They argued that the size of the effect and the projected trajectory for the children in the earliest implanted group suggested that they would reach 6 years of age with near-normal language skills.

Lesinki-Scheidtat, Illg, Heerman, Bertram, and Lenarz (2004) reported that mean speech perception scores were significantly better for a group of 27 children who were implanted before the age of 12 months than for a group of 89 children who were implanted between 12 and 24 months. Nicholas and Geers (2006) assessed the language skills of 76 children who received a CI between 12 and 38 months of age and had used the implant for at least 7 months. They found that those children who were implanted at an earlier age exhibited significantly better spoken language at age 3.5 years. In such studies as these, however, there is a problem with isolating the effects of age of implantation from the effects of length of experience with the device. In some cases the younger implanted group had a longer period of use of the device—up to 18 months longer in some cases.

Dettman et al. (2007) retrospectively compared the outcomes for 11 children who had received their implants before the age of 12 months (mean age at implantation 0.88 years) and 36 who were implanted between

12 and 24 months (mean age at implantation, 1.6 years). They collected the children's scores on two or more yearly administrations of expressive and receptive language measures to calculate average rates of growth over time. They found a significant difference in favor of the early implant group for the average rate of language comprehension growth (1.12 versus 0.71) and for language reception (1.01 versus 0.68). The mean growth rates for the 11 profoundly deaf children who received CIs before the age of 12 months were consistent with the growth rates expected for hearing children (i.e., 1.00).

It would appear that expectations of faster and more age-appropriate language acquisition are increasingly appropriate for many deaf children who receive a CI at a young age. In the context of earlier identification through newborn hearing screening, the potential for early implantation to account for such outcomes for an increasing proportion of deaf children is very considerable. On the evidence of the prevailing situation in Australia, this confluence of circumstances is likely to account for a dramatic shift in both intervention strategies and educational options for deaf children. Indeed, it might be argued that, if one parameter is likely to account for a new landscape for the education of DHH children, it is the age at which they receive a CI and the associated improved probability of outcomes for spoken language acquisition as a consequence of that earlier implantation.

The Confluence of Early Identification and Cochlear Implantation: The Changing Profile of Hearing Loss

The Australian state of New South Wales provides a good illustration of the potential relationship between newborn screening and earlier cochlear implantation. The New South Wales UNHS program was introduced in 2002, and rapidly achieved effective coverage of more than 95% of all births across the state (New South Wales Health Department, 2006). Since that time, the average age of diagnosis of children with permanent bilateral hearing loss across the state has fallen from approximately 18 months to just 1.6 months (New South Wales Health Department, 2006).

Even before the introduction of newborn hearing screening, New South Wales had already made the availability of cochlear implantation an option for most, if not all, children identified with severe or profound hearing loss. Using figures from the largest CI program in the state, it is possible to examine the pattern of implantation for children up to the age of 24 months over an extended period spanning the introduction of newborn hearing screening. Statistics from the Sydney Cochlear Implant Centre for the period 1992–2005 indicate that 162 children under the age of 24 months received a CI through that Centre (accounting for more than

95% of the state's CIs). Figure 2–1 shows the relative ages at which those implants were received. The majority (80%) of children in that group were over 1 year of age, and the vast majority were closer to 2 years of age. Since the advent of UNHS, however, the average age of implantation has changed.

If those groups of children identified through UNHS and those identified by more traditional means are separated, then the trend becomes very apparent. Perhaps not surprisingly, there is an obvious trend toward much younger implantation among the children identified through UNHS. Figure 2–2 shows the relative proportions of children in each of the two groups—UNHS and non-UNHS—who were implanted at various ages. For the non-UNHS group, just 14% received their implant by the age of 12 months. However, for the UNHS group, 65% were implanted by the same age. The average age of first implantation for early identified children is falling to below 12 months of age, with the youngest recipient just 3 months of age.

This apparent nexus between earlier identification and earlier implantation is undoubtedly not unique to Australia. Indeed, over time, this situation has the potential to be the norm in many, if not most countries in the Western world—if indeed it is not already the case. Such a situation changes the profile of service delivery for deaf children and presents both challenges and questions to providers of habilitation and educational services for DHH children and, in particular, for researchers in this field. In the remainder of this chapter, some of those issues will be addressed.

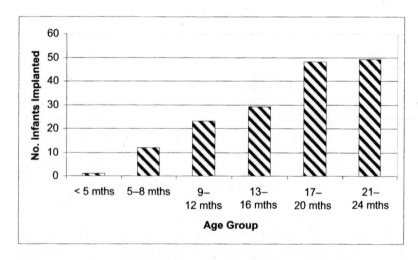

Figure 2–1. Infant children (< 24 months) implanted at Sydney Cochlear Implant Centre, 1992–2005 (n = 162).

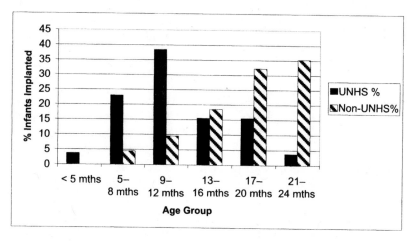

Figure 2–2. Percentage of infant children implanted by identification strategy: UNHS and non–UNHS.

Issues for Consideration/Research

Expanding the Evidence Base for the Benefits of Earlier Implantation

All of the studies so far considered in regard to the effect of age of implantation on speech communication and language outcomes fall short of the evidentiary standard of a randomized clinical trial. Given the strong theoretical arguments that now exist for earlier implantation, however, any research methodology that deliberately withheld the procedure from some children would undoubtedly be considered to be ethically unacceptable. By any description, cochlear implantation is now a mainstream procedure that is recognized as being both safe and effective—a distant position from the 1980s, when implantation was still viewed as an experimental procedure in many countries. Even if a randomized clinical trial were deemed to be ethical, it would be extremely difficult to organize, at least in the Australian context, where the prominence of cochlear implantation as a known clinical intervention makes it a high-priority option for almost all children who receive a diagnosis of significant hearing loss. Persuading a sufficiently large group of parents of matched children to be part of a trial that would delay implantation is inconceivable.

Accepting, therefore, the compelling theoretical logic for a "sensitive period" that would suggest the benefits of earlier implantation, several issues warrant consideration. The first goes to the basis for this perspective in theory, the second to the basis in evidence.

In regard to a theoretical sensitive period, as it might apply to cochlear implantation, there remains a valid question as to whether any such period that may apply to normal language processing and normal language acquisition would necessarily apply to the processing of speech and development of language through a cochlear implant. Without question, the neural signal produced by a CI is qualitatively different (and relatively degraded) to that received by hearing children. It may be that the processes that relate to the development of speech perception via normal peripheral and/or central auditory processing differ from those involved for perception through a cochlear implant. Such possibilities make the second issue all the more relevant and important; that is, the need for clearer empirical evidence of the actual benefits of earlier implantation.

Currently, the available empirical evidence base for earlier implantation remains incomplete and equivocal. As has been already noted, some of the research into the question of relative efficacy of earlier implantation has employed methods that fail to control for the possible effect of length of experience with implant as a factor independent of age of implantation. Some studies have, however, been designed to control for such possible confounding factors. Svirsky et al. (2004) and Tomblin et al. (2005) sought to isolate the effect of age of implantation on their language outcome measures by using developmental trajectory or growth curve analysis (i.e., plotting the curve representing the change in children's outcomes measures over time and/or considering the area under that curve or between the curves for two different groups of implanted children). Dettman et al. (2007) accounted for the effect of experience with the implant by considering each child's rate of progress on various language development outcome measures rather than net progress.

In each of these studies, however, a potentially confounding variable was either not identified and/or not controlled. Specifically, that variable was the difference between the earlier and later implanted groups in regard to their average age of diagnosis and first hearing-aid fitting. Dettman et al. (2007) acknowledged that their two groups differed significantly in regard to age of diagnosis and age of first hearing-aid fitting (i.e., 0.41 years for the early implanted group and group 0.92 years for the later implanted group). This issue warrants much closer attention. It may indeed be the case that the effect being attributed to earlier implantation is partially or wholly a function of the early identification process and of early hearing-aid fitting rather than being entirely a function of early implantation. As has already been discussed, there is an apparently robust effect of earlier identification for children with hearing loss (Yoshinaga-Itano, 2004).

As noted by Dettman et al. (2007), the most effective means of addressing such issues would be to undertake a study with a multifactorial design to account for a range of combinations of possible circumstances in regard to aiding and implantation, namely: (a) early aiding/early implantation; (b) late aiding/early implantation, and (c) early aiding/late implantation. Without the ability to ethically provide randomized assignment to such conditions, however, the likelihood of such studies being conducted is minimal, because serendipity is unlikely to provide for a quasi-experimental design with participatory groups of sufficient magnitude.

Another area in which the evidence base for earlier implantation remains open to alternative interpretation is in regard to the considerable intersubject variability in many of the studies. In the studies conducted by both Svirsky et al. (2004) and Dettman et al. (2007), for example, high-level outcomes were achieved by at least some children in the late-implanted groups whereas some children in the early-implanted groups showed lower-level or relatively poor outcomes. In the study by Svirsky et al., some children in the youngest implant group had language development curves that were more than 2 standard deviations below the mean, and a small group of children in each of the higher age groups had outcomes in the normal range or above. In the Dettman et al. study, individual results were not reported. However, the reported range in language growth rates for the children in the older (12–24 month) age group indicated that at least one child had a growth rate of 2.00 for language comprehension (i.e., double the rate that would be expected under normal developmental conditions for a child with normal hearing). The questions that must be answered in the light of such large variability relate to the conditions under which such high-level outcomes are achieved by some later-implanted children; and, whether such conditions are available or achievable for other children who come to implantation later?

Such questions suggest the need for more and better-controlled research. In the current environment, such research will clearly need to be quasi-experimental in nature. Nevertheless, there is a need to consider the control of a number of potentially confounding variables and to seek better and more sensitive language outcome measures across all of the domains of language, including syntactic, semantic, and pragmatic abilities, not just speech reception and global expressive and receptive abilities. It may be that differences exist between the language acquisition of children with implants and children with either normal hearing or alternative access modes for spoken language. At very least, a particular case can be made for the closer examination of lexical development by children with implants, given the predictive capacity of this measure in regard to literacy development (Kelly, 1996, 2003).

Apart from stimulating a particular line of research questions, the significant inter-subject variability that is observable among implant recipients (Geers, 2006) should give cause for thought in regard to the design of interventional models for early implanted children and, in particular, the potential difficulties associated with any "one size fits all" responses in regard to choice of language and communication modes and intervention strategies. This issue warrants particular attention.

Newborn Screening, Early Implantation, and Alternative Communication Approaches

For the vast majority of children who receive a CI at a young age, the therapeutic/educational environment of their family's choice is most commonly one in which a strong emphasis is placed on the development of spoken language exclusively through speaking and listening. Indeed, in New South Wales, such a response is almost universal—notably, even among signing deaf parents who have elected to have their deaf children receive implants. From a caregiver's perspective, such an emphasis on speaking and listening development is not surprising, given the motivations that underlie the decision to have a child receive an implant, namely to "help their child learn to talk, to understand speech, and participate in the family social environment and the world at large" (Moog & Geers, 2003, p. 124S).

For the most part, no form of signed communication is used in these programs. However, for some children in such programs, the response to what are often described as "poor outcomes" (i.e., lack of progress in spoken language development) may involve the introduction of some form of signed communication. Typically, however, such a response is much later in the child's development—usually much later than the sensitive period for language acquisition.

The obvious question here is whether a preference for exclusively auditory–oral intervention strategies as a first line of response is appropriate for *all* early identified/early implanted children. If not, what is the role for the use of signed communication in such a context, and how, when, and for whom, should it be introduced?

As noted earlier, the confluence of a number of drivers has seen the educational service-delivery profile for DHH children change significantly over the last 30 years. Nevertheless, a range of educational options continues to use sign language as an alternative first language (i.e., sign bilingual programs) or signed communication as a form of simultaneous augmentative communication to spoken language (i.e., total communication programs), particularly at the school-age level. Enrollments in these types of programs have, however, decreased steadily over a long period of time. There has also been an apparent rise in the age at which children are first entering such programs. A quick case-study example of a particular program's experiences may assist in establishing the developmental/educational point that is at issue here.

In recent years, an examination of the principles, practices, and outcomes of a sign language–based program for deaf children has occurred in New South Wales (Johnston, Leigh, & Foreman, 2002; Leigh & Johnston, 2004). The program operated from early intervention to the lower secondary school level. The investigations considered the outcomes of the program in regard to language and literacy development of the enrolled students. Notably, it was concluded that several factors appeared to be working against positive outcomes for many of the children in the program. Among a number of negative influences was the delayed entry into the program by many students and the associated delay in their ability to gain sufficient access to sign language communication to sustain their development of that language.

Under the curriculum model adopted by the program, it was intended that children entering the preschool section should have age-appropriate— or near age-appropriate—communication skills in sign language. Such skills were to have been developed through a program of early intervention, with families and children being exposed to extensive opportunities to develop those language skills. What was discovered, however, was that the majority of the children entered the program at preschool or school age—as opposed to the early-intervention level. Consequently, they (and their families) only began learning sign language at that time and were therefore unable to commence their preschool or school program with *any* sign language skills, much less with age-appropriate skills. By most definitions, they had missed the opportunity for engagement with the language during any sensitive or optimal period for language acquisition. It was concluded that, rather than being a population of learners who brought a viable language to the task of learning in school, the majority of children in the program were learning their primary language and communication skills *in* school. The effect of coming late to the learning of sign language was deemed to be related to a range of delayed language and educational outcomes experienced by those children.

If the argument that has been used for the introduction of earlier implantation in regard to ensuring access to language during a sensitive period is valid, then the argument for ensuring early engagement with sign language (or a least with some form of signed communication) by children who require that access is clearly just as valid. For many deaf children, including many who have CIs, a need exists for access to an alternative language and communication approach at a much earlier stage than during preschool or at the point of school entry. The assurance of a viable early communication mode is critical for both cognitive and linguistic development.

The point here is a simple one and returns to the central theme of this chapter: there remains a significant level of diversity among deaf children in terms of their communication and subsequent educational needs, including among those who receive CIs at an early age. For some deaf children, as for those just described, a clear indication of their need for access to sign language is proven. For others, circumstances may suggest the need for access to spoken language with augmentative communication in sign in a bimodal language situation. Toward this point, Marschark and Spencer (2003) noted "that no single method of communication is going to be appropriate for all deaf children" (p. 492). It would appear critical therefore to recognize that, even in the post-newborn hearing screening world of early cochlear implantation, there will likely continue to be children for whom the assumption of complete auditory access to spoken language is not going to be valid. Specifically, there will be children whose only viable access to social, cognitive, and language development will be via sign language, or at least through some form of manual supplement to their use of spoken language. For such children, waiting until they fail to achieve language and communication skills in spoken language before providing access to a viable communication mode will create a delay in their access to language and learning that will squander the real benefits offered by newborn hearing screening (early identification and early intervention). Given the potential benefits of very early identification and intervention, such a delay, it might be argued, is indefensible.

The literature on this issue is limited but unequivocal. It does not appear to matter what language a deaf child will ultimately develop; the consequences of early versus later intervention and provision of language learning opportunities *in that language* are significant. This fact is highlighted in the work of Yoshinaga-Itano and others (summarized by Yoshinaga-Itano, 2004), who found beneficial effects of early identification for both spoken and signed language acquisition. Mayberry and Eichen (1991) and Mayberry, Locke, and Kazmi (2002) argued from the evidence of early and late sign language and spoken language learners that the ability to learn either language "arises from a synergy between early brain development and language experience, and is seriously compromised when language is not experienced during early life" (Mayberry et al., 2002, p. 38). There is a clear message here in regard to the provision of early intervention services: The need remains for at least some deaf children, whether they have implants or not, to have access to communication alternatives other than exclusively auditory–oral communication. To this end, there is an associated need to ensure that all children are engaged as early as possible with the particular mode of communication that is fully accessible to them and best suits their needs. The issues at stake here are clear. The nature of the appropriate response to those issues is much less so.

Matching Communication Approaches to Individual Learners: Responding to Diversity

Given the continuing potential for diversity in the communication needs of DHH children—including those with CIs—several possible responses might ensure that all children have a fully accessible language and communication mode during their sensitive period for linguistic development. One possible response would be to routinely provide all newly identified children, whether they receive an implant or not, with access to both spoken and signed language. Such an approach could be argued to effectively ensure that all early identified children have the opportunity to develop their spoken language skills while, at the same time, ensuring that they have a fully accessible language and communication system as a basis for early (and continuing) cognitive development and for the important early processes of attachment and bonding. Another possible response would be to adopt a spoken language intervention model for most children but to seek to identify children for whom signed communication *might* be necessary to ensure their linguistic, social, cognitive, and emotional development and then to provide those children with a program focusing on the development of both spoken and signed language (or communication).

In the context of the increasing application of CIs and a field in which professionals show a very strong preference for intervention strategies that emphasize auditory information over visual sources of information for children with implants, these two possible alternatives focus attention on an inevitable question. Does early exposure to sign language limit or otherwise impact on spoken language development by deaf children, particularly those with CIs?

Typically, the argument underpinning the view that sign language use will limit spoken language development is that children with less-than-perfect auditory processing abilities will tend to focus almost exclusively on signs rather than the spoken language when both are available to them. Certainly, some evidence supports this view in the case of simultaneous exposure to speech and signed communication—at least in the case of older children. Hyde and Power (1992) found that for profoundly deaf students responding to simultaneous communication in speech and sign, the signed communication component was so robust in nature that the perception of the spoken components (listening and lip-reading) was virtually not required. They concluded that, under conditions of simultaneous communication, profoundly deaf students direct their attention primarily toward the signed component. Notably, however, they also found this effect to be less observable in children with lower levels of hearing loss and/or better speech perception abilities (i.e., as would be expected when the children concerned have access to audition through a cochlear implant).

In their extensive review of the literature, Spencer and Marschark (2003) concluded that most children tend to show improved outcomes in speech and language skill development after receiving a cochlear implant, regardless of type of language programming (auditory–oral, total communication, or cued speech), if there is sufficient exposure to and direct intervention in the development of the spoken language. They also concluded, however, that more rapid progress is typically made by children who are enrolled in one of the various forms of exclusively oral programs than by those enrolled in sign language programs.

Marschark (2001) considered the issue of coincidental learning of signed and spoken language in his extensive review of the literature on early communication and language development by deaf children. He concluded that "there is no evidence to suggest that the early use of gestures or signs by deaf children hampers their development of spoken English... nor is there any evidence that early introduction to spoken English negatively affects later acquisition of signing" (p. 15). From the specific perspective of children with CIs, however, the literature surrounding this issue is more limited in quantity and also in the rigor with which factors such as children's hearing levels and communication abilities prior to implantation have been controlled. There is also, perhaps not surprisingly, very little literature that addresses this issue from the perspective of children who were implanted at very young ages.

In some studies that have sought to compare outcomes for children with implants in exclusively oral programs (auditory–oral or auditory–verbal) with those for children for whom there is exposure to signed language (or communication), it has been found that children in oral programs make faster progress in their development of both speech perception (Dawson, McKay, Busby, Grayden, & Clark, 2000; Miyamoto, Kirk, Svirsky, & Sehgal; 1999; Osberger, Fisher, Zimmerman-Phillips, Geier, & Barker, 1998) and speech intelligibility (Miyamoto et al., 1999; Osberger, et al., 1994; Svirsky, Sloan, Caldwell, & Miyamoto, 2000; Tobey et al., 2000). Geers, Spehar, and Sedey (2002) studied 27 children (aged 8–9 years) who had received an implant as young children and found that placement in a program that provided for both signed and spoken communication development did not preclude the children's development of spoken language skills. The most significant issue was not their exposure to two modes of communication but the quality of their spoken language learning environment. Moog and Geers (2003) noted that spoken language acquisition is most significantly related to the availability of "an educational environment that provides a consistent emphasis on developing speech, auditory, and spoken language skills" (p. 124S).

On the basis of the available evidence (see Marschark, 2001; Spencer & Marschark, 2003 for more detailed reviews), a case could certainly be made for a model of intervention for young, early identified and implanted children that includes the use of signed and spoken language (or at least signed communication)—for all or at least some children. Given the strong propensity in the field to avoid any use of signed communication with young children with implants, however, there is a need to add to the available research evidence on which the potential merits of dual language and communication routes for children with CIs might be fairly judged. Clearly, the question of linguistic and cognitive outcomes associated with the simultaneous development of both spoken and signed language by very young deaf children with CIs remains very much open to investigation. In particular, the efficacy of a fully bilingual approach to language acquisition for deaf children who may otherwise have good access to spoken language communication will need to be empirically demonstrated if it is to be advocated as a viable educational approach for *all* children.

Researching Alternative Language Paradigms

As Marschark (2001) noted, no collective evidence in the literature yet suggests that signed communication (or any other form of visual communication for that matter) will *prevent* the development of oral language and communication by children with hearing loss, including those who receive CIs. Nevertheless, it is clear that the process of developing speech communication and spoken language through the use of a CI requires focused therapy and practice, and that faster progress in these areas tends to be made by children in oral rather than in sign language programs (see above and also Spencer & Marschark, 2003). In this regard, there remains a question as to how much exposure to, and practice with, spoken language is necessary for children with implants to *optimally* benefit from the device. Unlike children with normal hearing, it may be that, for children with CIs, there is some potential limitation of the rate or ultimate outcomes available in their acquisition of spoken language as a result of their splitting their "time on task" in the language learning process with another language. Although acquisition of two languages is clearly possible, the outcomes in neither may be optimal relative to those that may be achieved in a monolingual language learning situation where greater access to and experience with spoken language is available.

Spencer and Marschark (2003) noted that the amount of spoken language exposure and practice necessary for children to benefit optimally from a CI remains unknown. Clearly, if that threshold is unknown, then the impact of dividing exposure and attention between a signed and a spoken language on the achievement of that threshold also remains unknown. In addressing the latter question, evidence from spoken language bilingualism— where unequivocal access to both languages is typically assured from birth for children with normal hearing—cannot be taken as a reliable indicator of likely outcomes for children with CIs in environments where both signed and spoken language are used. Rather, specific research into the circumstances of DHH children with CIs in sign bilingual or multiple-communication-mode environments is required.

As already noted in regard to other research issues, it would be unethical for research into this issue to be pursued through randomized assignment of children with CIs to monolingual or bilingual language learning circumstances. Rather, such investigations must be quasi-experimental in nature and conducted in situations, for example, that permit the comparison of outcomes for children with CIs whose families actively chose a bilingual educational option (i.e., spoken language—through speech and audition—and sign language) or bimodal option (simultaneous communication) with matched children in a monolingual environment. To avoid confounding issues, children who were enrolled in a bilingual or bimodal program because of their real or potential difficulties in accessing spoken language communication would need to be excluded. The groups of particular interest in such research are pairs of children who have patently similar spoken language access via their implants but who are nevertheless pursuing alternative (bilingual/bimodal versus monolingual) paths to language acquisition.

Appropriate quasi-experimental research designs with groups of sufficient sizes would provide the opportunity to address several important questions. Specifically, what are the relative short- and long-term outcomes for children with CIs who receive their early language experiences and educational interventions in a monolingual (spoken language) environment as opposed to those who receive their early experiences in a bilingual (signed and spoken language) environment? The dependent variables of interest in such a study would not only be in the area of speech processing and language acquisition but would also include cognitive and social-emotional outcomes—both short- and long-term.

One area that clearly warrants consideration in any such investigation is that of memory processes (see Dye, Hauser, & Bavelier, this volume; Pisoni et al., this volume, for further discussion of these issues). How are the encoding, rehearsal, storage, and retrieval of information impacted by the use of two communication modalities and/or two language systems by young deaf children? Specifically in regard to lexical development and lexical access processes, how does the opportunity to access language visually impact the breadth and depth of lexical development by young deaf children? Do children who experience dual language input demonstrate differences in lexical retrieval processes? How do children with implants access the meaning of a spoken word? Is there any reason to believe that these processes are affected by access to a visual communication system? Such differences may be subtle but may indeed prove to be significant in the longer term.

Another area of interest is metalinguistic ability (see Hauser, Lukomski, & Hillman, this volume; Pisoni et al., this volume). Do children who have access to more than one communication and language system demonstrate any different abilities in regard to their capacity to monitor their own language abilities as symbolic and structured processes (see Marschark & Wauters, this volume)? These abilities are of particular interest because of their identification in the literature as being a strong predictor of early reading success (Strassman, 1997). It can only be through controlled investigation of such issues that the question of relative benefits and/or relative detriments of access to one or two languages and/or modes of communication could be answered.

Providing for Alternatives

As already outlined in detail, the need to ensure that all children have a fully accessible language and communication mode during the sensitive period for linguistic development suggests that at least two possible strategic responses might be considered: (a) a bilingual approach for all children or (b) a targeted dual language (or at least dual communication) approach for those children who are deemed at risk of failing to achieve optimal spoken language outcomes. Pragmatically, the latter approach seems much more likely to be viable given that the vast majority of children who receive CIs early are already enrolled in programs using auditory oral communication and that a strong propensity exists within such programs to de-emphasize sources of visual information unless an evidence-based strategy suggests otherwise.

The need for further evidence of the potentially positive contribution of signed communication to assuring positive language outcomes for at least some children has already been discussed. If the second approach is to be viable, it clearly also depends on the availability of alternative strategies and pathways for different children. There is certainly nothing new in the notion of different options being available for deaf children at any level of education. The challenge in such an approach, however, is in the need to develop effective strategies for identifying which option is best for which children. Such decision-making must be evidence-based. Given the arguments already advanced for a sensitive period for language acquisition and the relative cognitive benefits of early effective communication (see Pisoni et al., this volume), it would appear critical to ensure that such decision-making occurs at the earliest possible time. Currently, as already indicated, too many children who require an alternative language or mode of communication are identified too late and only by default—that is, after their unsuccessful engagement with a program focusing exclusively on spoken language development.

A range of factors *may* account for potential difficulties with exclusively auditory access to communication and for less than optimal outcomes for spoken-language children who receive a cochlear implant. In children with auditory neuropathy, for example, speech discrimination abilities and subsequent speech and language development outcomes may be less than optimal. Increasingly, the use of specialized electrophysiologic assessment techniques is delivering improved capacity to identify specific neuropathies and to predict which children will likely have the greatest difficulty with accessing spoken language communication, with or without a cochlear implant. A need exists for very early and consistent diagnosis of these circumstances so that all early identified children gain maximal access to language and communication opportunities—whether exclusively through hearing devices and spoken language or through bimodal or bilingual language input.

Space constraints prohibit consideration of the full range of factors accounting for variation in auditory processing ability in DHH children and the various potential diagnostic strategies. There is, however, a developing literature around the issue of differential identification of various hearing losses and their potential impacts on spoken language development in children. Gardner-Berry, Gibson, and Sanli (2005), for example, have discussed the diagnoses of auditory neuropathy and the differential diagnosis of auditory neuropathy and "auditory dys-synchrony." They argued that electrophysiologic evaluation allows for the early differential diagnosis of these conditions. Their experience suggests that such diagnostic information should be considered in counselling families about potential language and communication development outcomes for their deaf children and in making decisions about alternative or augmentative communication approaches that may need to be provided.

Gardner-Berry et al. noted that, by using a combination of electrophysiologic diagnostic tests (i.e., the combined use of electrocochleography, auditory brainstem response to acoustic stimuli, and auditory brainstem response to electrical stimuli) in conjunction with computed tomography (CT) and magnetic resonance imaging (MRI) scans and some specific functional evaluations, it is possible to better identify children's potential for successful cochlear implantation and outcomes for speech and spoken language development. Specifically, they have described four categories of deaf children based on each group's potential for development of speech discrimination ability and subsequent spoken language development following cochlear implantation. These groups are children with (a) *sensory hearing loss* (i.e., primarily a cochlear pathology)—with high potential for positive outcomes, (b) *auditory dys-synchrony* (believed to be primarily a peripheral or cochlear pathology)—with similarly high potential for positive outcomes, (c) *auditory neuropathy* (consistent with auditory nerve pathology)—with low potential for positive outcomes, and (d) *brainstem auditory neuropathy* (consistent with auditory brainstem pathology)—with low potential for positive outcomes. In identifying these categories and advocating such careful consideration of outcome potentials, Gardner-Berry et al. noted that, for families of deaf children, "knowing what can be realistically expected beforehand helps them to weigh the risks versus the benefits [of cochlear implantation] and ensures that the most appropriate type of intervention is in place for optimal language development" (p. 31).

The best possible analysis of children's audiologic status is a critical consideration in determining which children would benefit from exposure to an alternative language and/or mode of communication in early intervention. In addition, a range of other factors should be considered in determining a child's potential need or preference for access to alternative communication approaches. Not least among such issues are the family's language background and linguistic preference. Without going into the full discussion of such factors, the important point here is that all likely indicators must be considered at the earliest possible stage so that families are in a position to make a decision about their child's particular pathway. Ensuring that families have the best possible information on which to base such a decision is critical.

Summary and Implications

Developments in a number of related fields are providing greater opportunities for deaf children to access spoken language than at any time in history. Of particular note have been the advent of UNHS and the increasing accessibility of cochlear implantation. Independently, each of these developments offers considerable potential advantages for deaf children. In a succession of studies, children identified through UNHS within the first weeks of life have been shown to have superior development on a wide range of measures, both linguistic and social-emotional, when compared with children whose hearing loss was identified at later ages. Similarly, the literature provides compelling evidence of an improved rate and level of spoken language development for most children with severe to profound sensory-neural deafness who receive a cochlear implant, provided that they receive consistent input in spoken language.

As positive as the potential benefits of cochlear implantation may be, there continues to be significant variability in outcomes among children who receive implants. Numerous factors have been associated with this variability. The literature considered in this chapter—particularly that examining the impacts of very early implantation—suggests that age of implantation warrants particular attention as a significant source of the variance in outcomes. This view is reinforced, at least in theory, when the considerable theoretical and evidence-based support for the concept of an optimal (or sensitive) period for development of speech perception abilities and other language-related abilities in very early infancy is also considered.

Given the increasing availability of UNHS and the strong indications of improved outcomes associated with earlier cochlear implantation, the confluence of these two developments represents a substantial change in the governing paradigm for early intervention and education for deaf children. Indeed, it has been argued in this chapter that expectations of much faster and more age-appropriate language acquisition are increasingly appropriate for most children who have their hearing loss identified very early in life and receive a CI at a very early stage of development. Nevertheless, it has also been noted that more research is required to confirm the real nature of the relationship between earlier implantation and improved linguistic and other developmental outcomes.

Regardless of the overall positive effects associated with earlier identification and early implantation, there will continue to be children for whom the assumption of complete access to spoken language is not going to be valid. As has historically been the case, diversity of communication needs among DHH children continues to be a defining feature of this population. For some DHH children—albeit perhaps a decreasing minority—the most viable access to social, cognitive, and language development will continue to be via sign language or some form of manual supplement to their use of spoken language. An important issue addressed in this chapter is that, for such children, waiting until they fail to achieve language and communication skills in spoken language before providing access to such an alternative communication mode will create a delay in access to language and learning that will squander the benefits offered by newborn hearing screening and early identification of their of hearing loss.

The literature on this issue is unequivocal. Regardless of the language that a deaf child will ultimately develop, the consequences of early versus later intervention and the provision of language learning opportunities in that language are significant. This suggests the need to address the question of accessibility of spoken language communication at the earliest possible stage for all children, including those who receive CIs early in their development. Specifically, this chapter has argued for the merits of an alternative approach to early intervention. This approach seeks to identify, at the earliest possible stage, those children for whom spoken communication may not be entirely accessible and for whom signed communication will likely be necessary to ensure their linguistic, social, cognitive, and emotional development; it then seeks to provide those children with a program focusing on the development of both spoken and signed language (or communication).

Having argued the merits of a dual language (or communication) approach with at least some deaf children, it has also been noted in this chapter that there remains an open question as to how much engagement with spoken language use and practice is necessary or sufficient for a children with a CI to optimally benefit from the use of the device. In this regard, it has been argued that a need exists for research into the specific circumstances of DHH children with CIs who are in sign-bilingual or simultaneous communication environments in order to identify the relative impacts of such dual exposure on their linguistic outcomes. Such research, it is argued, will provide the opportunity to address several important questions. Specifically, what are the relative short- and long-term outcomes for children with CIs who receive their early language experiences and educational interventions in a monolingual (spoken language) environment as opposed to those who receive their early experiences in a bilingual (signed and spoken language) environment? The dependent variables of interest in such studies should not be only in the area of speech processing and language acquisition but should also include cognitive and social-emotional outcomes—both short- and long-term.

In the current zeitgeist, in which there is strong advocacy for children who receive CIs to use exclusively auditory–oral communication, any approach that seeks to use different combinations of spoken and signed language for some children will need to have some particular characteristics. Those characteristics include:

- the provision of clear and precise information to ensure parents' understanding of the indications for successful outcomes associated with cochlear implantation;
- close collaboration between educational, audiologic, and medical professionals to identify all indications (and any contraindications) of potential for effective access to spoken language;
- clear and precise information provision to ensure the parents' understanding of the development processes for spoken and signed languages, and, in particular, existing and emerging research evidence regarding the relative impact of simultaneous development of spoken and signed languages (as suggested earlier);
- a commitment to an inclusive educational environment in which the use of sign language (by at least some children) is recognized and valued; and
- a commitment to the provision of conditions that are conducive to the development of the language or languages targeted for particular children's development. In the case of spoken language, this means a consistent emphasis on developing speech, auditory, and spoken language skills—whether or not there is simultaneous development of sign language skills.

In conclusion, it is perhaps important to note again that, even within the context of such paradigm-changing developments as UNHS and very early cochlear implantation, the continuing diversity among the population of DHH children ensures continuing heterogeneous outcomes. In the context of this continuing diversity, every new development places new demands upon service delivery systems, available pedagogies and, most notably, researchers to account for the differential effects of those developments across children. The challenge to respond to those demands must be accepted if the needs of all deaf children are to be accounted for effectively.

References

Apuzzo, M., & Yoshinaga-Itano, C. (1995). Early identification of infants with significant hearing loss and the Minnesota Child Development Inventory. *Seminars in Hearing, 16*(2), 124–139.

Blamey, P., & Sarant, J. (2000). Speech perception and language criteria for paediatric cochlear implant candidature. *Audiology and Neuro-Otology, 7,* 114–121.

Connor, C. M., Hieber, S., Arts, H. A., & Zwolan, T. A. (2000). Speech, vocabulary, and the education of children using cochlear implants: Oral or total communication. *Journal of Speech, Language, and Hearing Research, 43,* 1185–1204.

Conrad, R., & Weiskrantz, B. C. (1981). On the cognitive ability of deaf children with deaf parents. *American Annals of the Deaf, 126,* 995–1003.

Dawson, P. McKay, C., Busby, P., Grayden, D., & Clark, G. (2000). Electrode discrimination and speech perception in young children using cochlear implants. *Ear and Hearing, 21*(6), 597–607.

DeCasper, A. J., & Fifer, W. P. (1980). Of human bonding: Newborns prefer their mothers' voices. *Science, 208*(4448), 1174–1176.

Dettman, S. J., Pinder, D., Briggs, R. J. S., Dowell, R. C., & Leigh, J. R. (2007). Communication development in children who receive the cochlear implant younger than 12 months: Risks versus benefits. *Ear and Hearing, 28*(2), 11S–17S.

Gardner-Berry, K., Gibson, W. P., & Sanli, H. (2005). Pre-operative testing of patients with neuropathy or dys-synchrony. *The Hearing Journal, 58*(11), 24–31.

Geers, A. E. (2002). Factors affecting the development of speech, language, and literacy in children with early cochlear implantation. *Language, Speech, and Hearing Services in the Schools, 33,* 172–183.

Geers, A. E. (2003). Predictors of reading skill development in children with early cochlear implantation. *Ear and Hearing, 24,* 59S–68S.

Geers, A. E. (2006). Factors influencing spoken language outcomes in children following early cochlear implantation. *Advances in Oto-Rhino-Laryngology, 64,* 50–65.

Geers, A. E., Brenner, C., & Davidson, L. S. (2003). Factors associated with development of speech perception skills in children implanted by age five. *Ear and Hearing, 24,* 24S–35S.

Geers, A. E., Brenner, C., Nicholas, J., Uchanski, R., Tye-Murray, N., & Tobey, E. (2002). Rehabilitation factors contributing to implant benefit in children. *Annals of Otolaryngology, Rhinology, and Laryngology, 111,* 127–130.

Geers, A. E., Nicholas, J. G., & Sedey, A. L. (2003). Language skills of children with early cochlear implantation. *Ear and Hearing, 24,* 46S–58S.

Geers, A., Spehar, B., & Sedey, A. (2002). Use of speech by children from total communication programs who wear cochlear implants. *American Journal of Speech–Language Pathology, 11,* 50–58.

Hammes, D. M., Novak, M. A., Rotz, L. A., Willis, M., Edmondson, D. M., & Thomas, J. F. (2002). Early identification and cochlear implantation: Critical factors for spoken language development. *Annals of Otology, Rhinology, and Laryngology—Supplement, 189,* 74–78.

Holt, R. F., & Kirk, K. I. (2005). Speech and language development in cognitively delayed children with cochlear implants. *Ear and Hearing, 26*(2), 132–148.

Hyde, M. B., & Power, D. J. (1992). The receptive communication abilities of deaf students under oral, manual, and combined methods. *American Annals of the Deaf, 137,* 389–398.

Johnston, T., Leigh, G., & Foreman, P. (2002). The implementation of the principles of sign bilingualism in a self-described sign bilingual program: Implications for the evaluation of language outcomes. *Australian Journal of Education of the Deaf, 8,* 38–46.

Karchmer, M. A., & Mitchell, R. E. (2003). Demographic and achievement characteristics of deaf and hard-of-hearing students. In M. Marschark & P. E. Spencer (Eds.), *Oxford handbook of deaf studies, language, and education* (pp. 21–37). New York: Oxford University Press.

Karchmer, M. A., & Trybus, R. J. (1977). *Who are the deaf children in "mainstream" programs? (Series R, No. 4).* Washington, DC: Gallaudet College, Office of Demographic Studies.

Kelly, L. (1996). The interaction of syntactic competence and vocabulary during reading by deaf students. *Journal of Deaf Studies and Deaf Education, 1,* 75–90.

Kelly, L. (2003). Considerations for designing practice for deaf readers. *Journal of Deaf Studies and Deaf Education, 8,* 171–186.

Khan, S., Edwards, L., & Langdon, D. (2005). The cognition and behaviour of children with cochlear implants, children with hearing aids and their hearing peers: A comparison *Audiology and Neuro-otology, 10,* 117–126.

Kirk, K., Miyamoto, R., Lento, C., Ying, E., O'Neill, T., & Fears, B. (2002). Effects of age at implantation in young children. *Annals of Otology, Rhinology and Laryngology, 111,* 69–73.

Kral, A., & Tillein, J. (2006). Brain plasticity under cochlear implant stimulation. *Advances in Oto-Rhino-Laryngology. 64,* 89–108.

Leigh, G., & Johnston, T. (2004). First language learning in a sign bilingual program: An Australian study. *NTID Research Bulletin, 9*(2/3), 1–5.

Lesinski-Schiedat, A., Illg, A., Heermann, R., Bertram, B., & Lenarz, T. (2004). Paediatric cochlear implantation in the first and second year of life: A comparative study. *Cochlear Implants International, 5,* 146–154.

Marschark, M. (2001). *Language development in children who are deaf: A research synthesis.* Alexandria, VA: National Association of State Directors of Special Education.

Marschark, M., & Spencer, P. (2003). Epilogue—What we know, what we don't know, and what we should know. In M. Marschark & P. Spencer (Eds.), *Oxford handbook of deaf studies, language, and education* (pp. 491–494). New York: Oxford University Press.

Mayberry, R. I., & Eichen, E. B. (1991). The long–lasting advantage of learning sign language in childhood: Another look at the critical period for language acquisition. *Journal of Memory and Language, 30,* 486–512.

Mayberry, R. I., & Locke, E. (2003). Age constraints on first versus second language acquisition: Evidence for linguistic plasticity and epigenesis. *Brain and Language, 87,* 369–384.

Mayberry, R. I., Locke, E., & Kazmi, H. (2002). Linguistic ability and early language exposure. *Nature, 417,* 38.

Mehler, J., Bertoncini, J., & Barriere, M. (1978). Infant recognition of mother's voice. *Perception, 7*(5), 491–497.

Miyamoto, R., Kirk, K., Svirsky, M., & Sehgal, S. (1999). Communication skills in pediatric cochlear implant recipients. *Acta Otolaryngologica, 119,* 219–224.

Moog, J. S., & Geers, A. E. (2003). Epilogue: Major findings, conclusions and implications for deaf education. *Ear and Hearing, 24,* 121S–125S.

Moon, C., Cooper, R. P., & Fifer, W. P. (1993). Two-day-olds prefer their native language. *Infant Behavior and Development, 16*(4), 495–500.

New South Wales Health Department (2006). Ministerial standing committee on hearing annual report 2004–2005. Retrieved November 24, 2006, from http://www.health.nsw.gov.au/hearing/pdf/annual_report.pdf

Nicholas, J., & Geers, A. E. (2006). Effects of early auditory experience on the spoken language of deaf children at 3 years of age. *Ear and Hearing, 27,* 286–298.

Osberger, M., Fisher, L., Zimmerman-Phillips, L., Geier, L., & Barker, M. (1998). Speech recognition performance of older children with cochlear implants. *American Journal of Otology, 19,* 152–175.

Osberger, M., Robbins, A., Todd, S., & Riley, A. (1994). Speech intelligibility of children with cochlear implants. *Volta Review, 96*(5), 169–180.

Pisoni, David B. (2000). Cognitive factors and cochlear implants: Some thoughts on perception, learning, and memory in speech perception. *Ear and Hearing, 21*(1), 70–78.

Pressman, L., Pipp-Siegel, S., Yoshinaga-Itano, C., & Deas, A. (1999). The relation of sensitivity to child expressive language gain in deaf and hard-of-hearing children whose caregivers are hearing. *Journal of Deaf Studies and Deaf Education, 4,* 294–304.

Pressman, L., Pipp-Siegel, S., Yoshinaga-Itano, C., Kubicek, L., & Emde, R. N. (2000). A comparison of the links between emotional availability and language gain in young children with and without hearing loss. *The Volta Review, 100,* 251–278.

Ruben, R. J. (1997). A time frame of critical/sensitive periods of language development. *Acta Otolaryngologica, 117,* 202–205.

Sharma, A., Dorman, M. F., and Spahr, A. J. (2002). A sensitive period for the development of the central auditory system in children with cochlear implants: Implications for age of implantation. *Ear and Hearing, 23,* 532–539.

Spencer, P. E., & Marschark, M. (2003). Cochlear implants: Issues and implications. In M. Marschark & P. E. Spencer (Eds.), *Oxford handbook of deaf studies, language, and education* (pp. 434–448). New York: Oxford University Press.

Stokoe, W. C. (1960/2005). *Sign language structure: An outline of the visual communication systems of the American deaf. Studies in Linguistics: Occasional Papers 8.* Buffalo, NY: University of Buffalo, Department of Anthropology and Linguistics. Reprinted in *Journal of Deaf Studies and Deaf Education, 10,* 3–37.

Strassman, B. K. (1997). Metacognition and reading in children who are deaf: A review of the research. *Journal of Deaf Studies and Deaf Education, 2*(3), 140–149.

Svirsky, M., Sloan, R., Caldwell, M., & Miyamoto, R. (2000). Speech intelligibility of prelingually deaf children with multichannel cochlear implants. *Annals of Otology, Rhinology, and Laryngology (Suppl. 185), 109*(12), 123–125.

Svirsky, M., Robbins, A., Iler-Kirk, K., Pisoni, D., & Miyamoto, R. (2000). Language development in profoundly deaf children with cochlear implants. *Psychological Science, 11*, 153–158.

Svirsky, M. A., Teoh, S-W., & Neuberger, H. (2004). Development of language and speech perception in congenitally, profoundly deaf children as a function of age at cochlear implantation. *Audiology and Neuro-otology, 9*, 224–233.

Sydney Cochlear Implant Centre. (2006). Sydney Cochlear Implant Centre. Retrieved December 1, 2006, from http://www.scic.nsw.gov.au/showarticle. asp?faq=2andfldAuto=43andheader=header4

Tobey, E. A., Geers, A. E., Brenner, C., Altuna, D., & Gabbert, G. (2003). Factors associated with development of speech production skills in children implanted by age five. *Ear and Hearing, 24*, 36S–45S.

Tobey, E., Geers, A., Douek, B., Perrin, J., Skillet, R., Brenner, C., & Toretta, G. (2000). Factors associated with speech intelligibility in children with cochlear implants. *Annals of Otology, Rhinology, and Laryngology (Suppl. 185), 109*(12), 28–30.

Tomblin, J. B., Baker, B. A., Spencer, L. J., Zhang, X, & Gantz, B. J. (2005). The effect of age at cochlear implant initial stimulation on expressive language growth in infants and toddlers. *Journal of Speech, Hearing, and Language Research, 48*, 853–867.

Tomblin, J. B., Spencer, L., Flock, S., Tyler, R., & Gantz, B. (1999). A comparison of language achievement in children with cochlear implants and children using hearing aids. *Journal of Speech, Language, and Hearing Research, 42*, 497–511.

Werker, J. F., & Tees, R. C. (2005). Speech perception as a window for understanding plasticity and commitment in language systems of the brain. *Developmental Psychobiology, 46*(3), 233–251.

Yoshinaga-Itano, C. (2004). From screening to early identification and intervention: Discovering predictors to successful outcomes for children with significant hearing loss. In D. Power & G. Leigh (Eds.), *Educating deaf students: Global perspectives* (pp. 69–84). Washington, DC: Gallaudet University Press.

Yoshinaga-Itano, C., Coulter, D., & Thomson, V. (2000). The Colorado Hearing Screening Program: Effects on speech and language for children with hearing loss. *Journal of Perinatology (Supplement), 20*(8), S132–142.

Yoshinaga-Itano, C., Sedey, A., Coulter, D., & Mehl, A. (1998). Language of early- and later-identified children with hearing loss. *Pediatrics, 102*, 1161–1171.

Chapter 3

Efficacy and Effectiveness of Cochlear Implants in Deaf Children

David B. Pisoni, Christopher M. Conway, William G. Kronenberger, David L. Horn, Jennifer Karpicke, and Shirley C. Henning

One direction of our research program at the Indiana University School of Medicine has been concerned with understanding the large individual differences in speech and language outcomes in deaf children who have received cochlear implants (CIs). We are interested in explaining and predicting the enormous variability observed in a wide range of conventional measures of speech and language following cochlear implantation. The degree of variation in clinical outcome measures is enormous and is a robust finding observed universally at all implant centers around the world. The variability observed in outcome and benefit following cochlear implantation remains a significant problem for both clinicians and researchers alike. Why do some profoundly deaf children do so well with their CIs, and why do other children do more poorly? The problem of individual differences in outcome and benefit is a major clinical issue in the field, one which has been addressed repeatedly over the years by the two earlier National Institutes of Health (NIH) Consensus Conferences on Cochlear Implants (1988, 1995).

Despite the importance of understanding and explaining variability and individual differences following CI, very little solid progress has been made in identifying the neurobiologic substrates and neurocognitive factors that are responsible for individual variation in speech and language outcomes. Knowledge and understanding of these factors and the information processing subsystems that are affected by profound deafness and language delay is critical for diagnosis, prediction, and treatment and for explaining why some children do poorly with their CIs. Several reasons can be proposed for the unsatisfactory state of affairs concerning variability and individual differences.

First, most of the people who work in the field of hearing impairment and CIs are clinicians. The CI surgeons, audiologists, and speech-language pathologists are primarily interested in the medical care of the patient and documenting the efficacy of CIs as a medical treatment for profound deafness. For them, individual differences and variability in speech and language outcome are viewed as a source of undesirable noise, a "nuisance variable" so to speak, that must be reduced or eliminated in order to reveal the true underlying benefits of cochlear implantation. When a child does well with her CI, the family, clinical team, teachers, and other professionals are all delighted with the outcome. However, when a child does poorly with an implant, the clinical team is at a loss to explain the anomaly or suggest alternatives about what to do next. At present, given the nature of the clinical research carried out on CIs, it is unclear even how to approach the study of individual differences in this clinical population. What factors are responsible for the individual differences in outcome and benefit? What behavioral and neurocognitive domains should be investigated? What kinds of new measures should be obtained? What theoretical approach should be adopted to study this problem?

Second, the conventional battery of speech and language tests that is routinely administered to measure clinical outcome and benefit was developed by the CI manufacturers to establish efficacy as part of the clinical trials for U.S. Food and Drug Administration (FDA) approval. These behavioral tests were never designed to measure individual differences or assess variability in outcome. Moreover, and perhaps more importantly, the foundational assumptions and theoretical framework underlying the selection and use of the conventional speech and language outcome measures—the idea that speech perception and spoken language processing recruit formal rules and use context-free symbolic representations—is now being seriously questioned and undermined (see Gaskell, 2007). The formalist assumption that every child comes up with the same grammar of language despite vastly different individual developmental histories has been questioned in recent years in light of new knowledge about brain structure and function and the development of adaptive self-organizing systems like speech and language. The old static views of language as an idealized homogeneous context-free system of abstract linguistic knowledge are now being replaced by new conceptions linking mind, body, and world together in a complex interactive system (Clark, 1997).

Third, because the primary focus of most of the research on CIs has been clinical in nature—that is, demonstrating efficacy and safety and establishing that CIs work well under quiet testing conditions in the clinic or research laboratory—the typical battery of conventional behavioral tests only provides measures of the final "product" or "end-point" of a long series of neural and neurocognitive processes. All of the current outcome measures routinely used in the clinic and research laboratory rely on accuracy and percent-correct as the primary dependent variable to assess performance and document benefit following cochlear implantation. Unfortunately, end-point measures of performance, although they have strong face validity and have been used successfully to demonstrate efficacy of CIs, are fundamentally unable to measure and assess the basic underlying elementary information processing variables like speed, capacity, learning and memory, inhibition, attention, cognitive control, and the neurocognitive operations that are used in performing the specific individual behavioral tasks used to assess the benefits of CIs.

In addition, because the field of clinical audiology is an applied science drawing knowledge and methods from several different disciplines, no common integrated theoretical framework motivates the choice of specific outcome measures and tests, interprets the results and findings, provides explanations, or makes predictions. Without the benefit of a well-defined conceptual framework and additional theoretically motivated "process-based" measures of performance, it is impossible to gain any new knowledge about the underlying neural and neurocognitive factors that are responsible for the observed variability in the traditional audiologic outcome measures of performance. Without knowing what factors are responsible for the individual differences and understanding the basis for variation in performance, it is difficult to motivate and select a specific approach to habilitation and therapy after cochlear implantation. Moreover, all of the clinical research on CIs has been primarily descriptive in nature and not experimentally motivated by hypothesis-testing or specific predictions that would lead to understanding and explanation of process and mechanism. The bulk of CI research has focused on medical, demographic, and educational factors, not the underlying neurobiologic and neurocognitive processes that link brain and behavior.

Given what we know about population variability in biology, it is very likely that deaf children who are performing poorly with their CIs are a heterogeneous group that differ in numerous ways from each other, reflecting dysfunction of multiple processing systems associated with deafness and language delays (see Leigh, this volume). Adopting a common, uniform approach to assessment, therapy, and habilitation after cochlear implantation will be inadequate to accommodate a wide range of individual differences and subtypes in outcome and benefit. Without knowing how and why poorer performers differ from each other and from the exceptionally good performers, as well as typically developing hearing children, it is difficult to establish realistic goals and generate expectations for treatment and intervention following implantation. Moreover, it is unlikely that an individual child will be able to achieve optimal benefits from her implant without knowing about the problems and what specific neurocognitive domains are involved.

Deaf Children as a "Model System" for Development

Two reasons motivate our interest in studying deaf children with CIs. The first is clinical in nature. Cochlear implants provide a medical treatment for profound deafness and have been shown to facilitate the development of spoken language. Without some kind of medical or behavioral intervention, profoundly deaf children will not learn language normally from caretakers in their surrounding environment and will be unable to achieve their full intellectual potential as productive members of society. No one argues with this reason for studying deaf children. Sensory deprivation is a significant neurodevelopmental problem that has lasting and permanent effects on brain development and intellectual achievement (Riesen, 1975). A profound hearing loss at birth is viewed by hearing people as a clinically significant sensory disability, an impairment that affects cognitive, social, and intellectual development. Almost all of the clinical research on CIs has been concerned with device efficacy; that is, demonstrating that CIs work and provide benefit to profoundly deaf children and adults. In contrast, very little research has been devoted to effectiveness, specifically, to understanding the reasons for the enormous variability in outcome and benefit following implantation.

When considering the *efficacy* of a treatment or intervention, we mean the power to produce a desired effect in an individual; that is, does a CI work and provide benefit to a profoundly deaf person? In contrast, when considering the *effectiveness* of a treatment or intervention, we mean actually producing the expected effect; that is, does a CI work equally well and provide the desired benefit in everyone who is a candidate and receives a CI?

A second major reason for our interest in studying deaf children with CIs is more basic in nature, in terms of theoretical implications for gaining fundamental new knowledge about learning, development, and neural plasticity. Deaf children with CIs represent a unique and unusual clinical population, because they provide an opportunity to study brain plasticity and neural reorganization after a period of auditory deprivation and a delay in language development. In some sense, the current research efforts involving deaf children with CIs can be thought of as the modern equivalent of the so-called "forbidden experiment" in the field of language development, but with an unusual and somewhat unexpected and positive consequence. The forbidden experiment refers to the proposal of raising a child in isolation, without exposure to any language input, to investigate the effects of early experience and sensory deprivation on language development. These kinds of isolation experiments are not considered ethical with humans although they are a common experimental manipulation with animals to learn about brain development and neural reorganization in the absence of sensory input.

Following a period of auditory deprivation from birth, a medical intervention is now available that can be used to provide a form of "electrical" hearing to a congenitally deaf child. A CI provides electrical stimulation to the auditory system, the brain, and nervous system, therefore facilitating development of the underlying neurobiologic and neurocognitive systems used in speech and language processing as well as other domains of neuropsychological function.

The current population of deaf children who use CIs also provides an unusual opportunity for developmental scientists to study the effects of early experience and activity-dependent learning and to investigate how environmental stimulation and interactions with caretakers shape the development of perception, attention, memory, and a broad range of other neurocognitive processes such as sensory–motor coordination, visual–spatial processing, and cognitive control. All of the latter may be "delayed" or "reorganized" as a consequence of a period of early auditory deprivation resulting from congenital or prelingual deafness prior to implantation and the associated delays in language development. When viewed in this somewhat broader context, the clinical and theoretical implications of research on deaf children with CIs are quite extensive. Research on this clinical population will contribute new knowledge and understanding about important contemporary problems in cognitive development and developmental cognitive neuroscience.

Perceptual Robustness of Speech

Research on deaf children who use CIs will also contribute new knowledge about perceptual learning and adaptation in speech perception and spoken language understanding. The most distinctive property of human speech perception is its perceptual robustness in the face of diverse physical stimulation over a wide range of environmental conditions that produce significant changes and perturbations in the acoustic signal. Hearing listeners adapt very quickly and effortlessly to changes in speaker, dialect, speaking rate, and speaking style and are able to adjust rapidly to acoustic degradations and transformations such as noise, filtering, and reverberation that introduce significant physical changes to the speech signal without apparent loss of performance (Pisoni, 1997). Investigating the perceptual, neurocognitive, and linguistic processes used by deaf listeners with CIs, and understanding how hearing listeners recognize spoken words so quickly and efficiently despite enormous variability in the physical signal and listening conditions, will provide fundamental new knowledge about the sources of variability in outcome and benefit in patients who use CIs.

What Is a Cochlear Implant?

A CI is a surgically implanted electronic device that functions as an auditory prosthesis for a patient with a severe to profound sensorineural hearing loss. The device provides electrical stimulation to the surviving spiral ganglion cells of the auditory nerve, bypassing the damaged hair cells of the inner ear to restore hearing in both deaf adults and children. This intervention/treatment provides patients with access to sound and sensory information via the auditory modality.

The current generation of multichannel CIs consist of an internal multiple-electrode array and an external processing unit. The external unit consists of a microphone that picks up sound energy from the environment and a signal processor that codes frequency, amplitude, and time and compresses the signal to match the narrow dynamic range of the ear. Cochlear implants provide temporal and amplitude information. Depending on the manufacturer, several different place-coding techniques are used to represent and transmit frequency information in the signal.

For postlingually profoundly deaf adults, a CI provides a transformed electrical signal to an already fully developed auditory system and an intact, mature language processing system. Postlingually deaf patients have already acquired spoken language under typical listening conditions, so it is more likely that their central auditory system and brain have developed normally (Luria, 1973). In the case of a congenitally deaf child, however, a CI provides novel electrical stimulation through the auditory sensory modality and an opportunity to perceive speech and develop spoken language for the first time after a period of auditory deprivation.

Congenitally deaf children have not been exposed to the auditory correlates of speech and do not develop spoken language in a typical manner. Although the brain and nervous system continue to develop and mature in the absence of auditory stimulation, increasing evidence suggests that substantial cortical reorganization has already taken place during the period of sensory deprivation before implantation and that several aspects of speech and language, as well as other cognitive processes and neural systems, may be delayed and/or disturbed and develop in an atypical fashion after implantation. Although both peripheral and central differences in neural and cognitive function are likely to be responsible for the wide range of variability observed in outcomes following implantation, increasing evidence suggests that the enormous variability in outcome and benefit following cochlear implantation cannot be explained as a simple sensory impairment in detection and/or discrimination of auditory signals. Other more complex cognitive and neural processes are involved.

Cochlear Implants Do Not Restore Normal Hearing

Although CIs work reasonably well with a large number of profoundly deaf children and adults under quiet listening conditions, it is important to emphasize that CIs do not restore normal hearing, and they do not provide support for the highly adaptive robust speech perception and spoken language processing routinely observed in hearing listeners under a wide range of challenging listening conditions. The difficulties consistently reported by CI patients under difficult listening conditions are both theoretically and clinically important because they reflect fundamental differences in perceptual processing between acoustic hearing and electrical stimulation of the auditory system. These difficulties demonstrate that the rapid adaptation, tuning, and continuous adjustment of the perceptual processes that are the hallmarks of robust speech perception by hearing listeners have been significantly compromised by the processing and stimulation strategies used in the current generation of CIs and any neural reorganization that may have taken place before implantation.

Although everyone working in the field fully acknowledges the difficulties that CI patients have when listening in noisy environments, these problems are not explicitly discussed in the literature nor are they considered to be major research questions. Because of their fundamental design, CIs create highly degraded, "underspecified" neural representations of the phonetic content and indexical properties of speech that propagate and cascade to higher processing levels. Although the degraded electrical signal can often be interpreted by most deaf listeners as human speech and can support spoken word recognition and lexical access under quiet listening conditions, the fine episodic acoustic–phonetic details of the original speech waveform are not reliably reproduced or transmitted to the peripheral auditory nerve, central pathways, or higher cortical areas that are used for recognition, categorization, and lexical discrimination and selection. Moreover, the internal perceptual spaces that are used to code and represent linguistic contrasts are significantly warped and deformed in idiopathic ways by the unique pathology of each individual patient (Harnsberger et al., 2001). When confronted with different sources of variability that transform and degrade the speech signal, patients with CIs often have great difficulty perceiving speech and understanding the linguistic content of the talkers' intended message.

The speech perception and spoken word recognition problems experienced by patients with CIs also reflect impairments and disturbances in the neural circuits and categorization strategies that are routinely used to compensate and maintain perceptual constancy in the face of variability in the speech signal. Hearing listeners routinely have similar problems in noise under high cognitive load, but they can cope and overcome the variability and degradation. In some cases, such as listening in high levels of noise or against a background of multitalker babble, patients are unable to derive any benefits at all from their CI and often turn their device off because the speech signal is unpleasant or becomes an aversive stimulus to them.

Key Findings on Outcome and Benefit Following Cochlear Implantation

What do we know about outcome and benefit in deaf children with CIs? Table 3–1 lists seven key findings that have been observed universally at all implant centers around the world. These findings indicate that a small number of demographic, medical, and educational factors are associated with speech and language outcome and benefit following implantation. In addition to the enormous variability observed in these outcome measures, several other findings have been consistently reported in the clinical literature on CIs in deaf children. An examination of these findings provides some initial insights into the possible underlying cognitive and neural basis for the variability in outcome and benefit among deaf children with CIs. When these contributing factors are considered together, it is possible to begin formulating some more specific hypotheses about the reasons for the variability in outcome and benefit.

Much of the past research on CIs has been concerned with questions of assessment and device efficacy using outcome measures that were based on traditional audiological criteria. These clinical outcome measures included a variety of hearing tests, speech discrimination, word recognition, and comprehension tests, as well as some standardized vocabulary and language assessments and other assessments of speech production, articulation, and speech intelligibility. The major focus of most clinical research has been concerned with the study of demographic variables as predictors of these outcome measures. The available evidence suggests that age

Table 3–1.   Key Findings on Outcome and Benefit Following Cochlear Implantation

Large individual differences in outcomes

Age of implantation (sensitive periods)

Effects of early experience (auditory–oral versus total communication)

No preimplant predictors of outcome

Abilities "emerge" after implantation (learning)

"Cross-modal plasticity" and "neural reorganization"

Links between speech perception, and production

at onset of deafness, length of deprivation, age at implantation, and early linguistic experience ("auditory–oral" versus "total communication") are all strongly associated with the traditional audiological outcome measures (Fryauf-Bertschy, Tyler, Kelsay, Gantz, & Woodworth, 1997; Kirk, Pisoni, & Miyamoto, 2000; Osberger, Robbins, Todd, & Riley, 1994; Staller, Pelter, Brimacombe, Mecklenberg, & Arndt, 1991; Waltzman et al., 1994, 1997).

Preimplant Predictors

Until recently, clinicians and researchers were unable to find reliable pre-implant predictors of outcome and success with a CI (see, however, Berge-son & Pisoni, 2004; Horn, Davis, Pisoni, & Miyamoto, 2005a; Horn, Pisoni, Sanders, & Miyamoto, 2005; Tait, Lutman, & Robinson, 2000). The absence of preimplant predictors is a theoretically significant finding, because it suggests that many complex interactions take place between the newly ac-quired sensory capabilities of a child after a period of auditory deprivation, properties of the language-learning environment, and various interactions with parents and caregivers that the child is exposed to after implanta-tion. More importantly, however, the lack of reliable preimplant predictors of outcome and benefit makes it difficult for clinicians to identify those children who may be at risk for poor outcomes at a time in perceptual and cognitive development when changes can be made to modify and improve their language-processing skills.

Learning, Memory, and Development

Finally, when all of the outcome and demographic measures are consid-ered together, the available evidence strongly suggests that the underly-ing sensory, perceptual, and cognitive abilities for speech and language "emerge" after implantation. Performance with a CI improves over time for almost all children. Success with a CI therefore appears to be due, in part, to perceptual learning and exposure to language models in the en-vironment. Because outcome and benefit with a CI cannot be predicted reliably from conventional clinical audiological measures obtained before implantation, any improvements in performance observed after implan-tation must be due to sensory and cognitive processes that are linked to maturational changes in neural and cognitive development (see Sharma, Dorman, & Spahr, 2002).

Our current working hypothesis about the source of individual differ-ences in outcome following cochlear implantation is that, while some pro-portion of the variance in performance is associated with peripheral factors related to audibility and the initial sensory encoding of the speech signal into information-bearing sensory channels in the auditory nerve, several additional sources of variance are associated with more central cognitive and linguistic factors that are related to perception, attention, learning, memory, and cognitive control. As summarized in the following sections, several converging sources of evidence suggest that other neural systems and circuits secondary to deafness and hearing loss may also be disturbed by the absence of sound and auditory stimulation early in development before implantation takes place. Because of the rich interconnections of sensory and motor systems and auditory and visual signals in the brain, there are numerous reasons to suspect that the absence of sound and delays in language during early development produce effects on processes that are not necessarily related to the early sensory processes of hearing and audition (Luria, 1973). These processes are uniquely associated with the development of those neural circuits in the frontal cortex that are involved with executive function and cognitive control processes, such as allocation of conscious attention and control; self-regulation; monitoring of working memory; temporal coding of patterns, particularly memory, for sequences and temporal order information; inhibition; planning and problem solving; and the ability to act on and make use of prior knowledge and experiences in the service of perception, learning, memory, and action.

To investigate individual differences and the sources of variation in outcome, we began by analyzing a set of clinical data from a group of exceptionally good CI users (Pisoni, Cleary, Geers, & Tobey, 2000; Pisoni, Svirsky, Kirk, & Miyamoto, 1997). These deaf children, often referred to as the "Stars," acquire spoken language quickly and easily after implantation and show a developmental trajectory that parallels normal-hearing children (see Svirsky, Robbins, Kirk, Pisoni, & Miyamoto, 2000). Clinical outcome measures of speech perception and language in these exceptionally good users were all found to be strongly intercorrelated with each other, suggesting the existence of a common underlying source of variance. These conventional clinical outcome measures of a child's speech and language skills reflect the final product or "end-point" of a long series of sensory, perceptual, cognitive, and linguistic analyses. "Process measures" of performance designed to assess how well a child uses the sensory information provided by a CI were not included in any of the standard clinical protocols at the time these data were collected, so it was impossible to assess information capacity, processing speed, memory and learning, inhibition, or organizational-integrative processes—neurocognitive factors that may be central for determining which children will become good CI users.

In light of these findings, our research program has explored process measures of performance that assess what a child does with the sensory information provided by a CI in terms of information processing (see Pisoni, 2000). We began by investigating working memory in deaf children with CIs. One reason for pursuing this particular research direction is that working memory has been shown to play a central role in human information processing (Cowan, 2005). Working memory serves as the primary "interface" between sensory input and stored knowledge and procedures in long-term memory. Another reason is that working memory has also been found to be a major source of individual differences in processing capacity across a wide range of information processing domains from perception to memory to language (Ackerman, Kyllonen, & Roberts, 1999; Baddeley, Gathercole, & Papagno, 1998; Carpenter, Miyake, & Just, 1994; Engle, Kane, & Tuholski, 1999; Gupta & MacWhinney, 1997; see Bavelier, Hauser, & Dye, this volume).

Process Measures of Performance

Immediate Memory Capacity

Measures of immediate memory capacity were obtained from a group of 176 deaf children following cochlear implantation in a study carried out in collaboration with Ann Geers and her colleagues at the Central Institute for the Deaf (CID) in St. Louis (Geers, Brenner, & Davidson, 2003; Pisoni & Geers, 2001). Geers and colleagues had a large-scale clinical research project already under way, and they collected a large number of different outcome measures of speech, language, and reading skills from 8- and 9-year-old children who had used their CIs for at least 3.5 years. Thus, chronological age and length of implant use were controlled in their study.

Using the test lists and procedures from the WISC III (Wechsler, 1991), forward and backward auditory digit spans were obtained from four groups of 45 deaf children who were tested separately during the summers of 1997–2000. Forward and backward digit spans were also collected from an additional group of 45 age-matched hearing 8- and 9-year-old children who were tested in Bloomington, Indiana, and served as a comparison group.

The WISC-III memory span task requires the child to repeat back a list of digits spoken live-voice by an experimenter at a rate of approximately one digit per second. In the "digits-forward" condition, the child was required to repeat the list as heard. In the "digits-backward" condition, the child was told to "say the list backward." In both subtests, the lists begin with two items and increase in length until a child gets two lists incorrect at a given length, at which time testing stops. Points are awarded for each list correctly repeated with no partial credit for incorrect recall.

A summary of the digit span results for all five groups of children is shown in Figure 3–1. Forward and backward digit spans are shown separately for each group. The children with CIs are shown in the four panels on the left by year of testing; the hearing children are shown on the right.

WISC Digit Span

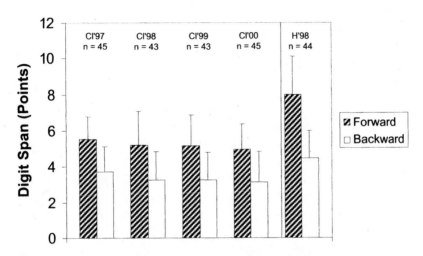

Figure 3–1. WISC digit spans scored by points for the four groups of 8- and 9-year-old children with cochlear implants and for a comparison group of 8- and 9-year-old hearing children. Forward digit spans are shown by the shaded bars, backwards digit spans by the open bars. Error bars indicate one standard deviation from the mean (adapted from Pisoni & Cleary, 2003).

Each child's digit span in points was calculated by summing the number of lists correctly recalled at each list length.

The forward and backward digit spans obtained from the group of age-matched hearing children are shown in the right-hand panel of Figure 3–1. These results show that the digit spans for the hearing children differ in several ways from the spans obtained from the children with CIs. First, whereas the digit spans for the hearing children are age-appropriate and fall within the published norms for the WISC III, those obtained from the children with CIs are atypical. That is, both forward and backward digit spans are longer for the hearing children than for the children with CIs. Second, the difference between the two groups is especially marked in the case of forward digit spans. The average difference between the forward and backward digit span scores was significantly larger in the normal-hearing group compared with the children with CIs.

Numerous studies have suggested that forward digit spans reflect coding strategies related to phonological processing and rehearsal mechanisms used to maintain verbal information in short-term memory for brief periods of time before retrieval and output response. Differences in backward digit spans, on the other hand, are thought to reflect the contribution of controlled attention and the operation of higher-level "executive" processes that are used to transform and manipulate verbal information for later processing operations (Rosen & Engle, 1997; Rudel & Denckla, 1974).

These findings are important because they demonstrate for the first time that the short-term immediate memory capacity of deaf children with CIs is atypical and suggests several possible differences in the underlying processing mechanisms that are used to encode and maintain verbal information in immediate memory (Pisoni & Cleary, 2003; Pisoni & Geers, 2001). These differences may cascade and influence other information processing tasks that make use of working memory and verbal rehearsal processes. Because all of the clinical tests routinely used to assess speech and language outcomes in this clinical population rely heavily on component processes of working memory, verbal rehearsal, and cognitive control, it seems reasonable to assume that these tasks will also reflect variability due to basic differences in immediate memory and processing capacity.

Correlations with Digit Spans

Several studies of hearing children have demonstrated close links between working memory and learning to recognize and understand new words (Gathercole, Hitch, Service, & Martin, 1997; Gupta & MacWhinney, 1997). Other research has found that vocabulary development and several other important milestones in speech and language acquisition are also associated with differences in measures of working memory—specifically, measures of digit span, which are commonly used as estimates of processing capacity of immediate memory (Gathercole & Baddeley, 1990).

To determine if immediate memory capacity was related to spoken word recognition, we correlated the WISC forward and backward digit span scores with three different measures of spoken word recognition that were obtained from the same children. A summary of the correlations between digit span and the spoken word recognition scores based on these 176 children is shown in Table 3–2.

The Word Intelligibility by Picture Identification Test (WIPI) is a closed-set test of word recognition in which the child selects a word's referent from among six alternative pictures (Ross & Lerman, 1979). The LNT is an open-set test of word recognition and lexical discrimination that requires the child to imitate and reproduce an isolated word (Kirk, Pisoni, & Osberger, 1995). Finally, the BKB is an open-set word recognition test in which key words are presented in short meaningful sentences (Bench, Kowal, & Bamford, 1979). The correlations for both the forward and backward spans reveal that children who had longer WISC digit spans also had higher word recognition scores on all three word recognition tests. This

Table 3–2. **Correlations Between WISC Digit Span and Three Measures of Spoken Word Recognition**

	Simple Bivariate Correlations	
	WISC Forward Digit Span	WISC Backward Digit Span
Closed-set word recognition (WIPI)	.42***	.28***
Open-set word recognition (LNT)	.41***	.20**
Open-set word recognition in sentences (BKB)	.44***	.24**

*** $p < 0.001$, ** $p < 0.01$
Adapted from Pisoni & Cleary, 2003.

finding was observed for both forward and backward digit spans. The correlations were all positive and reached statistical significance.

In addition, partial correlations were obtained after statistically controlling for differences due to seven other contributing variables, including chronological age, communication mode, and duration of deafness. Even after these other sources of variance were removed, forward digit span scores were still positively and significantly correlated with the three word recognition scores; however, the correlations with backward digit span scores were much weaker and no longer reached significance. These results demonstrate that children who have longer forward WISC digit spans also show higher spoken word recognition scores. The present results suggest a common source of variance, shared between forward digit span and measures of spoken word recognition, and independent of other mediating factors that have been found to contribute to the variation in these outcome measures.

Digit Spans and Verbal Rehearsal Speed

As part of the research project, speech production samples were obtained from each child to assess her speech intelligibility and measure changes in articulation and phonological development following implantation (see Tobey et al., 2000). The speech samples consisted of three sets of meaningful English sentences that were elicited using the stimulus materials and experimental procedures originally developed by McGarr (1983) to measure intelligibility of "deaf speech." All of the utterances produced by the children were originally recorded and stored digitally for playback to groups of naïve adult listeners who were asked to transcribe what they thought the children had said. In addition to the speech intelligibility scores, the durations of the individual sentences in each set were measured and used to estimate each child's speaking rate.

The sentence durations provided a quantitative measure of a child's articulation speed, which we knew from a large body of earlier research in the memory literature was closely related to speed of subvocal verbal rehearsal (Cowan et al., 1998). Numerous studies over the past 30 years have demonstrated strong relations between speaking rate and memory span for digits and words (for example, Baddeley, Thompson, & Buchanan, 1975). The results of these studies with hearing children and adults suggest that measures of an individual's speaking rate reflect articulation speed, and this measure can be used as an index of rate of covert verbal rehearsal for phonological information in working memory. Individuals who speak more quickly have been found to have longer memory spans than individuals who speak more slowly (see Baddeley et al., 1975).

Scatterplots of the forward digit span scores for the 168 children are shown in Figure 3–2 along with estimates of their speaking rates obtained from measurements of their productions of meaningful English sentences. The digit spans are plotted on the ordinate; the average sentence durations are shown on the abscissa. The top panel shows mean sentence durations; the bottom panel shows the log sentence durations. The pattern of results in both figures is very clear: children who produce sentences with longer durations speak more slowly and, in turn, have shorter forward digit spans. The correlations between forward digit span and both measures of sentence duration were strongly negative and highly significant. It is important to emphasize once again that the relations observed here between digit span and speaking rate were selective in nature and were found only for the forward digit spans. No correlation was observed between backward digit span scores and sentence duration in any of these analyses.

The dissociation between forward and backward digit spans and the correlation of the forward spans with measures of speaking rate suggests that verbal rehearsal speed is the primary underlying factor responsible for the variability and individual differences observed in deaf children with CIs on a range of behavioral speech and language tasks. The common feature of each of these clinical outcome measures is that they all make use of the storage and processing mechanisms of verbal working memory (Archibald & Gathercole, 2007).

Verbal Rehearsal Speed and Word Recognition

To determine if digit span and sentence duration share a common process and the same underlying source of variance that relates them both to word recognition performance, we analyzed the intercorrelations between each pair of variables with the same set of the demographic and mediating variables systematically partialled out. When sentence duration was partialled out of the analysis, the correlations between digit span and each of the

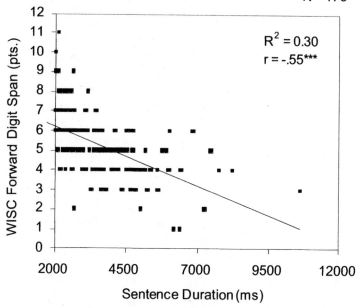

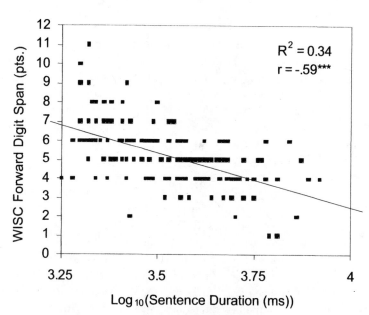

Figure 3–2. Scatterplots illustrating the relationship between average sentence duration for the seven-syllable McGarr Sentences (*abscissa*) and WISC forward digit span scored by points (*ordinate*). Each data-point represents an individual child. Measured duration scores are shown in the top panel, log-transformed duration scores in the bottom panel. R-squared values indicate percent of variance accounted for by the linear relation (adapted from Pisoni & Cleary, 2003).

three measures of word recognition essentially approached zero. However, sentence duration and word recognition were significantly negatively correlated even after digit span was partialled out of the analysis, suggesting that processing speed is the common factor shared between these two measures.

The results of these analyses confirm that the underlying factor shared in common with speaking rate is related to the rate of information processing; specifically, the speed of the verbal rehearsal process in working memory. This processing component of verbal rehearsal could reflect either the articulatory speed used to maintain phonological patterns in working memory or the time to retrieve and scan verbal information already in working memory, or both (see Cowan et al., 1998). In either case, the common factor linking word recognition and speaking rate is the speed of information processing operations used to store and maintain phonological representations in working memory (see Pisoni & Cleary, 2003).

Scanning of Information in Immediate Memory

In addition to our studies on verbal rehearsal speed, we also obtained measures of memory scanning during the digit recall task from a group of deaf children with CIs and a comparison group of typically developing age-matched hearing children (see Burkholder & Pisoni, 2003; 2006). Our interest in studying scanning of verbal information in short-term memory in these children was motivated by several earlier findings reported by Cowan and his colleagues, who have carefully measured the response latencies and interword pause durations during recall tasks in children of different ages (Cowan, 1992; Cowan et al., 1994; 1998). Articulation rate and subvocal rehearsal speed were measured using sentence durations elicited with meaningful English sentences. To assess differences in speech timing during recall, the response latencies, durations of the test items, and interword pauses were also measured in both groups of children.

Our findings showed that interword pause durations in recall differed significantly between the two groups of children. The average of individual pauses that occurred during digit recall in the forward condition was significantly longer in the deaf children with CIs than in the hearing children at list lengths three and four. Although the deaf children with CIs correctly recalled all the items from the three- and four-digit lists, their scanning and retrieval speeds were *three times slower* than the average retrieval speed of age-matched hearing children (Burkholder & Pisoni, 2003). Longer interword pauses reflect slower serial scanning processes, which affects the retrieval of phonological information in short-term memory (Cowan, 1992; Cowan et al., 1994). Taken together, the pattern of results indicates that both slower subvocal verbal rehearsal and slower serial scanning of short-term memory are associated with shorter digit spans in the deaf children with CIs.

The effects of early auditory and linguistic experience found by Burkholder and Pisoni (2003) suggest that the development of subvocal verbal rehearsal and serial scanning processes may be related to developmental milestones in cognitive control processes, such as the ability to effectively organize and utilize these two processes in tasks requiring immediate recall. Efficient subvocal verbal rehearsal strategies and scanning abilities also appear to be experience- and activity-dependent, reflecting the development of basic sensory-motor circuits used in speech perception and speech production.

Because the group of deaf children examined in the Burkholder and Pisoni (2003) study fell within a normal range of intelligence, the most likely developmental factor responsible for producing slower verbal rehearsal speeds, scanning rates, and shorter digit spans is an early period of auditory deprivation and associated delay in language development prior to receiving a CI. Sensory deprivation results in widespread developmental brain plasticity and neural reorganization, further differentiating deaf children's perceptual and cognitive development from the development of hearing children (Kaas, Merzenich, & Killackey, 1983; Riesen, 1975; Shepard & Hardie, 2001). Brain plasticity affects not only the development of the peripheral and central auditory systems but other higher cortical areas as well, both before and after cochlear implantation (Ryugo, Limb, & Redd, 2000; Teoh, Pisoni, & Miyamoto, 2004a, b).

Sequence Memory and Learning

All of the traditional methods for measuring memory span and estimating the capacity of immediate memory use recall tasks that require a subject to explicitly repeat a sequence of test items using an overt articulatory–verbal motor response (Dempster, 1981). Because deaf children may also have disturbances and delays in other neural circuits that are used in speech motor control and phonological development, it is possible that any differences observed in performance between deaf children with CIs and age-matched hearing children using traditional full-report memory span tasks could be due to the nature of the motor response requirements used during retrieval and output. Differences in articulation speed and speech motor control could magnify other differences in encoding, storage, rehearsal, or retrieval processes.

To eliminate the use of an overt articulatory–verbal response, we developed a new experimental methodology to measure immediate memory span in deaf children with CIs based on the Simon memory game developed by Milton-Bradley. Figure 3–3 shows a display of the apparatus, which we

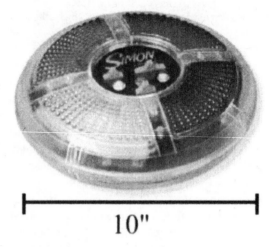

Figure 3–3. The memory game response box based on the popular Milton Bradley game "Simon."

modified so it could be controlled by a PC. In carrying out the experimental procedure, a child is asked to simply "reproduce" a stimulus pattern by manually pressing a sequence of colored panels on the four-alternative response box.

In addition to eliminating the need for an overt verbal response, the sequence memory task methodology permitted us to manipulate the stimulus presentation conditions in several systematic ways while holding the response format constant. This particular property of the experimental procedure was important, because it provided us with a novel way of measuring how auditory and visual stimulus dimensions are analyzed and processed alone and in combination, and how these stimulus manipulations affected measures of sequence memory span. This methodology also offered us an opportunity to study learning processes—specifically, sequence learning and the relationships between working memory and learning—using the identical experimental procedures and response demands (see Conway, Karpicke, & Pisoni, 2007; Karpicke & Pisoni, 2004).

Simon Sequence Memory Spans

In our initial studies with the Simon apparatus, three different stimulus presentation formats were employed (Cleary, Pisoni, & Geers, 2001; Cleary, Pisoni, & Kirk, 2002; Pisoni & Cleary, 2004). In the first condition, the sequences consisted only of spoken color names (A). In the second condition, sequences of colored lights (L) were presented in the visual modality. In the third presentation condition, the spoken color names were presented simultaneously with correlated colored lights (A+L). Thirty-one deaf children with CIs were tested using the Simon memory game apparatus; 31 hearing children who were matched in terms of age and gender with the group of children with CIs were also tested. Finally, 48 hearing adults were recruited to serve as an additional comparison group (see Pisoni & Cleary, 2004).

Sequences used for the Simon memory game task were generated pseudorandomly by a computer program, with the stipulation that no single item would be repeated consecutively in a given list. A memory span score was computed for each subject by finding the proportion of lists correctly reproduced at each list length and averaging these proportions across all list lengths.

A summary of the results from the Simon immediate memory task for the three groups of subjects is shown in Figure 3–4, presented on the left-hand side of each graph (called "memory span"). Examination of these memory span scores for the hearing adults reveals several findings that can serve as benchmarks for comparing and evaluating differences in the performance of the two groups of children. First, as in other studies of verbal short-term memory (Penny, 1989; Watkins, Watkins, & Crowder, 1974), we found a "modality effect" for presentation format. Auditory presentation (A) of sequences of color names produced longer immediate memory spans than did visual presentation (L) of sequences of colored lights. Second, we found a "redundancy gain." When information from the auditory and visual modalities was combined together and presented simultaneously (A+L), the memory spans were longer compared to presentation using only one sensory modality, reflecting the efficient use of cross-modal redundancies between stimulus dimensions (Garner, 1974).

Overall, the pattern of the Simon memory span scores for the group of hearing 8- and 9-year-old children is similar to the findings obtained with the hearing adults. However, the absolute memory spans for all three presentation conditions were lower for the hearing children; furthermore, both the modality effect and the cross-modal "redundancy gain" were smaller in magnitude, suggesting possible developmental differences in processing sequential patterns.

Examination of the pattern of the memory spans for the deaf children with CIs reveals several striking differences from the memory spans obtained from the hearing children and adults. First, the memory spans for all three presentation conditions were consistently lower overall than were the spans from the corresponding conditions obtained for the age-matched hearing children. Second, the modality effect observed in both the hearing adults and hearing children was reversed for the deaf children with CIs. The memory spans for the deaf children were longer for visual-only sequences than for auditory-only sequences. Third, although the cross-modal "redundancy gain" found for both the adults and hearing children was also

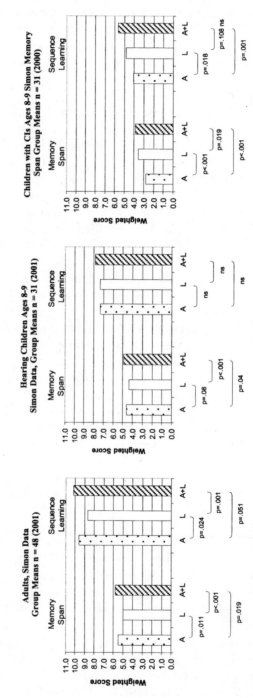

Figure 3–4. Mean immediate memory spans and sequence learning scores in each of the three conditions tested using the "Simon" memory game (adapted from Pisoni & Cleary, 2004). A, Auditory-only; L, Lights-only; A+L, Auditory+Lights.

observed for the deaf children and was statistically significant for both conditions, the absolute size of the redundancy gain was smaller in magnitude than the auditory–visual gain observed with the hearing children.

The results obtained for the visual-only presentation conditions are of particular theoretical interest, because the deaf children with CIs displayed shorter memory spans for visual sequences than did the hearing children. This finding adds additional support to the hypothesis that phonological recoding and verbal rehearsal processes in working memory play important roles in perception, learning, and memory in these children (Pisoni & Cleary, 2004). Capacity limitations of working memory are closely tied to speed of information processing even for visual patterns that can be rapidly recoded and represented in memory in a phonological or articulatory code for certain kinds of sequential processing tasks. Verbal coding strategies may be mandatory in memory tasks that require immediate serial recall of temporal patterns that preserve item and order information (Gupta & MacWhinney, 1997). Although the visual patterns were presented using only sequences of colored lights, both groups of children appeared to recode these sequential patterns using verbal coding strategies to create stable phonological representations in working memory for maintenance and rehearsal prior to response output.

The deaf children with CIs also showed much smaller redundancy gains under the multimodal presentation conditions (A+L), which suggests that, in addition to differences in working memory and verbal rehearsal, automatic attention processes used to perceive and encode complex multimodal stimuli are atypical and disturbed relative to age-matched hearing children. The smaller redundancy gains observed in these deaf children may also be due to the reversal of the typical modality effects observed in studies of working memory that reflect the dominance of verbal coding of the stimulus materials. The modality effect in short-term memory studies is generally thought to reflect phonological coding and verbal rehearsal strategies that actively maintain the temporal order information of stimuli sequences in immediate memory for short periods of time (Watkins et al., 1974). Taken together, the present findings demonstrate important differences in both automatic attention and working memory processes in this population. These basic differences in information processing skills may be responsible for the wide variation in the traditional clinical speech and language outcome measures observed in deaf children following cochlear implantation (Cleary, Pisoni, & Kirk, 2002).

Simon Sequence Learning Spans

In addition to measuring immediate memory capacity, we have also used the Simon memory game procedure to study sequence learning and investigate the effects of long-term memory on coding and rehearsal strategies in working memory (Cleary & Pisoni, 2001; Conway, Karpicke et al., 2007; Karpicke & Pisoni, 2004). To accomplish this goal and to directly compare the gains in learning and the increases in working memory capacity to our earlier Simon memory span measures, we examined the effects of sequence repetition on immediate memory span by simply repeating the same pattern over again if the subject correctly reproduced the sequence on a given trial. In the sequence learning conditions, the same stimulus pattern was repeated on each trial for an individual subject and the sequences gradually increased in length by one item after each correct response until the subject was unable to correctly reproduce the pattern. This change in the methodology provided an opportunity to study nondeclarative learning processes based on simple repetition and to investigate how repetition of the same pattern affects the capacity of immediate memory (see Hebb, 1961; Melton, 1963).

Figure 3–4 also displays a summary of the results obtained from the Simon learning conditions that investigated the effects of sequence repetition on memory span for the same three presentation formats used in the earlier conditions, auditory-only (A), lights-only (L), and auditory+lights (A+L). Examination of the two sets of memory span scores shown within each panel reveals several consistent findings. First, repetition of the same stimulus sequence produced large learning effects for all three groups of subjects. The sequence repetition effects can be seen clearly by comparing the three scores on the right-hand side of each panel of Figure 3–4 to the three scores on the left-hand side. For each of the three groups of subjects, the learning span scores on the right were higher than the memory span scores on the left. Although a repetition effect was also obtained with the deaf children who use CIs (shown in the right panel), the size of their repetition effect was about half the size of the repetition effect found for the hearing children.

Second, the rank ordering of the three presentation conditions in the sequence learning conditions was similar to the rank ordering observed in the memory span conditions for all three groups of subjects. The repetition effect was largest for the A+L conditions for all three groups. For both the hearing adults and hearing children, we also observed the same modality effect in learning that was found for immediate memory span. Auditory presentation was better than visual presentation. And, as before, the deaf children also showed a reversal of this modality effect for learning. Visual presentation was better than auditory presentation.

To assess the magnitude of the repetition learning effects, we computed difference scores between the learning and memory conditions by subtracting the memory span scores from the learning span scores for each subject. The data for individual subjects in each group for the three presentation formats are displayed in Figure 3–5, which reveals a wide range of

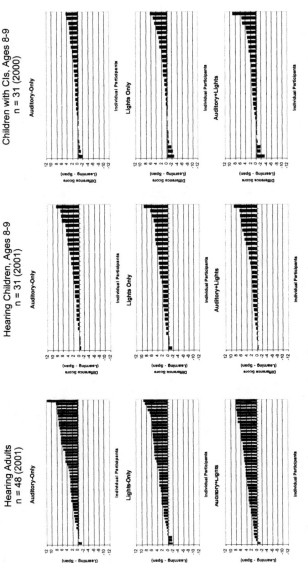

Figure 3–5. Difference scores for individual subjects showing sequence learning score minus memory span score. Data for the auditory-only (A) condition is shown on the top, lights-only (L) condition in the middle, and auditory-plus-lights (A+L) condition on the bottom. Data from hearing adults are shown on the left, scores for hearing 8- and 9-year-old children in the center, and scores for 8- and 9-year-old cochlear implant users on the right (adapted from Pisoni & Cleary, 2004).

performance for all three groups of subjects. Although most of the subjects in each group displayed some evidence of learning in terms of showing a positive repetition effect, a few subjects in the tails of the distributions either failed to show any learning at all or showed a small reversal of the predicted repetition effect. Although the number of subjects who failed to show a repetition effect was quite small in the adults and hearing children, about one-third of the deaf children with CIs showed no evidence of a repetition learning effect at all and failed to benefit from having the same stimulus sequence repeated on each trial.

Sequence Learning and Outcome Measures

To study the relations between sequence learning and speech and language development in these children, Cleary and Pisoni (2001) computed a series of correlations between the three learning scores obtained from the Simon learning task and several of the traditional audiological outcome measures of benefit that were obtained from these children as part of the larger CID project (see Geers, Nicholas, & Sedey, 2003). None of the demographic variables was found to be correlated with any of the Simon sequence learning scores. However, moderate positive correlations were obtained for three measures of spoken word recognition, the WIPI, BKB sentences, and the LNT and the auditory-only Simon learning condition. Moreover, the auditory-only Simon learning span was also found to be correlated with the Test for Auditory Comprehension of Language-Revised (TACL-R), a measure of receptive language, as well as the backward WISC digit span.

Thus, sequence learning in the auditory-only condition was positively correlated with outcome measures that involve more complex neurocognitive processing activities that reflect executive functions and controlled attention (Engle et al., 1999; Miller & Cohen, 2001). In a follow-up study, Pisoni and Davis (2003) assessed two additional sequence learning measures in a different group of deaf children who use CIs: a redundancy gain score that assessed how much gain the child received from the addition of redundant auditory information to a visual pattern, and a sequence learning gain score that assessed changes in the rate of sequence learning over time. These measures were found to be significantly correlated with several traditional speech and language outcome measures, including Common Phrases (auditory-alone) scores and vocabulary knowledge as assessed by the Peabody Picture Vocabulary Test-III (PPVT; Dunn & Dunn, 1997). These results show that measures of sequence learning in deaf children with CIs are associated with changes over time in several traditional clinical outcome measures of speech and language.

Together with the other Simon memory and learning results, these findings are of interest both clinically and theoretically, because they suggest that the individual differences in outcome of deaf children who receive CIs may reflect fundamental learning processes that affect the encoding and retention of temporal information in both short- and long-term memory. These findings suggest that differences in the development of basic sequence learning mechanisms in this population may contribute an additional unique source of variance to the overall variation observed in a range of different outcome measures following cochlear implantation. Additional studies of sequence learning and memory in hearing children and adults and deaf children with CIs have been carried out recently and are reported elsewhere (Conway, Karpicke et al., 2007; Conway, Pisoni, Anaya, Karpicke, & Henning, 2008).

Interim Summary

Examination of the findings described thus far on immediate memory capacity, speed of verbal rehearsal, and scanning of items correctly retrieved from short-term memory, suggests that the verbal coding strategies and automatized phonological processing skills of deaf children with CIs are atypical and differ in several significant ways from age-matched, typically developing hearing children. Deaf children with CIs demonstrated shorter digit spans, slower verbal rehearsal speeds and significant processing delays in scanning and retrieval of verbal information from short-term memory even for items that were successfully retrieved and correctly recalled. Disturbances were also found in visual sequence memory and learning. In particular, deaf children with CIs showed significant declines in sensitivity to sequence repetition effects in the Simon learning conditions, which suggests fundamental differences in repetition priming, procedural learning, and processes involved in encoding and retention of temporal sequences in long-term memory. Furthermore, the memory and learning results obtained with the Simon task suggest that the effects of deafness and delay in language development, the cognitive and behavioral sequelae following a period of auditory deprivation before implantation, are not modality-specific nor are they restricted to only the perception and processing of auditory signals. The effects of deafness appear to be much broader and more global in scope, involving the processing of sequences and temporal patterns independently of input modality and the allocation of attentional resources to perceptual dimensions of complex multidimensional stimuli (see Marschark & Wauters, this volume; Pelz, Marschark, & Convertino, this volume).

The present findings suggest that multiple information processing systems and the neural circuits underlying their operation are affected by a period of deafness and associated delay in language development prior to implantation. The memory, attention, and sequence learning effects observed in these studies are not directly related to the peripheral coding and sensory aspects of hearing or the perception of auditory signals, although these factors contribute to establishing and maintaining distinctiveness and discriminability of phonological information at the time of initial encoding and registration in sensory and short-term memory.

It is very likely that many of the deaf children with CIs tested in our studies have comorbid disturbances and delays in the development of neural circuits that underlie other information processing systems that are secondary to their profound hearing loss and delay in language development. The absence of sound and auditory experience during early development prior to implantation affects neurocognitive development in a wide variety of ways. Differences resulting from deafness and language delays and subsequent neural reorganization of multiple brain systems may be responsible for the enormous variability observed in speech and language outcome measures following implantation.

To explore these findings further, we shifted our research efforts in two new directions. First, we began searching for preimplant predictors of outcome and benefit that did not involve any direct measures of speech or language processing or perception of auditory signals. Second, adopting a broader integrated functional systems approach to brain, behavior, and development (Luria, 1973), we collected several new sets of data using several standardized neuropsychological measures of visual–motor integration and sensory–motor processes, as well as executive function and cognitive control, so that age-equivalent comparisons can be made based on normative data. Finally, we have recently obtained some preliminary data using the Behavior Rating Inventory of Executive Functions (BRIEF) (Gioia, Isquith, Guy, & Kenworthy, 2000), a behavioral rating inventory filled out by a parent or caretaker to study behavioral regulation, meta-cognition, and executive function in real-world environments outside the clinic and research laboratory. We have also obtained several additional measures of learning, memory, and attention using the Learning, Executive, and Attention Functioning (LEAF) (Kronenberger, 2006) and the Conduct-Hyperactive-Attention Problem-Opposition Scale (CHAOS) (Kronenberger, Dunn, & Giauque, 1998) rating scales that were developed in our attention deficit-hyperactivity disorder (ADHD) clinic to assess learning, executive function, and attention-hyperactivity. We present a summary of these new findings in the sections below.

Development of Motor Skills

In our research center, as part of the process for determining candidacy prior to implantation, a battery of standardized psychological tests is administered to each child by a clinical psychologist who has extensive experience working with deaf children. Historically, these tests were not considered as research data because they were administered prior to implantation and were designed primarily to rule out mental retardation and other developmental disorders that were thought to be possible risks for cochlear implantation. One of the parental reports used in our psychological assessments is the Vineland Adaptive Behavior Scales (VABS) (Sparrow, Balla, & Cicchetti, 1984), which we use to obtain information about the child's adaptive functioning in three functional domains: daily living skills, socialization, and motor skills. These three domains on the VABS provide valuable normative information about the child's adaptive behaviors prior to implantation and offered an opportunity to assess whether a period of profound deafness and language delay prior to cochlear implantation affects adaptive behaviors in these areas.

We examined data for 43 deaf children from the VABS for the motor development, daily living, and socialization scales as a function of duration of deafness prior to implantation (Horn et al., 2005). All of the children subsequently received a CI at our center, and all of them also provided scores on a range of traditional speech and language outcome measures obtained at several test intervals following implantation. Because the children in this study received their CIs at different ages, we were able to assess the effects of length of deprivation (i.e., duration of deafness) prior to implantation on these three adaptive behaviors to determine whether these skills developed in an age-appropriate fashion before cochlear implantation.

For each of the three VABS domains, children were divided into two groups based on a median split. Using this design, spoken language outcomes were compared for each group. If a given VABS domain is predictive of spoken language outcomes after implantation, children in the high group should show higher scores on spoken language measures than children in the low group.

When compared to the results obtained from the daily living skills and socialization domains, the effect of the median split on spoken language outcomes was more robust for the motor domain. Children in the high motor domain group demonstrated significantly better performance on all spoken language measures than did children in the low motor domain group. For the Grammatical Analysis of Elicited Language-Presentence Level (GAEL-P), a closed-set test of spoken word recognition, the estimated mean score of children in the high motor domain group was 60.5% words correct compared with 34.1% for children in the low motor domain group. Children in the high motor domain group also demonstrated language and vocabulary skills that were closer to their chronological age peers than did children in the low motor domain group, as shown by the differences between the two groups on several other outcome measures.

We also found that the average motor domain score was age-appropriate and within the typical range of variability compared to the other two domains of the VABS. This finding differs from earlier studies that have reported delays in motor skills of deaf children compared with hearing children. The earlier studies of motor development used children attending residential schools for the deaf who used American Sign Language rather than oral or manual English (Wiegersma & Van der Velde, 1983). Moreover, these studies did not report or control for etiology of deafness or other potential confounding variables such as neurological impairment or age at diagnosis. These findings suggest that deaf children who present for a CI in infancy or early childhood do not display evidence of general motor impairments, as measured by the VABS.

Multivariate analyses also revealed that nonmotor VABS scores were negatively related to chronological age at testing. Children who were older at the time the VABS data were obtained showed greater delays in socialization and daily living skills than did children who were younger. These results suggest that motor development proceeds more typically in these children than do the other two developmental domains. Because age at testing and duration of auditory deprivation are highly correlated in this population of infants and children, the relations observed between age at testing and VABS domain scores can be recast in terms of duration of auditory deprivation; longer periods of profound deafness before cochlear implantation are associated with greater delays in socialization and daily living skills, but not motor development.

This pattern of results indicates that not all VABS domains were related to the development of spoken language skills. Motor development was related to performance on spoken word recognition, receptive language, expressive language, and vocabulary knowledge tests obtained over a 3-year period after implantation. Links between motor development and perceptual and linguistic skills have been widely reported in the developmental literature on both hearing and deaf children. In hearing children, motor development assessed in infancy has been shown to be strongly associated with language outcomes in later childhood. The study carried out by Horn et al. (2005) was the first to demonstrate that preimplant measures of motor development can be used to predict post-implant language outcomes in profoundly deaf infants and young children who have received a CI.

One explanation of the relationships observed between motor development and spoken language acquisition in deaf children with CIs is that motor and language systems are closely coupled in development and share common cortical processing resources that reflect the organization and operations of an integrated functional system used in language processing. This hypothesis is not new. Eric Lenneberg (1967), one of the first theorists to propose a biological explanation for the links between motor and language development, argued strongly that correlations between motor and language milestones in development reflected common underlying rates in brain maturation. Recently, a number of studies have explored the basic neural mechanisms behind these links in greater depth (Iverson & Fagan, 2004). These findings suggest an articulatory or motor-based representation of speech in which brain areas traditionally known to be involved in regulating motor behavior are also recruited during language processing tasks (Teuber, 1964; Wilson, 2002).

Divergence of Fine Versus Gross Motor Skills

In a follow-up study, Horn, Pisoni, and Miyamoto (2006) assessed whether gross or fine motor skills on the VABS showed any evidence of a developmental divergence. Horn et al. also investigated whether preimplant measures of fine or gross motor skills predict spoken language outcomes in prelingually deaf children with CIs. In the earlier VABS paper, we found that preimplant motor development scores were significantly correlated with postimplant scores on tests of word recognition, receptive and expressive language, and vocabulary knowledge. In the second study, fine and gross motor skills were analyzed separately using correlational analyses with several different postimplant spoken language scores.

As in the earlier study, three spoken language outcome measures were collected longitudinally at various times after implantation. The first test assessed closed-set spoken word recognition, the second assessed both receptive and expressive language skills, and the third assessed vocabulary knowledge. Correlations between gross motor scores and the three outcome measures were weakly positive, whereas correlations between fine motor scores and the three language outcome measures were more strongly positive. The only correlations to reach significance were between fine motor scores and expressive language quotients obtained at the 1- and 2-year postimplant intervals. In contrast, the correlations between gross motor scores and expressive language scores were all lower and nonsignificant. That is, preimplant fine motor skills predict postimplant expressive language acquisition. Infants and children with more advanced fine motor behaviors on the VABS prior to implantation demonstrated higher expressive language scores after 1 or 2 years of CI use than did children with less advanced fine motor behaviors. In contrast, gross motor skills measured prior to implantation were not related to postimplant expressive language skills.

An additional dissociation in development between gross and fine motor skills in prelingually deaf children was also found. Although the average differences for fine and gross motor skills did not differ, the two motor subdomains showed a developmental divergence as a function of chronological age. For gross motor skills, a positive relationship between age and motor development was observed: older deaf children tended to show more advanced gross motor behaviors compared with younger deaf children. In contrast, the opposite trend was observed for fine motor skills: older deaf children tended to show less advanced fine motor behaviors than did younger deaf children. Although these findings are correlational, they are consistent with the hypothesis that a period of auditory deprivation and associated language delay affects the development of fine motor skills in a way different from gross motor skills.

In sum, these results provide new evidence that fine motor development and spoken language acquisition are closely coupled processes in deaf infants and children with CIs. Our findings suggest that a common set of cortical mechanisms may underlie both the control of fine manual motor behaviors and spoken language processing, especially the development of expressive language skills in this population.

Links Between Visual–Motor Integration and Language

Numerous researchers have recognized that perceptual–motor development and language acquisition are closely linked and develop together in a predictable fashion with several behavioral milestones correlated across systems (Lenneberg, 1967; Locke, Bekken, McMinn-Larson, & Wein, 1995; Siegel et al., 1982). In addition to motor development, visual–motor integration skills have also been found to be closely linked to spoken language development in numerous studies. Traditionally, visual-motor integration is measured using design-copying and construction tasks in which adults and children are asked to copy a series of increasingly complex geometric figures (Beery, 1989). Performance on design copying tasks has been shown to be correlated with language development, reading ability, and general academic achievement in hearing children (Taylor, 1999) as well as deaf children who use American Sign Language (Bachara & Phelan, 1980; Spencer & Delk, 1985).

In addition, several studies have reported that deaf children display atypical performance on visual–motor integration tasks as well as other perceptual–motor tasks involving balance, running, throwing, and figure drawing (Erden, Otman, & Tunay, 2004; Savelsbergh, Netelenbos, & Whiting, 1991; Wiegersma & Van der Velde, 1983). In fact, more than 50 years ago, Myklebust and Brutten (1953) carried out one of the earliest studies investigating the visual perception skills of deaf children. They found that performance on the marbleboard test, which required children to reproduce visual patterns using marbles on a 10 × 10 grid was significantly lower for deaf children than for hearing age-matched controls. They concluded that deafness disturbs the visual perceptual processes required for constructing continuous figures from models consisting of discrete elements and causes an alteration in the normal response modes of the organism, including disruptions in visual perceptual organization. Myklebust and Brutten (1953) argued further that deafness should not be viewed as an isolated autonomous sensory-perceptual impairment but rather as a modification of the total reactivity of the organism.

Many of these early studies included deaf children who had other neurological and cognitive sequelae. And, all of the earlier studies were conducted before deaf children could be identified at birth through universal newborn hearing screening (NIH, 1993). Other studies tested deaf children who were immersed in a manual language environment in which auditory–oral spoken language skills were not emphasized. Thus, the results from these earlier studies cannot be generalized easily to the current population of prelingually deaf children who present for a CI. Two recent studies carried out in our center (Horn, Davis, Pisoni, &, Miyamoto, 2004; Horn, Fagan, Dillon, Pisoni, & Miyamoto, 2007) addressed several questions about the development of visual–motor integration skills.

In the first study, the Beery Test of Visual Motor Integration (VMI; Beery, 1989), was administered prior to implantation to children who were identified from the large cohort of pediatric CI patients followed longitudinally at our center. The Beery VMI test contains a sequence of 24 geometric forms of increasing complexity, ranging from a simple vertical line to a complex three-dimensional star. Children are asked to copy each item as accurately as they can. Several clinical spoken language measures were also obtained at 6-month intervals in this longitudinal study. Open-set word recognition was measured using the Phonetically Balanced Kindergarten (PBK) test. Sentence comprehension was assessed with the Common Phrases (CP) test (Osberger et al., 1994), using auditory-only, live voice presentation. Speech intelligibility scores were obtained using the Beginner's Intelligibility Test (BIT). Vocabulary knowledge was assessed with the PPVT. Finally, the Reynell Developmental Language Scales (RDLS) was administered to assess receptive and expressive language skills. The receptive scales (RDLS-r) measured 10 skills, including spoken word recognition, sentence comprehension, and verbal comprehension of ideational content. The expressive language scales (RDLS-e) assessed skills such as spontaneous expression of speech and picture description.

The speech and language measures were obtained during the preimplant period, within 6 months before implantation, and then at 6-month intervals after implantation. Scores were collapsed into one of five intervals of CI use: preimplant, 1-year post, 2-years post, 3-years post, and 4-years post. The mean preimplant VMI score for the 40 deaf children was 0.98, which did not differ significantly from the expected mean of 1.0 for hearing children. For all of the language outcome measures, the scores increased significantly as a function of CI use. Moreover, children with higher preimplant VMI showed higher percent correct scores on the postimplantation word recognition, comprehension, and intelligibility tests.

Several new findings were obtained in this study. First, the preimplant visual–motor integration scores of the deaf children in this study were age-appropriate when compared with the normative data. This result contrasts with earlier reports showing delays in deaf children compared with hearing children (Erden, Otman, & Tunay, 2004; Tiber, 1985). The differences may be due to several factors. First, the sample of deaf children used in our studies was likely to have been diagnosed earlier and received earlier audiological and speech-language intervention than the children used in the earlier studies. Second, children with gross cognitive or motor delays were excluded from the present study.

Additionally, the longitudinal analyses revealed that VMI scores were robust predictors of postimplant outcomes of speech perception, sentence comprehension, and speech intelligibility. Children with higher preimplant VMI scores displayed better performance on all of the outcome measures following CI. Higher VMI scores were also associated with larger increases in speech intelligibility scores over time than were lower VMI scores. Thus, preimplant VMI not only predicts overall performance, but it also predicts rate of improvement with CI experience.

One limitation of the first VMI study reported by Horn et al. (2004) was that the children were only tested at early ages before implantation as part of their initial preimplant psychological assessment. Variability of visual–motor integration skills in prelingually deaf children and the associations observed with spoken language outcomes might not be fully realized until children are a little older and have had more experience using their CI. To pursue these questions further, a second study was carried out with prelingually deaf children who had used their implants for longer periods of time. The Design Copying and Visual–Motor Precision tests from the NEPSY (Korkman, Kirk, & Kemp, 1998), a standardized battery of neuropsychological tests widely used in clinical settings to assess neurocognitive functions of children between 3 and 12 years of age, were administered to determine if the preimplant findings obtained in the first study would generalize to other visual–motor tasks obtained postimplantation. The measures reported here were collected as part of a larger study investigating neuropsychological functioning, phonological processing, and reading skills in prelingually deaf children with CIs (Dillon, 2005; Fagan, Pisoni, Horn, & Dillon, 2007; Horn et al., 2007).

Design Copying is very similar to the Beery VMI test used in our first study. This test is a pencil-and-paper test that measures a child's ability to copy two-dimensional geometrical figures of increasing complexity, under no time limits. Visual–Motor Precision is a timed maze-tracing task containing two mazes, a Simple Maze and a Complex Maze. Children were instructed to draw a line down the track as fast as they could without crossing the lines or rotating the paper. Composite raw scores for each maze reflected number of errors (number of times the line crossed the track) and speed (time to complete the task). Fewer errors and faster speed contributed to higher raw scores.

Several conventional speech and language outcome measures were also obtained from each child. Open-set word recognition was assessed with the PBK test. The PPVT was administered to assess receptive vocabulary knowledge. The Forward Digit Span and Backward Digit Span subtests of the WISC-III were also administered to measure information processing capacity. Test sentences developed by McGarr (1983) were used to estimate verbal rehearsal speed (Baddeley et al., 1975; Pisoni & Cleary, 2003). The children were asked to repeat the sentences aloud, and their utterances were recorded and then later measured for length of utterance in seconds.

The results of the Design Copying performance showed that, although most children fell within normal limits, the mean performance on Design Copying was lower than would be expected from a sample of age-matched hearing peers. The same pattern was observed for the Visual–Motor Precision scores. In addition, correlations were carried out on both sets of visual–motor scores. The only demographic factor found to correlate significantly with these scores was age at implantation. Children who received a CI at an earlier age tended to show higher Design Copying and Visual–Motor Precision scores than did children implanted at later ages. Several correlations were also carried out on the language measures. For the correlations that were significant, partial correlations were conducted to control for the effect of age at implantation. Design Copying showed significant correlations with PPVT, PBK, and backward digit-span scores. Each of these relationships remained significant after partial correlations were carried out to control for age at implantation. Visual–Motor Precision scores were also significantly correlated with PBK scores.

Overall, performance on both Design Copying and Visual–Motor Precision tasks was below the scores reported for hearing peers based on the NEPSY norms. Unlike the first study, in which preimplant VMI scores were not significantly below normative data, the present results replicate earlier findings showing that visual–motor integration skills of deaf children are delayed compared to hearing children (Erden, Otman, & Tunay, 2004; Tiber, 1985). When administered prior to implantation, it is possible that VMI and design copying tests are not sensitive enough to pick up differences between prelingually deaf children and hearing peers. It is also possible that visual–motor integration skills display a slower developmental trajectory in prelingually deaf children compared with hearing children and, thus, delays in visual–spatial processing skills may only become apparent at later ages.

As in the first VMI study, longer periods of deafness prior to implantation were associated with greater delays on the Design Copying and Visual–Motor Precision. Children implanted at later ages showed lower Design Copying and Visual–Motor Precision standard scores than did children implanted at earlier ages. Although the above correlations are not causal, they suggest that a period of auditory deprivation and language delay may lead to atypical development of nonverbal, visual–spatial skills such as those assessed in the VMI tests. Although recent neuroimaging work has begun to reveal mechanisms of auditory cortical plasticity underlying speech perception and production outcomes (Lee, D. et al., 2001; Sharma, Dorman, & Spahr, 2002), little is currently known about how nonverbal processes such as visual–spatial coding and sensory–motor processes are affected by a period of profound deafness and delay in language. In a recent paper by H. Lee et al. (2005), increased preimplant positron emission tomography activity in the frontal and parietal cortex, brain areas involved in behavioral control and visual–spatial processing, was found to be a predictor of postimplant speech perception scores.

These findings suggest that early auditory experience not only affects speech perception and language processing skills but also affects the development of attentional and behavioral inhibition systems. Several investigators have reported that deaf children with CIs show more age-typical performance on visual-only tests of sustained attention than do deaf children without CIs who use hearing aids (Quittner, Smith, Osberger, Mitchell, & Katz, 1994; Smith, Quittner, Osberger, & Miyamoto, 1998). Sustained attention has also been shown to improve with length of CI use (Horn, Davis, Pisoni, & Miyamoto, 2005b). Furthermore, the ability of prelingually deaf children with CIs to regulate and delay premature behavioral responses has been shown to increase with CI use and to be related to performance on several spoken language measures (Horn et al., 2005a). The findings obtained with the Visual Motor Precision task provide additional converging support for these earlier findings on the development of attention and behavioral regulation, processes that reflect the operation of cognitive control and executive function.

The studies by Horn et al. demonstrate that visual–motor integration skills in prelingually deaf children are influenced by early auditory and linguistic experience. The findings suggest that early experience and activity affects the development of several basic elementary information processing operations that are independent of the sensory domain. Although the precise underlying neurobiological mechanisms behind these findings are still unclear, the results suggest that working memory, subvocal verbal rehearsal, and behavioral inhibition, neurocognitive processes typically associated with frontal lobe executive function, may play important roles in cognitive control and self-regulation used in a wide range of behavioral tasks commonly used to assess speech and language outcomes in both hearing children and deaf children with CIs (see Hauser, Lukomski, & Hillman, this volume).

The results reported by Horn et al. also demonstrate that several visual–motor integration tests, such as the Beery VMI, the NEPSY, and the Design Copying and Visual–Motor Precision tests, can be used clinically to predict outcomes following implantation. These standardized neuropsychological tests, which can be easily administered to deaf children because they do not require auditory processing skills, should be considered as potential additions to assessment batteries used with this clinical population both pre- and postimplantation.

Cognitive Control and Executive Function

When compared with findings obtained on behavioral tests of hearing children, our findings suggest that several aspects of executive function and frontal lobe activity may be disrupted or delayed and may underlie the differences we have observed in traditional outcome measures. "Executive function" is an umbrella term in neuropsychology and cognitive neuroscience that includes several different processing domains such as attention, cognitive control, working memory, and inhibition (see Hauser et al., this volume).

Many cognitive neuroscientists believe that executive function involves using prior knowledge and experience to predict future events and modulate the current contents of immediate memory (Goldman-Rakic, 1988). There is general agreement that several different aspects of executive function play important roles in receptive and expressive language processes via top-down feedback and control of information processing activities in a wide range of behavioral tasks. The study of executive function and frontal lobe processes may provide new insights into the neurobiological and neurocognitive basis of individual differences following cochlear implantation.

BRIEF, LEAF, and CHAOS Rating Scales of Executive Function

We are now engaged in a series of new studies to assess the contribution of executive function and self-regulation in the development of speech and language processes in deaf children following cochlear implantation. To obtain measures of executive function as they are realized in the real-world home, school, or preschool settings, outside the highly controlled conditions of the audiology clinic or research laboratory, we have been using a neuropsychological instrument called the BRIEF (Behavior Rating Inventory of Executive Function; Psychological Assessment Resources, Inc., 1996). The BRIEF consists of rating scales that are filled out by parents, teachers, and daycare providers to assess a child's executive functions and self-regulation. These rating scales measure specific aspects of executive function related to inhibition, shifting of attention, emotional control, working memory, planning, and organization among others. Scores from these clinical subscales are then used to construct several aggregate indexes of behavioral regulation, inhibitory self-control, flexibility, and metacognition. Each rating inventory also provides a global executive composite score.

The BRIEF has been shown in a number of recent studies to be useful in evaluating children with a wide spectrum of developmental and acquired neurocognitive conditions, although it has not been used yet with deaf children who use CIs (Gioia, Isquith, Kenworthy, & Barton, 2002). From our preliminary work so far, we believe that this instrument may provide new measures of executive function and behavior regulation that are associated with conventional speech and language measures of outcome and benefit in this clinical population. Some of these measures can be obtained preimplant and therefore may be useful as behavioral predictors of outcome and benefit after implantation.

Our initial analysis of recent data obtained on the BRIEF from 15 hearing 5- to 8-year-old children and 12 deaf 5- to 10-year-old children with CIs revealed elevated scores in the CI group on several subscales (see Conway, Pisoni, Geers, Kronenberger, & Anaya, 2007). The group means on the Behavioral Regulation Index (BRI), Metacognition Index (MCI), and the Global Executive Composite (GEC) scores were all higher for deaf children with CIs than for hearing children, although none of them fell within the clinically significant range.

Examination of the eight individual clinical subscales showed significant differences in shifting, emotional control, and working memory. The elevated scores on the BRI suggest that a period of profound deafness and associated language delay before cochlear implantation not only affects basic domain-specific speech and language processes but also affects self-regulation and emotional control, metacognitive processes not typically considered to be sequela of deafness and sensory deprivation in this population (see Schorr, 2005). The BRIEF scores from this new study provide additional converging evidence that multiple processing systems are linked together in development and that disturbances resulting from deafness are not domain-specific and restricted only to hearing and auditory signal processing by the peripheral auditory system (Conway, Pisoni et al., 2007).

Analysis of the scores obtained on both the Learning Executive Attention Functioning (LEAF), which was developed to measure executive function in the context of learning environments, and the Conduct-Hyperactive-Attention Problem-Oppositional Scale (CHAOS), which was designed to screen for ADHD and disruptive behavior symptoms, also revealed elevated scores on the clinical subscales for the children with CIs compared with the hearing comparison group. In particular, significant differences were observed in learning, memory, attention, speed of processing, sequential processing, complex information processing, and novel problem-solving subscales on the LEAF; and attention, hyperactivity, and opposition problems on the CHAOS. No differences were observed on the conduct disorder subscale of the CHAOS.

These additional results reflecting real-world behaviors demonstrate the involvement of several parallel information processing systems and neural circuits involved in learning, memory, attention, and processing of complex sequential information. Deaf children with CIs show evidence of disturbances in cognitive and emotional control, monitoring behavior, self-regulation, planning, and organization. These differences are not isolated domain-specific symptoms but reflect domain-general properties of an integrated system used in language and cognition, linking brain function and behavior with the executive control processes that monitor and regulate ongoing behavior and social functioning in novel environments where highly robust adaptive behaviors are routinely required (Luria, 1973).

Summary and Implications

The results from a large number of studies covering a range of information processing domains have been presented. In this section, we provide a brief overview and summary of the major findings of these studies and suggest several conclusions about what these findings mean. We then offer several suggestions for how to understand and interpret these diverse findings in terms of both their direct clinical significance and more basic theoretical relevance.

What do all of these diverse behavioral measures have in common? At first glance, the diverse pattern of differences observed across these tasks may seem unrelated and anomalous. However, more careful examination reveals they have links in common and show several important similarities with the extensive clinical literature on frontal lobe disturbances and executive dysfunction in other clinical populations. These frontal lobe disturbances are associated with differences in controlled attention, monitoring and manipulating of verbal information in working memory, functional integration, organization and coordination, self-regulation, inhibition, planning, and using prior knowledge and experience to predict future events and actions in the service of speech and language processing as well as other processing domains.

One of the hallmarks of research on CIs is the enormous variability and individual differences in outcome and benefit. Given this problem, which is observed at all implant centers around the world, how can we begin to identify the underlying neurobiological and cognitive factors and explain the heterogeneity in speech and language outcomes? Are there a set of "core" attributes or common "defining features," or are there several different distinct subgroups of CI users? At this point, we cannot provide a definite answer to this question, but understanding the sources of variability in outcome has both clinical and theoretical significance, and additional research using new methods and experimental techniques will provide answers to these questions.

Some of the best CI users overlap on specific behavioral measures with hearing children on the low end of a distribution of scores. In contrast, other children with CIs do more poorly and get little benefit from their CIs. At present, it is unclear whether these individual differences lie on a continuum or whether there are specific subtypes of poor users. We also do not know what neurocognitive processes and underlying neural circuits are responsible for these differences. Are the low performers simply poor on all outcome measures, or is their performance restricted more selectively to only certain subtests and specific domains? These are important problems to explore in the future, because basic knowledge and understanding of the sources of variability in outcome will have several direct implications for diagnosis, treatment, and assessment.

Theoretical and Clinical Issues

One of the major problems of past research efforts on CIs, especially research on variability and individual differences in outcome, is that the field of CIs has been and continues to be intellectually isolated from the mainstream of research in cognition and neural sciences and is narrowly focused on clinical issues surrounding efficacy and outcomes. Cochlear implant researchers and clinicians have adopted an approach to hearing loss that ignores the role of functional connectivity and global systems-level integrative processes in speech and language (Luria, 1973).

A growing consensus among speech scientists and psycholinguists believes that speech perception and spoken language processing do not take place in isolation. Rather, these processes are heavily dependent on the contribution of multiple brain systems. All behavioral responses in any psychological task are a function of long sequences of processing operations. No part of the brain, even for sensory systems like vision and hearing, ever functions in isolation without multiple connections and linkages to other parts of the brain and nervous system. As Nauta (1964) pointed out many years ago, "It seems that if we try to discover the ways in which any part of the brain functions, it is only logical to try to find out in what way it acts within the brain as a whole . . . no part of the brain functions on its own, but only through the other parts of the brain with which it is connected" (p. 125). These observations apply equally well today in terms of research on CIs. We cannot continue to view profound deafness as merely a sensory loss that is disconnected from the rest of mind and brain.

Automatized and Controlled Processing

Our recent findings involving deaf children with CIs suggest that, in addition to the traditional demographic, medical, and educational variables that have been found to predict some proportion of the variance in traditional audiological measures of outcome and benefit, several additional sources of variance reflect the contribution of basic information processing skills commonly used in a wide range of language processing tasks, specifically, those which rely on rapid phonological encoding of speech and verbal rehearsal strategies in working memory and executive function. Thus, some proportion of the variability and individual differences in outcome following cochlear implantation is related to central auditory, neurocognitive, and linguistic factors that reflect how the initial sensory information transmitted by the CI is subsequently encoded and processed and how it is used by the listener in specific behavioral tasks that are routinely used to measure speech and language outcomes and assess benefit.

Can we identify a common factor that links these diverse sets of findings together? A coherent picture is beginning to emerge from all of these results. At least two factors contribute to success with a CI. One factor is the development and efficient use of "automatized" phonological processing skills (see Marschark & Wauters, this volume), typically carried out rapidly without conscious awareness or processing efforts. A second factor is the development of "controlled" processing, operations that require active attention, processing resources and mental effort, working memory, cognitive control, and executive function (similar findings are discussed by Hauser and Lukomski, this volume). Some children can adapt and overcome the first problem, which is related to encoding and registration of early sensory information, by using "controlled" conscious processes, but other children may have more difficulty overcoming basic sensory limitations. Deaf children who have delays or disturbances in both processing domains may be at much greater risk for doing poorly with their CIs.

The use of automatized phonological processing skills is a significant contributor above and beyond the traditional demographic, medical, and educational variables that have been found to be associated with outcome and benefit following cochlear implantation. Phonological analysis involves the rapid encoding and decomposition of speech signals into sequences of discrete, meaningless phonetic segments and the assignment of structural descriptions to these sound patterns that reflect the linguistically significant sound contrasts of words in the target language.

For many years, both clinicians and researchers have considered open-set tests of spoken word recognition performance to be the "gold standard" of outcome and benefit in both children and adults who have received CIs. The reason open-set tests are viewed in this way is because they require the use and coordination of several component processes including speech perception, verbal rehearsal, retrieval of phonological representations from short-term memory, and phonetic implementation strategies required for speech production, motor control, and response output. All of these subprocesses rely on rapid, highly automatized phonological processing skills for analysis and decomposition of the input signal in perceptual analysis and the reassembly and synthesis of these units into action sequences as motor commands and articulatory gestures for output and speech production. All of these open-set tests also load heavily on cognitive control processes and executive function. They require organization, integration, coordination, planning, inhibition, attention, monitoring, and manipulation of symbolic phonological representations in working memory, and they make extensive use of past experiences and immediate context to predict, modulate, and control future behavior.

When prelingually deaf children receive a CI as a treatment for their profound hearing loss, they do not simply have their hearing restored at the auditory periphery. After implantation, they receive novel stimulation to those specialized cortical areas of their brain that are critical for the development of spoken language and, specifically, for the development of automatized phonological processing skills that are used to rapidly encode, process, and reproduce speech signals linking up sensory and motor systems in new ways. Moreover, many different neural circuits in other areas of the brain also begin to receive inputs from the auditory cortex and brainstem, and these contribute to the global connectivity and integrative functions linking multiple brain regions in regulating speech and language processes in a highly coordinated manner.

The present set of findings permits us to identify a specific information processing mechanism—the verbal rehearsal process in working memory—that is responsible for the limitations on processing capacity (see also chapters in this volume by Marschark & Wauters and Hauser et al.). Processing limitations are present in a wide range of clinical tests that make use of verbal rehearsal and phonological processing skills to rapidly encode, store, maintain, and retrieve spoken words from working memory. These fundamental information processing operations are components of all of the current clinical outcome measures routinely used to assess receptive and expressive language functions. Our findings suggest that the variability in performance on the traditional clinical outcome measures used to assess speech and language processing skills in deaf children after cochlear implantation reflects fundamental differences in the speed of information processing operations such as verbal rehearsal, scanning of items in short-term memory, and the rate of encoding phonological and lexical information in working memory.

Controlled Processing and Executive Dysfunction

A second factor uncovered in our research reflects differences in behavioral regulation, cognitive control, and executive function, domain-general meta-cognitive processes that are slow, effortful, and typically thought to be under conscious control of the individual. One of the reasons we have focused our recent research efforts on executive function in deaf children with CIs is that executive functions are domain-general processes that are involved in regulating, guiding, directing, and managing cognition, emotion and behavioral response, and actions across diverse environments, especially novel contexts in which active problem solving and adaptive skills are typically required. Our recent findings suggest that the sequela of deafness and delay in language are not domain-specific and restricted to only hearing and auditory processing. Other neurocognitive systems display disturbances, and these differences appear to reflect the operation of domain-general processes of cognitive control, self-regulation, and organization.

Another reason for our interest in cognitive control processes in spoken language processing is that executive function develops in parallel with other aspects of neural development, especially in the development of neural circuits in the frontal lobe, which are densely interconnected with other brain regions. The development of bidirectional connections among multiple brain regions suggests that the development of speech and spoken language processing may be more productively viewed within the broad context of development as an integrated functional system rather than a narrow focus on the development of hearing and the peripheral auditory system.

Moreover, large individual differences have been observed in the development of executive function within and across cognitive, emotional, and behavioral domains. Thus, variability in outcome and benefit following implantation may not only reflect contributions from basic domain-specific sensory, cognitive, and linguistic processes related directly to the development of hearing, speech, and language function but may also reflect domain-general control processes that are characteristic of global cognitive control, emotional regulation, and behavioral response and action.

Focusing new research efforts on executive function and frontal lobe disturbances in deaf children with CIs also provides a neurally grounded conceptual framework for understanding and explaining a diverse set of behavioral findings on attention and inhibition, memory and learning, visual–spatial processing, and sensory–motor function, traditional neurocognitive domains that have been studied extensively in other clinical populations that have acquired or developmental syndromes that reflect brain-behavior dysfunctions in these processing systems. Speech and language processing operations make extensive use of these neurocognitive domains, and it seems entirely appropriate to include these in any future investigations seeking to understand and explain the basis of variability and individual differences in speech and language outcome following cochlear implantation.

Recent theoretical developments in cognitive neuroscience have established the utility of viewing the development and use of speech and language as embodied processes linking brain, body, and world together as an integrated system (Clark, 1997). There is every reason to believe that these new theoretical views will provide fundamental new insights into the enormous variability and individual differences in outcome and benefit following cochlear implantation in profoundly deaf children and adults. Without knowing what specific biological and cognitive factors are responsible for the enormous individual differences in CI outcomes or understanding the underlying neurocognitive basis for variation and individual differences in performance, it is difficult to motivate and select a specific approach to habilitation and therapy after a child receives a CI. Deaf children who are performing poorly with their CIs are not a homogeneous group and may differ in numerous ways from each other, reflecting the dysfunction of multiple brain systems associated with congenital deafness and profound hearing loss. Moreover, it seems very unlikely that an individual child will be able to achieve optimal benefits from her CI without researchers and clinicians knowing why a specific child is having problems and what particular neurocognitive domains and information processing subsystems underlie these problems.

Acknowledgments

The research described in this chapter was supported by NIH-NIDCD Training Grant T32DC00012 and NIH-NIDCD Research Grants R01DC00111 and NIH-NIDCD R01DC00064 to Indiana University. We thank Luis Hernandez and Darla Sallee for their help and assistance on various phases of this work over the years.

References

Ackerman, P. L., Kyllonen, P. C., & Roberts, R. D. (1999). *Learning and individual differences.* Washington, DC: American Psychological Association.
Archibald, L. M. D., & Gathercole, S. E. (2007). The complexities of complex memory span: Storage and processing deficits in specific language impairment. *Journal of Memory and Language, 57,* 177–194.

Bachara, G., & Phelan, W. (1980). Visual perception and language levels of deaf children. *Perceptual and Motor Skills, 51,* 272.

Baddeley, A., Gathercole, S., & Papagno, C. (1998). The phonological loop as a language learning device, *Psychological Review, 105,* 158–173.

Baddeley, A. D., Thomson, N., & Buchanan, M. (1975). Word length and the structure of short-term memory. *Journal of Verbal Learning and Verbal Behavior, 14,* 575–589.

Beery, K. (1989). *The VMI developmental test of visual motor integration* (3rd revision). Cleveland: Modern Curriculum Press.

Bench, J., Kowal, A., & Bamford, J. (1979). The BKB (Bamford-Kowal-Bench) sentence lists for partially-hearing children. *British Journal of Audiology, 13,* 108–112.

Bergeson, T., & Pisoni, D. B. (2004). Audiovisual speech perception in deaf adults and children following cochlear implantation. In G. Calvert, C. Spence, & B. E. Stein (Eds.), *Handbook of Multisensory Integration.* Cambridge: MIT Press.

Burkholder, R. A., & Pisoni, D. B. (2003). Speech timing and working memory in profoundly deaf children after cochlear implantation. *Journal of Experimental Child Psychology, 85,* 63–88.

Burkholder, R. A., & Pisoni, D. B. (2006). Working memory capacity, verbal rehearsal speed, and scanning in deaf children with cochlear implants. In P. E. Spencer & M. Marschark (Eds.), *Advances in the spoken language development of deaf and hard-of-hearing children,* (pp. 328–357). New York: Oxford University Press.

Carpenter, P. A., Miyake, A., & Just, M. A. (1994). Working memory constraints in comprehension. In M. A. Gernsbacher (Ed.), *Handbook of psycholinguistics,* (pp. 1075–1122). San Diego: Academic Press.

Clark, A. (1997). *Being there: Putting brain, body, and world together again.* Cambridge, MA: MIT Press.

Cleary, M., & Pisoni, D. B. (2001). *Sequence learning as a function of presentation modality in children with cochlear implants.* Poster presented at CID New Frontiers Conference, St. Louis, MO.

Cleary, M., Pisoni, D. B., & Geers, A. E. (2001). Some measures of verbal and spatial working memory in eight- and nine-year-old hearing-impaired children with cochlear implants. *Ear, and Hearing, 22,* 395–411.

Cleary, M., Pisoni, D. B., & Kirk, K. I. (2002). Working memory spans as predictors of spoken word recognition and receptive vocabulary in children with cochlear implants. *The Volta Review, 102,* 259–280.

Conway, C. M., Karpicke, J., & Pisoni, D. B. (2007). Contribution of implicit sequence learning to spoken language processing: Some preliminary findings with hearing adults. *Journal of Deaf Studies and Deaf Education, 12,* 317–334.

Conway, C. M., Pisoni, D. B., Anaya, M., Karpicke, J., & Henning, S. (2008). *The role of implicit learning in spoken language development: Data from typically-developing children and deaf children with cochlear implants.* Manuscript in preparation.

Conway, C. M., Pisoni, D. B., Geers, A., Kronenberger, W. G., & Anaya, E. M. (2007). *Effects of cochlear implantation on executive function: Some preliminary findings.* Abstract submitted to the 10th International Conference on Cochlear Implants and other Implantable Auditory Technologies. San Diego, CA, April, 2008.

Cowan, N. (1992). Verbal memory and the timing of spoken recall. *Journal of Memory and Language, 31,* 668–684.

Cowan, N. (2005). *Working memory capacity.* New York: Psychology Press.

Cowan, N., Keller, T., Hulme, C., Roodenrys, S., McDougall, S., & Rack, J. (1994). Verbal memory span in children: Speech timing clues to the mechanisms underlying age and word length effects. *Journal of Memory and Language, 33,* 234–250.

Cowan, N., Wood, N. L., Wood, P. K., Keller, T. A., Nugent, L. D., & Keller, C. V. (1998). Two separate verbal processing rates contributing to short-term memory span. *Journal of Experimental Psychology: General, 127,* 141–160.

Dempster, F. N. (1981). Memory span: Sources of individual and developmental differences. *Psychological Bulletin, 89,* 63–100.

Dillon, C. (2005). Phonological processing skills and the development of reading in deaf children who use cochlear implants. *Research on Spoken Language Processing, Technical Report No. 14:* Indiana University, Bloomington, IN.

Dunn, L., & Dunn, L. (1997). *Peabody picture vocabulary test* (3rd ed.). Circle Pines, MN: American Guidance Service.

Engle, R. W., Kane, M. J., & Tuholski, S. W. (1999). Individual differences in working memory capacity and what they tell us about controlled attention, general fluid intelligence and functions of the prefrontal cortex. In A. Miyake & P. Shah. (Eds.), *Models of working memory: Mechanisms of active maintenance and executive control.* London: Cambridge Press.

Erden, Z., Otman, S., & Tunay, V. (2004). Is visual perception of hearing-impaired children different from healthy children? *International Journal of Pediatric Otorhinolaryngology, 68,* 281–285.

Fagan, M. K., Pisoni, D. B., Horn, D. L., & Dillon, C.M. (2007). Neuropsychological correlates of vocabulary, reading, and working memory in deaf children with cochlear implants. *Journal of Deaf Studies and Deaf Education, 12,* 461–471.

Fryauf-Bertschy, H., Tyler, R. S., Kelsay, D. M. R., Gantz, B. J., & Woodworth, G. G. (1997). Cochlear implant use by prelingually deafened children: The influences of age at implant and length of device use. *Journal of Speech, Language, and Hearing Research, 40,* 183–199.

Garner, W. R. (1974). *The processing of information and structure.* Potomac, MD: Lawrence Erlbaum.

Gaskell, M. G. (2007). *The Oxford handbook of psycholinguistics.* New York: Oxford University Press.

Gathercole, S., & Baddeley, A. (1990). Phonological memory deficits in language disordered children: Is there a causal connection? *Journal of Memory and Language, 29,* 336–360.

Gathercole, S. E., Hitch, G. J., Service, E., & Martin, A. J. (1997). Phonological short-term memory and new word learning in children. *Developmental Psychology, 33,* 966–979.

Geers, A., Brenner, C., & Davidson, L. (2003). Factors associated with development of speech perception skills in children implanted by age five. *Ear and Hearing, 24,* 24S–35S.

Geers, A., Nicholas, J., & Sedey, A. (2003). Language skills of children with early cochlear implantation. *Ear and Hearing, 24,* 46S97–58S.

Gioia, G. A., Isquith, P. K., Guy, S. C., & Kenworthy, L. (2000). *BRIEF™: Behavior Rating Inventory of Executive Function.* Psychological Assessment Resources, Inc.

Gioia, G. A., Isquith, P. K., Kenworthy, L., & Barton, R. M. (2002). Profiles of everyday executive function in acquired and developmental disorders. *Child Neuropsychology, 8,* 121–137.

Goldman-Rakic, P. S. (1988). Topography of cognition: Parallel distributed networks in primate association cortex. *Annual Reviews of Neuroscience, 11,* 137–156.

Gupta, P., & MacWhinney, B. (1997). Vocabulary acquisition and verbal short-term memory: Computational and neural bases. *Brain and Language, 59,* 267–333.

Harnsberger, J. D., Svirsky, M. A., Kaiser, A. R., Pisoni, D. B., Wright, R., & Meyer, T. A. (2001). Perceptual "vowel spaces" of cochlear implant users: Implications for the study of auditory adaptation to spectral shift. *Journal of the Acoustical Society of America, 109,* 2135–2145.

Hebb, D. O. (1961). Distinctive features of learning in the high animal. In J. F. Delafresnaye (Ed.), *Brain mechanisms and learning* (pp. 37–51). London and New York: Oxford University Press.

Horn, D., Davis, R. A. O., Pisoni, D. B., & Miyamoto, R. T. (2004). Visuomotor integration ability of pre-lingually deaf children predicts audiological outcome with a cochlear implant: A first report. *International Congress Series, 1273,* 356–359.

Horn, D., Davis, R., Pisoni, D., & Miyamoto, R. (2005a). Behavioral inhibition and clinical outcomes in children with cochlear implants. *Laryngoscope, 115,* 595–600.

Horn, D., Davis, R., Pisoni, D., & Miyamoto, R. (2005b). Development of visual attention skills in prelingually deaf children who use cochlear implants. *Ear and Hearing, 26,* 389–408.

Horn, D., Pisoni, D., Sanders, M., & Miyamoto, R. (2005). Behavioral assessment of pre-lingually deaf children prior to cochlear implantation. *Laryngoscope, 115,* 1603–1611.

Horn, D. L., Fagan, M. K., Dillon, C. M., Pisoni, D. B., & Miyamoto, R. T. (2007, in press). Visual-motor integration skills of prelingually deaf children: Implications for pediatric cochlear implantation. *Laryngoscope, 117.*

Horn, D. L., Pisoni, D. B., & Miyamoto, R. T. (2006). Divergence of fine and gross motor skills in prelingually deaf children: Implications for cochlear implantation. *Laryngoscope, 116,* 1500–1506.

Iverson, J. M. & Fagan, M. K. (2004). Infant vocal-motor coordination: Precursor to the gesture-speech system? *Child Development, 75,* 1053–1066.

Kaas, J. H., Merzenich, M. M., & Killackey, H. P. (1983). The reorganization of somatosensory cortex following peripheral nerve damage in adult and developing mammals. *Annual Review of Neuroscience, 6,* 325–356.

Karpicke, J. D. & Pisoni, D. B. (2004). Using immediate memory span to measure implicit learning. *Memory, and Cognition, 32,* 956–964.

Kirk, K. I., Pisoni, D. B., & Miyamoto, R. T. (2000). Lexical discrimination by children with cochlear implants: Effects of age at implantation and communication mode. In S. B. Waltzman & N. L. Cohen (Eds.), *Cochlear implants* (pp. 252–254). New York: Thieme.

Kirk, K. I., Pisoni, D. B., & Osberger, M. J. (1995). Lexical effect on spoken word recognition by pediatric cochlear implant users. *Ear and Hearing, 16,* 470–481.

Korkman, M., Kirk, U., & Kemp, S. (1998). *NEPSY: A developmental neuro-psychological assessment.* China: PsychCorp.

Kronenberger, W. G. (2006). *Learning Executive Attention Functioning (LEAF).* Department of Psychiatry, Indiana School of Medicine, Indianapolis, IN.

Kronenberger, W. G., Dunn, D. W., & Giauque, A. L. (1998). *Conduct-Hyperactive-Attention Problem-Oppositional Scale (CHAOS).* Department of Psychiatry, Indiana School of Medicine, Indianapolis, IN.

Lee, D., Lee, J., Oh, S. H., Kim, H., et al. (2001). Cross-modal plasticity and co-chlear implants. *Nature, 409,* 149–150.

Lee, H., et al. (2005). Preoperative differences of cerebral metabolism relate to the outcome of cochlear implants in congenitally deaf children. *Hearing Research, 203,* 2–9.

Lenneberg, E. (1967). *Biological foundations of language.* New York: Wiley.

Locke, J., Bekken, K., McMinn-Larson, L., & Wein, D. (1995). Emergent con-trol of manual and vocal-motor activity in relation to the development of speech. *Brain and Language, 51,* 498–508.

Luria, A. R. (1973). *The working brain: An introduction to neuropsychology.* New York: Basic Books.

McGarr, N. S. (1983). The intelligibility of deaf speech to experienced and inex-perienced listeners. *Journal of Speech and Hearing Research, 26,* 451–458.

Melton, A. W. (1963). Implications of short-term memory for a general theory of memory. *Journal of Verbal Learning and Verbal Behavior, 2,* 1–21.

Miller, E. K., & Cohen, J. D. (2001). An integrative theory of prefrontal cortex function. *Annual Reviews in Neuroscience, 24,* 167–202.

Myklebust, H. R. & Brutten, M. (1953). A study of the visual perception of deaf children. *Acta Oto-laryngol, Suppl. 105. p. 126.*

Nauta, W. J. H. (1964). Discussion of 'Retardation and facilitation in learning by stimulation of frontal cortex in monkeys.' In J. M. Warren & K. Akert (Eds.), *The Frontal Granular Cortex and Behavior* (p. 125). New York: McGraw-Hill.

NIH. (1988). *Cochlear implants.* NIH Consensus Statement, May 4, Vol. 7.

NIH. (1993). *Early identification of hearing impairment in infants and young children.* NIH Consensus Statement, March 1–3, Vol. 11.

NIH. (1995). *Cochlear implants in adults and children.* NIH Consensus State-ment 1995 May 15–17; 13, 1–30.

Osberger, M., Robbins, A., Todd, S., & Riley, A. (1994). Speech intelligibility of children with cochlear implants. *Volta Review, 96,* 169–80.

Penny, C. G. (1989). Modality effects and the structure of short-term verbal memory. *Memory, and Cognition, 17,* 398–422.

Pisoni, D. B. (1997). Some thoughts on "normalization" in speech perception. In K. Johnson, and J. W. Mullennix (Eds.), *Talker variability in speech processing* (pp. 9–32). San Diego: Academic Press.

Pisoni, D. B. (2000). Cognitive factors and cochlear implants: Some thoughts on perception, learning, and memory in speech perception. *Ear and Hearing, 21,* 70–78.

Pisoni, D. B., & Cleary, M. (2003). Measures of working memory span and verbal rehearsal speed in deaf children after cochlear implantation. *Ear and Hearing, 24,* 106S–120S.

Pisoni, D. B., & Cleary, M. (2004). Learning, memory, and cognitive processes in deaf children following cochlear implantation. In F. G. Zeng, A. N. Popper, & R. R. Fay (Eds.), *Springer handbook of auditory research: Auditory prosthesis,* SHAR Volume X, 377–426. New York: Springer.

Pisoni, D. B., Cleary, M., Geers, A., & Tobey, E. (2000). Individual differences in effectiveness of cochlear implants in children who are prelingually deaf: New process measures of performance. *The Volta Review, 101,* 111–164.

Pisoni, D. B., & Davis, R.A.O. (2003). Sequence learning as a predictor of outcomes in deaf children with cochlear implants. In *Research on spoken language processing progress report no. 26* (pp. 319–330). Bloomington, IN: Speech Research Laboratory, Indiana University.

Pisoni, D. B., & Geers, A. (2001). Working memory in deaf children with cochlear implants: Correlations between digit span and measures of spoken language processing. *Annals of Otology, Rhinology, and Laryngology, 109,* 92–93.

Pisoni, D. B., Svirsky, M. A., Kirk, K. I., & Miyamoto, R. T. (1997). Looking at the "Stars": A first report on the intercorrelations among measures of speech perception, intelligibility, and language development in pediatric cochlear implant users. *Research on Spoken Language Processing Progress Report No. 21* (pp. 51–91). Bloomington, IN: Speech Research Laboratory.

Quittner, A., Smith, L., Osberger, M., Mitchell, T., & Katz, D. (1994). The impact of audition on the development of visual attention. *Psychological Science, 5,* 347–53.

Riesen, A. H. (1975). *The developmental neuropsychology of sensory deprivation.* New York: Academic Press.

Rosen, V. M., & Engle, R. W. (1997). Forward and backward serial recall. *Intelligence, 25,* 37–47.

Ross, M., & Lerman, J. (1979). A picture identification test for hearing-impaired children. *Journal of Speech and Hearing Research, 13,* 44–53.

Rudel, R. G., & Denckla, M. B. (1974). Relation of forward and backward digit repetition to neurological impairment in children with learning disability. *Neuropsychologia, 12,* 109–118.

Ryugo, D. K., Limb, C. J., & Redd, E. E. (2000). Brain plasticity: The impact of the environment on the brain as it relates to hearing and deafness. In J. K. Niparko (Ed.), *Cochlear implants: Principles and practices* (pp. 33–56). Philadelphia, PA: Lippincott Williams, and Wilkins.

Savelsbergh, G., Netelenbos, J., & Whiting, H. (1991). Auditory perception and the control of spatially coordinated action of deaf and hearing children. *Journal of Child Psychology and Psychiatry, 32,* 489–500.

Schorr, E. A. (2005). *Social and emotional functioning of children with cochlear implants.* Unpublished Master's Thesis, University of Maryland, College Park, MD.

Sharma, A., Dorman, M. F., & Spahr, A. J. (2002). A sensitive period for the development of the central auditory system in children with cochlear implants: Implications for age of implantation. *Ear and Hearing, 23,* 532–539.

Shepard, R. K., & Hardie, N. (2001). Deafness-induced changes in the auditory pathway: Implications for cochlear implants. *Audiology and Neuro-Otology, 6,* 305–318.

Siegel, L., Saigal, S., Rosenbaum, P., Morton, R. A., Young, A., Berenbaum, S., & Stoskopf, B. (1982). Predictors of development in preterm and full-term infants: A model for detecting the at risk child. *Journal of Pediatric Psychology, 7,* 135–148.

Smith, L., Quittner, A., Osberger, M., & Miyamoto, R. (1998). Audition and visual attention: The developmental trajectory in deaf and hearing populations. *Developmental Psychology, 34,* 840–850.

Sparrow, S., Balla, D., & Cicchetti, D. (1984). *Vineland Adaptive Behavioral Scales.* Circle Pines, MN: American Guidance Service.

Spencer, P., & Delk, L. (1985). Hearing-impaired students' performance on tests of visual processing: Relationships with reading performance. *American Annals of the Deaf, 134,* 333–337.

Staller, S. J., Pelter, A. L., Brimacombe, J. A., Mecklenberg, D., & Arndt, P. (1991). Pediatric performance with the Nucleus 22-Channel Cochlear Implant System. *American Journal of Otology, 12,* 126–136.

Svirsky, M. A., Robbins, A. M., Kirk, K. I., Pisoni, D. B., & Miyamoto, R. T. (2000). Language development in profoundly deaf children with cochlear implants. *Psychological Science, 11,* 153–158.

Tait, M., Lutman, M. E., & Robinson, K. (2000). Preimplant measures of preverbal communicative behavior as predictors of cochlear implant outcomes in children. *Ear, and Hearing, 21,* 18–24.

Taylor, K. (1999). Relationship between visual motor integration skill and academic performance in kindergarten through third grade. *Optometry and Vision Science 76,* 69–73.

Teoh, S. W., Pisoni, D. B., & Miyamoto, R. T. (2004a). Cochlear implantation in adults with prelingual deafness: I. Clinical results. *Laryngoscope, 114,* 1536–1540.

Teoh, S. W., Pisoni, D. B., & Miyamoto, R. T. (2004b). Cochlear implantation in adults with prelingual deafness: II. Underlying constraints that affect audiological outcomes. *Laryngoscope, 114,* 1714–1719.

Teuber, H. L. (1964). The riddle of frontal lobe function in man. In J. M. Warren & K. Akert (Eds.), *The frontal granular cortex and behavior* (pp. 410–444). New York: McGraw-Hill.

Tiber, N. (1985). A psychological evaluation of cochlear implants in children. *Ear and Hearing, 6,* 48S–51S.

Tobey, E. A., Geers. A. E., Morchower, B., Perrin, J., Skellett, R., Brenner, C., & Torretta, G. (2000). Factors associated with speech intelligibility in children with cochlear implants. *Annals of Otology, Rhinology and Laryngology Supplement, 185,* 28–30.

Watkins, M. J., Watkins, O. C., & Crowder, R. G. (1974). The modality effect in free and serial recall as a function of phonological similarity. *Journal of Verbal Learning and Verbal Behavior, 13,* 430–447.

Waltzman, S. B., Cohen, N. L., Gomolin, R. H., Green, J. E., Shapiro, W. H., Hoffman, R. A., & Roland, J. T., Jr. (1997). Open-set speech perception in congenitally deaf children using cochlear implants. *American Journal of Otology, 18,* 342–349.

Waltzman, S. B., Cohen, N. L., Gomolin, R. H., Shapiro, W. H., Ozdamar, S. R., & Hoffman, R. A. (1994). Long-term results of early cochlear implantation in congenitally and prelingually deafened children. *American Journal of Otology, 15,* 9–13.

Wechsler. D. (1991). *Wechsler Intelligence Scale for Children, Third Edition* (WISC-III). San Antonio, TX: The Psychological Corporation.

Wiegersma, P., & Van der Velde, A. (1983). Motor development of deaf children. *Journal of Child Psychology and Psychiatry 24,* 103–111.

Wilson, M. (2002). Six views of embodied cognition. *Psychonomic Bulletin and Review, 9,* 625–636.

Chapter 4

Achieving Efficient Learning

*Why Understanding Theory of Mind Is Essential
for Deaf Children . . . and Their Teachers*

Cyril Courtin, Anne-Marie Melot, and Denis Corroyer

Theory of Mind (ToM), originally defined as the ability to consider the human mind as a generator of representations, is now more broadly presented as a cornerstone in social interactions, because it corresponds to developing an awareness of how mental states (beliefs, desires, wishes, etc.) govern the behavior of self and others. In research about theory of mind, the "theory" is the one the child develops about human minds, which goes from something like "the 'mind' just mirrors reality" up to an adult-like theory such as "the mind is based on mental representations."

In this chapter, we want to explore relations between these theories and teaching–learning. We first explain these relationships and present the state-of-the-art findings about ToM in deaf children. We then address the main objective of the chapter: that is, to discuss how cognitive processes underlying ToM may differ among deaf children and in deaf children compared to hearing children. We also present ways in which some key aspects of hearing children's ToM might differ from researchers' conceptions about ToM development. This leads to a discussion of learning by deaf students and the need for teachers to be conscious of different learning styles.

Theory of Mind and Learning: An Introduction

There are several ways to relate ToM and teaching–learning. One possibility is to examine both sides of the dyad—the student and the teacher. In practice, learners (especially children) usually are the main locus of research, although Wellman and Lagattuta (2004, p. 480) considered ToM in teachers: "Teachers' theory-of-mind—their background conceptions of ignorance, misconception, knowledge acquisition, and belief change—demonstrably shape their pedagogical practice (Strauss, 2001)."

Children's learning of how to learn is a second way to approach ToM and, in fact, it was the first one from an historical perspective. That research was part of the early work on metacognition during the 1970s. It first dealt with the way children understand memory (e.g., How to be sure to remember something the next day? What strategies to use to this end?, Gordon & Flavell, 1977) and had been labelled *metamemory*. Over time, this work progressively focused on how children understand cognitive processes more generally and, by the 1980s, was labelled *metacognition* (for details, see Flavell, Miller, & Miller, 1993). One area of metacognitive research involving children recently has attracted most attention, that pertaining to children's understanding of the mind. It has become prominent under the label of "theory of mind"

Note that the relations between ToM and learning do not include the way to learn ToM; several studies have consistently demonstrated that ToM is not learned and cannot be taught (e.g., Flavell, Everett, Croft, & Flavell, 1981). Children naturally acquire ToM via listening, observing, and interacting with others, and this will be one of the likely reasons for deaf children's delay in ToM development—because they often are constrained in their interpersonal exchanges unless they have early access to an effective language.

For our part, in this chapter, we consider ToM development and its role in reaching efficient learning. That is, since teachers should have a theory about children's ToM, it would be important to determine whether the ToM in deaf children corresponds to what teachers expect. To this end, there are several ways to address the question. One could assume that deaf and hearing children react and develop in the same way, that there are only possible differences as a function of age or stage of development, and thus the observation of results (pass or fail) on a given test should be enough to draw conclusions. Of course, most researchers and, surely, most parents and teachers alike, do not think in this seemingly oversimplistic way (although the recent results reported by Peterson and colleagues could lead to the conclusion that we *should,* in fact, think like this; see below). Instead, many believe that differences exist in the manner in which deaf children think, relative to hearing peers—a position that Marschark has advocated for a long time, with the proviso that it does not mean better or worse, just different (e.g., Marschark, 2003).

An alternative is to consider that scores on ToM and related tasks are useful if they are used to determine performance patterns that may provide information about possible differences in the way deaf children develop.

This method has been espoused by a few authors, including Peterson et al. in Australia (Peterson & Slaughter, 2006; Peterson, Wellman, & Liu, 2005) and Courtin and Melot (2005, submitted) in France. The idea is to compare the performance patterns on different ToM tasks and see whether deaf children succeed in the tasks in the same order as hearing children.

Finally, one could assume that ToM scores and patterns, in fact, may not be sufficient, and that one should also work on understanding why children choose one or the other response to a given problem. This is the idea we will introduce in this chapter. We will present, apparently for the first time, work on the justifications provided by deaf children on false-belief (FB) tasks as an example of this third possible way to investigate ToM. This constitutes a new and complementary avenue to other approaches to ToM development of deaf children. However, for historical coherence, we will briefly report results relevant to the two first approaches.

Theory-of-Mind in Deaf Children: The State of the Art

Theory of mind in deaf children has been explored quite extensively for more than 10 years, from the seminal work of Peterson and Siegal (1995) to Schick, de Villiers, de Villiers, and Hoffmeister (2007). More than 30 papers have been published on the topic, and we will not go into detail on all of them here. The present chapter is not aimed at providing a meta-analysis of the earlier studies, but instead to propose a new perspective from which to consider ToM. Thus, we will only describe the general trends and conclusions of the earlier work.

The main task that has been used in studying deaf children's metarepresentational development is the *FB paradigm*, taken from Wimmer and Perner (1983). It can be described as follows: After a short scenario during which two dolls are playing with a marble, one of the dolls puts the marble in one of two or three boxes and "leaves the scene." While she is gone, the other doll decides to resume playing and takes the marble out of the first box and puts it in one of the remaining boxes. The first doll, "who has not seen the marble change boxes," then comes back, and the child is asked, "Where will she look for the marble?" Thus, to answer correctly and pass the task, children must disregard their knowledge of the actual location of the marble and consider the first doll's knowledge, which entails that the marble is still in the first box.

Using various forms of the FB paradigm, many authors have found that deaf children born to deaf parents and hearing children born to hearing parents do not differ in terms of success on ToM tasks (e.g., Courtin & Melot, 2005; Peterson & Siegal, 1999; Schick et al., 2007; Woolfe, Want, & Siegal, 2002). Only one study, on 10 very young second-generation deaf children (age range of 3 years-10 months to 5 years-6 months), revealed a delay in native signers compared to hearing children, on visual perspective taking (Remmel, 2003). Thus it seems that, at least from age 5 onwards (i.e., the youngest age group tested by Courtin, 2000) or even 4 years-6 months (the mean age of the youngest group tested by Schick et al., 2007), native signers show no delay in the beginnings of their metarepresentational development (but see Meristo et al., 2007, Experiment 1, for conflicting results with older native signers).

According to Remmel, the primary factor explaining the delay of young deaf children in ToM is the absence of overseeing (overhearing) and limited incidental learning. However, it is important to note that native signers will not de facto perform on par to hearing children; that is, simple exposure to sign language from birth may not be enough. As noted by Meristo et al. (2007), in many parts of the world deaf children, native signers included, have no choice but to attend "oral" schools because of the paucity of "signing" schools. In an important and innovative study, Meristo et al. compared the performances of deaf native signers who attended either bimodal–bilingual schools or oral schools in Italy, Estonia, and Sweden. The authors found that, on several ToM tasks, native signers who attended bimodal–bilingual schools did not differ from hearing children, but outperformed native signers who were enrolled in oral classes. Meristo et al. concluded that intensive and continuous exposure to sign language—throughout the day and not only at home—is essential for native signers' typical metarepresentational development.

Deaf children born to hearing parents have consistently been found delayed in ToM when compared with native signers and with hearing children (e.g., Courtin, 2000; Meristo et al., 2007; Peterson & Siegal, 1995; Schick et al., 2007; Woolfe et al., 2002). Possible reasons for this delay have been exhaustively presented by Remmel, Bettger, and Weinberg (2001). Most authors agree that early access to an accessible language is the important variable for metarepresentational development (see Hauser, Lukomski, & Hillman, this volume). This is not to say that spoken language necessarily is to be avoided. In fact, no clear differences in performance exist between late signing and speaking deaf children, as reported in the ToM literature. The only notable exception appears in the results reported by Peterson and Siegal (1999). Their sample of oral deaf children demonstrated ToM results at the same level as hearing children and native signers, outperforming late signers. However, the oral children in that study were not deaf, but hard-of-hearing, whereas the signing children were deaf.

Possible confounds of hearing loss and language orientation are an important issue in the remaining literature (see Peterson, 2004, for discussion about oral deaf children). However, we still await research involving deaf children whose hearing parents have been informed early of their children's hearing loss, how to communicate with them, and so on (see Leigh, this volume). Still to be determined, therefore, are the nuances of ToM development in those deaf children of hearing parents who demonstrate normal early linguistic and cognitive development, owing to early detection and parental awareness of their cognitive and linguistic needs (Bebko, Calderon, & Treder, 2003; Prezbindowski & Lederberg, 2003; Spencer, Meadow-Orlans, Koester, & Ludwig, 2004). Apparently the group of deaf children born to hearing parents involved in the Schick et al. (2007) study includes many children of this sort (Schick, personal communication, 17 July 2007). Their status is not entirely clear, however, because their language fluencies were not described fully, and these children were still delayed compared to native signers in their development of ToM. Also at issue in ToM research is the continuing emphasis on the FB attribution task, one which has been overused in past research to the point at which some authors consider it as a kind of "neurotic task fixation" (Gopnik, Slaughter, & Metlzoff, 1994, p. 157). What about the success of deaf children on ToM tasks other than FB?

We must look further at ToM and metarepresentation via other paradigms, as we actually know very little about metacognitive development in deaf children (see Marschark & Wauters, this volume). Even if we focus on the FB task, some authors have questioned that the task fully assesses the understanding of metarepresentational abilities. Marschark, Green, Hindmarsh, and Walker (2000), for example, found that, on an implicit level, 7- to 15-year-old deaf children of hearing parents clearly demonstrated ToM and an understanding of the FB concept, providing examples of both in storytelling based on imaginative themes (e.g., being picked up by a UFO). Yet, Russell et al. (1998) demonstrated that such children in Scotland did not pass the FB task until age 13.

Other authors, using nonverbal paradigms (for a review, see Woolfe et al., 2002), have obtained some interesting findings. For example, Morgan and Kegl (2006) reported that exposure to sign language only after the age of 10 may be damaging for (long-term) success on the FB task (see Akamatsu, Mayer, & Hardy-Braz, this volume). In their research involving 22 deaf Nicaraguans, one of the adults (26 years old) who had been exposed to sign language since age 12 failed the FB task despite his access to sign language for 14 years. Morgan and Kegl's results suggest that 10 years could be a critical age, after which introduction to an accessible language would not be sufficient to ensure success on the FB task. However, according to Morgan and Kegl, FB attribution understanding may still be possible under some other, more ecologically supported conditions.

Beyond the False Belief Task

Theory-of-mind development, separate from FB, has been studied by several researchers relating to desires (Steeds, Rowe, & Dowker, 1997) and emotions (Rieffe & Terwogt, 2000), but none has been as complete as the studies by Peterson, Wellman, and Liu (2005) and Peterson and Slaughter (2006), which we focus on in this section. Peterson, in collaboration with Siegal, had already explored several tasks beyond the FB paradigm, such as biological thinking (Peterson & Siegal, 1997; see also Peterson, 2007, on children's representations of the mind versus the brain), in order to circumscribe children's knowledge and difficulties in their thinking about psychological entities.

Peterson et al. (2005) addressed the question of desires, real and false beliefs, and hidden emotions. Clearly, this broader method should lead to a more fine-grained understanding of ToM abilities than would focusing solely on the FB task. Let us briefly consider those different tasks.

In the first task, the *diverse desires task,* the experimenter explicitly tells the child that a doll prefers, for example, carrots over cookies. What will the doll choose to eat when both a cookie and a carrot are available? To answer this question correctly, the child must disregard his own preference for the cookie and consider the doll's desires; that is, understand that the doll will behave according to her own preferences.

In the second task, the *diverse belief task,* the child must disregard his own belief, consider the doll's, and understand that she will react according to her belief. For example, the doll believes her cat is in the kitchen, whereas the child himself thinks it is in the bedroom. Where will the doll look for her cat? Thus, the principle is close to that of the FB task, except that the child does not infer the belief—it is stated by the adult. No false or correct belief is possible, because it is not stated, in the scenario, where the cat is really.

The third task addresses knowledge access, taken from Wellman and Liu (2004). The experimenter assesses the child's understanding that, for example, if a doll has not looked in a drawer, she does not know what is in it. This task refers back to the "seeing equals knowing" stage established by Flavell (1988; Flavell et al., 1981), and does not necessarily involve an understanding of the concept of metarepresentation. However, Wellman and Liu (2004) found that "the concept assessed by this task, namely, that a protagonist who has not seen something will be ignorant of it, develops immediately before (FB) understanding in typical preschoolers" (Peterson & Slaughter, 2006, p. 162).

Finally, the *hidden emotion task* addresses two different issues using a storytelling paradigm. First, it determines that the children are able to infer the real emotion of a child who has been teased. Second, it assesses whether the children are able to infer the apparent emotion (versus hidden emotion) that the child wants other children to think he feels.

It is clear that this research is much more detailed than previous studies, extending FB research to show how true belief, desires, and emotions influence behaviors. Nevertheless, on these tasks, the results obtained by native and late signers are fully in accordance with previous work: native signers are at the same level as hearing children, whereas late signers are delayed. The aim of the Peterson et al. study, however, was not so much to look at score levels, but to establish performance patterns, an issue to which we return in the next section.

Peterson and Slaughter (2006) also addressed the relationships of ToM and expressive abilities in a study involving hearing children and deaf children of hearing parents. In their Experiment 2, Peterson and Slaughter used the standard FB task and the knowledge access task. They also presented the children two different pictures about two imaginative story lines, a "Head in the Clouds" theme and a "Ghost" theme. The authors compared success on the ToM tasks to the expressive abilities in relation to mental states, either simple (e.g., "he is dreaming") or elaborated (e.g., "he is dreaming that he is playing with a dog"). The results obtained on the ToM tasks are in accordance with past research, as the late signers (mean age of 9.75 years) performed on a par with hearing children who were about 5 years younger. We discuss performance patterns in the next section.

Courtin and Melot (submitted) have also tried to work on ToM in general, rather than only on the FB task, using up to five tasks. According to Wellman, Cross, and Watson (2001), however, all the Courtin and Melot tasks are to be considered FB tasks. We think this point is questionable for one main reason: it would result in only one class of cognitive processes, those involved in the FB task, which would be of little help in the other paradigms. For example, in the usual FB task (unexpected location), it is assumed that the child understands that a belief, even if false, is the basis for others' actions. In the other tasks, such as the representational change or "unexpected content," one just assumes the children's understanding that another child can hold a FB. This is possibly an important difference; in fact, we have ourselves regularly observed that results on the FB task differ when one asks, "What does the doll think?" or "Where will she look for the chocolate?" The child can understand that the doll holds a FB but nonetheless state that she will look for her chocolate at the place where it is really, not where the doll thinks it is (Marschark et al., 2000; but see Yazdi, German, Defeyter, & Siegal, 2006, Experiment 3, for opposite results when using a question about "Where will she look first?" instead of the usual "Where will she look for the chocolate?").

Our tasks involved three test items each. First was the classic FB task, involving an "unexpected location." Second, we included the classic appearance-reality (AR) task. In this task, children are shown visually misleading items (e.g., a candle that looks like an apple, a box that looks like a book), and are asked "When you look at this, what is it, what does it look like?" After the children respond with the intended appearance (an apple), they are confronted with the real identity of the item and their feeling that the item is in fact a candle is agreed to by the experimenter.

The children are then asked two questions: "What is it really? Is it really an apple or really a candle?," and "When you look at this right now, does it look like an apple or does it look like a candle?" Note that Wellman et al. (2001) call this task an "unexpected identity" FB task.

Our third task was the classic representational change (RC) task. This task consists in showing a box whose contents the child should know even before opening it (e.g., a box of Smarties or, for North-American children, an M&M box) but which, in fact, has secretly been changed before presentation. The box is shown closed, and the child is asked what it contains. After the child has said it contains sweets, he is shown the true contents—a pencil. The experimenter then closes the box, and the child is asked, "When I asked you first, before I opened up the box, what did you think was inside the box? Did you think there was a pencil inside or candies inside?" (e.g., Gopnik & Astington, 1988). Note that the RC task is now often considered as a FB task, but about oneself instead of others (e.g., Wellman et al., 2001). In fact, when the question is not about the self but relates to others' beliefs, the task is traditionally labelled as an "unexpected content" FB task (Perner, Leekam, & Wimmer, 1987). However, contrary to the "unexpected location" FB task, the RC task addresses the understanding by children that their own beliefs and representations can change, hence the term "representational change." Early research by Gopnik and Astington (1988) found that the understanding by children of their own representations was not as well developed as their understanding of representations in others, but later research did not replicate this finding (Gopnik & Slaughter, 1991; Wimmer & Hartl, 1991).

A modified appearance-reality task (AR2), which is a false-belief paradigm using the AR items, was our fourth task. After the child has passed the classic AR task, he is asked what a doll who has never seen the item will think it is when she sees it for the first time. Thus, the child must attribute a false belief on the basis of an AR item. Finally, the fifth task was a modified representational change task (RC2), which uses a false-belief paradigm with the RC items. After the child has passed the classic RC task, he is asked what a doll that has never seen the item will think it contains when she sees it for the first time. This task thus corresponds to the "unexpected content" FB one.

On the five tasks we have used, deaf native signers do not differ from hearing children of the same ages. The comparisons of native versus late signers are always in favor of native signers. In fact, late signers consistently reach an above-chance level of performance on only one task, the AR2, and that only from age 8 onward. On the four other tasks, a global trend for improvement with age is noted, but with no consistent success through age 10, even if the performances on the RC2 task seem better than those on the three classic tasks. We did not compare late signers to hearing children, because the comparison was not really interesting because of age differences and because of the fact that our aim was not to prove once again that late signers are delayed.

With regard to success on individual tasks, we go no further in describing our empirical findings other than noting a massive failure of late signers, failure which most surely originates in the lack of early exposure to language, although which part of language is involved remains unclear. It is often claimed that immersing children in a rich conversational sharing of ideas in a community of mind (Nelson, 2004) should lead to an awareness of others' mental states and to metarepresentational ToM. Nevertheless, several theories exist emphasizing either the role of early access to language-communication (Peterson & Siegal, 1999, Siegal, 2007), of discussions on mental entities (Dunn, 1994), or of grammatical skills (e.g., embedded components, deVilliers & deVilliers, 1999; for a recent review on the relationships between language and ToM, see Milligan, Astington, & Dack, 2007).

Patterns of Development

We now turn to the second research perspective, that of the way in which deaf children develop their ToM abilities. This issue has been seldom addressed, since it is necessary first to include children within a rather large age range and, second, to make use of several ToM tasks. The nature of such a perspective has been clearly stated by Peterson et al. (2005, p. 508): "The key question for our research . . . concerns not age trends or group differences but rather sequences of understanding." Thus, here, one does not focus on the age at which children pass or fail this or that task, but on the route and order (e.g., which task comes first, second, third, etc.) that they pass the different ToM tasks. Then, one can compare deaf children to hearing children and see whether their development follows the same pattern.

Four main studies, already mentioned, are informative in this regard: Peterson et al. (2005), Peterson and Slaughter (2006), Courtin and Melot (2005), and Courtin and Melot (submitted). In their research, Peterson et al. (2005) found that the performance patterns of deaf native signers, deaf children of hearing parents, and hearing children were similar, although deaf children of hearing parents developed ToM skills later. However, and this is the important point, the metacognitive structure seems to be the same in the three groups: desires are understood before beliefs, and hidden emotion is the most difficult task.

Peterson and Slaughter (2006) found that the two groups of children involved in their study (deaf late signers and hearing children) did not differ from each other in their development of ToM. In their narratives, children first begin to mention affect and/or perceptions. Then, as they get older, children begin to mention imaginative and/or realistic cognition; finally, they develop a mental state using causality, contrastives, and/or elaboration. Only after the latter stage of narrative skills is reached do children pass the FB task. This means that children can speak of false beliefs in their narratives, but nonetheless fail on the standard FB task (Marschark et al., 2000).

Thus, if one focuses on the results reported by Peterson and colleagues, it would seem that no difference exists in the course of metacognitive development between deaf and hearing children. Late signers may be delayed, but their developmental pattern is nonetheless identical to that of native signers and hearing children. This constitutes an important result for the discussion about the possible differences (or lack thereof) in deaf children's cognitive development relative to hearing peers.

We have tried to address ToM developmental patterns in speaking and signing deaf children on the AR versus FB tasks (Courtin & Melot, 2005) and, using another sample of signing deaf children, on the three classic ToM tasks and two modified ones (Courtin & Melot, submitted). Looking at the AR and FB tasks (Courtin & Melot, 2005), we first were led to the conclusion that deaf children of deaf parents tend to develop their ToM abilities in a different way than hearing children, succeeding on the FB task before the AR one. The reverse pattern was observed for late signers, for speaking deaf children of hearing parents, and for hearing children.

However, extending the research to five tasks, we found that hearing children, deaf native signers, and deaf late signers have specific and different development patterns when one focuses on success performances (Courtin & Melot, submitted). For hearing children, all of the tasks except FB (for a reason that remains unclear and seems peculiar to French children) lead to the same results: that is, they all emerge at about age 5, whereas the FB task is not yet mastered at age 6. The case is a little different for deaf children. Native signers first pass the AR2 task, by age 5, and the remainder by age 6. Late signers first succeed on AR2, by age 8, then seem to pass the RC2 by age 9, and then the remaining tasks. We do not know at which age or in which order late signers pass the other tasks, since these children still fail at the older age range we have tested, up to 10 years.

Courtin and Melot (submitted) have presented several possible reasons for these differences. Here, we present the two main reasons, those that seem the most likely when relating to previous work. First, we do not know the level of response to the task. That is, researchers on ToM generally have taken it for granted that, when the child passes the FB task, he is able to attribute some false belief from which the protagonist's behavior is based. Nevertheless, several authors have raised some doubts on this point. They suggest that the success on the FB task can be grounded on several different levels: behavioral, linguistic, and metarepresentational (Clements, Rustin, & McCallum, 2000; Courtin & Melot, 2005; Marschark et al., 2000; Perner & Clements, 1998). One way to disentangle this question is to address children's justifications for their answers, which is the aim of the next section of this chapter. Second, there could be difficulties with the ToM tasks that require consideration of two dimensions (i.e., two representations) of the same item at the same time (FB, AR, and RC). Tasks for which this need is less salient (AR2) would lead to better performances for deaf children. This idea is not new, and was presented first by Ottem (1980) in the context of a variety of learning, memory, and problem-solving tasks.

We are thus faced with conflicting results about ToM development in deaf children, although the comparisons are difficult because of the differing tasks used by the authors (Courtin and Melot on the one side, Peterson and colleagues on the other). Courtin and Melot have used only "FB-like" tasks, following Wellman et al.'s (2001) terminology, and thus work within a narrow scope of tasks and abilities. The underlying question in their work is whether children pass these tasks; that is, do they reach and use the relevant abilities all in the same way and in the same order. Peterson and her colleagues have explored a larger range of abilities closely related to ToM, enabling a clearer approach to the development of and access to a meta-representational ToM, with the underlying question of whether these are the same among different groups of children. According to Peterson et al., deaf children of deaf parents, deaf children of hearing parents, and hearing children of hearing parents all follow the same developmental pattern in acquiring ToM. According to Courtin and Melot, the three groups differ from one another on their patterns of success on different FB-like tasks.

Beyond ToM tasks: ToM Justifications and the Case of the False Belief Attribution Task

It is quite obvious that we understand some aspects of ToM development. However, for some other aspects, even using several different ToM tasks, we have too little information to know how children develop. It appears that working on children's justifications could be a complementary methodology that might prove enlightening. We propose using this approach in the present section for the FB "unexpected location" task, because it is the most widely used ToM paradigm. Two questions are addressed. First, do differences exist in the justifications in case of success versus failure on the FB task? Second, do hearing children, deaf native signers, and deaf late signers differ from one another in their justifications?

The children and the tasks have been presented earlier as those involved in the Courtin and Melot (submitted) study. In that investigation, three groups of children were studied: 36 4- to 6-year-old hearing children, 22 4- to 9-year-old native signers, and 62 5- to 10-year-old late signers. We will concentrate only on the children's justifications on the FB task; the other classic ToM tasks (AR and RC) do not naturally lead to justification questions, whereas the modified tasks are not as informative as the FB task on these justifications. To investigate these justifications in the hope that they would help us to understand the (meta) cognitive processes at work when the child passes (or fails) the FB task, the child was simply asked, after having correctly passed or failed a given item, "Why (does the doll look here)?," and his response was recorded. There are three items in this FB task.

For example, when confronted with the "Maxi" item, directly taken from Wimmer and Perner (1983), the child is presented with two dolls [a boy (Maxi) and his mother], a chocolate bar, and two boxes. The child is told (and the experimenter acts out) that "they have bought some chocolate and are back home. They put the chocolate here [in box A] and Maxi leaves the room, he goes out to play. While he is out, his mother takes the chocolate, breaks it into two pieces, takes one to use in baking a cake, and puts the second one here [in box B]. Then, Maxi comes back. He wants to eat the chocolate. Where will he look for his chocolate?" After the child has signed or shown box A or B, he is asked "Why? Why does Maxi look for his chocolate here?"

We then tried to classify the responses collected. To this end, we looked at all of the 120 children's responses, and we eventually found that these responses could be grouped into five main classes. We do not claim for the moment that some justifications are better than others, although the epistemic value of some may be more powerful than others. Examples of justifications following our classification method are presented in Table 4–1, with five main classes observed for the three items.

Mental states. In this type of justification, the child overtly refers to some cognitive activity. These justifications would be expected according to ToM theories developed by authors for decades to explain success on the

Table 4–1.   Examples of Justifications According to Failure or Success On the False Belief Task

	Success	Failure
Mental states	"he thinks (or believes) that the chocolate is here"	"he thinks that the chocolate is here" (verbs also used: believe, guess)
Behavioral	"he had put it here before he left the room".	"his mother has put it here".
Linguistic (role taking)	The child takes the role of the protagonist and explains (sometimes may only describe) what he would do when coming back in the room.	
Realism	"the chocolate was here before (points the first box)"	"the chocolate is here (points the second box)!"
Other (examples)	Because I don't know	He's bright His mother has told him.

FB task. But, as we will see, these very justifications also hold for erroneous answers. In this first exploratory analysis, we have not separated arguments on the basis of whether they are simple (e.g., "he thinks it is here"),
elaborate ("he thinks that the chocolate is here since he left it there"), or
contrastive ("he thinks it is here *but* in reality it is in the other box").

Behavior. The child here focuses on Maxi's action, or on the action of
Maxi's mother. In case of success with the FB task, the underlying rationale
is that, when you look for an object, you go and search where you put it on
the last time (cf. Clements et al., 2000).

Realism. This justification was not part of the primary theoretical
model underlying the research. However, during the response classification
process, we realized that this third class should be added. Here, children
do not focus on the protagonists' behavior, but instead on reality itself,
whether it pertains to the primary state or, on the contrary, to the final state
of the scenario. It is essentially simply a description of the state of affairs.

Note that, for the two latter categories of justification, some children
also add a second part to their explanations, such as ". . . thus Maxi *thinks*
that. . . ." We decided to avoid classifying one answer under two different categories. Therefore, these responses have been classified under the
"mental states" category only.

Linguistic. This type of justification has been included in order to investigate further the ideas of Courtin (2000) and Courtin and Melot (2005), and
subsequently rejected by Courtin and Melot (submitted), that native signers
could pass the FB task solely on the basis of a linguistic strategy, rather
than a metarepresentational one. In this linguistic strategy, which refers to
role-taking (e.g., Poulin & Miller, 1995; Sallandre, 2007), children take the
role of the protagonist and imagine what they would do if they were he.
This strategy was labeled "linguistic" to differentiate it from the "simulation
theory," according to which children use their own experience to simu-
late, understand, and predict the experiences of others (e.g., Harris, 1989).
In the linguistic strategy, the native signing child (hearing or deaf) would
be prone to consider the other's perspective, not in a real simulation perspective but in a role-taking one, owing to a frequent exposure to visual
perspective-taking in sign language. Although the results of these two strategies look similar, with the child taking the role of the protagonist, the two
cognitive processes are different. Note also that the use of perspective-taking
may not be equally frequent in American Sign Language (ASL) and Langue
des Signes Française (LSF). Cross-linguistic research would be welcome on
this point; at the very least, the importance of this perspective-taking structure is obviously much greater in French linguistic analyses of sign language
[under the name of "highly iconic structure" (Cuxac, 2000; Sallandre, 2006,
2007)] than in American analyses.

Other. The remaining possible "justifications," grouped under the category "Other," are quite diverse. These can involve a mere "I do not know"

or "because." We have also included in this category answers that could not be classified. These answers, such as "his mother told him" or "he is really bright," and some justifications off the subject, could be interesting to detail, but have not been evaluated for the present chapter.

The resulting raw scores and percentages from these categorizations are shown in Table 4–2. The table presents all the justifications of all children, and is given only for the information it provides about the general trends. Several points are worth mentioning on descriptive grounds.

In all three groups of children, correct choices are justified mainly through two types of justifications, totaling 60%–70% of responses: mental states and behaviors. These two types are roughly at the same percentage for deaf native signers, but mental states dominate for hearing children, whereas the reverse appears for late signing children, with behaviors being invoked twice as often as mental states. Reference to reality is the third most often-mentioned class of justification for both hearing children and native signers, whereas it is the fourth for late signers. Note also that the linguistic arguments, via role-taking, occur in only 4% of the cases in native signers, but in 18% in late signers. That is, what Courtin (2000) thought could help native signers and, to a lesser extent, late signers in their strategies for problem solving when confronted to the FB task is not really used for this particular task (even if it seems to be used for other tasks, such as the AR2).

The three groups differ in their pattern of justification, with hearing children stressing the mental states over any other class of justification,

Table 4–2. Justifications on the False Belief Task, According to Success and Group. Raw Scores (and Percentages)

		Mental states	Behavior	Realism	Linguistic	Other
Native signers	Pass	16 (34.04)	17 (36.17)	7 (14.90)	2 (4.25)	5 (10.64)
	Fail	5 (31.25)	0 (0)	7 (43.75)	0 (0)	4 (25.00)
Late signers	Pass	12 (19.67)	26 (42.62)	5 (8.20)	11 (18.03)	7 (11.48)
	Fail	19 (20.43)	0 (0)	49 (52.69)	3 (3.23)	22 (23.66)
Hearing	Pass	19 (42.22)	13 (28.89)	6 (13.33)	0 (0)	7 (15.55)
	Fail	13 (19.70)	28 (42.42)	21 (31.82)	0 (0)	3 (4.54)

native signers referring as often to mental states as to behaviors, and late signer stressing behaviors over any other class. Therefore, at first glance, these descriptive results argue against Peterson et al.'s (2005) and Peterson and Slaughter's (2006) reports of identical development among the three groups of children and support Courtin and Melot (2005, submitted) hypotheses (but see below).

When considering the justifications in case of failures on the FB task, deaf children's justifications are mainly (about 70%) divided into two classes: realism (between 40% and 50% or more) and mental states. The remaining responses are mainly scattered in nonpertinent classes (do-not-know, not justified, and not classifiable). For hearing children, three classes total almost 100% of justifications: behaviors (about 40%), then realism (30%), then mental states (20%).

A correlational analysis of these results reveals that, for hearing children, the more successful they are on the FB task, the more likely they are to provide mental state justifications (although the relation is moderate). As for deaf children, whether native or late signers, the differences of mental state justifications between success and failure on the FB task are almost nonexistent. That is, native signers refer to mental states about 30% of the time, and late signers about 20%, whatever their performance on the FB task. Instead, it appears that, as deaf children become more successful, they abandon realistic justifications and opt for behavioral ones.

It is noteworthy that there were no behavioral justifications for native or late signers' failures. This should be compared to what Marschark (1993, p. 139) wrote on traditional views about studies of intelligence in deaf children: "preoperational children are characterized as being *egocentric* . . . and constrained by *perceived appearances.* Because children focus on states rather than changes during this period of development . . ." (italics added). Is it just what happens when deaf children fail on the FB task? Are they attending to states (realism) instead of changes (behavioral justifications)? We will discuss this point later.

To analyze the data further, we divided children first according to their success or failure on the FB task. A child is considered to have passed the task when he correctly answers to at least two out of the three items; otherwise, he is said to fail. Then we looked at the justifications; we once again chose a criterion of two out of three. That is, a child who correctly passes the FB task and justifies his choices with at least two "mental states" out of the three justifications is classed in the "mental states" category. In practice, this led to relatively little loss of data, since the vast majority of children are consistent in their justifications and almost never use three different justifications for the three different items. Thus, of the 22 native signers, only two are not included in the final summary, one because of scattered justifications and a second because of relatively few justifications due to shyness in a 4-year-old. In fact, shyness was also involved for four of the late signers; two others had scattered justifications. Justifications from four other children were lost due to experimenter error. Finally, two hearing children are not included due to scattering in their justifications.

Table 4–3 presents the repartitioning of children according to the criteria just presented. No real new information is present, when compared to Table 4–2, even if some trends appear more pronounced. For example, all of the justifications given by deaf children of deaf parents who fail on the FB task now fall into two different classes only: mental states and behaviors, as no child consistently gave "other" justifications.

We have tried several intragroup comparisons (using nonparametric statistics because of small sample sizes), contrasting mental states to all other justifications in case of failure versus success. The only significant comparison relates to the repartitioning between behavioral and realistic justifications of the late signers in successes versus failures. It appears that when they pass the FB task, late signers refer much more often to behaviors than to realism, whereas the reverse appears in the case of failure on the task. Supporting this result, the only difference observed in the between-group comparisons lies in the repartitioning between mental states, behaviors, and realism in hearing versus late signers failing on the FB task. Both groups of children refer to mental states to the same extent. However, as mentioned earlier, late signers for the most part justify their choices with realistic arguments and no behavioral ones, whereas hearing children use both arguments, with a preference for behaviors over realism.

The remaining comparisons yielded no significant results. Therefore, it would seem that hearing children and deaf children of hearing or deaf parents do not really differ from one another, and that success or failure on the FB task does not lead to differences in justifications. This is counterintuitive to what is observed on descriptive grounds, in Tables 4–2 and 4–3; consequently, we are currently exploring other statistical designs in order to get a better understanding of the data collected. The fact is that

Table 4–3.   Patterns of Justifications, According to Success and Group

		Mental states	Behavior	Realism	Linguistic	Other
Native signers	Pass	6	5	2	1	1
	Fail	2	0	3	0	0
Late signers	Pass	6	9	1	4	1
	Fail	5	0	16	1	9
Hearing	Pass	6	4	2	0	1
	Fail	4	9	7	0	1

we might have samples that are too small to effectively use the usual statistical tools.

In summary, what does this study tell us? First, that although the FB task is a valid and reliable paradigm for investigating ToM development, children are far from providing clear and rational justifications for their answers, correct or not, on this task. One and the same justification—for example, references to mental states—can be invoked by children in case of success as well as in case of failure. In case of success justified by arguments other than mental states, it could be claimed that the mental state response is so obvious for children that they consider it hardly worth mentioning: the mental state may be implicit; it may emerge more or less clearly in children's minds but not be overtly expressed. Children only state what they think may be a pertinent explanation for Maxi's behavior. Importantly, we have prompted only one justification from the children. Perhaps if we had asked them for a second possible argument, children would have mentioned mental states (and mentioned behavior for justifying an erroneous choice).

Keeping these possibilities in mind, we focus on three main points in the following section. First, we address the case of mental states arguments and then attend to the possible ways to pass the FB tasks. Last, we discuss the differences of justifications between hearing children, deaf children of deaf parents, and deaf children of hearing parents.

Mental States Arguments and Metarepresentational ToM

The reference to mental states in case of failure on the FB task may seem counterintuitive. If one considers theories about ToM, it would give the impression that our findings are inconsistent with and invalidate the original theoretical rationale. This is not the case, however, and our findings are not as inconsistent as they appear if considered within the context of the existing literature.

For some few (deaf and hearing) children, it happens that, when engaged in FB tasks, they are sometimes thinking in terms of "magic worlds" in which, when you *think hard* you will find the object you are looking for. Nevertheless, the situation appears quite rare. Instead, children more often provide us with explanations, expressing themselves without any doubt, such as "he knows it is here." Some other children have justified their choices stating that "he thinks it is here"—*thinks* here refers to the French verb *penser*, which involves a part of uncertainty, whereas the prior expression *thinks hard* refers to the French verb *réfléchir*, which implicates mental efforts but implies firmer conclusions than *penser*. Thus, in metarepresentational development, it is not the reference to mental states that matters for determining ToM achievement; nor do mental states, or mental representations, govern actions since (in children's justifications) they govern actions on the ToM task in case of success and failure as well. It may be that children who refer to mental states while failing on the FB task are at the threshold of success, but it is not clear at present. It also is not yet clear whether the results might be different in languages that, unlike French and LSF, do not have two such readily accessible verbs as *penser* and *réfléchir*.

If the critical point in the access to a metarepresentational ToM does not seem to lie in the reference to mental representations, it may instead lie in the way children use these representations. This notion is related to the discussion of Wellman and Bartsch (1994) about the contrastive use of mental terms when discussing the age at which children understand the concepts underlying words. As addressed by Peterson et al. (2006, Experiment 2), the simple use of a mental verb such as "think" appears first in children's narrative development. Later comes the contrastive use, just prior to—not at the same time as—success on the FB task. Our results of mental states justifications in case of failure on the FB task are in clear accordance with the findings reported by Wellman and Bartsch (1994) and Peterson and Slaughter (2006) in this regard.

Possible Bases for Success on the False-Belief Task

As for our results, it appears obvious that the success on the FB task does not necessarily entail a mental states justification; that is, it is not always explicitly metarepresentationally based. More than half of the successes are justified in terms of behaviors, realism, or other arguments. It is as though children focused on some parts of the scenario, parts that appear more salient to them, in order to pass the FB questions. Thus, our work empirically supports the suggestions of Perner and Clements (1998), Clements et al. (2000), and Courtin and Melot (2005): the success on the FB task can be grounded on different levels of response, such as metarepresentations, realism, or behaviors. Deaf and hearing children do not differ on this point of diversity, at least when considering our three samples. The results should be replicated with much larger samples, but that might prove difficult as our initial group of 120 children apparently was not sufficient to yield consistent, significant results.

Do Deaf Children Differ from Hearing Children?

What about the comparisons between the three groups of children? Overall, as mentioned earlier, deaf and hearing children who correctly pass the FB task answer in the same general way, referring to the same three general categories of justifications. However, hearing children seem to have better internalized the fact that mental states govern behaviors and that these mental states may be more powerful than other arguments to explain some-one's actions. Late signers seem to be delayed in this regard, and native signers stand between late signers and hearing children.

If the three groups refer to mental states to approximately the same extent when they fail the FB questions (and, in this regard, they can be said to be similar), they obviously differ in their reference to reality versus behaviors. This absence of behavioral justification for deaf children in the case of failure, whereas it is the preferred justification for hearing children, may constitute the most striking result in the present work. There are two possible interpretations, not mutually exclusive, of these trends.

First, deaf children may have difficulty managing the relation of the tasks to reality. The reality category is in fact important for the justifica-tions of success. In the FB tasks in general, children need to smoothly go back and forth from a "world reality" (the one that leads to failure on the FB attribution task question, but to success on the FB control questions[1]) to a "representational reality," the one used in case of success: the reality for Maxi, the state of affairs in his mental representation, is that the chocolate is still in the first box. Hence, the epistemic value of the realism option depends on what reality refers to and on the question to answer.

Thus, perhaps deaf children focus on the actual state of affairs (i.e., the box where the chocolate really is) while hearing children would be more, or also, turned toward behaviors (that of Maxi's mother, who removed the chocolate). However, and this constitutes the second possible interpreta-tion, one may also argue the reverse. Deaf children also could be focused on behaviors and, when they consider this feature, they do not fail on the subsequent question (the FB task). This second interpretation supposes that deaf children have a better understanding of behaviors, at least in their causal links to other behaviors, than do hearing children. This would ex-plain why deaf children never justify an erroneous choice via behaviors and, for this reason, seem to get bogged down in reality justifications. On this point, the difference between hearing and deaf children would be in the domain of differential approaches to problem solving, instead of delay, as may be the case for the mental states mentioned earlier. This would mean that, instead of gaining a more and more mature ToM, in the sense of a ToM that mirrors that of hearing children, deaf children gain knowledge on how to use clues for solving ToM tasks. This argument is consistent with one suggested by Marschark, Lang, and Albertini (2002, p. 115), who claim that "although cognitive differences are observed between deaf and hearing children, these often are related more to how they go about various tasks than to absolute differences in ability."

---

1. Two control questions are asked in the classic FB task: the first pertains to the chocolate's current location; the second is about the chocolate's initial location.

A question arises, however: is there any ToM delay in deaf children or, rather, do they simply have a different way of thinking about the mind that is a function of the age of first exposure to an effective language? To answer this question, it would be necessary to know whether signing deaf adults react like hearing adults on ToM tasks. The delay observed on the classic FB task in fact might not be overcome when signing begins after age 10, if one looks at Morgan and Kegl's (2006) results, yet the issue should be addressed with other ToM tasks. Noteworthy enough, even healthy hearing adults are usually led to bias when evaluating someone else's knowledge, due to the influence of their own experience—just as are young children in the FB task (cf. Bernstein, Atance, Loftus, & Meltzoff, 2004; Birch & Bloom, 2004). This possibility would entail cognitive inhibition of one's own beliefs or knowledge (cf. Carlson & Moses, 2001; but, for an opposite interpretation of these relations see Perner & Lang, 2000; and Hauser et al., this volume).

It appears that there is an urgent need for testing older children, teenagers, and adults on ToM tasks suited to their ages. Only limited research up to now has involved these older age ranges. Russell et al. (1998) tested children up to age 17 on a FB task, and concluded that not until age 13 do deaf children of hearing parents correctly pass the test. Clark, Schwanenflugel, Everhart, and Bartini (1996) tested deaf adults of hearing parents on the mental organization of 17 cognitive verbs (e.g., thinking, memorizing, knowing). They were led to the conclusion that this mental organization was close to that of hearing adults, and that "deaf adults may possess a very similar theory of mind indeed [as hearing adults]" (p. 188).

Older work on cognitive or social perspective taking (e.g., Bachara, Raphael, & Phelan, 1980; Cates & Shontz, 1990; Couch, 1985), have included children up to 14 years of age, but results are difficult to interpret because of methodological concerns (see Marschark, 1993). Nonetheless, Couch (1985, cited by Marschark, 1993, p. 70), using a cognitive perspective-taking task such as the three-mountains task designed by Piaget and Inhelder (1948) found that deaf adults lagged significantly behind hearing controls. The latter results, on a task that in fact belongs within the ToM domain, conflict with the conclusion of Clark et al. (1996). Therefore, it is important to resume work with teenagers and adults to get a clearer idea of their ToM sociocognitive abilities.

Another interesting point in our results is the almost complete absence of any obvious effect of the "linguistic variable" on deaf children's justifications. The fact is that, for native signers, this role-taking possibility appeared only twice when children succeeded (4.25% of the total justifications) and never when they failed. For late signers, it occurred on 18% of successes and 3% of failures. The absence of any justification of this kind would have definitively invalidated the hypothesis we raised in past work, which claimed that native signers could pass the FB task on the basis of a linguistic role-taking strategy rather than a metarepresentational one

(Courtin, 2000; Courtin & Melot, 2005). Although this hypothesis is not totally ruled out, it certainly fails to be convincing. The question remains open for the justifications on the other tasks we have used based on the FB paradigm (Courtin & Melot, submitted).

All the trends discussed here must be confirmed by the analysis of justifications on the representational change task for others. This has often been a FB task in the literature but is one which, going back to basics, we have decided to separate, in order to be clearer in our discussion. Obviously, in this task, children's arguments cannot be the same as in the FB task, for there is no place for justifications based on behaviors. Thus, although the results are usually the same on both tasks in the literature, the cognitive processes underlying the successes may be different. At the very least, the features on which children base their justifications should differ. For example and at first glance, in the representational change task for others, children seem to relate more on visual cues (e.g., "he has not seen what is inside the box"), hence they are more turned toward knowledge access, the critical point of the scenario. Surprisingly enough, this argument was seldom used by children in the FB task.

Summary and Implications

Reconsidering Assessment . . .

Several conclusions can be drawn from the research presented here that apply to children in general (hearing as well as deaf). First, several different possible explanations exist for an identical result among children. The same result on a test is not a guarantee that children react in the way we think they should. The point here is somewhat different from the argument put forward by Kelly, Lang, Mousley, and Davis (2003; see Kelly, this volume), who demonstrated how the results on a test differ from what would be expected from students due to confounding factors such as reading abilities or executive functions in mathematics assessment, to use Kelly et al.'s example. Instead, we think that there may be differences in the cognitive processes among children that do not preclude success on a test. Even if the ToM results of deaf and hearing children are roughly the same in terms of scores and the developmental patterns observed, as nicely demonstrated by Peterson et al. (2005) and Peterson and Slaughter (2006), children might rely on idiosyncratic features of the problem (such as mental states or behaviors) or distinct cognitive strategies. This would extend to our ideas about metacognition what has already been suspected for memory (Bebko, 1998), visual perception (see Dye, Hauser, & Bavelier, this volume), or learning (Marschark et al., 2002). In Marschark's (2003, p. 466) words, more broadly dealing with cognitive functioning, "most results suggest that [deaf and hearing individuals] simply vary in their approaches to cognitive tasks . . . and differ in their amount of relevant knowledge (including strategic knowledge)."

Second, a seemingly logical rationale (e.g., the protagonist's mental states) can be invoked by children in order to justify an erroneous choice. The corollary proposition is that an erroneous choice sometimes can hide mature cognitive processes. The latter idea has been well known for a decades, arising from reconsiderations of Piaget's early findings in the context of modern methods (e.g., the visual perspective-taking abilities as studied by Flavell et al., 1981, or the numerical protoabilities of infants, see Wynn, 1992). In fact, it seems that ToM, or more exactly FB attribution, is also in need of reconsideration because of recent findings that 2-year-olds and even 15-month-olds already have some understanding of false beliefs (Onishi & Baillargeon, 2005; Southgate, Senju, & Csibra, 2007; for a discussion, see Siegal, 2007). Alternatively, but not unrelated, erroneous choices hiding mature cognitive processes are an issue when considering how inhibitory difficulties can lead to ineffective choices while children hold a logical rationale (see Hauser et al., this volume). That is, children may first need cognitive inhibitory abilities in order to distance themselves from the immediate situation and to depart from salient and misleading knowledge, so as to demonstrate their understanding of others' perspective or belief. This explains why some authors (e.g., Clements & Perner, 1994) have shown that the age at which the children pass the FB task depends on the criterion selected (and the cognitive inhibitory processes it requires): eye gaze (as in Onishi & Baillargeon, 2005), pointing, verbal justifications, or the epistemic content of these justifications.

As for the first part of the premise, the logical rationale invoked when justifying an erroneous choice, a distinction must be made between knowledge (i.e., the logical rationale), and its application to real cases, the "know how," pragmatics, or "strategic knowledge" as mentioned by Marschark (2003), which we have often stressed following Wellman and Bartsch (1994). Note, however, that this distinction between knowledge and pragmatics is not involved in the partition between simple versus elaborate usage of mental states in Peterson and Slaughter's (2006) terminology. Some children justify their erroneous choice as "Maxi knows that his mother has put the chocolate here," using what is considered as an elaborate sentence according to Peterson and Slaughter. Instead, the distinction we refer to lies in the contrastive usage, when the child begins to fully and explicitly understand the outcomes of the rationale he owns. At present, however, it is not really clear when and how the child passes from an erroneous to a correct usage of a logical rationale in the FB task.

A further remaining question is whether ToM tasks simply assess metacognition less effectively in deaf children as compared with hearing children (Akamatsu et al., this volume). We think that the literature about ToM in deaf native signers and hearing children (e.g., Courtin & Melot,

2005[2]; Peterson et al., 2005; Schick et al., 2007), which suggests that these two groups of children pass the same tasks at the same ages, demonstrate that the tasks address essentially the same ToM abilities in the two populations. However, this need not entail that ToM abilities, attested to by success on FB-like tasks, are processed alike by the two groups. More generally, facing an identical problem and reaching seemingly identical results, deaf children may nonetheless differ from hearing ones on the cognitive processes leading to these results (Marschark, 2003).

Deaf children, at least in terms of the research presented in this chapter, have some thinking that differs from that of their hearing peers. Because of our relatively small sample sizes, we are still considering alternative ways to evaluate children's justifications in "FB-like" tasks. It is possible that we will eventually find no difference at all. Nonetheless, some other authors, working on other research domains, have been led to similar conclusions (e.g., Marschark, Convertino, & LaRock, 2006). At present, we could simply say that reality and behaviors seem to be more anchored in young deaf children's mind than in any case of young hearing children. Crucially, however, our test was not designed to assess abstract versus concrete skills, but to evaluate whether deaf and hearing children explain actions in the same way. Keeping in mind this point, it is important to note that the above-mentioned "anchorage" is not a problem per se, since reality and behaviors, when they pertain to the representational world, are effective methods for understanding others' actions. Only if children were unable to go further would this realism be a problem. Research about imagination, creativity, and fancy is consistent (at least when methods are adapted to deaf children) and clearly demonstrates normal abilities in deaf children (for a review see Marschark, 1993).

. . . and Teaching?

It is sometimes claimed that teaching for deaf students is more turned toward a "concrete and focused approach to problem solving, hoping that students will have a clear understanding of a particular strategy" (cf. Marschark et al., 2002, p.132). In addition, Power and Leigh (2003) suggested that teachers need to go beyond the mere teaching of particular course content (e.g., mathematics) and instead opt for some more global approaches, in order to boost language and concept development as well as background

---

2. The results presented in Courtin (2000) and Courtin and Melot (2005) in fact show that native signers outperform hearing children on the FB task. However, we now think these results are the consequence of a surprising difficulty encountered by French hearing children on this particular task, as opposed to other classic ToM tasks (Courtin and Melot, submitted). This performance of French hearing children has been replicated several times and remains unanswered.

knowledge and relationships. These concreteness and local approaches possibly relate to uneasiness in communication with deaf students, which is likely to exist among teachers for deaf children in France at present. Results reported by Meristo et al. (2007) on ToM performances in native signers attending either bilingual or oral schools may be thought as an evidence for the importance of constant and consistent exposure to sign language. But, following Marschark et al.'s (2002) and Power and Leigh's (2003) arguments, Meristo et al.'s results may also be considered as the consequence of teaching and communication strategies that are more concrete in oral schools, where communication is not likely to be so easy as it would be in other settings with native signers who share an accessible language.

Could these different points explain the high percentages of realistic arguments in case of failure on the FB task? If this were the case, then deaf children of deaf parents might show some more advanced patterns compared to late signers since, at least at home, they are supposed to be immersed in a context that offers optimal communication. At first blush, this seems to be the case. With some caution due to the few children involved, deaf children of deaf parents more frequently refer to mental states and less to reality compared to deaf children born to hearing parents. However, Marschark, Sapere, Convertino, Seewagen, and Maltzan (2004) did not observe such differences among deaf college students as a function of parental hearing status, as both groups appeared to present lesser metacognitive and learning skills as compared with hearing students.

If it is reasonable to think that deaf children progressively abandon, or depart from, this preponderance of realism, and turn to mental states in a metacognitive way, the causal relationship remains to be determined. Is it that, when teaching or family discussions are less concrete and more global, children reach more mature metacognitive stages? Should the reverse relationship also be advanced? In fact, higher metacognitive skills should lead to a difference in the mechanisms of learning. As children gain knowledge about effective learning strategies and about memorizing (the metamemory studied by Gordon & Flavell, 1977, and presented earlier) and cognitive processes in general, they should become aware of which strategy to apply in solving one or another cognitive–academic problem. Likewise, these growing metacognitive skills should enable students to know what they do not know, to analyze their own past errors, owing to their ability to consider from other perspectives, previous mental states, and cognitive strategies. Thus, higher metacognitive skills should lead to more effective thinking on self-progression and self-efficiency in learning, and in the efficiency of a student's approach of social life and relationships to other students. More research, including teachers, is needed although the point seems logical.

Could these differences be overcome and, if so, how? As mentioned in the first part of this chapter, it does not seem that ToM can be taught, nor that metacognitive development can really be boosted. The fact that native signers differ from hearing children on their justifications in ToM tasks suggests that the "problem" does not originate (or not only) in early communication. Besides, we would like to consider our results in an alternative way: that there is, in fact, no problem, at least for native signers. There is nothing to overcome, nothing to teach or to boost, but instead we simply face some differences that we should be aware of, and we must adapt ourselves to these differences in how deaf children think the human mind.

Acknowledgments

We are most thankful to Harry Lang, Marc Marschark, and Peter Hauser for their helpful comments and discussions about earlier drafts of this chapter.

References

Bachara, G. H., Raphael, J., & Phelan, W. J. (1980). Empathy development in deaf preadolescents. *American Annals of the Deaf, 125*, 38–41.

Bebko, J. M. (1998). Learning, Language, Memory, and reading: The role of language automatization and its impact on complex cognitive activities. *Journal of Deaf Studies and Deaf Education, 3*, 4–14.

Bebko, J. M., Calderon, R., & Treder, R. (2003). The Language Proficiency Profile-2: Assessment of the global communication skills of deaf children across languages and modalities of expression. *Journal of Deaf Studies and Deaf Education, 8*, 438–451.

Bernstein, D. M., Atance, C., Loftus, G. R., & Meltzoff, A. (2004). We saw it all along: Visual hindsight bias in children and adults. *Psychological Science, 15*, 264–267.

Birch, S. A. J., & Bloom, P. (2004). Children are cursed: An asymmetric bias in mental-state attribution. *Psychological Science, 14*, 283–286.

Carlson, M. S., & Moses, L. J. (2001). Individual differences in inhibitory control and children's theory of mind. *Child Development, 72*, 1032–1053.

Cates, D. S., & Shontz, F. C. (1990). Role taking ability and social behavior in deaf school children. *American Annals of the Deaf, 135*, 217–221.

Clark, M. D., Schwanenflugel, P. J., Everhart, V. S., & Bartini, M. (1996). Theory of mind in deaf adults and the organization of verbs of knowing. *Journal of Deaf Studies and Deaf Education, 1*, 179–189.

Clements, W. A., & Perner, J. (1994). Implicit understanding of belief. *Cognitive Development, 9*, 377–395.

Clements, W. A., Rustin, C. L., & McCallum, S. (2000). Promoting the transition from implicit to explicit understanding: A training study of false belief. *Developmental Science, 3*, 81–92.

Couch, C. G. (1985). *A test of Kohlberg's theory: The development of moral reasoning in deaf and hearing individuals.* Unpublished doctoral dissertation, University of North Carolina at Greensboro.

Courtin, C. (2000). The impact of sign language on the cognitive development of deaf children: the case of theories of mind. *Journal of Deaf Studies and Deaf Education, 5*, 266–276.

Courtin, C., & Melot, A.-M. (2005). Metacognitive development of deaf children: Lessons from the appearance—reality and false belief tasks. *Developmental Science, 8*, 16–25.

Courtin, C., & Melot, A.-M. (submitted). Metacognitive development in deaf children, in search of linguistic relativism.

Cuxac, C. (2000), La langue des signes française. Les voies de l'iconicité. *Faits de Langues, 15/16*, 1–391.

DeVilliers, J. G., & DeVillier, P. A. (1999). Linguistic determinism and the understanding of false beliefs. In H. P. Mitchell and K. Riggs (Eds.), *Children's reasoning and the mind* (pp. 191–228). Hove, U.K., Psychology Press.

Dunn, J. (1994). Changing minds and changing relationships. In C. Lewis and P. Mitchell (Eds.), *Children's early understanding of mind* (pp. 297–310). Hillsdale, NJ: Erlbaum.

Flavell, J. H. (1988). The development of children's knowledge about the mind: From cognitive connections to mental representations. In J. W. Astington, P. L. Harris, and D. R. Olson (Eds.), *Developing theories of mind* (pp. 244–267). New York: Cambridge University Press.

Flavell, J. H., Everett, B. A., Croft, K., & Flavell, E. R. (1981). Young children's knowledge about visual perception: further evidence for the level 1– level 2 distinction. *Developmental Psychology, 17*, 99–103.

Flavell, J. H., Miller, P. H., & Miller, S. (1993). *Cognitive Development* (3rd ed.). Englewood Cliffs, NJ, Prentice Hall.

Gopnik, A., & Astington, J. W. (1988). Children's understanding of representational change and its relation to the understanding of false belief and the appearance-reality distinction. *Child Development, 59*, 26–37.

Gopnik, A., & Slaughter, V. (1991). Young children's understanding of changes in their mental states. *Child Development, 62*, 98–110.

Gopnik, A., Slaughter, V., & Meltzoff, A. (1994). Changing your views: how understanding visual perception can lead to a new theory of mind. In C. Lewis and P. Mitchell (Eds.), *Origins of an early understanding of mind*, (pp. 157–181). Hove, U.K.: Erlbaum.

Gordon, F. R., & Flavell, J. H. (1977). The development of intuitions about cognitive cuing. *Child Development, 48*, 1027–1033.

Harris, P. L. (1989). *Children and emotion: The development of psychological understanding.* Oxford: Basil Blackwell.

Kelly, R. R., Lang, H. G., Mousley, K., & Davis, S. (2003). Deaf college students' comprehension of relational language in arithmetic compare problems. *Journal of Deaf Studies and Deaf Education, 8*(2), 120–132.

Marschark, M. (1993). *Psychological development of deaf children.* New York: Oxford University Press.

Marschark, M. (2003). Cognitive functioning in deaf adults and children. In M. Marschark & P. E. Spencer (Eds.), *Oxford handbook of deaf studies, language, and education* (pp. 464–477). New York: Oxford University Press.

Marschark, M., Convertino, C., & LaRock, D. (2006a). Optimizing academic performance of deaf students: Access, opportunities, and outcomes. In D. F. Moores and D. S. Martin (Eds.), *Deaf learners: New developments in curriculum and instruction* (pp. 179–200). Washington, DC: Gallaudet University Press.

Marschark, M., Green, V., Hindmarsh, G., & Walker, S. (2000). Understanding theory of mind in children who are deaf. *Journal of Child Psychology, Psychiatry and Allied Disciplines, 41*, 1067–1073.

Marschark, M., Lang, H. G., & Albertini, J. A. (2002). *Educating deaf students: From research to practice.* New York: Oxford University Press.

Marschark, M., Sapere, P., Convertino, C., Seewagen, R. & Maltzan, H. (2004). Comprehension of sign language interpreting: Deciphering a complex task situation. *Sign Language Studies, 4*, 345–368.

Meristo, M., Falkman, K. W., Hjelmquist, E., Tedoldi, M., Surian, L., & Siegal, M. (2007). Language access and theory of mind reasoning: Evidence from deaf children in bilingual and oralist environments. *Developmental Psychology, 43*, 1156–1169.

Milligan, K., Astington, J., & Dack, L. A. (2007). Language and theory of mind: Meta-analysis of the relation between language ability and false-belief understanding. *Child Development, 78*, 622–646.

Morgan, G., & Kegl, J. (2006). Nicaraguan Sign Language and Theory of Mind: The issue of critical period and abilities. *Journal of Child Psychology and Psychiatry, 47*, 811–819.

Nelson, K. (2004). Commentary. The future of ToM lies in CoM. *International Society for the Study of Behavioural Development Newsletter, 45*, 16–17.

Onishi, K. H., & Baillargeon, R. (2005). Do 15-month-old infants understand false beliefs? *Science, 308*, 255–258.

Ottem, E. (1980). An analysis of cognitive studies with deaf subjects. *American Annals of the Deaf, 125*, 564–575.

Perner, J., & Clements, W. A. (1998). From an implicit to an explicit 'theory of mind.' In Y. Rossetti and A. Revonsuo (Eds.), *Beyond dissociation: Interaction between implicit and explicit processing* (pp. 273–293). Amsterdam: John Benjamins.

Perner, J., & Lang, B. (2000). Theory of mind and executive function: Is there a developmental relationship? In S. Baron-Cohen, H. Tager-Flusberg, and D. Cohen (Eds.), *Understanding other minds: Perspectives from autism* (pp. 155–186). Oxford: Oxford University Press, 155–186.

Perner, J., Leekam, S., & Wimmer, H. (1987). 3-year-olds' difficulty with false belief: The case of conceptual deficit. *British Journal of Developmental Psychology, 5*, 125–137.

Peterson, C. C. (2004). Theory-of-mind development in oral deaf children with cochlear implants or conventional hearing aids. *Journal of Child Psychology, Psychiatry, and Allied Disciplines, 45*, 1096–1106.

Peterson, C. C. (2007). Le développement métacognitif des enfants sourds [Metacognitive development of deaf children]. *Enfance, 59*(3).

Peterson, C. C., & Siegal, M. (1995). Deafness, conversation and theory of mind. *Journal of Child Psychology, Psychiatry and Allied Disciplines, 36*, 458–474.

Peterson, C. C., & Siegal, M. (1997). Domain specificity and everyday biological, physical, and psychological thinking in normal, autistic, and deaf children. In H. M. Wellman and K. Inagaki (Eds.). *The emergence of core domains of thought: Children's reasoning about physical, psychological, and biological phenomena* (pp. 55–70). San Francisco: Jossey-Bass.

Peterson, C. C., & Siegal, M. (1999). Insight into Theory of Mind from deafness and autism. *Mind and Language, 15*, 77–99.

Peterson, C. C., & Slaughter, V. (2006). Telling the story of theory of mind: Deaf and hearing children's narratives and mental states understanding. *British Journal of Developmental Psychology, 24*, 151–179.

Peterson, C. C., Wellman, H. M., & Liu, D. (2005). Steps in theory-of-mind development for children with deafness or autism. *Child Development, 76*, 502–517.

Piaget, J., & Inhelder, B. (1948). *La representation de l'espace chez l'enfant.* Paris: Presses Universitaires de France.

Poulin, C., & Miller, C. (1995). On narrative discourse and point of view in Quebec Sign Language. In K. Emmorey & J. S. Reilly (Eds.), *Language, gesture, and space* (pp. 117–131). Hillsdale N.J.: Lawrence Erlbaum.

Power, D., & Leigh, G. R. (2003). Curriculum: Cultural and communicative contexts. In M. Marschark & P. E. Spencer (Eds.), *Oxford handbook of deaf studies, language, and education* (pp. 38–51). New York: Oxford University Press.

Prezbindowski, A. K., & Lederberg, A. R. (2003). Vocabulary assessment of deaf and hard-of-hearing children: From infancy through the preschool years. *Journal of Deaf Studies and Deaf Education, 8*, 383–400.

Remmel, E. (2003). *Theory of mind development in signing deaf children.* Unpublished doctoral dissertation. Stanford University, California.

Remmel, E., Bettger, J. G., & Weinberg, A. M. (2001). Theory of mind development in deaf children. In M. D. Clark, M. Marschark, & M. Karchmer (Eds.). *Context, Cognition, and Deafness* (pp. 113–134). Washington, DC: Gallaudet University Press.

Rieffe, C., & Terwogt, M. (2000). Deaf children's understanding of emotions: Desire takes precedence. *Journal of Child Psychology, Psychiatry and Allied Disciplines, 41*, 601–608.

Russel, P. A., Hosie, J. A., Gray, C. D., Scott, C., Hunter, N., Banks, J. S., & Macaulay, M. C. (1998). The development of theory of mind in deaf children. *Journal of Child Psychology, Psychiatry, and Allied Disciplines, 39*, 903–910.

Sallandre, M.-A. (2006). Iconicity and Space in French Sign Language. In H. Maya & S. Robert (Eds.), *Space in languages: linguistic systems and cognitive categories* (pp. 239–255). Amsterdam: John Benjamins.

Sallandre M.-A. (2007). Simultaneity in French Sign Language Discourse. In M. Vermeerbergen, L. Lorraine, & O. Crasborn (Eds.), *Simultaneity in signed languages: Form and function* (pp. 103–125). Amsterdam: John Benjamins.

Schick, B., de Villiers, P, de Villiers, J., & Hoffmeister, R. (2007). Language and theory of mind: A study of deaf children. *Child Development, 78*, 376–396.

Siegal, M. (2007). Accès au langage et théorie de l'esprit [Language access and theory of mind reasoning]. *Enfance, 59*(3).

Southgate, V., Senju, A., & Csibra, G. (2007). Action attribution through anticipation of false beliefs by two-year-olds. *Psychological Science, 18*, 587–592.

Spencer, P., Meadow-Orlans, K., Koester, L., & Ludwig, L. (2004). Relationships across developmental domains and over time. In K. Meadow-Orlans,

P. Spencer, and K. Koester (Eds.), *The world of deaf infant* (pp. 205–217). New York: Oxford University Press.

Steeds, L., Rowe, K., & Dowker, A. (1997). Deaf children's understanding of beliefs and desires. *Journal of Deaf Studies and Deaf Education, 2*, 185–195.

Strauss, S. (2001). Folk psychology, folk pedagogy, and their relations to subject matter. In B. Torff (Ed.), *Understanding and teaching the intuitive mind* (pp. 217–242). Mahwah, NJ: Erlbaum Associates.

Wellman, H. M. & Bartsch, K. (1994). Before belief: Children's early psychological theory. In C. Lewis & P. Mitchell (Eds.), *Children's early understanding of mind* (pp. 331–354). Hove, U.K.: Lawrence Erlbaum.

Wellman, H. M., Cross, D., & Watson, J. (2001). Meta-analysis of theory-of-mind development: The truth about false belief. *Child Development, 72*, 655–684.

Wellmann, H. M., & Lagattuta, K. H. (2004). Theory of mind for learning and teaching: The nature and role of explanation. *Cognitive Development, 19*, 479–497.

Wellman, H. M., & Liu, D (2004). Scaling of theory-of-mind tasks. *Child Development, 75*, 523–541.

Wimmer, H., & Hartl, M. (1991). Against the Cartesian view on mind: Young children's difficulty with own false beliefs. *British Journal of Developmental Psychology, 9*, 125–138.

Wimmer, H., & Perner, J. (1983). Beliefs about beliefs: Representation and constraining function of wrong beliefs in young children's understanding of deception. *Cognition, 13*, 103–128.

Woolfe, T., Want, S. C., & Siegal, M. (2002). Signposts to development: Theory of mind in deaf children. *Child Development, 73*, 768–778.

Wynn, K. (1992). Addition and subtraction by human infants. *Nature, 358*, 749–750.

Yazdi, A. A., German, T. P., Defeyter, M. A., & Siegal, M. (2006). Competence and performance in belief-desire reasoning across two cultures: The truth, the whole truth and nothing but the truth about false belief? *Cognition, 100*, 343–368.

Chapter 5

Why Considerations of Verbal Aptitude Are Important in Educating Deaf and Hard-of-Hearing Students

C. Tane Akamatsu, Connie Mayer, and Steven Hardy-Braz

The common wisdom in deaf education circles is that *verbal intelligence* or *verbal ability* is inappropriate to measure because language acquisition conditions cannot be assumed to apply for deaf and hard-of-hearing (DHH) students, given their highly varied opportunities (or lack thereof) for language acquisition and development (Maller, 2003). Even if "equivalent" language acquisition conditions exist—the closest example being that of deaf children of deaf adults who acquire a natural signed language from birth—the use of standardized measures is only appropriate if the standardization sample is drawn from the same natural signed language.

Yet, mathematics and science require skills in logical thinking, consideration of evidence, categorical thinking, manipulation of information, hypothesis generation, hypothesis testing, and argumentation, which are all highly symbolic and language-loaded activities, some of which are learned incidentally by normally hearing children before they even enter school (Lang & Albertini, 2001; Nunes et al., 2007; Yore, 2000). Therefore, the assessment of language abilities of DHH students is also necessary for understanding their potential for achievement in mathematics and science.

Deaf and hard-of-hearing students are found in ever-increasing numbers in integrated settings, either for part or most of their school day. For example, in the Toronto District School Board, the largest school board in Canada, there are some 280,000 students. Of these, about 780 students are identified as having some level of hearing loss. Around 90% of these students use spoken language as their primary means of communication. Many have cochlear implants (CIs), and most of the rest have digital hearing aids. The vast majority of these students are placed either in mainstream settings with itinerant specialist teacher support or in congregated classes for DHH students within hearing neighborhood schools (where only about 50 use signing as their primary mode of communication). Fewer than 20 are at the school for the deaf (a bilingual-bicultural school).

Where infant hearing screening and CI programs are in place, this distribution is not uncommon, nor is it occurring because of unwillingness on the education system's part to offer instruction in sign language. Indeed, in this school board, American Sign Language (ASL)[1] is offered as an official language of instruction, and sign language interpretation is offered to students whose primary placement is in congregated classes when they take classes in the mainstream. What this distribution tells us is that the vast majority of today's DHH students are functioning as auditory learners and that, with good amplification and auditory management, they are functioning in mainstream hearing classes with English as their only or preferred language. As such, these students are expected to function as if their language development were similar to those of normally hearing students (see Marschark & Wauters, this volume; Pisoni et al., this volume). The assumption that most DHH children have severely limited access to spoken language is no longer viable.

At the same time, increasingly large numbers of deaf children have complex needs. Many of these children were born at extremely early gestational age, with their lives being saved only through intensive medical intervention. In consequence, they often enter school with a number of developmental disabilities, including deafness, and cognitive and neurological impairments are not uncommon.

It is clear that with these changes in school population, the range of needs that teachers are being asked to meet, and the kinds of information required to address these needs, is changing. Because the nature of the deaf school-age population is changing so quickly, anything held as a truism even 5 years ago seems obsolete. In this vein, a review of the literature even from the 1990s seems dated; however, it is important to examine the field, in order to chart a way into the future without repeating too many mistakes of the past.

Intelligence, Aptitude/Ability, and Achievement

Before proceeding with a discussion of issues around "verbal intelligence," it is necessary to discuss the relationships among intelligence, aptitude/ability, and achievement. These concepts are different, but overlap occurs

---

1. Our discussion focuses on the languages in which we work, ASL and English, but could equally well apply to other spoken and signed language pairings.

and, for the purposes of this chapter, it is important to disambiguate them for a theoretical discussion to proceed.

At a theoretical level, "there is no generally agreed upon meaning of 'intelligence'" (Jensen, 1997, p. 55). However, there seems to be some consensus that the ability to use information for learning, judgment, adaptation, rational thinking, creativity, and problem solving is fundamental to the concept of intelligence, but whether there is a single general intelligence factor (g) or different kinds of intelligences is still under discussion. The measurement of intelligence, therefore, is also a contentious issue. Tests of intelligence (IQ tests) themselves were initially devised to predict who would do well in school and who would have trouble. Operationally, however, intelligence is that which IQ tests measure.

The cognitive revolution of the 1970s provided the opportunity to study and measure more specific cognitive abilities such a visual perception, memory, psychomotor speed, reaction time, and such. Although different kinds of cognitive abilities had been hinted at earlier (e.g., Horn & Cattell, 1966), it was not until the latter part of the twentieth century that a more unified theory of cognitive abilities emerged.[2] The notions of crystallized and fluid intelligence introduced by Horn and Cattell implied that intelligent behavior (or more intelligent people?) used both what they already had learned and their ability to gather and apply new information to problem-solve.

The recognition of measurement of cognitive abilities, still codified in intelligence tests, included measuring both acquired information (crystallized intelligence and academic achievement) and more fundamental cognitive abilities (fluid intelligence, other cognitive processes such as visual/auditory perception, memory, etc.).

In his commentary on a special edition of *School Psychology Review,* Braden (1997) noted that the one thing that all the authors agreed on was that the notion of a general intelligence factor, or g, "exhibits a profound impact on educational outcomes" (p. 245). From that point, considerable controversy arose over whether more specific factors or abilities would be worthy of consideration and, if so, what these might be and how these abilities might be measured. It would seem, based on the literature in deafness and the contributions to this volume, that researchers take it as given that examinations of more specific abilities are necessary. Lopez (1997), writing in the same issue as Braden, suggested that because school functioning involves complex cognitive demands, the understanding of both global and specific constructs is crucial for the practitioner of school psychology. He also reminded us that "group and individual differences exist, and

2. Here, we are not referring to "multiple intelligences" in either Gardner's (1983) sense or in Sternberg's "triarchic" sense (1985).

one type of educational practice is not likely to work for every student" (Lopez, 1997, p. 250). Although Lopez was speaking particularly of second-language students, what he said certainly rings true for deaf students as well. To better inform practice in the education of DHH students, it will be necessary for school psychologists and others who assess this population to find ways to better measure and identify individual differences, especially in areas of obvious complex cognitive demand such as the development of literate thought and literacy.

Language for Communication, Thinking, and Literacy

With respect to the education and assessment of DHH children, it is critical to focus on verbal abilities, as they are central to gaining an understanding of how well any learner can use language to "do school." In other words, it is not sufficient to say that an individual has (or has not) acquired a first language, but rather it is necessary to identify whether the level of language acquired is sufficient for operating across the full range of functions in contexts both in and out of school. Halliday (1973) categorized these functions in a hierarchical fashion from the early developing instrumental stage (e.g., requesting, persuading) to the later developing heuristic (e.g., clarifying, solving, predicting) and informative (e.g., explaining, comparing, discussing) stages. Our intent in referring to this hierarchy is not to privilege one use of language over another, but rather to highlight those uses of language (heuristic and informative) that are most closely tied to school-based learning and to note that they are not uniquely tied to any modality in that each can be realized via spoken, signed, or written language.

Making a related distinction, Cummins (1979, 1981) identified two kinds of language proficiency—Basic Interpersonal Communication Skills (BICS) and Cognitive Academic Language Proficiency (CALP).[3] Basic Interpersonal Communication Skills refers to the face-to-face language that children typically develop first, as a matter of course, through interactions in their first language. Included are such things as the ability to maintain a face-to-face conversation; communicate, read, and write about familiar topics; employ basic/high-frequency vocabulary; and use basic sentence structures and grammar. Typically CALP develops after BICS have been established, and unlike the conversational proficiency that characterizes BICS, CALP refers to the use of language in less familiar contexts and/or for academic purposes. It denotes the ability to understand when there is

---

3. We acknowledge that there have been critiques of the BICS/CALP distinction (see discussions in Cummins, 2000; Edelsky, 2006), however for the purposes of this discussion, they provide a useful framework for distinguishing between language for communication and language for schooling.

less opportunity for face-to-face interaction; communicate, read, and write about topics that are abstract or more distant in time and space; employ more sophisticated/low-frequency vocabulary; and use more complex sentence structures and grammar. Whereas BICS are necessary for everyday communication and provide the prerequisite linguistic foundation for the subsequent development of CALP, they are not sufficient for doing school.

In terms of Halliday's functions of language, it could be argued that CALP is closely associated with the heuristic and informative functions—those functions that are intimately tied to academic learning and closely associated with text-based literacy. Although a strong link exists between CALP and print literacy (i.e., academic information is often best represented in a written mode), it should also be emphasized that the development of language for academic purposes can occur in any language (ASL or English) and in any mode (spoken, signed, or written). In a spoken or signed mode, this level of language use is often referred to as *literate discourse.*

This said, it is our contention that a measure of verbal abilities is central in sorting out the extent to which DHH learners are able to make use of language for literate discourse and literacy in order to solve problems, explain concepts, justify claims, and discuss issues (Halliday's heuristic and informative functions and Cummins' notion of CALP). This information is central and critical for educators of DHH students in planning programs and setting appropriate learning goals. Yet it is often the case that such information is unavailable, given the ongoing concerns with respect to administering tests of verbal abilities to DHH individuals.

Further complicating the situation for all concerned is the fact that many DHH children can face challenges in acquiring BICS in any first language (L1), leaving them with a shaky foundation on which to develop literate discourse and literacy (Mayer, in press). And, even when a DHH learner has had access to a language learning environment that has allowed for the development of an L1 (spoken or signed) for everyday interaction, it is often the case that she is not able to use this language to engage effectively in literate discourse or to develop literacy (Mayer, Akamatsu & Stewart, 2002). Although this is a challenge for DHH learners who use either a spoken or a signed language as their L1, the issues for those who sign become even more complex.

Given that a positive interdependence exists between the development of literacy and the development of CALP within and among languages (Cummins, 1991, 2000), it has been argued that deaf children, whose L1 is ASL or another natural signed language, can exploit CALP developed in their L1 to support the development of literacy in a second language (L2) such as English. However, Mayer and Wells (1996), while agreeing that although CALP could be developed in a natural signed language, challenged the assumption that the L1 competence would transfer wholesale to allow the development of text-based language in L2 when access to the L2 is limited by modality and when the L1 does not have its own written form. Thus, even when students have highly developed ASL as an L1, this may not provide the appropriate cognitive resources to develop proficient literacy in English as an L2.

Although positive benefits can and do accrue from CALP developed in a signed L1, developing text-based literacy in L2 also requires knowledge of the language being represented in written form, including the ability to make sense of the phonological system of that language in order to map it onto the written form (Mayer, 2007). And for students whose L1 is some form of signed and/or spoken English, we need to better understand how to develop higher levels of CALP in L2 and how to exploit the affordances and constraints of the various alternative routes to English that students may have used (e.g., mouthing, fingerspelling, signed forms of English). In both cases, we also need to recognize what kinds of cognitive skills in addition to language that a student is able to harness, keeping in mind that some of these are the skills (e.g., phonological processing, auditory short-term, and working memory) that have typically been viewed by school psychologists as difficult to assess in DHH learners (Hornberger, 1989; Mayer & Wells, 1996). On this point, it is useful to consider the relationship of language and literacy in the development of both hearing and deaf learners. Mayer and Wells (1996) provided a framework for how learners move from the basic face-to-face use of language to full literacy (see Figure 5–1). They suggested that, in learning the first language, it does not matter which language one learns, as long as there are interactions with competent users of sufficient quantity and quality to allow language acquisition to occur.

The internal transformation from social to inner speech is where language begins to be used as a tool for thinking (Vygotsky, 1978). It is where cognitive sequelae begin to manifest themselves (see Hauser, Lukomski, & Hilllman this volume). Since the social language forms the foundation for the inner language, the quality of the language used in social interactions as well as the nature of these interactions, has a direct bearing on the quality of the language and thought that becomes the substance of inner speech.

The move from inner speech to writing is where a number of questions arise with respect to how deaf children develop literacy. At this stage, knowledge of the language they know and knowledge of the language that is represented in print must be reconciled (Mayer & Wells, 1996; Olson, 1994). Given the extensive literature that indicates that "a broadly conceived notion of language skills, which includes vocabulary, syntax, discourse, and phonemic awareness, is fundamental for early and long-term literacy success" (Mayer, 2007), it becomes clear that deaf children have unique hurdles to overcome.

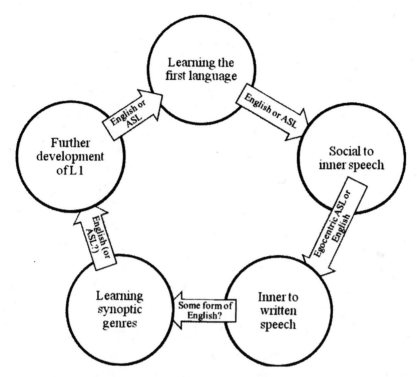

Figure 5–1. Deaf children's development from face-to-face language to literacy and literate thought (adapted from Mayer & Wells, 1996).

Although a natural signed language might be a perfectly serviceable L1, no natural signed language has a standard writing system, so continued development of CALP through text-based literacy in L1 is impossible. Secondly, DHH children may not have access to a threshold level of comprehensible input in a spoken L2 and therefore may not develop a level of language proficiency even at the BICS level that is necessary to develop L2 literacy. And, it is also the case that this L2 BICS serves as the linguistic foundation for inner speech upon which text-based literacy must be built (Mayer, 2009).

A number of researchers (e.g., Harris & Moreno, 2006; Leybaert, 1993; Mayer, 1999; Trezek & Wang, 2006) have suggested alternate routes through which deaf children might access some features of spoken language, including mouthing, fingerspelling, visual phonics, signed forms of English, or contact sign. Each of these relies on the visual and/or kinaesthetic modalities as a substitute for audition and, as such, probably interacts with other cognitive abilities in unique ways that are different from audition alone.

In the move from basic literacy to gaining control over the academic discipline-based synoptic genres[4] of expository writing literate discourse and literacy come together. Discipline-based knowledge is encoded within these genres, whether this occurs in speech, sign, or print. These genres are typified by the use of complex language, low-frequency vocabulary, and grammatical metaphor (Halliday, 1973) and are the hallmarks of the educated, literate person (Mayer, 2007). Although it has been argued that literate thinking can develop in the absence of a written tradition (Olson & Torrance, 1991), it is also true that literacy in a particular language does influence the face-to-face language that is used by people who are literate in that language, where speakers "[appropriate] the means for rational, abstract thinking in the medium of inner speech" (Mayer & Wells, 1996, p. 101). In this sense, it could be argued that learners who have CALP in both a face-to-face and written mode may think differently from individuals who do not.

In any event, it is clear that a richer understanding of how a DHH learner is developing CALP, or indeed if this development is even possible in all cases, is critical if teachers and other educational workers are to plan and program effectively. The challenge for those in the field of assessment is to find ways to examine CALP in the DHH population—an examination that has traditionally been fraught with controversy.

Does Eliminating "Verbal IQ" Eliminate Deaf People's Verbal Thinking Skills?

Evidence-based practice demands that we have evidence that the measurement of deaf people's VIQs is both valid and reliable, and that this information contributes to an understanding of the cognitive functioning of deaf students. Ample evidence suggests that standardized measures of VIQ are not adequate to the task (Braden, 1994; Maller, 2003). The most obvious is that the conditions under which most children learn spoken language simply do not apply to deaf children.

Certainly, the size and complexity of any language that deaf children acquire is affected by conditions of its acquisition. Signed language must be seen, and even the few children who are fortunate enough to be born into signing households do not see as much language as normally hearing children hear, because they cannot "overhear" conversations. Spoken language must be heard, and limited hearing and the reliance on vision

---

4. Synoptic genres are characterized by the language of epistemology, in which actions and processes grammatically become objects, and in which nouns (representing "things") are privileged over verbs (representing actions). Much of scientific writing is done in a synoptic genre.

and properly working amplification systems limit both the quantity and the quality of language exposure. We know about the delay in exposure to any language for the vast majority of deaf children. This situation is improving as a consequence of earlier identification and intervention with greater numbers of children having meaningful access to language from an earlier age (Yoshinaga-Itano, 2003). That said, it is still the case that many children continue to experience delayed exposure to linguistic input. The result may be that, by adulthood, many deaf people actually have "smaller languages" (lexically, morphologically, and syntactically) than most hearing people (Berent, 1996, p. 501).

Some evidence suggests that prolonged auditory deprivation and/or lack of (enough) access to language may result in permanent deficits in verbal reasoning ability. The acquisition of language has been shown to be time-sensitive, regardless of the modality of the language being acquired. In a series of studies, Mayberry and her colleagues found that deaf people who were first exposed to signed language in adolescence, after they had shown that acquisition of spoken language was not possible for them, did more poorly on tests of ASL syntax and comprehension than did deafened adolescents who had already acquired spoken English and who were learning ASL as a second language (Mayberry, 2003). They also did more poorly on these tests than people who had learned ASL either from birth or a very young age (Mayberry & Eichen, 1991; Mayberry & Fischer, 1989).

Although recent technological advances may minimize these difficulties, it may be the case that we are in fact working with a population that has not developed adequate reasoning skills in any language—skills referred to in an educational context as CALP. But knowing that there will potentially be a weakness in this area should not negate the utility of testing these language abilities. "Eliminating IQ is different from eliminating intelligence" (Braden, 1997, p. 244), and we would contend that eliminating the testing of VIQ is different from eliminating verbal intelligence. Rather, it behooves us to assess cognitive abilities in a way that taps the processes underlying spoken, signed, and written language to try and describe the strengths to be exploited, specify which weaknesses are susceptible to improvement, and which are simply to be accommodated.

Challenges in Assessing BICS and CALP

Conversational interviews. Although the BICS–CALP distinction is not one that is often made in the literature on assessment, it could be argued that several methods exist for examining BICS skills in deaf children (Akamatsu & Musselman, 1998; Bebko, Calderon, & Treder, 2003; Bebko & McKinnon, 1993, 1998; Newell, Caccamise, Boardman, & Holcomb, 1983). There is also a fair amount of research on deaf children's BICS, and this research has been done within the contexts of natural signed language, spoken language, and everything in between, using structured interview scales to measure global language development, including vocabulary, syntax, and pragmatics.

However, because these interviews are somewhat open-ended, they do not measure the breadth and depth of the same items across interviews. That is, while a rating about an interviewee's breadth and depth of vocabulary is made, specific vocabulary items are not sampled. Therefore, direct comparisons between two individuals' ability to define words, use these words in sentences, and identify these words based on their definitions are not possible, and similar comparisons at the syntactic level also cannot be made. Discourse-level comparisons, in contrast, such as the ability to introduce oneself, describe, compare/contrast ideas, hypothesize, and make reasoned argument can typically be completed, since structured interviews are designed around these categories. Such structured interviews have a certain face validity (Singleton & Supalla, 2003), as they are authentic language samples. Examples of research done on structured interviews include adapting language proficiency interviews for use in sign language with adults who are learning sign language (Newell et al., 1983); with adolescents to compare their conversational skills across oral, simultaneous speech and sign, and sign-only modalities using a modified version of this interview (Akamatsu & Musselman, 1998); and with children to evaluate their conversational skills either across modalities or in ASL (Kendall Demonstration Elementary School, 1985; Maller, Singleton, Supalla, & Wix, 1999).

The Conversational Proficiency Interview (CPI), for example, is an adaptation of the Sign Language Proficiency Interview (Newell et al., 1983). The CPI is actually a series of three interviews conducted separately in ASL, simultaneous English and signing, and spoken English, with three different trained interviewers (a deaf one, a strong simultaneous communicator, and a nonsigning hearing individual, respectively). These communication conditions are commonly encountered by deaf youth, and it was anticipated (and confirmed) that they would function differently in the three different situations (Akamatsu & Musselman, 1998; Musselman & Akamatsu, 1999). In a study of 67 deaf adolescents ranging in age from 14.5 years to 19.5 years and enrolled in a variety of settings across Ontario, including provincial schools, segregated classes in public schools, resource room programs, and mainstream settings, scores on the CPI in these students' strongest modality/language were strongly related to the Wechsler Intelligence Scales for Children (WISC-III; Wechsler, 1991) verbal IQ (VIQ) scores, but not to the performance IQ (PIQ) scores (Nizerro, Musselman, & MacKay-Soroka, 1993). It is worth noting that the signing deaf teens in these studies who scored at Intermediate+ or higher level in the ASL version of the CPI also tended to have significantly higher VIQs (but similar

PIQs) than those scoring at or lower than the Intermediate range, suggesting that at least some CALP skills are measurable in both ASL and English (Musselman & Akamatsu, 1997).

Although the VIQ standard scores of the group as a whole averaged in the high 70s (mean = 78.45, SD = 11.36), some of the teenagers in these studies were able to attain VIQ scores within the average range, regardless of whether their strongest language/modality on the CPI was ASL or spoken English, thus suggesting that they were able to mobilize their language abilities for verbal problem solving. However, those students whose highest CPI scores are in the developing range may not yet have the necessary control over the kind of decontextualized language that is used in school (i.e., CALP) and may be at academic risk, even when their PIQ is within average limits (Akamatsu & Musselman, 1998).

There are two shortcomings with this prior work, however. First, at the time it was conducted (data were collected from 1989 to 1993), it was not known whether the items on the WISC-III verbal scales functioned similarly for deaf signing students as they did for normally hearing students. Subsequent research by Maller (1997) indicated that they do not. Second, the psychometric properties of the CPI were not researched, other than by comparison to the verbal scales of the WISC-III and an achievement test.

The Language Proficiency Profile-2 (Bebko et al., 2003; Bebko & McKinnon, 1993, 1998) uses parent and teacher reports to estimate a child's proficiency in "expressive pragmatic/semantic skills that would be common to spoken and signed languages and other non-standard systems used by deaf or hearing children" (Bebko et al., 2003, p. 439). The LPP-2 has been shown to be developmental in nature, with older children scoring higher than younger children. However, there are no standardized age norms. The researchers found that hearing children tend to reach maximum scores at younger ages than do deaf children (Bebko & McKinnon, 1998). When they compared years of relevant language experience for deaf children to chronological age in hearing children (which can be assumed to be synonymous with years of relevant language experience), they found that the delays were effectively reduced or eliminated.

Several attempts have been made at developing ASL assessment instruments, none of which has been developed to the point of publication as test batteries or formal assessments (American Sign Language Assessment Instrument, Hoffmeister, Bahan, Greenwald, & Cole, 1990; American Sign Language Proficiency Assessment (ASL-PA), Maller et al., 1999; Test of ASL, Prinz, Strong, & Kuntze, 1994). By and large, these instruments include comprehension and production measures for linguistic structures specific to ASL and were intended for use with children ranging in age from 5 to 18, depending on the test. These tests are intended only to measure ASL skills, and no claims about verbal abilities or more general thinking abilities are made.

Similarly, rating scales measuring spoken language have been in use with both hearing and deaf children for quite some time. Measures developed specifically for deaf children include the Pragmatics Profile of Everyday Communication Skills (Dewart & Summers, 1988), Story Narrative Assessment Procedure (Nottingham Early Assessment Package, 2004), and the Profile of Actual Linguistic Skills (Nottingham Early Assessment Package, 2004). Again, none of these addresses verbal cognition, although the developers of the Nottingham Early Assessment Package say that unduly slow progress on any of their measures is cause for concern and referral for a more detailed cognitive assessment (Archbold & Harbor, 2007).

One of the difficulties with all these rating scales is the degree to which abilities can be differentiated. Most of these scales have only a few anchor points, making correlations to other scales with wide distributions (e.g., IQ scores) difficult. Converting IQ scores to z-scores helps in this regard. However, the rating scales are descriptive rather than normative in nature. At best, we can say that if higher scores on one scale are associated with higher scores on another scale, then they might be measuring the same phenomenon.

Although the assessment tools just described tell us a fair bit about the early language and communication development of deaf children, they do not adequately separate language abilities from verbal thinking skills. At best, they show that good communicators, that is, those who develop their BICS well, use whatever tools they have, from actual language, to good pragmatics, to general intelligence, personality, and temperament. It is CALP, however, that allows a learner to do well in school, as evidenced by the fact that hearing children with language delays/disorders often do have BICS in place, but not CALP. These are children who can identify colors but when asked "How are red and yellow alike?" answer "They're not alike; they're both different colors" or "They're orange."

Standardized tests of verbal intelligence or verbal abilities. Psychometric information on verbal or language-based tests is woefully inadequate in the field of deaf education. Reasons for this are fairly obvious. First, deaf students are often not administered tests of VIQ because these tests contain huge amounts of construct-irrelevant variance (e.g., hearing ability, knowledge of English). Second, nonstandard translations of the tests into either ASL or a signing system render the norms tables invalid. Third, very few school psychologists know much about deafness. The list goes on.

In spite of this, a few studies have investigated the role of VIQ in deaf students' achievement. Correlations between IQ and achievement in the DHH population have been mixed. Reynolds (1976) found that IQ did not correlate with reading achievement once hearing level was accounted for.

Elsewhere, high correlations have been reported between the WISC-III Verbal scales and academic achievement (Davis, Elfenbein, Schum, & Bentler, 1986; Maller & Braden, 1993; Nizerro et al., 1993). Nizerro et al. (1993) showed the presence of a very strong relationship between early PIQ and adolescent VIQ (smarter kids learn language better?), stronger than that of early PIQ and adolescent PIQ. They also found stronger relationships between reading comprehension and VIQ than with PIQ; adolescent IQ measures and math computation were moderate to strong.

However, it is important to note that, although VIQ and academic performance were highly correlated in these studies, tests of both kinds of abilities may actually be reflecting other factors such as hearing ability, comorbidity with neurological deficits, access to language of any kind, access to English, and opportunities to learn (Maller & Braden, 1993). Additionally, several studies have shown weak to moderate correlations between tests of *nonverbal* abilities and scores on standardized achievement tests (Allen, 1986; Jastak & Wilkinson, 1984; Kelly & Braden, 1990; Maller & Braden 1993; Phelps & Branyan, 1990; Ulissi, Brice, & Gibbins, 1989). To some extent this is not remarkable: smarter kids tend to do better academically.

Up to this point, verbal skills have been discussed as if they are a unitary whole. Yet, "VIQ" tests are known to be made up of different subtests that sample a variety of language and problem-solving tasks. Therefore, a "global" verbal abilities (e.g., the Verbal Comprehension Index on the WISC-IV, Wechsler, 2003) does not yield useful enough information for the classroom teacher, although it might reveal whether language/verbal abilities need more detailed examination. Since in the case of deaf children this is a given, what more detailed information would be useful? Even the reliable, although not necessarily valid, finding of deaf people's VIQ being approximately one standard deviation below that of the hearing population (Braden, 1994; Maller & Braden, 1993; Moores, 2001) does not illuminate the nature of deaf people's verbal reasoning abilities.

To further complicate matters, Maller (1996, 1997) found that even when a translated, signed version of the WISC-III was administered, differential item functioning occurred on the verbal scales of this test. Item-level analyses show that on the WISC-III verbal subtests, deaf students find item difficulties to be different from those for hearing students, suggesting that their VIQs *could* be higher than the test scores suggest, thereby calling into question the validity of the scores that they demonstrate. Interestingly, the structure of deaf people's nonverbal IQ also might be different (Maller, 1997; Zweibel & Mertens, 1985). Whether this is a result of language-related issues, lack of auditory stimulation, test construction, education, or other factors is unknown. Maller therefore recommended that the verbal scales not be administered to deaf students for the purposes of estimating intellectual abilities. "Although the Verbal Scale may seem to provide useful information regarding a deaf examinee, tests should not be used in the absence of sufficient validity evidence for a given purpose" (Maller, 2003, p. 453).

Estimating *g* without information about verbal abilities. Because *g* is the most robust predictor of academic achievement, it is important that the reader understand that best practices continue to support the use of nonverbal IQ as the best estimate of general intelligence (*g*) in the DHH (particularly deaf) population. And while we do not dispute this practice, some difficulties arise when translating that idea into the classroom and world of academic achievement. Nonverbal aptitude tests of *g* may rule out global cognitive delays, but they tell us precious little about the strengths and weaknesses a particular student brings to the learning enterprise, nor about an individual's language capacity.

The critical question for school psychologists working with deaf students is this: If deaf people's intelligence as estimated by nonverbal IQ has roughly the same mean and standard deviation as that of hearing people, then why is the median academic achievement of deaf high school leavers still around the Grade 4 level? One of the roles of the school psychologist is to explain why students are not achieving academically and to suggest changes either in curriculum or practice to enable students to better access and learn the curriculum.

Spencer (2004) suggested that general cognitive ability, which can be accurately estimated in deaf children with nonverbal/PIQ scores, may be correlated with the ability to acquire and sustain pragmatic language skills, make sense of imperfect auditory information, and reflect non–modality-specific strengths in sequencing and patterning that is required of any language (see also Lindsay, Shapiro, Musselman, & Wilson, 1988). In her study of language measures associated with age of cochlear implantation and duration of implant use, Spencer found that younger age at implantation was significantly correlated with better scores on a measure of English language (CELF-preschool, Wiig, Secord, & Semel, 1992), even when the effects of nonverbal IQ were statistically removed. Clearly, nonverbal IQ, even as the best estimate of *g*, does not say it all. Information is missing.

If *g* is so good at predicting academic achievement, and if certain abilities are not assessed because of known third-factor issues (e.g., testing auditory processing of people with measurable hearing loss), then how can *g* be estimated? Whereas the use of nonbiased nonverbal tests such as the Universal Nonverbal Intelligence Test (UNIT; Bracken & McCallum, 1998) does give a reliable and valid estimation of *g*, the fact is that *g* in the rest of the population is estimated by a variety of verbal and nonverbal measures. On the surface, it would seem that we are advocating for the very practice that has been shown to contribute to invalid results. And appropriate test accommodations and the robust findings that nonverbal tests of

IQ (or *g*) speak to the continued practice of estimating IQ in this fashion. But, it is not enough to say to a teacher, "Well, this child has measured intelligence within (or even above) the average range," when the child is patently several years behind not only in the obvious language skills of reading and writing, but also in academic areas such as mathematics, science, and social studies. Does this mean that the teacher is deficient in his practice? Hardly. The robust findings that, on average, deaf children remain academically behind cannot suggest that *that* many teachers are unskilled practitioners.

Nonstandard administration of any of the verbal tests immediately calls into question the validity of the scores at the item, subtest, and scale level (Maller, 2003). There are occasional calls for proper (blind back-translated) ASL versions of tests on the assumption that by testing language skills in a natural signed language, a more accurate measure of verbal abilities will be obtained. This is a curious solution because there are so few children for whom a natural signed language is truly the L1 and, that said, it seems they would not fare much better in a test administered in ASL than one given in English.

The first, stronger, and possibly only language a particular child knows might be some version of home sign or school sign that is English-based, but because they are signing, people might be fooled into thinking that they are poor users of a natural signed language. However, any signer will use three dimensions and space in the way that native signers do. An abundant literature says that both home-signers and contact signers do this (Goldin-Meadow & Feldman, 1977; Goldin-Meadow & Mylander, 1984; Lucas & Valli, 1992). Just because signers use spatial mechanisms does *not* mean they are signing in a natural signed language. It means they are signing. We cannot allow ourselves to get bogged down classifying the kind of signing someone is doing. We need to concentrate on what kinds of *thinking* they are able to do with their language (Akamatsu, Stewart, & Mayer, 2002; Mayer, et al., 2002) and communicate with them accordingly.

Perhaps what needs to happen is a wider sampling of cognitive skills under ideal testing conditions (i.e., appropriate accommodations, well-translated tests, using tests with appropriate item functioning, examiners who understand the effects of deafness and can interpret the results appropriately) and more research analyzing the results of those students who score within or above the average range on tests that tap CALP. One possible solution to these testing challenges may be a reconsideration of verbal abilities in terms of BICS and CALP. This is not to suggest that BICS and CALP supplant anything in current intelligence theory, but that it would be instructive to consider whether tested skills are "BICS-like" or "CALP-like." As Mayer and Wells (1996) pointed out, it is in the learning of the synoptic genres that literate thought can occur, and this literate thought can be tapped using carefully selected tests.

Cattell-Horn-Carroll Theory and Academic Achievement

The Cattell-Horn-Carroll (CHC) theory of cognitive abilities (Carroll, 1993, 1996; Cattell, 1943, 1963; Horn, 1988, 1991; Horn & Cattell, 1966) is supported by over 50 years of "factor analytic, developmental, heritability, external outcome validity, and neurocognitive research evidence" (Floyd, Evans, & McGrew, 2003, p. 156), much of which is summarized and reviewed in McGrew and Flanagan (1998). Briefly, CHC theory is a three-stratum hierarchical framework of cognitive abilities that postulates a general factor (g) and 10 broad factors: crystallized intelligence (Gc), fluid reasoning (Gf), auditory processing (Ga), visual processing (Gv), short-term memory (Gsm), long-term retrieval (Glr), processing speed (Gs), reaction time (Gt), literacy (Grw), and quantitative abilities (Gq). These 10 broad abilities subsume over 70 narrow-stratum abilities (see Figure 5–2). For the purposes of this chapter, we will focus on crystallized intelligence (Gc), which is most closely aligned with language abilities, and briefly consider fluid intelligence (Gf), which can be easily measured nonverbally and is therefore considered to be a good estimate of deaf people's general intelligence. Additionally, we will consider the roles of auditory processing (Ga) in the light of increased access to auditory information through technology such as digital hearing aids and CIs, and memory (short-term and working memory (Gsm) and long-term retrieval (Glr)).

It is important to note that, for the purposes of schooling, not all narrow abilities need to be developed to an equal extent, and indeed, not all narrow abilities are needed to live a full and productive life. Rather, the narrow abilities identified so far have been shown to be associated in particular ways with the broad category abilities listed here. Therefore, in the context of this chapter, it might be helpful to understand which narrow abilities are most useful for the development of BICS and CALP and how these abilities align with literacy development.

CHC Broad-stratum Abilities, BICS, CALP, and Literacy

Print literacy requires knowledge of the phonological, lexical, and syntactic systems of a language. Therefore, it would make sense that the narrow abilities subsumed under crystallized intelligence (Gc), including language development, lexical development, listening ability, communication ability, oral production and fluency, and grammatical sensitivity be considered, at least for early literacy within spoken languages. In the context of English-based signing, whether "listening" ability, "oral" production, and fluency actually need to be auditory/oral is debatable, but at minimum, some form of "running English in the head" would seem to be necessary.

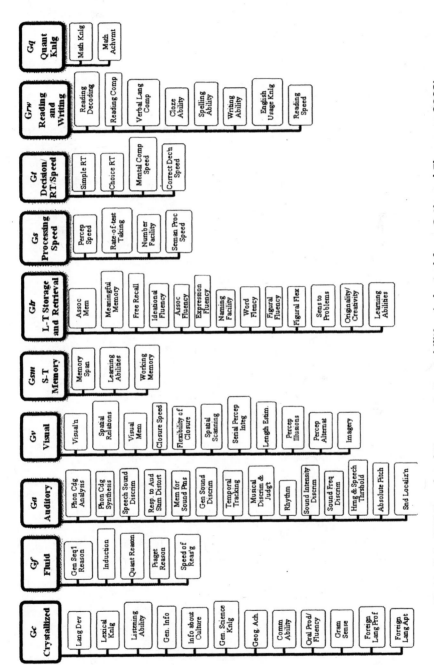

Figure 5–2. CHC Broad and Narrow stratum abilities (adapted from Ortiz and Flanagan, 2002).

Gc
Crystallized
- Lang Dev
- Lexical Knlg
- Listening Ability
- Gen. Info
- Info about Culture
- Gen. Science Knlg
- Geog. Ach
- Comm Ability
- Oral Prod/ Fluency
- Gram Sense
- Foreign Lang Prof
- Foreign Lang Apt

Gf
Fluid
- Gen Seql Reason
- Induction
- Quant Reason
- Piaget Reason
- Speed of Reas'g

Ga
Auditory
- Phon Cdg Analysis
- Phon Cdg Synthesis
- Speech Sound Discrim
- Resp to Aud Stim Distort
- Mem for Sound Ptns
- Gen Sound Discrim
- Temporal Tracking
- Musical Discrim & Judgt
- Rhythm
- Sound Intensity Discrim
- Sound Freq Discrim
- Hrng & Speech Thrshld
- Absolute Pitch
- Snd Localiz'n

Gv
Visual
- Visual'n
- Spatial Relations
- Visual Mem
- Closure Speed
- Flexibility of Closure
- Spatial Scanning
- Serial Percep Integ
- Length Estim
- Percep Illusions
- Percep Alternat
- Imagery

Gsm
S-T Memory
- Memory Span
- Learning Abilities
- Working Memory

Glr
L-T Storage and Retrieval
- Assoc Mem
- Meaningful Memory
- Free Recall
- Ideational Fluency
- Assoc Fluency
- Expression Fluency
- Naming Facility
- Word Flency
- Figural Fluency
- Figural Flex
- Sens to Problems
- Originality/ Creativity
- Learning Abilities

Gs
Processing Speed
- Percep Speed
- Rate-of-test Taking
- Number Facility
- Seman Proc Speed

Gt
Decision/ RT-Speed
- Simple RT
- Choice RT
- Mental Comp Speed
- Correct Dccn Speed

Grw
Reading and Writing
- Reading Decoding
- Reading Comp
- Verbal Lang Comp
- Cloze Ability
- Spelling Ability
- Writing Ability
- English Usage Knlg
- Reading Speed

Gq
Quant Knlg
- Math Knlg
- Math Achvmt

The CALP skills are clearly culturally and discipline-based, and would be developed once the synoptic genres are also developed.

This division into BICS and CALP skills may be criticized as too simplistic, and for the purposes in the classroom, that criticism is valid. What is closer to the truth, at least in practice, is that the kinds of narrow-stratum skills in Figure 5–2 interact in complex ways with each other, and a clear division into BICS and CALP skills becomes increasingly difficult to disentangle. Similarly, the broad-stratum cognitive skills do not act independently from one another, nor are they all equally important for any particular endeavor. However, for a first pass at this idea, we will continue to maintain a theoretical distinction.

The implications of CHC theory are daunting in the context of deafness (Hardy-Braz & Miller, 2004). If Gc and Ga (auditory processing), for starters, are ignored, and measures of auditory working memory (a narrow ability under Gsm) cannot be obtained, then educators find themselves with the explanation that deaf children are not achieving because they cannot hear, and the best way for them to access the curriculum is by being put into a school for the deaf or by finding ways to help them hear. Fuller explanations are needed of how these sensory deficits interact with cognitive abilities in general and the development of CALP in particular.

The first implication of CHC theory, as originally postulated, is that deaf people can never have "normal" cognition by dint of the fact that their auditory systems do not work in the same way as they do in hearing people. We fully understand resistance to this idea, particularly after decades of argument and scientific research that would suggest that (a) deaf people have average intelligence (g), and (b) that ASL, as a bona fide language, allows verbal cognition in deaf people. If we were to ignore Ga and Gc because tests for these broad abilities introduce construct-irrelevant variance, then we would have a cognitive system with holes in it. An examination of the kinds of skills that are tested under Gc suggests that many of those skills could well be tested in ASL or some form of English-based signing, as long as construct-irrelevant variance is eliminated. Similarly, the skills tested under Ga are actually often tested by audiologists.

There is, however, a second implication from this theory. Although we have presented it as if all broad-stratum skills are of equal value and separate from each other, in fact, they interact in various ways. The most obvious interaction is that of Gc, Ga, and Grw (reading and writing achievement). That is, one's ability to process the spoken form of a language, including developing phonological and phonemic awareness (all included in Ga), which impacts on one's ability to acquire and use that language for a number of purposes (Gc), including learning to read and write (Grw). Examination of narrow-stratum skills clearly points to the very skills upon which both encoding and decoding of a spoken language is critical to the development of literacy in that language. That being said, it is instructive to consider how the notions of BICS and CALP align themselves within the CHC model. BICS and CALP are clearly language-related concepts and, since Gc is most closely aligned with verbal abilities, it follows that language-based tasks are use to measure this broad-stratum ability. An examination of the narrow abilities represented here reveals that both BICS and CALP skills are represented. However, since BICS and CALP come from a different theoretical tradition, it is likely that other kinds of cognitive skills interact in producing both BICS and CALP skills.

However, to look only at Gc as if it were synonymous with VIQ or CALP as a predictive variable in deaf children's academic achievement is both limited and limiting in conception. Indeed, a developing body of research (aptly summarized in Fiorello & Primerano, 2005) points to specific cognitive abilities that are associated with specific academic achievements, beyond the general explanatory power of g. Understanding the relationship between Gc and reading development, we must be careful to ensure that the definition of specific learning disabilities in reading among culturally and linguistically diverse populations includes cognitive processing weaknesses that are separate from the Gc factor (Wexler & Fiorello, 2002). To aid us in this process, Flanagan and Ortiz (2001, see also Flanagan, Ortiz, & Alfonso, 2007) have developed Culture–Language matrices, which categorize subtests by how heavily loaded they are with cultural and linguistic information that could disadvantage examinees whose native culture/language is not American English. Using these matrices, it is possible to consider and tap into various narrow abilities with low to moderate culture/language loadings across broad ability areas such as fluid reasoning (Gf), quantitative reasoning (Gq), visual spatial processing (Gv), and short-term memory (Gsm) (Hardy-Braz & Miller, 2004).

Academic Achievement and Other Cognitive Factors

Reading difficulties have been associated with difficulties in Ga (auditory processing, particularly phonological analysis and synthesis), Gc (broad: crystallized intelligence, particularly knowledge of the language being read), Gsm (broad: short-term memory, particularly working memory), and Gs (broad: processing speed, particularly speed and automaticity of making sound/symbol correspondences) in the hearing population (Wexler & Fiorello, 2002). It is clear that these skills can be problematic in the deaf population, but they need to be accounted for somehow (Mayer, in press, 2007). It is becoming clear that "phonological" awareness does not have to be auditory in nature. For example, evidence of phonological awareness was found in deaf children who use cued speech with French (Leybaert & Charlier, 1996) and English (LaSasso & Metzger, 1998). Similarly, visual phonics (International Communication Learning Institute, 1996) has been shown to be an effective intervention tool for developing phonemic aware-ness in beginning deaf readers (Plesko-DuBois, Jones-Oleson, & Shreckhise, 2007; Trezek, Wang, Woods, Gampp, & Paul, 2007). Moreover, some deaf people are able to construct an idiosyncratic phonological code that is use-ful for literacy learning (Lichtenstein, 1998), although the neurological mechanisms for doing this are poorly understood.

In hearing children, writing is associated with Gc (broad: crystal-lized intelligence, therefore knowledge of the language being written), Gs (broad: processing speed, therefore automaticity of executing mechanics such as spelling), Ga (broad: auditory processing, therefore phonological analysis and synthesis, acquisition of the spoken form), and Gf (broad: fluid intelligence, therefore planning what to say, deciding how to make an argument, etc.) (McGrew & Knopik, 1993). Caveats similar to those for reading apply here, as well. Similarly, in hearing children, math calcu-lation is significantly predicted by Gc, Gf, Gq (quantitative knowledge), and Gsm, and math reasoning by Gc, Gf, Gq, Gsm (Floyd, Shaver, & Mc-Grew, 2003). The predictive value of other cognitive abilities [e.g., Gs, Gsm, Glr (long-term retention and retrieval)] varies by age, but also factors in to these academic achievements, although the cognitive mechanisms for how working memory contributes to math achievement are not well-understood (Nunes et al., this volume; Nunes et al., 2007).

Testing a Broad Range of Cognitive Abilities

Balancing issues of fairness in testing—particularly around the language issues involved in Gc—and the need to sample a broad range of cognitive abilities is tricky. Publishers of a number of commonly used tests have begun to incorporate procedures such as reviewing items during the test develop-ment phase for fairness for DHH students, collecting validity information for DHH students and presenting them in the test manuals, including va-lidity studies and the performance of DHH students in their manuals, and providing administration accommodations, subtest caveats, or suggestions by communication modality, and/or a sign language translation (Hardy-Braz, 2003a; 2003b, 2004; Hardy-Braz, Elliott, Fulton-Behrens, & Kushal-nagar, 2007). This information is summarized in Table 5–1. It is important to note that, although test publishers are beginning to provide additional information to aid in testing DHH individuals, appropriate interpretation of their test results requires an extensive knowledge of deafness and how DHH individual's medical, educational, social/emotional, and communi-cation history impact on test performance. Additionally, because most of these tests do not sample the full range of cognitive abilities, even when they do include measures of Gc, being able to test a wide range of abilities

Table 5–1. Comparisons of Commonly Used Tests for Use with DHH Students

Comments	KABC2[7]	WISC-IV[8]	SB5[9]	RIAS[10]	DAS2[11]	WPPSI[12]	WJIII[13]
Factors not measured	Gs, Ga	Ga, Glr	Gs, Ga, Glr	Gf, Glr, Ga, Gs	None	Ga, Glr, Gsm	none
Test items reviewed in development for fairness for D/HH students	Yes	Yes	Yes	No	Yes	No	no
D/HH Validity Study Data Collected and Presented in manual	Yes	None	None	Yes	Yes	None	none
D/HH Administration Guidelines by communication modality	In press	Yes	Yes	None	Yes	None	possibilites suggested
Subtest Caveats for D/HH administration provided	In press	Yes	Yes	None	Yes	None	none

(continued)

Table 5–1. (Continued)

Comments	Test						
	KABC2[7]	WISC-IV[8]	SB5[9]	RIAS[10]	DAS2[11]	WPPSI[12]	WJIII[13]
Sign Language Translation Provided	None	None	None	None	Partial	None	none
Other caveats	Different subtests used at different ages; if MPI model used, then Gc not measured in an attempt for greater fairness	PRI measures alone just measure 1 Gv and 2 Gf	Only the "nonverbal" subtests gives one subtest level measure of four areas	the nonverbal index test you get just three measures of Gv	Special Nonverbal Composite cannot be calculated at youngest ages; only two Gv and two Gf at other ages	PIQ only measures: one Gv and two Gf, (two optional Gv available, too)	

7. Kaufman, A. S., and Kaufman, N. L. (2004). KABC-II : *Kaufman Assessment Battery for Children, 2nd edition: Manual*. Circle Pines, MN (4201 Woodland Rd., Circle Pines 55014–1796): American Guidance Service.

8. Wechsler, D. (2003). *Wechsler Intelligence Scales for Children®—4th edition*. San Antonio: Harcourt.

9. Roid, G. H. (2003). *Stanford Binet Intelligence Scales* (5th ed.). Itasca, IL: Riverside Pub.

10. Reynolds, C. and Kamphaus, R. (2007). *Reynolds Intellectual Assessment Scales™*. Lutz, FL: Psychological Assessment Resources, Inc.

11. Elliott, C. D. (2006). *Differential Ability Scales 2*. San Antonio: Harcourt Assessment Inc.

12. Wechsler, D. (2002). *Wechsler Preschool and Primary Scales of Intelligence™, 3rd edition*. San Antonio: Harcourt.

13. Woodcock. R. W., McGrew, K. S., and Mather, N. (2001). *Woodcock-Johnson III Tests of Cognitive Abilities*. Itasca, IL: Riverside Publishing.

typically requires the use of multiple instruments, which can be costly and time-consuming.

However, the techniques of cross-battery assessment, in which carefully selected subtests from large, well-known standardized tests are administered and scored, allows the examiner to use selected subtests from multiple tests in a cost- and time-efficient manner, and to compare the results of these subtests in a meaningful way. Cross-battery assessment has made not simply predictive, but explanatory testing possible (Flanagan, Ortiz, & Alfonso, 2007). Cross-battery assessment calls for selecting two subtests per broad-stratum ability, each of which taps different narrow-stratum abilities. The rationale for the selection of specific subtests rests in the empirical literature on the relationships of the kinds of abilities being tested, the broad-stratum cognitive domain, and academic achievement. Because only two narrow-stratum abilities need to be tested to arrive at an estimate of the broad-stratum ability, efficient testing is possible. If an individual's performance on the two narrow-stratum abilities diverges widely, additional focused testing is required. Procedures for this kind of testing are outlined (Flanagan and Ortiz, 2001, 2002; Flanagan, Ortiz, & Alfonse, 2007). Table 5–2 shows how seven broad-range cognitive abilities (Gc, Gf, Ga, Gv, Glr, Gsm, and Gs) are sampled using the subtests tests commonly used with DHH students.[5]

Critics of cross-battery assessment note that not all subtests are created equal, nor are all subtests that have been shown to be strongly associated with particular narrow-stratum abilities equally predictive of academic achievement. The reliability and validity of comparing subtests from different test batteries are also at issue (Watkins, Glutting, & Youngstrom, 2002; Watkins, Youngstrom, & Glutting, 2002). Therefore, school psychologists must continue to research the predictive value of various tests on the market (Ortiz & Flanagan, 2002a, 2002b).

The Continuing Struggle for Literacy and Literate Thinking in DHH Students

Now that so many DHH children are receiving auditory information that is far superior to that of a generation ago, it would be useful to understand exactly what kind of sense these children are making of this auditory information. It is no longer enough to say "This child has a mild-moderate hearing loss" and simply report aided and unaided dB hearing levels. It is also not enough to say, "Most children with CIs function like children

---

5. This is not to suggest that all of these subtests test each cognitive factor in the same way, but merely to show which cognitive factors these subtests have been shown, through research, to tap.

Table 5–2. Commonly Used Subtests Measuring Seven Broad-stratum Cognitive Factors

Test	Subtest	Gc	Gf	Ga	Gv	Gsm	Glr	Gs
DAS-2	Early number concepts	x						
DAS-2	Verbal comprehension	x						
DAS-2	Verbal similarities	x						
DAS-2	Word definitions	x						
KABC-2	Expressive vocabulary	x						
KABC-2	Riddles	x						
KABC-2	Verbal knowledge	x						
RIAS	Guess what	x						
RIAS	Verbal reasoning	x						
SB-5	Nonverbal knowledge	x						
SB-5	Verbal knowledge	x						
WISC-IV	Comprehension	x						
WISC-IV	Information	x						
WISC-IV	Similarities	x						
WISC-IV	Vocabulary	x						
WISC-IV	Word reasoning	x						
WJ-III	General information	x						
WJ-III	Verbal comprehension	x						
WPPSI-III	Comprehension	x						
WPPSI-III	Information	x						
WPPSI-III	Picture naming	x						
WPPSI-III	Receptive vocabulary	x						
WPPSI-III	Similarities	x						
WPPSI-III	Vocabulary	x						
WPPSI-III	Word reasoning	x						
DAS-2	Matrices		x					
DAS-2	Picture similarities		x					
DAS-2	Sequential and quantitative reasoning		x					
KABC-2	Story completion		x					
SB-5	Nonverbal fluid reasoning		x					
SB-5	Nonverbal quantitative reasoning		x					
SB-5	Verbal fluid reasoning		x					
SB-5	Verbal quantitative reasoning		x					

Table 5–2. *(Continued)*

Test	Subtest	Gc	Gf	Ga	Gv	Gsm	Glr	Gs
					Broad Cognitive Factor			
WISC-IV	Matrix reasoning		x					
WISC-IV	Picture concepts		x					
WJ-III	Analysis–synthesis		x					
WJ-III	Concept formation		x					
WPPSI-III	Matrix reasoning		x					
WPPSI-III	Picture concepts		x					
DAS-2	Phonological processing			x				
WJ-III	Auditory attention			x				
WJ-III	Sound blending			x				
DAS-2	Copying				x			
DAS-2	Matching letter-like forms				x			
DAS-2	Pattern construction				x			
DAS-2	Recall of designs				x			
DAS-2	Recognition of pictures				x			
KABC-2	Block counting				x			
KABC-2	Conceptual thinking				x			
KABC-2	Face recognition				x			
KABC-2	Gestalt closure				x			
KABC-2	Pattern reasoning				x			
KABC-2	Rover				x			
KABC-2	Triangles				x			
RIAS	Nonverbal memory				x			
RIAS	Odd-item out				x			
RIAS	What's missing				x			
SB-5	Nonverbal visual–spatial processing				x			
SB-5	Verbal visual–spatial processing				x			
WISC-IV	Block design				x			
WISC-IV	Picture completion				x			
WJ-III	Picture recognition				x			
WJ-III	Spatial relations				x			
WPPSI-III	Block design				x			
WPPSI-III	Object assembly				x			
WPPSI-III	Picture completion				x			

(continued)

Table 5–2. *(Continued)*

		Broad Cognitive Factor						
Test	Subtest	Gc	Gf	Ga	Gv	Gsm	Glr	Gs
DAS-2	Recall of digits					x		
DAS-2	Recall of sequential order					x		
KABC-2	Hand movements					x		
KABC-2	Number recall					x		
KABC-2	Word order					x		
RIAS	Verbal memory					x		
SB-5	Nonverbal working memory					x		
SB-5	Verbal working memory					x		
WISC-IV	Arithmetic					x		
WISC-IV	Digit span					x		
WISC-IV	Letter-number sequencing					x		
WJ-III	Memory for words					x		
WJ-III	Numbers reversed					x		
DAS-2	Rapid naming						x	
DAS-2	Recall of objects						x	
KABC-2	Atlantis						x	
KABC-2	Atlantis delayed						x	
KABC-2	Rebus delayed						x	
KABC-2	Rebus						x	
WJ-III	Visual–auditory learning						x	
WJ-III	Retrieval fluency						x	
DAS-2	Speed of information processing							x
WISC-IV	Cancellation							x
WISC-IV	Coding							x
WISC-IV	Symbol search							x
WJ-III	Decision speed							x
WJ-III	Visual matching							x
WPPSI-III	Coding							x
WPPSI-III	Symbol search							x

with mild hearing losses." Some children seem to do well linguistically and academically with their implants and others continue to struggle (see Pisoni et al., this volume; Leigh, this volume). Further, a few children somehow manage to create a phonological system of a spoken language based on very little auditory information. Children who receive CIs very early in life (1 to 3 years old) vary tremendously in terms of language development, even when nonverbal IQ is accounted for (Spencer, 2004). Some children have age-appropriate vocabulary development (a domain in which deaf children have historically scored very poorly), whereas others still experience delays.

In this context, it makes sense for school psychologists, speech-language therapists, and audiologists to work together to better understand a child's learning needs. Although the broad-stratum ability of auditory processing (Ga) seems tantamount to measuring hearing, an understanding of how auditory processing fits into the general cognitive picture will help parents and teachers understand any learning difficulties a child might be having. Much of the recent research on very young children, particularly those with CIs, focuses on their auditory and speech perception skills, speech production skills, and early language and communication abilities. Some of these abilities fall under the Gc category, others are narrow Ga abilities, whereas others might arguably be Gf abilities. The research consistently says two things: children who have CIs have better auditory and speech perception than those with conventional hearing aids, and the younger a child receives an implant, the better the spoken language (Tait, 2007; Tait, Lutman, & Nikolopoulos, 2001; Tait, Lutman, & Robinson, 2000). What is sorely lacking is information about how these children use their language not only for communicating, but also for thinking and reasoning.

This is not advocating for a return to solely auditory/oral practices in educating deaf children, nor to advocate against the use of ASL, but to recognize that many more deaf children now have somewhat useable hearing, and there is no particular reason why they should not or could not use it, cross-modally in combination with vision and general intelligence, for developing either spoken or bimodal English not only for cognition, but also for literacy (see Leigh, this volume). Indeed, all the research on "total communication" and "simultaneous communication" suggests that deaf children process this kind of English-based information in cognitively appropriate ways (reviewed in Akamatsu et al., 2002). Further to the point, Mayer (2007) noted that the necessary "bridges" to literacy that have been investigated since Mayer and Wells (1996) first published their analysis have all been through various forms of English. She argues that "it is not the presence of ASL but the absence of some form of face-to-face English that is at issue" with respect to what is necessary for the development of text-based literacy.

It would seem that a child whose amplification system allows full-time or nearly full-time mainstreaming and who does not use signing for communication with hearing parents, teachers, or peers, can and should be tested in spoken language. Similarly, even for those children whose education is occurring with English-based signing or contact language, it is unclear why the results of a language or IQ test administered in ASL would be more valid than one administered in English-based signing (leaving a precise definition to the side for the moment).

Children who are good communicators, whether nonverbally or with some level of BICS in any language, prior to receiving their implants, tend to be the most successful spoken language learners post-implantation (Tait et al., 2000). This suggests that hearing, while certainly a necessary component, is not the sole contributor in learning spoken language. Other cognitive factors such as Gv (visual processing) and Gf (on-the-ground problem solving) may also play an important role. Noncognitive factors such as temperament and family communication style, apart from the specific language or modality, also are important. Moreover, individuals who are able to mobilize a number of environmental and personal resources (including cognition) are likely to be not only good communicators, but also good first-language learners.

Of course, there are children who, despite all efforts to provide language in any modality, do not acquire it well, for whatever reason. Some of these students appear to have BICS skills, and it is only when their language is specifically challenged that difficulties with CALP appear. Vocabulary and conceptual development are influenced by literacy abilities (Olson, 1994; Stanovich, 1993), which in turn are based on both underlying cognitive abilities as well as knowledge of the *spoken* form of the language one is trying to read.[6] Could this be a case of reduced CALP development? A considerable body of research on vocabulary development reveals that giving formal definitions in decontextualized settings is quite a complex task and not mastered until fairly late (see Snow, 1990; Watson, 1985, for reviews). For example, delays in vocabulary development and general expressive language are well-documented in the literature, and vocabulary development in most deaf children remains limited over time (Lederberg, 2003). How much of this difficulty is the result of true language deprivation and how much is the result of any number of other factors remains a question. However, as accessibility to language becomes less of an issue, other cognitive factors will come to the fore, especially given the changing nature of the school-age population (Edwards, 2007).

Some Applications to Math and Science

According to CHC theory, mathematical ability is defined as a broad-stratum ability (Gq, quantitative knowledge), with narrow strata including

---

6. It is possible that the spoken form of a language, as represented through another modality (e.g., cued speech, visual phonics, certain forms of English-based signing, contact language) could be substituted for the actual *spoken* form of that language. Future research efforts might clarify this issue.

such skills as Math Knowledge and Math Achievement. These abilities are generally tested for separately from language ability, yet it is obvious that language plays a key role in some of these areas. Floyd, Evans, and McGrew (2003) investigated the validity of the broad cognitive clusters (broad-stratum abilities) tested by the Woodcock-Johnson Test of Cognitive Abilities, Third Edition (WJIII-COG; Woodcock, McGrew, & Mather, 2001) against mathematical achievement outcomes as tested by the Math Calculation and Math Reasoning subtests of the Woodcock-Johnson Tests of Achievement, Third Edition (WJIII-ACH; Woodcock, McGrew, & Mather, 2001). They found that Gc (crystallized intelligence) was strongly correlated with outcomes on Math Reasoning, particularly after age 10, and moderately correlated with Math Calculation after age 9. In addition, Gf (fluid intelligence) was moderately to strongly correlated with Math Reasoning and moderately correlated with Math Calculation.

In terms of other cognitive processes, working memory (specifically, and more so than short-term memory in general) was moderately correlated to both Math Calculation and Math Reasoning throughout childhood and adolescence. Auditory processing (Ga) and long-term retrieval (Glr) were moderately correlated with Math Calculation or Math Reasoning only in the very early stages of learning. Importantly, Gv (visual processing) was not significantly correlated to either outcome. These results suggest that thinking about math achievement outcomes solely in terms of PIQ or nonverbal IQ/abilities (largely measured by tests that tap Gv) is wrongheaded and highlights the large role that language and other cognitive factors play both in the acquisition of general as well as specific mathematical reasoning abilities.

Drawing on the work of Gregory (1998) and Pau (1993), Power and Leigh (2003, p. 46) noted that the "specialist language of mathematics and the linguistic sequencing and manipulation of events in written mathematics problems" pose particular difficulty for deaf students. They suggest that teachers make use of opportunities throughout the curriculum to expand on and elaborate mathematics concepts, thereby expanding the linguistic and conceptual understandings of deaf students (Marschark & Hauser, this volume).

Perhaps because of the difficulties that language poses, mathematics instruction historically focused on the four arithmetic operations (Daniele, 1993; Pagliaro, 1998) and less on the application of mathematics principles in real-world settings. Indeed, studies of mathematics achievement have consistently shown much higher achievement in arithmetic operations than in word problems or applied problem solving. In some sense, this is a chicken-and-egg problem. Arithmetic operations are easier to teach and learn with less language and, if instruction has focused on this area, it is no surprise that students achieve more (Bull, this volume).

The study of science requires the application of several other disciplines, most notably language and mathematics. Studies of scientific concepts development in science education in hearing students reveal the tension between having students do "hand-on" work and asking them to write about their developing conceptualizations (Yore, 2000). Among deaf students, difficulties with literacy in general are reflected in their science writing, and specific strategies for overcoming these difficulties have been suggested (Lang & Albertini, 2001; Roald, 2002; Yore, 2000). These strategies focus, not surprisingly, on enabling students to discuss their ideas using scientific language (in both sign and speech), teaching specialist vocabulary, and introducing students to scientific writing as a specific genre (see Hermsen & Franklin, this volume).

Summary and Implications

"Since sign language has been integrated into many programs for deaf students, it is now high time to look at the attendant verbal thought development and processes in deaf students" (Akamatsu, 1998, p. 28). This sentiment remains relevant a decade later. Moreover, now that hearing loss can be detected so early, interventions can be instituted in the critical months or even weeks before there is evidence of language delay. Indeed, deaf infants are receiving amplification at increasingly young ages, often within the first weeks of life. In some locales, they receive CIs between 6 and 12 months of age. Research on children who received CIs prior to 24 months of age has revealed that these children overwhelmingly become auditory learners within a year, and while some may have used some form of gestural communication or sign language prior to implantation, they no longer use it for the purposes of communicating with hearing people (e.g., their parents, teachers, classmates) and learning spoken language (Tait, 2007).

Because Vygotsky (1962, 1978) was making the case that everyone's cognitive functioning had its origins in interpersonal meaning making, he took issue with individual psychological testing because it focused too highly on the intrapersonal—what an individual had acquired—rather than using it to measure what an individual might acquire in the future (Wertsch & Stone, 1985). The challenge of mediating meaning and learning is acute for deaf children because of the difficulties of establishing the necessary inner speech to be used for thinking, regardless of the external language and/or modality that is used to develop inner speech. Vygotsky (1962, 1978) posited that it is this inner speech that serves as the basis for language becoming rational and thought verbal.

Cattell-Horn-Carroll theory, a three-stratum hierarchical framework of cognitive abilities, postulates a general factor (g) and 10 broad factors: crystallized intelligence (Gc), fluid reasoning (Gf), auditory processing (Ga), visual processing (Gv), short-term memory (Gsm), long-term retrieval (Glr), processing speed (Gs), reaction time (Gt), literacy (Grw), and quantitative abilities (Gq). These 10 broad abilities subsume over 70 narrow-stratum abilities. Because CHC theory has been supported by nearly a half-century of research, it is one that is favored by practitioners for its ability to describe cognitive functioning, diagnose cognitive dysfunction, and predict academic achievement.

Although controversy exists over the utility of a general intelligence factor (g), the 10 broad-stratum factors have received considerable attention by practitioners. In this chapter, we focused on the level of broad-stratum abilities, particularly that of crystallized intelligence (Gc), which is most closely aligned with language abilities and verbal intelligence. We briefly considered fluid intelligence (Gf), which can be measured nonverbally and has therefore been considered a valid estimate of deaf people's general intelligence. Additionally, we gave some consideration to the role of auditory processing (Ga), particularly for spoken language acquisition, and considered the role of memory—particularly short-term memory (Gsm)—in learning.

Using CHC theory will aid in understanding the cognitive processes underlying language and literacy weaknesses that are unusual even within the deaf population. The CHC theory in combination with BICS/CALP conceptualization, not only in basic research but also in applied educational psychology, allows for the possibility that teachers and psychologists can create learning opportunities that capitalize on individual strengths while ameliorating cognitive weaknesses. For example, we have investigated certain classroom practices that might influence the kinds of CALP or verbal reasoning skills that are so important in cognitive development (Mayer et al., 2002).

Studies that examine the interactive nature of language acquisition and knowledge building (Mayer et al., 2002) must be balanced with studies of the qualities that deaf learners bring to the learning task. The argument that deaf learners are cognitively like hearing learners ends up placing undue burden on parents and teachers when the deaf learner, on average, ends up achieving much less than the hearing learner (Hauser et al., this volume; Marschark & Wauters, this volume). Teaching practices to enhance functioning in specific narrow-stratum abilities could serve to strengthen the broad-stratum abilities as well. Evidence is already available to show enhanced functioning of visual processing in signers (see Dye, Hauser, & Bavelier, this volume; Emmorey, 2003, for a review).

Consideration must also be given to both existing technology, such as CIs and digital hearing aids, and cutting edge technology, such as electroacoustic hearing aids and brainstem implants. These technologies are making possible the assessment of abilities that were practically inaccessible a decade ago.

We have not reviewed in depth other cognitive factors that might be related to language and learning, such as working memory, nor the neuropsychological functioning that underpins functions such as planning and speed, nor educational practices that can enhance language and knowledge building. And, although it is beyond the scope of this chapter to talk about noncognitive abilities and other factors that also influence language development, clearly parenting style/abilities, the child's personality, and the amount of hearing experience do influence language development and learning (reviewed in Spencer, 2004).

As in all intelligence testing, the greater the sampling of skills, the greater the likelihood of arriving at a correct estimation of *g*. An understanding of *g* must be fleshed out with an understanding of how specific abilities influence specific kinds of learning. New tests and assessment techniques must continue to tap intellectual abilities as defined by intelligence theory, and "the nature of those abilities creates a content validity standard for intelligence tests" (Braden, 1997, p. 244), even for deaf children. Future research must include information about cognitive correlates of language achievement to determine if this early intervention makes any appreciable difference in deaf children's ability to acquire the necessary CALP skills to "do school," regardless of the modality in which this language is conveyed.

References

Akamatsu, C. T. (1998). Thinking with and without language: What is necessary and sufficient for school-based learning? In A. Weisel (Ed.), *Issues unresolved: New perspectives on language and deaf education* (pp. 27–40). Washington, DC: Gallaudet Press.

Akamatsu, C. T., & Musselman, C. (1998). Development and use of a conversational proficiency interview with deaf adolescents. In M. Marschark & M. D. Clark (Eds.), *Psychological perspectives on deafness*, Vol. 2 (pp. 265–301). Mahwah, NJ: Lawrence Erlbaum.

Akamatsu, C. T., Stewart, D., & Mayer, C. (2002). Is it time to look beyond teachers' signing behavior? *Sign Language Studies, 2,* 230–254.

Allen, T. E. (1986). Patterns of academic achievement among hearing impaired students: 1974 and 1983. In A. N. Schildroth & M. A. Karchmer (Eds.), *Deaf children in America* (pp. 161–206). San Diego, CA: College Hill.

Archbold, S., & Harbor, D. (2007, May). *Assessing deaf/hard of hearing children using the Nottingham Early Assessment Package (NEAP)*. Workshop presented at York University, Toronto, ON, Canada.

Bebko, J. M., Calderon, R., & Treder, R. (2003). The Language Proficiency Profile-2: Assessment of the global communication skills of deaf children across languages and modalities of expression. *Journal of Deaf Studies and Deaf Education, 8,* 438–451.

Bebko, J. M., & McKinnon, E. E. (1993). *The Language Proficiency Profile-2.* Unpublished assessment tool. Toronto: York University.

Bebko, J. M., & McKinnon, E. E. (1998). Assessing pragmatic language skills in deaf children: The Language Proficiency Profile. In M. Marschark &

M. D. Clark (Eds.), *Psychological perspectives on deafness* (2nd ed., pp. 243–264). Mahwah, NJ: Lawrence Erlbaum.

Berent, G. P. (1996). The acquisition of English syntax by deaf learners. In W. Ritchie & T. Bhatia (Eds.), *Handbook of second language acquisition* (pp. 469–506). San Diego, CA: Academic Press.

Bracken, B. A., & McCallum, R. S. (1998). *Universal Nonverbal Intelligence Test*. Itasca, IL: Riverside Publishing Co.

Braden, J. P. (1994). *Deafness, deprivation, and IQ*. New York: Plenum Press.

Braden, J. P. (1997). The practical impact of intellectual assessment issues. *School Psychology Review, 26*, 242–248.

Carroll, J. B. (1993). *Human cognitive abilities: A survey of factor analytic studies*. New York: Cambridge University Press.

Carroll, J. B. (1996). The three-stratum theory of cognitive abilities. In D. P. Flanagan, J. L. Genshaft, & P. L. Harrison (Eds.), *Contemporary intellectual assessment: Theories, tests, and issues* (pp. 122–130). New York: Guilford Press.

Cattell, R. B. (1943). The measurement of adult intelligence. *Psychological Bulletin, 40*, 153–193.

Cattell, R. B. (1963). Theory for fluid and crystallized intelligence: A critical experiment. *Journal of Educational Psychology, 54*, 1–22.

Cummins, J. (1979). Cognitive academic language proficiency, linguistic interdependence, the optimum age question and other matters. *Working Papers on Bilingualism, 19*, 121–129.

Cummins, J. (1981). The role of primary language development in promoting educational success for language minority students. In California State Department of Education (Ed.), *Schooling and language minority students: A theoretical framework* (pp. 3–49). Los Angeles, CA: Evaluation, Dissemination and Assessment Center, California State University.

Cummins, J. (1991). Language development and academic learning. In L. Malave & G. Duquette (Eds.), *Language, culture and cognition* (pp. 266–283). Clevedon, U.K.: Multilingual Matters.

Cummins, J. (2000). *Language, power and pedagogy: Bilingual children in the crossfire*. Clevedon, U.K.: Multilingual Matters.

Daniele, V. (1993). Quantitative literacy. *American Annals of the Deaf, 138*, 76–81.

Davis, J. M., Elfenbein, J., Schum, R., & Bentler, R. A. (1986). Effects of mild and moderate hearing impairments on language, educational, and psychosocial behavior of children. *Journal of Speech and Hearing Disorders, 51*, 53–62.

Dewart, H., & Summers, S. (1988). *The pragmatics profile of early communication skills*. Windsor, U.K.: NFER Nelson.

Edelsky, C. (2006). *With literacy and justice for all: rethinking the social in language and education (3rd ed.)* Mahwah, NJ: Erlbaum.

Edwards, L. C. (2007). Children with cochlear implants and complex needs: A review of outcome research and psychological practice. *Journal of Deaf Studies and Deaf Education, 12*, 258–268.

Emmorey, K. (2003). Neural systems underlying sign language. In M. Marschark & P. E. Spencer (Eds.), *The Oxford handbook of deaf studies, language, and education* (pp. 361–376). New York: Oxford University Press.

Elliott, C. D. (2006). *Differential Ability Scales-II.* San Antonio: Harcourt.

Fiorello, C. A., & Primerano, D. (2005). Research into practice: Cattell-Horn-Carroll cognitive assessment practice: Eligibility and program development issues. *Psychology in the Schools, 42,* 525–536.

Flanagan, D. P., & Ortiz, S. O. (2001). *Essentials of Cross-Battery Assessment.* New York: Wiley Press.

Flanagan, D. P., & Ortiz, S. O. (2002). Best practices in intellectual assessment: Future directions. In A. Thomas and J. Grimes (Eds.), *Best practices in school psychology IV* (Vol. 2, pp. 1351–1372). Washington, DC: National Association of School Psychologists.

Flanagan, D. P., Ortiz, S., & Alfonso, V. C. (2007). *Essentials of cross-battery assessment with CD/Rom,* (2nd ed.). New York: Wiley Press.

Floyd, R. G., Evans, J. J., & McGrew, K. (2003). Relations between measures of Cattell-Horn-Carroll (CHC) cognitive abilities and mathematics achievement across the school-age years. *Psychology in the schools, 40,* 155–171.

Floyd, R. G., Shaver, R. B., & McGrew, K. S. (2003). Interpretation of the Woodcock-Johnson III Tests of Cognitive Abilities: Acting on evidence. In F. A. Schrank & D. P. Flanagan (Eds.)., *WJ III clinical use and interpretation* (pp. 1–46, 403–408). New York: Academic Press.

Gardner, H. (1983). *Frames of mind: The theory of multiple intelligences.* New York: Basic Books.

Goldin-Meadow, S., & Feldman, H. (1977). The development of language-like communication without a language model. *Science, 197,* 401–403.

Goldin-Meadow, S., & Mylander, C. (1984). Gestural communication in deaf children: The effects and noneffects of parental input on early language development. *Monographs of the Society for Research in Child Development, 49,* (Serial nos. 3–4).

Gregory S. (1998) Mathematics and deaf children. In S. Gregory, P. Knight, W. McCracken, S. Powers, & L. Watson (Eds.). *Issues in Deaf Education* (pp. 119–128). London: Fulton.

Halliday, M. A. K. (1973). *Explorations in the functions of language.* London: Edward Arnold.

Hardy-Braz, S. T. (2003a). Appendix E: Use of the Stanford-Binet Intelligence Scales, Fifth edition, with deaf and hard of hearing individuals: General considerations and tailored administration. In G. H. Roid (Ed.), *Stanford-Binet Intelligence Scales* (5th Ed.)., *Examiner's Manual.* Itasca, IL: Riverside Publishing.

Hardy-Braz, S. T. (2003b). Testing children who are deaf or hard of hearing. In D. Wechsler (Ed.), *WISC-IV Manual* (pp. 12–18): San Antonio, TX: Psychological Corporation.

Hardy-Braz, S. T. (2004). Using the WISC-IV with deaf or hard of hearing students. In D. P. Flanagan & A. S. Kaufman (Eds.), *Essentials of WISC-IV Assessment* (pp. 208–214). Hoboken, NJ: John Wiley and Sons.

Hardy-Braz, S. T., Elliott, C., Fulton-Behrens, S., & Kushalnagar, P. (2007, March). *Developing and using the DAS-II with deaf and hard of hearing students.* Paper presented at the National Association of School Psychologists, New York.

Hardy-Braz, S. T., & Miller, B. D. (2004, April). Matters of the deaf mind: Assessing students who are deaf or hard of hearing using CHC cross-battery assessment. Presentation at the National Association of School Psychologists Annual Convention, Dallas, TX

Harris, M., & Moreno, C. (2006). Speech reading and learning to read: A comparison of 8-year-old profoundly deaf children with good and poor reading ability. *Journal of Deaf Studies and Deaf Education, 11(2)*, 189–201.

Hoffmeister, R., Bahan, B., et al. (1990). *American Sign Language Assessment Instrument (ASLAI)*. Unpublished test, Center for the Study of Communication and the Deaf, Boston University.

Horn, J. L. (1988). Thinking about human abilities. In J. R. Nesselroade (ed.), *Handbook of multivariate psychology* (pp. 645–685). New York: Academic Press.

Horn, J. L. (1991). Measurement of intellectual capabilities: A review of theory. In K. S. McGrew, J .K. Werder, & R.W. Woodcock, *WJ-R Technical Manual* (pp. 197-232). Chicago, IL: Riverside.

Horn, J. L., & Cattell, R. B. (1966). Refinement and test of the theory of fluid and crystallized intelligence. *Journal of Educational Psychology, 57*, 253–270.

Hornberger, N. (1989). Continua of biliteracy. *Review of Educational Research, 59*, 271–296.

International Communication Learning Institute. (1996). *See the sound/Visual phonics*. Webster, WI: ICLI.

Jastak, S., & Wilkinson, G. S. (1984). *Wide Range Achievement Test—Revised administration manual*. Wilmington, DE: Jastak Associates.

Jensen, A. (1997). The puzzle of nongenetic variance In R. Sternberg & E. Grigorenko (Eds.). *Intelligence, Heredity, and Environment* (pp. 42–88). New York: Cambridge University Press.

Kaufman, A. S., & Kaufman, N. L. (2004). KABC-II : *Kaufman Assessment Battery for Children, second edition: Manual*. Circle Pines, MN: American Guidance Service.

Kelly, M., & Braden, J. P. (1990). Criterion-related validity of the WISC-R performance scale with the Stanford Achievement Test-Hearing Impaired Edition. *Journal of School Psychology, 28*, 147–151.

Kendall Demonstration Elementary School. (1985). *Kendall Communicative Proficiency Scale*. Washington, DC: Author.

Lang, H. G., & Albertini, J. A. (2001). Construction of meaning in the authentic science writing of deaf students. *Journal of Deaf Studies and Deaf Education, 6*, 258–284.

LaSasso, C., & Metzger, M. (1998). An alternate route for preparing deaf children for BiBi programs: The home language as L1 and Cued Speech for conveying traditionally-spoken languages. *Journal of Deaf Studies and Deaf Education, 3*, 265–289.

Lederberg, A. (2003). Expressing meaning: From communicative intent to building a lexicon. In M. Marschark & P. E. Spencer (Eds.), *Oxford handbook of deaf studies, language, and education* (pp. 247–260). New York: Oxford University Press.

Leybaert, J. (1993). Reading in the deaf: The role of phonological codes. In M. Marschark & D. Clark (Eds.), *Psychological perspectives on deafness* (pp. 269–309). Hillsdale, NJ: Erlbaum.

Leybaert, J., & Charlier, B. (1996). Visual speech in the head: The effect of cued speech on rhyming, remembering, and spelling. *Journal of Deaf Studies and Deaf Education, 1*, 234–248.

Lichtenstein, E. (1998). The relationships between reading processes and English skills of deaf college students. *Journal of Deaf Studies and Deaf Education, 3*, 80–134.

Lindsay, P. H., Shapiro, A., Musselman, C., & Wilson, A. (1988). Predicting language development in deaf children using subscales of the Leiter International Performance Scale. *Canadian Journal of Psychology, 42*, 144–162.

Lopez, R. (1997). The practical impact of current research and issues in intelligence test interpretation and use for multicultural populations. *School Psychology Review, 26*, 249–254.

Lucas, C., & Valli, C. (1992). *Language contact in the American Deaf community.* San Diego: Academic Press.

Maller, S. J. (1996). WISC-III Verbal item invariance across samples of deaf and hearing children of similar measured ability. *Journal of Psychoeducational Assessment, 14*, 152–165.

Maller, S. J. (1997). Deafness and WISC-III item difficulty: Invariance and fit. *Journal of School Psychology, 35*, 299–314.

Maller, S. (2003). Intellectual assessment of deaf people: A critical review of core concepts and issues. In M. Marschark & P. Spencer (Eds.), *Oxford handbook of deaf studies, language, and education* (pp. 451–463). New York: Oxford University Press.

Maller, S. J., & Braden, J. P. (1993). The construct and criterion-related validity of the WISC-III with deaf adolescents. *Journal of Psychoeducational Assessment, Monograph Series: WISC-III*, 104–113.

Maller, S., Singleton, J. L., Supalla, S. J., & Wix, T. (1999). Development and psychometric properties of the American Sign Language Proficiency Assessment (ASL-PA). *Journal of Deaf Studies and Deaf Education, 4*, 249–269.

Mayberry, R. (2003). Cognitive development in deaf children: The interface of language and perception in neuropsychology. In F. Boller & J. Grafman (Series Eds.) and S. J. Segalowitz & I. Rapin (Vol. eds.), *Handbook of neuropsychology: Vol. 8, Part II: Child Neuropsychology, Part II* (pp. 71–107). Amsterdam: Elsevier.

Mayberry, R., & Eichen, E. (1991). The long-lasting advantage of learning sign language in childhood: Another look at the critical period for language acquisition. *Journal of Memory and Language, 30*, 486–512.

Mayberry, R., & Fischer, S. D. (1989). Looking through phonological shape to lexical meaning: The bottleneck of non-native sign language processing. *Memory and Cognition, 17*, 740–754.

Mayer, C. (1999). Shaping at the point of utterance: An investigation of the composing processes of the deaf student writer. *Journal of Deaf Studies and Deaf Education, 4*, 37–49.

Mayer, C. (2007). What really matters in the early literacy development of deaf children. *Journal of Deaf Studies and Deaf Education, 12*, 411–431.

Mayer, C. (in press). All language is not created equal. *Proceedings from Building Bridges through Access: International Conference on Deaf Education.* Johannesburg: University of Witswatersrand.

Mayer, C. (2009). Issues in second language literacy education with learners who are deaf. *International Journal of Bilingualism and Bilingual Education.*

Mayer, C., Akamatsu, C. T., & Stewart, D. (2002). A model for effective practice: Dialogic inquiry in the education of deaf students. *Exceptional Children, 68,* 485–502.

Mayer, C., & Wells, G. (1996). Can the linguistic interdependence theory support a bilingual-bicultural model of literacy education for Deaf Students? *Journal of Deaf Studies and Deaf Education, 1,* 93–107.

McGrew, K., & Flanagan, D. P. (1998). *The intelligence test desk reference (ITDR): Gf-Gc cross-battery assessment.* Boston: Allyn and Bacon.

McGrew, K., & Knopik, S. N. (1993). The relationship between WJ-R Gf-Gc cognitive clusters and writing achievement across the life span. *School Psychology Review, 22,* 687–695.

Moores, D. F. (2001). *Educating the Deaf: Psychology, Principles, and Practices* (5th ed.). Boston: Houghton Mifflin.

Musselman, C., & Akamatsu, C. T. (1999). Interpersonal communication skills of deaf adolescents and their relationship to communication history. *Journal of Deaf Studies and Deaf Education, 4,* 305–320.

Newell, W., Caccamise, F., Boardman, K., & Holcomb, B. R. (1983). Adaptation of the Language Proficiency Interview (LPI) for assessing sign communicative competence. *Sign Language Studies, 41,* 311–351.

Nizerro, I., Musselman, C., & MacKay-Soroka, S. (1993, June). *Verbal and nonverbal IQs as predictor of academic achievement in deaf teenagers.* Paper presented at the Convention of American Instructors of the Deaf, Baltimore.

Nunes, T., Bryant, P., Evans, D., Bell, D., Gardner, S., Gardner, A., & Carraher, J. (2007). The contribution of logical reasoning to the learning of mathematics in primary school. *British Journal of Developmental Psychology, 25,* 147–166.

Olson, D. R. (1994). *The world on paper: Conceptual and cognitive implications of reading and writing.* Cambridge: Cambridge University Press.

Olson, D. R., & Torrance, N. (1991). *Literacy and orality.* Cambridge, MA: Cambridge University Press.

Ortiz, S. O., & Flanagan, D. P. (2002a). Cross-battery assessment revisited: Some cautions about "Some cautions" (Part I). *NASP Communiqué, 30*(7), 32–34.

Ortiz, S. O., & Flanagan, D. P. (2002b). Some cautions concerning "Some cautions concerning cross-battery assessment" (Part 2). *NASP Communiqué, 30*(8), 36–38.

Pagliaro, C. (1998). Mathematics preparation and professional development of deaf education teachers. *American Annals of the Deaf, 143,* 373–379.

Pau, C. S. (1993). The deaf child and solving the problems of arithmetic. *American Annals of the Deaf, 149,* 287–290.

Phelps, L., & Branyan, B. J. (1990). Academic achievement and nonverbal intelligence in public school hearing-impaired children. *Psychology in the Schools, 27,* 210–217.

Plesko-DuBois, R., Jones-Oleson, L., & Shreckhise, L. (2007, March). *Oral reading fluency in students who use sign language.* Paper presented at the National Association of School Psychologists, New York.

Power, D., & Leigh, G. (2003). Curriculum: Cultural and communicative contexts. In M. Marschark & P. Spencer (Eds.), *Oxford handbook of deaf studies, language, and education* (pp. 38–51). New York: Oxford University Press.

Prinz, P., Strong, M., & Kuntze, M. (1994). *The test of ASL*. Unpublished test, San Francisco State University, San Francisco, CA.

Reynolds, C., & Kamphaus, R. (2007). *Reynolds Intellectual Assessment Scale.* Lutz, FL: Psychological Assessment Resources, Inc.

Reynolds, H. N. (1976). Development of reading ability in relation to deafness. *Proceedings of the Seventh World Congress of the World Federation of the Deaf.* Silver Spring, MD: National Association of the Deaf.

Roald, I. (2002). Norwegian deaf teachers' reflections on their science education: Implications for instruction. *Journal of Deaf Studies and Deaf Education, 7,* 57–73.

Roid, G. H. (2003). *Stanford Binet Intelligence Scales* (5th ed.). Itasca, IL: Riverside Pub.

Singleton, J., & Supalla, S. (2003). Assessing children's proficiency in natural signed languages. In M. Marschark and P. E. Spencer (Eds.). *Oxford handbook of deaf studies, language, and education* (pp. 289–302). New York: Oxford University Press.

Snow, C. E. (1990). The development of definitional skill. *Journal of Child Language, 17,* 697–710.

Spencer, P. (2004). Individual differences in language performance after cochlear implantation at one to three years of age: Child, family, and linguistic factors. *Journal of Deaf Studies and Deaf Education, 9,* 395–412.

Stanovich, K. E. (1993). Does reading make you smarter? Literacy and the development of verbal intelligence. In H. W. Reese (eds.), *Advances in child development and behaviour* (Vol. 2) (pp. 133–180). San Diego: Academic Press.

Sternberg, R. J. (1985). *Beyond IQ: A triarchic theory of human intelligence.* New York: Cambridge University Press.

Tait, M. (2007). *Implantation at 1+ compared with 2+ and 3+ does this give children an early auditory advantage?* http://www.earfoundation.org.uk/research/tait (Retrieved 27 August 2007).

Tait, M., Lutman, M. E., & Nikolopoulos, T. P. (2001). Communication development in young children: Review of the video analysis method. *International Journal Pediatric Otorhinolaryngology, 61,* 105–112.

Tait, M., Lutman, M. E., & Robinson, K. (2000). Predictive value of measures of pre-verbal communicative behavior in young children with cochlear implants. *Ear and Hearing, 21,* 18–24.

Trezek, B., & Wang, Y. (2006). Implications of utilizing a phonics-based reading curriculum with children who are deaf or hard of hearing. *Journal of Deaf Studies and Deaf Education, 11,* 202–213.

Trezek, B., Wang, Y., Woods, D. G., Gampp, T. L., & Paul, P. (2007). Using visual phonics to supplement beginning reading instruction for students who are deaf or hard of hearing. *Journal of Deaf Studies and Deaf Education, 12,* 373–384.

Ulissi, S. M., Brice, P. J., & Gibbins, S. (1989). Use of the Kaufman-Assessment Battery for children with the. hearing impaired. *American Annals of the Deaf, 134,* 283-287.

Vygotsky, L. S. (1962). *Thought and language.* Cambridge: MIT Press.

Vygotsky, L. S. (1978). *Mind in society: The development of higher psychological processes.* Cambridge, MA: Harvard University Press.

Watkins, M. W., Glutting, J. J., & Youngstrom, E. A. (2002). Cross-battery assessment: Still concerned. *NASP Communiqué, 31*(2), 42–44.

Watkins, M. W., Youngstrom, E. A., & Glutting, J. J. (2002). Some cautions concerning cross-battery assessment. *NASP Communiqué, 30*(5), 16–20.

Watson, R. (1985). Towards a theory of definition. *Journal of Child Language, 12*, 181–197.

Wechsler, D. (1991). *Wechsler Intelligence Scales for Children* (3rd ed.). San Antonio: Harcourt.

Wechsler, D. (2002). *Wechsler Preschool and Primary Scales of Intelligence* (3rd ed.). San Antonio: Harcourt.

Wechsler, D. (2003). *Wechsler Intelligence Scales for Children* (4th ed.). San Antonio: Harcourt.

Wertsch, J. V., & Stone, C. A. (1985). The concept of internalization in Vygotsky's account of the genesis of higher mental functions. In J. V. Wertsch (Ed.), *Culture, communication and cognition: Vygotskian perspectives* (pp. 162–179). Cambridge: Cambridge University Press.

Wexler, M. B., & Fiorello, C. A. (2002, March). *Diagnostic validity of CHC theory based cross-battery assessment for reading disability.* Paper presented at the Annual Convention of the National Association of School Psychologists, Chicago, IL.

Wiig, E., Secord, W., & Semel, E. (1992). *Clinical Evaluation of Language Fundamentals—Preschool.* San Antonio, TX: Psychological Corporation, Harcourt Brace.

Woodcock, R. W., McGrew, K. S., & Mather, N. (2001). *Woodcock-Johnson III Tests of Cognitive Abilities.* Itasca, IL: Riverside Publishing.

Yore, L. D. (2000). Enhancing science literacy for all students with embedded reading instruction and writing-to-learn activities. *Journal of Deaf Studies and Deaf Education, 8*, 105–122.

Yoshinaga-Itano, C. (2003). Earlier identification for earlier intervention. In D. Power and G. Leigh (Eds.), *Educating deaf students: Global perspectives* (pp. 69–84). Washington, DC: Gallaudet University Press.

Zweibel, A., & Mertens, D. M. (1985). A comparison of intellectual structure in deaf and hearing children. *American Annals of the Deaf, 130*, 27–31.

Chapter 6

Deafness, Numerical Cognition, and Mathematics

Rebecca Bull

Numerical understanding is involved in many aspects of our lives, not just as we learn mathematical skills in school, but also as we advance as adults into a technologically advanced society. Numerical skills are core to many occupations, such as those involving science, technology, and finance, but are also required to some extent in many professions: handling money, estimating discounts, projecting resource needs, to name but a few examples (see McCloskey, 2007, for more examples). Basic quantitative skills, such as the ability to estimate, are also essential for dealing with commercial matters in everyday life. However, not all of us find engaging with numerical concepts easy, and indeed around 5%–10% of hearing children and adolescents experience a learning deficit in at least one area of mathematics (see Shalev, 2007, for a recent review), with many more "underachieving" in mathematics even if they are not classified as having a learning deficit. There are many reasons why an individual may struggle to learn numerical and mathematical concepts. Studies of children and adults with mathematical difficulties, and children with neurodevelopmental disorders (for a review see Mazzocco, Murphy, & McCloskey, 2007) have provided insights about subtypes of specific numerical and more general cognitive difficulties that may result in difficulties learning about numbers and how early developing numerical skills feed into the continued development of formal complex mathematical reasoning.

The aim of this chapter is to apply the knowledge we have about the development of numerical cognition in hearing individuals to understand the often-observed lag in arithmetical and mathematical performance of deaf children and adults (Allen, 1986; Hine, 1970; Lang, 2003; Nunes & Moreno, 1998; Traxler, 2000; Wollman, 1965; Wood, Wood, Kingmill,

French, & Howarth, 1984). On standardized tests of academic achievement (e.g., on the *Stanford Achievement Test—Ninth Edition,* or SAT9), lags in mathematical achievement are apparent from approximately 8 years of age (Traxler, 2000) and remain relatively constant at "below basic" levels of performance. Studies examining specific aspects of mathematical understanding have revealed deaf students to have a delay in measurement and number concepts (Austin, 1975), fraction concepts (Titus, 1995), and arithmetic compare problems (Kelly, Lang, Mousley, & Davis, 2003).

Clearly, the early educational and learning experiences of deaf children may play a profound role in how skills such as numeracy develop (Marschark, Lang, & Albertini, 2002; Swanwick, Oddy, & Roper, 2005), although few studies have specifically considered how fundamental differences in information processing by deaf individuals may influence learning and representation of numerical knowledge and concepts (Marschark, 2003; Schick, 2005; Tharpe, Ashmead, & Rothpletz, 2002). Many studies examining mathematical skills in deaf populations have only considered mathematical achievement as part of broader studies of general educational performance, in which often the main focus is literacy (Swanwick et al., 2005). Language skills are important for allowing access to mathematical information, and studies from both deaf and hearing populations typically show a strong association between language and mathematical abilities (e.g., Hyde, Zevenbergen, & Power, 2003; Kelly & Mousley, 2001), with some researchers arguing that language is the key barrier to success, particularly in mathematics word problems. Others argue that such a perception has led to a neglect of the complete process of problem solving (Kelly, Lang, & Pagliaro, 2003; see Kelly, this volume). Furthermore, there is clearly more to numerical understanding and mathematical development than language.

We perform some numerical tasks without recourse to language, and there is clear neuropsychological evidence to show that separable areas of the brain deal with verbally based numerical skills (such as exact calculation) and nonverbally based skills (such as estimation and magnitude comparison). The ability of preverbal infants to respond to numerical properties is also testament to the fact that some aspects of numerical processing are not reliant on verbal or language skills (see Butterworth, 2005, for a brief review of infant capacities).

In addressing some of these issues, findings from studies of numerical cognition in hearing individuals will be discussed, with consideration given to how the information processing strategies of deaf individuals may influence the learning, representation, and retrieval of numerical and mathematical knowledge. The focus here will be on basic numerical processes that underlie mathematics and that subsequently feed into our understanding of related topics in science and technology. Information from a range of tasks assessing quantity recognition, magnitude representation, and magnitude retrieval will provide a solid starting point for identifying whether these basic numerical skills account for the development of mathematical difficulties in deaf individuals, or equally importantly, can be eliminated as contributory factors to mathematical difficulties.

Representation of and Access to Magnitude Information: The Mental Number Line

One of the most fundamental aspects of numerical cognition is the ability to represent and manipulate approximate numerical quantities in a nonverbal format. This ability remains at the core of many numerical tasks, even once symbolic representations such as Arabic digits have been learned (Dehaene, 1997; Dehaene, Molko, Cohen, & Wilson, 2004). Evidence from studies of both acquired (for a review see Dehaene, Spelke, Pinel, Stanescu, & Tsivkin, 1999; Zamarian, Lopez-Rolon, & Delazer, 2007) and developmental disorders (e.g., Donlan, 2007, children with Specific Language Impairment) reveals that certain aspects of numerical understanding are relatively independent of language (for example, numerosity and magnitude judgments and approximation) and are supported by specific areas in the parietal cortices of the left and especially the right hemispheres. Such skills have been described within the realm of rudimentary "number sense" that is present early in development and is elaborated through incidental mathematical learning without explicit instruction (see Berch, 2005; Dehaene, 1997), thus providing the foundational structure for elementary numerical abilities (e.g., Butterworth, 1999, 2005; Jordan, Kaplan, Olah, & Locuniak, 2006; Mazzocco, 2005). Ability to judge the relative value of numerical symbols plays an important role in numerous aspects of number processing, including rapid and accurate calculation, comparison of magnitude, and estimation of numerosity (Dehaene, 1992; Delazer & Butterworth, 1997; Fischer, 2003; Gelman & Gallistel, 1978; Girelli, Lucangeli, & Butterworth, 2000; Griffin, Case, & Capodilupo, 1995; Nunes & Bryant, 1996), and with increasing exposure to numbers in school these key aspects of basic numerical processing become automatic (Berch, Foley, Hill, & Ryan, 1999; Girelli et al., 2000; Rubinsten, Henik, Berger, & Shahar-Shalev, 2002).

Dehaene's "triple-code theory" assumes that when Arabic or verbal numerals are identified, this information is automatically translated into a nonverbal analog magnitude representation that conveys semantic information such as relative amount and contributes to mathematical performance (Dehaene, 1992). An impaired nonverbal representation of approximate magnitude may constrain the typical development of exact number abilities across time (Ansari & Karmiloff-Smith, 2002), and researchers suggest that dyscalculia (a deficit in the processing of numerical and arithmetical information associated with neurodevelopmental abnormalities) may involve an impairment in quantity representation or its access via symbolic representations (Berch, 2005; Butterworth, 1999, 2005; Gersten, Jordan, & Flojo, 2005). A less clear and/or less accurate representation may result in more difficulty establishing robust links between Arabic numerals and their associated semantic information, resulting in difficulties with estimation and magnitude comparison, or more variability between the boundaries of different magnitudes along the mental number line. Rubinsten and Henik (2005) found that adults with developmental dyscalculia had problems in the automatic activation of magnitudes by digits, showing less interference on a physical size comparison task when the physical size of the digit was incongruent with its magnitude. Based on this finding, they suggested that intensive practice associating magnitudes with their Arabic numerals might help in the rehabilitation of developmental dyscalculia. Furthermore, Jordan, Hanich, and Kaplan (2003) speculated that weaknesses in spatial representations of numerical magnitude, in particular difficulties manipulating visual representations on a number line, are particularly influential during the early acquisition of calculation skills and may underpin arithmetical retrieval deficits observed in many populations with mathematical difficulties.

Various methods have been used to examine how magnitude information is represented, and how automatically it can be retrieved. One commonly used method in studies with hearing participants is the Stroop paradigm (see MacLeod, 1991, for a review), which assesses interference from an irrelevant aspect of the stimulus. Participants are presented with two-dimensional stimuli (e.g., a color word typed in a particular ink color), and are asked to focus on one dimension (ink color) and ignore the other dimension (the color word). Many participants cannot ignore the irrelevant dimension, which interferes with their processing of the relevant dimension. This is considered an indication for the automatic nature of the irrelevant dimension and as a failure of selective attention. A example of a numerical Stroop-like task requires participants to indicate which number is physically larger when presented with stimuli that are congruent (physical size and magnitude match, e.g., 1 3), incongruent (1 3) or neutral (3 3). Results show that incongruent (yet task irrelevant) numerical magnitude interferes with physical size judgments, resulting in a congruity effect; that is, slowing of response times on incongruent compared to neutral trials, and/or faster response times on congruent compared to neutral trials (size congruity effects; e.g., Girelli et al., 2000; Rubinsten et al., 2002; Rubinsten & Henik, 2005).

Studies of typically achieving hearing children show that congruity effects are not present in first grade, but are present in children in third grade and older, suggesting a gradual process of automatization in number processing as numerical skills progress (Girelli et al., 2000). Many

researchers argue that differences between deaf and hearing individuals
in early incidental exposure to numerical ideas and later mathematical instruction might result in a difference or lag in both number processing and
calculation between deaf and hearing individuals (Epstein, Hillegeist, &
Grafman, 1994; Gregory, 1998). If deaf children have less opportunity to
practice numerical skills, there may be a delay in automatization, resulting in no congruity effects. Findings from Bull and Theodorou (in preparation) provide some evidence to support this. Deaf children (N = 18, from
10 to 13 years of age) were tested on the Stroop-like number paradigm
just described. Response-time differences between incongruent and neutral trials allowed an examination of interference effects, which provides
evidence for the degree of automatic activation of magnitude information.
Deaf children overall showed a similar level of interference as hearing
peers, indicating that magnitude information was accessed with equal automaticity as in hearing children. However, the results from the deaf children were highly variable, and subsequent analysis examining whether
the level of interference was significantly different from 0 revealed that
only the interference effect for the hearing children was significant. Neither group showed a significant facilitation effect (faster responses to
congruent compared to neutral stimuli), in line with findings from Girelli
et al. (2000). Therefore, we cannot rule out the possibility that some deaf
children show a delay in the automatization of numerical processing, although this is certainly not the case for all deaf children. Of those deaf
children tested, three used British Sign Language (BSL) as their main form
of communication in school, and only one of these children showed interference effects. All remaining children used spoken language, and 12
out of the 15 latter children showed interference effects. We do not have
the information to indicate which of these children also have deaf parents
or the main mode of communication between parents and children in the
home.

Although it is difficult to draw firm conclusions on the basis of such
observations from a small sample, possible differences according to language use should be examined in more detail, particularly if this impacts
on opportunities early in development for incidental learning of numerical knowledge. Bandurski and Gałkowski (2004) found clear differences
between deaf children of deaf parents compared with deaf children of
hearing parents on relational processing tasks that required the use of linguistic or mathematical symbols, symbolic knowledge that can only really
be acquired through socially mediated activities. There was no difference
between these groups on a figural-geometric version of the task, suggesting
that differences between the groups were not generally related to differences in relational processing per se, but were due instead to the lack of opportunity of deaf children of hearing parents to have incidental exposure
to linguistic and mathematical symbols.

Congruity effects have also been examined in deaf students (Bull, Blatto-Vallee, & Fabich, 2006). In this study, all deaf students used American Sign Language (ASL) as their primary means of communication. As well as using the Arabic numeral condition described earlier, hand-shapes were also used (as would be used to indicate numerals in ASL; examples can be seen in Figure 6–1). Because ASL numerals should be processed relatively automatically by deaf individuals, performance with the ASL numerals for deaf individuals might equate to performance with Arabic numerals for hearing individuals (i.e., the preferred format/mode for which each hearing status group would be most adept at processing numerical information). For Arabic symbols, both deaf and hearing adults showed a congruity effect when making both physical size and magnitude judgments, with the size of the congruity effect comparable for deaf and hearing students. Identical analyses were performed on the ASL numerals but revealed no significant congruity or hearing status effects.

The Stroop-like paradigm used to examine automatic access to magnitude information also allows an examination of other aspects of number representation. Numerous studies report that magnitude information is represented conceptually in the form of a visual number line, with small magnitudes associated with the left side of space, and large magnitudes with the right side of space; that is, an association exists between numerical and spatial codes. This is referred to as the SNARC effect (Spatial Numerical Association of Response Codes; Dehaene, Bossini, & Giraux, 1993). SNARC tasks typically require participants to make a judgment, unrelated to magnitude, about a presented number (e.g., parity or physical size). Patterns of response times show that participants are faster to make responses to lower-magnitude numbers with a left-sided response and higher-magnitude numbers with a right-sided response. This has been

Size incongruent   Size congruent

Figure 6–1. Example of ASL stimuli for the numerical stroop task.

taken as an indication that magnitude information is being activated and influences nonmagnitude judgments, even when this is irrelevant to the task. So, the SNARC effect tells us not only about the spatial format in which numerical information is represented, but also the automaticity with which it is activated.

Additional evidence for this form of magnitude representation and the automatic translation of written or auditory numbers into analog magnitudes comes from studies of distance effects in the comparison of numbers (e.g., Dehaene & Akhavein, 1995; Dehaene & Changeux, 1993; Dehaene, Dehaene-Lambertz, & Cohen, 1998; Dehaene, Dupoux, & Mehler, 1990; Duncan & McFarland, 1980; Moyer & Landauer, 1967; Tzelgov, Meyer, & Henik, 1992). Where numbers are in close proximity on the mental number line (e.g., 4 and 5), the time to decide which is the larger number will be greater relative to numbers that are more distant on the number line (e.g., 1 and 5). This is due to the inexactness of these magnitude representations, which results in a degree of overlap or "fuzziness" at the magnitude boundaries, making it particularly difficult to compare magnitudes that are close together.

Given what we know about the experiences and cognitive processing of deaf individuals, how might performance on such tasks differ and what might this mean for mathematical development? As noted earlier, the development of such skills may be dependent on opportunities for incidental learning, which allow our magnitude representations to become more exact and activated more automatically. Furthermore, studies conducted by Marschark et al. have shown that deaf university students have different organization of their semantic and conceptual knowledge, relative to hearing peers, and utilize such knowledge differently in problem-solving tasks (Marschark, Convertino, McEvoy, & Masteller, 2004; Marschark & Everhart, 1999; McEvoy, Marschark, & Nelson, 1999; see Marschark & Wauters, this volume). McEvoy et al. (1999), for example, found that hearing students showed a greater associative strength between concepts than did deaf students and were more likely to produce the same associates in response to a particular category compared with deaf individuals, who produced a wider spread of category associates. Relational processing, in particular, appears to be less automatic, or less easy, for deaf than hearing students in both verbal and nonverbal tasks (e.g., Banks, Gray, & Fyfe, 1990; Ottem, 1980; Richardson, MacLeod-Gallinger, McKee, & Long, 2000). A focus on individual item information can impede learning and performance in academic domains from mathematics to history, as multiple factors must be considered in order to understand the causes and outcomes of problems and events. Marschark et al. (2004) found that deaf students had more difficulty with analogy tasks that involved considering the relations between category exemplars, between superordinate and subordinate categories, and between part–whole relations, suggesting qualitative differences between hearing and deaf in both the organization and application of knowledge [although the findings from Bandurski and Gałkowski (2004) discussed earlier suggest that these differences may be partially dependent on early incidental learning and exposure to symbolic knowledge]. Mathematics in particular relies on relational knowledge to make judgments of more, less, faster, slower, taller, shorter, and so on (Wiese, 2003), exactly the type of comparatives with which deaf students generally lack experience (Serrano Pau, 1995).

In two studies, Bull, Marschark, and Blatto-Vallee (2005) and Bull et al., (2006) examined the strength and nature of numerical magnitude representation in deaf adults. If deaf adults process numerical information on an item-specific basis, or if they have weak associative links between different types of numerical knowledge (e.g., between symbolic and nonsymbolic forms), we might anticipate a less marked SNARC effect, as the relations to other magnitudes will be processed more slowly or less automatically. Both studies included deaf and hearing students enrolled as university undergraduates. All of the deaf students used sign language, sometimes accompanied by speech, as the primary means of communication. Deaf students' scores on the American College Test (ACT) entrance examinations indicated them to have an average mathematics subtest corresponding to approximately the 21st percentile relative to national norms for all students taking the test.

In our first study of numerical representation (Bull et al., 2005), we examined whether intentional processing of magnitude would result in the typical SNARC and distance effect findings. That is, we were specifically interested in whether deaf adults showed the same spatial representation of magnitude. Participants were asked to perform a simple magnitude judgment task: they were presented with numbers 1–4 and 6–9 and, in one condition, were asked to respond with the left-hand key if the number was below 5 and the right-hand key if the number was above 5. In the second condition, these response mappings were reversed. If deaf students held the left–right number line representation, we expected that they would show typical SNARC effects (faster responses to low number with the left hand and higher numbers with the right hand). We also expected to find distance effects, that is, a longer response time to those numbers closest to the target comparison (4 and 6) compared with those farther away (1 and 9). In line with findings from a large number of studies examining the SNARC effect in hearing adults, deaf adults showed the same pattern of results. Figure 6–2 shows the difference in response times (left—right hand) to each number, revealing that responses to number 1–4 were indeed faster with the left hand, and 6–9 were faster with the right hand. Both deaf and hearing adults also showed a distance effect, being significantly slower to respond to 4 and 6 (when the target comparison was 5) compared to all other numbers.

In our second study (Bull et al., 2006), we used the numerical Stroop paradigm, with participants asked to indicate which number was physically

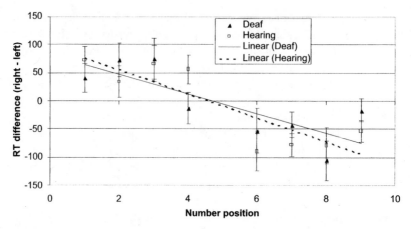

Figure 6–2. SNARC effects (right hand – left hand RT) for intentional magnitude decisions.

larger in one condition, and to indicate which number was larger in magnitude in a second condition. Asking participants to respond to physical size provides a more robust assessment of whether magnitude information is activated even when it is irrelevant to the task (i.e., magnitude information is unintentionally processed). This study also used the ASL numerals of different physical size as described earlier. If magnitude information is being activated even though it is irrelevant, again we would expect to see SNARC and distance effects indicative of a left–right orientated mental number line.

Analysis of distance effects (differences of 1, 2, 3, or 4) revealed that both groups showed distance effects only when asked to make magnitude judgments, not physical size judgment. As distance between the numbers increased, participants were faster to state which number was the larger in magnitude. Accuracy was significantly lower when the numerals presented differed only by a distance of one, but overall accuracy levels were very high. Previous studies have also found distance effects when participants are asked to make judgments of the numbers unrelated to magnitude (e.g., Dehaene & Akhavein, 1995), although recent developmental studies (e.g., Rubinsten et al., 2002) have only shown a numerical distance effect when magnitude judgments were being made. The current findings also extend the effect typically found with Arabic numerals, finding the same distance effect with the ASL numerals for both deaf and hearing adults. It was anticipated that the retrieval of magnitude information from ASL numerals would be more automatic for deaf participants, although the interaction of distance by hearing status indicated that the distance effect was slightly more pronounced for hearing adults. The ASL numerals 1–5 do represent the actual number of items shown in the set and as such may automatically activate information about magnitude for hearing as well as deaf individuals.

Unfortunately, in this study, we were unable to replicate the SNARC effect findings in either deaf or hearing adults. Both groups showed SNARC effects in the appropriate direction, but analysis revealed that the regression slopes were not significantly different from 0. However, there were approximately equal numbers of deaf and hearing students showing the expected negative slope. Iverson, Nuerk, and Willmes (2004) did find typical SNARC effects when deaf native signing adults were asked to make parity judgments. This indicates that numerical magnitude information was activated even though it was irrelevant to the task.

It was anticipated that if deaf adults had a lower associative strength between the various forms of numerical representations, for example, between an Arabic digit and the spoken word form or the nonverbal magnitude representation, or if deaf adults were less likely to consider relations (more than, less than) between numerical magnitudes, then we would be less likely to witness the typical SNARC and distances effects found in many studies from hearing children and adults. The comparative findings from hearing and deaf adults on tasks designed to examine the automaticity of accessing magnitude information and the spatial format of the representation reveal that there are no obvious idiosyncratic differences. Both groups showed results indicating a left–right spatial number line, as illustrated by distance and SNARC effects, and automatic activation of magnitude information, as shown by congruity effects. Therefore, it is unlikely that resulting difficulties in learning mathematics stem from a basic problem in the representation of or access to magnitude information. The findings from deaf children do suggest wide individual differences in the automaticity of retrieval early in development, suggesting that more in-depth analysis is needed of factors that may result in a developmental delay and the impact that this may subsequently have on early counting and arithmetic skills.

Enumeration

In some aspects of cognitive processing, deaf individuals (particularly deaf signers) show distinct advantages. This is particularly the case for some aspects of visual cognition, for example, in speed of shifting visual attention and visual scanning (Rettenback, Diller, & Sireteaunu, 1999), peripheral detection of motion (Bavelier et al., 2000; Corina, Kritchevsky, & Bellugi, 1992; Neville & Lawson, 1987; Proksch & Bavelier, 2002; Stevens & Neville, 2006; Swisher, 1993; see Pelz, Marschark, & Convertino, this volume), and in the generation and manipulation of mental images (Chamberlain & Mayberry, 1994; Emmorey & Kosslyn, 1996; Emmorey, Kosslyn, &

Bellugi, 1993; Talbot & Haude, 1993). These advantages may influence the numerical skills of deaf individuals at a number of levels (see Marschark & Wauters, this volume).

The ability to enumerate is captured by two processes. For arrays containing a small number of items (up to four, also termed the *subitizing range*), individuals are able to apprehend rapidly and accurately the numerosity (Mandler & Shebo, 1982; Peterson & Simon, 2000; Trick & Pylyshyn, 1993). Response times suggest that all items are concurrently apprehended, as there is little difference in the time to respond to one item and the time to respond to four items. Beyond the subitizable range, response times increase in a linear fashion, depending on the number of items to be apprehended, thus suggesting a sequential counting process.

A handful of studies have considered subitizing in hearing children with mathematical difficulties. Koontz and Berch (1996) found that those with arithmetic learning disabilities had difficulty subitizing, instead using time-consuming counting strategies for set sizes as small as three items. Landerl, Bevan, and Butterworth (2004) also found that response times increased linearly and were steeper within the subitizing range for children with mathematical difficulties only and those with both math and reading difficulties, suggesting a counting process rather than concurrent apprehension within the subitizable range. However, the comparisons to control groups (normally achieving and with reading difficulties) showed no significant effects.

Bull et al. (2006) examined subitizing skills of deaf and hearing college students. Stimulus displays containing between one and six items were shown in three formats, either a random arrangement in the center of the display, as skewed dot arrangements (with two dot subgroups, presumably requiring separate eye fixations), or in a canonical arrangement, as they would appear on dice. Each display was shown for a very short amount of time (50 ms) to avoid the possibility that participants counted the items. Because deaf individuals show enhanced abilities in some aspects of visual and spatial processing, it was anticipated that deaf participants would perform well on the subitizing task, particularly in conditions where stimuli were not presented in well-known canonical patterns, and where the subitizing process may require a rapid refocus of attention to a second group of dots or attention to the periphery. In fact, the patterns of results were very similar for both deaf and hearing participants in the tasks employed here. If participants are able to rapidly enumerate small set sizes (i.e., subitize), then we would expect overall accuracy to be higher for set sizes within the subitizable range (1–4) compared to outside the subitizing range (5–6). For all presentation formats, accuracy was very high in the subitizing range (85%–97%). Accuracy remained high for larger item sets in the dice presentation format, presumably because all participants were able to use knowledge of dice patterns to accurately estimate the number presented.

For the dot and skew dot formats, both hearing status groups showed a significant drop in performance (to approximately 70% accuracy). Deaf participants did not show the anticipated advantage on the skew dot format, but showed completely typical subitizing effects, with performance not significantly different from the hearing group. Recent research from Hauser, Dye, Boutla, Green, and Bavelier (2007) also supports this finding. Deaf native signers of ASL showed the typical enumeration results of fast speed and accuracy within the subitizable range and an increase in response time and errors for displays containing between five and ten items. The performance was entirely comparable to their hearing peers in displays in which presentation of the array was either in the center or periphery. Hauser et al. (2007) also calculated the "breakpoint," defined as the number of items at which a switch occurs from subitizing to a counting response. Again, there was no significant difference in the breakpoint, with both deaf and hearing groups showing a breakpoint of approximately four items.

Finally, recent results with deaf children (aged 10–13 years) indicate no difference between the hearing status groups in subitizing skills (Bull & Theodorou, in preparation). In this study, children were presented with brief displays (200 ms) containing between two and eight items, and they simply had to say how many items they thought were in the display. Performance on two to four items was very accurate, with the degree of error (difference between children's estimates and actual number presented) increasing with increasing numbers of items in the display. Overall, it appears that the early enhancements in aspects of visual attention caused by deafness do not lead to similar changes in the number of objects that can be attended. If this were the case, we might expect the subitizing range to increase. However, the results do show that, in contrast to the findings of Koontz and Berch (1996) and Landerl et al. (2004) with hearing participants, deaf individuals do not have a deficit in the ability to enumerate arrays of objects, suggesting that subitizing skills do not contribute to the mathematical difficulties of deaf individuals.

Estimation

One aspect of basic number sense that has been the focus of recent research is the development of numerical estimation, the skills necessary to complete tasks such as approximating answers to arithmetic problems, estimating the number of objects in an array when they are outside the subitizable range, or locating numerical magnitudes along a number line (Barth et al., 2006; Booth & Siegler, 2006). A number of studies show strong positive relationships between good number estimation skills and better counting and arithmetic abilities (LeFevre, Greenham, & Waheed, 1993), better understanding of mathematical concepts (LeFevre et al., 1993; Petitto, 1990), and better overall scores on maths achievement tests from kindergarten through to third grade (Booth & Siegler, 2006; Siegler & Booth, 2004).

Our internal number magnitude system conforms to the natural logarithm of the number, resulting in number line placement of magnitude that becomes progressively compressed as number magnitude increases (Dehaene, 1997; Feigenson, Dehaene, & Spelke, 2004; Siegler & Opfer, 2003). Studies with adults and children and habituation studies with infants have shown that speed and accuracy in comparing numerical magnitudes decreases logarithmically as the ratio of the number approaches 1 (distance effects; e.g., Dehaene et al., 1990; Lipton & Spelke, 2003) and with numerical magnitude when comparing numbers separated by equal distance (size effects; e.g., Moyer & Landauer, 1967; Starkey & Cooper, 1980). With schooling, children's number line judgments gradually conform to the linear mathematical system (Siegler & Booth, 2004), where the difference between consecutive numbers is identical regardless of position on the number line. For an understanding of mathematical concepts, children need to recognize the linear nature of quantity and the idea that all parts of the range are equally important if they are to accurately make approximations, verify arithmetical answers, and so on.

Siegler's (1996) multiple-representations model suggests that both linear and logarithmic representations are available interchangeably to humans, and a choice is made regarding the best representation to use for a particular task, in a particular context. In some cases, a logarithmic style would be more suitable over a linear one (e.g., estimating food quantity), whereas in other cases, a linear representation would be more beneficial, for instance, when all parts of a set are equally important (e.g., in the structure of the number system for understanding arithmetic, decimal notation). It is believed that because of the unfamiliarity of some larger numbers, children (and adults in the context of high-magnitude numbers) tend to rely on a more intuitive logarithmic representation for numerical estimation tasks. Over time and with experience, this logarithmic representation is replaced with the more appropriate linear representation.

One direct method of measuring these mental representations is to examine accuracy on numerical estimation in number-to-position (NP) tasks. In an NP task, a line is presented with the number 0 at one end and 10, 100, or 1000 at the other, depending on the context. A target number is provided, and the participant is asked to estimate where its position would be located on the number line. This task provides a clear physical measure of one's mental representations of distances between numbers on a number line. Using the NP task, Siegler and Booth (2004) observed a developmental change over time from logarithmic to linear representations, with the period of developmental change depending on familiarity with the number range used. For example, kindergartners (aged 5–6 years), who had limited experience with numbers 1–100, showed a clear logarithmic pattern of number representation. First grader (ages 6–7 years) best–fits were divided, with half of the age group showing logarithmic patterns and the other half fitting a linear pattern. Second graders (ages 7–8 years), who had a greater familiarity with the numbers of that range, were more likely to reveal numerical representations that were best fit by a linear function. In the context of a 0–1000 line, this shift appears around the fourth grade, reinforcing the idea that the shift from logarithmic to linear representations is facilitated by greater experience and familiarity with the number range (Siegler & Opfer, 2003), which may include opportunities for incidental learning through, for example, playing number board games that provide a combination of spatial, temporal, kinanesthetic, and verbal/auditory cues to numerical magnitude (see e.g., Whyte & Bull, 2008).

If deaf children have difficulty making the transition from the natural logarithmic representation to the school-taught linear system, then there should be evidence of more frequent logarithmic representations. In deaf adults, if exposure to larger-value numbers (up to 10,000) occurs less frequently, or if there is difficulty inhibiting the natural logarithmic representation of number (see Geary, Hoard, Nugent, & Bryd-Craven, 2007b, for such a proposal with hearing children), then we might expect either fewer linear representation of magnitude or less accuracy in making number placements on a linear scale.

Bull, Marschark, and Convertino (in preparation) examined estimation skills in deaf (N = 50) and hearing (N = 36) adults enrolled at RIT. Students were shown a number line with end-points labelled 0–100, 0–1000, or 0–10,000. For each line, they were shown a number and asked to make a mark on the line where they thought that number would come. The position marked on the line was then converted into the actual number that would be represented by that point on the line. To measure estimation accuracy, the percentage absolute error for each requested number was calculated as: ([actual estimate—requested estimate]/scale of estimates) × 100. For example, if the participant was asked to estimate the position of 70 on the 0–1000 line, and he placed a mark at a location that corresponded to 100, the percent absolute error would be 3%: ([100 – 70]/1000) × 100.

On the 0–100 number line, comparisons of mean absolute errors for deaf and hearing participants revealed a significant difference. Deaf participants showed a higher mean absolute error (4.76%) compared with hearing participants (3.64%). Deaf participants also showed a higher absolute error on the 0–1000 number line (Deaf = 5.38%, Hearing = 4.46%), although this difference was not significant; on the 0–10,000 line (Deaf = 6.05%, Hearing = 3.79%), the difference was significant. Therefore, it appears that, overall, deaf participants are less accurate, particularly in the context of higher-magnitude numbers, in their numerical approximations.

Despite this difference in accuracy, numerical representations for all number lines for both deaf and hearing participants were best fit by linear functions. On the 0–100 line, 84% of deaf participants and 86.1% of hearing participants showed a linear regression slope. On the 0–1000 line, 92% of deaf participants and 83.3% of hearing participants showed a linear function. Finally, on the 0–10,000 line, 80% of deaf participants showed a linear function, very similar to the findings from hearing individuals where 80.6% showed a linear function. So, whereas deaf individuals appear to show no difference in the representational format (i.e., frequency of linear or logarithmic functions) compared with hearing individuals, the percentage of absolute error between estimates and actual position on the number line is higher.

Outcome measures of math ability were available for deaf students [National Technical Institute for the Deaf (NTID) mathematics placement test, N = 27] and for hearing students (SAT scores, N = 34). Median scores for each hearing status group on each outcome measure were calculated and participants placed into one of two groups, depending on whether their scores fell above or below the median. Analyses were conducted to examine whether the estimation skills of those students in the above- and below-median ability groups differed. Based on the median split on the NTID placement scores, those deaf students scoring below the median were significantly less accurate compared with those above the median on 0–100 estimation, 0–1000 estimation, and marginally less accurate on the 0–10,000 estimation. However, this finding was not specific to deaf students. The same analysis of hearing students based on a median split on the SAT scores revealed similar findings, with those students in the below-median group being less accurate on the 0–100 and 0–1000 estimation. Mean performance levels on the estimation task are shown in Figure 6–3. These results, based on a conservative median split, concur with the findings from hearing children that individuals who are less mathematically able have less precise representations of number. In first grade, hearing children with mathematical learning difficulties are less accurate in their placement of numbers on the number line and are delayed in the development of a linear, mathematical representation of the number line (Geary, Hoard, Byrd-Craven, Nugent, & Numtee, 2007). They are also less accurate in their placement of magnitudes conforming to a logarithmic representation, suggesting that even before formal schooling, the magnitude representation of children with mathematical learning difficulties is less precise (Geary et al., 2007b).

The ability to estimate also has been examined using nonsymbolic tasks. In studies examining children's mathematical difficulties, it has been argued that a problem may exist in accessing numerical magnitude from symbols rather than in processing numerosity per se. Rousselle and Noel (2007) found that children with mathematical difficulties were only

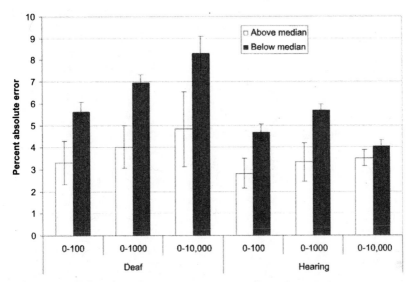

Figure 6–3. Mean absolute error on each number line for deaf and hearing students above and below median on mathematics outcome measure.

impaired when comparing Arabic digits (symbolic number comparison), but not when comparing collections of items (nonsymbolic number magnitude). Numerical abilities observed in studies of animals, infants, and adults suggest a preverbal number sense or rough estimation of magnitude that is present prior to the emergence of symbolic number representations. This provides a characteristic pattern of results showing that when the ratio between the two quantities being considered gets closer to one, the accuracy of estimation judgments decreases (see Barth et al., 2006 for studies with infants and adults). In these studies, participants are asked to perform approximations, discriminations, or even arithmetical calculations following brief presentations of arrays of objects where counting using traditional symbolic means is not possible. The importance of such nonsymbolic representations is apparent from neuroimaging studies, in which it has been shown that tasks dealing with exact symbolic numerosities automatically activate nonsymbolic number representations (Dehaene et al., 1990).

Masataka (2006) compared deaf and hearing adults in their performance on tasks like those used by Barth et al. (2006). On a comparison task, participants were shown two arrays that varied by a ratio of 0.75, 0.8, 0.83, and 0.86, and were asked which array of the two contained more elements. Participants also completed a nonsymbolic subtraction task, in which they were asked to subtract a second array from a first array, compare this to the number of elements in the third array, and decide whether array three contained more or fewer elements compared to the subtracted array.

Participants also performed a formal mathematics task in which the stimulus set used for the nonsymbolic subtraction task was presented with Arabic symbols. Overall mean accuracy scores for the comparison task were not significantly different between the hearing and deaf participants. However, deaf participants were significantly more accurate on the nonsymbolic subtraction task. Both groups showed the typical ratio effects, with accuracy declining as the ratio difference between the two arrays approached one. Deaf participants were significantly less accurate on the formal (symbolic) mathematics task.

Taken together, these results suggest that reduced accuracy in estimation, for both deaf adults and hearing children with mathematical difficulties, may only be apparent when number meaning has to be accessed from symbols (referred to as the "access deficit hypothesis" by Rouselle & Noel, 2007). When estimation is based on nonsymbolic items, accuracy is increased. Further insights into the estimation abilities of deaf individuals should be made, including tasks that involve both symbolic (e.g., answers to arithmetic problems, amount of money) and nonsymbolic estimation (e.g., estimating distance, number of discrete objects). This seems particularly important in light of findings showing that good estimation skills are positively related to a host of mathematical outcomes (Booth & Siegler, 2006; LeFevre et al., 1993; Petitto, 1990; Siegler & Booth, 2004). The ability to make accurate estimations may be in part reliant on the ability to monitor one's own responses, consider the appropriateness of the estimation, and adjust it accordingly, a skill that may not be used to the same extent by deaf individuals (see later discussion on metacognition and self-regulation).

The Next Step?

In identifying a useful next stage at which to focus our attention, it makes sense to work to the next level of complexity in mathematical processing—the development of counting strategies in arithmetical problem solving. The stages of development of arithmetical problem solving have been widely studied in hearing children. Initially, children may count both addends in an arithmetical problem (e.g., counting all; starting the count from 1 when presented with a problem like 5 + 3), using finger or verbal counting, and gradually add the more efficient counting-on strategy to the repertoire (given 5 + 3 starting the count from 5). The repeated use of such counting procedures and the production of the same answer to the problem gradually results in the development of memory representations of basic facts (Siegler & Shrager, 1984). The long-term representations support the use of memory-based problem-solving procedures such as direct retrieval and decomposition. Siegler (1988) also argues that the use of retrieval-based processes is moderated by a confidence criterion against which the child can gauge confidence in correctness of the retrieved answer. Children with a lenient criterion may report any retrieved answer, correct or not, whereas those with a rigorous criterion will only state answers that they are certain are correct. The use of memory-based procedures results in quick solution to problems and a decrease in the demands made on working memory in solving these problems. This makes solving more complex problems, in which the simple problems are embedded (e.g., word problems), less error-prone (e.g., Geary & Widaman, 1992).

Children with mathematical difficulties tend to show a delay in the development of efficient counting strategies and tend to commit more counting errors (see Geary, Hoard, Nugent, & Bryd-Craven, 2007a for a review). It has also been reported that children with mathematical difficulties do not show adaptive strategy choices. Whereas children who show typical math skills adapt their strategy according to the complexity of the problem (e.g., direct retrieval for easy problems and counting for complex problems), children with mathematical difficulties tried to rely on direct retrieval (often incorrect) of arithmetic answers for complex problems (Geary, Hoard, Bryd-Craven, & DeSoto, 2004).

An impairment in working memory may underlie the frequent counting errors and the subsequent failure to construct a reliable network of arithmetic facts in semantic memory (Geary, 2004, 2005). The central executive function controls the attentional and inhibitory processes needed to select, use, and monitor procedures during problem solving. The information supporting procedural and conceptual competencies is represented in the language or visual-spatial systems. The language system is important in the articulation of number words and counting. The visual-spatial system supports the representations already discussed, such as number magnitude and representing information in a spatial form, as in a mental number line (Zorzi, Proftis, & Umilta, 2002). The frequent counting errors and reliance on immature counting strategies shown by children with mathematical difficulties may be due to deficits in the information representation within the language system. To develop long-term representations, both problem and answer must be simultaneously active in working memory. If information decays too quickly in working memory, the terms of the problem are no longer accessible when the answer is reached, and a long-term memory association cannot be created.

Working memory is also responsible for the allocation of attentional resources during problem-solving monitoring. Reduced ability to monitor the problem-solving process may result in procedural errors and incorrect associations being formed in long-term memory. Many models of arithmetical processing assume that associations are formed in semantic memory between problems and answers through repeated exposure. Where frequent errors are made, these associations are weaker and "fuzzier," resulting in less frequent retrieval of answers or retrieval of incorrect answers directly

from long-term memory. This established pattern of associations also results in errors that are associated with the correct answer: table errors (correct answer for another entry in the multiplication table, e.g., $4 \times 8 = 27$,
because 27 is the answer for 3×9), operation errors (answer is correct for
a different operation, e.g., $3 \times 4 = 7$), and operand errors (given answer is
correct for another example with a shared operand, e.g., $3 \times 4 = 16$). If the
semantic association of number bonds were weak or different in deaf individuals, we may not see evidence of these typical types of errors.

Only a handful of studies have examined patterns of response times
and errors for arithmetical processing in deaf individuals. Hitch, Arnold,
and Phillips (1983) found the same pattern of response times in deaf and
hearing children, with response time to arithmetic problems fitting what
is referred to as the "min" model. This is a counting strategy in which
response time to solve the problem is related to the value of the minimum
number in the problem. Accuracy and pattern of response times were also
found to be similar for deaf and hearing adults on judgments of magnitude
and correctness of arithmetic, but deaf individuals were slower in both
tasks (Epstein et al., 1994). However, arithmetic verification may be solved
through approximation rather than precise calculation, and the examination
of error types for both hearing and deaf individuals revealed no consistent
pattern.

More in-depth studies should be undertaken to the analyze the development of arithmetic processing strategies and retrieval in deaf children
and adults, particularly in light of findings that memory span in natural
sign languages tends to be shorter than verbal memory span. Through a series of carefully controlled studies, Boutla, Supalla, Newport, and Bavelier
(2004) argued that shorter ASL span cannot be explained by the phonological properties of signs (such as visual similarity), the articulatory duration
of signs compared to speech (Marschark & Mayer, 1998), or by a fundamental reduction in memory capacities in deaf individuals (see Dye, Hauser, &
Bavelier, this volume). Instead, they argue that differences in encoding for
deaf individuals (visual versus phonological) might result in different rates
of decay of information, proposing that speech-like information processing
through echoic memory decays at a slower rate than signed information,
which is most likely to be processed using iconic memory. This would
mean that signed information would need to be rehearsed more frequently
to stop it decaying from working memory and that, without rehearsal,
signed information would be lost from memory more rapidly. In terms of
arithmetic, this may result in more information being lost from short-term
memory, and without both problem and answer active in memory at the
same time, representations will not be established in long-term memory.
Based on this, we would expect to see the typical findings present in hearing children with mathematical difficulties—reliance on less efficient and

more error-prone counting strategies, and higher frequency of fact retrieval errors.

Boutla et al. (2004) also provide an alternative explanation for the shorter ASL span, related to the differences in retention of serial order information across modalities. Whereas the auditory system is highly efficient in retaining the order of occurrence of words, the visual system is more limited in its retention of visual order information, being more efficient in the maintenance of spatial structure. Others have proposed that speakers and signers encode order information in different manners, speakers predominantly using verbal coding and signers using spatial coding (see Marschark, 2003, for a review). This finding is supported by the result that signers show equivalent recall to speakers in free recall tasks in which temporal ordering is not necessary. However, in tasks like arithmetic or mathematical problem solving, often a number of pieces of information (e.g., the addends and operation) need to be held in memory in relevant order to ensure the correct procedure and calculation are carried out. So, a combination of faster decay of iconic information coupled with the necessity for temporal coding, which does not easily lend itself to spatial information, may influence the likelihood of automatization of arithmetic fact learning as deaf children progress through school. Systematic investigation of the development of counting strategies and arithmetic fact retrieval is required (see Frostag & Ahlberg, 1999, for an interesting qualitative analysis of children's solution strategies to arithmetical problems).

Coupled with a potential short-term memory limitation is an apparent inability among deaf students to monitor their learning and appreciate the level of knowledge they have acquired. Metacognition refers to awareness and monitoring of one's own cognitive system and functioning, and allows students to better comprehend, monitor, or assess conceptual and procedural knowledge related to a domain. Self-regulation refers to those processes that coordinate cognition, including the ability to use metacognitive knowledge strategically to achieve goals, especially if one has to overcome cognitive obstacles, and being conscious of cognitive capacities, strategies for processing information, and task variables that influence performance (see Panaoura & Philippou, 2007). Studies by Marschark and colleagues (Marschark, Sapere, Convertino, Seewagen, & Maltzan, 2004; Marschark, Sapere, Convertino, & Seewagen, 2005a,b) have found that deaf students comprehend less than hearing peers in mathematics and science classrooms and, perhaps more interestingly, have less (or less accurate) awareness of their level of learning/comprehension (Maki, 1995; Thiede, Anderson, & Therriault, 2003) than do their hearing classmates. Current research exploring deaf students' self-monitoring with regard to learning science from text versus sign language is yielding similar results

(Marschark et al., 2006). Deaf students are less likely than hearing students to consider alternative approaches to a task prior to undertaking it or while working through it. In domains such as reading and mathematics, deaf students frequently are unaware of their performance, apply strategies that are inappropriate, or fail to apply strategies known to be in their repertoires (Kelly & Mousley, 2001; Marschark & Everhart, 1999; Mousley & Kelly, 1998; see Strassman, 1997).

Again, the overlap of results from hearing children is apparent. Children with mathematical difficulties do not adapt their problem-solving strategies in line with the demands of the task, tending to rely on (often incorrect) retrieval of answers from long-term memory with no apparent check of the appropriateness of the answer (Geary et al., 2004). Few studies have considered whether this is a result of lack of metacognitive monitoring (but see Panaoura & Philippou, 2007), although findings do suggest that hearing children with learning difficulties also perceive their abilities to be better than they actually are (e.g., Meltzer, Roditi, Houser, & Perlman, 1998), suggesting that such children may not monitor their own learning adequately or may not be aware of their own capabilities and when strategies should be put into play to help them learn.

Summary and Implications

The main aim of this chapter was to bring together findings from recent research examining basic and in some cases automatic aspects of numerical processing to determine whether this might help to explain the frequently observed lag in arithmetical and mathematical skills in deaf individuals. The focus here was on basic aspects of number processing—fast and accurate enumeration of small set sizes, automaticity of activation of semantically related numerical information (magnitude), the nature of the visual–spatial representation of number, and estimation using symbolic and nonsymbolic means. If hearing status differences were found on such skills, then these may feed into developing mathematical competencies, which, when coupled with the higher language demands of more complex mathematical processing, may have made understanding even more difficult for deaf individuals.

Overall, data from deaf adults indicate that the format of numerical representation and the level of automatic activation of magnitude information are not idiosyncratically different in deaf individuals and do not represent the basis of later developing difficulties with arithmetic and mathematics. Because sign language is a visually–spatially organized language, it may lend itself particularly well to the establishment of connections between Arabic numerals and spatial representations of magnitude. Difficulties that were found, for example, on the number line estimation task, appear to be general to all participants who are lower-functioning in math, not just those who are deaf, and this may be restricted only to conditions that involve symbolic knowledge.

A focus on adult mature numerical functioning does not tell us anything about the processes by which that level of functioning was achieved, and whether any differences in the early developmental progression of these skills impact on other aspects of mathematical development. Our small studies of deaf children suggest wide variability in performance on tasks of basic number processing, suggesting that we need to look much more closely at the factors leading to individual differences in performance. Given the heterogeneity of the experiences of deaf children, it may be appropriate to consider in-depth cases studies that closely examine factors such as opportunities for incidental learning dependent on form of communication. Other studies of children's performance on basic aspects of numerical functioning have not revealed significant problems. Zafarty, Nunes, and Bryant (2004), for example, found no difficulties in representing and discriminating number in deaf preschool children. Children were presented with a number of items either spatially (all items at one time) or temporally (one item at a time). The visual representation was then taken away, and children were asked to reproduce the same number of items. Deaf children showed a distinct advantage when the tasks were spatial rather than temporal in nature, and showed no difference from their hearing peers on the temporal task. Furthermore, despite deaf children showing age-related lags in their knowledge of the number sequence, their performance on an object-counting and cardinality task was similar to that of hearing children (Leybaert & Van Custem, 2002), suggesting that deaf children's conceptual understanding of counting was on a par with their hearing peers, despite poorer procedural understanding. Leybaert and Van Custem argued that hearing children may produce a longer count sequence simply because of rote learning, but with little conceptual understanding of the application of these higher numbers. Other studies have shown that computational skills (Hitch, Arnold, & Phillips, 1983) and problem-solving abilities (Nunes & Moreno, 1997) appear to follow the same pattern as that seen in hearing children, albeit at a slower pace.

These findings support the idea that deaf children, at least measured by these tasks, do not begin school with any particular problem in accessing or representing number, or in their general understanding of counting principles. The main findings discussed in this chapter relate to the visual–spatial representation of number with minimal involvement from language functions other than being able to recognize Arabic digits. Given the strength that deaf children and adults appear to show in this nonverbal representation of number, it highlights the potential importance of playing to these processing strengths when teaching and assessing the understanding of numerical concepts.

Results from an intervention study by Nunes and Moreno (2002) high-light the benefits of visually presenting mathematical concepts to deaf children, which potentially plays to their preferred (and more experienced) mode of information processing (see Nunes & Bryant, this volume). That study addressed skills that hearing children are thought to learn informally through incidental learning before entry into school, such as additive composition (any number can be seen as the sum of other numbers). The aims of the intervention were to strengthen pupils' understanding of additive composition, to strengthen their understanding of how numbers are used to measure (expanding the use of additive composition), and to introduce the number line as a working visual tool for representing and solving problems. The intervention program, designed to meet the need for visual support in the mathematics classroom, and the need for systematic teaching of concepts that hearing children might learn informally, was successful in raising the standardized mathematics performance of deaf children. Although tools for supporting visual representations of number, such as the number line, have proved beneficial, they are not the definitive answer to supporting mathematical learning. Studies with older deaf children and adolescents (e.g., Blatto-Vallee, Kelly, Gaustad, Porter, & Fonzi, 2007) show that they fail to utilize spatial–relational representations reflecting conceptual and mathematical aspects of mathematic problems. Instead, they relied on "pictorial" representations, which included incidental aspects of the problems but not quantitative/conceptual relations important to their solution (Hegarty & Kozhevnikov, 1999). Kelly et al. (2003) comment that, whereas concrete visualization is an excellent strategy for understanding variables in a problem, it is insufficient by itself for advanced problem solving, an argument supported by results from Blatto-Vallee et al. (2007), showing that deaf students' mathematics problem solving was limited by their dependence on visual representations. Kelly et al. argued that teachers of deaf children need to place more emphasis on critical thinking, synthesis of information, and abstraction of known knowledge to novel situations, to allow deaf students to go beyond simple repetition and application of procedures (see Kelly, this volume).

There is clearly still much to learn about the development of numerical cognition in deaf individuals. Only by detailed systematic investigation will we be able to pinpoint the reasons underlying the mathematical learning difficulties of some deaf individuals, be they cognitive or experiential in nature. As with research in hearing children, studies examining mathematical development have taken a back seat in comparison to the detailed studies of children's reading and language skills. However, quantitative understanding is required in virtually every workplace, and is critical in many aspects of our day-to-day lives. In providing deaf individuals with the best opportunities to engage fully in our technologically advancing environment, it is essential that we continue with a detailed analysis of mathematical skills, considered in relation to experiential factors, differences in cognitive organization and functioning, and differences in exposure to language and teaching.

Certain mathematical tasks may be more difficult for deaf individuals, but learning should be accomplished if we more fully understand the processing limitations of these individuals, which should be taken into consideration in both the teaching and assessment of quantitative skills. We also know that not all deaf individuals have problems learning quantitative skills, with Wood, Wood, and Howarth (1983) reporting that approximately 15% of profoundly deaf children perform at average or above average in standardized mathematics tests. By considering individual differences within deaf populations, rather than just comparing them to hearing populations, progress will be made in determining those factors that result in individual differences in numerical skills.

References

Allen, T. E. (1986). Patterns of academic achievement among hearing impaired students: 1974–1983. In A. N. Shildroth & M. A. Karchmer (Eds.), *Deaf children in America* (pp. 161–206). San Diego, CA: College-Hill Press.

Ansari, D., & Karmiloff-Smith, A. (2002). Atypical trajectories of number development: A neuroconstructivist perspective. *Trends in Cognitive Sciences, 6,* 511–516.

Austin, G. F. (1975). Knowledge of selected concepts obtained by an adolescent deaf population. *American Annals of the Deaf, 120,* 360–370.

Bandurski, M., & Galkowski, T. (2004). The development of analogical reasoning in deaf children and their parents' communication mode. *Journal of Deaf Studies and Deaf Education, 9,* 153–175.

Banks, J., Gray, C., & Fyfe, R. (1990). The written recall of printed stories by severely deaf children. *British Journal of Educational Psychology, 60,* 192–206.

Barth, H., La Mont, K., Lipton, J., Dehaene, S., Kanwisher, N., & Spelke, E. (2006). Non-symbolic arithmetic in adults and young children. *Cognition, 98,* 199–222.

Bavelier, D., Tomann, A., Hutton, C., Mitchell, T., Corina, D., Liu, G., & Neville, H. (2000). Visual attention to the periphery is enhanced in congenitally deaf individuals. *Journal of Neuroscience, 20,* 1–6.

Berch, D. B. (2005). Making sense of number sense: Implications for children with mathematical disabilities. *Journal of Learning Disabilities, 38,* 333–339.

Berch, D. B., Foley, E. J., Hill, R. J., & Ryan, P. M. (1999). Extracting parity and magnitude from Arabic numerals: Developmental changes in number processing and mental representation. *Journal of Experimental Child Psychology, 74,* 286–308.

Blatto-Vallee, G., Kelly, R. R, Gaustad, M. G., Porter, J., & Fonzi, J. (2007). Spatial-relational representation in mathematical problem-solving by

deaf and hearing students. *Journal of Deaf Studies and Deaf Education,*
12, 432–448.

Booth, J. L., & Siegler, R. S. (2006). Developmental and individual differences
in pure numerical estimation. *Developmental Psychology, 41,* 189–201.

Boutla, M., Suppalla, T., Newport, E. L., & Bavelier, D. (2004). Short term
memory span: Insights from sign language. *Nature Neuroscience, 7,*
997–1002.

Bull, R., Blatto-Vallee, G., & Fabich, M. (2006). Subitizing, magnitude representation, and magnitude retrieval in deaf and hearing adults. *Journal of*
Deaf Studies and Deaf Education, 11, 289–302.

Bull, R., Marschark, M., & Blatto-Vallee, G. (2005). SNARC hunting: Examining number representation in deaf students. *Learning and Individual Dif-*
ferences, 15, 223–236.

Bull, R., Marschark, M., & Convertino, C. (in preparation). Numerical estimation in deaf and hearing adults.

Bull, R., & Theodorou, G. (in preparation). Numerical automaticity and enumeration skills in deaf children.

Butterworth, B. (1999). *The mathematical brain.* London: Macmillan.

Butterworth, B. (2005). The development of arithmetical abilities. *Journal of*
Child Psychology and Psychiatry, 46, 3–18.

Chamberlain, C., & Mayberry, R. I. (1994). *Do the deaf "see" better? Effects of*
deafness on visual-spatial skills. Poster presented at TENNET V meetings, Montreal, May.

Corina, D. P., Kritchevsky, M., & Bellugi, U. (1992). Linguistic permeability
of unilateral neglect: Evidence from American Sign Language. *Proceed-*
ings of the Cognitive Science Conference (pp. 384–389). Hillside, NY:
Erlbaum.

Dehaene, S. (1992). Varieties of numerical abilities. *Cognition, 44,* 1–42.

Dehaene, S. (1997). *The number sense: How the mind creates mathematics.*
New York: Oxford University Press.

Dehaene, S., & Akhavein, R. (1995). Attention, automaticity and levels of representation in number processing. *Journal of Experimental Psychology:*
Learning, Memory, and Cognition, 21, 314–326.

Dehaene, S., Bossini, S., & Giraux, P. (1993). The mental representation of parity and number magnitude. *Journal of Experimental Psychology: General,*
122, 371–396.

Dehaene, S., & Changeux, J. (1993). Development of elementary numerical abilities: A neuronal model. *Journal of Cognitive Neuroscience, 5,* 390–407.

Dehaene, S., Dehaene-Lambertz, G., & Cohen, L. (1998). Abstract representation of number in the animal and human brain. *Nature Neuroscience, 21,*
355–361.

Dehaene, S., Dupoux, E., & Mehler, J. (1990). Is numerical comparison digital:
Analogical and symbolic distance effects in two-digit number comparison. *Journal of Experimental Psychology: Human Perception and Perfor-*
mance, 16, 626–641.

Dehaene, S., Molko, N., Cohen, L., & Wilson, A. J. (2004). Arithmetic and the
brain. *Current Opinion in Neurobiology, 14,* 218–224.

Dehaene S., Spelke, E., Pinel, P., Stanescu, R., & Tsivkin, S. (1999). Sources of
mathematical thinking: Behavioral and brain imaging evidence. *Science,*
284, 970–974.

Delazer, M., & Butterworth, B. (1997). A dissociation of number meanings. *Cognitive Neuropsychology, 14,* 613–636.

Donlan, C. (2007). Mathematical developmental in children with specific language impairments. In D. B. Berch & M. M. M. Mazzocco (Eds.), *Why is math so hard for some children? The nature and origins of mathematical learning difficulties and disabilities* (pp. 151–172). Baltimore: Paul H. Brookes.

Duncan, E. M., & McFarland, C. E. (1980). Isolating the effects of symbolic distance and semantic congruity in comparative judgments: An additive-factor analysis. *Memory and Cognition, 8,* 612–622.

Emmorey, K., & Kosslyn, S. (1996). Enhanced image generation abilities in deaf signers. A right hemisphere effect. *Brain and Cognition, 32,* 28–44.

Emmorey, K., Kosslyn, S., & Bellugi, U. (1993). Visual imagery and visual-spatial language: Enhanced imagery abilities in deaf and hearing ASL signers. *Cognition, 46,* 139–181.

Epstein, K. I., Hillegeist, E. G., & Grafman, J. (1994). Number processing in deaf college students. *American Annals of the Deaf, 139,* 336–347.

Feigenson, L., Dehaene, S., & Spelke, E. (2004). Core systems of number. *Trends in Cognitive Sciences, 8,* 307–314.

Fischer, M. H. (2003). Spatial representations in number processing— evidence from a pointing task. *Visual Cognition, 10,* 493–508.

Frostad, P., & Ahlberg, A. (1999). Solving story-based arithmetic problems: Achievement of children with hearing impairment and their interpretation of meaning. *Journal of Deaf Studies and Deaf Education, 4*(4), 283–293.

Geary, D. C. (2004). Mathematics and learning disabilities. *Journal of Learning Disabilities, 37,* 4–15.

Geary, D. C. (2005). Role of cognitive theory in the study of learning disability in mathematics. *Journal of Learning Disabilities, 38,* 305–307.

Geary, D. C., Hoard, M. K., Byrd-Craven, J., Nugent, L., & Numtee, C. (2007). Cognitive mechanisms underlying achievement deficits in children with mathematical learning disability. *Child Development, 78,* 1343–1359.

Geary, D. C., Hoard, M. K., Nugent, L., & Bryd-Craven, J. (2007a). Strategy use, long-term memory, and working memory capacity. In D. B. Berch & M.M.M. Mazzocco (Eds.), *Why is math so hard for some children? The nature and origins of mathematical learning difficulties and disabilities* (pp. 83–105). Baltimore: Paul H. Brookes.

Geary, D. C., Hoard, M. K., Nugent, L., & Bryd-Craven, J. (2007b). Development of number line representations in children with mathematical learning disability. *Developmental Neuropsychology.*

Geary, D. C., & Widaman, K. F. (1992). Numerical cognition: On the convergence of componential and psychometric models. *Intelligence, 16,* 47–80.

Geary, D. C., Hoard, M. K., Bryd-Craven, J., & DeSoto, C. M. (2004). Strategy choices in simple and complex addition. Contributions of working memory and counting knowledge for children with mathematical disability. *Journal of Experimental Child Psychology, 88,* 121–151.

Gelman, R., & Gallistel, C. R. (1978). *The child's understanding of number.* Cambridge, MA: Harvard University Press.

Gersten, R., Jordan, N. C., & Flojo, J. R. (2005). Early identification and intervention for students with mathematical difficulties. *Journal of Learning Disabilities, 38,* 293–304.

Girelli, L., Lucangeli, D., & Butterworth, B. (2000). The developmental of automaticity is accessing number magnitude. *Journal of Experimental Child Psychology, 76*, 104–122.

Gregory, S. (1998). Mathematics and deaf children. In S. Gregory, P. Knight, W. McCracken, S. Powers, & L. Watson (Eds.), *Issues in Deaf Education* (pp. 119–128). London: Fulton.

Griffin, S., Case, R., & Capodilupo, A. (1995). Teaching for understanding: The importance of central conceptual structure in the elementary mathematics curriculum. In A. McKeough, J. Luppart, & A. Marini (Eds.), *Teaching for transfer: Fostering generalization in learning* (pp. 123–151). Mahwah, NJ: Erlbaum

Hauser, P. C., Dye, M.W.G., Boutla, M., Green, C. S., & Bavelier, D. (2007). Deafness and visual enumeration: Not all aspects of attention are modified by deafness. *Brain Research, 1153*, 178–187.

Hegarty, M. & Koshevnikov, M. (1999). Types of visual-spatial representation and mathematical problem solving. *Journal of Educational Psychology, 91*, 684–689.

Hine, W. D. (1970). The attainment of children with partial hearing. *Journal of the British Association of Teachers of the Deaf, 68*, 129–135.

Hitch, G. J., Arnold, P., & Phillips, L. J. (1983). Counting processes in deaf children's arithmetic. *British Journal of Psychology, 74*, 429–437.

Hyde, M., Zevenbergen, R., & Power, D. (2003). Deaf and hard of hearing students' performance on arithmetic word problems. *American Annals of the Deaf, 148*(1), 56–64.

Iverson, W., Nuerk, H. C., & Willmes, K. (2004). Do signers think differently? The processing of number parity in deaf participants. *Cortex, 40*, 176–178.

Jordan, N. C., Hanich, L. B., & Kaplan, D. (2003). A longitudinal study of mathematical competencies in children with specific math difficulties versus children with comorbid mathematics and reading difficulties. *Child Development, 74*, 834–850.

Jordan, N. C., Kaplan, D., Olah, L. N., & Locuniak, M. N. (2006). Number sense growth in kindergarten: A longitudinal investigation of children at risk for mathematics difficulties. *Child Development, 77*, 153–175.

Kelly, R. R., Lang, H. G., Mousley, K., & Davis, S. M. (2003). Deaf college students' comprehension of relational language in arithmetic compare problems. *Journal of Deaf Studies and Deaf Education, 8*, 120–132.

Kelly, R. R., Lang, H. G., & Pagliaro, C. M. (2003). Mathematics word problem solving for deaf students: A survey of practices in Grades 6–12. *Journal of Deaf Studies and Deaf Education, 8*, 104–119.

Kelly, R. R., & Mousley, K. (2001). Solving word problems: More than reading issues for deaf students. *American Annals of the Deaf, 146*(3), 253–264.

Koontz, K. L. & Berch, D. B. (1996). Identifying simple numerical stimuli: Processing inefficiencies exhibited by arithmetic learning disabled children. *Mathematical Cognition, 2*, 1–23.

Landerl, K., Bevan, A., & Butterworth, B. (2004). Developmental dyscalculia and basic numerical capacities: A study of 8–9 year old students. *Cognition, 93*, 99–125.

Lang, H. G. (2003). Perspectives on the history of deaf education. In M. Marschark & P. E. Spencer (Eds.), *Oxford handbook of deaf studies, language, and education* (pp. 9–20). New York: Oxford University Press.

LeFevre, J. A., Greenham, S. L., & Waheed, N. (1993). The development of procedural and conceptual knowledge in computational estimation. *Cognition and Instruction, 11,* 95–132

Leybaert, J., & Van Custem, M–N. (2002). Counting in sign language. *Journal of Experimental Child Psychology, 81,* 482–501.

Lipton, J. S., & Spelke, E. S. (2003). Origins of number sense: Large number discrimination in human infants. *Psychological Science, 14,* 396–401.

MacLeod, C. M. (1991). Half a century of research on the Stroop effect: An integrative review. *Psychological Bulletin, 109,* 163–203.

Maki, R. H. (1995). Accuracy of metacomprehension judgments for questions of varying importance levels. *American Journal of Psychology, 108,* 327–344.

Mandler, G., & Shebo, B. J. (1982). Subitizing: An analysis of its component processes. *Journal of Experimental Psychology: General, 11,* 1–22.

Marschark, M. (2003). Cognitive functioning in deaf adults and children. In M. Marschark & P. E. Spencer (Eds.), *Oxford handbook of deaf studies, language, and education* (pp. 464–477). New York: Oxford University Press.

Marschark, M., Convertino, C., McEvoy, C., & Masteller, A. (2004). Organization and use of the mental lexicon by deaf and hearing individuals. *American Annals of the Deaf, 149,* 51–61.

Marschark, M., & Everhart, V.S. (1999). Problem solving by deaf and hearing children: Twenty questions. *Deafness and Education International, 1,* 63–79.

Marschark, M., Lang, H., & Albertini, J. (2002). *Educating deaf students: From research to practice.* New York: Oxford University Press.

Marschark, M., Leigh, G., Sapere, P., Burnham, D., Convertino, C., Stinson, M., Knoors, H., Vervloed, M.P.J., & Noble, W. (2006). Benefits of sign language interpreting and text alternatives to classroom learning by deaf students. *Journal of Deaf Studies and Deaf Education, 11,* 421–437.

Marschark, M., & Mayer, T. S. (1998). Interactions of language and memory in deaf children and adults. *Scandinavian Journal of Psychology, 39,* 145–148.

Marschark, M., Sapere, P., Convertino, C., & Seewagen, R. (2005a). Access to postsecondary education through sign language interpreting. *Journal of Deaf Studies and Deaf Education, 10,* 38–50.

Marschark, M., Sapere, P., Convertino, C., & Seewagen, R. (2005b). Educational interpreting: Access and outcomes. In M. Marschark, R. Peterson, & E. A. Winston (Eds.), *Interpreting and interpreter education: Directions for research and practice* (pp. 57–83). New York: Oxford University Press.

Marschark, M., Sapere, P., Convertino, C., Seewagen, R., & Maltzan, H. (2004). Comprehension of sign language interpreting: Deciphering a complex task situation. *Sign Language Studies, 4,* 345–368.

Masataka, N. (2006). Differences in arithmetical subtraction of nonsymbolic numerosities by deaf and hearing adults. *Journal of Deaf Studies and Deaf Education, 11,* 139–143.

Mazzocco, M. M. M. (2005). Challenges in identifying target skills for math disability screening and intervention. *Journal of Learning Disabilities, 38,* 318–323.

Mazzocco, M. M. M., Murphy, M. M., & McCloskey, M. (2007). The contribution of syndrome research understanding mathematical learning disability: The case of Fragile X and Turner Syndromes. In D. B. Berch & M.M.M. Mazzocco (Eds.), *Why is math so hard for some children? The nature and origins of mathematical learning difficulties and disabilities* (pp. 173–193). Baltimore: Paul H. Brookes.

McCloskey, M. (2007). Quantitative literacy and developmental dyscalculias. In D. B. Berch & M.M.M. Mazzocco (Eds.), *Why is math so hard for some children? The nature and origins of mathematical learning difficulties and disabilities* (pp. 415–429). Baltimore: Paul H. Brookes.

McEvoy, C., Marschark, M., & Nelson, D. L. (1999). Comparing the mental lexicons of deaf and hearing individuals. *Journal of Educational Psychology, 91,* 1–9.

Meltzer, L. J., Roditi, B., Houser, R. F., & Perlman, M. (1998). Perceptions of academic strategies and competence in students with learning disabilities. *Journal of Learning Disabilities, 31,* 437–451.

Mousley, K., & Kelly, R. R. (1998). Problem-solving strategies for teaching mathematics to deaf students. *American Annals of the Deaf, 143,* 325–336.

Moyer, R. S., & Landauer, T. K. (1967). The time required for judgments of numerical inequality. *Nature, 215,* 1519–1520.

Neville, H. J., & Lawson, D. (1987). Attention to central and peripheral visual space in a movement detection task: An event-related potential and behavioral study. II. Congenitally deaf adults. *Brain Research, 405,* 268–283.

Nunes, T., & Bryant, P. (1996). *Children doing mathematics.* Oxford: Blackwell.

Nunes, T., & Moreno, C. (1998). Is hearing impairment a cause of difficulties in learning mathematics? In C. Donlan (Ed.), *The development of mathematical skills* (pp. 227–254). Hove, U.K.: Psychology Press.

Nunes, T., & Moreno, C. (1997). Solving word problems with different ways of representing the task: How do deaf children perform? Equals. *Mathematics and Special Educational Needs, 3,* 15–17.

Nunes, T., & Moreno, C. (2002). An intervention program to promote deaf pupil's achievement in mathematics. *Journal of Deaf Studies and Deaf Education, 7,* 120–133.

Ottem, E. (1980). An analysis of the cognitive studies with deaf subjects. *American Annals of the Deaf, 125,* 654–575.

Panaoura, A., & Philippou, G. (2007). The developmental change of young pupils' metacognitive ability in mathematics in relation to their cognitive abilities. *Cognitive Development, 22,* 149–164.

Peterson, S., & Simon, T. J. (2000). Computational evidence for the subitizing phenomenon as an emergent property of the human cognitive architecture. *Cognitive Science, 24,* 93–122.

Petitto, A. L. (1990). Development of numberline and measurement concepts. *Cognition and Instruction, 7,* 55–78.

Proksch, J., & Bavelier, D. (2002). Changes in the spatial distribution of visual attention after early deafness. *Journal of Cognitive Neuroscience, 14,* 687–701.

Richardson, J. T. E., McLeod-Gallinger, J., McKenn, B. G., & Long, G. L. (2000). Approaches to studying in deaf and hearing students in higher education. *Journal of Deaf Studies and Deaf Education, 5,* 156–173.

Rettenback, R., Diller, G., & Sireteaunu, R. (1999). Do deaf people see better? Texture segmentation and visual search compensate in adult but not in juvenile subjects. *Journal of Cognitive Neuroscience, 11,* 560–583.

Rouselle, L., & Noel, M-P. (2007). Basic numerical skills in children with mathematical learning disabilities: A comparison of symbolic vs non-symbolic number magnitude processing. *Cognition, 102,* 361–395.

Rubinsten, O., & Henik, A. (2005). Automatic activation of internal magnitudes: A study of developmental dyscalculia. *Neuropsychology, 19,* 641–648.

Rubinsten, O., Henik, A., Berger, A., & Shahar-Shalev, S. (2002). The development of internal representations of magnitude and their association with Arabic numerals. *Journal of Experimental Child Psychology, 81,* 74–92.

Schick, B. (2005). Educational interpreting and cognitive development in children: Potential relationships. In E. Winston (Ed.), *Educational interpreting: The questions we should be asking* (pp. 73–87). Washington, DC: Gallaudet University Press.

Serrano Pau, C. (1995). The deaf child and solving problems in arithmetic: The importance of comprehensive reading. *American Annals of the Deaf, 14,* 287–291.

Shalev, R. S. (2007). Prevalence of developmental dyscalculia. In D.B. Berch and M.M.M. Mazzocco (Eds.), *Why is math so hard for some children? The nature and origins of mathematical learning difficulties and disabilities* (pp. 49–63). Baltimore: Paul H. Brookes.

Siegler, R. S. (1988). Strategy choice procedures and the development of multiplication skill. *Journal of Experimental Psychology: General, 117,* 258–275.

Siegler, R. S. (1996). *Emerging minds: The process of change in children's thinking.* New York: Oxford University Press.

Siegler, R. S., & Booth, J. (2004). Development of numerical estimation in young children. *Child Development, 75,* 428–444.

Siegler, R. S., & Opfer, J. E. (2003). The development of numerical estimation: Evidence for multiple representations of numerical quantity. *Psychological Science, 14,* 237–243.

Siegler, R. S., & Sharger, J. (1984). Strategy choice in addition and subtraction: How do children know what to do? In C. Sophian (Ed.), *Origins of cognitive skills* (pp. 229–293). Hillside, NJ: Erlbaum.

Starkey, P., & Cooper, R. G. (1980). Perception of numbers by human infants. *Science, 210,* 1033–1035.

Stevens, C., & Neville, H. (2006). Neuroplasticity as a double-edged sword: Deaf enhancements and dyslexic deficits in motion processing. *Journal of Cognitive Neuroscience, 18,* 710–714.

Strassman, B. (1997). Metacognition and reading in children who are deaf: A review of the research. *Journal of Deaf Studies and Deaf Education, 2,* 140–149.

Swanwick, R., Oddy, A., & Roper, T. (2005). Mathematics and deaf children: An exploration of barriers to success. *Deafness and Education International, 7,* 1–21.

Swisher, M. V. (1993). Perceptual and cognitive aspects of recognition of signs in peripheral vision. In M. Marschark & M. D. Clark (Eds.), *Psychological perspectives of deafness* (pp. 229–265). Hillside, NJ: Lawrence Erlbaum Associates.

Talbot, K. F., & Haude, R. H. (1993). The relationship between sign language skill and spatial visualizations ability: Mental rotation of three-dimensional objects. *Perceptual and Motor Skills, 77,* 1387–1391.

Tharpe, A., Ashmead, D., & Rothpletz, A. (2002). Visual attention in children with normal hearing, children with hearing aids, and children with cochlear implants. *Journal of Speech, Hearing and Language Research, 45,* 403–413.

Thiede, K. W., Anderson, M.C.M., & Therriault, D. (2003). Accuracy of the cognitive monitoring affects learning of texts. *Journal of Educational Psychology, 95,* 66–73.

Titus, J. C. (1995). The concept of fraction number among deaf and hard of hearing students. *American Annals of the Deaf, 140,* 255–263.

Traxler, C. B. (2000). Measuring up to performance standards in reading and mathematics: Achievement of selected deaf and hard-of-hearing students in the national norming of the 9th Edition Stanford Achievement Test. *Journal of Deaf Studies and Deaf Education, 5,* 337–348.

Trick, L. M., & Pylyshyn, Z. W. (1993). What enumeration studies can show us about spatial attention: Evidence for limited capacity preattentive processes. *Journal of Experimental Psychology: Human Perception and Performance, 19,* 331–351.

Tzelgov, J., Meyer, J., & Henik, A. (1992). Automatic and intentional processing of numerical information. *Journal of Experimental Psychology: Learning, Memory, and Cognition, 18,* 166–179.

Whyte, J. C., & Bull, R. (2008). Number games, magnitude representation, and basic number skills in preschoolers. *Developmental Psychology, 44,* 588–596.

Wiese, H. (2003). Iconic and non-iconic stages in number development: The role of language. *Trends in Cognitive Sciences, 7,* 385–390.

Wollman, D. C. (1965). The attainments in English and arithmetic of secondary school pupils with impaired hearing. *The Teacher of the Deaf, 159,* 121–129.

Wood, D., Wood, H., & Howarth, P. (1983). Mathematics abilities of deaf school leavers. *British Journal of Developmental Psychology, 1,* 67–73.

Wood, H., Wood, D., Kingsmill, M. C., French, J.R.W., & Howarth, S. P. (1984). The mathematical achievement of deaf children from different educational environments. *British Journal of Educational Psychology, 54,* 254–264.

Zamarian, L., Lopez-Rolon, A., & Delazer, M. (2007). Neuropsychological case studies on arithmetical processing. In D. B. Berch and M.M.M. Mazzocco (Eds.), *Why is math so hard for some children? The nature and origins of mathematical learning difficulties and disabilities* (pp. 245–263). Baltimore: Paul H. Brookes.

Zarfaty, Y., Nunes, T., & Bryant, P. (2004). The performance of young deaf children in spatial and temporal number tasks. *Journal of Deaf Studies and Deaf Education, 9,* 315–326.

Zorzi, M., Priftis, K., & Umilta, C. (2002). Brain damage: Neglect disrupts the mental number line. *Nature, 417,* 138–139.

Chapter 7

Deaf Children's Understanding of Inverse Relations

Terezinha Nunes, Peter Bryant, Diana Burman, Daniel Bell, Deborah Evans, Darcy Hallett, and Laura Montgomery

The Importance of Logic

Philosophers of science, psychologists, and teachers will readily agree that logical reasoning is important for children's learning of science and mathematics. Children need to use logic in order to understand mathematical and scientific concepts. In spite of this general agreement, there was, until recently, no conclusive evidence to show a causal connection between children's logical reasoning and their achievements in mathematics or science in school. Piaget (1952), the pioneer of this hypothesis, contributed to the identification of logical relations that might be important for children's mathematics and science learning and also to the development of measures of children's logical understanding of these relations. However, unambiguous support for a causal connection between children's understanding of specific logical principles and mathematics learning has only been provided recently.

Using a combination of longitudinal and intervention studies, Nunes et al. (2007b) showed that a measure of children's logical reasoning taken when they have just started school is a longitudinal and specific predictor of their mathematics achievement, after controlling for the differences in the children's age, general intelligence, knowledge of arithmetic facts, and working memory. In that study, we measured the children's logical reasoning by giving them problems to solve about (a) inverse relations between addition and subtraction, (b) the additive composition of number,

(c) one-to-one and one-to-many correspondence, and (d) serial order. We found that these logical tasks predicted the children's success about 1 year later in a mathematics assessment that we devised and also in a test of mathematics achievement designed by the government and administered by teachers, given about a year and a half later.

A longitudinal study, like that just described, may indicate that, in natural conditions not influenced by the researchers, the development of children's logical reasoning is related to their progress in mathematical learning. However, the weakness of longitudinal data on their own is that, although many controls can be included, some third unknown and there-fore unmeasured factor may yet exist, which might have influenced the children's logical reasoning and also mathematics learning. In that case, the relation between logical reasoning and mathematics that was charted in the longitudinal study would not be a causal one. The relation between the two variables could simply be due to the fact that both were influenced by the same third factor. To avoid this danger, intervention studies can be used in combination with longitudinal studies. If an intervention that successfully enhances children's logical reasoning also has an impact on their mathematical achievement, then the support for a causal connection between the two is strengthened (see Bradley & Bryant, 1983, for the full explanation of this argument).

Nunes et al. (2007b) complemented their longitudinal study by also carrying out an intervention with children who were at risk for under-achieving in mathematics. Their intervention consisted of teaching the children about the logical principles that had formed part of the logical reasoning assessment. The intervention group out-performed a control group both in an immediate post-test of the understanding of the logical prin-ciples and, about 1 year later, in the government administered mathematics achievement tests.

The Importance of Inversion

This chapter focuses on the inverse relation between addition and subtrac-tion, which is one of the logical principles investigated by Nunes et al. (2007b). Piaget (1952) argued that children cannot be credited with under-standing either addition or subtraction if they do not realize that they are the inverse of each other. They lack conceptual understanding of these op-erations if they do not realize that $a + b - b$ must necessarily equal a. Many aspects of Piaget's theory have been disputed since his groundbreaking work on children's understanding of number, but this claim has been ac-cepted by many and has formed the basis for much research on children's conceptual knowledge of arithmetic (see, for example Bryant, Christie, & Rendu, 1999; Canobi, Reeve, & Pattison, 1998; Siegler & Stern, 1998; Stern,

1992; Vilette, 2002). For instance, Bryant et al. (1999) argued that children can only understand the decomposition of number (if a + b equal c, then c − a must equal b) if they also grasp the inverse relation between addition and subtraction.

The understanding of this inverse relation also must play a crucial part in mathematical development in older children, when they start to learn algebra in school. For example, if students are asked to solve even the simplest of the equations, such as $x - 3 = 5$, they need to use their understanding of the inverse relation between addition and subtraction. Failing to understand the inverse relation between addition and subtraction might lead students to develop an incomplete understanding of the meaning of the equal sign (see, for example, Kieran, 1981, 1997). If students are taught to make equivalent changes to both sides of the equation in order to solve it (i.e., transform the initial equation $x - 3 = 5$ into $x - 3 + 3 = 5 + 3$), and they do not see that they now do not need to subtract 3 from x, then the method they were taught is mysterious to them. Consistently with this analysis, Stern (2006) found that children's understanding of inversion assessed when they were aged 8 years was the best predictor of their performance in an algebra test when they were in university.

The understanding of the inverse relation between addition and subtraction may also be a precursor to the understanding of the inverse relation between multiplication and division. Geary (1994) suggested that children's conceptual knowledge in arithmetic "allows the child to see similarities across problems that have different superficial structures" (p. 270). If this is the case, children's understanding of the inverse relation between addition and subtraction should be significantly related to their understanding of the inverse relation between multiplication and division. Although properly controlled studies are still lacking, a medium-sized and significant correlation ($r = .59$) between the understanding of these two sorts of inverse relation has been reported (Robinson, Ninowski, & Gray, 2006).

Understanding of the inverse relation between multiplication and division is crucial for solving algebra problems but also of great importance for the concepts of function and predicting values from functional relations (Lafon, Chasseigne, & Mullet, 2004). In the context of multiplication and division situations, understanding inverse relations consistently has been found to be more difficult for children than understanding direct relations (e.g., Lafon, Chasseigne, & Mullet, 2004; Nunes, Desli, & Bell, 2003). Stavy and Tirosh (2000) argued that children often fail to understand inverse relations both in science and mathematics because they overextend the rule "the more A − the more B," which is relevant to many situations, by applying it to situations in which the rule is not relevant or is incomplete. For example, when comparing the concentration of sugar in two glasses with mixtures of sugar and water, children aged 4–8 years may say that the water in the glass with two lumps of sugar tastes sweeter than the one in the glass with only one lump, even though the glass with two lumps has twice as much water. They correctly judge that "the more sugar, the sweeter the taste will be," but do not consider the inverse relation between the amount of water and the concentration—the more water, the less sweet the taste will be.

How Well Do School Children Understand Inversion?

Since the understanding of inversion must play a significant part in children's learning about arithmetic and algebra, we need to know whether this concept causes children any particular difficulty. This is a controversial issue.

Piaget's theory made the clear prediction that children in their early years at school might be quite unable to grasp the fact that addition and subtraction cancel each other out. He claimed that the thought processes of children who are in the early part of the concrete operations period (up to the age of roughly 5 or 6 years) are characterized by "irreversibility," by which he meant that, when they saw some transformation, they could not envisage if the results of the opposite transformation would exactly cancel the fist one. If a set of counters was spread out, they could not imagine exactly what it would be like if it were bunched up again, and similarly, if counters were added to the set young children would find it hard to work out how many counters would be left if the same quantity were removed from the set.

Although Piaget often made the claim that young children do not grasp the inversion of arithmetical operations, he only tested this idea toward the end of his life, and reported it in one of his last books (Piaget & Moreau, 2001), in which he and Moreau described an ingenious experiment with children whose ages ranged from 6 to 11 years. Piaget and Moreau asked each child to put together a set of bricks without showing or telling the experimenters how many bricks were in this set. Then they asked the child to carry out a series of transformations on this set, which again only the child could see; they asked the child sometimes to add a number of bricks to the set, sometimes to subtract from it, and also occasionally to multiply the set by a certain number. Finally, the experimenters asked the child how many counters there were in the set, and worked out (by inversion) how many bricks the child had collected in the first place. Having done this and told the children about their conclusion, the experimenters asked the child to explain how they knew the correct number of bricks in the original set when they had never set eyes on these bricks at any stage of the task. Most of the younger children were quite unable to provide an explanation for this apparently uncanny insight. Only children of around 10 years in age or more could invoke the principle of inversion to account for the experimenters' successful inferences.

These results certainly suggest that the inversion principle is not immediately obvious to many young children, but the study did not establish that these children had no understanding of this principle at all. At least two alternative possibilities exist, both of which loom large in subsequent work on children's understanding of inversion. The first, which is usually referred to as a "competence-performance gap" (Stern, 1992), is that children do have a basic understanding of inversion, but are not always able to take complete advantage of it. In some situations, they spot the relevance of inversion; in others they miss it entirely. They may, for example, have a basic grasp of inversion and may use it themselves when solving arithmetical problems, and yet may be unable to realize that, in Piaget and Moreau's indirect task, someone else was making inferences based on inversion.

Stern (1992) herself came to the conclusion that, as far as inversion is concerned, children's competence is prone to outstrip their performance, on the basis of a study in which she gave 7- to 9-year-old children some addition/subtraction sums $(a + b - b)$ that could be solved on the basis of inversion. A child who understands the inverse relation of addition and subtraction should in principle be able work out, for example, that $24 + 17 - 17 = 24$ without having to do any calculation. Stern found that children were more likely to use this inversion "shortcut" when she gave them blocks of sums, all of which took the $a + b - b$ form and therefore could be solved by the inversion shortcut, than when she gave them "mixed" blocks, in which some sums took the $a + b - b$ form and others did not $(a + b - c)$. She concluded that 7-year-olds do have some understanding of the inversion principle, but use it more effectively in some contexts than in others. This led her to argue that their underlying understanding of inversion (their competence) was strong, but that their actual use of this principle (their performance) was fragile.

The second alternative to Piaget's view that inversion is a principle that young children simply cannot grasp is that they understand and use the principle implicitly but have no explicit knowledge of inversion. This, too, would explain their failure to account for the experimenters' inferences in the Piaget and Moreau task. The argument that implicit knowledge of inversion precedes explicit knowledge was made most forcefully by Siegler and Stern (1998) on the basis of the results of a microgenetic study of 7-year-old children solving $a + b - b$ problems. In this study, Siegler and Stern worked with selected children who had shown no sign of using the inversion principle—the "shortcut strategy"—in a pretest. During the course of seven following experimental sessions, many of the children began to take the inversion shortcut with $a + b - b$ problems. However, Siegler and Stern noted that initially the children were usually quite unable to give them an explicit reason for their use of inversion. Explicit justifications tended to come later on, usually in a subsequent session. The authors therefore concluded that children's understanding of inversion is at first entirely implicit.

The evidence for a competence-performance gap in the understanding of inversion and for a developmental progression from implicit to explicit knowledge of the principle certainly provides us with different possible reasons for the children's difficulties with the problem that Piaget and Moreau set them. However, in a general way, these studies reinforce the idea that young children do have a great amount of difficulty in taking advantage of the inversion principle, even if they do have some basic understanding of this principle. In Siegler and Stern's pretest, for example, the majority of the 7-year-old children showed no sign of understanding inversion. It is worth noting too that Piaget almost certainly would have been quite happy to accept Siegler and Stern's claim for a progression from implicit to explicit knowledge, since the main claim in his book *Reflecting Abstraction,* which contained the Piaget and Moreau study, was for a general development by means of reflection from implicit to explicit understanding in all forms of cognitive development.

Even children's successes in inversion problems have sometimes proved dubious. Bisanz, Lefevre, and Gilliland (1989) measured how long it took 6- to 11-year-old children to answer a set of addition and subtraction problems, some of which (a + b − b) could be solved by inversion while others (a + b − c) needed some computation. They argued that children who understood the inversion principle should spend less time in dealing with the inversion problems than with the control problems because they could solve the inversion problems without having to make any calculations. They found that only a small number of children in the 6- to 9-year-old range were noticeably faster on the inversion than on the control problems, and that the number of these children who used the inversion shortcut did not increase between the ages of 6 and 9 years. Children older than this were much more likely to take advantage of the invariance principle.

This result seemed to confirm that most young children are reluctant to use the inversion principle when doing arithmetic and may not show any knowledge about it. But the most remarkable claim made by Bisanz et al. (1989) was that even those children who solved inversion sums more rapidly than control sums may not have had a genuine understanding of inversion. They suggested that some of the children used a strategy that they called "negation," and which they argued was based on a much lower level of understanding than the understanding of inversion. The authors noticed that these children used finger-counting to represent the problems and when, for example, they had to add and then subtract the number 3, they simply put three fingers up to represent the addend and then down again to represent the subtraction, which left them with the number of fingers that they had used to represent the initial quantity. Bisanz et al. argued that these children did not understand the quantitative significance of the addend and the subtrahend being the same number. They simply understood that when you introduce some objects (in this case fingers) and then you remove the same objects, you restore the status quo. This observation does not definitely establish that these children were in fact using this lower-level approach, but Bisanz et al. were right to raise the possibility that they were doing so.

The contrast between the inversion of identity (if you add some objects to x and then take them away, x is as it was in the first place) and the inversion of quantity (if you add a number of objects to x and then subtract the same number of objects from x, x is the same number as it was at the start) is an absorbing one. Bisanz and his colleagues considered this contrast in the context of finger counting, but also pointed out that the issue of identity versus quantity stretches far beyond this particular form of representation.

How can one distinguish between these two forms of understanding inversion? A child who understands the inversion of identity, but not the inversion of quantity, will realize that adding some bricks to an initial set and then removing the identical bricks that were just added (identity) will leave you the same bricks as before. However, this child will not understand that adding a certain number of bricks and then removing different bricks, but the same number as had just been added, leaves you with the same quantity of bricks as you started with. Bryant, Christie, and Rendu (1999, Study 1) set out to compare children's performance in these two kinds of problem. Their aim was to test whether young children understand both kinds of inversion, or only the inversion problems that involve identity.

These experimenters gave 5- and 6-year-old children inversion (a + b − b) and control (a + a − b) problems with sets of Unifix bricks in which they either added and subtracted the same bricks (Identity Condition) or added some bricks and then subtracted completely different bricks (Quantity Condition). They argued that if the children understand the inversion of identity but not of quantity, they should do better in the inversion than in the control problems in the Identity Condition only. In the Quantity Condition, they should do no better with the inversion problems than with the control problems, because they would not be able to understand that equal addends and subtrahends cancel each other out when addends and subtrahend involve different objects. On the other hand, if they understand the inversion of quantity they should solve the inversion problems more easily than the control problems in both conditions.

Both predictions turned out to be right, and the results suggest a more interesting developmental pattern than the authors had imagined. With impressive consistency, the children in both age groups were more successful in solving the inversion than the control problems. This certainly suggests that even at the age of 5 years, many English children do understand and use the inversion principle at a genuinely quantitative level, at any rate with concrete material. On the other hand, the difference between the children's success in the inversion and control problems and the level of their success in the inversion problems were both reliably higher in the Identity than in the Quantity conditions. This second result suggests a developmental pattern. It now seems likely that children progress from understanding inversion in the sense of identity ("if I get mud on my shirt and my Mum washes it off, the shirt is as it was before it got dirty") and quantity ("if I have seven sweets and someone gives me three more, and then I eat three of the original sweets, I'm left with exactly as many sweets as I started with").

In their next study, Bryant et al. (1999, Study 2) showed that many 7-, 8-, and 9-year old children can also use the principle of inversion to help them to solve problems in which the addend and subtrahend are not actually equal. In this study, the experimenters gave the children some quantitative inversion problems (again with bricks) in which the addend and the subtrahend differed by 1 (e.g., 24 + 10 − 9). Although these problems were harder for the children to solve than when the addend equaled the subtrahend (e.g., 24 + 9 − 9), they were still significantly easier than control problems in which the children had to carry out some computation (e.g., 18 + 18 − 11) and could not use the inversion principle. The children's relative success with the new inversion problems (24 + 10 − 9) led Bryant and colleagues to conclude that many of them actually transformed such problems into inversion problems by decomposing either the addend or subtrahend. For example, given the problem 24 + 10 − 9, they would decompose 10 into 9 + 1 and transform the problem into 24 + 9 − 9 + 1.

These two studies produced another result that has been replicated many times since (e.g., Gilmore, 2005; Rasmussen, Ho, & Bisanz, 2003). In each study, a factor analysis of the different inversion tasks and the different control tasks was carried out. Both of these factor analyses, in studies 1 and 2, produced two significant factors, and in each analysis the inversion tasks loaded heavily on one of these factors and the control task on the other. This clear division strongly suggests that two separate and relatively different variables were at play. One variable was the strength of the children's knowledge about the inversion principle and the other their relative ability to compute. The factor on which the inversion scores loaded quite highly represents the first of these variables, and the other factor on which the scores in the control problems loaded represents the second.

The two studies by Bryant et al. (1999) established a much stronger grasp of quantitative inversion in young hearing children than previous work had suggested. This rather optimistic conclusion, which was strongly supported by the results of a later study by Rasmussen et al. (2003), raises a pressing question about deaf children. Do they have as strong a grasp of the crucial inversion principle as do young hearing children?

It is clear that deaf children are at a relative disadvantage in mathematics (Nunes, 2004; Traxler, 2000; Wood, Wood, & Howarth, 1983), but little is known about their understanding of specific mathematical principles (see also Bull, this volume, and Zarfaty, Nunes, & Bryant, 2004). There is, to our knowledge, no investigation to date of deaf children's understanding of the inverse relation between addition and subtraction. Many studies have compared deaf children's performance on arithmetic story problems with the performance of hearing children.

Among the different types of story problems, some are called "direct" and some are called "inverse." In direct problems, the story mentions a particular transformation—for example, getting some more sweets—and the problem is solved through addition. An example for a direct story problem would be: "A girl had six sweets; her Grandmother gave her five sweets; how many does she have now?" In inverse story problems, the operation that represents the solution is the inverse of the transformation referred to in the story. For example: "A girl had some sweets; her Grandmother gave her five sweets; now she has 11 sweets; how many did she have before her Grandmother came to visit?" Comparisons between hearing and deaf children's performance show that the order of difficulty of problems is the same for both groups (e.g., Frostad & Ahlberg, 1999; Hyde, Zevenbergen, & Power, 2003; Nunes & Moreno, 1998): inverse story problems are more difficult than direct problems.[11] However, this does not indicate whether deaf children find it considerably more difficult than hearing children to understand the inverse relation between addition and subtraction or not.

In view of the importance of understanding inversion and the lack of information about deaf children's performance, we designed and recently completed two studies: the first was a comparison of deaf and hearing children's performance on the inverse problems; the second was an intervention study aimed at improving deaf children's performance on inversion problems.

Problem Type Affects Inversion Performance

Inverse problems, as we have shown, can be presented to children in many ways. Items can be presented within the context of concrete situations (for

---

1. Ansell and Pagliaro (2006) found some differences between hearing and deaf children in order of difficulty of problems, but the set of problems they analyzed did not include "start unknown" problems, which are the inverse problems mentioned here.

example, a row of bricks hidden under a cloth, to which a number of bricks is added and then subtracted), of word problems (for example, there were some objects in a box, and then some items were added and the same number was subtracted), or simply as numerical problems (for example, "what is 8 + 6 − 6?").

Young children, aged 3–5 years, solve problems in the context of concrete situations significantly better than when equivalent sums are presented only verbally (e.g., Hughes, 1986; Levine, Jordan, & Huttenlocher, 1992). Bryant et al. (1999) also found that children were significantly more successful with inversion problems that involved concrete material than with story problems presented only verbally. So, it was decided to use in this study the relatively cautious approach of using concrete situations and word problems when administering the inversion questions to deaf children.

Nunes, Bryant, and Pretzlik (2006) found that deaf children perform significantly better on story problems when these are presented with the support of pictures that display the sequence of events as in a cartoon, where all pictures are presented simultaneously. Thus, the method chosen in this study for the story problems was to complement the linguistic information with drawings that depicted each step in the story and which were simultaneously available to the children while the story problem was presented.

This first study involved 23 deaf and 130 hearing children in their first year of primary school. All the deaf children were attending either a special school for the deaf or a mainstream school with a special unit; none of them was fully integrated in a mainstream school without additional support. Six of them were moderately to severely deaf and seven were profoundly deaf; 10 of the deaf children had cochlear implants. The mean age of the children in the deaf group was 6;7 (range 5;2 to 8;3). The hearing children's mean age was 5;8 (range 5;0 to 6;7). These age differences reflect the fact that deaf children's entry into primary school is often delayed by their teachers and parents for a variety of reasons (e.g. to allow them to develop language and communication further). The deaf children were tested in their preferred mode of communication by a fluent signer. Although some of them used oral communication in the classroom, they often signed during problem solving.

In fact, in this study the inversion items were only part of a collection of varied tasks that measured several different aspects of the children's mathematical knowledge, but only the inversion items are considered here. The children had to try to solve six inversion problems, three in the context of a concrete situation and three as part of a story problem presented along with drawings.

In the concrete situation, the children were shown a row of Unifix bricks joined together and were asked to count the bricks. Then the experimenter partially hid the row, so that it was no longer possible for the children to count the bricks, but each end of the row was left exposed, so that the additions and subtractions would be seen by the children. The experimenter added one lot of bricks to one side of the row and subtracted the same number from the other side. These problems measure the understanding of quantitative inversion, and Bryant et al. (1999) have shown them to be more difficult than problems in which the same bricks, and not just the same number of bricks, are added and taken away (identity problems). The children were asked how many bricks remained after the experimenter added and took away bricks. The problems presented with bricks were: $7 + 5 - 5$; $9 + 4 - 4$; and $6 + 5 - 5$.

In the story problems, the experimenter talked to the children about some objects (ice lollies, books, and marbles, respectively for each of the problems) that had been placed in a box and showed them a picture of the box. In this picture, the total number of objects that were inside the box was marked with a numeral on the outside. Then the experimenter told them that a teacher came and put some more objects in the box (of the same type already in the box) and that some children came later and took the same number of items out. The children were asked how many objects were left. The problems were: $8 + 6 - 6$; $9 + 5 - 5$; $7 + 4 - 4$.

The addition facts involved in the first sequence (e.g., $7 + 5$) were too difficult for children in their first year in school. So, if they succeeded in obtaining the correct answer, they were very likely to have used their understanding of inversion. The children were given one point for each correct answer. In order not to put the deaf children at a disadvantage, no explanation for the strategy used was required in order for the child to pass the item.

In the analyses of these results, the difference between the children's performance in the items presented with bricks and those presented as story problems was not significant, and so, thenceforth we pooled the two kinds of item. Another point to make about the analysis was that they routinely controlled and adjusted for age differences. This was because the deaf children were on average older than the children in the hearing group. Since this difference was significant, age differences were controlled in subsequent analyses.

The mean number of correct responses in the inversion problems (out of 6) was 2.05 for the hearing children and 1.87 for the deaf children. Thus, even though the hearing children were younger, they performed better than the deaf children. The effect size for this difference was a large one.

The deaf children were behind in understanding the inverse relation between addition and subtraction, despite the fact that many of the problems were given to them under conditions that previous research (Nunes et al., 2006) had shown to be helpful to deaf children. This delay is serious, because children's understanding of the inverse relation between addition and subtraction is one of the logical principles that predicts mathematics achievement.

Past research (Nunes et al., 2007b) has also shown that hearing children who were identified as being at risk for difficulties in mathematics by their low performance in an assessment of their understanding of logical principles made significant progress if taught about these logical principles. They also showed significant gains in mathematics achievement, in comparison to a control group that did not receive this teaching. So, it is important to see whether deaf children too would benefit from instruction about the inversion principle. A second study provided an answer to this question.

Inversion Intervention

Intervention studies are valuable in at least two ways. First, they allow for a test of a causal hypothesis about why some children have difficulties in mathematics, as discussed earlier. Second, they open the way for teachers to use findings from research more readily in the classroom. But intervention studies involve at least two steps and for that reason they are time–consuming and costly. The first and crucial one is to show that a specific intervention is successful. If an intervention is not successful, it does not mean that the children cannot learn—only that the particular method used is not effective. In the case of interventions to improve deaf children's mathematics skills, it is necessary to show that the intervention provided to the deaf children improves their performance in inversion problems. The second, equally important step is to find out whether this improvement has an impact on the children's general mathematics achievement. The study described here only took the first step toward improving deaf children's mathematical learning: it was a test of the effectiveness of a particular inversion intervention. The second step, which will assess whether the improvement on inversion also affects mathematics learning, is still under investigation.

The design of the intervention to improve deaf children's understanding of inversion, described here, took into account the results of earlier work with hearing children. Nunes et al. (2007a) compared two different ways of demonstrating the inversion principle to hearing children. The children who took part in this earlier study were in their second and third years in school, aged 7 and 8 years.

The aim of the previous study with hearing children was to see how well two different methods of teaching the inversion principle worked. These two intervention methods were (a) a concrete and visual demonstration, in which the children saw bricks being added to a row, which was partially hidden under a cloth (further details of this procedure are presented later in this chapter), and received feedback by counting the bricks in the row after the two operations had been carried out; and (b) a verbal, calculator demonstration, in which the children, after answering the question, entered the operations into a calculator as they said the arithmetic sentence and checked the result.

The effectiveness of these two methods was measured by randomly assigning the participant children to two intervention groups and also to a control group. The children in both intervention groups were taught individually by an experimenter in two intervention sessions, using one or the other of the two methods just described. The children in the control group also participated in two individual sessions with the experimenter, during which they memorized the results of the first additions and subtractions included in the intervention trials. So, the children in the control group had the benefit of working with the experimenter on a numerical task, but this task did not involve thinking about inversion. This was considered an ideal control group because several studies (Bryant et al., 1999; Gilmore, 2005; Rasmussen et al., 2003) had shown previously that knowledge of sums and understanding inversion load on different factors that describe children's arithmetic competence.

All the children in the study were given a pretest before the two individual sessions with the experimenter and a post-test soon after these two sessions. The aim of these two tests was to assess the effects of the three different kinds of experiences that were given to the children in the two intervening sessions. The pre- and post-tests were identical and consisted entirely of two types of abstract number problems: these were exact inverse problems (e.g., $8 + 7 - 7$) and inverse plus decomposition problems (e.g., $8 + 7 - 6$) in which the difference between the number added and the number subtracted is 1. An earlier study (Bryant et al., 1999) had shown that the latter problems are relatively hard, and significantly harder than straightforward inversion problems, even though only one extra step is required to solve this type of problem. The added step is to realize that the value will change by 1 if the difference between what was added and what was subtracted is 1.

All the groups did better in the post-test after the two intervening sessions than in the pretest. However, the improvement from pre- to post-test was markedly, and significantly, greater in the two intervention groups than in the control group; the extent of this improvement was roughly the same for two intervention groups (there was no significant difference between the children in the two groups). So, it was concluded that both intervention methods were effective and that, in principle, either one could be adopted in a study with deaf children. However, during the intervention sessions, there were signs that the verbal-calculator method might be difficult for deaf children: it was sometimes necessary to repeat the verbal-calculator procedure for the children in this group to realize that they had returned to the starting number in the inversion items, or to $n +/-1$ in the inversion plus decomposition items. This method seemed to place greater demands on the children's working memory, and thus might not be as effective with deaf children, who have consistently shown lower scores on working-memory verbal tasks than their hearing cohorts (for a review, see Marschark, 1993). Therefore, in the new intervention with deaf children, only the visual-concrete demonstration training procedure was used.

In designing this new intervention, it was also borne in mind the fact that children's understanding of inversion is relatively independent of their calculation ability. This clear and consistent pattern of results prompted us to include in the new intervention study with deaf children a set of control items that could not be solved by understanding inversion. We predicted that the children receiving the intervention would make significant progress on the inversion items but not on the control items.

The intervention study with deaf children consisted of a pretest, two sessions of intervention, immediate post-test, and delayed post-test design. The pretest came just before the first of the two intervention sessions, and the immediate post-test soon after the second intervention session. The length of time between the immediate and the delayed post-test varied between the children and depended on their availability for the final test. The time from the first to the second post-test varied from 2 to 4 weeks.

In the pretest, the children were given a set of inversion problems and also several control items that they could solve only by computation and not through applying the inversion principle. They also answered the matrices subtest of the British Abilities Scale (BASII; Elliott, 1997), which provides a measure of their nonverbal intelligence. In this test, the children are presented with 2×2 and 3×3 matrices that contain drawings that vary in one or more dimensions. The dimensions used in the initial items, which would be those that such young children would solve, are form, size, number, orientation, or a combination of these dimensions (e.g., boat-like drawings may have different forms for the hull and different numbers of banners). The children are presented with the sequence of items until they reach a stopping point, determined by the number of items that they fail. Our reason for giving this subtest was to use the children's scores on it as a covariate in the analysis of the effect of the intervention. In the immediate post-tests, we gave the children the same inversion and control problems as in the pretest. In the delayed post-test, for reasons described later, the children were only asked to solve the inversion problems that they had been given in the pretest and immediate post-test.

The deaf children, who participated in the first of the studies described in this chapter, also took part in this intervention study, along with four more children who had recently joined the schools where the project was carried out. A total of 27 children were randomly assigned either to an inversion intervention group ($n = 14$) or to a control group ($n = 13$), with randomization carried out within each school so that the number of children in each condition by school was approximately the same.

The pretest and the immediate post–test contained the six items about the inverse relation between addition and subtraction that were given to the children in Study 1: three in the context of the bricks and three in the context of story problems. Figure 7–1 shows an example of the drawings that we used for the story problems.

The children were also given six inversion-plus-decomposition items in each of these tests, three in the context of bricks and three in the context of story problems. These items serve an important function in the measure of children's understanding of inversion. Children cannot solve them simply by repeating the first number (i.e., $8 + 5 - 4$ is not equal to 8): they have to be able to combine inversion with decomposition (i.e., by combining their understanding of inversion with the realization that 5 is the same as $4 + 1$, they will realize that the answer has to be $8 + 1$). So, these items are a measure of the understanding of the principle of inversion, but they are more difficult than simple inversion because they require the children to consider two mathematical principles at the same time.

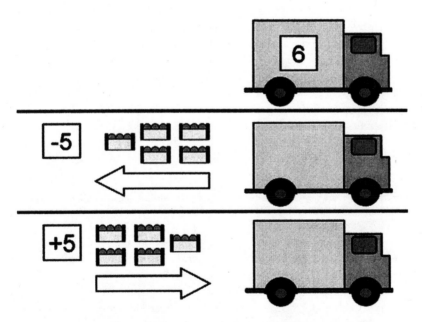

Figure 7–1. Example of a cartoon used to support the presentation of an inversion story problem in the pre- and post-tests. The oral presentation was: There were 6 boxes of fruit in a lorry. The men unloaded 5 at one stop and loaded 5 at the next stop. How many boxes of fruit are in the lorry now?

Finally, the children were also given a series of control problems that could not be solved by using their knowledge of the inverse principle. The control problems were: $7 + 7 - 4$; $9 + 8 - 3$; $6 + 5 - 2$; $7 + 6 - 2$; $8 + 9 - 3$; and $9 + 9 - 3$. Three of these were presented in a concrete way using bricks and the other three as word problems. In the delayed post-test, the children were given all the inversion problems that were in the pretest and the immediate post-test, but none of the control problems.

A final note about the pre- and post-tests: the story problems are considered as transfer items because, during the training sessions, the children were not presented with story problems. All the problems during the training sessions involved concrete objects.

The children were randomly assigned to two groups: one was the intervention group and the other the control group. Two intervention sessions were held, and the total amount of time taken for the two sessions (around 20 minutes for each session) was approximately the same across the two groups. During these intervention sessions, the children in the intervention group worked on inversion problems and the children in the control group worked on another mathematical task, in which they were taught how to compose sums of money using coins of different denominations (different combinations of 2 and 1, 5 and 1, 10 and 1, and 20 and 1 coins). These problems did not make any demands on the children's understanding of inversion. All the children were taught on a one-to-one basis—one child, one instructor—and all went through the two sessions with the same experimenter-instructor.

Each child in the intervention group was given a total of 33 inversion problems, 21 in the first and 12 in the second session. After the child had offered a solution to any problem, the child was allowed to count the objects in order to establish whether the answer had been correct or not. The instructor then constructed with the child an explanation for why, in the inversion items, the amount was the same, and in the inversion plus decomposition items, why the amount differed from the original by one. These guided explanations aimed to offer each child the opportunity to learn by experiencing concrete inversion problems and construct an explicit verbal account of inversion.

The numbers used in the addition and subtraction for each trial in the intervention sessions were always either the same or they differed by 1. In each of the first nine problems, the instructor showed the child a column of bricks of one color and counted them. The bricks were then partially covered with a cloth, so that the ends of the column still showed. Thus, the child could still see how many bricks were added or subtracted, but could not see all the bricks in the column. Then the instructor added some bricks to and subtracted some from it. The bricks that were added were of a different color from those in the initial row. Because the number of bricks added and subtracted was sometimes the same but sometimes it differed by 1, the children could not simply repeat the initial number as the answer but needed to keep thinking about the transformations made to the initial row of bricks for each problem. After the addition and subtraction, the instructor asked the child how many bricks there were in the column, and after the child had answered, the cloth was removed so that the child could count the bricks to see whether the answer was right or not. Then the explanations were jointly constructed, with the tutor complementing the child's explanation when it was necessary. This process proved of value in clarifying some later results, in the case of inversion plus decomposition items. Many of the children who could see with no difficulty that, for example, adding 5 and subtracting 4 would not lead back to the same number of bricks, could not make the second inversion required in these problems: if the number subtracted is one *less*, the number in the row is one *more*. The often knew that the number was different but could not decide whether it should be greater or smaller than the initial number.

In some of the problems, the bricks were added to and subtracted from the same end of the initial row. In this case, the difference in color allowed the child to see that identical bricks had been added and then subtracted. The reason for giving these problems was to help each child to make a connection between identity problems and inversion problems, in which the number is the same but the items different. In the other problems in this set of nine problems, the instructor added bricks to one end of the row and then subtracted bricks from the other end. Thus the addend and the subtrahend were different bricks, and also differently colored bricks. In these problems, the children were encouraged to place the bricks that had been removed next to those that had been added at the feedback stage. They did this before they were allowed to count all the bricks in the column. Thus, the children could see that the number added and subtracted made a row of bricks of the same length.

The children then continued to work with bricks for a further set of six problems, but no color cues were available in these last trials: all the bricks were the same color. The final block of problems in the first session consisted of carrying out a similar procedure using other objects (e.g., pencils, marbles, cards) that were placed into opaque containers; further items were then added and subtracted. The second session was carried out on a different day. Whenever possible, this was the day after the first session. It consisted of six trials with bricks and six trials with objects, and the same methods were used.

The immediate post-test was carried out on a different day, again if possible, the day after the end of the training, and the delayed post-test 2–4 weeks later, depending on the child's availability. There was a loss of two participants for the immediate post-test and one for the delayed post-test, all from the control group.

Table 7–1.   Pretest Results by Intervention Group

	Control ($n = 10$)		Intervention ($n = 14$)	
	Mean	SD	Mean	SD
Age in fractional years	7.01	1.00	6.72	1.27
BAS matrices raw score	8.33	3.68	9.00	5.46
Inversion	1.75	1.60	1.87	1.30
Inversion plus decomposition	1.00	0.85	0.93	1.14
Control items	0.01	0.00	0.86	1.17

For all three inversion tasks, maximum score = 6.

None of the children achieved a perfect score in the inversion items at pretest. Table 7–1 presents the results for each of the groups at pretest, excluding the children who did not attend the post-test sessions. Small differences were noted between the two groups at pretest but only one of the differences was significant: the difference in performance on the control items. As the difference in the BAS-matrices score was in favor of the intervention group, it was decided to enter the BAS score and the relevant pretest score as covariates in the comparison between the intervention and the control group at post-test. This would provide the most stringent test of the effectiveness of the intervention for the number of participants in the study (with just over 20 participants, no more than two covariates could be used).

Preliminary analyses established that there were no significant gender differences on any of the three testing occasions, which allowed us to pool the boys' and girls' results. The reliability of our measures was good and, as the reliability for the post-tests was high when bricks and story problems were considered as part of the same measure, the analyses use a total score, combining the two types of problem.

The most important result was that the intervention group significantly out-performed the control group in the inversion items both at the immediate and delayed post-tests. Table 7–2 displays the adjusted means (controlling for pretest performance on the BAS-matrices and score in the inversion items), the standard error of the means, and the confidence intervals by group. It shows that the children in the intervention group managed much better in these post-tests than did the control group children. Thus, the instruction about inversion was successful and effective.

In contrast, the comparison between the control and intervention groups did not produce a significant result when the dependent measure was the number of correct answers to the control items. As predicted, the children in the intervention group made progress in the inversion but not in the control items. However, there was no significant difference between the groups in the inversion plus decomposition items. The intervention group showed some progress in the inversion plus decomposition items,

Table 7–2.   Adjusted Means and Standard Error of the Mean by Group

Group			95% Confidence Interval	
	Mean	Standard Error	Lower Bound	Upper Bound
Inversion Items				
Immediate Post-test				
Control Group	0.82	0.42	−.050	1.68
Intervention Group	2.56	0.35	1.83	3.29
Delayed Post-test				
Control Group	1.54	0.38	0.74	2.34
Intervention Group	3.47	0.33	2.79	4.16
Control Items				
Immediate Post-test				
Control Group	0.50	0.10	0.28	0.71
Intervention Group	0.54	0.09	0.35	0.73

Adjusted means and standard error of the mean by group was calculated by controlling for BAS-matrices and inversion score at pretest; results are for the immediate and delayed post-test on the inversion and control items (maximum score = 6).

going from 0.9 correct answers at pretest, to 1.3 at immediate post-test, to 1.7 at delayed post-test, whereas the control group's means were equal to 1 on all three occasions. However, this small improvement in the intervention group did not lead to a significant difference between the groups.

Thus, the deaf children in our intervention did much better after the intervention than before it in inversion items but not on control problems, as predicted. This pattern establishes that the intervention children's superiority over the control group in the inversion problems was specifically due to an improvement in their understanding of inversion as a direct result of the intervention and cannot be dismissed as the product of a newly acquired computation skill.

This positive result demonstrates that it is possible to promote deaf children's understanding of the inverse relation between addition and subtraction by using the approach that we adopted in this intervention. This approach was to choose the inversion items carefully so that they followed the order in which they are learned, to provide adequate support in the form of visual cues, to require the children to think continuously about the transformations performed to the numbers of objects by using both inversion and inversion plus decomposition items, and to construct jointly with the children inversion accounts for the solutions.

It is not clear why no equivalent effects of our intervention were observed in the inversion plus decomposition items. We think that the best explanation is that this task involves inversion twice. First, the children have to think of the inverse relation between addition and subtraction, and then they also need to consider the inverse relation of the difference between the addend and the subtrahend to the final result: if one less brick is taken away, there will be one more brick left in the row. Our informal observations during the intervention support this idea. For example, one boy, seeing the transformations $+ 5 - 4$, said "you took less," but when he was asked how many items were now left, he seemed unable to carry out the second inversion and produce the answer $a - 1$. Some children spontaneously said that the amount now would be "not the same" as before but were then in doubt about what the correct answer was. Thus, children may well need extra help, over and above the help provided in the intervention, to learn to solve this kind of problem.

Summary and Implications

The research described in this chapter is relevant to the study of children's mathematical development in two ways. One concerns deaf children's understanding and use of the principle of inversion. The other concerns the understanding of inversion by children in general.

Two new studies reported here tell us something about deaf children's mathematical reasoning. The first study showed that deaf children found it relatively difficult to use the inversion principle. Their scores in the basic inversion problems were significantly lower than those of a comparable group of hearing children who were given the same tasks. This difference could have two explanations. One, which is perhaps simpler, is that their logical reasoning in general, and including their understanding of inversion, is delayed for one or more possible reasons—for example, as a consequence of a linguistic delay or lack of stimulation. A less straightforward interpretation, but one which is entirely plausible, is that the difference was one of performance, not of competence. Deaf children's entry into school is delayed, as indicated earlier, and school is one of the environments in which their use of logical principles such as inversion would be stimulated.

Whatever the reasons for the deaf children's difficulties with inversion in the first study, the results from a second, intervention study established that they cannot be due to a serious conceptual impairment in this group. The strong effect of only two short intervention sessions on the children's solutions to the inversion problems shows that the concept of inversion poses no insurmountable barrier to deaf children. This suggests that they were ready to learn about inversion and had all the necessary logical abilities to do so—that is, their difficulties were due to some peripheral, perhaps even trivial, obstacle, and not to any central cognitive difficulty. This supports the interpretation of their weak results in terms of performance rather than competence.

Irrespective of the interpretation of these findings, it is widely recognized that the inversion principle lies at the heart of additive reasoning. The discovery that deaf children under-perform in inversion problems in relation to their age and intelligence suggests that something must be done about this so that they have a good chance for a sound start in their mathematics learning in school.

This conclusion raises an obvious, more general question. This question, which takes us to the second of the two issues in this discussion, is about the cognitive basis for children's understanding of the inversion principle. The results of our two studies are relevant to this question in various ways. One clear point is that the relatively high scores of the 5-year-old hearing children in the first study confirms the claim made by Bryant et al. (1999) that many children in their first year at school typically have some understanding of inversion and are able to use this understanding to solve some inversion problems. This consistent early success suggests that the origin of the understanding may be already set by the informal experiences that the children have had before they ever go to school.

Yet, this optimistic finding contrasts with the rather dismal performance of children of this age and even of older children in several other studies. For example, the children in the studies by Stern and by Siegler and Stern described earlier were actually older than those in our first study, and yet they made many errors in the inversion tasks they were given. Our explanation for this apparent discrepancy is about the material used in these other studies. The children were given abstract sums in the Stern and Sigler and Stern studies, whereas most of the problems in our studies were about concrete material. These discrepancies between children's performance in problems presented as abstract symbols and with concrete materials or with real situations was documented in the introduction and was used to help make decisions about the design of the studies reported here. In the case of inversion problems, the explanation for the difference between concrete problems and those with number only may very well have something to do with the origin of the understanding of the inversion principle. The Bryant et al. (1999) study suggests that children understand the inversion of identity (the same thing added and then subtracted) earlier and that this eventually leads to the understanding of the inversion of quantity (the same amount added and then subtracted). The inversion of identity is about concrete material, and if inversion of identity leads to inversion of quantity, it is highly likely that children's first understanding of inversion of quantity should be about concrete material.

The next issue to be considered here is the significance of the intervention study for theories about the understanding of inversion by children in general and by deaf children in particular. The same intervention techniques used in this study were used successfully with hearing children (Nunes et al., 2007a). This intervention was effective in both studies in that it did improve the children's scores in inversion tasks. However, only this study included in the post-tests problems about which the children had not received instruction. Therefore, this study could show that the children in the intervention group learned about inversion in a specific, but flexible and abstract way, as they were able to use their new knowledge in the novel context of story problems, which had not been included in the intervention.

The fact that the children in this instance were all deaf does not reduce the general implications of this finding. We think that it is safe to assume that the same instruction would produce at least as good effects with children who are not deaf. After all, the performance of the deaf children in the first experiment showed that they had a relatively hard time with inversion problems, which means that they would be less likely to benefit from the experiences and explanations in our two intervention sessions.

There are several possible reasons why this training was so effective. One reason might be that the effect of the intervention was to teach them about the logical principle itself. Many of the children in the intervention group may have had no inkling, implicit or explicit, about the inversion principle. This suggestion may be true, but it seems improbable to us given that the children improved so much after so little teaching. It is hard, though not impossible, to believe that children can learn about a basic logical principle so easily and quickly.

Another possibility is that the intervention bridged the gap between competence and performance that Stern (1992) originally suggested as the main feature of children's answers—particularly their incorrect answers—to inversion problems. In other words, the children might not have been learning the inversion principle, which they knew already, but rather about how to put it into effect.

A final possibility is that the intervention helped the children to make their implicit knowledge of inversion explicit through the connections that they made between the easier idea of inversion when the items added and subtracted are the same and the more sophisticated idea that a number remains the same if the transformations cancel each other even though the items added and subtracted are not the same. This is a plausible explanation, since the children could have become progressively more aware that, by adding and subtracting the same number of objects to a set, the initial number did not change. However, as yet no direct evidence suggests that the teaching worked by helping children to cross the implicit-explicit divide. This idea should be the subject of new research. If further research shows this third idea to be correct, one would conclude that there may be two different ways in which children's implicit knowledge can become explicit. One is through the children reflecting on their own knowledge and experiences, as Piaget (2001) suggested in his last great book. The other is through some form of instruction, as seems to have happened in our intervention study.

Finally, the implications of the negative results in the inversion plus decomposition items should be considered. Negative results in an intervention study are often impossible to explain. Usually, one cannot say whether they happened because the hypothesis (that children learn some concept through certain kinds of experience) was wrong or because the teaching method was not a good one. However, the intervention produced a combination of positive and negative results, since the intervention did work with the inversion problems but not with inversion plus decomposition problems. The fact that the intervention improved the children's scores in the inversion, but not in the inversion plus decomposition problems can, as already suggested, be explained quite plausibly. The two sessions of training were just enough for inversion but not for the extra step of decomposition: adding that new step made the more complex problems inaccessible to intervention effects. This idea can, of course, be tested.

In conclusion, these studies confirm the value of looking at highly specific aspects of deaf children's mathematical understanding in order to enhance their progress in mathematics. Interventions specifically targeted to help deaf children (and probably hearing children as well) overcome particular mathematical difficulties can be of great value. In the work with deaf children, it still is necessary to investigate, as Nunes et al. (2007b) did with hearing children, whether overcoming these particular difficulties with logical reasoning will have an impact on their mathematical learning in school.

Acknowledgments

This study was supported by Grant #G21 from the RNID. We are extremely grateful for their support and also to the children and teachers whose generous participation made this study possible.

References

Ansell, E., & Pagliaro, C. (2006). The relative difficulty of signed arithmetic story problems for primary level deaf and hard-of-hearing students. *Journal of Deaf Studies and Deaf Education, 11,* 154–170.

Bisanz, J., Lefevre, J.-A., & Gilliland, S. (1989). *Developmental changes in the use of logical principles in mental arithmetic.* Paper presented at the Society for Research in Child Development, Kansas.

Bradley, L., & Bryant, P. (1983). Categorising sounds and learning to read—a causal connection. *Nature, 301,* 419–421.

Bryant, P., Christie, C., & Rendu, A. (1999). Children's understanding of the relation between addition and subtraction: Inversion, identity and decomposition. *Journal of Experimental Child Psychology, 74,* 194–212.

Canobi, K. H., Reeve, R. A., & Pattison, P. E. (1998). The role of conceptual understanding in children's addition problem solving. *Developmental Psychology, 34,* 882–891.

Elliott, C. D. (1997). *British ability scales (BAS II): early years* (2nd ed.). Windsor: NFER-Nelson.

Frostad, P., & Ahlberg, A. (1999). Solving story-based arithmetic problems: Achievement of children with hearing impairment and their interpretation of meaning. *Journal of Deaf Studies and Deaf Education, 4,* 283–298.

Geary, D. (1994). *Children's mathematical development: Research and practical applications.* Washington, DC: American Psychological Association.

Gilmore, C. K. (2005). Children's understanding of the inverse relationship between addition and subtraction. Doctoral dissertation, University of Oxford, UK.

Hughes, M. (1986). *Children and number.* Oxford: Blackwell.

Hyde, M., Zevenbergen, R., & Power, D. (2003). Deaf and hard of hearing students' performance on arithmetic word problems. *American Annals of the Deaf, 148,* 56–64.

Kieran, C. (1981). Concepts associated with the equality symbol. *Educational Studies in Mathematics, 12,* 317–326.

Kieran, C. (1997). Mathematical concepts at the secondary school level: The learning of algebra and functions. In T. Nunes & P. Bryant (Eds.), *Learning and teaching mathematics. An international perspective* (pp. 133–158). Hove, U.K.: Psychology Press.

Lafon, P., Chasseigne, G., & Mullet, E. (2004). Functional learning among children, adolescents and young adults. *Journal of Experimental Child Psychology, 88,* 334–347.

Levine, S. C., Jordan, N. C., & Huttenlocher, J. (1992). Development of calculation abilities in young children. *Journal of Experimental Child Psychology, 53,* 72–203.

Marschark, M. (1993). *Psychological development of deaf children.* New York: Oxford University Press.

Nunes, T. (2004). *Teaching mathematics to deaf children.* London: Whurr.

Nunes, T., Bryant, P., Bell, D., Evans, D., & Hallett, D. (2007a). Teaching Children about the Inverse Relation between Addition and Subtraction. *Mathematical Thinking and Learning,* under review.

Nunes, T., Bryant, P., Evans, D., Bell, D., Gardner, S., Gardner, A., & Carraher, J. (2007b). The contribution of logical reasoning to the learning of mathematics in primary school. *British Journal of Developmental Psychology, 25,* 147–166.

Nunes, T., Bryant, P., & Pretzlik, U. (2006) *Using deaf children's visual skills to promote mathematics learning.* Paper presented at the 19th Meeting of the International Society for the Study of Behavioural Development, August, Melbourne.

Nunes, T., & Moreno, C. (1998). Is hearing impairment a cause of difficulties in learning mathematics? In C. Donlan (Ed.), *The development of mathematical skills* (pp. 227–254). Hove, U.K.: Psychology Press.

Nunes, T., Desli, D., & Bell, D. (2003). The development of children's understanding of intensive quantities. *International Journal of Educational Research, 39,* 652–675.

Piaget, J. (1952). *The child's conception of number.* London: Routledge and Kegan Paul.

Piaget, J. (2001) *Studies in reflecting abstraction.* Hove UK: Psychology Press.

Piaget, J., & Moreau, A. (2001). The inversion of arithmetic operations (R. L. Campbell, Trans.). In J. Piaget (Ed.), *Studies in reflecting abstraction* (pp. 69–86). Hove U.K.: Psychology Press.

Rasmussen, C., Ho, E., & Bisanz, J. (2003). Use of the mathematical principle of inversion in young children. *Journal of Experimental Child Psychology, 85,* 89–102.

Robinson, K. M., Ninowski, J. E., & Gray, M. L. (2006). Children's understanding of the arithmetic concepts of inversion and associativity. *Journal of Experimental Child Psychology, 94,* 349–362.

Siegler, R. S., & Stern, E. (1998). Conscious and unconscious strategy discoveries: A microgenetic analysis. *Journal of Experimental Psychology-General, 127,* 377–397.

Stavy, R., & Tirosh, D. (2000). *How students (mis-)understand science and mathematics. Intuitive rules.* New York: Teachers College Press.

Stern, E. (1992). Spontaneous used of conceptual mathematical knowledge in elementary school children. *Contemporary Educational Psychology, 17,* 266–277.

Stern, E. (2006). *Transitions in mathematics: from intuitive quantification to symbol-based mathematics.* Paper presented at the ISSBD meeting, July, Melbourne.

Traxler, C. B. (2000). The Stanford Achievement Test, 9th Edition: National norming and performance standards for deaf and hard-of-hearing students. *Journal of Deaf Studies and Deaf Education, 5,* 337–348.

Vilette, B. (2002). Do you children grasp the inverse relation between addition and subtraction? Evidence against early arithmetic. *Cognitive Development, 17,* 1365–1383.

Wood, D., Wood, H., & Howarth, P. (1983). Mathematical abilities of deaf school leavers. *British Journal of Developmental Psychology, 1,* 67–73.

Zarfaty, Y., Nunes, T., & Bryant, P. (2004). The performance of young deaf children in spatial and temporal number tasks. *Journal of Deaf Studies and Deaf Education, 9,* 315–326.

Chapter 8

Deaf Learners and Mathematical Problem Solving

Ronald R. Kelly

One could take a number of approaches in discussing the kind of cognitive underpinnings that deaf[1] students need in order to facilitate their learning and thinking skills across all learning environments, from K–12 and post-secondary settings to future jobs. The focus here will be on the *cognitive tools* suggested by the work of Vygotsky (1962, 1978), who emphasized the importance of children incorporating into their thinking processes the concepts, symbols, mental strategies, and problem-solving procedures that are shared and used by others. As children grow and mature, they need to acquire a variety of cognitive tools that will enable them to think about, discuss, and respond to situations and problems effectively (Ormrod, 2006), so that they can interact with their instructors and peers in educational settings as well as understand pertinent reading materials.

Problem solving for all content domains is an integrative cognitive process that draws upon a broad range of one's knowledge and skills to understand a problem and successfully devise a solution. For example, mathematical word problems describe situations involving numerical relationships that must be interpreted and grasped, followed by computations to obtain the answer (Whimbey & Lochhead, 1991). Successful problem solving requires that one understands and spells out precisely what numerical relationships are being described so that the problem solution can be set up properly to guide the computations (p. 239). Although this description for solving mathematical word problems appears to be relatively straightforward, it requires a depth and integration of relevant knowledge

---

1. The term *deaf* refers to both deaf and hard-of-hearing students. *English* refers to any spoken/written language.

(Ormrod, 2006). Mayer (1992) demonstrated that solving a mathematical word problem involves knowledge of the English language, facts about the world, different problem types, strategic techniques for planning and monitoring the solution, and procedures or a sequence of operations to compute the answer (pp. 458–459). All this, in addition to quantitative reasoning, which considers the numerical information presented and uses the rules of mathematics to deduce a numerical answer. Thus, it can be seen that mathematical problem solving is a complex thinking process that involves (a) comprehension skills to understand specific problem tasks at hand and (b) drawing upon one's integrated relevant knowledge to develop appropriate solutions.

The importance of developing good problem-solving skills is widely accepted. However, considerable evidence indicates that deaf students are not developing sufficient skills with respect to reading comprehension and mathematical procedures. Qi and Mitchell (2007) recently reported on three decades of large-scale, nationwide, academic-achievement testing of K–12 deaf students in the United States, conducted by the Gallaudet Research Institute. For the reading comprehension subtests, their data show that, from 1974 to 2003, five cohorts (1974, 1983, 1990, 1996, 2003) of deaf students' performance increased slightly each year from ages 8–17, but at age 17 their median performance never exceeded the fourth grade equivalent (age 9) for any of the five cohorts. For the mathematics performance of the same cohorts over the three decades, 17-year-olds achieved the equivalent of sixth grade in mathematics problem solving—two grade equivalents higher than for reading comprehension. Results were similar for mathematics procedures where, by the ages of 16–17, the deaf students generally achieved about the sixth grade level during these three decades, except for the 1983 and 1990 samples, when they reached the grade equivalent of 7.5.

Qi and Mitchell found that three patterns emerged from the 30-year historical trends. First, deaf students' performance has been consistently below hearing students. Second, this achievement gap is larger for reading than for mathematics. And third, these gaps between deaf students and hearing students have not closed over the past three decades. Almost no change has occurred in the central tendency of academic achievement among the deaf student population from 1974 to 2003, based on their Stanford Achievement Test (SAT) performance.

The reality of deaf students' academic readiness for college-level study has long been known. Allen (1994) reported data showing that, although two-thirds of the severely to profoundly deaf students leaving high school from 1992–1994 attended some type of postsecondary institution, only one-fourth read at the fifth grade level or above. Furthermore, Allen estimated that only about 8% of these college-bound deaf students read at the eighth-grade level or higher. More recently, data show that for college-bound deaf students who took the American College Test (ACT), five entering freshman cohorts from 2002–2006 had average ACT composite scores at least one standard deviation below the general population of students (NTID Annual Report, 2006). For these deaf students, only 20%, on average, met or exceeded the ACT College Readiness Benchmarks (ACT, 2005) for English and Reading, while 10% and 15%, on average, met or exceeded the benchmarks for science reasoning and mathematics, respectively. Deaf students' academic readiness for college is a factor that most certainly influences their performance in mathematics and problem solving, as well as all other academic subjects.

Mathematical Problem Solving of Deaf Students

In 1995, an initial study was designed and implemented that became the catalyst for a decade of related research studies to better understand deaf students' mathematical problem solving and what related skills might contribute to their success in that domain. This modest study by Mousley and Kelly (1998) examined deaf college students' abilities to explain their understanding of a problem and its solution in both sign language and in writing. The participating students were given two types of challenging problems to solve: mathematical word problems and a manipulative visual puzzle that did not require reading. The latter provided a nonverbal problem-solving experience that would contrast with solving problems presented in text format. The nonverbal Tower of Hanoi is a game puzzle consisting of three towers, or pegs, and a stack of four doughnut-shaped disks of different diameters. The goal is to move all the disks from one tower to another target tower and end up with the same ordered stack of disks (progressively smaller disks stacked on the largest disk) by moving only one disk at a time and never placing a larger disk on top of a smaller disk. The mathematical problems were typical word problems requiring the students to calculate the cost of shirts at "buy two shirts, get a third one free" versus single shirts at a 30% discount, and to calculate the best price for grass seed at a sale price versus regular price when the weight of the bags is different. After completing each task, students had to explain their answer.

The results showed that deaf students with higher reading abilities provided the best explanations of their problem-solving strategies and solutions for both the Tower of Hanoi and the mathematical word problems, whether they were communicating in sign language or in writing. Although not suggesting a causal effect, these findings indicated that reading skills contributed in part to how deaf students analyzed problem information and organized the explanation of their problem solutions for a nonverbal visual puzzle and typical mathematical word problems regardless of communication mode (see Akamatsu, Mayer, & Hardy-Braz, this volume).

Two recently completed studies conducted from 2004 to 2007 involved deaf and hearing students' performance in mathematics across a range of age and grade levels. The first study examined deaf and hearing students in middle school, high school, and college for their ability to create and use visual–spatial relational representations in solving mathematical word problems. The second study was a secondary analysis that utilized the published technical documentation for the Mathematics Procedures and Problem-solving subtests, levels Primary 1 through Advanced 2 (grade 1 through 8), and the Mathematics tests, levels TASK 1 through 3 (grade 9 through 12) from the 2002 general (hearing) population norms for the SAT Series, Tenth Edition (SAT10, Harcourt Educational Measurement, 2003). For this secondary analysis, data were also included from the original student-level dataset of the 2003 deaf student norms (Gallaudet Research Institute, 2004; Mitchell, Qi, & Traxler, 2007) on the same SAT Series.

Using Visual–Spatial Representation in Mathematical Problem Solving

The positive relationship between spatial ability and achievement in mathematics has long been documented as one of the main factors affecting students' mathematical performance (Battista, 1990; Hegarty & Kozhevnikov, 1999; Sherman, 1979). The need to recognize and utilize relationships in mathematics is vital to successful problem solving. *The Compact Oxford English Dictionary, Second Edition* (2000) defines mathematics as "the abstract science which investigates deductively the conclusions implicit in the elementary concepts of spatial and numerical relations" (p. 1048). Because deaf individuals who use sign language have been shown to have an advantage in a number of visual–spatial domains (Dye, Hauser, & Bavelier, this volume; Emmorey, Kosslyn, & Bellugi, 1993; Marschark, 2003; Talbot & Haude, 1993), one might hypothesize that this would be helpful to their mathematical performance.

Blatto-Vallee, et al. (2007) replicated and developmentally extended the research of Hegarty and Koshevnikov (1999). They examined deaf ($n = 149$) and hearing ($n = 156$) students' ability to see, generate, and use visual–spatial relationships in mathematical problem solving at the middle school, high school, and college associate degree and baccalaureate degree levels. All student participants were given three paper-and-pencil tests. One test included the 15 mathematical problems used by Hegarty and Koshevnikov, modified only for terminology from the original British English to American English usage (e.g., lorry to truck). The other two tests assessed students' visual–spatial abilities: The *Primary Mental Abilities Spatial Relations Test* (Optometric Extension Program, 1995), a 25-item form completion task, and the *Revised Minnesota Paper Form Board Test*

(Likert & Quasha, 1994), a 64-item test designed to test part–whole relationship skills. Additionally, every student's shown work for each of the 15
mathematical problems was assigned to one of three categories of representation reflected in their solutions (visual–spatial schematic with numerical relationships shown, pictorial only with no numerical relationships
shown, and nonvisual representation), or it was assigned "no answer" or
"no work shown." Inter-rater reliabilities were .96 and .97 for the second
and third raters, respectively, with the primary rater (Borg & Gall, 1983).

To provide an idea of the problem situations used in this study and
how the students' problem representations were evaluated, following are
two typical examples:

> *Example 1.* A hitchhiker set out on a journey of 60 miles. He walked the first 5
> miles, then got a lift from a truck driver. When the driver dropped him off, he
> still had half of his journey to travel. How far had he traveled in the truck?

> *Example 2.* Four young trees were set out in a row 10 meters apart. A well was
> located by the last tree. A bucket of water is needed to water two trees. How
> far would a gardener have to walk altogether if he had to water the four trees
> using only one bucket?

For either of the above two examples, if a student drew only the objects
from the problem situation with no indication of distance relationships
between the objects, then it would be judged as a "pictorial representation"
with no numerical relationships shown. If a student drew the objects in the
problem situation and showed the distance relationships among the objects, then it would be judged as "visual–spatial schematic representation"
that included the numerical relationships of the problem situation.

Figure 8–1 shows each deaf and hearing participant group's mean score
by educational grade level, on the 15-item mathematical problem-solving
task (columns) along with their mean number of visual–spatial schematic
relational representations (superimposed line graph) that they developed
in solving the problems. The deaf participant groups' performance on the
mathematical problem-solving task was essentially the same at the middle
school, high school, and college associate degree program level, with only
the baccalaureate students showing a significantly higher performance.
This same pattern occurred for the average number of visual–spatial schematic relational representations that individuals in each deaf participant
group self-generated in solving these mathematical problems. In contrast,
the hearing participants' performance was significantly higher at all three
educational grade levels for both the mathematical problem-solving task
and the use of visual–spatial schematic representations.

The use of visual–spatial schematic representations was a strong predictor of mathematical problem-solving performance for the deaf students
across all four participant groups. A multiple regression analysis showed
that when deaf students used visual–spatial schematic representations in

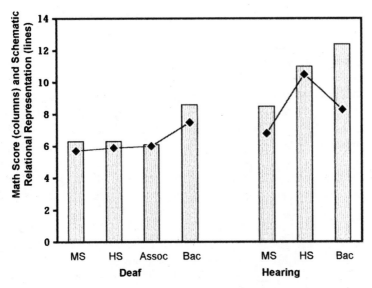

Figure 8–1. Deaf and hearing students' mathematical problem-solving performance with use of visual–spatial schematic representation.

solving the mathematical word problems, it predicted from 40% to 67% of their total score (middle school R^2 = .67, high school R^2 = .54, associate level R^2 = .49, and baccalaureate level R^2 = .40). R^2 is the proportion of variance predicted or accounted for in the dependent measure (i.e., their score in this case). In contrast, the use of visual–spatial schematic representations was an educationally important predictor of problem-solving performance only for the hearing middle school students (R^2 = .41). For hearing students at both the high school (R^2 = .06) and college baccalaureate level (R^2 = .12), the use of visual–spatial schematic representations was no longer as important a predictor of their mathematical problem-solving performance, suggesting that other factors were coming into play.

Although the use of visual–spatial schematic relationships was a stronger predictor for the deaf than hearing students, their actual performance scores for correctly solving the 15 mathematical problems were consistently and significantly lower than the hearing students' scores at all grade levels. Post hoc comparisons showed that the hearing students performed significantly higher than their deaf counterparts on both the mathematical problem-solving tasks and in generating and using more visual–spatial schematic representations that described the relationships in the problem situations. Only the comparison between the deaf and hearing baccalaureate students for generating schematic representations was not significantly different. Furthermore, the hearing students consistently scored higher than their deaf counterparts on the two visual–spatial ability tests across all grade level groupings.

Two findings of this study should raise educators' concerns. First is the similar performance of middle school, high school, and associate degree level deaf students in solving these mathematical word problems, as well as their use of visual–spatial schematic representations. The deaf students' problem-solving performance from middle school through associate degree programs in college suggests they may have reached a plateau in their mathematical word problem-solving skills (also observed in the SAT data, Traxler, 2000). The second concern is that deaf, baccalaureate level students performed very similarly to hearing middle school students in terms of mathematical problem solving and visual–spatial schematic representation. Although the deaf baccalaureate students' problem-solving performance was significantly better than the other deaf participant groups in this study, as a group they performed similar to the hearing middle school students for this type of mathematical word problem-solving task.

Nonetheless, the results of the Blatto-Vallee et al. (2007) research are clear. When deaf students generated and used visual–spatial schematic representation that showed the numerical relationships in the word problem situation, it was a very strong predictor of problem-solving success.

Mathematics Performance on the Stanford Achievement Test, Tenth Edition

Mitchell et al. (2007) conducted a secondary analysis of published technical documentation for the Mathematics Procedures and Problem-solving subtests, levels Primary 1 through Advanced 2, and the Mathematics tests, levels TASK 1 through 3 from the 2002 general hearing population norms for the SAT10. Their analysis also included the original student-level dataset from the 2003 deaf student norms (Gallaudet Research Institute, 2004; Mitchell, Qi, & Traxler, 2007) on the same SAT10. The number of general population, age-grade-typical respondents with valid scores ranged from 3717 to 7073, depending on test level (higher participation at the lower test levels). The number of deaf, frequently out-of-level, 8- to 18-year-old respondents with valid scores ranged from 207 to 563 (total $n = 2448$), depending on test level, with higher student numbers at lower levels. The deaf norms were derived from nonstandard testing conditions from a psychometric perspective, but standard conditions from a legal perspective. That is, the norms were based on deaf students' performance under IEP-mandated testing conditions, which are not necessarily identical to those experienced by the general population.

The Mitchell et al. results indicated that deaf students who were older than the typical age for their grade had a performance profile different from those who were "on grade" for their age. Deaf students are considered "on grade" if their age does not exceed by 2 years what would be expected for the typical age–grade correlation in the general hearing population. For the older students, higher computational accuracy came with more schooling, but it did not result in improved performance on word problem-solving tasks.

For the text readability of word problems, Mitchell et al. found very few associations between item-level test difficulty and item readability at any level of the SAT10, for either the general population of hearing students or deaf students. Based on the Dale-Chall readability scale (Chall & Dale, 1995), there was no indication that readability of the text material was differentially important for deaf or hearing students. More importantly, there were also no strong associations with the mathematics-specific Kane Formula II readability scale (Kane, Byrne, & Hater, 1974) on any test items regardless of hearing status. Rather than text readability, items on the SAT10 mathematical procedures were more difficult for both hearing and deaf students when they were presented as word problems compared to problems presented in mathematical symbolic notation with no English text.

Mathematics test items on the SAT10 do function differentially for deaf and for hearing students, but Mitchell et al. could not identify a clear explanation for the differential based on their available data. Differential item difficulty was estimated by examining the correlation between item level difficulties and then regressing the performance of deaf students onto the performance of hearing students. Although the regression analyses indicated a systematic difference in performance between deaf and hearing students, individual-level item responses were not available from the test publisher to further explore the actual source of the differential. However, their results showed no performance distribution biases due to out-of-level testing. As explained earlier, deaf students testing "on grade" are allowed to be up to 2 years older than the typical age–grade in the general population. Therefore, the test results of older deaf students testing out-of-level are potentially contaminated by factors such as maturation or other age- or time-in-school-related learning effects. Nevertheless, the analyses showed no distribution biases associated with older students testing out-of-level. Item difficulty, however, was related to the presence of English text. For all students, regardless of hearing status, responding accurately to mathematical problems presented in English text was, on average, more difficult than responding correctly to symbolic computation problems.

The Mitchell et al. secondary analysis of SAT10 data from a national sample of deaf and hearing students revealed that the inherent difficulties of mathematics academic achievement tests are similar for both the general population of hearing students and deaf students. Although recognizing similar difficulties for both populations, Mitchell et al. nonetheless found that "...deaf students clearly are not performing as well as the general population. Not only are items more difficult, on average, they function differentially as well.... [Whereas] it remains possible that reading English is one of the primary barriers to equal performance, there are a number of confounding issues, including inadequate opportunity to learn (either as a result of curriculum coverage or instructional shortcomings), inappropriate test accommodations, and other circumstances that would interfere with test performance..." (pp. viii–ix). Mitchell et al. suggested that further research is required to carefully parse the potential causes of mathematics performance differences between the general hearing student population and the deaf student population (see Bull, this volume).

Relational Language in Mathematical *Compare* Problems

Kelly, Lang, Mousley, and Davis (2003) examined deaf college students' (associate degree level) performance for solving *compare word problems,* in which the relational statements were either consistent or inconsistent with the arithmetic operation. This study replicated a study by Lewis and Mayer (1987) with hearing college freshman. There were eight types of target problems, described as follows:

1a. *Addition Consistent* (requires adding two numbers and the problem says *more*)
1b. *Addition Inconsistent* (requires adding two numbers and the problem says *less*)
2a. *Subtraction Consistent* (requires subtracting the second number from the first and the problem says *less*)
2b. *Subtraction Inconsistent* (requires subtracting the second number from the first and the problem says *more*)
3a. *Multiplication Consistent* (requires multiplying two numbers and the problem says *n times as many*)
3b. *Multiplication Inconsistent* (requires multiplying two numbers and the problem says *1/n as many*)
4a. *Division Consistent* (requires dividing two numbers and the problem says *1/n as many*)
4b. *Division Inconsistent* (requires dividing two numbers and the problem says *n times as many*)

Each word problem had three sentences with an average length of 31.6 words and an average readability grade level of 3.6. The following example shows the differential wording for consistent versus inconsistent problems that required addition (see Nunes et al., this volume):

Addition Consistent
At SuperFood, milk sells for $2.43 per gallon. Milk at Big M is 5 cents more per gallon than milk at SuperFood. How much do 4 gallons of milk cost at Big M Grocery?
Addition Inconsistent
At SuperFood, milk sells for $2.43 per gallon. This price is 5 cents less per gallon than milk at Big M Grocery. How much do 4 gallons of milk cost at Big M Grocery?

Table 8–1 shows the percentage of correct responses of the deaf students by their measured reading ability grade level for the consistent versus inconsistent experimental conditions. Across all reading ability levels, the deaf students' performance was higher for word problems in which relational language was consistent with the arithmetic function, and their performance dropped dramatically when the relational language of the word problem was inconsistent with the arithmetic function. These results were similar to the findings of Lewis and Mayer (1987) for hearing college freshmen. Table 8–1 also shows the impact of the students' reading ability on their performance in correctly solving these word problems, as well as the percentage of reversal errors they made in their problem solutions and on self goal-monitoring to be sure that they included all of the problem information and procedural steps in their solution. A *reversal error* occurs when one reverses the arithmetic operation of the initial step (i.e., addition for subtraction, subtraction for addition, multiplication for division,

Table 8–1. Percentage of Correct Answers and Errors of Participants for Consistent and Inconsistent Word Problems per Reading Grade Levels

	Reading Grade Level Groups			
Response Categories	5.0–6.9 $n = 21$	7.0–7.8 $n = 19$	8.0–8.9 $n = 25$	9.1–12.0 $n = 15$
Correct Answers				
Consistent	22.6	44.6	62.0	80.0
Inconsistent	1.2	15.9	27.0	46.5
Reversal Errors				
Consistent	0	0	1.0	1.7
Inconsistent	22.6	38.2	36.0	35.0
Goal-monitoring Errors				
Consistent	51.2	38.2	28.0	13.3
Inconsistent	67.9	43.3	35.0	13.9

and division for multiplication). A *goal-monitoring error* occurs when one of the two procedural steps is omitted from the calculation, including the related numerical information.

The hearing students in the Lewis and Mayer study were freshmen undergraduate students in baccalaureate degree programs. Only the deaf students in the highest reading level group of the Kelly et al. study are typical of deaf students who go on to complete baccalaureate degrees. How do they compare? First, these better deaf readers made 35% reversal errors in contrast to 6.9% by the hearing students. Second, the higher reading deaf students produced goal-monitoring errors, in which they left out one of the procedural steps in their problem solution, at the rate of 13.3% for consistent word problems and 13.9% for inconsistent word problems, whereas the hearing freshmen students' total rate for goal-monitoring errors across both conditions was less than 1%.

The results of the Kelly et al. study show that the students' reading ability level is associated with both their performance on the relational language of compare word problems and their ability to self-monitor the inclusion of all procedural steps in the problem situation. However, there is one caveat to this interpretation, and that is reading ability may not be the sole explanation for deaf students' poor goal-monitoring in problem solving (e.g., checking carefully to include all the procedural steps and related numerical information in the solution). For the deaf students with reading abilities in the 9.1–12.0 grade level range, their goal-monitoring error rates of 13.3%–13.9% may be due in part to careless reading or checking, rather than a reading problem per se. However, for the deaf college students with much lower reading ability—that is, those reading at the 5.0–6.9 reading level—their higher goal monitoring errors of 51%–67.9% may be due to multiple factors such as general academic ability, cognitive processing of the problem situation, reading ability and lack of reading precision, or carelessness.

Poor goal-monitoring or careless reading, however one wishes to describe it, is also an issue for deaf college students' comprehension of science texts. Kelly, Albertini, and Shannon (2001) examined deaf college students' reading comprehension of short science passages. After reading the science passages, each student was asked to underline or circle any words, phrases, or sentences they did not understand or that did not make sense. Although the students' self-assessment generally indicated that they understood everything they had just read, 90% did not pick up on an embedded sentence in the text that was topically incongruent with the entire passage. Furthermore, almost all of the student participants had difficulty identifying key points while referring to the passage. These results suggest that deaf students profess a better understanding of what they read (or see signed, see Marschark & Wauters, this volume) than they are able to demonstrate. An intervention component in this study showed that a refresher in comprehension strategies was beneficial to higher reading level deaf college students, but not lower level readers.

Morphological Knowledge, Reading, and Mathematical Performance

Reading ability is one, but not the only, cognitive tool important to deaf college students' performance for solving mathematical problems. In addition to reading ability, Kelly and Gaustad (2007) examined specific predictive relationships between deaf college students' assessed skills in language and knowledge of English morphology and their mathematical performance. This study built on previous research by Gaustad, Kelly, Payne, and Lylak (2002) and Gaustad and Kelly (2004), which examined deaf and hearing students' morphological knowledge specific to word meaning and word segmentation. Although Gaustad et al. (2002) showed that deaf college students' performance on both the word meaning and word segmentation tasks of the morphological knowledge assessment was similar to the performance of hearing middle school students, Gaustad and Kelly (2004) demonstrated that significant nuanced differences existed between the deaf college students and the hearing middle school students, even though their performance scores were similar.

The two tests of morphological knowledge developed by Gaustad are described fully in Gaustad and Kelly (2004) and Gaustad et al. (2002). The Split Decisions Test, with 75 items, measures students' skills in segmenting English words into morphemes. The Meaningful Parts Test, with 40 multiple-choice items, measures students' knowledge of the meaning associated with specific English morphemes. The test–retest reliabilities for these two tests are $r = .81$ and $.71$, respectively. Gaustad and Paul (1998) established the content validity of these two tests consisting of three levels of morpheme difficulty. The other assessments used in this study were the Michigan Test of English Language Proficiency for grammar, vocabulary, and reading (English Language Institute, 2003), and the California Achievement Test for Comprehension (Tiegs & Clark, 1963), a standardized reading ability test that has been administered to all entering students at the National Technical Institute for the Deaf (NTID) since 1972. These tests of reading, language proficiency, and morphological knowledge were used as predictor variables for the deaf college students' performance on the ACT Mathematics Subtest and the NTID Mathematics Placement Test.

The ACT Mathematics Subtest is a 60-minute, 60-item multiple-choice part of the ACT standardized college entrance exam. It consists of the following mathematical content areas: pre-algebra 23%, elementary algebra 17%, intermediate algebra 15%, coordinate geometry 15%, plane geometry 23%, and trigonometry 7% (ACT 2000, p. 3). The NTID Mathematics

Placement Test is a 48-item test designed and administered by the NTID Department of Science and Mathematics to determine course placement in their curriculum. This direct measure of students' calculation ability consists of the following mathematical content: general mathematics 45%, algebra 40%, and geometry and trigonometry 15%.

Regression analyses showed that deaf college students' language proficiency, reading ability, and knowledge of English morphology for segmenting words and understanding word meaning all significantly predicted both the ACT Mathematics Subtest score and the NTID Mathematics Placement Test score. Subsequent multiple regression analyses revealed that deaf college students' reading ability level and word segmentation skills (as measured by the Split Decisions Test) together predicted 63% of the deaf students' ACT mathematics score variance, while their word meaning skills (as measured by the Meaningful Parts Test) and word segmentation skills combined predicted 52% of their ACT score in mathematics. The results of the regression analyses for the NTID Mathematics Placement Test closely paralleled those of the ACT Mathematics Subtest analyses. Together, these results, showing that the combinations of significant predictors were similar for both a national standardized assessment of mathematics (ACT) and a "locally" developed direct measure of students' calculation ability, strengthens the efficacy of the findings. In addition, deaf students' actual grade performance in their college mathematics courses showed a significant association with their reading ability levels and knowledge of morpheme meanings.

Since regression studies are based on correlations of existing student characteristics rather than experimentally manipulated treatment variables, one cannot draw any conclusions about cause and effect. However, the results showed that the deaf participating students' reading ability and morphological knowledge had a predictive relationship to their performances on two mathematical tests, and was also significantly associated with their classroom grades. These findings provide evidence that reading ability and morphological skills are positive contributors to deaf students' mathematical problem-solving performance.

Mental Calculation Related to Reading Ability

Davis and Kelly (2003) examined deaf and hearing college students' mental calculation abilities for verifying the accuracy of solutions to addition and multiplication problems. The deaf participants were divided into two groups representing higher and lower reading skills as assessed by their combined performance on the California Reading Test and the California Vocabulary Test; this resulted in a percentile score based on both tests ranging from 0 to 200 (Crandall, 1997). Students with a combined percentile score of 150 or above are excused from the NTID reading curriculum requirements. In this study, the lower reading group of deaf students had a mean percentile score of 81.3, with individual scores ranging from 59 to 103. The higher deaf reading group had a mean percentile score of 151.5, with individual scores from 116 to 200.

Each participant in this study was administered the experimental task individually. They viewed individual mathematical problems with answers presented in random sequence on a 17-inch computer screen and responded to each problem by pressing one of two buttons to indicate whether the answer shown was correct or incorrect. Their response times were measured in milliseconds from the moment a problem was presented on the computer screen. In addition to the practice problems, the actual experimental task involved a total of 80 arithmetic verification problems, half true and half false.

The similarities and differences between deaf and hearing college students on the mental calculation verification tasks pertain to both speed of response and accuracy. First, the hearing students' response times were significantly faster than those of the lower reading deaf students, but not the higher reading deaf students (although numerically, the hearing students' mean response times were greater). In terms of accuracy, the lower reading deaf students had significantly poorer performance scores than either the hearing students or the higher reading deaf students. In contrast, the higher reading deaf college students exhibited similar performance patterns to the hearing college students for both response times and accuracy. These results suggest a positive association between reading ability and mental calculation tasks, with the caveat, of course, that no conclusions about causation can be drawn. To reiterate, reading ability is an existing subject characteristic and not an experimentally manipulated treatment variable.

Mathematical Word Problems More Than Reading

In an earlier study consistent with the findings of Mitchell et al. (2007), Kelly and Mousley (2001) showed that deaf college students performed better with mathematical symbolic problems as compared to word problems. Figure 8–2 compares the performance of deaf college students in associate degree level programs on mathematical problems presented graphically and numerically with the same problems (different values) presented in word format. Note that the comparison group of hearing college students (who were not mathematics majors) performed at the same level regardless of problem format. Although there were no statistically significant differences between the deaf and hearing students' performance for the mathematical problems presented in numeric/graphic

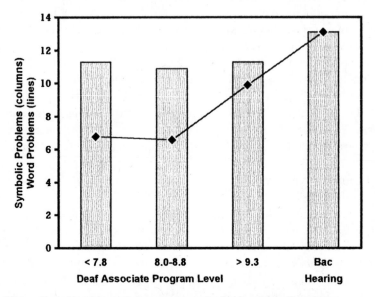

Figure 8–2. Deaf associate program students versus hearing baccalaureate program students for solving mathematical symbolic and mathematical word problems.

format, significant differences were noted for their word problem-solving performances.

Figure 8–2 shows that, for the deaf college students, reading ability level was related to their problem-solving performance. The deaf students with reading abilities at eighth grade or below had the most difficulty with the word problems, whereas the students who read at ninth grade or higher performed significantly better. Although these results were not surprising, what was puzzling is that even when the deaf students accurately represented the components of the word problem situations in their shown work, they had a lower performance for problem-solving accuracy. When the comparison group of hearing students accurately represented the word problems, their performance scores remained high. However, across all three groups, even when the deaf students shown work accurately represented the word problem situations, their problem-solving performance was only correct on the easiest problems. Scores were significantly lower on the more complex problems. This finding is even more puzzling because the students demonstrated their problem-solving accuracy for the same problems (different values) presented in numeric/graphic format (i.e., mathematic symbolic) during the same testing session. For some students, perhaps their self-monitoring skills became stressed with the text presentation of the problem situation, thus affecting their computational accuracy; for others, it may be that the presentation of mathematical word problems stimulated an anxiety or a previously learned avoidance behavior that influenced their problem-solving performance.

In addition to the reading comprehension factors associated with solving mathematical word problems, other characteristics and generic thinking skills influence problem-solving performance. For example, Woditsch (1991) described "failure prone" behaviors that negatively influence problem solving, such as the inability to sustain focus on the critical variables of the problem, scanning information haphazardly, failure to test prior knowledge against potential relationships in the problem by using analogies, jumping from the first "lead" to an answer without incorporating all available data, and not reviewing and checking the solution. In contrast, "good problem solvers" were described as those who give conscious, focused, and undivided attention to a problem. They persist in considering all relevant information and use analogies to relate known information to better understand a problem situation. Finally, they assess all available problem information before making a conclusion, and they evaluate their potential solution before affirmation (p. 21). Marzano et al. (1988) similarly highlighted the importance of focused attention and persistence to analytical problem solving, as well as the value of commitment to do well. Closely related to commitment is the attitude that "I can perform the task," which influences how efficiently one approaches the task (Marzano et al., p. 10). Such factors as low confidence, unfocused attention, or lack of commitment to do well may have affected the deaf students' performance on the word problems in the Kelly and Mousley study. Further research should be conducted with respect to these kind of factors possibly influencing problem-solving performance.

Teaching Practices in Grades 6–12 for Mathematics Word Problem Solving

In an effort to understand the kind of teaching and learning opportunities for mathematical problem solving that deaf students may experience in grades 6–12, Kelly, Lang, and Pagliaro (2003) surveyed 253 educational programs consisting of 185 mainstreamed schools and 68 public and private residential and day schools. The 133 responding teachers who taught mathematics to deaf students were about equally divided, with 51.5% from residential and day schools and 48.5% from mainstreamed programs representing both integrated and self-contained classrooms. Approximately 41% of teachers from residential and day schools were certified in mathematics education. For the mainstreamed programs, 76% of the teachers in the regular integrated classrooms were certified in mathematics or mathematics education, whereas only 9% of the teachers in the self-contained classrooms were mathematics certified.

In this survey study, the teachers were asked a series of questions about what they taught and emphasized in teaching problem-solving skills to deaf students, especially with respect to mathematical word problems. The survey instrument was divided into multiple sections asking about the time they spent teaching problem-solving skills and word problems, as well as what their instructional emphases were for teaching general problem-solving strategies and skills specific to solving mathematical word problems. Finally, the survey asked for the teachers' perceptions of their students' capabilities for solving word problems.

In terms of the instruction and learning time spent on mathematical problem solving, 84% of the teachers responded that they allocated 6 hours or less per week for a weekly average of 3.7 hours, with only approximately 1.6 hours allocated to teaching mathematical word problems each week. Homework assignments pertinent to word problems averaged only 25%.

For "general problem-solving strategies," the teachers' indicated their frequency of instruction on a 6-point equal-interval Likert scale from 1 = Never to 6 = Very Often for eight general strategies worded as follows:

- Identifying the target goal (what is to be solved)
- Making a plan
- Identifying the key information
- Evaluating one's plan and solution
- Hypothesis testing
- Estimating
- Testing trial-and-error approaches
- Dividing a problem into subproblems (two or more procedural operations)

The results of the teachers' responses showed that their primary instructional emphasis for general problem-solving strategies was on comprehension of the problem situation. The teachers' highest-rated strategies focused on identifying the target goal (what has to be solved) and key information, making a plan, and dividing the problem situation into subproblems. Their responses also indicated that they gave significantly less instructional emphasis to evaluating one's plan and solution, estimating potential answers, testing trial-and-error approaches, and hypothesis testing.

With respect to instructional emphases for strategies specific to solving mathematical word problems, the teachers were asked to respond (using the same 6-point Likert rating scale just described) to 20 randomized statements that were categorized as "concrete visualizing strategies" or "analytical strategies. The teachers' responses indicated that they instructionally emphasized significantly more concrete visualizing strategies (visual and sign representations, modeling, signing/talking their thoughts out loud, active engagement), compared to analytical strategies (teaching problems for specific domain areas, writing problem representations, posing new problems from given facts and information, analogical reasoning, relating problem situations to knowledge and information already known).

In the final section of the survey, the teachers were asked about their perceptions of their deaf students' capabilities for solving mathematical word problems. The items read "My deaf students...

1. ...are capable of reading a word problem and representing it in their thoughts before solving it.
2. ...are capable of reading a word problem and representing it on paper using illustrations, diagrams, relational charts, etc.
3. ...are capable of reading a word problem and representing it in writing on paper by identifying the target goal and organizing the relevant information for analysis.
4. ...English skills are the primary barrier to their being able to successfully solve word problem situations."

Figure 8–3 shows a line graph of the teachers' responses to these four perceptions of their deaf students' capabilities for solving mathematical word problems. The teacher responses were on a 6-point equal-interval Likert Scale ranging from Strongly Disagree (1) to Strongly Agree (6). As shown in Figure 8–3, teachers of the deaf in both residential and self-contained programs perceived their students' capabilities to be relatively

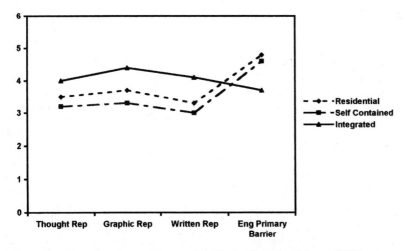

Figure 8–3. Teacher perceptions of their deaf students' capabilities to cognitively handle thought, graphic, and written representations of word problem situations and whether English was the primary barrier.

low for thought, graphic, and written representation of mathematical word problem situations, while perceiving that English was the primary barrier to their deaf students' lack of success in solving word problems. The mathematics teachers in regular classrooms with mainstreamed deaf students had a relatively higher perception of their deaf students' capabilities and perceived that English was less of a barrier to deaf students successfully solving mathematical word problems. Although recognizing residential and self-contained programs may have a different population of deaf students than do mainstreamed settings, nonetheless, the generally low perceptions of the teachers of their deaf students' capabilities to solve mathematical word problems suggests that teacher expectancies may influence the mathematical problem-solving instruction of deaf students and become a fulfilling prophesy—sort of a reverse *Pygmalion effect*. The Pygmalion effect, first proposed by Rosenthal and Jacobson (1968) and discussed in further detail more by Rosenthal (2002), derived from an experiment in which teachers' higher expectations resulted in their students' improved academic performance. Conversely, teachers' low expectations of their students have the potential to negatively influence their instructional approach and thus, possibly limit students' learning opportunities.

The responses of teachers providing mathematics instruction to deaf students in the Kelly et al. survey suggest that the deaf students in their classes were generally exposed more to comprehension strategies while receiving relatively less exposure, experience, and practice with analytical-oriented strategies.

Summary and Implications

Data have been presented and discussed that show deaf students in the United States, in K–12 programs and at entry to college, exhibit a level of knowledge and abilities in the areas of reading comprehension, mathematics performance, and knowledge of mathematics procedures that potentially affects their development of good problem-solving skills. Furthermore, based on standardized measures, deaf students' English and reading skills, as well as their knowledge of mathematics and science, suggest that they are considerably under-prepared for advanced studies at the postsecondary level. At entry to college, only about 20% of deaf students meet or exceed the ACT college readiness benchmarks for English and reading. For science reasoning and mathematics, only 10%–15% meet or exceed the ACT college readiness benchmarks, respectively.

The research findings presented and discussed here indicate that deaf students generally perform differently from their hearing peers on mathematical problem-solving tasks, especially problem situations presented in English text (i.e., word problem format). When deaf students generated visual–spatial schematic representations of the numerical relationships in mathematical word problems, it was a strong predictor of their problem-solving success. When the mathematical problem-solving tasks required deaf students to explain their strategies and solutions for both nonverbal and text problems, conduct mental calculations, process relational language consistent and inconsistent with the arithmetic operation, or to solve similar problems presented in symbolic versus word format, the students' reading ability levels were associated with their problem-solving performance. Deaf students' goal-monitoring ability for including all the procedural steps and numeric information of a word problem situation was also associated with their reading ability.

Both reading level and morphological knowledge were significant predictors of deaf students' performance on a national standardized mathematics test and a "locally" developed direct measure of computation skills, as well as being associated with grade performance in college mathematics courses. However, as cautioned throughout the discussion of this research, deaf students' reading abilities cannot be interpreted as having a causal influence on their problem-solving skills. Yes, reading ability is associated with deaf students' problem-solving performance, but it may only be a reflection or proxy variable for their underlying conceptual development and experience with problem solving. A national survey of teachers providing mathematics instruction to deaf students revealed that they gave less instructional emphasis to analytical-oriented problem-solving strategies and more to comprehension strategies. Students obviously need exposure, experience, and practice with a balance of both. And finally, the text readability of word problems was not found to be a significant factor in deaf students problem-solving performance on a national standardized test.

Good problem-solving skills are developed through direct instruction and with practice in solving increasingly challenging problem situations (Ormrod, 2006; Whimbey & Lochhead, 1991). The research findings discussed here suggest a number of areas deserving increased focus in the problem-solving instruction provided to deaf students in K–12, along with further research at all educational levels. Briefly, the areas are:

- More instructional emphasis on analytical strategies for solving problem situations described in mathematical word problems
- Increased direct instruction on how to write descriptions of numerical relationships in mathematical problems
- Specific instruction on how to graphically create visual–spatial representations that show numerical relationships in mathematical problem situations

- More allocation of time on task for problem-solving practice and opportunities to learn and apply analytical strategies, as well as to build students' confidence in their abilities to be analytical and successful in solving increasingly more difficult problems, especially mathematical word problems
- Teaching a variety of analytical strategies such as:
  o Hypothesis testing
  o Estimation
  o Trial-and-error
  o Evaluating one's problem solution
- More instruction on developing students' morphological knowledge, particularly with respect to the meaning of morphemes and their implications for different component parts of a word
- Emphasizing reading precision and accuracy at all ability levels by using age-grade appropriate self-monitoring and self-evaluation strategies

Although these suggestions are not the only areas deserving increased focus, they are areas of need identified by consistent research findings. If deaf students are to interact successfully with their instructors and peers, and understand more sophisticated text materials in their educational pursuits, they need to develop in their thinking processes the concepts, symbols, mental strategies, and problem-solving procedures commonly shared and used by others, as suggested by the work of Vygotsky (1962, 1978). These are cognitive tools critical to good thinking skills and advanced academic study.

Equally important would be the initiation of a national program of intervention research designed to engage deaf students with analytical strategies and problems at their true ability level, and then increasingly challenge them as they develop and progress with their problem-solving skills. The deaf students who meet or exceed the ACT minimum benchmarks for college preparedness in English, reading, science reasoning, and mathematics are not the ones who need the most help. Deaf students at this level are comparatively easy to teach, and they learn readily. It is the 80%–90% of deaf students who fall below the ACT minimum academic readiness benchmarks who truly need the attention. The challenge for educators and researchers is to identify and focus on the most effective instructional methodologies to best serve deaf students who have not fully developed their cognitive tools for mathematical problem solving, as well as general problem-solving skills that apply to a broad range of academic learning.

Acknowledgments

Material in this chapter is based in part upon work supported by the National Science Foundation under grant 0350277. Any opinions, findings and conclusions, or recommendations expressed in this material are those of the author and do not necessarily reflect the views of NSF.

References

ACT (2000). ACT assessment: User handbook 2000–2001. Iowa City, IA: ACT, Inc.

ACT (2005). *What are ACT's college readiness benchmarks?* Iowa City, IA: ACT, Inc. Available online at http://www.act.org/path/policy/pdf/benchmarks.pdf.

Allen, T. E. (1994). Who are the deaf and hard-of-hearing students leaving high school and entering postsecondary education? http://gri.gallaudet.edu/AnnualSurvey/whodeaf.html

Battista, M. T. (1990). Spatial visualization and gender differences in high school geometry. *Journal of Research in Mathematics Education, 21,* 47–60.

Blatto-Vallee, G., Kelly, R. R., Gaustad, M. G., Porter, J., & Fonzi, J. (2007). Visual-spatial representation in mathematical problem solving by deaf and hearing students. *Journal of Deaf Studies and Deaf Education, 12,* 432–448.

Borg, W. R., & Gall, M. D. (1983). *Educational research: An introduction* (4th ed.). New York: Longman, Inc.

Chall, J. S. & Dale, E. (1995). *Readability revisited: The new Dale-Chall readability formula.* Cambridge, MA: Brookline Books.

Crandall, K. A. (1997). *Review and selection of tests for placement of deaf college students in NTID's nonfiction reading curriculum: A curriculum development Team Report.* Rochester, NY: National Technical Institute for the Deaf at the Rochester Institute of Technology.

Davis, S. M., & Kelly, R. R. (2003). Comparing deaf and hearing college students' mental arithmetic calculations under two interference conditions. *American Annals of the Deaf, 148*(3), 213–221.

English Language Institute. (2003). *The Michigan Test of English Language Proficiency (MTELP).* Ann Arbor: University of Michigan.

Emmorey, K., Kosslyn, S. M., & Bellugi, U. (1993). Visual imagery and visual-spatial language: Enhanced imagery abilities in deaf and hearing ASL signers. *Cognition, 46*(2), 139–181.

Gallaudet Research Institute. (2004). *Norms booklet for deaf and hard-of-hearing students: Stanford Achievement Test, 10th Edition, Form A.* Washington, DC: Gallaudet University.

Gaustad, M. G., & Kelly, R. R. (2004). The relationship between reading achievement and morphological word analysis in deaf and hearing students matched for reading level. *Journal of Deaf Studies and Deaf Education, 9*(3), 269–285.

Gaustad, M. G., Kelly, R. R., Payne, J. A., & Lylak, E. (2002). Deaf and hearing students' morphological knowledge applied to printed English. *American Annals of the Deaf,* 147(5), 5–21.

Gaustad, M. G. & Paul, P. (1998). Instruction and first-language literacy. In P. Paul (Ed.), *Literacy and deafness* (pp. 181–235). Boston: Allyn and Bacon.

Hegarty, M. & Kozhevnikov, M. (1999) Types of visual-spatial representation and mathematical problem solving. *Journal of Educational Psychology, 91*(4), 684–689.

Harcourt Educational Measurement (2003). *Stanford Achievement Test, Tenth Edition: Spring technical data report.* San Antonio: Author.

Kane, R. B., Byrne, M. A., & Hater, M. A. (1974). *Helping children read mathematics.* New York: American Book Company.

Kelly, R. R., Albertini, J. A., & Shannon, N. B. (2001). Deaf college students' reading comprehension and strategy use. *American Annals of the Deaf, 146*(5), 385–400.

Kelly, R., & Gaustad, M. (2007). Deaf college students' mathematical skills relative to morphological knowledge, reading level, and language proficiency. *Journal of Deaf Studies and Deaf Education, 12*(1), 25–37.

Kelly, R. R., Lang, H. G., Mousley, K., & Davis, S. (2003). Deaf college students' comprehension of relational language in arithmetic compare problems. *Journal of Deaf Studies and Deaf Education, 8*(2), 120–132.

Kelly, R. R., Lang, H. G., & Pagliaro, C. M. (2003), Mathematics word problem solving for deaf students: A survey of practices in grades 6–12. *Journal of Deaf Studies and Deaf Education, 8,* 104–119.

Kelly, R. R., & Mousley, K. (2001). Solving word problems: More than reading issues for deaf students. *American Annals of the Deaf, 146*(3), 253–264.

Lewis, A. B., & Mayer, R. E. (1987). Students' miscomprehension of relational statements in arithmetic word problems. *Journal of Educational Psychology, 79,* 363–371.

Likert, R., & Quasha, W. H. (1994). *Revised Minnesota paper form board test, Second Edition.* San Antonio: The Psychological Corporation, Harcourt Brace and Company.

Marschark, M. (2003). Cognitive functioning in deaf adults and children. In Marschark, M., and Spencer, P.E., (Eds.), *Oxford handbook of deaf studies, language, and education* (pp. 264–277). New York: Oxford University Press.

Marzano, R. J., Brandt, R. S., Hughes, C. S., Jones B. F., Presselsen, B. Z., Rankin, S. C., & Suhor, C. (1988). *Dimensions of thinking: A framework for curriculum and instruction.* Alexandria, VA: Association for Supervision and Curriculum Development.

Mayer, R. E. (1992). *Thinking, problem solving, cognition* (2nd ed.). New York: W. H. Freeman and Company.

Mitchell, R. E., Qi, S., & Traxler, C. B. (2007). *Stanford Achievement Test, 10th Edition, national performance norms for deaf and hard of hearing students: A technical report.* Washington, DC: Gallaudet Research Institute, Gallaudet University.

Mitchell, R. E., Young, T. A., Hochgesang, J. A., Bachleda, B., & Karchmer, M. A. (2007). *Relationship between mathematics test item difficulty and English text for deaf and hard of hearing students: A technical report.* Washington, DC: Gallaudet Research Institute, Gallaudet University.

Mousley, K., & Kelly, R. R. (1998). Problem-solving strategies for teaching mathematics to deaf students. *American Annals of the Deaf, 143*(4), 325–336.

National Technical Institute for the Deaf. (2006). *Annual report: October 1, 2005–September 30, 2006*. Rochester, NY: National Technical Institute for the Deaf at the Rochester Institute of Technology.

Optometric Extension Program. (1995). *Primary mental abilities: Spatial relations and perceptual speed*. Reprinted by permission of Macmillan/McGraw Hill School Publishing Co. Adapted for OEP by S. Groffman and H. Solan. Santa Ana, CA: Optometric Extension Program Foundation, Inc.

Ormrod, J. E. (2006). *Essentials of educational psychology*. Upper Saddle River, NJ: Pearson Education, Inc.

Oxford University Press. (2000). *The compact Oxford English dictionary* (2nd ed.). New York: Oxford University Press Inc.

Qi, S., & Mitchell, R. E. (April, 2007). *Large-scaled academic achievement testing of deaf and hard-of-hearing students: Past, present, and future*. Paper presented at the Annual Meeting of the American Education Research Association, Research on the Education of Deaf Persons SIG Business Meeting, April 10, 2007, Chicago, Illinois.

Rosenthal, R. (2002). The Pygmalion effect and its mediating mechanisms. In J. Aronson (Ed.), *Improving academic achievement* (pp. 26–36). San Diego, CA: Academic Press.

Rosenthal, R., & Jacobson, L. (1968). *Pygmalion in the classroom*. New York: Holt, Rinehart, and Winston.

Sherman, J. A. (1979). Predicting mathematical performance in high school girls and boys. *Journal of Educational Psychology, 71,* 242–249.

Talbot, K. F., & Haude, R. H. (1993). The relationship between sign language skill and spatial visualizations ability: Mental rotation of three-dimensional objects. *Perceptual and Motor Skills, 77,* 1387–1391.

Tiegs, E. W., & Clark, W. (1963). *California Achievement Tests (Reading Comprehension, Junior High Level, Form Z)*. Monterey, CA: CTB/McGraw-Hill.

Traxler, C. B. (2000). Measuring up to performance standards in reading and mathematics: Achievement of selected deaf and hard-of-hearing students in the national norming of the 9th Edition Stanford Achievement Test. *Journal of Deaf Studies and Deaf Education, 5,* 337–348.

Vygotsy, L. S. (1962). *Thought and language* (E. Haufmann and G. Vakar, eds. and trans.). Cambridge, MA: MIT Press.

Vygotsy, L. S. (1978). *Mind in society: The development of higher psychological processes*. Cambridge, MA: Harvard University Press.

Whimbey, A., & Lochhead, J. (1991). *Problem solving and comprehension* (5th ed.). Hillsdale, NJ: Lawrence Erlbaum Associates, Inc.

Woditsch, G. A. (1991). *The thoughtful teacher's guide to thinking skills*. Hillsdale, NJ: Erlbaum.

Chapter 9

Visual Attention in Deaf Children and Adults

Implications for Learning Environments

Matthew W.G. Dye, Peter C. Hauser, and Daphne Bavelier

> *Think you of the fact that a deaf person cannot hear. Then, what deafness may we not all possess? What senses do we lack that we cannot see and cannot hear another world all around us?*
> —Frank Herbert, *Dune*

The world we live in is overwhelmingly rich and complex. As human agents living in such a world we are constantly bombarded with large amounts of sensory information through multiple channels such as vision, audition, and olfaction. Our ability to filter, select, and focus upon different aspects of the environment is termed *attention*. Indeed, an initial level of filtering occurs at the sensory level—our senses are only able to process some of that information which bombards us. We cannot see the infrared light emitted by our remote controls, or hear the sound of a bat as it echo-locates in search of food. Some species, of course, can detect such signals—however, the human visual system has evolved in such a way that it cannot. When psychologists talk of attention, however, they do not refer to this kind of information selection. Rather, the emphasis is on selecting information that is made available to us via our senses.

Attention can be construed as the mechanism or mechanisms that allow us to select from the information those aspects we need in order to act appropriately—detect an oncoming vehicle in order to cross a road safely—or simply as a way to reduce incoming information to make it manageable for a brain that is limited in its capacity to process that information. Whatever the role of attention, it is clear that an ability to filter out irrelevant information and focus upon specific aspects of our environment in a goal-directed manner is an essential tool for survival. In this chapter, we focus upon visual attention—the ability to select and concentrate on information entering the brain via the visual pathway—and how significant hearing loss may have an effect upon how visual information is selected and attended.

Attention and Behavior Problems in Deaf Children

Deaf children have been reported to have behavioral problems related to impulsivity and an inability to focus attention. These reports have come from both subjective ratings of teachers and caregivers, as well as from clinical tests of attention skills. For example, mothers have been reported to rate deaf children as having greater distractibility–hyperactivity problems than hearing children using the Parenting Stress Index (Quittner, Glueckauf, & Jackson, 1990), and Reivich and Rothrock (1972) suggested that impulsivity and lack of inhibition accounted for a significant amount of the problem behavior in deaf pupils reported by teachers in their study. On the other hand, Altshuler et al. (1976) noted that teachers demonstrated little agreement in their ratings of impulsivity in their deaf adolescent pupils. Meadow (1976), using the Behavior Symptom Checklist with mothers of deaf and hearing children, reported little evidence of deaf–hearing differences in short attention spans, with few mothers reporting problems eliciting and maintaining eye gaze and joint attention with their deaf children. The lack of consistent findings is perhaps not surprising given the subjective nature of such rating scales.

Of more interest then, are the results obtained using more objective, clinical measures of attention. Altshuler et al. (1976) report that deaf children in their study performed on average worse than hearing controls on the Porteus Mazes and the Time to Draw a Line tests. Specifically, deaf children tended to make more wrong turns in the maze task and took significantly less time to draw a straight line across a sheet of paper, suggesting a lack of planning and an inability to consider decisions.

Other studies have examined lower-level visual skills underpinning attention behavior and the visuo-motor skills that may also influence problems coordinating action within the environment. An early study by Myklebust and Brutten (1953) reported that deaf children had low-level visual deficits, as measured by the Keystone Visual Survey, as well as poor levels of performance on visual tasks such as the marble boards test, a test of visuo-motor skills developed by Werner and Strauss (1941). Attempts to replicate these findings, however, found either no difference between deaf and hearing children (Keystone Visual Survey; Hayes, 1955) or slightly better performance by deaf children (marble boards test; Larr, 1956; McKay, 1952). Finally, Hauser and colleagues (Hauser, Cohen, Dye, & Bavelier, 2007) reported no differences between deaf and hearing college students on a range of tests of visuo-motor tasks, including the Rey–Osterrieth Complex Figure Test (Osterrieth, 1944; Rey, 1941) and the Wechsler Memory Scale Visual Reproduction subtest (Wechsler, 1997).

Recently, deficits in continuous performance tasks (CPTs) have been reported in deaf children (Mitchell & Quittner, 1996; Quittner, Smith, Osberger, Mitchell, & Katz, 1994; Quittner, Leibach, & Marciel, 2004; Smith, Quittner, Osberger, & Miyamoto, 1998). Continuous performance tasks are computerized measures of attention that typically require children to sustain their attention to a rapidly changing visual display and make responses to targets while withholding responses to nontargets. In one commonly used CPT, the Gordon Diagnostic System (Gordon & Mettleman, 1987), digits appear one at a time in rapid succession in the center of a display—children are usually required to make a response to a target number when it is preceded by a specific number, but not otherwise. For example, children may be asked to press the response button upon seeing the target number 9 if it has been preceded by the number 1, but not otherwise. In this case, the sequence 1–9 would require a response to the 9, whereas the sequence 4–9 would require the child to withhold a response to the 9 and the sequence 1–4 would require the child not to make an impulsive response on the basis of seeing the number 1 alone.

Several different versions of this CPT have been used with deaf children. In one version, a *delay* task, children are required to press a button and then wait before pressing it again in the absence of any numerical stimuli. If they wait long enough, they receive a reward (a point), providing a measure of the efficiency with which children obtain rewards, taken to be an index of impulsivity. In a second version, a *vigilance* task, correctly pressing the button to a 9 preceded by a 1 is an index of vigilance or sustained attention, whereas pushing the button at any other time (a commission error) is taken as a measure of impulsivity. A third version of CPT, a *distractibility* task, involves irrelevant numbers appearing to the left and right of the central numbers. Poor performance is attributed to the child being distracted by the flanking numbers. Using these tasks, deaf children have been reported to be more impulsive (Quittner et al., 1994) and to suffer from increased distractibility (Mitchell & Quittner, 1996). Furthermore, Smith et al. (1998) reported data suggesting that cochlear implants (CIs) diminish the strength of these deficits, although the children with CIs did not achieve the performance levels of hearing controls. The authors suggest that their data indicate a deficit in visual selective attention stemming from poor multimodal sensory integration as a result of early, profound hearing loss. Such a position can be termed a deficiency hypothesis and, generally stated, it proposes that integration of information from the different senses is an essential component to the development of normal attentional functioning within each individual sensory modality.

Parasnis, Samar, and Berent (2003) administered another version of CPT—called the Test of Variables of Attention (T.O.V.A., Leark, Dupuy, Greenberg, Corman, & Kindschi, 1999)—to deaf and hearing college students. In the T.O.V.A., targets and nontargets are randomly presented to observers in quick succession, and they are asked to respond to the targets only. Their data suggested that deaf observers had increased impulsivity when selecting the appropriate response, accompanied by decreased perceptual sensitivity (i.e., they found it harder to distinguish between targets and nontargets). Parasnis et al. argued that both of these factors contributed to the apparent increased impulsivity in deaf samples, but that both reflect adaptations to the environment and not attentional pathology. Specifically, a less conservative response selection reflects a reliance upon vision for alerting in the absence of auditory input. In the absence of auditory cues to objects and events in the environment, more reliance is placed upon visual information for bringing such objects and events to the attention of the deaf observer. The decreased perceptual sensitivity in central vision, they argue, results from redistribution of attention away from the center and toward peripheral vision, as initially proposed by Neville and her collaborators (Neville, Schmidt, & Kutas, 1983; Neville & Lawson, 1978a,b). This possibility was also considered by Mitchell and Quittner (1996) in regard to their findings on distractibility. This idea, that a redistribution of attention occurs across visual space in deaf individuals, is the focus of the next section. However, before considering that hypothesis, it is important to consider other limitations in the work just reviewed, with a particular focus upon the selection of appropriate stimuli and careful consideration of what is meant by a "deaf child" in the context of such studies.

The Importance of Etiology and Communication

Lesser and Easser (1972) suggested that the impulsivity that had been reported in early studies of behavior problems in deaf children might have been a result of a lack of self-regulation stemming from difficulties in communication and expressing needs. Thus, early on, the importance of language in the development of attentional skills had been acknowledged (see Hauser, Lukomski, & Hillman, this volume). Furthermore, Meadow (1980) cited a study by Chess, Korn, and Fernandez (1971) that showed that maternal rubella was related to hyperactivity, thus establishing the importance of examining comorbidity in deaf children. That is, many deaf children have learning and other disabilities, in addition to their hearing losses, that are often associated with the same etiological cause. Indeed, deaf individuals in general vary greatly in the etiology of their deafness, its severity, and age of onset.

Over 20 million people in the United States have been diagnosed with hearing loss, representing a prevalence rate of 9% (Ries, 1994). The etiology of hearing loss can be hereditary (~50%) or acquired by several mechanisms such as prenatal or perinatal infections (cytomegalovirus, rubella, and herpes simplex), postnatal infections (meningitis), premature birth, anoxia, trauma, or as a result of ototoxic drugs administered during pregnancy. Many of these causes have been associated with other, sometimes severe, neurological sequelae that affect behavioral, cognitive, and psychosocial functioning (Hauser, Wills, & Isquith, 2006; King, Hauser, & Isquith, 2006). Hereditary deafness is associated with over 350 genetic conditions (Martini, Mazzoli, & Kimberling, 1997), and about a third of these genetic conditions are associated with syndromes (Petit, 1996). Although not all hereditary cases of deafness are nonsyndromic, hereditary-deafened individuals are more likely to have unremarkable neurological and psychiatric histories.

In the United States, many individuals who have severe to profound hearing loss before the age of 3 years use American Sign Language (ASL) as their first language, and thus may also be less likely to have self-regulatory issues resulting from communicative stress and an inability to express themselves. This group relies on visual routes to learning and language access, and has similar values, beliefs, and behaviors that usually reflect Deaf culture. The community of ASL users is often referred to in the literature as a *linguistic minority community* because of the similarities it has with other minority communities in terms of language and culture (Ladd, 2003; Padden & Humphries, 2005). The body of research considered next has focused largely upon such deaf individuals, often referred to as *deaf native signers*, minimizing potential confounds due to comorbid disorders or difficulties and problems stemming from communication problems in early childhood.

Altered Distribution of Visual Attention in Deaf Individuals: Behavioral Studies

In contrast to studies reporting examples of visual deficits, studies using homogenous samples of deaf native signers have demonstrated changes in visual function that could be considered more adaptive, in that they show a compensation in the visual modality for the lack of auditory input. In such individuals, a selective enhancement for stimuli that are peripheral or in motion and require attentional selection has been demonstrated using a variety of paradigms.

One of the key attributes of attention is that, when allocated to a position in space, an object occupying that space receives enhanced processing. Put another way, when attention is allocated to an object, an observer demonstrates increased sensitivity to that object. An early study by Loke and Song (1991) demonstrated that deaf observers responded more rapidly to targets flashed at locations in the periphery, a finding replicated recently by Chen, Zhang, and Zhou (2006). Importantly, in these studies, the location of the peripheral target is unpredictable (i.e., they do not always appear at the same peripheral location), and the targets are presented for brief durations so that the observer cannot make a visual saccade and redirect their fixation to the target location. The conclusion, therefore, is that the deaf observers had allocated more of their attention to the whole of the peripheral field prior to the onset of the target.

Another common technique for analyzing how attention is distributed across the visual field is the *flanker compatibility paradigm*. In this paradigm, participants are required to identify a target (usually presented at fixation in the center of a screen). The decision is typically a two-alternative forced choice, using stimuli such as shapes (square or diamond), letters (H or S), or arrows (← or →). Accompanying the target are peripheral distractors, located at varying degrees of visual angle (usually to the left and right of the target). These distractors can be congruent with the target (e.g., square target and square distractors) or incongruent (e.g., square target and diamond distractors). By measuring how long it takes an observer to respond accurately to the target and how many mistakes they make, the degree of processing of the distractors can be measured. Typically, congruent distractors will speed responses (or have little effect), whereas incongruent distractors will slow down responses and lead to more errors. The more attention that an observer allocates to peripheral vision, the greater their sensitivity to the distractors, and the greater the influence of those distractors on response times and errors. Although this greater influence can be considered as a sign of greater distractibility, fundamentally it reflects greater processing resources allocated to the distractors.

In a task employing a flanker compatibility paradigm, enhanced processing of peripheral distractors located at 4.2 degrees of visual angle from a concurrent target has been reported for deaf native signers relative to hearing participants (Proksch & Bavelier, 2002). In this experiment, participants were asked to identify shapes positioned in a circular pattern around fixation, while ignoring distractors placed peripherally to the circular pattern. The proposal that deaf individuals have greater attentional resources in the periphery predicts that peripherally located distractors will receive more attentional resources and thus be more distracting for deaf than for hearing individuals. This peripheral condition was contrasted with a condition in which the distractor was presented centrally. Results confirmed the known finding that, in hearing individuals, central distractors are more distracting than peripheral distractors. In contrast, deaf individuals were more distracted by peripheral distractors than were hearing individuals, and, interestingly, less so by central distractors.

These findings establish that, whereas in hearing individuals attention is at its peak in the center of the visual field, deaf individuals show greater attention at peripheral locations. Subsequently, Sladen et al. (2005) confirmed greater processing of peripheral distractors in deaf individuals by showing that the responses of deaf individuals were more influenced by distractor letters positioned at ~1.5 degrees from a letter target than were hearing controls. Following the same logic, Dye, Baril, and Bavelier (2007) recently showed that nonletter distractors (arrows) positioned at increasing eccentricities (1.0, 2.0, and 3.0 degrees) increasingly affected target performance in deaf individuals as compared with hearing individuals. Finally, using peripheral kinetic and foveal static perimetry—where observers are asked to respond when they can see a moving or static light point, respectively—deaf individuals were reported to be better than hearing controls at detecting moving lights in the periphery, manifested as a difference in field of view (Stevens & Neville, 2006). No difference was observed in their sensitivity to static points of light presented in central vision. What all of these "compensation" studies have in common is that they focus upon visual attention skills—how the deaf individuals allocate limited processing resources to the visual scene—and report enhanced attention to the periphery for deaf native signers across a range of visual angles (from 1.5 to over 60 degrees).

In the previous literature, this greater peripheral processing has often been interpreted as greater distractibility in deaf individuals. Here, we argue that it is better understood as a difference in allocation of attentional resources between deaf and hearing observers, with enhanced peripheral processing in deaf people and enhanced central processing in hearing people. This view predicts that deaf individuals should be more distracted by irrelevant peripheral information, but hearing individuals should be more distracted by irrelevant central information. Accordingly, in tasks where the target is slightly off-center, deaf individuals are more distracted by peripheral distractors but hearing individuals by central distractors (Proksch & Bavelier, 2002). In terms of adaptation to the environment, the attentional change observed in deaf individuals makes intuitive sense—a redistribution of visual attention to the periphery can compensate for the lack of peripheral auditory cues provided by the environment, such as the sound of an approaching vehicle or the creak of an opening door.

Importantly, such enhanced peripheral attention has been observed in deaf signers, but not in hearing individuals who are native signers (Bavelier et al., 2001; Neville and Lawson, 1987c; Proksch and Bavelier, 2002). The lack of a similar effect in hearing native signers demonstrates that using a visuo-manual signed language such as ASL is not sufficient to induce changes in peripheral attention. Rather, deafness appears to be the leading factor in this reorganization of the attentional system.

In contrast to these changes in visual attention, in which the onset and location of stimuli are unknown, attempts to demonstrate changes in basic visual skills among deaf native signers using psychophysical methods (where target location and onset are known a priori) have been unsuccessful. For example, in a task measuring contrast sensitivity thresholds across different spatial frequencies, temporal frequencies, and spatial locations, Finney, Fine, and Dobkins (2001a) reported no differences between deaf and hearing individuals. An absence of overall population effects has also been found in measures of visual flicker (Bross & Sauerwein, 1980), brightness discrimination (Bross, 1979), and temporal discrimination (Mills, 1985; Poizner & Tallal, 1987). Even psychophysical thresholds for motion processing have been found to be equivalent in deaf and hearing individuals. Sensitivity for motion direction and for small changes in motion velocity was compared in deaf native signers and hearing individuals, and no detectable difference was reported (Bosworth & Dobkins, 2002a,b; Brozinsky & Bavelier, 2004). This lack of effect stands in contrast to other studies, such as the kinetic perimetry study mentioned earlier, which document enhanced processing of motion information in deaf native signers when presented under conditions of attention.

The same dissociation between attentional changes but little to no perceptual change has been observed in the domain of touch: deaf individuals have been shown to have equivalent thresholds for detecting differences in vibration frequency, but a superior ability to detect a change in vibration frequency under conditions of attention, when the time of onset of the change in vibration is unknown (Levanen & Hamdorf, 2001). One working hypothesis is that a sensory loss leads to changes in higher-level attentional processing, especially in domains in which information from multiple senses is integrated (Bavelier, Dye, & Hauser, 2006; Bavelier & Neville, 2002). It thus appears that early deafness results in a redistribution of attentional resources to the periphery, most commonly observed when input from peripheral and central space competes for privileged access to processing resources.

Altered Distribution of Visual Attention in Deaf Individuals: Imaging Studies

Given the observed changes in the distribution of visual attention that have been observed behaviorally among deaf native signers, it makes sense to ask whether we can observe associated neurological changes. There is now a substantial body of work looking at compensational changes in brain activation following early auditory deprivation. One well-studied brain area is the medial temporal area/medial superior temporal area (MT/ MST), an area of visual cortex involved in the detection and analysis of movement. When viewing unattended moving stimuli, deaf and hearing individuals do not differ in the amount of activation in MT/MST cortex. However, when required to attend to peripheral movement and ignore concurrent central motion, enhanced recruitment of MT/MST is observed in deaf native signers as compared with hearing controls (Bavelier et al., 2000, 2001; Fine, Finney, Boynton, & Dobkins, 2005). This pattern echoes a general trend in the literature, whereby the greatest population differences have been reported for motion stimuli in the visual periphery under conditions that engage selective attention, such as when the location or time of arrival of the stimulus is unknown or when the stimulus has to be selected from among distractors (Bavelier et al., 2006).

There are several potential ways in which cross-modal reorganization could support the changes observed in the spatial distribution of visual attention in deaf individuals. One possibility is that an expansion occurs in the representation of the peripheral visual field in early visual cortex. However, currently, little data supports this hypothesis (Fine et al., 2005). Another possibility is that, in deaf individuals, multimodal associative cortex—parts of the brain that combine information from different sensory modalities—may display a greater sensitivity to input from remaining modalities such as vision and touch. Evidence for this hypothesis comes from studies reporting changes in the posterior parietal cortex of deaf individuals (Bavelier et al., 2000, 2001), an area known to be involved in the integration of information from different sensory modalities. Finally, it is possible that in deaf individuals the lack of input from audition causes the auditory cortex—which is multimodal in nature—to reorganize and process visual information. Indeed, there is some evidence that auditory areas in the superior temporal sulcus show greater recruitment in deaf than in hearing individuals for visual, tactile, and signed input (Bavelier et al., 2001; Finney, Fine, & Dobkins, 2001b; Finney, Clementz, Hickok, & Dobkins, 2003; Levanen, Jousmaki, & Hari, 1998; Neville et al., 1998).

To conclude, behavioral studies suggest that a redistribution of attentional resources occurs in deaf individuals, with an enhancement of peripheral space that can be accompanied by a reduction at competing central locations. These behavioral differences are accompanied by neural changes suggesting cross-modal reorganization in areas that integrate information from different modalities and possible recruitment of multimodal cortex in auditory regions for the processing of visual information.

Summary and Implications

Deaf children have been reported to be inattentive and easily distracted. However, this may be a reflection of how they allocate attentional resources, as well as other factors such as linguistic competence and teacher–parent attributions, as opposed to a state of inattentiveness and attentional pathology per se. With respect to attentional allocation, problems may arise when there is a conflict between the demands of the environment and the default allocation of resources. For example, in structured learning environments, such as classrooms, a deaf child's attention has to be focused upon an instructor or an interpreter. When sources of visual distraction occur in the periphery, a deaf child may appear to be inattentive, as their attention is constantly being drawn toward those peripheral events. Note, however, that in other environments such an adaptation in resource allocation may be beneficial. For example, a research report published by the California Department of Motor Vehicles suggested that deaf drivers had driving records the same as or better than hearing drivers,[1] and the ability to better process peripheral information may also confer certain advantages in team sports (Knudson & Kluka, 1997), although reports to date are only anecdotal.[2]

The concern, here, is with learning environments and how best to construct learning environments in which deaf children are less distracted by events in the periphery, allowing them to focus their resources upon the task at hand. The behavioral research cited here suggests that deaf individuals cannot help but be distracted by visual information in their peripheral vision. This is perhaps unintuitive for the hearing reader, who experiences distraction more commonly from visual input in the center of their visual field. Imagine your frustration, for example, if every word on this page were to change color as soon as you fixated upon it. But for the deaf individual, inattention may occur more easily as a result of visual activity that is away from the direction of their overt gaze. It is not that they are being inattentive toward what they are looking at directly, but rather that they cannot help but allow peripheral input to draw their covert attention away from the task at hand, in much the same way that hearing individuals cannot help but be distracted by central distractors.

Any modification of the learning environment that aims to counteract these sources of visual distraction must also be sensitive to the psychological and cultural needs of the deaf child. It appears that the change observed in their attentional system is an adaptive change—it allows them to adapt to their environment, given the lack of an auditory sense to inform them about the environment and guide the focus of their attention. Thus, positioning a deaf child at the front of the classroom with their classmates behind them, or in a position where they cannot see out of windows or

---

1. State of California DMV Research Report No. 42, see http://www.dmv.ca.gov/about/profile/rd/rde2.htm.
2. See Stiles, J. (March 24–30, 2004) Deaf player excels through field vision and skill. *The Villager, 73* (47), published online at http://www.thevillager.com/villager_47/deafplayersexcels.html.

through the classroom door, may actually exacerbate the difficulties they encounter in the formal learning environment. Positioning of the child in this manner will in effect serve to counter the adaptation that has arisen in their visual system and may be disconcerting and lead to greater distraction. This is because the enhancement in their peripheral vision is attentional and thus more evident when the timing and location of events in the periphery is unknown. Indeed, when the onset time and location of a peripheral stimulus is known a priori, deaf and hearing individuals do not differ in their sensitivity to those stimuli.

With this in mind, one approach may be allowing the deaf child or college student to "learn" their visual environment. Small class sizes, with a semicircular arrangement of seats, and consistent seating positions for each student across the term of instruction may result in a more predictable learning environment, one in which the deaf student can successfully learn to ignore abrupt onset stimuli at specific locations in their peripheral space. Unpredictable distraction may also be minimized by reducing the ebb-and-flow of traffic through the learning environment. Further classroom research involving the active participation of deaf children, deaf adults, and teachers will be required in determining how best to arrange the physical layout of learning environments to maximize the ability of the deaf child to attend to formal instruction. The literature on visual attention in deaf children and adults suggests, however, that the best practices will be those that produce a visually predictable environment in which deaf students can learn to predict and therefore ignore task-irrelevant stimuli that may distract them from attending to their instructor or other learning resource.

References

Altshuler, K. Z., Deming, W. E., Vollenweider, J., Ranier, J. D., & Tendler, R. (1976). Impulsivity and early profound deafness: A cross-cultural inquiry. *American Annals of the Deaf, 121*, 331–345.

Bavelier, D., Brozinsky, C., Tomann, A., Mitchell, T., Neville, H., & Liu, G. (2001). Impact of early deafness and early exposure to sign language on the cerebral organization for motion processing. *The Journal of Neuroscience, 21* (22), 8931–8942.

Bavelier, D., Dye, M.W.G., & Hauser, P. C. (2006). Do deaf individuals see better? *Trends in Cognitive Sciences, 10*, 512–518.

Bavelier, D., & Neville, H. J. (2002). Cross-modal plasticity: Where and how? *Nature Review Neuroscience, 3*, 443–452.

Bavelier, D., Tomann, A., Hutton, C., Mitchell, T., Corina, D., Liu, G., & Neville, H. (2000). Visual attention to the periphery is enhanced in congenitally deaf individuals. *The Journal of Neuroscience, 20* (17), RC93, 1–6.

Bosworth, R. G., & Dobkins, K. R. (2002a). The effects of spatial attention on motion processing in deaf signers, hearing signers, and hearing nonsigners. *Brain and Cognition, 49* (1), 152–169.

Bosworth, R. G., & Dobkins, K. R. (2002b). Visual field asymmetries for motion processing in deaf and hearing signers. *Brain and Cognition, 49* (1), 170–181.

Bross, M. (1979). Residual sensory capacities of the deaf: A signal detection analysis of a visual discrimination task. *Perceptual and Motor Skills,* 48, 187–194.

Bross, M., & Sauerwein, H. (1980). Signal detection analysis of visual flicker in deaf and hearing individuals. *Perceptual and Motor Skills,* 51, 839–843.

Brozinsky, C. J., & Bavelier, D. (2004). Motion velocity thresholds in deaf signers: Changes in lateralization but not in overall sensitivity. *Cognitive Brain Research, 21,* 1–10.

Chen, Q., Zhang, M., & Zhou, X. (2006). Effects of spatial distribution of attention during inhibition of return (IOR) on flanker interference in hearing and congenitally deaf people. *Brain Research, 1109,* 117–127.

Chess, S. Korn, S. J., & Fernandez, P. B. (1971). *Psychiatric disorders of children with congenital rubella.* New York: Brunner-Mazel.

Dye, M. W. G., Baril, D. E., & Bavelier, D. (2007). Which aspects of visual attention are changed by deafness? The case of the attentional network task. *Neuropsychologia, 48* (8), 1801–1811.

Fine, I., Finney, E. M., Boynton, G. M., & Dobkins, K. R. (2005). Comparing the effects of auditory deprivation and sign language within the auditory and visual cortex. *Journal of Cognitive Neuroscience, 17* (10), 1621–1637.

Finney, E. M., Clementz, B. A., Hickok, G., & Dobkins, K. R. (2003). Visual stimuli activate auditory cortex in deaf subjects: Evidence from MEG. *Neuroreport, 14* (11), 1425–1427.

Finney, E. M., Fine, I., & Dobkins, K. R. (2001a). Visual contrast sensitivity in deaf versus hearing populations: Exploring the perceptual consequences of auditory deprivation and experience with a visual language. *Brain Research and Cognitive Brain Research, 11,* 171–183.

Finney, E. M., Fine, I., & Dobkins, K. R. (2001b). Visual stimuli activate auditory cortex in the deaf. *Nature Neuroscience, 4* (12), 1171–1173.

Gordon, M., & Mettleman, B. B. (1987). *Technical guide to the Gordon Diagnostic System (GDS).* DeWitt, NY: Gordon Systems.

Hauser, P., Cohen, J., Dye, M.W.G., & Bavelier, D. (2007). Visual constructive and visual-motor skills in deaf native signers. *Journal of Deaf Studies and Deaf Education, 12* (2), 148–157.

Hauser, P. C., Wills, K., & Isquith, P. K. (2006). Hard of hearing, deafness, and being deaf. In J. D. Farmer and S. Warschausky (Eds.), *Neurodevelopmental disabilities: Clinical research and practice* (pp. 119–131). New York: Guilford Publications, Inc.

Hayes, G. M. (1955). A *study of the visual perception of orally educated deaf children.* Amherst, MA: University of Massachusetts.

King, B. H., Hauser, P. C., & Isquith, P. K. (2006). Psychiatric aspects of blindness and severe visual impairment, and deafness and severe hearing loss in children. In C. E. Coffey and R. A. Brumback (Eds.), *Textbook of pediatric neuropsychiatry* (pp. 397–423). Washington, DC: American Psychiatric Association.

Knudson, D., & Kluka, D. A. (1997). The impact of vision and vision training on sport performance. *The Journal of Physical Education, Recreation and Dance, 68* (4), 17–24.

Ladd, N. P. (2003). *In search of deafhood.* Clevedon, U.K.: Multilingual Matters.

Larr, A. L. (1956). Perceptual and conceptual ability of residential school deaf children. *Exceptional Children, 23,* 63–66, 88.

Leark, R. A., Dupuy, T. R., Greenberg, L. M., Corman, C. L., & Kindschi, C. L. (1999). *T.O.V.A. test of variables of attention.* Los Alamitos, CA: Universal Attention Disorders, Inc.

Lesser, S. R., & Easser, B. R. (1972). Personality differences in the perceptually handicapped. *Journal of the American Academy of Child Psychiatry, 11,* 458–466.

Levanen, S., & Hamdorf, D. (2001). Feeling vibrations: Enhanced tactile sensitivity in congenitally deaf humans. *Neuroscience Letters, 301,* 75–77.

Levanen, S., Jousmaki, V., & Hari, R. (1998). Vibration-induced auditory-cortex activation in a congenitally deaf adult. *Current Biology, 8* (15), 869–872.

Loke, W. H., & Song, S. (1991). Central and peripheral visual processing in hearing and nonhearing individuals. *Bulletin of the Psychonomic Society, 29*(5), 437–440.

Martini, A., Mazzoli, M., & Kimberling, W. (1997). An introduction to genetics of normal and defective hearing. *Annals of the New York Academy of Sciences, 830,* 361–374.

McKay, B. E. (1952). *An exploratory study of the psychological effects of severe hearing impairment.* Syracuse, NY: Syracuse University, Syracuse.

Meadow, K. P. (1976). Behavior problems of deaf children. In H. S. Schlesinger and K. P. Meadow (Eds.), *Studies of family interaction, language acquisition and deafness* (pp. 257–293). San Francisco: University of California.

Meadow, K. P. (1980). *Deafness and child development.* Berkeley, CA: University of California Press.

Mills, C. (1985). Perception of visual temporal patterns by deaf and hearing adults. *Bulletin of the Psychonomic Society, 23,* 483–486.

Mitchell, T. V., & Quittner, A. L. (1996). Multimethod study of attention and behavior problems in hearing-impaired children. *Journal of Clinical Child Psychology, 25*(1), 83–96.

Myklebust, H. R., & Brutten, M. A. (1953). A study of the visual perception of deaf children. *Acta Otolaryngologica,* Supplement 105.

Neville, H. J., Bavelier, D., Corina, D., Rauschecker, J., Karni, A., Lalwani, A., Braun, A., Clark, V., Jezzard, P., & Turner, R. (1998). Cerebral organization for language in deaf and hearing subjects: Biological constraints and effects of experience. *Proceedings of the National Academy of Sciences USA, 95* (3), 922–929.

Neville, H. J., & Lawson, D. S. (1987a). Attention to central and peripheral visual space in a movement detection task: An event-related potential and behavioral study. I. Normal hearing adults. *Brain Research, 405,* 253–267.

Neville, H. J., & Lawson, D. S. (1987b). Attention to central and peripheral visual space in a movement detection task: An event related potential and behavioral study. II. Congenitally deaf adults. *Brain Research, 405,* 268–283.

Neville, H. J., & Lawson, D. S. (1987c). Attention to central and peripheral visual space in a movement decision task. III. Separate effects of auditory deprivation and acquisition of a visual language. *Brain Research, 405,* 284–294.

Neville, H. J., Schmidt, A. L., & Kutas, M. (1983). Altered visual-evoked potentials in congenitally deaf adults. *Brain Research, 266,* 127–132.

Osterrieth, P. A. (1944). Le test de copie d'une figure complex: Contribution a l'etude de la perception et de la memoire [The test of copying a complex figure: A contribution to the study of perception and memory]. *Archives de Psychologie, 30*, 206–356.

Padden, C., & Humphries, T. (2005). *Inside Deaf culture*. Cambridge, MA: Harvard University Press.

Parasnis, I, Samar, V. J., & Berent, G. P. (2003). Deaf adults without attention deficit hyperactivity disorder display reduced perceptual sensitivity on the Test of Variables of Attention (T.O.V.A.). *Journal of Speech, Language, and Hearing Research, 46*(5), 1166–1183.

Petit, C. (1996). Genes responsible for human hereditary deafness: Symphony of a thousand. *Nature Genetics, 14*, 385–391.

Poizner, H., & Tallal, P. (1987). Temporal processing in deaf signers. *Brain and Language, 30*, 52–62.

Proksch, J., & Bavelier, D. (2002). Changes in the spatial distribution of visual attention after early deafness. *Journal of Cognitive Neuroscience, 14*(5), 687–701.

Quittner, A. L., Glueckauf, R. L., & Jackson, D. N. (1990). Chronic parenting stress: Moderating versus mediating effects of social support. *Journal of Personality and Social Psychology, 59* (6), 1266–1278.

Quittner, A. L., Leibach, P., & Marciel, K. (2004). The impact of cochlear implants on young deaf children: New methods to assess cognitive and behavioral development. *Archives of Otolaryngology and Head and Neck Surgery, 130(5)*:547–554.

Quittner, A. L., Smith, L. B., Osberger, M. J., Mitchell, T. V., & Katz, D. B. (1994). The impact of audition on the development of visual attention. *Psychological Science, 5*(6), 347–353.

Reivich, R. S., & Rothrock, I. A. (1972). Behavior problems of deaf children and adolescents: A factor-analytic study. *Journal of Speech and Hearing Research, 15*, 84–92.

Ries, P. W. (1994). Prevalence and characteristics of persons with hearing trouble: United States, 1990–91. *Vital Health Statistics, 10* (188), 1–75.

Rey, A. (1941). L'examen psychologique dans les cas d'encephalopathie tramatique (Les problemes) [Psychological examination in cases of traumatic encephalopathy]. *Archives de Psychologie, 28*, 286–340.

Sladen, D. P., Tharpe, A. M., Ashmead, D. H., Wesley Grantham, D., & Chun, M. M. (2005). Visual attention in deaf and normal hearing adults: Effects of stimulus compatibility. *Journal of Speech, Language, and Hearing Research, 48*(6), 1529–1537.

Smith, L. B., Quittner, A. L., Osberger, M. J., & Miyamoto, R. (1998). Audition and visual attention: The developmental trajectory in deaf and hearing populations. *Developmental Psychology, 34*(5), 840–850.

Stevens, C., & Neville, H. (2006). Neuroplasticity as a double-edged sword: Deaf enhancements and dyslexic deficits in motion processing. *Journal of Cognitive Neuroscience, 18*, 701–714.

Wechsler, D. (1997). *Wechsler memory scale, third edition*. San Antonio: The Psychological Corporation.

Werner, H., & Strauss, A. A. (1941). Pathology of figure-background relation in the child. *Journal of Abnormal and Social Psychology, 36*, 236–248.

Chapter 10

Visual Gaze as a Marker of Deaf Students' Attention During Mediated Instruction

Jeff B. Pelz, Marc Marschark, and Carol Convertino

Deaf and hard-of-hearing (DHH) students are now enrolled at a majority of colleges and universities in the United States (National Center for Education Statistics, 1999). Consequently, instruction mediated through sign language interpretation has become more and more common in higher education. At the same time, it is increasingly common for instructors to augment traditional lectures with visual displays, encouraged by research demonstrating that memory and learning are enhanced by engaging multiple modalities (Hegarty & Just, 1989; Iding, 2000; Paivio, 1971, 1986; Presno, 1997; Tiene, 2000). But integrating what is a "parallel" presentation of visual and verbal information to hearing students requires the concurrent input of multiple visual streams for DHH students. Despite evidence that some DHH individuals may have enhanced performance in the visual periphery (e.g., Bavelier et al., 2000; Dye, Hauser, & Bavelier, this volume; Swisher, 1993), the design of the visual system precludes the use of peripheral vision to gather high-acuity information.

Because of neural limitations, acuity varies dramatically across the visual field. Dropping by orders of magnitude from central vision to the far periphery, we are typically unaware of this severe *anisotropy* because the eyes move to compensate. The spatial limitation can be demonstrated by fixing your gaze on the first word of a line of text and trying to read the rest of the line without moving your eyes. The fovea covers approximately 1 degree of visual angle, only enough to cover an average word at typical reading distance. Because only a small part of the field is imaged with high acuity at any given time, observers must move their gaze about the scene to sample the environment with the high-acuity fovea. So, while hearing students can take advantage of multiple, concurrent streams of information in the modern classroom, the sign language interpreter is actively converting the instructor's voice into another visual input. In this environment of multiple visual inputs, DHH students need to rapidly shift their attention between the instructor, the sign language interpreter, and the visual display.

In two separate experiments, described later, wearable eyetracking devices were used to monitor the gaze of DHH and hearing students in a classroom environment that included instruction mediated through sign language. While traditional eye-tracking systems have been limited to simple tasks performed in a reduced laboratory setting, the new instrumentation allows the study of the attentional strategies of students in the classroom. This environment, which provides special challenges for the DHH student population, is especially challenging because some sign language information (e.g., finger spelling) may indeed require *foveation*—that is, focusing on the hand with central vision.

In each experiment, three groups of students participated: hearing students who did not know sign language, skilled signers, and new signers— DHH students with varying but very limited levels of experience with sign language. The DHH students were categorized as "skilled" or "new" based on self-report and review by an educational sign language interpreter. More than half of the new signers learned sign language when they arrived at the Rochester Institute of Technology (RIT); others learned in high school, and two students were exposed to sign language at a young age but did not remain immersed in it enough to become skilled signers (mean age of acquisition = 14.1 years, SD = 6.8).

The Oculomotor System

The oculomotor system, comprised of six muscles attached to each eye, moves the eyes over 100,000 times every day, alternately shifting the central, high-acuity fovea to new regions of interest, then stabilizing the retinal image for a period typically lasting 100–500 milliseconds before shifting again. The oculomotor system therefore performs two functions: (a) it maintains a stable gaze while information is gathered from a point in the visual scene, referred to as *fixation;* and (b) it moves the point of gaze to the next point of interest. The simplest viewing condition involves a stationary observer viewing a static scene. Maintaining fixation on an object in this case requires only that the eyes be motionless. Moving the gaze from one point of interest to another is accomplished with *saccadic* eye movements. These very rapid (>500 deg/sec), ballistic movements of the eyes are made several times per second to bring the fovea to regions requiring high acuity. Saccades are also made to regions of a scene to which attention is deployed, even when foveal acuity is not required for a given task.

This foveation behavior provides an opportunity to probe the temporal and spatial deployment of attention by using gaze as a marker of attention. By monitoring DHH and hearing students' gaze, it is possible to infer the manner in which they distributed their visual attention among the instructor, sign language interpreter (when present), and a projected display.

Measuring Visual Gaze

In these experiments, students were seated but free to move their heads during the lectures. Because of the head movements, and because the instructor and interpreter were moving, students made *smooth-pursuit* and *vestibular-ocular reflex (VOR)* eye movements in addition to the saccadic eye movements. Smooth-pursuit eye movements stabilize the retinal image of objects that move with respect to the observer, while VOR eye movements compensate for head movements by counter-rotating the eyes to stabilize the retinal image.

The eye-movement records of DHH and hearing college students were made up of (a) fixations, when the eyes were essentially stationary in the head, as when watching the instructor's face; (b) saccades, when moving gaze among instructor, interpreter, and display; reading text on the visual display; or looking between the interpreters' face and hands; (c) smooth pursuit, when tracking the interpreter's hand motions; and (d) VOR, during head movements. Since the term *fixation* is more typically used to refer to a brief duration when the eyes are fixed on a single target, for the purposes of this study, the term "gaze" is used to describe one or more temporally contiguous fixations within a small region. So, for example, if a student made a series of 15 individual fixations while reading text and looking at an image within the computer display for a total of 5400 msec, then made a large saccade to the interpreter, analysis would yield a single gaze to the computer display lasting 5.4 seconds followed by a gaze to the interpreter.

Implications of Live Versus Videotaped Presentations

Only two students can be tracked at a time, so the challenge of presenting repeated live lectures makes it preferable to use videotaped lectures. But this leads to the concern that the use of videotaped lectures and interpreting might suffer from the loss of 3D cues present in the live lecture/interpreting setting and the loss of feedback between students and interpreter. Sign language inherently entails grammatical use of three-dimensional space, raising the concern that two-dimensional displays could lose information critical to student performance. The effects of student–interpreter feedback might also affect student performance.

These questions were considered in experiments reported in Marschark et al. (2005). In one experiment, the value of interpreter–student feedback and 3D cues were examined by manipulating both variables in four conditions. Feedback was varied from *full* to *no-feedback* in two live conditions by adjusting the lighting on the interpreter in a performing-arts classroom. In the full condition, the lighting was normal, allowing the students and interpreter normal feedback. In the no-feedback condition, lighting was arranged so that the students could see the interpreter and had access to full 3D cues, but the interpreter could not see the students' faces, thus preventing the feedback that is normally available in a classroom setting. The two videotaped conditions varied the playback size of the interpreter. In the *life-sized* condition, the videotaped interpreter was projected life size on a screen; in the *television* condition, the interpreter was shown on a television monitor. Analysis of the learning outcomes in the four conditions showed that there were no statistically significant differences due to the availability of feedback or 3D cues among the 145 DHH students who viewed the live and videotaped lectures.

Eye Tracking Gaze Behavior

A second experiment in the Marschark et al. (2005) study was conducted using lightweight, head-mounted RIT Wearable Eyetrackers to monitor the gaze behavior of both DHH and hearing students as they viewed prerecorded lectures. The RIT Wearable Eyetracker is a video-based eyetracker with two miniature video cameras mounted on eyeglass frames (see Figure 10–1). One camera images the participant's eye and the second camera is mounted

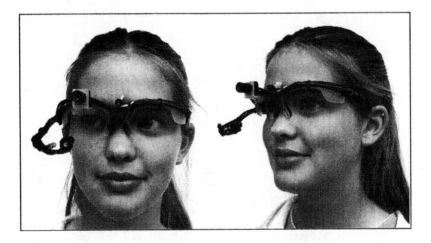

Figure 10–1. RIT Wearable Eyetracker headgear.

above the eye being tracked to image the scene from the participant's perspective. A low-power infrared LED illuminates the eye. The video from
the eye and scene cameras were multiplexed into a single NTSC video signal and recorded to videotape for off-line analysis. See Babcock and Pelz
(2004) for a full description of the eyetracker.

Off-line analysis provided important benefits over traditional real-time
gaze tracking. Calibration, which normally takes several minutes to complete before a trial can begin, is completed off-line after the trial has ended.
This is especially important in these experiments, in which two participants
were tracked at the same time. The synchronized eye and scene records can
be paused during off-line calibration, making it unnecessary to stabilize the
head during calibration. This essentially eliminates the tedious and often
frustrating calibration procedure that would otherwise have to take place
before each trial. Additionally, the off-line calibration can be repeated as
often as necessary to achieve a reliable gaze pattern record. Before each trial,
participants were instructed to follow a spot projected on the wall by a laser
pointer forming a five-point calibration pattern. The calibration pattern was
displayed again at the end of the lecture to verify calibration.

After the trial was completed and the participants left the classroom,
the multiplexed video containing the eye and scene video records was
demultiplexed and input to a traditional dark-pupil eyetracker (ISCAN
726-PCI). After calibration, the eyetracker provided a video output showing the participant's viewpoint, with a cursor overlaid showing gaze position, as seen in Figure 10–2. Because the scene camera is attached to the

**Figure 10–2. Frame from eyetracker output; crosshair indicates
gaze position.**

headgear and participants were free to move their heads, the scene image was sometimes rotated, as in Figure 10–2, where the head is rotated approximately 10 degrees. The eyetracker monitors gaze position by locating the pupil center and the first-surface corneal reflection of the infrared illuminator in each video frame of the eye image and mapping it to the observer's point-of-regard in the scene image. The tracker has an accuracy of approximately 1 degree of visual angle in the central field and 2–3 degrees near the periphery; calibration was optimized in the regions including the instructor and interpreter.

The participants' eye movements were analyzed by examining the video records manually using a computer-controlled VCR. The videotape could be moved forward or backward at variable speed, and moved frame-by-frame under computer control. A frame-accurate timecode was read by the lab computer to correlate gaze changes to the time at which they occurred. A complete discussion of the data analysis system can be found in Pelz and Canosa (2001).

The scene was divided into three regions of interest (ROIs)—the *Instructor*, the *Interpreter*, and the *Display*, as shown in Figure 10–3. The timecode was marked whenever the track moved in or out of one of the ROIs. Track losses, blinks, and fixations to areas outside the three defined areas totaled less than 2% of the trial duration and were excluded from analysis. Metrics included the distribution and duration of students' gaze as they viewed the instructor, interpreter, and display.

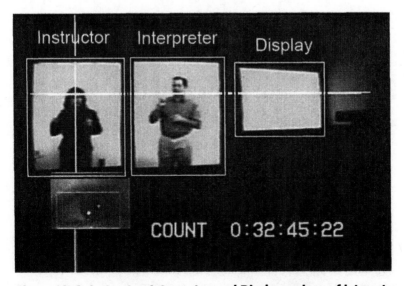

Figure 10–3. Instructor, Interpreter, and Display regions of interest.

Live Versus Videotaped Presentations: Gaze Behavior

Before describing the two new experiments, a second experiment reported in Marschark et al. (2005), which measured both learning outcomes and gaze behavior for live and videotaped lectures, will be reviewed. Thirty-two students were recruited for the study; 10 hearing students and 22 DHH students. Eleven DHH students were categorized as "skilled" and 11 as "new" signers based on self-report and review by an educational sign language interpreter. The skilled signers had learned sign language at a mean age of 2.8 years (SD = 2.8); the new signers at a mean age of 14.9 years (SD = 6.4), an average skewed by the fact that two of the students reported "learning" to sign as young children but not having used it since. None of the hearing students knew sign language. Two hearing faculty members presented 15-minute introductory lectures that included PowerPoint® slides. The lectures were interpreted by an experienced educational sign language interpreter. Each participant saw one lecture presented and interpreted in real time (the "Live" condition) and the same lectures presented from videotape, projected life-size in the same classroom (the "*Memorex*®" condition; see Figure 10–2). Analyses again showed no statistically significant differences due to live or videotaped presentation, so analyses were collapsed across presentation condition.

The eyetracking records were analyzed to determine the ROI throughout the trial. Figure 10–4 shows the relative time that gaze was deployed into the Instructor, Interpreter, and Display regions by group. The hearing

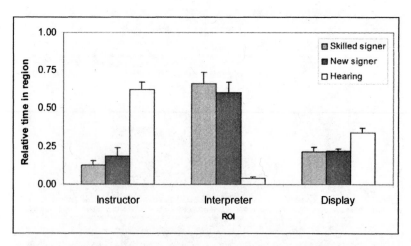

Figure 10–4. Fraction of time gaze spent in each region for skilled signer, new signer, and hearing students. Error bars represent 1 SEM (after Marschark et al., 2005).

students spent approximately 62% of the trial looking toward the instructor, 34% looking at the display, and 4% looking at the interpreter. The skilled and new signers' gaze behavior was nearly the reverse in terms of the instructor and interpreter; they spent between 60% and 66% of the time looking toward the interpreter, 12%–18% looking at the instructor, and 22% of the time looking to the display.

Note that Figure 10–4 represents the relative time spent in each area and does not carry information about the duration of individual gaze segments. Figure 10–5 shows the mean gaze duration in each region for skilled signers, new signers, and hearing students. Recall that "gaze duration" in this context refers to the total time a subject's gaze remains within one of the three regions, and typically contains a number of individual fixations. The basic pattern between hearing and DHH students' gaze behavior in the Instructor and Interpreter regions is reflected in gaze duration. When hearing students did look to the interpreter, they maintained their gaze in that region for less than 1 second on average before moving to the instructor or display regions, whereas the DHH students remained in the interpreter region for 4.5 seconds (skilled signers) and 6.0 seconds (new signers).

Paralleling the results for relative time in each area, the opposite trend was true for gaze in the Instructor region; hearing students' average gaze duration was over 4 seconds, while DHH students averaged only half that long: 2.4 seconds for new signers and 1.6 seconds for skilled signers. There was less variability between hearing and DHH students in the average duration of gaze in the Display region; skilled signers' average gaze duration

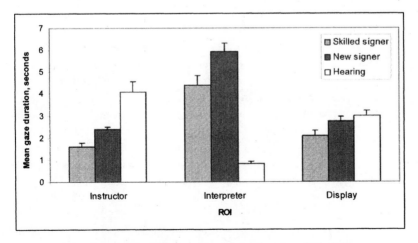

Figure 10–5. Mean gaze duration in each region for skilled signer, new signer, and hearing students. Error bars represent 1 SEM (after Marschark et al., 2005).

was 2.1 seconds, new signers' was 2.7 seconds, and hearing students averaged 3.0 seconds. Comparing Figure 10–4 and Figure 10–5 reveals, however, that while the trends in relative time and average gaze duration are similar, the ratios are quite different. Although the DHH students spent nearly 16 times as much time in the interpreter region than did the hearing students, their average duration of each individual gaze was only six times as long as the hearing students'. Similarly, although hearing students spent four times as much time looking in the instructor region as did the DHH students, their average gaze duration in that region was only twice as long as the DHH students'.

The students were free to move their heads during the task, and care was taken not to limit head movements by instruction. One advantage of the off-line calibration is the fact that participants do not need to hold their heads still while following the calibration laser spot. Previous experience has shown that individuals often are reluctant to make natural head movements after they have been told to hold their heads still for a calibration procedure, even when told that the calibration procedure is complete.

Although there was significant variability in the degree of head movements observed in this task, head movements were typically small and limited to gaze changes to the display region at the extreme right of the classroom. Wide variation in head movements has been reported in other situations (e.g., Bard, Fleury, & Paillard, 1992; Pelz, Hayhoe, & Loeber, 2001).

The results of these preliminary experiments are easily summarized. First, combined with the results from two learning tasks (see Marschark et al., 2005), the eyetracking data indicated that the deaf students were able to coordinate allocation of visual gaze in a way that resulted in comparable levels of comprehension with live and videotaped presentations. Contrary to assumptions by some educators and interpreters, learning was not affected by either the availability of three-dimensional visuospatial cues or student-interpreter feedback. This result is a positive sign for the future of remote interpreting, the utility of increasingly popular video relay services, and the potential accessibility of distance learning for DHH students. Video-based education might help to reduce deaf students' eye fatigue, provide opportunities for the review of previously interpreted material, and offer the possibility of rest breaks in the case of asynchronous presentation.

Although preliminary, the second important finding from this present study was that, although skilled signers might demonstrate enhanced visuospatial sensitivity in the periphery under carefully controlled conditions (Dye et al., this volume), those abilities do not appear to offset limitations of the visual system with regard to acuity in the periphery. The lack of reliable differences in patterns of gaze duration and transitions between skilled and new signers suggests that the real world may be too complex and information-rich for a simple bridge to exist between the modest enhancements of visual abilities observed among skilled deaf and hearing signers.

Of primary interest in this chapter are two new experiments that extend our earlier work, examining the effects of lecture speed; distance between the visual display, instructor, and interpreter; and mode of instruction.

Lecture Speed Versus Display Distance

In the first experiment, the effects of lecture speed and the distance between the visual display and the instructor and interpreter were examined. For this experiment, the lectures were manipulated along two dimensions: the speed of the lectures was varied to 85% and 115% of their original speed, and the distance between the visual display and the interpreter was varied during each presentation as shown in Figure 10–6 (the outline frames are shown for reference in the figure and were not visible during the trials). The interpreter was always presented next to the instructor. For half the students, the visual display started at the Near position (as in Marschark et al., 2005) and moved to the Middle position approximately one-third of the way through the lecture, then to the Far position for the final third of the lecture. The order was reversed for the remaining students.

The videotaped lectures were manipulated using Final Cut Pro 5.0 (Apple, Inc.). This software allows the speed of the videos to be manipulated without affecting the pitch of the audio. The 85% (*Slow*) and 115% (*Fast*) values were selected as the minimum and maximum values at which the interpreter's arm motion and finger spelling still appeared natural.

Three DLP projectors were prearranged in the classroom and connected to the display video by a three-way video switch, so that the presentation could be quickly switched at the same point for each participant. Although the order (Near-Middle-Far versus Far-Middle-Near) was counterbalanced, the point at which the display position was switched was held constant.

Two hearing faculty members were recruited for the study. They each developed a 15-minute introductory lecture that included PowerPoint® slides that they considered "moderately important" for comprehension of their lectures. One lecture was on the development of the Internet and the

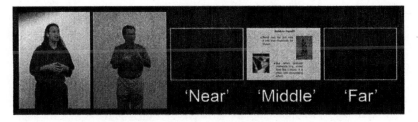

Figure 10–6. Near, Middle, and Far display positions.

other on granular physics. Each lecture was videotaped for presentation. A single, experienced interpreter interpreted both lectures and was also videotaped. To maximize the spatial resolution of the projected images, particularly for the "new" signers who might depend on speechreading, the instructor and interpreter were videotaped on separate Canon ZR-80 digital miniDV video cameras that were rotated 90 degrees into portrait mode. The videotapes were then projected on DLP projectors rotated to the same orientation. This methodology provided maximum pixel density and utilization of the visual frame. The PowerPoint slides were captured to digital videotape via S-video with a TView Gold Model 444–3700 (Focus Enhancements, Inc.) scan converter. Each video was edited to include a traditional film rotary countdown to simplify synchronization for playback. Each tape was paused at the same location, and then all three were started with a single Play command at the start of each trial.

Forty-eight students were recruited; 16 hearing students and 32 DHH students. Sixteen of the DHH students were categorized as skilled and 16 as new signers, based on self-report and review by an educational sign language interpreter. The skilled signers all began learning sign language by 3 years of age (mean = 1.6 years, SD = 0.9). Six of the new signers reported that they did not know sign language, nine learned between the age of 18 and 22, and the final participant reported using sign language only for 1 year at age 5. The mean age at which the 10 new signers with some sign-language experience first learned sign was 17.6 years (SD = 4.9). If the final participant (with just 1 year of sign language at age 5) is excluded, the mean age increases to 19.0 years (SD = 1.3). None of the hearing students knew sign language.

Each of the hearing, skilled signing, and new signing students saw one fast and one slow lecture in a within-subjects (Fast/Slow × Near/Middle/Far) design. Before each lecture, the students were fitted with the eyetrackers and instructed to "follow the laser pointer spot" as it was moved around the front of the classroom for off-line calibration. After each lecture, the students completed a post-test to assess their learning.

Figure 10–7 shows the relative time that the skilled signers spent in each of the three regions based on display position (Near/Middle/Far) and lecture speed (Fast/Slow). As is evident from the figure, neither variable had a significant effect on gaze distribution of the skilled signers, and the values were very similar to those reported in Marschark et al. (2005) for the normal speed presentation (compare to Figure 10–4). More variation occurred in gaze performance among hearing students, as seen in Figure 10–8. Again, the mean values were similar to those reported when the videotapes were viewed at normal speed, but there was a marked reduction in gaze to the Display in the Far condition regardless of playback speed. The extra time was shifted to the Instructor region.

Analysis of the new signers' gaze performance showed that their patterns looked very similar to the hearing students,' as seen in Figure 10–9.

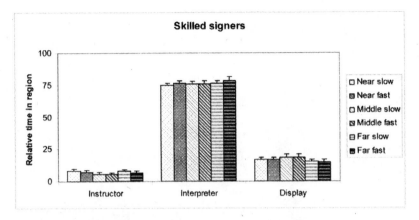

Figure 10–7. Fraction of time gaze spent in each region for skilled signer in the Near, Middle, and Far conditions for Fast and Slow presentations. Error bars represent 1 SEM.

This is quite different from the results reported in Marschark et al. (2005), where distribution of the new signers' gaze was most similar to the skilled signers (compare to Figure 10–4). Examination of the standard deviations of the relative time in each region shows that significantly more variation occurred within the new signer group than within the skilled signer or hearing groups. The standard deviations for new signers ranged from 19% to 25% and from 22% to 25% in the Interpreter and Instructor regions, respectively, compared to 6% to 11% and 3% to 7% for the skilled signers and 5% to 11% and 11% to 15% for the hearing students.

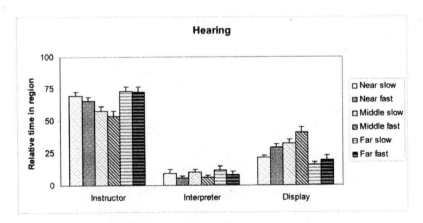

Figure 10–8. Fraction of time gaze spent in each region for hearing students in the Near, Middle, and Far conditions for Fast and Slow presentations. Error bars represent 1 SEM.

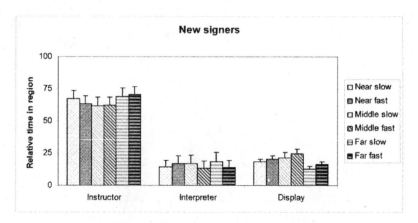

Figure 10–9. Fraction of time gaze spent in each region for new signers in the Near, Middle, and Far conditions for Fast and Slow presentations. Error bars represent 1 SEM.

Again, the variation in lecture speed, from 85% to 115%, had very little effect on the relative time students spent in each area. Recall that this metric describes the total time spent in each area and is not affected by the number or duration of individual gaze events into each region. Figure 10–10 shows the mean gaze duration for skilled signers across Near, Middle, and Far display positions for the Fast and Slow playback conditions. Note that in contrast to the relative time spent in the three regions (Figure 10–7), both display position and playback speed affect gaze duration in the Interpreter region.

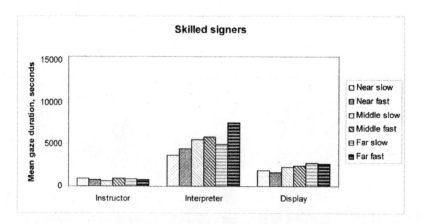

Figure 10–10. Mean gaze duration in each region for skilled signers in the Near, Middle, and Far conditions for Fast and Slow presentations.

Figure 10–11 shows the mean gaze duration for hearing students across display position and playback speed. The overall shift in gaze toward the instructor in the Far display condition is mirrored in the mean gaze duration, where the mean gaze duration approaches 8 seconds. The increase is even more pronounced among the new signers, where the average gaze duration in the Far display condition is over 13 seconds (see Figure 10–12).

In summary, the present results replicated our earlier findings, at least in the case of the lectures presented at normal speed. When shifting of gaze became "more costly," however, due to a greater distance between the primary source of information (interpreter or instructor) and the instructor's slides, deaf students reduced attention to the latter in favor of the former. The new signers showed a pattern closer to that displayed by the hearing students than the skilled signers, perhaps reflecting a greater reliance on speechreading of the instructor or utilization of residual hearing. Alternatively, that result might simply indicate that the newer signers have not developed optimal gaze allocation strategies, as they were much more variable than either the hearing students or the skilled signers. For all of the deaf students, however, varying the lecture speed, at least within the limits utilized here, had little if any effect on student gaze allocation (or learning), suggesting some amount of flexibility in the usual attention system.

The findings also suggest that deaf individuals, even if they are not skilled signers, have sufficient visual resources to deal with the learning situations encountered in the typical mainstream education classroom. The lack of a decrement in learning with video-based materials or with greater angular deviations between the primary source of information (interpreter/instructor) and visual displays provides some support for this suggestion.

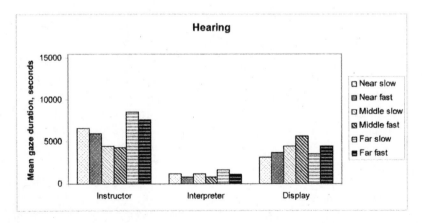

Figure 10–11. Mean gaze duration in each region for hearing students in the Near, Middle, and Far conditions for Fast and Slow presentations.

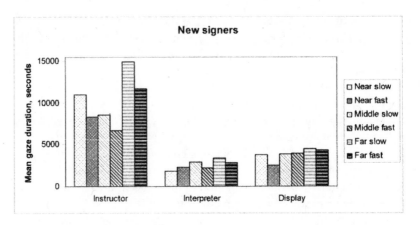

Figure 10–12. Mean gaze duration in each region for new signers in the Near, Middle, and Far conditions for Fast and Slow presentations.

Direct Instruction Versus Interpreted Lectures

To directly examine the effects of mediated (interpreted) instruction on gaze behavior, the second experiment compared lectures that were either signed by the instructors themselves using simultaneous communication or SimCom (simultaneous speech and signing) and Interpreted conditions in which the lectures were presented by the same instructors but spoken only and interpreted by an experienced educational sign language interpreter. Twelve hearing students who did not know sign language, 12 skilled signers, and 12 new signers participated as observers. The skilled signers were all exposed to sign language by the age of 3 (mean = 1.2 years, SD = 0.6). Ten of the 12 new signers reported first learning sign language between the ages of 18 and 21, and one reported learning "only a little" at age 10 (mean = 18.2 years, SD = 2.9). The final DHH student and the 12 hearing students had no sign language experience.

Short, introductory-level lectures were prepared by two National Technical Institute for the Deaf (NTID) faculty members; one on mathematics, the second on computer programming. The faculty were selected in part for their communication skills, in part for their teaching skills (both had won the university award for outstanding teaching), and the mathematics lecturer is frequently described as among the best communicators on the faculty.

The lectures were videotaped under studio conditions, once using simultaneous communication, then repeated using voice only. The spoken lectures were then interpreted by an experienced educational interpreter, who was also videotaped. The lectures were presented to two students at a time, sitting in the same classroom used in the first experiment. In each testing session, participants were given instructions regarding the eyetracking equipment and then were fitted with the eyetracker. Calibration was performed as described earlier. Analysis of the eyetracking record was identical to that described earlier, except that in the SimCom condition no Interpreter region was present.

Coding of individual students' eye movement records required several hours each. After 10 students' tracks were analyzed in full, the full data were compared to the data from the middle 4 minutes of each lecture. No reliable differences were found for any factors, so subsequent coding and analyses were conducted using only the middle 4-minute segments to simplify the analysis.

Figure 10–13 shows the relative time gaze is spent in each region for skilled signers in the SimCom and Interpreted conditions. In the SimCom condition, skilled signers spent 60% of their time looking at the instructor and 40% at the display, approximately the same distribution as the hearing students in the Marschark et al. (2005) study (compare to Figure 10–4). When the interpreter was present, skilled signers dropped to less than 5% of the time looking toward the instructor, and the time spent looking to the display fell as well.

The new signers' gaze distribution in the SimCom condition was very similar to the skilled signers: 62% to the instructor and 38% to the display. Their distribution in the Interpreted condition, however, was dramatically different. As seen in Figure 10–14, the gaze was distributed widely among

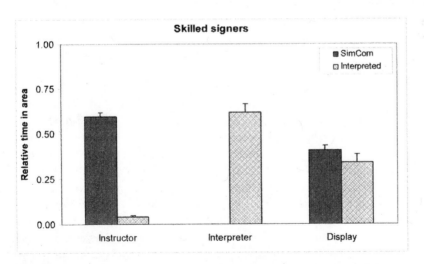

Figure 10–13. Fraction of time gaze spent in each region for skilled signers in the SimCom and Interpreted conditions. Error bars represent 1 SEM.

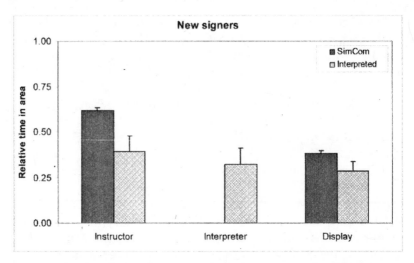

Figure 10–14. Fraction of time gaze spent in each region for new signers in the SimCom and Interpreted conditions. Error bars represent 1 SEM.

the three regions; 39%, 32%, and 29% to the Instructor, Interpreter, and Display, respectively.

Figure 10–15 shows the distribution for the hearing students, who spent the majority of their time looking to the display region in both conditions.

The results of this experiment were consistent with our earlier findings, showing that deaf students adapt to the visual demands of the classroom in allocating their gaze (and presumably their attention) to the location of their primary source of information. Skilled signers attended to the instructors when they were signing for themselves and the interpreters when they were the primary source of information. The average performance of the new signers, in contrast, was to split their time approximately equally between looking at the instructor and the interpreter in the interpreted condition, reflecting either their attempt to utilize speechreading of the instructor or perhaps being unsure of the best place to look to maximize information reception. Note that the result also reflects a variation between observers within the new signers group, with some of the DHH students spending more time looking toward the interpreter and others toward the instructor. In any case, the strategies adopted by the deaf students apparently were sufficiently effective that the two deaf groups did not differ in their learning under any condition (Marschark, Sapere, Convertino, & Pelz, submitted). From a learning perspective, it is noteworthy that although the deaf students came into the classroom with less content knowledge and scored lower on learning assessments, they learned just as much, proportionally, as their hearing peers (see Marschark & Wauters, this volume).

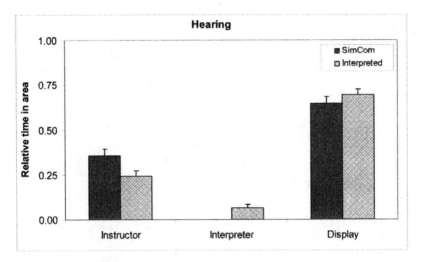

Figure 10–15. Fraction of time gaze spent in each region for hearing students in the SimCom and Interpreted conditions. Error bars represent 1 SEM.

This finding suggests that, by college age, deaf students have developed cognitive as well as visuo-spatial strategies that enable them to function in mainstream educational settings. Better understanding of their strengths and needs will allow educators to adjust teaching methods and classroom/technology organization so as to optimize their learning.

Summary and Implications

The experiments described here offer the first glimpse into the gaze behavior of hearing and DHH students in the classroom. The results of the first experiment show that a single metric such as the relative time spent in each region may mask some differences that are revealed by higher-order metrics, such as the mean gaze duration within an area (or, equivalently, the number of times gaze returns to an area within a given period). For example, examination of Figure 10–7 might lead one to the conclusion that skilled signers were not affected by the speed of the lecture or the position of the display. Figure 10–10, however, reveals that the mean gaze duration was sensitive to both manipulations.

Data from the second experiment make it clear that skilled signers "follow the signs" when lecturers switch from SimCom to using an interpreter. Figure 10–16 illustrates the essentially complete shift from instructor to interpreter for skilled signers. Hearing students also shift attention away from the instructor in interpreted lectures, possibly also because they spend some time watching both interpreter and instructor signing (see

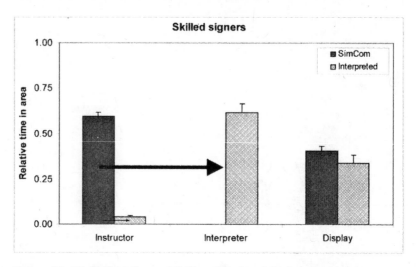

Figure 10–16. Skilled signers "follow the signs" from instructor to interpreter when a lecture is interpreted rather than presented in SimCom.

Figure 10–17). As noted earlier, new signers' gaze distribution does not reflect a simple shift, but rather indicates a division of the time previously spent in the instructor region between the instructor and the interpreter, as evident in Figure 10–18. Note that the distribution is due partly to variation within the group, as evidenced by the large standard error.

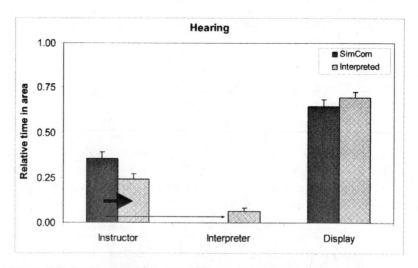

Figure 10–17. Hearing students shift some attention away from the instructor when a lecture is interpreted rather than presented in SimCom.

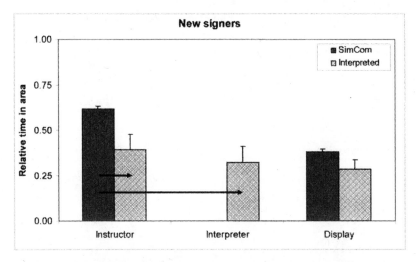

Figure 10–18. New signers' time is split between the instructor and interpreter when a lecture is interpreted rather than presented in SimCom.

Again, some of the new signers had patterns that looked like the skilled signers, shifting their gaze almost completely from the Instructor to the Interpreter; some kept their gaze on the Instructor; and some distributed their gaze more broadly among the three regions.

These results highlight the need for educators to consider the additional demands on DHH students in modern classrooms, especially those mediated by sign-language interpreters. Because they cannot take advantage of the same concurrent streams of information as their hearing counterparts, they must shift serially between multiple sources of information. In general, however, contrary to assumptions of some interpreters and deaf students, these and our previous results indicate that comprehension of sign language—as indexed by the amount learned from a lecture—is not affected by either the availability of three-dimensional visuo-spatial cues or student–interpreter feedback. That is, video-based interpreting appears to work just as well as live interpreting, at least in the college classroom.

Coupled with learning data not presented here (Marschark et al., 2005, submitted), the present results also are consistent with our earlier findings indicating that, despite demonstrations of enhanced visuo-spatial processing abilities on the part of skilled signers in carefully controlled laboratory demonstrations (e.g., Bavelier et al., 2001; Emmorey et al., 1993; Rettenbach et al., 1999), those abilities do not appear to have any obvious effect on learning in the classroom. This conclusion is certainly preliminary, as participants in the present experiments were not tested on their visuo-spatial abilities. Nevertheless, the lack of reliable differences—either in patterns of gaze duration and transitions or in learning from multiple visual displays between skilled and unskilled signers in Experiment 3—suggests that the real world may be too complex and information-rich for a simple bridge to exist between the modest enhancements of visual abilities observed among skilled deaf and hearing signers.

Acknowledgments

The research reported here was supported by Grant REC-0307602 from the National Science Foundation.

References

Babcock, J. S., & Pelz, J. B. (2004). Building a lightweight eyetracker headgear. *Proceedings of the 2004 ACM SIGCHI Eye Tracking Research and Applications Symposium,* San Antonio, TX. (pp. 109–114). New York: ACM Press.

Bard, C., Fleury, M., & Paillard, J. (1992). Different patterns in aiming accuracy for head-movers and non-head movers. In A. Berthoz, W. Graf, & P. P. Vidal (Eds.), *The head-neck sensori-motor system* (pp. 582–586). New York: Oxford University Press.

Bavelier, D., Tomann, A., Hutton, C., Mitchell, T., Liu, G., Corina, D., & Neville, H. (2000). Visual attention to the periphery is enhanced in congenitally deaf individuals. *Journal of Neuroscience, 20,* 1–6.

Bavelier, D., Brozinsky, C., Tomann, A., Mitchell, T., Neville, H., & Liu, G. (2001). Impact of early deafness and early exposure to sign language on the cerebral organization for motion processing. *Journal of Neuroscience, 21,* 8931–8942.

Emmorey, K., Kosslyn, S. M., & Bellugi, U. (1993). Visual imagery and visual-spatial language: Enhanced imagery abilities in deaf and hearing ASL signers. *Cognition, 46,* 139–181.

Hegarty, M., & Just, M. A. (1989). Understanding machines from text and diagrams. In H. Mandl & J. R. Stevens (Eds.), *Knowledge acquisition from text and pictures* (pp. 171–195). Amsterdam: Elsevier.

Iding, M. K. (2000). Is seeing believing? Features of effective multimedia for learning science. *International Journal of Instructional Media, 27,* 403–415.

Marschark, M., Pelz, J., Convertino, C., Sapere, P., Arndt, M. E., & Seewagen, R. (2005). Classroom interpreting and visual information processing in mainstream education for deaf students: Live or Memorex? *American Educational Research Journal, 42,* 727–761

Marschark, M., Sapere, P., Convertino, C. M., & Pelz, J. (submitted). Optimizing classroom learning by deaf students.

National Center for Education Statistics. (1999). *Integrated Postsecondary Education Data System, fall enrollment data file, fall 1997.* http://nces.ed.gov/Ipeds/ef9798/ (Retrieved April 20, 2005).

Paivio, A. (1971). *Imagery and verbal processes.* New York: Holt, Rinehart and Winston.

Paivio, A. (1986). *Mental representations: A dual coding approach.* New York: Oxford University Press.

Pelz, J. B., & Canosa, R. (2001). Oculomotor behavior and perceptual strategies in complex tasks. *Vision Research, 41,* 3587–3596.

Pelz, J. B., Hayhoe, M. M., & Loeber, R. (2001). The coordination of eye, head, and hand movements in a natural task, *Experimental Brain Research, 139,* 266–277.

Presno, C. (1997). Bruner's three forms of representation revisited: Action, pictures, and words for effective computer instruction. *Journal of Instructional Psychology, 24,* 112–118.

Rettenback, R., Diller, G., & Sireteaunu, R. (1999). Do deaf people see better? Texture segmentation and visual search compensate in adult but not in juvenile subjects. *Journal of Cognitive Neuroscience, 11,* 560–583.

Swisher, M. V. (1993). Perceptual and cognitive aspects of recognition of signs in peripheral vision. In M. Marschark & M. D. Clark (Eds.), *Psychological perspectives on deafness* (pp. 229–265). Hillsdale, NJ: Erlbaum.

Tiene, D. (2000). Sensory mode and information load: Examining the effects of timing on multisensory processing. *International Journal of Instructional Media, 27,* 183–198.

Chapter 11

Development of Deaf and Hard-Of-Hearing Students' Executive Function

Peter C. Hauser, Jennifer Lukomski, and Tara Hillman

Over the past decade, executive function (EF) has received substantial attention in neuropsychological, cognitive, and educational literature. This control and self-regulatory system has significant implications for everyday social and academic functioning. The understanding of the role of EF in the learning process is especially relevant for teachers and practitioners. This chapter provides an overview of the environmental factors that affect the development of EF, the research on deaf and hard-of-hearing (DHH) children's and adults' EF, and recommendations for classroom applications to facilitate EF development among DHH students.

Barkley (e.g., 2001) uses a neuropsychological behavioral model to describe EF and claims that response inhibition is the prerequisite to self-regulation, which is instrumental for purposive intentional behavior. He explains that *behavioral inhibition* is linked with four major metacognitive abilities, all of which moderate *behavioral/motor control*. The four metacognitive abilities are *sensing to the self* (e.g., nonverbal working memory), *speech to the self* (e.g., inner voice or verbal working memory), *emotion/motivation to the self* (e.g., intrinsic motivation), and *play to the self* (e.g., hypothesis testing and generativity). These EFs represent the major classes of behavior regulation or self-regulation. Barkley (2001) explains that the purpose of the four EFs "is to 'internalize' or make private certain self-directed behavior so as to anticipate and prepare for change (time) and the future, especially the social future" (p. 6). This perceiving and valuing of future over immediate outcomes requires self-control, which develops with maturity and experience.

There are substantial literatures on EF and the frontal system of the brain. Damage to this area of the brain has been shown to impair various components of executive functions (Anderson, 1998; Eslinger & Grattan, 1991). The dorsolateral prefrontal area has been associated with EF and working memory, and the ventromedial prefrontal area has been associated with emotional and social decision-making (MacPherson, Phillips, & Della Sala, 2002). Although the frontal lobe plays a major role in executive functions, EF cannot be localized solely in the frontal lobe as other areas of the brain (e.g., posterior cortical and subcortical systems) are also involved (Welsh & Pennington, 1988).

Whereas no one single EF disorder exists, different patterns of EF deficits have been found in psychological, psychiatric, neuropsychological, and neurological disorders among children and adolescents (e.g., Barkley, 1997; Gioia, Isquith, Guy, & Kenworth, 2000). The type of disorders that involve executive dysfunction are those that are *developmental*, such as learning disabilities (Siegal & Ryan, 1989) and attention deficit/hyperactivity disorder (ADHD; Pratt, Campbell-LaVoie, Isquith, Gioia, & Guy, 2000) and Tourette syndrome (Singer & Walkup, 1991), and *acquired*, such as traumatic brain injury (Fletcher, Ewing-Cobbs, Miner, Levin, & Eisenberg, 1990), lead poisoning (Goldstein, 1992), and effects of cranial radiation treatment for leukemia (Brouwers, Riccardi, Poplack, & Fedio, 1984).

Development of Executive Function

The maturation of EF is crucial to psychological adaptation and adjustment across the life span (i.e., Eslinger, Biddle, & Grattan, 1997). The development of EF, moreover, is a multistage process with different components developing at different times (Klenberg, Korkman, & Lahti-Nuuttila, 2001). Many of the major cognitive achievements of infancy and childhood appear to depend on the development of the prefrontal cortex (Diamond, Prevor, Callender, & Druin, 1997; Posner & Rothbart, 1998). In addition, experience has been shown to affect brain development at many levels of organization, from molecules to systems (McEwen, 2001; Rosenweig & Bennett, 1996). Developmental neuroscience literature has illustrated the rapid growth and modification of those brain areas that subserve self-regulation, including emotion, memory, and attention during infancy and early childhood (Nelson & Luciana, 2001).

Early intentional self-control behaviors, such as maintaining an intentional action and inhibiting irrelevant behavior, have been found in infants and toddlers during goal-directed problem solving (Vaughn, Kopp, & Krakow, 1984). Similarly, development of attention control and self-regulation of emotion and behavior is considered to begin in infancy (Haith, Hazen, & Goodman, 1988) and continue into the preschool period (Espy, Kaufmann, McDiarmid, & Glisky, 1999). Nonverbal working memory, as well, seems to arise within the first few months of human development and, by the age of 12–24 months, a human's nonverbal working memory exceeds that of all other primates (Hofstadter & Reznick, 1996; Zelazo, Reznick, & Piñon, 1995). Self-regulatory skills vary widely during infancy and become stable around 18–30 months of age (Ruff & Rothbart, 1996).

In the early years of elementary school, the ability to inhibit internal (e.g., emotions, hunger) and external distractors (e.g., flashing light, sudden movements in the periphery) and the ability to sustain attention are necessary for appropriate academic achievement. In the later elementary school grades and in middle school, the demand for EF becomes more evident when students are required to apply what they have learned to more complicated real-life situations and more advanced reading, writing, and mathematics (Bernstein & Waber, 1997). As the educational environment becomes less structured, students are required to perform more complicated tasks independently. At the same time, a greater EF demand arises for regulating complex social behaviors. Both the behavioral regulation (i.e., impulsivity, emotional control) and metacognitive (i.e., planning, judgment) aspects of EF continue to mature into late adolescence (Steinberg & Scott, 2003).

Effects of Environment on Executive Function

Systematic associations have been found between socioeconomic status (SES) and performance during the early school years on basic attentional and executive processes (Mezzacappa, 2004). Children who attend schools in low-income, urban neighborhoods have been found more likely to exhibit problems on measures of EF (Waber, Gerber, Turcios, Wagner, & Forbes, 2006). Low SES children have been found, on average, to have poorer abilities to regulate their attention, and this dysregulation may play a contributory role in their school success, even when they are motivated to succeed (Howese, Lange, Farran, & Boyles, 2003). Children from low SES families also tend to perform worse than children from the middle SES on neurocognitive measures involving the left perisylvian system (language) and the prefrontal system (EF) (Noble, Norman, & Farah, 2005).

Noble and colleagues (2005) found that SES and EF predict language ability independently, but SES does not account for any variance in EF ability over and above that predicted by language performance. They claim that the effect of SES on EF might be indirect, as SES appears to have an effect on language development and EF development is dependent on language advancing age-appropriately. Ardila and his colleagues (2005) investigated the effects of type of school (private versus public) and parents' education level on EF development. They found an effect of type of school, but further analyses revealed that this effect depended on parents' educational levels, not the school setting per se. Ardila and colleagues suggested that the parents' educational level may be associated with home environmental circumstances that establish early skills when solving problems or performing EF tasks.

A child's psychosocial development must be relatively unremarkable to not interfere with EF development. Investigations on the interface of cognitive and affective neuroscience have demonstrated that neurological processes associated with emotional reactivity interfere with or support higher-order cognitive processes (see Panksepp, 1998). Blair (2002) suggested emotionality can influence the development of neurological interconnections among structures underlying emotion and EF.

A child's language environment and language practices are also important for EF development. Effective use of language requires coordination of one's linguistic, cognitive, and social skills, and the EF is responsible for this coordination (Im-Bolter, Johnson, & Pascual-Leone, 2006). Individuals with aphasia (decreased functional communication ability) demonstrate difficulties on tests of EF (Fridriksson, Nettles, & Davis, 2006). Children with specific language impairment (SLI) often exhibit nonlinguistic cognitive (Lahey, Edwards, & Munson, 2001; Miller, Kail, Leonard, & Tomblin, 2001; Windsor & Hwang, 1999) and social cognitive deficits (Craig, 1995). For example, children with SLI demonstrate deficits in visuo-spatial memory, mental rotation, haptic recognition, and processing of nonlinguistic information (Lahey, et al., 2001; Miller et al., 2001; Windsor & Hwang, 1999). More generally, children with SLI perform poorly on measures of EF compared to age-matched peers (Marton, Schwartz, & Farkas, 2006).

Research on the Theory of Mind (ToM) sheds light on the relationship between language and EF. Preschoolers' ability to make sense of others' behaviors, taking into account their own mental and emotional states, is known as ToM (see Courtin, Melot, & Corroyer, this volume). These skills involve viewing the world from the perspective of another person. The ToM develops in parallel with the development of self-regulatory skills (Kochanska, Coy, & Murray, 2001). The ToM skills correlate with language skills (Lohmann & Tomasello, 2003) and mental-state talk at home and among friends (Ruffman, Slade, & Crowe, 2002). Carlson, Mandell, and Williams (2004) found that EF performance in children as young as 24 months significantly predicted ToM performance 1 year later, and that children's ability to talk about mental states predicted both EF and ToM skill. The development of ToM follows a similar age trajectory across many cultures, and the relation between EF and ToM is robust in cross-cultural studies, even among preschoolers (Sabbagh, Xu, & Carlson, 2006). The contribution of EF to the development of ToM is not surprising, because inhibiting one's own view or perspective is required to imagine an alternate view or perspective, and this type of imagination requires working-memory abilities (Carlson, Moses, & Breton, 2002).

Peterson (2004) found that deaf children performed worse than hearing age-matched peers on ToM tasks but similarly to age-matched hearing children with autism. Other studies have shown that deaf children born to hearing families (henceforth *deaf-of-hearing*) achieve ToM skills that are mastered by hearing preschoolers during elementary school or when they are older (de Villiers, Pyers, & Salkind, 1999; Remmel, 2002; Schick, Hoffmeister, de Villiers, & de Villiers, 2000; Woolfe, Want, & Siegal, 2002). Peterson (2004) suggested that peer interaction and fluent communication with peers and family would facilitate the growth of ToM and language early in a deaf child's life. This suggestion is supported by studies demonstrating that the performance of deaf children born to deaf signing parents (henceforth *deaf-of-deaf*) on ToM tasks are similar to that of hearing children (Courtin et al., this volume; Peterson & Siegal, 1999; Schick et al., 2000; Woolfe et al., 2002).

The cognitive and biological aspects of EF continue to develop through childhood and adolescence (Anderson, Anderson, Northam, Jacobs, & Catroppa, 2001). An event-related potential (ERP) study by Travis (1998) recorded brain activity of hearing students from three grade levels (fourth, eighth, and twelfth) who also completed EF tasks. Travis found that the maturation of EF predicts the developmental age of a child/adolescent. Toward the end of the adolescent years and the beginning of adulthood, prefrontal brain systems have been found to be among the last brain structures to completely develop (Dawson & Guare, 2004). The prefrontal brain system is also shaped by the environment for the longest period of time.

Deaf Children's Early Environment

Vygotky's (1978) sociocultural theory of development provides a useful framework to examine deaf children's early environment and the development of EF. Vygotsky believed that parents and school shape cognitive development to reflect cultural values (see also Rogoff, 2003). Students' social interactions and dialogue with older students and adults is believed to shape cognitive development. The difference between what a child can do independently and what can be accomplished with some assistance is known as the *zone of proximal development. Scaffolding* is how a more knowledgeable individual supports a child's learning. The effectiveness of the interaction between parent/teacher and the child/student depends on the model's ability to provide enough support to be challenging without frustrating or boring the child. In other words, the adult needs to challenge the child within their zone of proximal development and provide just enough scaffolding to further facilitate development.

The sociocultural environment of a deaf child is complicated. Among DHH children born to hearing families, with poor visual access to language, effective visual learning is often delayed as parents often do not immediately develop the skills to raise a DHH child, and medical professionals often are not educated about evidence-based communication and educational options (King, Hauser, & Isquith, 2006). Upon diagnosis of hearing loss, parents often go through a process of mourning for the idyllic hearing child whom they have lost (Meadow-Orleans, Dyssegaard, & Smith-Gray, 2004). For a typical hearing parent, at least initially, having a deaf child can seem like a tragedy. Feelings of grief, anger, and betrayal, as well as feelings of love and acceptance, are likely to alternate in "waves" rather than follow a set, predictable sequence with a clear timetable for resolution.

The processes parents go through are different when one or both parents are deaf or hard-of-hearing. Some deaf parents may hope for a child who is deaf like them, whereas others hope for a child who is hearing (Hauser, Wills, & Isquith, 2005). Deaf parents tend to be at least conscious of, and prepared for, the possibility that their child may be deaf. Most deaf-of-deaf toddlers develop secure attachments and independence from their parents as do hearing children of hearing parents (Meadow, Greenberg, & Erting, 1983). Hearing parents who have more positive attitudes about deafness in general, and those who communicate more successfully with their DHH child, tend to show more positive and mutually responsive parent–child interactions (Samuel, 1996).

Deaf individuals are visually oriented, and aspects of their visual attention and visuo-spatial skills are either the same or better than those of hearing individuals (Hauser, Cohen, Dye, & Bavelier, 2007; Hauser, Dye, Boutla, Green, & Bavelier, 2007; see Dye, Hauser, & Bavelier, this volume). There appear to be distinctive visually oriented communicative strategies used by deaf parents that may not come naturally to some hearing parents (Koester, Karkowski, & Traci, 1998; Singleton & Morgan, 2006; Waxman & Spencer, 1997). As a result, some researchers have recommended using communication strategies modeled upon those strategies used in deaf families (Koester, Papousek, & Smith-Gray, 2000; Singleton & Morgan, 2006). The studies reviewed in this section focus on families that use signed languages; however, deaf mothers' visual attention-getting and other communication techniques might similarly be necessary for a deaf infant who is to be raised orally (relying on lipreading) or using cued English.

Deaf mothers' attention-getting strategies for engaging their deaf infants have been found to be developmentally appropriate strategies that are coordinated with both the infant's attending behaviors and language use

(Swisher, 2000; Waxman & Spencer, 1997). For example, when an infant's eye gaze is directed toward a deaf mother in shared face-to-face interaction, the mother responds with visual behaviors such as facial exaggerations, nodding, finger play, and gestures (Koester, Papousek, & Smith-Gray, 2000). Deaf mothers, compared with hearing mothers, communicate in shorter periods to compensate for the deaf child's developing eye gaze coordination between an object and the mother (Spencer, Bodner-Johnson, & Gutfreund, 1992). In a way, deaf mothers intuitively provide visual communication to infants, which promotes the development of the visual attention skills that are later necessary for visual language dialogue (Singleton & Morgan, 2006).

Mothers who talk to their hearing children, at early ages, about their and others' thoughts and feelings (mental states) promote the subsequent development of ToM skills (Jenkins, Turrell, Kogushi, Lollis, & Ross, 2003; Ruffman, Slade, & Crowe, 2002). Moeller and Schick (2006) found that mothers who have proficient sign skills similarly had deaf children with the strongest language ability and ToM skills, and that these mothers commented on mental states to the same degree as mothers of hearing children. Mothers with limited sign skills (those who primarily used speech to communicate) made few references to mental states and had children with limited language and ToM skills. These results illustrate that it is possible for hearing mothers to comment on mental states in sign to the same degree as hearing mothers of hearing children, and that deaf children are able to develop ToM and language skills comparable to hearing peers (Courtin et al., this volume). Moeller and Schick (2006) also found the effect of maternal talk on language and ToM skills remained significant even when the deaf children were school-aged, despite the fact they all had been enrolled in early interventions and started preschool at 3 years of age. This illustrates the importance of communication within the family context.

Parents typically socialize with their children intuitively, which often reflects how their own parents engaged in socialization with them during their own childhood (Papousek & Papousek, 1987). Therefore, in hearing mother–deaf child dyads, a mismatch in the engagement process might hinder cognitive development (Kuntze, 1998; Meadow-Orlans, 1997; Singleton & Morgan, 1996), including EF development. Hearing mothers of deaf infants often attempt to start new, unrelated, activities that interrupt their deaf infant's attention (Meadow-Orlans & Spencer, 1996). Hearing mothers also often talk or sign when their deaf infant is not visually attending (Koester et al., 1998). Overall, a lower proportion of child-initiated linguistic constructions appears to occur in deaf child–hearing mother dyads (Jamieson, 1994). As a result, the language experience of deaf-of-hearing children is dramatically different from that of deaf-of-deaf children. The following section will discuss the impact this difference appears to have on their EF development as well as school readiness.

Deaf Individuals' Executive Function Development

Early studies claimed that deaf children are more impulsive than hearing children (Altshuler, Deming, Vollenweider, Rainer, & Tendler, 1976; Chess & Fernandez, 1980; Ouellette, 1988) and that deaf children's impulsivity remains the same as they mature, whereas hearing children's impulsive tendencies become more controlled over time (Campbell & Douglas, 1972; Kagen, 1965). However, these conclusions were not based on well-controlled experimental measures of impulse control, but on projective testing such as the Rorschach (e.g., Altshuler et al., 1976), the House-Tree-Person test (e.g., Ouellette, 1988), and other personality measures such as the Id-Ego-Superego Test (e.g., Ouellette, 1988). In addition, the participants in these studies were not carefully selected to represent the diversity of the deaf population. Some of the sample populations contained primarily individuals who lost their hearing from maternal rubella or those with additional disabilities (e.g., Chess & Fernandez, 1980). It is important to note that a study comparing the impulsivity rates of deaf-of-deaf and deaf-of-hearing children, found that deaf-of-deaf have lower impulsivity rates (Harris, 1978). This suggests that there might be family and school environmental factors that facilitate impulse control development and/or that the deaf-of-hearing children have a higher prevalence of EF difficulties secondary to the same factor that might have caused the hearing loss.

More recently, Marschark and Everhart (1999) failed to find differences in impulsivity between deaf and hearing students in any of four groups, from 7 years through college age, using two behavioral tests, Porteus Mazes (Porteus, 1965) and the Wisconsin Card Sorting Test (WCST; Berg, 1948; Heaton, Chelune, Talley, Kay, & Curtis, 1993). On Continuous Performance Tests (CPT), which are often used to assess an individual's ability to sustain attention, studies have shown that deaf children and adults obtain higher inattention scores than standardized normative samples (Parasnis, Samar, & Berent, 2003; Sporn, 1997, 1999). Using the Test of Variables of Attention (Leark, Dupuy, Greenberg, Corman, & Kindeschi, 1996), Parasnis et al. (2003) reported that young deaf adults (from hearing families) obtained elevations on CPT measures of impulsivity. Well-controlled experimental studies of attention tasks with distractors among deaf-of-deaf participants provide the opposite results (see Dye et al., this volume, for discussion).

The EFs of DHH individuals have been investigated in several studies using the Behavior Rating Inventory of Executive Functions that was developed to measure the everyday behavior associated with specific EFs in hearing children and adolescents aged 5–18 years (BRIEF; Gioia et al., 2000) and adults (BRIEF-A; Roth, Isquith, & Gioia, 2005). The test has strong psychometric properties, and a relationship was found between the BRIEF Global Executive Composite Index and language impairment in a study of hearing adolescents with and without language impairments, further supporting the relationship between language and EF (Hughes, 2006). Oberg (2007) administered the BRIEF and selected EF performance tests to 22 deaf students between ages 5 and 18 from a school for the deaf. She found significant correlations between the BRIEF forms completed by parents and teachers and the students' scores on the WCST (Heaton, 2005), Children's Color Trails Test (CCTT; D'Elia, Staz, Uchiyama, & White, 1996), and the Woodcock-Johnson-III Tests of Achievement Writing Fluency Subtest (WJ; Woodcock, McGrew, & Mathers, 2001).

Rhine (2002) found that deaf children obtained higher negative ratings on three of the eight BRIEF scales (Inhibit, Shift, and Working Memory) compared with hearing children; however, all the scores fell within the nonclinical range. Rhine-Kalback (2004) examined the relationship among language, EF, and social skills in deaf children between the ages of 6 and 14. She found that deaf children's language ability was significantly predictive of their EF performance. Specifically, performance-based measures of language predicted the performance-based measures of EF more than the language measures predicted BRIEF ratings. However, EF behavior, as rated by the BRIEF, was the strongest predictor of social skills ratings.

In the Oberg (2007) study, students born to deaf parents ($n = 5$), compared with those born to hearing parents ($n = 17$), obtained significantly more positive ratings on the BRIEF scales and performed significantly better on the WJ Visual Matching subtest, WJ Reading and Math Fluency subtests, CCTT (Trail 2), and the Kaufman Assessment Battery for Children–Second Edition Hand Movements subtest (Kaufman & Kaufman, 2004). It is not possible to determine whether the deaf-of-deaf children's language skills or the deaf-of-hearing group's inclusion of students with nonhereditary and unknown etiologies of deafness caused these differences.

Hauser, Lukomski, and Isquith (2007) administered the BRIEF-A to deaf and hearing college students. Preliminary results reveal that no population difference exists. However, when analyzing variation among deaf participants, deaf-of-deaf college students had better ratings than deaf-of-hearing students, with deaf-of-hearing who have deaf siblings obtaining ratings between the two other groups. None of the scales were within the clinical range. Rehkemper (2004) examined whether deaf college students with nonhereditary causes of deafness demonstrate differences in EF. Overall, Rehkemper found that on only one of five measures of EF did the nonhereditary deaf participants make significantly more commission errors than did hereditary deaf participants on a task requiring sustained attention, regardless of their parents' hearing status.

Possible Impact of Deaf Education on Deaf Students' Executive Function

During the preschool years, dramatic, interactive play with siblings and peers becomes increasingly important for the development of social skills, preacademic learning, vocabulary, syntax, pragmatic skills, and general knowledge. Deaf-of-hearing children who have not yet developed adequate signed or spoken language skills will have difficulties in self-regulation and social communication (Hauser et al., 2006; Rhine-Kahlback, 2004). Deaf-of-deaf children begin their schooling knowing where to look for essential linguistic information. They are more attuned to the timing patterns of the shifts of eye gaze between objects and the person talking to the child. Deaf-of-deaf children's conversations are similar to those of hearing children from hearing families, which typically involve questioning, symbolic references, and abstractly conversing about their own self and others, whether or not others are present (Meadow, Greenberg, Erting, & Carmichael, 1981). Deaf-of-deaf preschoolers' eye gaze behavior is often not observed in deaf-of-hearing children even at the fourth grade level (i.e., Ramsey & Padden, 1998). This is a serious educational and developmental issue that has not received much attention in deaf education.

When deaf-of-hearing children begin preschool, their teachers and other educational professionals need to further facilitate the visual, social, cognitive, and language skills of these children to the same level of their deaf-of-deaf age-peers. In addition, deaf-of-deaf children need teachers to continue to provide opportunities for them to exercise the EF, language, and ToM skills that their mothers may have shaped to age-appropriate levels. Teachers of the deaf frequently teach students with a wide range of language and cognitive skills. These teachers need to create tasks that are individualized based on where each child is within her EF development in order to scaffold and shape her advancement.

As the EF continues to develop throughout childhood and into early adulthood, deaf students need to "exercise" their EF. Tasks with novel materials that require active problem solving, especially those that require rapid performance speed, demand EF more than tasks that are more familiar, automatic, and simple (Gioia, Isquith, & Guy, 2001). It is possible that classroom tasks will not demand use of students' EF if they are not challenged enough (within their zone of proximal development) or provided with the right support. Inadequate amounts of novel activities and challenges could under-demand the use of EF and fail to appropriately facilitate its development.

Deaf children often do not receive the visual cues they need in the classroom to further the development of the EFs necessary to appropriately control visual attention. Erting (1988) observed a hearing teacher and a deaf teacher aide in a preschool classroom, noted that the hearing teacher often began signing before all the children were attending. In contrast, the deaf adult used visual and tactile signals to ensure that all children were visually attending before she signed. Mather (1989) investigated a hearing teacher's and a deaf teacher's eye gaze patterns and found that only the deaf teacher managed to use eye gaze to direct the children's attention to the person speaking. The hearing teacher used inappropriate eye gaze techniques that confused the students about where to look. It is important for teachers to appropriately guide deaf children's visual attention toward targets to maximize their learning and language development. Teacher difficulty with visual-orienting strategies that could scaffold deaf children's attention control and regulation could hinder both learning and EF development.

In addition to differences between hearing and deaf teachers' use of visual orienting strategies, the two groups of teachers have been found to differ in their communication discourse in the classroom. Hearing teachers have been observed to do most of the initiating of conversations with deaf children and exert considerable control over the conversation. Wood, Wood, and Kingsmill (1991) also found that hearing teachers requested that children repeat themselves and frequently asked questions, consequently controlling the content of discourse and narrowing what would be considered appropriate contributions from deaf students. The length of the turn-taking sequences was short. In another study, a deaf teacher aide averaged longer interactions (3 turns) with the preschool children than the hearing teacher (1.6 turns) (Erting, 1980). Wood et al. (1991) found that the grammatical complexity of the teacher's language did not increase with the age of deaf students in the classroom, as it has been shown to do with hearing students. The deaf students seldom contributed to the topic of the conversation, exercised listener control such as asking for clarification, or added to what their peers had said.

Mather (1989) observed that one deaf teacher scaffolded deaf children's language development by providing more clues and persisting with modified questions and discussions until the struggling students engaged in discourse at their own level of understanding. The deaf teacher frequently asked questions that required students to participate and think actively in discussion. In contrast, the hearing teacher asked questions that typically required a yes/no answer or asked for specific information. In one episode, the deaf teacher asked 41 questions, all of which were eventually answered by the students. The hearing teacher asked nine questions, only two of which were answered by the students. The deaf teacher engaged in role play, positioned himself at the toddler's eye gaze level for ease of perception, and produced miniature signs near or on the book to visibly connect the pictures to sign concepts, all of which were strategies rarely used by the hearing teacher. Together with the studies mentioned earlier, such findings indicate that both qualitative and quantitative differences exist in teacher–deaf student discourse depending on whether the teacher is deaf or hearing, suggesting that the educational practices of deaf teachers need to be studied to determine the educational effects of these differences.

Deaf-of-hearing children's visual tracking difficulties found in qualitative studies suggests that many of these children have not learned how to follow conversations at home (or in school). A lot of incidental learning must be absent. This would cause the child to be further behind in academic development even at school entry. In terms of EF development, children need to follow conversations not only to learn language but also to learn how older individuals think. Teachers also need to externalize their self-talk so DHH children can see how adults self-regulate. This might be interrelated with EF development and the development of ToM. Such linkages become important later in life, helping to make sense of others' perspectives and social planning (thinking ahead about social consequences). No studies have explored these interrelations yet. However, some qualitative studies have analyzed how teachers share their thoughts with deaf children.

Deaf teachers have been found to explicitly express in their everyday narratives what it means to be deaf and demonstrate by example how to interact effectively with hearing individuals (Singleton & Morgan, 2004). In an ethnographic study, Singleton and Morgan observed deaf preschool teachers making comments about everyday activities in their lives. For example, in one episode, a 5-year-old deaf-of-hearing child asked via gesture about a bracelet on the teacher's wrist. The teacher responded with a narrative that detailed how she acquired the bracelet, with role-play that revealed an emotional component of what it is like to discover something wonderful. Thus, this adult, influenced by the child's initiation, is using a culturally meaningful practice—narration—to reference her actions and reactions. Many deaf-of-hearing children lack this kind of "everyday talk" in their home settings.

Teachers must be able to converse with deaf students with ease, as well as to direct their attention. Teacher difficulty in communicating with DHH students visually likely has consequences on learning and development. Hearing teachers who do not have the indigenous knowledge and practices of many deaf teachers might find some challenges regardless of the language/mode of instruction. For example, it is possible that in settings that utilize only spoken language (or use cued speech), hearing teachers speak (and cue) before all of the deaf students are looking at the teacher's lips (and cues). Similarly, it is possible that in settings where deaf children are mainstreamed with or without a sign interpreter or cued speech transliterator, the same observation could be made. Ramsey (1997), in a study of a group of students who had both a mainstream and a self-contained classroom, concluded that deaf children were less engaged in the mainstream classroom than they were in the self-contained classroom. Also, hearing teachers were observed to direct fewer interactions toward deaf students compared with hearing students in mainstream settings (Cawthon, 2001).

This review of interdisciplinary literature on the environmental factors that influence EF development suggests that if language is not developing age-appropriately, it might have a negative effect on EF development. Many deaf children in the United States have delayed language development in both English and American Sign Language. Further, they appear to have underdeveloped executive skills to control their visual attention. Individuals with any degree of hearing loss rely on their vision more so than hearing individuals. The inability to adapt visually to compensate for the loss of auditory input can have negative consequences on age-appropriate learning. Teachers need to help all deaf students further develop their language(s) and EF abilities. They need to be aware of how to work within each child's zone of proximal development and present them with enough challenges to exercise their EF.

Summary and Implications

Executive function makes up the higher-order cognitive processes responsible for metacognition and behavior regulation, including the control of attention and impulses. The brain development of EF begins before birth and continues until early adulthood. The research reviewed here shows that EF is influenced by environmental factors such as language use at home and in the school. Deaf individuals' EF appears to be able to develop following the expected milestones if they receive effective access to language during the first few years of life and are trained how to use their eyes more effectively than hearing individuals to learn from their environment.

Teacher's habits and discourse patterns, like all humans, are strongly influenced by their social and cultural upbringing. These sociocultural behaviors have a role in the classroom because social and communication interactions shape students on how to develop learning and thinking skills (Borkowski & Muthukrishna, 1998; see Singleton & Morgan, 2006 for discussion related to the deaf classroom). The research reviewed here suggests such language and environmental factors shape EF development. It is argued here that deaf individuals, regardless of the level of their aided hearing loss, rely on visual learning more so than hearing individuals. Therefore, deaf individuals' development of visual attention control, which is not separate from EF development, is important for these students to be able to maximize their access to language and incidental learning. Evidence suggests that, with intensive training, hearing individuals can learn how to use visual engagement techniques that are used in deaf mother–deaf child dyads (Mohay, 2000). Such training should be available to all teachers of the deaf, from infant toddler programs to college programs for deaf students.

Such training would need to include instruction on how to moderate a classroom of visual learners. Participating in a few workshops is not sufficient for acquiring this skill (Mohay, 2000).

The Promoting Alternative Thinking Strategies (PATHS) curriculum is a well-researched classroom-wide prevention curriculum that incorporates many aspects of supporting the development of EF. Noteworthy is that Greenberg and Kusché (1998) initially developed the curriculum with the objective to teach DHH children effective interpersonal problem-solving skills. Their premise was that the means to achieving effective interpersonal problem-solving skills is to build emotional awareness and emotional regulation skills, so that the child automatically uses inner speech to serve as a mediator for behavioral self-control. The PATHS curriculum is based on a comprehensive model incorporating cognitive–behavioral principles, encompassing the dynamic relationships of cognition, behavior, and affect. The five domains that the PATHs curriculum addresses are self control, emotional understanding, interpersonal problem-solving skills, positive self-esteem, and peer communication/relationships. The lessons are taught three times a week for 20 to 30 minutes for most of the school year (see Greenberg & Kusché, 2006 for details of the curriculum).

The PATHS curriculum has shown long-term effectiveness with regular education classes (Kelly, Longbottom, Potts, & Williamson, 2004), special education (Kam, Greenberg, & Kusché, 2004), and DHH classrooms (Greenberg & Kusché, 1998). In a follow-up to their 1994 study, Greenberg and Kusché (1998) found that 1- and 2-year postintervention assessments showed that the deaf children who had participated in the PATHS program exhibited better problem-solving skills, better social emotional adjustment, and improvements in cognitive functioning, including less impulsive responding as well as verbal self-direction and planning. Teachers have commented that the program promoted language development (Curtis & Norgate, 2007). All of these positive outcomes are clearly related to EF.

In addition to curriculum changes, teachers can incorporate computerized training of EF skills as a part of the students' classroom activities. Klenberg et al. (2001) found that using computerized visual-spatial working memory tasks, while adjusting the difficulty level as performance increased, significantly improved performance on working-memory tasks and general reasoning tasks in hearing children with ADHD. Additionally, their parents reported decreases in attention difficulties. This type of computerized training has promise for DHH students who may be struggling with EF.

It is important for adults working with deaf students to learn how to work with deaf students within their visually oriented world (see Marschark & Wauters, this volume). Deaf individuals have a wider field of view and are sensitive to motion in the periphery (Bavelier, Dye, & Hauser, 2006), which most likely helps them attend to more of what is going around them (see Dye, Hauser, & Bavelier, in press, for discussion). The literature reviewed here illustrates differences between deaf and hearing parents and teachers in how they regulate visual attention and adult-child discourse patterns. Although deaf parents and deaf teachers appear to have indigenous knowledge on how to work within deaf students' zone of proximal development and provide the appropriate amount of scaffolding, research has shown that hearing mothers who are able to develop appropriate sign language competency can converse with their deaf children similarly to that of hearing mothers with hearing children (Moeller & Schick, 2006). It has also been demonstrated that visual attention-getting and use of visual communication strategies can be learned (Mohay, 2000).

Sociocultural approaches to instruction (Rogoff, 1990, 2003; Vygotsky, 1978) provide theoretical-based teaching methods that are evidence-based and shown to be successful for hearing children. These approaches focus on ways social interactions and language use shape students to become independent learners and facilitate their cognitive development. It is proposed here that the individualized attention involved in sociocultural approaches that focus on each child's development as social and cultural learners and thinkers is likely necessary to maximize the development of the EF. Although this is relevant to all learners, this is specifically relevant to deaf learners and deserves more attention in research and practice.

Acknowledgments

The authors wish to express their appreciation to members of the Deaf Studies Laboratory at NTID for their assistance in conducting the research described in this chapter and their comments on earlier drafts of the text.

References

Altshuler, K., Deming, W., Vollenweider, J., Rainer, J., & Tendler, R. (1976). Impulsivity and profound early deafness: A cross-cultural inquiry. *American Annals of the Deaf, 121,* 331–345.

Anderson, V. (1998). Assessing executive functions in children: Biological, psychological and developmental considerations. *Neuropsychological Rehabilitation, 8(3),* 319–349.

Anderson, V. A., Anderson, P., Northam E., Jacobs, R., & Catroppa, C. (2001). Development of executive functions through late childhood and adolescence in an Australian sample. *Developmental Neuropsychology, 20(1),* 385–406.

Ardila, A., Rosselli, M, Matute, E., & Guajardo, S. (2005). The influence of the parents' educational level on the development of executive functions. *Developmental Neuropsychology, 28(1),* 539–560.

Barkley, R. A. (1997). *ADHD and the nature of self-control.* New York: Guilford Press.

Barkley, R. A. (2001). The Executive Functions and Self-Regulation: An Evolutionary Neuropsychological Perspective. *Neuropsychology Review, 11,* 1–29.

Bavelier, D., Dye, M.W.G., & Hauser, P. C. (2006). Do deaf individuals see better? *Trends in Cognitive Science, 10,* 512–518.

Berg, E. A. (1948). A sample objective technique of measuring flexibility in thinking. *Journal of General Psychology, 39,* 15–22.

Bernstein, J. H., & Waber, D. P. (1997). Pediatric neuropsychological assessment. In T. E. Feinberg & M. J. Farah (Eds.), *Behavioral neurology and neuropsychology* (pp. 721–728). New York: McGaw-Hill.

Blair, C. (2002). School readiness: Integrating cognition and emotion in a neurobiological conceptualization of children's functioning at school entry. *American Psychologist, 57,* 111–127.

Borkowski, J. G., & Muthukrishna, M. (1998). Learning environments and skill generalization: How contexts facilitate regulatory processes and efficacy beliefs. In F. Weinert & W. Schneider (Eds.), *Memory performance and competencies: Issues in growth and development* (pp. 283–300). Mahwah, NJ: Erlbaum.

Brouwers, P., Riccardi, R., Poplack, D., & Fedio, P. (1984). Attentional deficits in long-term survivors of childhood acute lymphoblastic leukemia (ALL). *Journal of Clinical Neuropsychology, 6,* 325–336.

Campbell, S., & Douglas, V. (1972). Cognitive style and responses to the threat of frustration. *Canadian Journal of Behavioral Sciences, 4,* 30–42.

Carlson, S. M., Mandell, D. J, & Williams, L. (2004). Executive function and theory of mind: Stability and prediction from ages 2 to 3. *Developmental Psychology, 40(6),* 1105–1122.

Carlson, S. M., Moses, L. J., & Breton, C. (2002). How specific is the relation between executive function and theory of mind? Contributions of inhibitory control and working memory. *Infant and Child Development, 11,* 73–92.

Cawthon, S. W. (2001). Teaching strategies in inclusive classrooms with deaf children. *Journal of Deaf Studies and Deaf Education, 6,* 212–225.

Chess, S., & Fernandez, P. (1980). Neurologic damage and behavior disorder in rubella children. *American Annals of the Deaf, 125,* 505–509.

Craig, H. K. (1995). Pragmatic impairments. In P. Fletcher & B. MacWhinney (Eds.), *The handbook of child language* (pp. 623–640). Cambridge, MA: Blackwell.

Curtis, C., & Norgate, R. (2007). An evaluation of the promoting alternative thinking strategies curriculum at key stage 1. *Educational Psychology in Practice, 23(1),* 33–44.

D'Elia, L. F., Satz, P., Uchiyama, C. L., & White, T. (1996). *Color trails test.* Odessa, FL: Psychological Assessment Resources.

Dawson, P., & Guare, R. (2004). *Executive skills in children and adolescents: A practical guide to assessment and intervention.* New York: The Guilford Press.

de Villiers, P. A., Pyers, J., & Salkind, S. (1999, April). Language delayed deaf children understand "false" photographs but not false beliefs. Poster presented at the biennial meeting of the Society for Research in Child Development, Albuquerque, NM.

Diamond, A., Prevor, M. B., Callender, G., & Druin, D. P. (1997). Prefrontal cortex cognitive deficits in children treated early and continuously for PKU. *Monographs of the society for research in child development, 62,* 1–205.

Dye, M. W. G., Hauser, P. C., & Bavelier, D. (in press). Visual skills and cross-modal plasticity in deaf readers: Possible implications for acquiring meaning from print. *New York Annals of Science.*

Erting, C. J. (1980). Sign language and communication between adults and children. In C. Baker & R. Battison (Eds.), *Sign language and the Deaf community* (pp. 159–176). Silver Spring, MD: National Association of the Deaf.

Erting, C. J. (1988). Acquiring linguistic and social identity: Interactions of deaf children with a hearing teacher and a deaf adult. In M. Strong (Ed.), *Language learning and deafness* (pp. 192–219). New York: Cambridge University Press.

Eslinger, P. J., Biddle, K. R., & Grattan, L. M. (1997). Cognitive and social development in children with prefrontal cortex lesions. In N. A. Krasnegor, G. R. Lyon, & P. S. Goldman-Rakic (Eds.), *Development of the prefrontal cortex: Evolution, neurobiology, and behavior* (pp. 295–336). Baltimore: Paul H. Brooks.

Eslinger, P. J., & Grattan, L. M. (1991). Perspectives on the developmental consequences of early frontal lobe damage: Introduction. *Developmental Neuropsychology, 7,* 257–260.

Espy, K. A., Kaufmann, P. M., McDiarmid, M. D., & Glisky, M. L. (1999). Executive functioning in preschool children: Performance on A-not-B and other delayed response format tasks. *Brain and Cognition, 41,* 178–199.

Fletcher, J. M., Ewing-Cobbs, L., Miner, M. E., Levin, H. S., & Eisenberg, H. (1990). Behavioral changes after closing head injury in children. *Journal of Consulting and Clinical Psychology, 58,* 93–98.

Fridriksson, J., Nettles, C., & Davis, M. (2006). Functional communication and executive function in aphasia. *Clinical Linguistics and Phonetics, 20,* 401–410.

Gioia, G. A., Isquith, P. K., & Guy, S. C. (2001). Assessment of executive functions in children with neurological impairment. In R.J. Simeonsson & S.L. Rosenthal, (Eds.), *Psychological and developmental assessment: Children with disabilities and chronic conditions* (pp. 317–356). New York: Guilford Press.

Gioia, G. A., Isquith, P. K., Guy, S. C., & Kentworth, L. (2000). *Behavior Rating Inventory of Executive Function (BRIEF) professional manual.* Odessa, FL: Psychological Assessment Resources.

Goldstein, G. W. (1992). Developmental neurobiology of lead toxicity. In H. L. Needleman (Ed.), *Human lead exposure* (pp. 125–135). Anne Arbor, MI: CRC Press.

Greenberg, M. T., & Kusché, C. A. (1998). Preventive intervention for school-age deaf children: The PATHS curriculum. *Journal of Deaf Studies and Deaf Education, 3,* 49–63.

Greenberg, M. T., & Kusché, C. A. (2006). Building social and emotional competence: The PATHS curriculum. In S. R. Jimerson & M. J. Furlong (Eds.), *Handbook of school violence and schools safety: From research to practice* (pp. 395–412). Mahwah, NJ: Lawrence Erlbaum Associates.

Haith, M. M., Hazen, C., & Goodman, G. S. (1988). Expectation and anticipa-
    tion of dynamic visual events by 3.5 months-old babies. *Child Develop-
    ment, 59,* 467–479.

Harris, R. (1978). The relationship of impulse control to parent's hearing sta-
    tus, manual communication, and academic achievement in deaf children.
    American Annals of the Deaf, 123, 52–67.

Hauser, P. C., Cohen, J., Dye, M. W. G., & Bavelier, D. (2007). Visual construc-
    tive and visual-motor skills in Deaf native signers. *Journal of Deaf Stud-
    ies and Deaf Education, 12,* 148–157.

Hauser, P. C., Dye, M.W.G., Boutla, M., Green, C. S., & Bavelier, D. (2007).
    Deafness and visual enumeration: Not all aspects of attention are modi-
    fied by deafness. *Brain Research, 1153,* 178–187.

Hauser, P. C., Lukomski, J., & Isquith, P. (2007). *Deaf college students' perfor-
    mance on the BRIEF-A and Connors.* Manuscript in preparation.

Hauser, P. C., Wills, K., & Isquith, P. K. (2005). Hard of hearing, deafness, and
    being deaf. In J. E. Farmer, J. Donders, & S. Warschausky (Eds.), *Neuro-
    developmental disabilities: Clinical research and practice* (pp. 119–131).
    New York: Guilford Publications, Inc.

Heaton, R. K. (2005). *Wisconsin Card Sorting Test: Computer Version 4:
    Research Edition: User's Manual.* Florida: Psychological Assessment
    Resources, Inc.

Heaton, R., Chelune, G., Talley, J., Kay, G., & Curtis, G. (1993). *Wisconsin Card
    Sorting Test manual.* Odessa, FL: Psychological Assessment Resources.

Hofstadter, M. C., & Reznick, J. S. (1996). Response modality affects human
    infant delayed-response performance. *Child Development, 67,* 646–658.

Howese, R. B., Lange, G., Farran, D. C., & Boyles, C. D. (2003). Motiva-
    tion and self-regulation as predictors of achievement in economically
    disadvantaged young children. *Journal of Experimental Education, 71,*
    151–174.

Hughes, D. M. (2006). Parent and self-ratings of executive function in adoles-
    cents with language impairments and typically developing peers. *Disser-
    tation Abstracts International, 67*(5), 2515B.

Im-Bolter, N., Johnson, J., & Pascual-Leone, J. (2006). Processing limitations in
    children with specific language impairment: The role of executive func-
    tion. *Child Development, 77,* 1822–1841.

Jamieson, J. R. (1994). Instructional discourse strategies: Differences between
    hearing and deaf mothers of deaf children. *First Language, 14,* 153–171.

Jenkins, J. M., Turrell, S., Kogushi, Y., Lollis, S., & Ross, H. A. (2003). Longitu-
    dinal investigation of the dynamics of mental state talk in families. *Child
    Development, 74,* 905–920.

Kagan, J. (1965). Impulsive and reflective children: Significance of concep-
    tual tempo. In J. Krumboltz (Ed.), *Learning and the educational process*
    (pp. 133–161). Chicago: Rand McNally.

Kam, C., Greenberg, M. T., & Kusché, C. A. (2004). Sustained effects of the
    PATHS curriculum on the social and psychological adjustment of chil-
    dren in special education. *Journal of Emotional and Behavioral Disor-
    ders, 12*(2), 66–78.

Kaufman, A., & Kaufman, N. (2004). *Kaufman Assessment Battery for Chil-
    dren* (2nd ed.). Circle Pines, MN: American Guidance Services.

Kelly, B., Longbottom, J., Potts, F., & Williamson, J. (2004). Applying emotional intelligence: Exploring the Promoting Alternative Thinking Strategies curriculum. *Educational Psychology in Practice, 20*(3), 221–240.

King, B. H., Hauser, P. C., & Isquith, P. K. (2006). Psychiatric aspects of blindness and severe visual impairment, and deafness and severe hearing loss in children. In C. E. Coffey & R. A. Brumback (Eds.), *Textbook of pediatric neuropsychiatry* (pp. 397–423). Washington, DC: American Psychiatric Association.

Klenberg, L., Korkman, M., & Lahti-Nuuttila, P. (2001). Differential development of attention and executive functions in 3- to 12-year old Finnish children. *Developmental Neuropsychology, 20*, 407–428.

Kochanska, G., Coy, K. C., & Murray, K. T. (2001). The development of self-regulation in the first four years of life. *Child Development, 72*, 1091–1111.

Koester, L. S., Karkowski, A. M., & Traci, M. A. (1998). How do deaf and hearing mothers regain eye contact when their deaf infants look away? *American Annals of the Deaf, 143*, 5–13.

Koester, L. S., Papousek, H., & Smith-Gray, S. (2000). Intuitive parenting, communication, and interaction with deaf infants. In P. Spencer, C. Erting, & M. Marschark (Eds.), *The deaf child in the family and at school* (pp. 55–71). Mahwah, NJ: Lawrence Erlbaum.

Kuntze, M. (1998). Literacy and deaf children: The language question. *Topics in Language Disorders, 18*, 1–15.

Lahey, M., Edwards, J., & Munson, B. (2001). Is processing speed related to severity of language impairment? *Journal of Speech, Language, and Hearing Research, 44*, 1354–1361.

Leark, R. A., Dupuy, T. R., Greenberg, L. M., Corman, C. L., & Kindeschi, C. L. (1996). *T.O.V.A. Test of Variables of Attention: Professional manual* (Version 7.0). Los Alamitos, CA: Universal Attention Disorders Inc.

Lohmann, H., & Tomasello, M. (2003). The role of language in the development of false belief understanding: A training study. *Child Development, 74*, 1130–1144.

MacPherson, S. E., Phillips, L. H., & Della Sela, S. (2002). Age, executive function and social decision making: A dorsolateral prefrontal theory of cognitive aging. *Psychology and Aging, 17*, 598–609.

Marschark, M., & Everhart, V. S. (1999). Problem solving by deaf and hearing children: Twenty questions. *Deafness and Education International, 1*, 63–79.

Marton, K., Schwartz, R. G., & Farkas, L. (2006). Effect of sentence length and complexity on working memory performance in Hungarian children with specific language impairment. *International Journal of Language and Communication Disorders, 41*, 653–673.

Mather, S. M. (1989). Visually oriented teaching strategies with deaf preschool children. In C. Lucas (Ed.), *The sociolinguistics of the Deaf community* (pp. 165–187). San Diego, CA: Academic Press.

McEwen, B. S. (2001). From molecules to mind: Stress, individual differences, and the social environment. *Annals of the New York Academy of Sciences, 935*, 42–49.

Meadow, K. P., Greenberg, M. T., & Erting, C. (1983). Attachment behavior of deaf children with deaf parents. *Journal of the American Academy of Child Psychiatry, 22*, 23–28.

Meadow, K., Greenberg, M., Erting, C., & Carmichael, H. (1981). Interactions of deaf mothers and deaf preschool children: Comparisons with three other groups of deaf and hearing dyads. *American Annals of the Deaf, 126*, 454–468.

Meadow-Orlans, K. P. (1997). Effects of mother and infant hearing status on interactions at twelve and eighteen months. *Journal of Deaf Studies and Deaf Education, 2*, 26–36.

Meadow-Orlans, K. P., Dyssegaard, B., & Smith-Gray, S. (2004). Hearing parents reactions to the identification of deafness and cognitive or motor disabilities. In K.P. Meadow-Orlans, P.E. Spencer, & L. S. Koester, (Eds.), *The world of deaf infants: A longitudinal study* (pp. 66–91). New York: Oxford University Press.

Meadow-Orlans, K. P., & Spencer, P. E. (1996). Maternal sensitivity and the visual attentiveness of children who are deaf. *Early Development and Parenting, 5*, 1213–1223.

Mezzacappa, E. (2004). Alerting, orienting, and executive attention: Developmental properties and sociodemographic correlates in an epidemiological sample of young, urban children. *Child Development, 75*, 1373–1386.

Miller, C. A., Kail, R., Leonard, L. B., & Tomblin, J. B. (2001). Speed of processing in children with specific language impairment. *Journal of Speech, Language, and Hearing Research, 44*, 416–433.

Moeller, M. P., & Schick, B. (2006, May/June). Relations between maternal input and theory of mind understanding in deaf children. *Child Development, 77*, 751–766.

Mohay, H. (2000). Language in sight: Mothers' strategies for making language visually accessible to deaf children. In P. E. Spencer, C. J. Erting, & M. Marschark (Eds.), *The deaf child in the family and at school* (pp. 151–166). Mahwah, NJ: Lawrence Erlbaum.

Nelson, C. A., & Luciana, M. (Eds.). (2001). *Handbook of developmental cognitive neuroscience.* Cambridge, MA: MIT Press.

Noble, K. G., Norman, M. F., & Farah, M. J. (2005). Neurocognitive correlates of socioeconomic status in kindergarten children. *Developmental Science, 8(1)*, 74–87.

Oberg, E. (2007). *Assessing Executive Functioning in Children with a Hearing Loss.* Unpublished Master's Thesis. Rochester Institute of Technology, Rochester, NY.

Ouellette, S. (1988). The use of projective drawing techniques in the personality assessment of prelingually deafened young adults: A pilot study. *American Annals of the Deaf, 133*, 212–218.

Panksepp, J. (1998). *Affective neuroscience: The foundations of human and animal emotions.* New York: Oxford University Press.

Papousek, M., & Papousek, H. (1987). Didactic adjustments in fathers' and mothers' speech to their 3-month-old infants. *Journal of Psycholinguistics Research, 16*, 491–516.

Parasnis, I., Samar, V. J., & Berent, G. P. (2003). Deaf adults without attention deficit hyperactivity disorder display reduced perceptual sensitivity and elevated impulsivity on the Test of Variables of Attention (T.O.V.A.) *Journal of Speech, Language, and Hearing Research, 46,* 1166–1183.

Peterson, C. C. (2004). Theory-of-mind development in oral deaf children with cochlear implants or conventional hearing aids. *Journal of Child Psychology and Psychiatry, 45,* 1096–1106.

Peterson, C. C., & Siegal, M. (1999). Representing inner worlds: Theory of mind in autistic, deaf, and normal hearing children. *American Psychological Society, 10,* 126–129.

Porteus, S. D. (1965). *Porteus maze test.* Palo Alto, CA: Pacific Books.

Posner, M., & Rothbart, M. K. (1998). Attention, self-regulation and consciousness. *Transactions of the philosophical society of London, 353,* 1915–1027.

Pratt, B., Campbell-LaVoie, F., Isquith, P. K., Gioia, G. A., & Guy, S. C. (2000). The comparative development of executive function in elementary school with reading disorder and attention-deficit/hyperactivity disorder. *Journal of the International Neuropsychological Society, 6,* 127.

Ramsey, C. (1997). *Deaf children in public schools: Placement, context, and consequences.* Washington, DC: Gallaudet University Press.

Ramsey, C., & Padden, C. (1998). Natives and newcomers: Gaining access to literacy in a classroom for deaf children. *Anthropology and Education Quarterly, 29,* 5–24.

Rehkemper, G. M. (2004). Executive functioning and psychosocial adjustment in deaf subjects with non-hereditary and hereditary etiologies. *Dissertation Abstracts International, 64,* (11-B).

Remmel, E. (2002). *Theory of mind development in signing deaf children.* Unpublished doctoral dissertation. Stanford University, Stanford, CA.

Rhine, S. (2002). *Assessment of Executive Function.* Unpublished master's thesis, Gallaudet University, Washington, DC.

Rhine-Kahlback, S. (2004). *The Assessment of Developmental Language Differences, Executive Functioning, and Social Skills in Deaf Children.* Unpublished doctoral dissertation, Gallaudet University, Washington, DC.

Rogoff, B. (1990). *Apprenticeship in thinking: Cognitive development in social context.* New York: Oxford University Press.

Rogoff, B. (2003). *The cultural nature of human development.* New York: Oxford University Press.

Rosenweig, M. R., & Bennett, E. L. (1996). Psychobiology of plasticity: Effects of training and experience on brain and behavior. *Behavioural Brain Research, 78,* 57–65.

Roth, R. M., Isquith, P. I., & Gioia, G. A. (2005). *Behavior Rating Inventory of Executive Function-Adult Version.* Lutz, FL: Psychological Assessment Resources.

Ruff, H. A., & Rothbart, M. K. (1996). *Attention in early development: Themes and variations.* New York: Oxford University Press.

Ruffman, T., Slade, L., & Crowe, E. (2002). The relations between childrens' and mothers' mental state language and theory-of-mind understanding. *Child Development, 73,* 734–751.

Sabbagh, M. A., Xu, F., & Carlson, S. M. (2006). The development of executive functioning and Theory of Mind: A comparison of Chinese and U.S. preschoolers. *Psychological Science, 17,* 74–81.

Samuel, K. A. (1996). The relationship between attachment in deaf adolescents, parental sign communication and attitudes, and psychosocial adjustment. *Dissertation Abstracts International, 57,* 2182B. (UMI No. 9623718).

Schick, B., Hoffmeister, R., de Villiers, P. A., & de Villiers, J. (2000). *American sign language and theory of mind in deaf children with deaf or hearing parents.* Paper presented at the 7th Conference on Theoretical Issues in Sign Language Research, Amsterdam.

Siegel, L. S., & Ryan, E. B. (1989). The development of working memory in normally achieving and subtypes of learning disabled children. *Child Development, 60,* 973–980.

Singer, H. S., & Walkup, J. T. (1991). Tourette syndrome and other tic disorders. *Medicine, 70,* 15–32.

Singleton, J., & Morgan, D. D. (2004, April). *Becoming deaf: Deaf teachers engagement practices supporting deaf children's identity development.* Paper presented at the annual meeting of the American Educational Research Association, San Diego, CA.

Singleton, J. L., & Morgan, D. D. (2006). Natural signed language acquisition within the social context of the classroom. In B. Schick, M. Marschark, and P. E. Spencer (Eds.), *Advances in the sign language development of deaf children* (pp. 344–375). New York: Oxford University Press.

Spencer, P. E., Bodner-Johnson, B. A., & Gutfreund, M. K. (1992). Interacting with infants with a hearing loss: What can we learn from mothers who are deaf? *Journal of Early Intervention, 16,* 64–78.

Sporn, M. B. (1997). *The assessment of the Test of Variables of Attention with deaf children.* Unpublished Master's Thesis, Gallaudet University, Washington, DC.

Sporn, M. B. (1999). *The use of the Test of Variables of Attention to predict attention and behavior problems in deaf adults.* Unpublished doctoral dissertation, Gallaudet University, Washington, DC.

Steinberg, L., & Scott. E. (2003). Less guilty by reason of adolescence. *American Psychologist, 58,* 1009–1018.

Swisher, M. V. (2000). Learning to converse: How deaf mothers support the development of attention and conversational skills in their young deaf children. In P. E. Spencer, C. J. Erting, & M. Marschark (Eds.), *The deaf child in the family and at school* (pp. 21–39). Mahwah, NJ: Lawrence Erlbaum.

Travis, F. (1998). Cortical and cognitive development in 4th, 8th, and 12th grade students: The contribution of speed of processing and executive functioning to cognitive development. *Biological Psychology, 48,* 37–56.

Vaughn, B. E., Kopp, C. B., & Krakow, J. B. (1984). The emergence and consolidation of self-control form 18 to 30 months of age: Normative trends and individual differences. *Child Development, 55,* 990–1004.

Vygotsky, L. S. (1978). *Mind in society: The development of higher psychological processes* (M. Cole, V. John-Steiner, S. Scribner, and E. Soubernam, eds.). Cambridge, MA: Harvard University Press.

Waber, D. P., Gerber, E. B., Turcios, V. Y., Wagner, E. R., & Forbes, P. W. (2006). Executive functions and performance on high-stakes testing in children from urban schools. *Developmental Neuropsychology, 29,* 459–477.

Waxman, R. P., & Spencer, P. E. (1997). What mothers do to support infant visual attention: Sensitivities to age and hearing status. *Journal of Deaf Studies and Deaf Education, 2,* 104–114.

Welsh, M. C., & Pennington, B. F. (1988). Assessing frontal lobe functioning in children: Views from developmental psychology. *Developmental Neuropsychology, 4,* 199–230.

Windsor, J., & Hwang, M. (1999). Testing the generalized slowing hypothesis in specific language impairment. *Journal of Speech, Language, and Hearing Research, 42,* 1205–1218.

Wood, D., Wood, H., & Kingsmill, M. (1991). Signed English in the classroom, II. Structural and pragmatic aspects of teachers' speech and sign. *First Language, 11,* 301–315.

Woodcock, R. W., McGrew, K. S., & Mather, N. (2001). *Woodcock-Johnson Tests of Achievement* (3rd ed.). Itasca, IL: Riverside Publishing.

Woolfe, T., Want, S., & Siegal, M. (2002). Signposts to development: Theory of mind in deaf children. *Child Development, 73,* 768–778.

Zelazo, P. D., Reznick, J. S., & Piñon, D. E. (1995). Response control and the execution of verbal rules. *Developmental Psychology, 31,* 508–517.

Chapter 12

Language Comprehension and Learning by Deaf Students

Marc Marschark and Loes Wauters

Do deaf children learn in the same ways that hearing children learn?[1] If communication barriers in the mainstream classroom are removed, do they learn as much and as quickly as their age-matched peers? Alternatively, is there a benefit to an academic setting with a trained teacher of the deaf? Such questions involve aspects of language and cognition as well as pedagogy and academic curriculum issues. The fact that we do not yet have definitive answers to any of them also indicates that these questions are not simple.

In this chapter, we consider the possibility that interactions between language comprehension and cognition underlie the differences and challenges observed in learning by deaf students at a more basic level than has been considered previously. The notion of differences in the development of deaf learners relative to hearing learners, in addition to the considerable variability found among deaf learners, is an essential premise here. Early investigations involving deaf individuals often failed to account for the fact that deaf children had different language and experiential histories than their hearing peers. Those differences can create subtle and not-so-subtle differences in the cognitive and linguistic functioning of deaf individuals

---

1. Unless otherwise noted, in this chapter "deaf" is used generically to refer to individuals with a wide range of hearing thresholds, from those considered hard-of-hearing to those considered profoundly deaf. Similarly, unless otherwise noted, both "English" and "American Sign Language/ASL" are used to refer to any spoken/written vernacular or natural signed language. These conveniences notwithstanding, most research described in this chapter has involved deaf rather than hard-of-hearing individuals and individuals living in countries utilizing English and ASL.

which, at some times and places, have erroneously been interpreted as deficiencies. More recently, issues concerning deaf students' language comprehension generally are overlooked or ignored but nonetheless, these are of central importance if educational interventions are to be effective (Detterman & Thompson, 1997).

When language comprehension is factored into the literature relating to the academic achievement of deaf students, we see that it is less contradictory and more informative than is typically assumed. Further, doing so will result in a better understanding of the strengths and needs of deaf learners and in the emergence of specific directions for future research. Many deaf students do face challenges in academic and other domains, regardless of the preferred mode of their communication. Our contention is that some of those challenges might be eliminated by fuller explication of language comprehension in deaf students' learning, and other challenges will at least be better understood. As a concrete example that will be elaborated later, a recent study examined deaf college students' comprehension of each other's spoken and signed communication using a version of the Trivial Pursuit game (Marschark, Convertino, Macias, et al., 2007). Comprehension was assessed by having each student repeat the one-sentence Trivial Pursuit question to a partner sitting directly across a table, under auditorily and visually quiet conditions. The results indicated that students who were strongly oral[2] and used spoken language in playing the game understood each other only about 44% of the time. Students who reported being essentially life-long signers (in American Sign Language, ASL) understood each other only about 63% of the time. Students were encouraged to request repetitions when they were unsure of their comprehension, but they did so only rarely. The findings were interpreted as reflecting either metacomprehension failure—that is, failure to recognize that questions were not fully understood—or an unwillingness to request clarification of partially understood messages, even in a comfortable communication context. Coupled with low levels of language comprehension under ideal conditions, either alternative would have significant implications for classroom learning.

Educating Deaf Students: From Research to Practice

Detterman and Thompson (1997, p. 1083) argued that "lack of understanding of the cognitive skills underlying educational isnterventions is the fundamental problem in the development of special education. Without under-

---

2. "Oral" is really a misnomer for deaf individuals who utilize spoken language, but it is a traditional, convenient shorthand.

standing the full complexity of cognitive abilities, special educational methods can never be special." Evidence presented later in this chapter suggests that deaf and hearing students have somewhat different knowledge, that the organization of that knowledge is measurably different in the two populations, and that they employ different cognitive strategies in learning and memory tasks. Such variability makes educational research involving deaf learners far more complex than might be assumed (Marschark, Convertino, & LaRock, 2006). Issues associated with the debate over integrated versus separate schooling of deaf children are particularly relevant here. However, it is rare that investigators consider the role of either psychological factors or language skills in academic achievement. Some investigators have sought to identify the characteristics of optimal academic environments for deaf learners, but most of these have involved surveys of perceptions rather than direct empirical assessment (e.g., Lang, Dowaliby, & Anderson, 1994; Lang, McKee, & Conner, 1993; Long & Beil, 2005).

Lang et al. (1993), for example, found that deaf and hearing students valued the same characteristics in their teachers. Perhaps not surprisingly, both groups appreciate teachers who have extensive knowledge of course content, use visual materials, present information in an organized manner, and provide clear explanations. Deaf learners who use sign language also report a clear preference for teachers who sign for themselves (Long & Beil, 2005). These findings notwithstanding, other studies suggest that deaf college students, like those surveyed by Lang et al., may not be accurate in evaluating their comprehension and learning in various contexts. Deaf teachers and those who sign for themselves, for example, may make students more comfortable (e.g., Long & Beil, 2005), but they do not necessarily facilitate greater learning (Marschark, Leigh, Sapere, et al., 2006; Marschark, Sapere, Convertino, & Pelz, 2008).

Singleton and Morgan (2006) evaluated the situation of deaf children who grow up matched or mismatched in their mode of communication with their parents. They argued that "deaf children born to deaf parents could be characterized as *knowing how to learn* and are poised to make a successful transition from home to school. However, all of this presupposes a school teacher in the classroom who *knows how to teach*" (p. 352). Singleton and Morgan reviewed the literature relevant to conversation and communication in classrooms with deaf children and hearing teachers, concluding that deaf teachers are likely to utilize more effective conversational strategies than most hearing teachers. In considering more broadly what constitutes effective teaching for deaf students, Singleton and Morgan referred primarily to communication issues, but recognized the need for students and teachers to be actively engaged in the joint construction of knowledge through interactions that focus on meaningful, relevant problems. Indeed, recent studies concerning deaf children's mathematical problem-solving skills indicate that a failure to link problems presented in the classroom to real-world, meaningful scenarios is a significant impediment to problem-solving success (Ansell & Pagliaro, 2001; Blatto-Vallee, Kelly, Gaustad, Porter, & Fonzi, 2007; see Kelly, this volume). Such findings parallel more global cognitive differences observed between deaf and hearing learners (Marschark et al., 2006) and highlight the importance of deaf students' having teachers who know how they think.

Consistent with suggestions of Singleton and Morgan (2006), Mayer, Akamatsu, and Stewart (2002) articulated an approach to educating deaf students that focuses more on mutual understanding and cognitive interaction between teachers and students, rather than the mode or modality of instruction. Consistent with their Vygotskyian approach to language and learning, Mayer et al. identified dialogic educational practices among outstanding teachers of deaf children across several educational settings. Such practices included interactive turn-taking, in which teachers' responses related to and expanded upon students' statements (Cawthon, 2001). In seeking to appropriately match discourse to students' levels of cognitive and linguistic functioning, Mayer et al. observed teachers scaffolding classroom interactions so as to promote active student involvement in ongoing inquiry.

Despite its popularity, the notion of "active learning" for deaf students remains relatively ambiguous. To the extent that deaf and hearing students, as well as deaf students as a group, differ in their content knowledge and learning strategies, it may be difficult for a teacher to scaffold instruction effectively or promote active learning when there are multiple deaf students in the same class. Yet, active engagement with to-be-learned material in the learning environment can occur (or not) at many levels. Dowaliby and Lang (1999), for example, found that interspersing adjunct questions into a presented science text led to better retention than presenting the material in sign language or providing animated movies depicting the content. The investigators emphasized the importance of active involvement of the deaf students in the adjunct question condition, but those questions actually required only short-term rote retention of factual information. A recent investigation by Wauters, Marschark, Sapere, Convertino, and Sarchet (in preparation) extended the Dowaliby and Lang study by examining the effects of deaf and hearing college students' periodic responding to factual versus inferential questions while either seeing a passage presented via real-time text or the same passage signed by an interpreter. In parallel conditions, factual or inferential statements were inserted periodically (with no response necessary), so that two levels of active processing were examined. In neither case did more active processing of the content lead to better learning by either deaf or hearing students, but the manipulation may not have had an effect on their learning for different reasons. Hearing students may not have needed the additional "mental rehearsal," whereas deaf students might not have effectively utilized the opportunity (deaf students scored significantly below hearing students). In any case, the point is that educational interventions need to be developed in concert with research into their cognitive underpinnings (Detterman & Thompson, 1997).

Even if we cannot yet be sure what kinds of educational interventions would be optimal for deaf students, the difference in outcomes when teachers know how deaf students think and learn is now clear. Several studies have demonstrated that deaf students tend to learn significantly less in mainstream college classrooms than their hearing peers, despite having highly skilled interpreters and instructors who utilize appropriate classroom techniques for teaching deaf students (e.g., collaboration with interpreters, providing notes) (Jacobs, 1977; Marschark, Sapere, Convertino, Seewagen, & Maltzen, 2004; Marschark, Sapere, Convertino, & Seewagen, 2005; Marschark, Pelz, et al., 2005, Marschark, Leigh, et al., 2006). Marschark, Sapere, et al. (2008) conducted a series of experiments that yielded a somewhat different result from that found in earlier investigations. In contrast to previous studies involving mainstream instructors, each of the teachers in their four experiments had considerable experience and skill in teaching deaf students; all had won awards for excellence in teaching (deaf students). Independent of whether teachers were deaf or hearing, signed for themselves or used an interpreter, used simultaneous communication (speech and sign together) or voice-off ASL, the deaf students gained just as much as hearing students, despite the fact that pretests showed them to start at a significant disadvantage in content knowledge. We can only assume that if such teachers were available to deaf students in mainstream primary and secondary classrooms, disadvantage might never have developed in the first place. The challenge now is to determine precisely what teachers who are familiar with deaf students do differently from those who are not and then develop ways to impart that information efficiently and economically to teachers in mainstream classrooms (Antia, 2007).

Teaching, Learning, and Language

Regardless of educational histories, placement, and philosophy, effective teaching and learning demand shared communication between instructors and students. For deaf students, that shared communication is often mediated by an interpreter or technology. Perhaps the most obvious forms of technology-supported, mediated learning in deaf education are real-time text (e.g., captioning), synchronous or asynchronous distance learning, and computer-supported self-directed instruction. Hearing aids and cochlear implants (CIs) are also technologies that support learning, perhaps the most basic technologies employed by deaf students in educational settings (Harkins & Bakke, 2003; Leigh, this volume). What is common to all of these is that they serve simply as channels of communication, and the language transmitted through them, as well as the channels themselves, present potential barriers to learning.

Regardless of whether particular technologies facilitate or hinder learning, most teachers (and, we suspect, students themselves) assume that their students are fluent in the preferred language of instruction. Setting reading aside for the moment, most teachers would expect that deaf students who rely on spoken language will be fairly fluent in that language, even if their production and reception are not perfect. Similarly, and perhaps even more so because they are unable to judge for themselves, teachers who encounter signing deaf students will assume that those students have sign language fluencies comparable to the spoken language fluencies of their hearing classmates. Unfortunately, such assumptions often may be without basis.

Given the inconsistent and relatively impoverished language backgrounds of many deaf children, they frequently arrive at school lagging significantly behind hearing peers in their language fluencies. Deaf children who sign, in particular, face challenges because they typically come from hearing families and, relative to hearing children from hearing families and deaf children from deaf families, rarely are immersed in settings including fluent users of a shared language. Unlike the children of immigrants, who might nonetheless have access to a second language via incidental learning, most deaf children will receive classroom instruction in a language in which they lack both expertise and a strong cognitive–linguistic foundation (Mayer & Wells, 1996). In that situation, cognitive flexibility, cloze (i.e., gap-filling) skills, and language aptitude are extremely important. Yet beyond the Singleton and Morgan (2006) study noted earlier and some of our own research described later, we do not know of any programmatic efforts to evaluate the relationship between students' language fluencies and the effectiveness of access in the classroom.

Learning to Use Language and Using Language in Learning[3]

Given the long history of parents and educators focusing on deaf children's speech, the shorter but intensive history with regard to ASL and other natural sign languages, and the demonstrated academic challenges of deaf students, one would expect a considerable literature with regard to language comprehension in educational settings. Only limited attention has been given to the language competencies of school-age deaf children and adults,

---

3. Portions of this section draw from Marschark et al. (2007).

however, and relatively little is known about their language skills in real-world settings (versus in audiology booths).

Several studies have demonstrated the importance of deaf children's language to academic performance insofar as they have found a relationship between early ASL skills and later reading abilities (e.g., Padden & Ramsey, 1998, 2000; Singleton, Supalla, Litchfield, & Schley, 1998). These studies have all been correlational, however, demonstrating that high or low levels of performance in one of these domains are often accompanied by similar levels in the other. At the same time, other investigations have shown a similar link between spoken language and reading abilities (e.g., deVilliers, Bibeau, Ramos, & Gatty, 1993; Geers & Moog, 1989; see Pisoni et al., this volume), although that relationship likely is confounded by the amount of residual hearing. It thus appears that early access to fluent language explains all of these results, but the situation is more complex.

Consider the study most frequently cited as demonstrating that deaf children of deaf parents are academically superior to those with hearing parents as another empirical example. Jensema and Trybus (1978) reported an extensive study of academic achievement in deaf children involving 412 children with two hearing parents, 26 with one deaf parent and one hearing parent, and 14 with two deaf parents. Despite frequent citations to the study as indicative that deaf children of deaf parents read better than deaf children of hearing parents, the advantages observed for deaf children of deaf parents were not statistically significant. Perhaps more telling, achievement scores were *negatively* related to the use of sign language between parents and children and positively related to the use of speech between parents and children (although again not significantly). Many deaf adults are not fluent readers themselves (Traxler, 2000), however, so it may be that some of the advantages of early language fluency may be offset by having parents who are not good reading models. Moreover, other studies have indicated that those deaf children who have the best literacy skills are those who were exposed early to both sign language and the vernacular (Akamatsu, Musselman, & Zweibel, 2000; Brasel & Quigley, 1977; Spencer, Gantz, & Knutson, 2004; Strong & Prinz, 1997).

Research on deaf children's language currently focuses on the acquisition of sign language structures in children who grow up with a natural sign language, the acquisition of spoken language by children with CIs, and the development of print literacy. Throughout arguments about the benefits of different language modalities and claims about who might be to blame for deaf students' academic challenges, the protagonists have devoted relatively little attention to how language and achievement might be linked and enhanced. Case studies and investigations involving small samples of deaf children of deaf parents sometimes do demonstrate academic success and thus the potential of deaf children who are immersed in such linguistically and educationally rich environments (Chamberlain & Mayberry, 2000; Padden & Ramsey, 1998). Yet, other studies demonstrate similar success among deaf children reared with spoken language by hearing parents in environments that are comparably supportive (Geers & Moog, 1989; Moeller, 2000). Those studies, too, are often limited in their generality, but they also demonstrate the flexibility and potential of deaf children. The difficulty is that those who cite either of the two kinds of research too often ignore the other, as well as the majority of deaf children: those falling between those extremes and all too frequently "between the cracks" in public education.

Learning a language within an experientially and linguistically rich environment may seem relatively effortless for young children, but it is far from simple. Ample evidence suggests that at least younger deaf children of deaf parents go through the same stages of language development as hearing children of hearing parents, and at about the same rate (e.g., Anderson & Reilly, 2002), but evidence concerning social and academic language use is harder to come by. Current research on language development usually involves relatively brief language samples and small samples who are not necessarily representative of the larger population of deaf children. Marschark, Schick, and Spencer (2006) therefore concluded that the complexities of language learning by deaf children are often missed or ignored. They suggested that, in efforts to make definitive statements about deaf children's development of natural signed languages and demonstrate commonalities between deaf and hearing children, researchers have adopted simplistic accounts of development in which deaf children with deaf parents are presumed to be essentially identical to hearing children except for the modality of their communication. In other words, they treat deaf children as hearing children who cannot hear—and therefore sign. Little interest has been shown in assessing the validity of such assumptions, examining the linguistic diversity among deaf children, or determining how to know whether any particular deaf child is developing sign language normally (see Leigh, this volume).

The vast majority of hearing parents are unfamiliar with the implications of hearing loss, the viability of sign language as a first language, and the difficulty encountered by deaf children in acquiring spoken language. It therefore is not surprising that most of them eagerly embrace the recommendations of the early hearing detection and intervention (EHDI) professionals for "speech first." No evidence has ever shown that early sign language interferes with the acquisition of spoken language and, in fact, considerable evidence now suggests that deaf children's spoken language abilities are either independent of or supported by early use of sign language in the home (e.g., Moeller, 2000; Yoshinaga-Itano, 2003). Yet, the recent pragmatic emphasis on spoken language for deaf children, accompanying the increasing popularity of CIs, has not been accompanied by research concerning the acquisition of receptive versus production skills in real-world settings like the classroom.

In view of the wealth of information available concerning early language development in deaf children, as well as the fact that it is tangential to the focus of this chapter, we will not consider acquisition in any further detail here. If more were known about the cognitive foundations of language acquisition by deaf children, it certainly would be relevant to the present discussion. However, little consideration has been given of the possibility of cognitive differences underlying the two as a function of either modality or language users. Those interested in the acquisition of sign languages will find recent collections by Morgan and Woll (2002) and Schick, Marschark, and Spencer (2006) to provide the current state of the art. Those interested in the acquisition of spoken language will find the collection in Spencer and Marschark (2006) to capture the breadth of research in that area. Here, we will focus on two areas of language functioning that have included studies with school-age children and young adults. Studies in these areas also bear directly on the use of language for learning and the cognitive foundations of its comprehension.

Pragmatic Communication

Pragmatic communication refers to interpersonal interactions intended to communicate information for a particular purpose. The most common laboratory paradigm for studying pragmatic communication is the *referential communication task*. Most versions of the paradigm involve one individual describing a stimulus unseen by a second individual; the second individual then has to select the correct stimulus from within a group of similar distractors. Most studies involving referential communication and deaf individuals have focused on young children's interactions with their mothers. Of interest here are studies that have examined language production, receptive skills, and instances of communication breakdown. Such tasks provide insight into the coordination of cognitive and language abilities, as individuals take on the roles of both "speaker" and "listener" (see Courtin, Melot, & Corroyer, this volume). At different levels, they therefore entail metacognition, problem solving, and an awareness of conversational rules (i.e., social cognition).

Arnold, Palmer, and Lloyd (1999) used a referential communication task to examine the receptive language skills of oral deaf and hearing children aged 5–9 years. The task entailed selecting a picture that corresponded to an examiner's spoken description. Arnold et al. found that the hearing children significantly outscored their deaf peers in correct responses and were significantly more likely to ask the experimenter for repetitions and clarifications. The latter finding was taken as evidence of more sophisticated metacognitive and conversational abilities. No information was given, however, on whether requests for clarification were associated with task performance. Therefore, we do not know if the relative infrequency of deaf students' requests reflected a failure to recognize their lack of comprehension.

Lloyd, Lieven, and Arnold (2005) extended the Arnold et al. study, examining communication breakdowns in production and reception during a referential communication task. Deaf and hearing children, aged 7–12 years, took turns as describer and responder. Once again, the deaf children relied exclusively on spoken language, and the test was conducted orally. Overall, hearing students outperformed deaf students in terms of correct responding, but there was no significant difference in the frequency with which the groups asked for repetitions or clarifications. Assessments of the deaf students' language skills revealed a significant positive correlation between language and requests for clarification, but the relationship of requests to performance on the referential communication task was not examined. Taken together, these two studies suggest that deaf students who rely on spoken language lag significantly behind hearing peers in their receptive language skill, even in a one-on-one situation.

This conclusion is consistent with the results of the Marschark, Convertino, Macias, et al. (2007) Trivial Pursuit study described earlier, even if it did not include a hearing comparison group (preliminary testing showed the task to be too simple, with all respondents at 100%). In addition to ASL and oral dyads, that study also included "mixed" dyads containing one ASL student and one oral student who did not know sign language or was new to it within the past 2 months. Students in the mixed dyads asked for repetitions at about the same rate as those in the oral dyads (19% and 20%, respectively), and scored about the same number correct (46% and 44%, respectively). The fact that students in all three groups were relatively poor in repeating back a single sentence and yet failed to request repetitions even with encouragement suggests that deaf students might be relatively less adept than hearing peers in monitoring their ongoing language comprehension in sign as well as in spoken language (Marschark, Sapere, et al., 2004; Marschark, Pelz, et al., 2005). Given the inconsistency of their language experiences, perhaps that result should not be unexpected, but the results clearly indicate that the communication barrier in educational settings goes beyond access in the physical (auditory and visual) sense.

Jeanes, Nienhuys, and Rickards (2000) used referential communication tasks to investigate conversational interactions and repairs in deaf and hearing 11- to 17-year-olds. Half of the deaf students were enrolled in an oral school program and half in a program that utilized simultaneous communication. Jeanes et al. found that the oral deaf students made significantly more requests for clarification than either the signing deaf students or the hearing students. They concluded that deaf students who use spoken language are more likely to recognize and repair communication breakdowns because they are more accustomed to the necessity to do so. It was unclear, however, whether the signing students did not experience communication breakdowns as frequently, did not recognize them when they happened, or simply failed to request clarification when they did occur.

One alternative explanation of the Jeanes et al. results is that they reflect a lower criterion for comprehension among deaf and hearing students. Some tangential support exists for that suggestion, although it apparently has not been explored explicitly. Matthews and Reich (1993), for example, examined communication between teachers and deaf students as well as among students in high school classes at a school for the deaf. They found that when students were signing after being called on, their peers were looking at them only about 30% of the time. When teachers were signing to the class, students looked at them an average of only 44% of the time, only slightly less than when they were the target of a teacher's language production (50%). Similarly, in our studies of sign language comprehension conducted in college classrooms (both live and via video) deaf students spend a surprising amount of time looking elsewhere than at the instructor or interpreter. This contrasts with the behavior observed on the part of interpreters watching the same lectures (without audio) who reported an unwillingness to look away from the lecture for fear that they would miss information (Marschark, Pelz, et al., 2005; Experiment 2). It thus appears that deaf students sometimes assume that, if they understand a teacher's/interpreter's signs (when they are paying attention), they are fully comprehending the meaning. In fact, there may be only a superficial level of processing, and students may be aware of it (Napier, 2002) or not (Marschark, Sapere, et al., 2004). As described in later sections, there is support for this suggestion in the cognitive literature and from studies of classroom learning via sign language interpreting.

In contrast to the Jeanes et al. findings, MacKay-Soroka, Trehub, and Thorpe (1988) found that deaf children who used simultaneous communication showed significantly better receptive performance in a referential communication task than did deaf peers who used spoken language. Examining language production rather than reception, MacKay-Soroka, Trehub, and Thorpe (1987) found that deaf schoolchildren who used simultaneous communication provided clearer messages than deaf children who relied exclusively on spoken language. It is unclear whether these results are in some way related to using simultaneous communication, a reflection of sign language somehow allowing greater precision in referential communication than spoken language, or the product of educational differences in the United States (MacKay-Soroka et al.) and Australia (Jeanes et al.). Research that would help to clarify this issue is available from a limited number of studies that have compared the comprehension of spoken and signed communication in various settings.[4]

Comprehension and Learning via Signed and Spoken Language

Several studies have examined the reception of spoken and signed language by deaf individuals in carefully controlled audiological and laboratory settings. One body of literature has addressed the role of vision in deaf individuals' reception of spoken language (see Dodd & Campbell, 1987; Power & Hyde, 1997). Results from several studies indicate that the comprehension of spoken language by deaf individuals is enhanced by the simultaneous availability of visual as well as auditory input (see Power & Hyde, 1997, for a review). In contrast, there is no direct evidence that removal of correlated visual information is helpful in acquiring language fluency (see Eriks-Brophy, 2004; Marschark & Spencer, 2006, for reviews). Hyde and Power (1992), for example, conducted a study in which groups of severely and profoundly deaf students had to match pictures with sentences presented under 11 different communication conditions. Videotaped stimuli were utterances that included auditory and visual information (lipreading, fingerspelling, and signs) in all possible unisensory and multisensory combinations. Overall, performance was greater in all conditions that included visual information, relative to the condition that included auditory information alone.

Much less evidence exists concerning the effectiveness of communication in real-world settings for individuals varying in their hearing losses and language preferences. Most of what is available beyond studies of early mother–child communication (see Meadow-Orlans, Spencer, & Koester, 2004, for a review) has involved students' comprehension of instructors and/or interpreters in the classroom. Several studies, for example, have compared learning via sign language interpreting versus simultaneous communication from an instructor (e.g., Cokely, 1990; Leigh & Power, 1998; Marschark et al., 2007). Other studies of classroom learning by deaf students have compared the effectiveness of transliteration (English-based signing) and interpretation (in ASL) in the classroom, usually at the college level (e.g., Livingston, Singer, & Abramson, 1994; Murphy & Fleischer, 1977). Such studies have not demonstrated an advantage for any particular mode of signing by instructors (Marschark et al., 2008) or by interpreters (Marschark, Sapere, et al., 2004; Marschark, Sapere, et al., 2005), indicating

---

4. Some evidence suggests that children with CIs also benefit from total communication in terms of academic performance (Spencer et al., 2004; see Marschark, Rhoten, & Fabich, 2007, for a review), even if not in language performance (see Pisoni et al., this volume).

that deaf students have sufficiently flexible language skills to be able to utilize diverse modes of signed communication, at least by college age. Although these studies have indicated that deaf college students, on average, come away with less information from interpreted classes than do their hearing peers, results have indicated that not to be a consequence of either interpreting quality or student language/communication skills.

Several studies have also compared classroom learning by deaf students who use spoken language versus sign language. Those studies typically have utilized spoken lectures supported by sign language interpreting, so that students with both orientations are provided with both speech and sign. The studies of visual gaze allocation described by Pelz, Marschark, and Convertino (this volume) were focused on whether previous findings indicating that deaf signers have greater peripheral sensitivity to movement and illumination changes (see Dye, Hauser, & Bavelier, this volume) extend to learning. We therefore have included deaf students who are skilled signers and deaf and hearing students who rely exclusively on spoken language. Experiments have manipulated the nature of the signed message (e.g., two-dimensional or three-dimensional, simultaneous communication or sign only), the physical relationship of an instructor's lecture to visual materials (angular separation), and the complexity of signs produced in the periphery. Although Pelz et al. describe the results of the eye tracking part of these investigations, we have never observed significant differences in learning between the signing and oral students (e.g., Marschark, Pelz, et al. 2005; Marschark et al., 2008) despite a variety of studies suggesting that skilled deaf signers have greater acuity for peripheral visual stimuli (Dye et al., this volume). Marschark, Pelz, et al. (2005) therefore concluded that the enhanced visuo-spatial acuity that apparently accrues to signers in terms of sensitivity to stimulus change in the periphery may have little effect on functioning "in the real world."

The findings described in this section contradict many of the strong statements encountered about the advantages of one communication mode over the other. At the same time, they suggest that other studies may have failed to find differences between spoken language and sign language in various contexts, but their null findings remain unpublished. Unfortunately, without reports of such null results, anecdote and assumption continue to be taken as fact and influence parental decisions about educational placement for their deaf children. Clearly, more careful and diverse investigations are needed about language alternatives for learners of different ages and characteristics. Studies of the allocation of visual attention by deaf children also would be interesting because of the central role that such attention plays in early vocabulary learning and language acquisition at-large. Early intervention programming focusing on teaching hearing parents the visual communication and attention-getting strategies used by deaf parents has been helpful (Mohay, Milton, Hindmarsh, & Ganley,

1998), but its impact on language, cognitive, or even social development has not been evaluated.

Linking Language and Cognition Among Deaf Children

As noted in chapter 1, the link between cognitive functioning and language has been of interest to investigators for centuries, with deaf children frequently being seen as the ultimate example of how the two are necessarily intertwined, or not, depending on the theoretical orientation of the observer. Investigations concerning this convergence have typically compared deaf children's performance to that of hearing children. Deaf children were studied in order to test ideas from theory and research on hearing children and thus contribute to our knowledge base concerning language and language development or to identify aspects of language development and links between language and learning that were robust and could emerge without a child having full access to the sounds of language (e.g., Furth, 1966). More recently, studies have explored deaf students' knowledge and its underlying structure in order to better understand memory and problem solving (see Marschark, Convertino, McEvoy, & Masteller, 2004; McEvoy, Marschark, & Nelson, 1999), even if that work has not yet been extended to academic settings. Here, we touch on just a few areas of investigation to demonstrate the variety of links between cognition and language (both in print and "through the air").

Working Memory

Bavelier et al. (in press) and Pisoni et al. (this volume) provide overviews of current research concerning working memory in deaf individuals who are reared with sign language or spoken language, respectively. Although of theoretical utility with regard to cognition and language, the small minority of deaf individuals who have deaf parents and thus make up the "pure" population in the work of Bavelier and her colleagues may not be those who demonstrate memory functioning outside of the norm. "Norm" here necessarily refers to what is typical for hearing children. We do not believe that deaf children should be viewed as hearing children who cannot hear, and it may well be that the cognitive differences between deaf and hearing parents also affect the way that they rear and teach their young deaf (and perhaps hearing) children. Deaf children of either deaf or hearing parents who come to the classroom with different cognitive hardware and software may not benefit optimally from teaching methods intended for the majority of students in neighboring seats.

Wilson, Bettger, Niculae, and Klima (1997), for example, compared memory span performance of deaf children of deaf parents with that of hearing children of hearing parents. The deaf and hearing children were found to have comparable forward and backward digit span tasks, suggesting that encoding of serial information in ASL does not entail directional dominance in the same way that print does. The deaf children also showed better memory than hearing children with the Corsi blocks. These results suggest that memory in deaf individuals who are fluent in sign language may have different characteristics than that of hearing individuals and perhaps deaf individuals who rely on spoken language (Pisoni et al., this volume). Depending on the nature of the task and to-be-remembered materials, those differences can lead to deaf individuals having better, equal, or worse memory as compared with hearing individuals, but there are also large differences among deaf individuals (Boutla, Supalla, Newport, & Bavelier, 2004). Burkholder and Pisoni (2006), for example, found that slower verbal rehearsal and serial scanning resulted in decreased working memory among deaf children with CIs. Verbal rehearsal is known to underlie working memory in both hearing and deaf children (Bebko & Metcalfe-Haggert, 1997), and for nonverbal as well as verbal materials (Glucksberg & Krauss, 1967). So, such "lower-level" differences should not be deemed trivial.

Findings reported by Bavelier (2007) indicate that the earlier studies demonstrating poorer memory for sequential information among deaf than hearing individuals (see Marschark, 1993, chapters 8 and 9) may represent tendencies rather than limitations. Many such studies involve verbal materials such as word lists or digits. Krakow and Hanson (1985), for example, examined serial recall for printed, signed, and fingerspelled words by deaf college students who were either native signers (from deaf families or parents) or late sign language learners (from hearing families) as compared with recall of printed word lists by hearing college students. No differences were found between the two deaf groups, but the hearing students surpassed both in recall of printed words. Studies by Todman and Cowdy (1993) and Todman and Seedhouse (1994) later showed that such differences were not limited to verbal materials. They found that deaf children surpassed hearing peers in their memories for complex visual figures, but that the advantage disappeared when the figures were presented in parts and had to be recalled sequentially. More recently, Boutla et al. (2004) confirmed earlier findings suggesting that signers and speakers have comparable working memory capacities, even if signers tend to have shorter memory spans (Bavelier et al., in press). They argued that short-term memory and working memory operate differently in the two modalities, thus requiring separate digit span norms for deaf (native-signing) and hearing individuals.

Modality differences notwithstanding, Marschark, Convertino, et al. (2006) described a fairly large body of research indicating that deaf adults and children are less likely to adopt serial or sequential processing strategies than are hearing peers across a variety of tasks. Because such differences were never all or none, "tendency" is certainly a better label than "limitation." At the same time, some aspects of learning necessarily involve sequential presentation and recall, reading being the most obvious. Even if native sign language users have a tendency toward spatial–positional coding rather than sequential coding in memory (Bavelier, 2007; O'Connor & Hermelin, 1973), we need to understand how to help students recognize when alternative strategies are necessary and determine the tendencies in memory processing by the other 95% of deaf students who have hearing parents. It therefore is worth considering this issue in more detail.

Integration of Information and Learning

The past 25 years of research on cognition, language, and deaf individuals has yielded a robust pattern of results consistent with the Todman studies noted earlier. Ottem's (1980) review of cognitive research involving tasks such as concept learning, problem solving, memory, and classification revealed a marked difference in the cognitive behaviors of deaf adults and children relative to hearing peers. He showed that, across dozens of experimental comparisons, deaf and hearing individuals performed similarly when tasks involved only a single stimulus dimension (e.g., sorting on number or color). When responses depended on integrating, balancing, or selecting from among multiple dimensions (e.g., sorting on number and color), in contrast, deaf adults and children consistently performed more poorly than hearing age-matched peers. Similar results have been obtained with printed materials.

Banks, Gray, and Fyfe (1990), for example, examined the recall of reading-level appropriate texts by deaf and hearing children. The two groups recalled the same amount, overall, but hearing children's recall was consistent with the overall structure of the text. The deaf children, in contrast, tended to recall disconnected portions of the text, suggesting a lack of semantic integration or deeper processing of meaning. Marschark, De Beni, Polazzo, and Cornoldi (1993) presented texts to groups of deaf adolescents and hearing students matched either for age or reading ability. The deaf adolescents recalled significantly less than their hearing age-matched peers, but more than the younger, reading-matched children. More importantly, deaf students remembered proportionately fewer relations than words, whereas the reverse was true for both groups of their hearing peers. Insofar as this finding occurred with both age- and reading-matched hearing peers, it means that the effect could not be ascribed to reading difficulties per se nor to a developmental lag. Richardson, MacLeod-Gallinger, McKee, and Long (2000) obtained convergent results in an investigation involving deaf and hearing college students. They found that the two groups reported similar strategies in studying written materials, but the deaf students had significantly more difficulty than hearing students in integrating ideas across texts. This difficulty in relational processing has also been observed in the way that deaf students link material presented via video and accompanying captions, apparently because they "lag behind hearing students in their ability to generalize information or to use prior knowledge" (Jelinek Lewis & Jackson, 2001, p. 49).

Metacognition and Metacomprehension in Learning

The research just described can be interpreted in two ways. Most generally, it might be suggested that deaf students tend to engage in superficial processing of language relative to their hearing peers. Given the inconsistencies and outright errors contained in the language directed to deaf children growing up and their challenges in learning via incidental comprehension, a superficial level of language monitoring might serve as an effective strategy in many settings. A large part of language comprehension, however, depends on linking ongoing language to what is already known and recognizing when it is new. Research involving hearing students is informative in this regard.

A central component of learning involves recognition of when comprehension is successful and when it is not (Dunlosky, Rawson, & Middleton, 2005; Thiede, Anderson, & Therriault, 2003). The general finding is that students who know more are better able to distinguish what is known from what is new and, if anything, tend to underestimate their performance. Students who know less tend not to realize how much they do not know or comprehend and thus tend to learn less while overestimating their performance (Kruger & Dunning, 1999). In most studies involving hearing students, however, it is assumed that the participants are all language-fluent without any particular (or at least identified) learning difficulties. Many deaf children, in contrast, grow up with relatively impoverished language and educational experiences (Harrington, 2000; Ramsey, 1997). Limited access to good language models may leave them unable to judge accurately whether and how much they comprehend of classroom content or any other communication. Some deaf students recognize gaps in their comprehension in some settings, and may attempt to compensate through questions, reading, and meetings with tutors or instructors. Others either will be unaware of their comprehension failures (Strassman, 1997) or simply accept them as normal (Napier, 2002).

Similar findings have been obtained with regard to reading per se. Deaf students, on average, appear to be relatively poor at assessing their reading comprehension and often consider themselves to be good readers even when they are largely unaware of what that means (Ewoldt, 1986). Kelly, Albertini, and Shannon (2001), for example, had deaf college students read short science passages and identify anything they did not understand or that did not make sense. Students' self-assessments indicated that they understood essentially everything they had just read; 90% appeared not to notice a sentence embedded in the text that was topically incongruent with the entire passage (although still science-related).

Marschark (2007) suggested that perhaps because of the ways deaf children are taught, they may demonstrate instrumental dependence in their reading strategies, looking to teachers and peers for explanations of text rather than attempting to figure out the meaning themselves. Ewoldt, Israelite, and Dodds (1992), however, observed deaf adolescents using a variety of independent, metacognitive reading strategies, such as re-reading the text or looking up words in a dictionary. Their study suggested that it was the teachers who appeared to encourage more dependent strategies. Parents and teachers also may inadvertently foster dependent strategies in young deaf readers by underestimating their reading abilities and demonstrating the over-directiveness often seen in hearing parents of deaf children.

Another factor affecting classroom learning is students' prior knowledge, both about course-related content and more general world knowledge. Rawson and Kintsch (2002) demonstrated that, during reading, background information helps to organize new information through semantic associations. They noted that, to the extent that associations with prior knowledge are not activated quickly and automatically, overall comprehension will suffer (pp. 774–775). Using single-word association tasks, McEvoy et al. (1999) and Marschark, Convertino, et al. (2004) demonstrated that associative links among concepts are weaker and far more variable across deaf college students than hearing peers. Such differences help to explain why prior knowledge is less effectively applied by deaf than hearing students across academic contexts (Jelinek, Lewis, & Jackson, 2001; Strassman, 1997). Similar results are obtained for hearing students with literacy-related learning difficulties (e.g., Oakhill & Cain, 2000).

These findings suggest that deaf learners may be at risk in settings where new information is structured for hearing learners by hearing instructors who are unfamiliar with deaf students' knowledge and knowledge organization. At the same time, instructors and interpreters would find it more difficult to adjust their instruction to match several deaf students in the same classroom because of the heterogeneity of these students' knowledge and learning styles. This situation also suggests that some apparent differences between deaf and hearing students in language comprehension may be independent of the nature and quality of communication per se. Rather, inappropriate or incomplete language comprehension strategies may be holding deaf students back. At issue here is the ability to recognize when ongoing comprehension is successful or not and when information is new or not. Marschark, Sapere, et al. (2004), for example, had observed an apparent lack of awareness among deaf students concerning how much they were learning from interpreted classroom lectures. Their study examined deaf students' comprehension of interpreting (ASL) versus transliteration (signing with English word order but characteristics of ASL). In two experiments, students complained that the assessments of learning were too simple, although they were scoring only 50%–60% correct. In a third experiment, the investigators therefore asked students to predict how many questions they would get correct, after they had taken the test. Correlations of test scores and students' predictions were significant for the hearing students (indicating consistency between predictions and learning) but not for the deaf students.

It thus appears that differences in both knowledge and the strategies involved in accessing that knowledge between deaf and hearing students can have specific effects on learning. Although considerable overlap exists in their semantic structures for concepts varying widely in familiarity, there also appears to be a tendency of deaf students not to apply conceptual knowledge in some task situations that would benefit from such application (Marschark & Everhart, 1999; Marschark, Convertino, et al., 2004). Whether that situation is related to depth or breadth of semantic memory knowledge, a failure to strategically apply such knowledge spontaneously, or the use of alternative nonobvious strategies is unclear. To the extent that knowledge of the world is needed but either is not recognized in a particular task or is not used successfully, learning will suffer. This issue is particularly pertinent to the development of literacy skills, and we now turn to several aspects of reading that seem parallel to more general issues in language comprehension and cognition.

Language Skills and Literacy

Most research on language comprehension involving deaf learners relates to written language rather than "through-the-air" communication. Although several frequently cited studies describe relatively low reading comprehension skills among deaf students (Allen, 1986; Conrad, 1979; Holt, 1993; Traxler, 2000), relatively few studies have actually examined the overall comprehension of text. Most have focused on specific aspects of the reading process, such as vocabulary, grammar, or word recognition.

In this section, we discuss what is known about comprehension of printed language from the perspectives of both the smaller and the larger units of this process.

There has been a long history of assessing children's literacy skills through standardized tests. Reports on reading comprehension of deaf children are mostly based on data from such tests. Traxler (2000), for example, reported that the median reading level of 18- to 19-year-old deaf students on the Stanford Achievement Test, Ninth Edition (SAT9) matched the average level of 8- to 9-year-old hearing students, a level of performance that has not changed much over recent decades (Allen, 1986; Holt, 1993). Conrad (1979) reported a similar level for 15- to 16-year-old deaf students in the United Kingdom. In the Netherlands, Wauters, van Bon, and Tellings (2006) found that deaf secondary school students on average performed at the level of 8-year-old hearing students on a reading test similar to the SAT9.

Such findings have led to concerns in deaf education and to many studies on the reasons for these low levels of comprehension. In their discussions of factors affecting deaf children's reading comprehension, King and Quigley (1985) and Paul (2003) distinguished three groups of factors: text factors, reader factors, and task or context factors. Text factors include word identification, vocabulary, syntax, and figurative language; reader factors refer to prior knowledge, metacognition, working memory, and phonological coding; and task or context factors are the purpose of reading, the setting of reading, and the type of measurement. In the next sections, we consider several of these with an eye toward better understanding the link between language fluencies and literacy.

Phonological Awareness

For hearing children, phonological coding is an important factor in reading comprehension (Bradley & Bryant, 1983; Caravolas, Hulme, & Snowling, 2001). For deaf children, limited access to spoken language can obstruct their access to phonological information and therefore their word identification skill. Studies on deaf readers' use of phonological information have shown varying results (Perfetti & Sandak, 2000). Several studies have shown a significant positive relation between phonological awareness and reading-related tasks (Dyer et al., 2003; Hanson & Fowler, 1987; Harris & Beech, 1998), but other studies have failed to show this relation (Beech & Harris, 1997; Harris & Moreno, 2004; Kyle & Harris, 2006; Waters & Doehring, 1990). It thus appears that some but not all deaf students have access to phonology to varying degrees. Deaf students who do have access to phonology tend to be older, have better reading skills, better speech intelligibility, more residual hearing, and better speechreading skills. Leybaert

(1993) thus suggested that the codes underlying phonological processing by deaf students are constructed from auditory information (residual hearing), fingerspelling, kinesthetic feedback from speech, and orthography. The result is a mental representation that may be functionally equivalent to the phonological processing used by hearing readers, but is clearly different from it.

Consistent with Leybaert's theoretical perspective, Mayer (2007) suggested that we should try to find ways to solve the phonological barrier of spoken language for deaf children instead of imagining that we can bypass phonology. For her part, Leybaert and her colleagues have pursued this approach using cued speech (see Leybaert, 2003; Leybaert & Alegria, 2003). *Cued speech* is a system of hand positions and locations around the mouth designed to make speech unambiguous when cues and spoken language are co-articulated. The studies of Leybaert and colleagues have demonstrated that, for deaf children who are learning to read French, the availability of cued speech both at home and at school leads to significant improvement in literacy subskills. To date, however, little evidence has been obtained supporting cued speech for deaf children learning to read English, perhaps the result of its less regular correspondence between sound and orthography (Alegria & Lechat, 2005).

Another way to solve the problem of phonological processing for deaf readers might be through visual phonics. *Visual phonics* is a system of 46 moving hand cues and written symbols, used in conjunction with spoken language and speechreading, to represent aspects of the phonemes of a language and the grapheme-phoneme relationships (Trezek, Wang, Woods, Gampp, & Paul, 2007). Studies by Trezek and colleagues (Trezek & Malmgren, 2005; Trezek & Wang, 2006; Trezek et al., 2007) have started to explore visual phonics in teaching deaf children to read and claim that students who utilize it as a supplemental tool show improvement in their beginning reading skills. Their studies with kindergarten and first grade students did not include comparison groups without training, making it difficult to unequivocally attribute improvements to the use of visual phonics. For middle school–aged students, however, the use of the visual phonics approach (in combination with other approaches) led to better phonics knowledge compared with students who did not use the approach. Although more research is needed to be confident about the potential of visual phonics, its combination of phonemic information and visual information corresponding to how speech sounds are made seems a potentially new tool in teaching deaf children to read.

At its core, establishing a link between phonology and orthography is a problem-solving task that utilizes both bottom-up and top-down processing in much the same way as other reading processes (word identification, syntactic processing, discourse processing). Burkholder and Pisoni (2006) found that deaf children with CIs had significant difficulties in the rapid encoding and repetition of novel phonological patterns, indicating that the phonological processing observed in such children is not the same as in hearing children. Their findings of atypical memory encoding and serial scanning in short-term memory suggest a strong relationship between the cognitive underpinnings of language, exposure to auditory and linguistic stimuli, and literacy. To date, however, little attention has been given to such variability among deaf children without implants. Regardless of whether they utilize spoken language or sign language, differences in the amount of residual hearing, the availability of early language, and related opportunities for incidental learning will be of central importance in the establishment of the foundations for later language and literacy skills.

Word Identification

Studies on word identification skills among deaf readers have yielded varying results. In a study by Harris and Beech (1998), deaf 4- to 6-year-olds scored lower than their hearing peers on a task in which they had to match pictures with written words. Burden and Campbell (1994), however, found no differences between older deaf students (mean age = 14 years, 6 months) and age-matched hearing students on a lexical decision task (see Fischler, 1985, for similar findings with college students). Both groups scored higher than a reading level–matched group of (younger) hearing students. Merrills, Underwood, and Wood (1994) also used a lexical decision task and found that deaf 11- to 15-year-olds scored lower than same-age hearing students with good reading comprehension skills. However, the deaf students scored higher than younger hearing students who were matched on their reading comprehension skills, and they did not differ from same-age hearing students with poor reading comprehension skills. In a Dutch study with 7- to 20-year-old students, Wauters et al. (2006) found no overall differences between deaf and hearing students in word identification performance. However, some differences were found within individual age groups, especially beyond fifth grade.

These studies varied in the characteristics of the participants and in the tasks used, which makes it hard to draw any conclusions about the role word identification plays in reading achievement. The results from Burden and Campbell (1994) and Fischler (1985) suggest that it is not a major factor. Merrills et al. (1994) also concluded that word identification problems are not sufficient to explain the comprehension difficulties of deaf readers. Even though their word identification level is lower than it is for hearing students with good reading comprehension skills, it is not lower than hearing students with poor reading comprehension skills or younger hearing students, and yet they consistently show lower levels of achievement on reading comprehension assessments.

In the study by Wauters et al. (2006), word identification scores were insufficient to account for the deaf students' low reading comprehension scores. Although a significant relation was found between word identification and reading comprehension, the latter scores were still low when word identification scores were controlled for age. Vermeulen, van Bon, Schreuder, Knoors, and Snik (2007) further examined word identification and reading comprehension in deaf 7- to 22-year-olds with CIs compared to the deaf 7- to 20-year-olds without CIs in the Wauters et al. (2006) study. The deaf group with implants scored higher than the deaf group without implants on reading comprehension, but still scored significantly lower than the age-appropriate hearing norms. On their word identification task, secondary school students with implants scored higher than the students without implants, but there was no difference between similar groups of primary school children. Further, when word identification was statistically controlled, the differences in reading comprehension still existed, indicating that other reading-related skills were also contributing to the improved reading comprehension skills of the deaf students with implants.

It thus appears that word identification is a necessary skill underlying text comprehension, one that interacts with other linguistic and cognitive skills (Bebko & Metcalf-Haggert, 1997). Similar arguments could be mounted with regard to word identification in the comprehension of spoken language and for sign identification in the comprehension of sign language, but relevant studies have not yet been undertaken. The issue of sign identification might be particularly important within the larger context of language comprehension and learning. Even if young deaf children (e.g., of deaf parents) have early vocabularies comparable in size to those of their hearing peers, their word knowledge appears to develop somewhat differently (Anderson & Reilly, 2002). Further, differences in the size and structure of the lexicons for signed and spoken/printed languages may well create challenges to deaf learners' transition from signing to reading (Mayer & Wells, 1996; McEvoy et al., 1999).

Vocabulary Knowledge

King and Quigley (1985) and Paul (2003) described vocabulary as a text factor, referring to the kind of words that are used in texts. Consistent with our focus on language and cognitive foundations of comprehension and our concern about individual differences among learners, we will discuss vocabulary more as a reader factor, focusing on the relation between a deaf student's vocabulary knowledge and reading comprehension.

Vocabulary is a significant predictor of reading comprehension in hearing students (Adams, 1990; Dickinson, Anastasopoulos, McCabe, Peisner-Feinberg, & Poe, 2003) and in deaf students (Garrison, Long, & Dowaliby,

1997; Harris & Beech, 1998; Kelly, 1996; Kyle & Harris, 2006). Unfortunately, deaf students often have been found to have lower vocabulary skills than hearing age-matched peers. The size of their vocabulary tends to be smaller, the rate in which they acquire new vocabulary is lower, and they less easily develop new word meaning acquisition processes (Geers & Moog, 1989; Lederberg, 2003; Lederberg & Spencer, 2001; Paul, 2003; Waters & Doehring, 1990). Several researchers have pointed out that early identification of hearing loss has a positive effect on vocabulary development (Lederberg, 2003; Prezbindowski & Lederberg, 2003; Yoshinaga-Itano, 2003), presumably the result of early intervention services providing support for both language and cognitive development. Aside from studies of early vocabulary development as part of language acquisition, studies of vocabulary in deaf learners have focused on the relation between vocabulary and reading, with some attention to related student characteristics, such as having CIs.

Kelly (1996), for example, focused on the interaction of vocabulary and syntactic ability in deaf students' reading. He reported receptive vocabulary levels in adolescents and college students, but unfortunately did not indicate whether their performance was comparable to that of hearing students. Kelly found that vocabulary was a strong predictor of reading comprehension, with a stronger relation among college students than among adolescents. For both groups, he found an interaction with syntactic ability, as the relation between vocabulary and reading was stronger for students with higher syntactic abilities than for those with lower syntactic abilities. Apparently, when students have better syntactic skills, they can profit more from better vocabulary skills during reading than when they have lower syntactic skills.

Garrison et al. (1997) also studied the relation between vocabulary skills and reading comprehension in deaf readers. In addition to vocabulary (measured as knowledge of synonyms), world knowledge and text-integration skills were measured. Deaf college students scored lower than hearing students (seventh grade and college) on all three measures; for both deaf and hearing students, scores were lowest on world knowledge. Vocabulary and world knowledge were strong predictors for reading comprehension, whereas the ability to make inferences (i.e., integrate information within or across paragraphs) was predicted from these two measures.

More recently, Kyle and Harris (2006) found a relation between vocabulary and reading comprehension in younger deaf students. They studied predictors of reading development in 7- and 8-year-old deaf children (mean = 7 years, 10 months) and reading-age matched 5- to 8-year-old hearing children (mean = 6 years, 9 months). On their productive vocabulary measure, in which children were asked to give the correct name for an object (in speech, sign, or a combination of both), the deaf children scored lower than hearing children, demonstrating a mean vocabulary age of 3 years, 7 months compared to age-appropriate vocabulary for the hearing children. Regression analyses indicated that using the independent variables of productive vocabulary, speechreading, short-term memory, and phonological awareness, only the first two were significant predictors of reading achievement. After controlling for hearing loss and nonverbal IQ, productive vocabulary was the strongest predictor for sentence comprehension, whereas speechreading was the strongest predictor for single-word reading.

Wauters, Tellings, van Bon, and Mak (2008; see also Wauters, 2005) studied the effects on comprehension of Mode of Acquisition (MoA), a cognitive variable centrally related to vocabulary. Mode of Acquisition refers to the type of information children use in acquiring word meanings (Wauters, Tellings, van Bon, & van Haaften, 2003). Word meanings can be acquired through perception, language, or a combination of both. Although MoA correlates with word characteristics, such as concreteness and imageability, it does not coincide with them. Wauters et al. argued that concreteness and imageability are concept-relative dimensions whereas MoA is also context relative. The MoA of a word is not only determined by its abstractness or the imageability (both mainly concept characteristics), but also by the context in which the word is acquired. Children living in Egypt, for example, most likely will not acquire the meaning of "snow" perceptually, whereas children living in Greenland most probably will.

Both deaf 7- to 20-year-olds and hearing 7- to 12-year-olds in the Wauters (2005) and Wauters et al. (2008) studies showed longer reading times and lower comprehension scores on words for which the meanings have to be acquired through language than on words for which the meaning can be acquired through perception, consistent with theoretical arguments concerning language development by Paivio (2008). Words for which the meaning has to be acquired through language were harder to read and understand even after controlling for length and frequency. Reading times were no different for deaf and hearing students, but comprehension scores were lower for the deaf students. Comprehension of words for which the meaning has to be learned through language was extremely low for deaf students, with scores not significantly exceeding chance level (50%–58% correct, compared to 60%–85% correct for hearing students). Although comprehension of word meanings that can be learned through perception was better (60%–75% correct), it was still lower than it was for hearing children (88%–95% correct). Obviously, vocabulary is an obstacle for deaf students' reading achievement, with particular difficulty if word meanings are more abstract (Paivio, 2008) or are language-based (Wauters et al., 2008).

In the current zeitgeist, no discussion of the link between vocabulary and reading in deaf children would be complete without considering the effects of CIs. Studies bearing on this issue generally have not focused specifically on the relation between vocabulary and reading development, but have explicitly investigated vocabulary levels and vocabulary growth.

Geers (2006), for example, found that deaf children with implants showed an expressive vocabulary growth that was as fast as in hearing children and faster than in deaf children with hearing aids. Their receptive vocabulary growth, however, was not as fast as in hearing children and did not exceed the growth in deaf children with hearing aids. Paatsch, Blamey, Sarant, and Bow (2006) also compared receptive vocabulary skills of deaf children with CIs and those with hearing aids. They reported lower receptive vocabulary and slower vocabulary growth in deaf children than in hearing children, with no differences between deaf children with CIs or hearing aids. The rate of growth in their implant group was only two-thirds of the growth rate in hearing children. More generally, a review by Marschark, Rhoten, and Fabich (2007) showed that despite consistent findings that CIs can improve reading achievement for many deaf children, they usually still lag significantly behind hearing peers. Results vary with several factors, however, such as age of implantation and amount of language experience prior to implantation (which work in opposite directions), and it appears that total communication might be particularly facilitative for reading comprehension, even if it is not for speech and language (Spencer et al., 2004). Further research of the sort conducted by Pisoni and his colleagues (see Pisoni et al., this volume), exploring the intersection between cognitive and language development in children with (and without) implants, is clearly in order.[5]

Inferential Processes in Reading: Metacognition and Relational Processing Revisited

As noted earlier, self-monitoring of comprehension is an important aspect of reading and of learning more generally (Alexander & Jetton, 2000; Pressley, 2000; Theide et al., 2003; see Hauser et al., this volume). Several studies have found differences between skilled and unskilled readers in their metacognitive skills (Pressley & Afferbach, 1995; Snow, Burns, & Griffin, 1998). Skilled readers use their general world knowledge to comprehend text and to make inferences. Unskilled readers are less likely to make use of such monitoring strategies in order to detect inconsistencies or resolve misunderstandings. In short, they do not realize that they do not understand what they are reading (Mohktari & Reichard, 2002), a specific form of the "unskilled and unaware" phenomenon (Kruger & Dunning, 1999). These characteristics also have been observed in deaf students' reading.

---

5. Hauser (personal communication, 28 August 2007) suggested that deaf children who have CIs may receive more speech training inside and outside of school, thus contributing to their documented language and speech skills. This variable has rarely been considered in relevant studies.

They have been found to use fewer metacognitive strategies than hearing students, such as utilizing background information, context clues, or the title of the passage, and rereading or looking back in the text. When deaf students use strategies in their reading, they also tend to use less appropriate ones or use them for the wrong reasons (Marschark, Lang, & Albertini, 2002; Paul, 2003). In her review on metacognition and reading, Strassman (1997) noted that deaf students often use a look-back strategy as a visual-matching strategy instead of a strategy to improve comprehension. She also described deaf readers' difficulty with judging their feeling-of-knowing. The ability to know what you know and what you comprehend are important in guiding the reading process and using strategies to facilitate comprehension. At face value, the metacomprehension difficulties evidenced by deaf readers appear no different from those observed by Marschark, Sapere, et al. (2004) in deaf students' sign language comprehension.

Monitoring of ongoing language comprehension not only facilitates the linking of new information with what is already known, but also supports the text-based and knowledge-based inferential processing essential for full understanding. The integration of information in a text with a reader's knowledge allows the reader to go beyond the information given, both in terms of facilitating comprehension of individual words and in constructing the meaning of the larger discourse. Information that has to be inferred in a text is not explicitly stated, but may be more or less implied, thus implicating problem solving and cognitive flexibility as well as lower-level reading skills (e.g., grammar, word-finding). In drawing an inference, propositions within the text are linked either by text-specific information or by the reader's prior knowledge. The result is usually, but not always, a valid (i.e., content-consistent) conclusion (Noordman & Vonk, 1998). The inferred information (when valid) contributes to the coherence or completeness of the text representation. Although they do sometimes go wrong, inferences typically are necessary if a reader is to gain more than only a superficial understanding of the text.

Deaf learners have been found to have particular difficulty with drawing inferences from text. Wilson (1979, cited in King & Quigley, 1985) suggested that deaf students' difficulty with reaching a reading level above fourth grade may be related to the change in reading materials at that point. According to Wilson, reading materials from fourth grade on require use of prior knowledge to infer meanings that are not explicitly stated in the text. Wilson found that drawing inferences was much harder for deaf students than it was for hearing students. Garrison et al. (1997) also found lower scores for deaf college students than for hearing college students on inferences that required the integration of information from different parts of a text (Richardson et al., 2000). As noted earlier, they found a relation between the ability to make inferences and students' vocabulary and world knowledge. Jackson, Paul, and Smith (1997) measured reading comprehension in deaf high school students through three types of questions: text-explicit (literal) questions, text-implicit questions (inferences that integrate explicit information from different parts of text), and script-implicit questions (inferences that integrate information from the text with the reader's knowledge; i.e., the main source of information is not in the text). They found no significant difference between text-explicit and text-implicit questions, but scores on script-implicit questions were lower than on the other two question types. The ability to answer these script-implicit questions, and thus make the inferences based on the reader's prior knowledge and memory, was the strongest predictor of reading comprehension.

Several studies have examined the differences between skilled and less skilled deaf readers in drawing inferences. Sarachan-Deily (1985) had deaf and hearing high school students read a story written at the fourth-grade level and then reproduce it in writing. She measured the number of propositions that students recalled and the number of inferences they included in their writing. Deaf students recalled fewer propositions than hearing students, but included just as many inferences. However, when Sarachan-Deily looked at whether the inferences were valid or not, she found that deaf readers produced just as many invalid (wrong) as valid inferences. Sarachan-Deily also looked at deaf high school students performing at different reading levels. The mean reading level of the deaf students was grade level 5.3 and that of the hearing students was grade level 10.5. She found that the good deaf readers (mean grade level 6.9) recalled significantly more valid propositions—propositions that indeed occurred in the text—than the average deaf readers (mean grade level 5) and poor deaf readers (mean grade level 3.4). However, no differences were found among students from the three reading levels in the number of invalid propositions or in the number of valid and invalid inferences. Better deaf readers thus can more accurately recall information explicitly stated in texts, but they are not necessarily better than poor deaf readers in drawing inferences from implicit information.

Pinhas (1991) studied inference-making during reading by skilled deaf readers. She had a group of deaf college students reading at a mean grade level of 10.3 (mean age = 21.9 years) and a group of hearing students matched on their reading level (mean grade level = 10.4, mean age = 16.2 years) read four passages and answer factual and inferential questions about them. Both deaf and hearing students performed better on the factual than inferential questions, but there was no difference in accuracy between the two groups (there was a difference in speed, with the deaf students responding slower than the hearing students). Pinhas concluded that deaf skilled readers are able to draw inferences from text, although they seem to do it at the time of questioning, not during reading (i.e., not automatically). Inference-making thus does not support ongoing comprehension in her view, but can be reconstructed from memory. Unfortunately, Pinhas did not include a group of less skilled deaf readers, and it is unclear how they would have performed in this task.

In the recent study by Wauters et al. (in preparation), inference making was found to be difficult not only in print, but also in sign language. Deaf and hearing college students were compared on answering factual and inferential questions about written, signed, or spoken passages. Students each read two passages. The deaf students watched two other passages presented via sign and the hearing students saw two passages presented via spoken English. Independent of whether a text was read or watched (in ASL or spoken language), deaf students scored lower than hearing students. The hearing students performed at the same level, overall, in reading and in listening, whereas the deaf students performed the same overall in reading and in watching sign. For both groups, factual questions were easier than inferential questions independent of whether a text was read or watched in ASL or spoken language. However, the difference was slightly larger for deaf students (56% versus 71%) than for hearing students (71% versus 83%). Also, for the deaf students, the difference between the two question types was caused by a difference in ASL only. They answered factual questions after a passage was presented in ASL just as well as the hearing students answered them after a passage was presented in spoken or written language. Answering inferential questions after an ASL passage was harder for deaf students than answering them after reading a text. Apparently, deaf students' receiving information in sign language, relative to print, facilitates their comprehension or retrieval of explicit information after the fact, but not their processing of implicit information.

Doran and Anderson (2003) studied inference-making in both reading and comprehension of British Sign Language (BSL). Their study involved deaf 12- to 18-year-olds and hearing 12- to 13-year-olds who read short narratives. Key elements of the passages involved either temporal or causal relations. Even though no differences were found in reading rates between deaf and hearing students or between explicit or implicit information, the deaf students were found to draw fewer correct inferences than the hearing students. Inferences concerning temporal relations, in particular, were problematic for the deaf students, who scored at chance levels. In addition to reading the materials, the deaf students also watched the passages in BSL. No analyses were performed on the data from sign language, however, because the responses of the deaf students did not significantly differ from chance on the inferential (implicit) questions and even some of the factual (explicit) questions. Like the Wauters et al. (in preparation) study, these results suggest that deaf students have trouble deriving implicit information from signed passages as well as from print. It thus appears that going beyond the information given to link information from a passage to prior world or text knowledge—a form of relational problem solving—is less automatic or spontaneous in deaf students than in hearing students (Marschark et al., 2006), regardless of the language modality.

Several other studies have examined deaf students' sign language comprehension in the classroom, and several have contrasted natural sign languages with English transliteration, simultaneous communication, or spoken language alone (e.g., Cokely, 1990; Jacobs, 1977; Kurz, 2004; Livingston, Singer, & Abramson, 1994; Marschark, Sapere, et al., 2004, 2005; Murphy & Fleischer, 1977). In all of these studies that have included hearing comparison groups, deaf students scored significantly lower on tests of comprehension and learning relative to hearing peers, even when prior knowledge was controlled. Insofar as neither language modality, parental hearing status, nor language background/proficiency have been found to be consistently related to comprehension in those studies, it appears that the situation is more complex than may have been assumed previously and not necessarily specific to literacy, language, or even hearing loss. Yet, recent findings indicate that deaf students can learn as much as hearing peers when they have skilled instructors who are sensitive to the knowledge and learning strategies of deaf learners (Marschark, Sapere, et al., 2008).

Summary and Implications

Other chapters in this volume describe how various aspects of cognitive functioning by deaf students potentially affect learning in formal and informal settings. In this chapter, we have argued that, in addition to the need to understand individual differences and the cognitive tools underlying learning (Akamatsu, Mayer, & Hardy-Braz, this volume; Detterman & Thompson, 1997), basic issues of language and cognition must be understood and resolved if we are to optimize educational opportunities for deaf students (Hauser et al., this volume). Recent research has demonstrated three relevant findings that are consistent with a variety of previous studies, but have either been overlooked or ignored. First, language comprehension is clearly a significant challenge for many students in college-level as well as K–12 classrooms, even when that language is fluent, clear, and complete. All of the stakeholders in deaf education are aware of the fact that most deaf students come from backgrounds in which they did not have fully accessible language experiences. Yet, we frequently fail to consider how much language is fully accessible to deaf students in the typically noisy classroom and ensure that potential barriers due to language, cognition, and pedagogy are separately recognized. Second, several studies have now demonstrated that deaf students do not understand as much as both they and we think they do. Such barriers in language comprehension and metacognition may create significant impediments to learning and to improving education. At the very least, receptive language skills during the school years are in need of empirical and pedagogical attention. Third, it may be that the traditional focus on children's literacy in deaf education is somewhat misplaced, as many of the challenges encountered by deaf learners are more a function of more general language and cognitive issues rather than print literacy per se. Importantly, some of these may be more reflective of differences in the learning styles of deaf and hearing children and mismatches with teaching methods and materials, rather than indicative of any underlying problems.

Many of the errors that deaf students exhibit in reading and writing are the same as those made by people learning English as a second language. A variety of programs therefore have been developed to instruct teachers of deaf students in methods like those used in teaching English as a second language (see Marschark et al., 2002; Schirmer & Williams, 2003). Most deaf children also come to school without fluency in sign language, and yet for some reason, beyond early intervention programming, we do not teach them how to sign (or utilize interpreters). Without either English or sign language fluency, we thus deprive deaf children, at the outset, of an essential learning tool and access to the full richness of the world. This may help to explain the findings that deaf students are relatively poor in predicting how much they understand and learn in the classroom. Their reading behaviors and their writing may look similar to second language learners, but they do not have a fluent first language on which to construct a second. This means that second-language learning methods may be inappropriate or only address some of deaf students' needs (Mayer & Wells, 1996).

A large portion of the effort devoted to improving deaf children's literacy has gone into trying to teach them the skills and strategies that work for hearing children, even though it is apparent that deaf and hearing children often have very different background knowledge and learning strategies. Obviously, this approach has not worked very well, and most deaf children still progress far more slowly than hearing children in learning to read, regardless of their preferred language modality and whether or not they have a CI. This means that deaf students leaving school are at a relatively greater disadvantage, lagging farther behind hearing peers, than when they entered. At the same time, there are clearly many deaf adults and children who are excellent readers and writers.

The literature concerning deaf children's reading skills indicate that, although deaf children of deaf parents have been shown to be better readers than deaf children of hearing parents in some studies, others have shown no difference. Importantly, none of the studies to date have considered the reading skills of parents, and many of the investigations that have included deaf parents have been conducted in areas known for having relatively high numbers of educated deaf adults. If 50% of deaf high school graduates in the United States read at or below the fourth grade level, why would we expect them to be good language models for their deaf children?

It thus seems likely that any generalization about a link between children's reading abilities and parental hearing status per se will be extremely limited. Indeed, regardless of whether their parents are deaf or hearing, deaf children who are better readers turn out to be those who had their hearing losses diagnosed earlier, had early access to fluent language (via sign language or spoken language), and were exposed to both sign language and English. At the same time, having a mother who is a good signer appears to be more important than whether she is deaf or hearing or the precise age at which a child learns to sign, as long as it is early (Akamatsu et al., 2000; Strong & Prinz, 1997).

There are other differences between deaf and hearing parents, beyond their primary mode of communication, that might affect the development of literacy skills. For example, the two groups may have very different expectations for their deaf children in terms of academic achievement. They also may differ in their ability to help their children in reading-related activities—even for those parents who have good reading skills themselves—and we know that children whose parents spend time working with them on academic and extracurricular activities are more motivated and have greater academic success (see Marschark, 2007, chapter 8). So, parental hearing status does not seem likely to be a sufficient explanation for deaf children's literacy skills. This chapter has suggested that other cognitive skills, including visual attention, memory, metacognition, and relational processing all have roles in explaining deaf learners' language comprehension, regardless of language modality (see Hauser et al., this volume).

Marschark (2007) suggested that we may be devoting so much time and energy to teaching the fundamental skills underlying reading, that we may be overlooking the goals of reading. Reading and writing are labor-intensive, frustrating activities for many deaf individuals, and they are thus often reluctant to engage in them for pleasure. We know, however, that children who read more become good readers, and not the other way around, creating a "Catch 22" situation for young deaf readers. By not reading and not having the desire to read more, deaf children may not spontaneously develop the literacy-related metacognitive skills easily acquired by many of their reading, hearing peers. Some of those skills can be explicitly taught (Akamatsu, 1988), but their durability is likely to be far less than if they were actively acquired by children through their own reading.

If deaf students' reading difficulties are not the result of any particular orientation in their early language experience, early sign language can provide most deaf children with earlier access to the world. No evidence apparently suggests that learning to sign early interferes with the development of spoken language, and the reverse appears to be true, even for children with CIs. Sign languages have not yet been shown sufficient to provide effective bridges to print literacy (Mayer & Wells, 1996), but early access to language through signing or speech is necessary for providing children with a context for acquiring the cognitive tools that will, in turn, contribute to language development as well as literacy and other domains of academic achievement.

Most educators acknowledge that we have made relatively little progress in advancing deaf students' print literacy skills, despite decades of trying. To the extent that recent findings concerning deaf students' learning via sign language and real-time text indicate that neither of these provides full access in the classroom, it clearly is time to approach the education of deaf students from a new and different tack. That approach must be an objective one, letting go of assumptions and philosophical biases. It also has to be an empirically driven one, building on what works and perhaps re-examining methods previously abandoned because of our obsession with literacy as both the barrier and the solution.

Acknowledgments

Preparation of this chapter was supported by grants from the National Science Foundation (REC-0633928) and the Niels Stensen Foundation. Any opinions, findings and conclusions, or recommendations expressed in this material are those of the authors and do not necessarily reflect the views of either foundation.

References

Adams, M. J. (1990). *Beginning to read: Thinking and learning about print.* Cambridge, MA: Massachusetts Institute of Technology.

Akamatsu, C. T. (1988). Instruction in text structure: Metacognitive strategy instruction for literacy development in deaf students. *ACEHI/ACEDA, 14,* 13–32.

Akamatsu, C. T., Musselman, C., & Zweibel, A. (2000). Nature vs. Nurture in the development of cognition in deaf people. In P. Spencer, C. Erting, & M. Marschark (Eds.), *Development in context: The deaf children in the family and at school* (pp. 255–274). Mahwah, NJ: Lawrence Erlbaum Associates.

Alegria, J., & Lechat, J. (2005). Phonological processing in deaf children: When lipreading and cues are incongruent. *Journal of Deaf Studies and Deaf Education, 10,* 122–133.

Alexander, P. A., & Jetton, T. L. (2000). Learning from text: A multidimensional and developmental perspective. In M. Kamil, P. Mosenthal, P. D. Pearson, & R. Barr (Eds.), *Handbook of reading research* (Vol. 3, pp. 285–310). Mahwah, NJ: Lawrence Erlbaum Associates.

Ansell, E., & Pagliaro, C. M. (2001). Effects of a signed translation on the types and difficulty of arithmetic story problems. *Focus on Learning Problems in Mathematics, 23*(2), 41–69.

Allen, T. E. (1986). Patterns of academic achievement among hearing impaired students: 1974 and 1983. In A. N. Schildroth & M. A. Karchmer (Eds.), *Deaf children in America* (pp. 161–206). San Diego: College Hill Press.

Anderson, D., & Reilly, J. (2002). The Macarthur Communicative Development Inventory: Normative data for American Sign Language. *Journal of Deaf Studies and Deaf Education, 7*, 83–106.

Antia, S. (2007). Can deaf and hard of hearing students be successful in general education classrooms? *TCRecord.*, www.tcrecord.org/PrintContent.asp?ContentID=13461 (Retrieved 17 May 2007).

Arnold, P., Palmer, C., & Lloyd, J. (1999). Hearing-impaired children's listening skills in a referential communication task: An exploratory study. *Deafness and Education International, 1*, 47–55.

Banks, J., Gray, C., &Fyfe, R. (1990). The written recall of printed stories by severely deaf children. *British Journal of Educational Psychology, 60*, 192–206.

Bavelier, D. (2007, June). Similar working memory capacity but different serial short-term memory span in signers and speakers: Theoretical and practical implications. Presentation at Cognitive Underpinnings of Learning by Deaf and Hard-of-Hearing Students conference. Rochester, NY.

Bavelier, D., Newman, A., Mukherjee, M., Hauser, P., Kemeny, S., Braun, A., & Boutla, M. (in press). Encoding, rehearsal, and recall in signers and speakers: Shared network but different engagement. *Cerebral Cortex.*

Beech, J. R., & Harris, M. (1997). The prelingually deaf young reader: A case of reliance on direct lexical access? *Journal of Research in Reading, 20*, 105–121.

Bebko, J. M., & Metcalfe-Haggert, A. (1997). Deafness, language skills, and rehearsal: A model for the development of a memory strategy. *Journal of Deaf Studies and Deaf Education, 2*, 131–139.

Blatto-Vallee, G., Kelly, R. R, Gaustad, M. G., Porter, J., & Fonzi, J. (2007). Spatial-relational representation in mathematical problem-solving by deaf and hearing students. *Journal of Deaf Studies and Deaf Education, 12*, 432–448.

Boutla, M., Supalla, T., Newport, E. L., & Bavelier, D. (2004). Short-term memory span: Insights from sign language. *Nature Neuroscience, 7*, 997–1002.

Bradley, L., & Bryant, P. E. (1983). Categorizing sounds and learning to read: a causal connection. *Nature, 301*, 419–421.

Brasel, K., & Quigley, S. P. (1977). Influence of certain language and communicative environments in early childhood on the development of language in deaf individuals. *Journal of Speech and Hearing Research, 20*, 95–107.

Burden, V., & Campbell, R. (1994). The development of word-coding skills in the born deaf: An experimental study of deaf school-leavers. *British Journal of Developmental Psychology, 12*, 331–349.

Burkholder, R. A., & Pisoni, D. B. (2006). Working memory capacity, verbal rehearsal speed, and scanning in deaf children with cochlear implants. In P. E. Spencer & M. Marschark (Eds.), *Advances in the spoken language development of deaf and hard-of-hearing children*, (pp. 328–357). New York: Oxford University Press.

Caravolas, M., Hulme, C., & Snowling, M. J. (2001). The foundations of spelling ability: Evidence from a 3-year longitudinal study. *Journal of Memory and Language, 45*, 751–774.

Cawthon, S. W. (2001). Teaching strategies in inclusive classrooms with deaf students. *Journal of Deaf Studies and Deaf Education, 6*, 212–225.

Chamberlain, C., & Mayberry, R. I. (2000). Theorizing about the relationship between ASL and reading. In C. Chamberlain, J. Morford & R. I. Mayberry, (Eds.), *Language acquisition by eye* (pp. 221–260). Mahwah, NJ: LEA.

Cokely, D. (1990). The effectiveness of three means of communication in the college classroom. *Sign Language Studies, 69,* 415–439.

Conrad, R. (1979). *The deaf schoolchild.* London: Harper and Row.

Detterman, D. K., & Thompson, L. A. (1997). What is so special about special education? *American Psychologist, 52,* 1082–1090.

De Villiers, J., Bibeau, L., Ramos, E., & Gatty, J. (1993). Gestural communication in oral deaf mother-child pairs: Language with a helping hand. *Applied Psycholinguistics,* 14, 319–347.

Dickinson, D. K., Anastasopoulos, L., McCabe, A., Peisner-Feinberg, E. S., & Poe, M. D. (2003). The comprehensive language approach to early literacy: The interrelationships among vocabulary, phonological sensitivity, and print knowledge among preschool-aged children. *Journal of Educational Psychology, 95,* 465–381.

Dodd, B., & Campbell, R. (Eds.) (1987). *Hearing by eye: The psychology of lip-reading.* Hillsdale, NJ: Lawrence Erlbaum Associates.

Doran, J. & Anderson, A. (2003). Inferencing skills of adolescent readers who are hearing impaired. *Journal of Research in Reading, 26,* 256–266.

Dowaliby, F., & Lang, H. (1999). Adjunct aids in instructional prose: A multimedia study with deaf college students. *Journal of Deaf Studies and Deaf Education, 4,* 270–282.

Dunlosky, J., Rawson, K. A., & Middleton, E. L. (2005). What constrains the accuracy of metacomprehension judgments? Testing the transfer-appropriate-monitoring and accessibility hypotheses. *Journal of Memory and Language, 52,* 551–565.

Dyer, A., MacSweeney, M., Szczerbinski, M., Green, L., & Campbell, R. (2003). Predictors of reading delay in deaf adolescents: The relative contributions of rapid automatized naming speed and phonological awareness and decoding. *Journal of Deaf Studies and Deaf Education, 8,* 215–229.

Eriks-Brophy, A. (2004). Outcomes of auditory-verbal therapy: A review of the evidence and a call to action. *The Volta Review, 104,* 21–35.

Ewoldt, C. (1986). What does "reading" mean? *Perspectives for Teachers of the Hearing Impaired, 4,* 10–13.

Ewoldt, C., Israelite, N., & Dodds, R. (1992). The ability of deaf students to understand text: A comparison of the perceptions of teachers and students. *American Annals of the Deaf, 137,* 351–361.

Fischler, I. (1985). Word recognition, use of context, and reading skill among deaf college students. *Reading Research Quarterly, 2,* 203–218.

Furth, H. G. (1966). A comparison of reading test norms of deaf and hearing children. *American Annals of the Deaf, 111,* 461–462.

Garrison, W., Long, G., & Dowaliby, F. (1997). Working memory capacity and comprehension processes in deaf readers. *Journal of Deaf Studies and Deaf Education, 2,* 78–94.

Geers, A. E. (2006). Spoken language in children with cochlear implants. In P. E. Spencer & M. Marschark (Eds.), *Advances in the spoken language development of deaf and hard-of-hearing children* (pp. 244–270). New York: Oxford University Press.

Geers, A. E., & Moog, J. S. (1989). Factors predictive of the development of literacy in hearing-impaired adolescents. *Volta Review, 91,* 69–86.

Glucksberg, S., & Krauss, R. M. (1967). What do people say after they have learned how to talk? Studies of the development of referential communication. *Merrill-Palmer Quarterly, 13,* 309–316.

Hanson, V. L., & Fowler, C. A. (1987). Phonological coding in word reading: Evidence from hearing and deaf readers. *Memory and Cognition, 15,* 199–207.

Harkins, J. E., & Bakke, M. (2003). Technologies for communication: Status and trends. In M. Marschark & P. E. Spencer (Eds.), *Oxford handbook of deaf studies, language, and education* (pp. 406–419). New York: Oxford University Press.

Harrington, F. (2000). Sign language interpreters and access for deaf students to university curricula: The ideal and the reality. In R. P. Roberts, S. E. Carr, D. Abraham, & A. Dufour (Eds.), *The critical link 2: Interpreters in the community* (pp. 219–273). Amsterdam: John Benjamins.

Harris, M., & Beech, J. (1998). Implicit phonological awareness and early reading development in prelingually deaf children. *Journal of Deaf Studies and Deaf Education, 3,* 205–216.

Harris, M., & Moreno, C. (2004). Deaf children's use of phonological coding: Evidence from reading, spelling, and working memory. *Journal of Deaf Studies and Deaf Education, 9,* 253–268.

Holt, J. A. (1993). Stanford Achievement Test—8th edition: Reading comprehension subgroup results. *American Annals of the Deaf, 138,* 172–175.

Hyde, M. B., & Power, D. J. (1992). Receptive communication abilities of hearing-impaired students. *American Annals of the Deaf, 137,* 389–398.

Jackson, D. W., Paul, P. V., & Smith, J.C. (1997). Prior knowledge and reading comprehension ability of deaf adolescents. *Journal of Deaf Studies and Deaf Education, 2,* 172–184.

Jacobs, L. R. (1977). The efficiency of interpreting input for processing lecture information by deaf college students. *Journal of Rehabilitation of the Deaf, 11,* 10–14.

Jeanes, R. C., Nienhuys, T.G.W.M., & Rickards, F. W. (2000). The pragmatic skills of profoundly deaf children. *Journal of Deaf Studies and Deaf Education, 5,* 229–247.

Jelinek Lewis, M. S. & Jackson, D. W. (2001). Television literacy: Comprehension of program content using closed-captions for the deaf. *Journal of Deaf Studies and Deaf Education, 6,* 43–53.

Jensema, C. J., & Trybus, R. J. (1978). *Communicating patterns and educational achievements of hearing impaired students.* Washington, DC: Gallaudet College Office of Demographic Studies.

Kelly, L. (1996). The interaction of syntactic competence and vocabulary during reading by deaf students. *Journal of Deaf Studies and Deaf Education, 1,* 76–90.

Kelly, R. R., Albertini, J. A., & Shannon, N. B. (2001). Deaf college students' reading comprehension and strategy use. *American Annals of the Deaf, 146*(5), 385–400.

King, C. M., & Quigley, S. P. (1985). *Reading and deafness.* San Diego, CA: College Hill Press.

Krakow, R. A., & Hanson, V. L. (1985). Deaf signers and serial recall in the visual modality: Memory for signs, fingerspelling, and print. *Memory and Cognition, 13,* 265–272.

Kruger, J., & Dunning, D. (1999). Unskilled and unaware of it: How difficulties in recognizing one's own incompetence lead to inflated self-assessment. *Journal of Personality and Social Psychology, 77*(6), 1121–1134.

Kurz, K. B. (2004). *A comparison of deaf children's learning in direct communication versus an interpreted environment.* Unpublished doctoral dissertation, University of Kansas, Lawrence.

Kyle, F. E., & Harris, M. (2006). Concurrent correlates and predictors of reading and spelling achievement in deaf and hearing school children. *Journal of Deaf Studies and Deaf Education, 11,* 273–288.

Lang, H. G., Dowaliby, F. J., & Anderson, H. (1994). Critical teaching incidents: Interviews with deaf college students. *American Annals of the Deaf, 139,* 119–127.

Lang, H. G., McKee, B. G., & Conner, K. N. (1993). Characteristics of effective teachers: A descriptive study of perceptions of faculty and deaf college students. *American Annals of the Deaf, 138,* 252–259.

Lederberg, A. R. (2003). Expressing meaning: From communicative intent to building a lexicon. In M. Marschark & P. E. Spencer, *Oxford handbook of deaf studies, language, and education* (pp. 247–260). New York: Oxford University Press.

Lederberg, A. R., & Spencer, P. E. (2001). Vocabulary development of deaf and hard of hearing children. In M. D. Clark, M. Marschark, & M. Karchmer (Eds.), *Context, cognition, and deafness* (pp. 88–112). Washington, DC: Gallaudet University Press.

Leigh, G. R., & Power, D. J. (1998, August). Communicating with deaf students: Does simultaneous communication inhibit the development of oral skills? Paper presented at *6th Asia-Pacific Congress on Deafness,* Beijing, China.

Leybaert, J. (1993). Reading in the deaf: The roles of phonological codes. In M. Marschark & M. D. Clark (Eds.), *Psychological perspectives on deafness* (pp. 269–310). Mahwah, N.J.: LEA.

Leybaert, J., & Alegria, J. (2003). The role of cued speech in language development of deaf children In M. Marschark & P. E. Spencer (Eds.), *Oxford handbook of deaf studies, language, and education* (pp. 262–274). New York: Oxford University Press.

Livingston, S., Singer, B., & Abramson, T. (1994). A study to determine the effectiveness of two different kinds of interpreting. *Proceedings of the Tenth National Convention of the Conference of Interpreter Trainers— Mapping our course: A collaborative venture,* pp. 175–197. Sacramento, CA: CIT.

Lloyd, J., Lieven, E., & Arnold, P. (2005). The oral referential communication skills of hearing-impaired children. *Deafness and Education International, 7,* 22–42.

Long, G. L., & Beil, D. H. (2005). The importance of direct communication during continuing education workshops for deaf and hard-of-hearing professionals. *Journal of Postsecondary Education and Disability, 18,* 5–11.

MacKay-Soroka, S., Trehub, S. E., & Thorpe, L. A. (1987). Referential communication between mothers and their deaf children. *Child Development, 58,* 986–992.

MacKay-Soroka, S., Trehub, S. E., & Thorpe, L. A. (1988). Reception of mothers' referential messages by deaf and hearing children. *Developmental Psychology, 24,* 277–285.

Marschark, M. (1993). *Psychological development of deaf children.* New York: Oxford University Press.

Marschark, M. (2007). *Raising and educating a deaf child, Second edition.* New York: Oxford University Press.

Marschark, M., Convertino, C., & LaRock, D. (2006). Optimizing academic performance of deaf students: Access, opportunities, and outcomes. In D. F. Moores & D. S. Martin (Eds.), *Deaf learners: New developments in curriculum and instruction* (pp. 179–200). Washington, DC: Gallaudet University Press.

Marschark, M., Convertino, C. M., Macias, G., Monikowski, C. M., Sapere, P. M., & Seewagen, R. (2007). Understanding communication among deaf students who sign and speak: A trivial pursuit? *American Annals of the Deaf, 152,* 415–424.

Marschark, M., Convertino, C., McEvoy, C., & Masteller, A. (2004). Organization and use of the mental lexicon by deaf and hearing individuals. *American Annals of the Deaf, 149,* 51–61.

Marschark, M., De Beni, R., Polazzo, M. G., & Cornoldi, C. (1993). Deaf and hearing-impaired adolescents' memory for concrete and abstract prose: Effects of relational and distinctive information. *American Annals of the Deaf, 138,* 31–39.

Marschark, M., & Everhart, V. S. (1999). Problem solving by deaf and hearing children: Twenty questions. *Deafness and Education International, 1,* 63–79.

Marschark, M., Lang, H. G., & Albertini, J. A. (2002). *Educating deaf students: From research to practice.* New York: Oxford University Press.

Marschark, M., Leigh, G., Sapere, P., Burnham, D., Convertino, C., Stinson, M., Knoors, H., Vervloed, M.P.J., & Noble, W. (2006). Benefits of sign language interpreting and text alternatives to classroom learning by deaf students. *Journal of Deaf Studies and Deaf Education, 11,* 421–437.

Marschark, M., Pelz, J., Convertino, C., Sapere, P., Arndt, M. E., & Seewagen, R. (2005). Classroom interpreting and visual information processing in mainstream education for deaf students: Live or Memorex?® *American Educational Research Journal, 42,* 727–762.

Marschark, M., Rhoten, C., & Fabich, M. (2007). Effects of cochlear implants on children's reading and academic achievement. *Journal of Deaf Studies and Deaf Education, 12,* 269–282.

Marschark, M., Sapere, P., Convertino, C. M., & Pelz, J. (2008). Learning via direct and mediated instruction by deaf students. *Journal of Deaf Studies and Deaf Education.*

Marschark, M., Sapere, P., Convertino, C., & Seewagen, R. (2005). Access to postsecondary education through sign language interpreting. *Journal of Deaf Studies and Deaf Education, 10,* 38–50.

Marschark, M., Sapere, P., Convertino, C., Seewagen, R., & Maltzan, H. (2004). Comprehension of sign language interpreting: deciphering a complex task situation. *Sign Language Studies, 4,* 345–368.

Marschark, M., Schick, B., & Spencer, P. E. (2006). Understanding sign language development of deaf children. In B. Schick, M. Marschark, &

P. E. Spencer (Eds.), *Advances in the sign language development of deaf children* (pp. 3–19). New York: Oxford University Press.

Marschark, M., & Spencer, P. E. (2006). Spoken language development of deaf and hard-of-hearing children: Historical and theoretical perspectives. In P. E. Spencer & M. Marschark (Eds.), *Advances in the spoken language development of deaf and hard-of-hearing children* (pp. 3–21). New York: Oxford University Press.

Matthews, T. J., & Reich, C. F. (1993). Constraints on communication in classrooms for the deaf. *American Annals of the Deaf, 138,* 14–18.

Mayer, C., Akamatsu, C. T., & Stewart, D. (2002). A model for effective practice: Dialogic inquiry in the education of deaf students. *Exceptional Children, 68,* 485–502.

Mayer, C. (2007). What really matters in the early literacy development of deaf children. *Journal of Deaf Studies and Deaf Education, 12,* 411–431.

Mayer, C. & Wells, G. (1996). Can the linguistic interdependence theory support a bilingual-bicultural model of literacy education for deaf students? *Journal of Deaf Studies and Deaf Education, 1,* 93–107.

McEvoy, C., Marschark, M., & Nelson, D. L. (1999). Comparing the mental lexicons of deaf and hearing individuals. *Journal of Educational Psychology, 91,* 1–9.

Meadow-Orlans, K. P., Spencer, P. E., & Koester, L. S. (2004). *The world of deaf infants.* New York: Oxford University Press.

Merrills J. D., Underwood, G., & Wood, D. J. (1994). The word recognition skills of profoundly, prelingually deaf children. *British Journal of Psychology, 12,* 365–384.

Moeller, M. P. (2000). Early intervention and language development in children who are deaf and hard of hearing. *Pediatrics, 106*(3), 1–9.

Mohay, H., Milton, L., Hindmarsh, G., & Ganley, K. (1998). Deaf mothers as communication models for hearing families with deaf children. In A. Weisel (Ed.), *Issues unresolved: New perspectives on language and deaf education* (pp. 76–87). Washington, DC: Gallaudet University Press.

Mokhtari, K., & Reichard, C. A. (2002). Assessing students' metacognitive awareness of reading strategies. *Journal of Educational Psychology, 94,* 249–259.

Morgan, G., & Woll, B. (Eds.) (2002). *Current developments in child signed language research.* Amsterdam: John Benjamins.

Murphy, H. J., & Fleischer, L. R. (1977). The effects of Ameslan versus Siglish upon test scores. *Journal of Rehabilitation of the Deaf, 11,* 15–18.

Napier, J. (2002). University interpreting: Linguistic issues for consideration. *Journal of Deaf Studies and Deaf Education, 7,* 281–301.

Noordman, L. G. M., & Vonk, W. (1998). Memory-based processing in understanding causal information. *Discourse Processes, 26,* 191–212.

Oakhill, J., & Cain, K. (2000). Children's difficulties in text comprehension: Assessing causal issues. *Journal of Deaf Studies and Deaf Education* 5, 51–59.

O'Connor, N., & Hermelin, B. M. (1973). The spatial or temporal organization of short-term memory. *Quarterly Journal of Experimental Psychology, 25,* 335–343.

Ottem, E. (1980). An analysis of cognitive studies with deaf subjects. *American Annals of the Deaf, 125,* 564–575.

Paatsch, L. E., Blamey, P. J., Sarant, J. Z., & Bow, C. P. (2006). The effects of speech production and vocabulary training on different components of spoken language performance. *Journal of Deaf Studies and Deaf Education, 11*, 39–55.

Padden, C. A., & Ramsey, C. (1998). Reading ability in signing deaf children. *Topics in Language Disorders, 18* (4), 30–46.

Padden, C. A., & Ramsey, C. (2000). American Sign Language and reading ability in deaf children. In C. Chamberlain, J. P. Morford, & R. I. Mayberry (Eds.), *Language acquisition by eye* (pp. 165–190). Mahwah, NJ: Lawrence Erlbaum Associates.

Paivio, A. (2008). How children learn and retain information: The dual coding theory. In S. B. Newman (Ed.), *Literacy achievement for young children in poverty*. Baltimore: Paul H. Brookes

Paul, P. V. (2003). Processes and components of reading. In M. Marschark & P. E. Spencer, *Oxford handbook of deaf studies, language, and education* (pp. 97–109). New York: Oxford University Press.

Perfetti, C. A., & Sandak, R. (2000). Reading optimally builds on spoken language: Implications for deaf readers. *Journal of Deaf Studies and Deaf Education, 5*, 32–50.

Pinhas, J. S. (1991). Constructive processing in skilled deaf and hearing readers. In D. S. Martin (Ed.), *Advances in cognition, education, and deafness* (pp. 296–301). Washington, DC: Gallaudet University Press.

Power, D., & Hyde, M. (1997). Multisensory and unisensory approaches to communicating with deaf children. *European Journal of Psychology and Education, 12*, 449–464.

Pressley, M. (2000). What should comprehension instruction be the instruction of? In M. Kamil, P. Mosenthal, P. D. Pearson, & R. Barr (Eds.), *Handbook of reading research* (Vol. 3, pp. 545–561). Mahwah, NJ: Lawrence Erlbaum Associates.

Pressley, M., & Afflerbach, P. (1995). *Verbal protocols of reading: The nature of constructively responsive reading*. Hillsdale, NJ: Lawrence Erlbaum Associates.

Prezbindowski, A. K., & Lederberg, A.R. (2003). Vocabulary assessment of deaf and hard-of-hearing children from infancy through the preschool years. *Journal of Deaf Studies and Deaf Education, 8*, 383–400.

Ramsey, C. (1997). *Deaf children in public schools*. Washington, DC: Gallaudet University Press.

Rawson, K. A., & Kintsch, W. (2002). How does background information improve memory for text? *Memory and Cognition, 30*, 768–778.

Richardson, J. T. E., MacLeod-Gallinger, J., McKee, B. G., & Long, G.L. (2000). Approaches to studying in deaf and hearing students in higher education. *Journal of Deaf Studies and Deaf Education, 5*, 156–173.

Sarachan-Deily, A. B. (1985). Written narratives of deaf and hearing students: story recall and inference. *Journal of Speech and Hearing Research, 28*, 151–159.

Schick, B., Marschark, M., & Spencer, P. E., (Eds.) (2006). *Advances in the sign language development of deaf children*. New York: Oxford University Press.

Schirmer, B. R., & Williams, C. (2003). Approaches to teaching reading. In M. Marschark & P. E. Spencer (Eds.), *Oxford Handbook of deaf studies, language, and education* (pp. 110–122). New York: Oxford University Press.

Singleton, J. L., & Morgan, D. D. (2006). In B. Schick, M. Marschark, & P. E. Spencer (Eds.), *Advances in the sign language development of deaf children* (pp. 344- 375). New York: Oxford University Press.

Singleton, J. L., Supalla, S., Litchfield, S., & Schley, S. (1998). From sign to word: Considering modality constraints in ASL/English bilingual education. *Topics in Language Disorders, 18*(4), 16–29.

Snow, C. E., Burns, M. S., & Griffin, P. (1998). *Preventing reading difficulties in young children.* Washington, DC: National Academy Press.

Spencer, L. J., Gantz, B. J., & Knutson, J. F. (2004). Outcomes and achievement of students who grew up with access to cochlear implants. *Laryngoscope 114,* 1576–1581.

Spencer, P. E., & Marschark, M. (Eds.) (2006). *Advances in the spoken language development of deaf and hard-of-hearing children.* New York: Oxford University Press.

Strassman, B. K. (1997). Metacognition and reading in children who are deaf: A review of the research. *Journal of Deaf Studies and Deaf Education, 2,* 140–149.

Strong, M., & Prinz, P. M. (1997). A study of the relationship between American Sign Language and English literacy. *Journal of Deaf Studies and Deaf Education, 2,* 37–46.

Thiede, K. W., Anderson, M.C.M., & Therriault, D. (2003). Accuracy of the cognitive monitoring affects learning of texts. *Journal of Educational Psychology, 95,* 66–73.

Todman, J., & Cowdy, N. (1993). Processing of visual-action codes by deaf and hearing children: Coding orientation or capacity? *Intelligence, 17,* 237–250.

Todman, J., & Seedhouse, E. (1994). Visual-action code processing by deaf and hearing children. *Language and Cognitive Processes, 9,* 129–141.

Traxler, C. B. (2000). Measuring up to performance standards in reading and mathematics: Achievement of selected deaf and hard-of-hearing students in the national norming of the 9th Edition Stanford Achievement Test. *Journal of Deaf Studies and Deaf Education, 5,* 337–348.

Trezek, B. J., & Malmgren, K. W. (2005). The efficacy of utilizing a phonics treatment package with middle school deaf and hard-of-hearing students. *Journal of Deaf Studies and Deaf Education, 10,* 256–271.

Trezek, B. J., & Wang, Y. (2006). Implications of utilizing a phonics-based reading curriculum with children who are deaf or hard of hearing. *Journal of Deaf Studies and Deaf Education, 11,* 202–213.

Trezek, B. J., Wang, Y., Woods, D. G., Gampp, T. L., & Paul, P. V. (2007). Using Visual Phonics to supplement beginning reading instruction for student who are deaf of hard of hearing. *Journal of Deaf Studies and Deaf Education, 12,* 373–384.

Vermeulen, A. M., van Bon, W., Schreuder, R., Knoors, H., & Snik, A. (2007). Reading comprehension of deaf children with cochlear implants. *Journal of Deaf Studies and Deaf Education, 12,* 283–302.

Waters, G., & Doehring, P. G. (1990). Reading acquisition in congenitally deaf children who communicate orally. In T. Carr & B. Levy (Eds.), *Reading and its development: Component skills approaches* (pp. 323–373). London: Academic Press.

Wauters, L. N. (2005). *Reading comprehension in deaf children: The impact of mode of acquisition of word meanings.* Unpublished doctoral dissertation, Radboud University Nijmegen. Nijmegen: The Netherlands.

Wauters, L. N., van Bon, W. H. J., & Tellings, A. E. J. M. (2006). Reading comprehension of Dutch deaf children. *Reading and Writing: An Interdisciplinary Journal, 19,* 49–76.

Wauters, L. N., Marschark, M., Sapere, P., Convertino, C., & Sarchet, T. (in preparation). Inference-making in deaf students' comprehension of sign and text.

Wauters, L. N., Tellings, A. E. J. M., van Bon, W. H. J., & van Haaften, A. W. (2003). Mode of acquisition of word meanings: The viability of a theoretical construct. *Applied Psycholinguistics, 24,* 385–406.

Wauters, L. N., Tellings, A. E. J. M., van Bon, W. H. J., & Mak, W. M. (2008). Mode of acquisition as a factor in deaf children's reading comprehension. *Journal of Deaf Studies and Deaf Education, 13,* 175–192.

Wilson, M., Bettger, J. G., Niculae, I., & Klima, E. S. (1997). Modality of language shapes working memory: Evidence from digit span and spatial span in ASL signers. *Journal of Deaf Studies and Deaf Education, 2,* 152–162.

Yoshinaga-Itano, C. (2003). From screening to early identification and intervention: Discovering predictors to successful outcomes for children with significant hearing loss. *Journal of Deaf Studies and Deaf Education, 8,* 11–30.

Chapter 13

A Model of Learning Within an Interpreted K–12 Educational Setting

Brenda Schick

Academic achievement continues to be a challenge for many students who are deaf or hard-of-hearing (DHH), and language, cognitive, and literacy skills are often significantly delayed compared with hearing peers (Antia, Reed, & Kreimeyer, 2005; Blamey et al., 2001; Connor & Zwolan, 2004; Schick, de Villiers, de Villiers, & Hoffmeister, 2007; Traxler, 2000). For many DHH students, their hearing loss makes spoken communication undependable for learning, and educational interpreting services are required to provide access to the communication in the general education classroom.

As a profession in the United States, educational interpreting emerged in 1974, with the implementation of the first federal law protecting the educational rights of children receiving special services (Bolster, 2005), with large shifts in placement from residential schools to the general education setting (Moores, 1992). There is little published data on how many DHH students use an educational interpreter. The Gallaudet Research Institute Annual Survey of Deaf and Hard of Hearing Children and Youth (2006) shows that of 37,500 DHH students in their survey, 25% used an interpreter, and 47% were in a general education classroom the majority of the time. However, it is possible that the survey undersamples students in this setting. A survey of all DHH students in the state of Colorado conducted by the Colorado Department of Education (C. Johnson, 2005) showed that of 269 school-aged students with any degree of hearing loss, 35% used an interpreter. Seal (2004) estimates that 24,000 students in the K–12 setting use the services of an educational interpreter. Clearly, as an educational practice, educational interpreting is widespread, but it is not an evidence-based practice.

Standards for Educational Interpreters

Until about 10 years ago, very few states had established standards of qualifications for educational interpreters (Schick, Williams, & Bolster, 1999; Stuckless, Avery, & Hurwitz, 1989). In 1985, Kluwin and Moores, using a survey of 40 interpreters who worked in high schools, described a typical interpreter in the public schools as a person who is a high school graduate with some college work and a brief training period, but no certification or other assurance of skill. Since that time, many states have recognized the need to monitor the knowledge and skills of K–12 interpreters, and currently, more than 28 states have some type of minimum standard (L. Johnson, 2005; Lineham, 2000; Schick, Williams, & Kupermintz, 2006). These minimal standards are typically defined as scoring at least a 3.5 on the Educational Interpreter Performance Assessment, or EIPA (scale = 0–5/ Low–High; Schick et al., 1999), or certification from the Registry of Interpreters of the Deaf (RID, 2006b), both nationally recognized evaluations. A few states also have continuing education or coursework requirements. However, in some cases, a person can meet the minimum standards by completing a short training program or passing a written test without verification of interpreting skills. In addition, many states have provisional certification requirements that allow any individual to serve as an educational interpreter, regardless of qualifications, some without restrictions on length of time. Because these requirements are new in many states, there is widespread employment of interpreters who do not meet minimal standards.

Wide variations exist in interpreter's performance skills across states. Figure 13–1 shows the mean EIPA score by state, for states with more than five evaluations available ($n = 4939$ from 37 states and Canada). States with standards are indicated using black bars. As a point of reference, a common state standard is 3.5 on a 5-point scale. It is important to note that interpreters who are in states without standards typically volunteered to take the test, so results are likely skewed toward higher scores. In addition, no simplistic relationship exists between standards and scores, because there are widespread differences in terms of how long standards have been in place and the monitoring and enforcement of these standards.

Skill Levels of Educational Interpreters

Despite the important role that educational interpreters have in providing access to the general education curriculum, many interpreters do not have the skills to represent the teacher's and hearing students' communication, and cannot pass minimum requirements, as established by state standards. Reduced skill levels in many interpreters undoubtedly impact

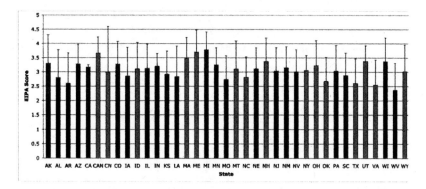

Figure 13-1. EIPA scores by state, with black bars representing some type of standard (*n* = 4939).

learning by DHH students, particularly in domains with abstract concepts and technical vocabulary, such as science and social studies.

Most investigations have surveyed the amount of training that interpreters typically receive, which is only an indirect, and somewhat poor, measure of performance skills (Burch, 2002; Dahl & Wilcox, 1990; Jones, 2004; Jones et al., 1997). Schick et al. (2006) investigated a group of 2091 educational interpreters on their ability to interpret authentic classroom teaching, at an elementary or secondary level, and their ability to interpret a signing child/youth into spoken English. Evaluations used the EIPA (Schick et al., 1999; Schick & Williams, 2004), a rating tool that has very good inter-rater reliability (.86–.94) as well as high internal consistency (Cronbach alpha = .93–.98). The interpreters were from across the United States (>35 states). Results showed that 45% of the educational interpreters did not meet common U.S. minimum standards (the 3.5 score on a 0–5 scale on the EIPA required in about 40% of states). The average EIPA score was 3.1 (*SD* = .86). The results were not greatly different from a study reporting data nearly a decade earlier (Schick et al., 1999). Thus, both elementary and high school DHH students are supported in classroom communication by interpreters who do not meet a common minimum standard. The data also were analyzed according to which sign language the interpreter was tested in: American Sign Language (ASL), nativized English signing, or Manually Coded English (MCE), three common language choices in schools.[1] Interpreters who use ASL and nativized English signing obtained slightly higher scores on the EIPA than those who use MCE. However, the

---

1. ASL, or American Sign Language and nativized English signing are used by the Deaf community. Manually Coded English is an invented form of signing that tries to replicate spoken English manually, and is sometimes used in the educational setting, but not by the adult Deaf community (see Marschark, 2007).

effect sizes were small (.001–.039), which indicates that the magnitude of the effect was not large, despite the significant differences. Regardless of language, it is likely that DHH students receive services from an interpreter who is underqualified to provide access to classroom communication.

Interpreter Training Programs and Performance

It would be easy to fault schools for hiring educational interpreters who are not qualified, but the lack of qualified interpreters is in large part due to training practices and emerging standards (Jones, 2004; Schick et al., 2006; Witter-Merithew & Johnson, 2005). Only a few states require formal training for interpreters at the postsecondary level. Surveys have repeatedly shown that the majority of interpreters who work in the public schools have not had postsecondary training, and very few have had training in K–12 settings (Dahl & Wilcox, 1990; Hayes, 1992; Jones et al., 1997). For example, in a survey of self-reported training of 221 educational interpreters in Kansas, Nebraska, Iowa, and Missouri, Jones et al. (1997) found that only 15% had an associate degree in interpreting. A higher figure was found by Hayes (1992), who reported that 14 of 32, or 44% of educational interpreters had completed an interpreter training program (ITP). The EIPA database has demographic information on 3619 interpreters who have taken the EIPA (as of October 15, 2006) that shows that 46% of the interpreters completed an interpreter training program, 27% had a BA degree, and 15% had accomplished both.

Research also shows that graduating from an interpreter training program does not mean that an educational interpreter is ready to work (Commission on Education of the Deaf, 1988; RID, 2006a; Schick et al., 2006; Stewart & Kluwin, 1996). Most training programs are 2-year programs in community colleges, trying to train both sign language skills and interpreting skills in a very short period of time (Burch, 2002; Witter-Merithew & Johnson, 2005). In an investigation of 2091 educational interpreters, individuals who had completed an interpreter training program outscored those who had not only in some skill areas (Schick et al., 2006). They were significantly better in grammar and vocabulary, but were no different in their ability to (voice) interpret a deaf student's sign communication or in their overall discourse skills, and there was a great deal of variability in both groups (Table 13–1). Based on the most conservative measure of effect size, graduating from an ITP has an effect size of .34, a bachelor's degree only has an effect size of .56, while both a bachelor's degree and ITP training gives a .77 effect. The effect size is a measure of the magnitude of difference, rather than just whether differences are significant or not. An effect size of .5 is considered a medium effect and .80 is a large effect (Portney & Watkins, 2000).

Table 13–1.   Average EIPA Score

	ITP (*SD*)	No ITP (*SD*)
BA degree	3.57 (.65)	3.19 (.80)
No BA	3.38 (.71)	2.89 (.88)

Average EIPA score (0–5 scale) for individuals who have attended an interpreter training program versus those who have not, and those with and without a bachelor degree (BA; *n* = 1505).

It should be noted that the national professional organization for interpreters, the Registry of Interpreters for the Deaf or RID (www.rid.org) only recently adopted a bachelor's degree requirement for certification (in addition to written and performance tests). The organization will require the degree in 2012, but in any content area. That is, the degree does not need to be in an area relevant to interpreting. At the current time, there is no regulation of ITPs. The RID, as a professional organization, is not involved in training curriculum or accreditation. A new national organization, the Commission on Collegiate Interpreter Education (http://www.cit-asl.org/ccie.htm) has been formed and is attempting to establish a system of accreditation for ITPs. Neither RID nor the accreditation organization has addressed student performance standards upon graduation; rather, the focus is on program evaluation.

It is clear that even the training programs and national organizations do not expect ITP graduates to be ready to work. The RID website states that after completing an ITP, "If you are active in the field and continue to upgrade your knowledge and skills, you should be able to pass the RID skills certification within three to five years" (RID, 2006a; see also Witter-Merithew & Johnson, 2005). Of course, "active in the field" means practicing on consumers and, in many instances, this practice is in the K–12 setting. Frishberg (1990) estimated that 60% of graduates of interpreter training programs first work in K–12 settings to gain experience to pass the national examination. A recent ethnographic study that included extensive interviews with 400 stakeholders concluded that the majority of graduates take their first job in the educational setting (Witter-Merithew & Johnson, 2005). Evidence suggests that interpreter training programs routinely advise graduating students to get a job in the public school system to prepare for adult community interpreting, as illustrated by several quotes from the study.

> "I understand that I will not be ready for a job I want when I graduate....My teachers have repeatedly emphasized that I will not be ready for community work...What does an entry-level interpreting job look like? The only things I am ever told is that it is a job in the public school system. But our program was not an educational interpreter program. We had some exposure to it but not enough to make me feel qualified." (p. 54; second-year student in a 2-year training program)

"I think I will start working in a K–12 setting initially because it is where there is a structured mentoring program available and therefore, the support to get certified quicker." (p. 56; senior in a 4-year training program)

"Most of us were going to be placed in school settings. I thought that was ironic since we had only given limited attention to interpreting for kids...I always got the impression that interpreting in a school setting was not a re-spected option, but more like a 'have to' kind of deal until you got yourself established." (p. 57; second-year student in a 2-year training program)

Witter-Merithew and Johnson concluded that, although practicum and in-ternships were typically in a K–12 setting, these placements were inconsis-tent with the curriculum emphasis in the program, which usually focuses on interpreting for adult consumers.

It is relevant to the profession of educational interpreting that most ITPs focus on interpreting for the adult community (Dahl & Wilcox, 1990; Davis, 2005; Stewart & Kluwin, 1996). Some programs include a single, three credit-hour course on interpreting in the educational setting, which means that K–12 interpreters often have very little information about educational systems, facilitating language development, working with educational teams and families, and the range of knowledge skills that are important when working in the K–12 environment. One survey found that 69% of the interpreter training programs did not have a single course on interpreting in an educational setting (Dahl & Wilcox, 1990), although the results are likely better today. However, current accredita-tion standards established by the Council of Interpreter Trainers (2006) do not mention educational interpreting at all, nor any competencies as-sociated with the K–12 setting.[2] The Council requires that programs use ASL and does not mention the range of English signing commonly used in schools, which Davis (2005) finds problematic. The Council's standard specifies that programs must adopt a sociolinguistic view of the Deaf community, which is admirable, but may leave educational interpreters confused about their role in the public school system as members of the educational team.

In summary, as a profession, educational interpreting is relatively new; training models cannot assure that graduates are qualified to work, and they provide little training specific to the K–12 setting. Issues related to interpreter quality are pervasive and, if anything, imposed on school systems by lack of standards and training, leaving schools to hire large numbers of individuals who lack essential qualifications to provide chil-dren and students access to the K–12 general education setting.

---

2. CIT has established standards for Interpreter Training Programs in 2002, now administered by the recently organized Council on Collegiate Interpreter Educa-tion, but no program has sought accreditation at this time.

Learning Through Interpreted Communication

It is a mantra within the interpreting profession that an interpretation is never the same as direct communication (Foster, 1989; Marschark & Sapere, 2005; Monikowski, 2004; Ramsey, 1997, 2004; Stewart & Kluwin, 1996; Winston, 1994, 2004). Even when an interpreter is highly competent, sign language interpreters are performing a simultaneous interpretation of one real-time language to another real-time language—a feat of cognitive and linguistic processing. Interpreting spoken English to English-like signing, rather than ASL, does not make this task easier, in that interpreters who took the MCE version of the EIPA scored lower than those who took the ASL version or the nativized English signing version (Schick et al., 2006). As Lang (2002, p. 271) states, "there is a dire need to examine the relationship of interpreting to learning." What we know supports the notion that it may be more difficult to learn through interpreted communication, and even that information largely pertains to college students and adults, not K–12 students.

Research on DHH adults indicates that they acquire less than hearing peers from interpreted college-level lectures (Marschark, Sapere, Convertino, & Seewagen, 2005; Marschark, Sapere, Convertino, Seewagen, & Maltzan, 2004). For example, Marschark and colleagues (2005) studied a group of 105 DHH college students and 22 hearing students at the Rochester Institute of Technology, a university with an extensive support program for the 10% of its students who are DHH. In the study, students watched two interpreted, college-level lectures in math and science, with a pre-test of knowledge and a post-test of learning. The participants attended a university with respectable entrance requirements, and clearly the students had language and cognitive skills well beyond those of a student in elementary or middle school. The results showed that the DHH students learned significantly less than their hearing peers even though the interpreters were highly qualified, had extensive experience with the subject matter, and worked to match their interpreting to the students' preferences. For the hearing college students, post-test scores ranged from 85% to 90%, but for the DHH students, scores were lower, 60%–75%, and the variability was greater among the DHH students ($SD = .18$) than their hearing peers ($SD = .12$). Although an effect size was not reported, a calculation reveals an effect size of 1.13, a very large effect. These results are consistent with those found in a similar study (Marschark et al., 2004), in which DHH students learned 59% of the lecture content and hearing students learned 87%, even with highly qualified interpreters.

Deaf and hard-of-hearing students appear aware that they do not fully understand college lectures about science topics. Napier (2004) interviewed four deaf college students (two native and two non-native signers) who reported that they understood between 50% and 90% of a lecture on language development. Kurz and Langer (2004) interviewed 20 DHH students about their experiences learning in an interpreted education environment and noted that as the students got older, their estimation of how much they learned from an interpreted classroom got lower, indicating that as they matured they were better able to recognize that they were not always understanding the material. It also appears that DHH students also are less aware of what they are missing. Marschark et al. (2004) reported that the DHH students were less able to predict their own level of comprehension after watching a lecture than were their hearing peers. Clearly, DHH students' ability to think metacognitively about their level of understanding may be skewed when learning through an interpreter. It seems that it can be more difficult to learn and to know what you know when you learn through an interpreted lecture. It certainly costs the DHH student some cognitive resources to have to maintain a cognitive watchdog regarding the communication breakdowns and errors that must be frequent with underqualified interpreters.

It is highly relevant to K–12 interpreting that research has not shown major differences in learning when an interpretation is in ASL as compared to a more English representation. That is, even when a student says he or she prefers an ASL interpretation to an English transliteration, learning is similar (Hatfield, Caccamise, & Siple, 1978; Livingston, Singer, & Abramson, 1994; Marschark et. al, 2004, 2005; Murphy & Fleischer, 1977). Deaf and hard-of-hearing students may prefer a particular type of signing style, but that does not seem to improve learning of abstract college materials, which were used in most of the studies.

Not surprising, much less information is available about how DHH K–12 students learn via an interpreter, although one study shows that children can learn in both direct and interpreted situations. Kurz (2004) investigated how much information deaf children learned when a science/social studies lesson was interpreted, compared with when a lesson was presented directly in ASL. She investigated a group of 19 deaf children (ages 11–15 years), with approximately half enrolled in direct-communication educational settings and the other half attending interpreted-educational settings. She compared how well the students learned new information from lessons presented by two certified secondary science teachers, one a deaf educator who was a deaf native signer, and the other a hearing teacher who taught science in a public school with experience with educational interpreters who worked in his classes. The hearing teacher's lessons were interpreted into ASL by an interpreter who had RID certification and RID-Legal certification, with more than 35 years of experience. She had grown up in a deaf family with deaf parents, siblings, and extended family. In short, she was extremely fluent and experienced.

Kurz (2004) used a within-subjects design in which each student saw three different lessons with direct communication and three other lessons in the interpreted condition. She found that all students were able to learn in the interpreted condition. Figure 13–2 shows the differences in the amount of learning in the direct communication condition when compared with the interpreted condition. For two of the six lessons, the students learned more information in the direct instruction condition; comparisons in the other lessons did not reach statistical significance. On average, the students learned 17% more information in the direct communication condition compared with the interpreted condition, but there was a great deal of individual variation, as shown in Figure 13–2. It is clear that for some students, learning through an interpreter was as effective as direct communication, whereas other students showed much better learning in the direct communication condition. Kurz also compared deaf students of deaf parents, assumed to have typical language development, with deaf students of hearing parents, who typically have language delays. She found that the deaf students from deaf families consistently learned more information in the lessons, learning 21% more content. This indicates that students with better language skills may be more likely to succeed in an interpreted classroom. Kurz also found that for all but one lesson, students learned abstract information better through direct communication, scoring 20% higher when compared to the interpreted lessons.

Although Kurz' (2004) data are interesting, the sample was small and the design did not allow investigation of students' abilities—that is their language, vocabulary, and reading skills, or how they relate to the

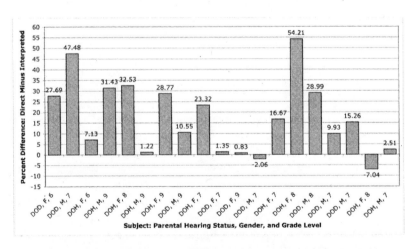

Figure 13–2. Difference scores between the percent of information learned from three lessons in direct communication and three lessons in interpreted communication for each student. Students are identified as having deaf families (DOD) or hearing families (DOH), gender, and age.

ability to learn. Another important finding was that signing in the direct communication condition took almost twice the time as the spoken English version, even though the deaf and hearing educators worked together to balance the content and vocabulary in the lessons. That is, the interpreter was constrained by the timing of the spoken communication of the hearing science teacher, but the deaf teacher was able to set a different pacing, which altered the learning task in the two conditions. Although Kurz did not examine the content of the two versions, the deaf teacher may have provided more information or more redundancy in his signed version. Despite these caveats, this study provides preliminary evidence that when the interpreter is highly qualified, even elementary-age students can learn in an interpreted setting, but that learning may be less than through direct communication. What factors mediate and moderate learning cannot be determined from this study.

Previous research has assumed the best-case scenario; that is, all interpreters were highly qualified, typically possessing RID certification, the "gold standard" for adult community interpreters, as well as extensive experience. In most cases, the interpreters in previous research should be considered master interpreters, far more qualified than an average adult community interpreter. This is not the case for the typical DHH student who receives services from an educational interpreter. As previously detailed, the average working interpreter, who has been evaluated on the EIPA, scores at a level 3.2 on a 5.0 scale. The RID certification is roughly equivalent to a 4.3 on the EIPA (Schick et al., 2006). This means that more than half of DHH students would receive interpreting services from an educational interpreter who does not meet minimum state standards nor has skills equivalent to those of a RID-certified individual. It is important to ask what a DHH student, likely with language, vocabulary, and reading delays, would learn from a less-than-qualified interpreter.

In an attempt to determine what students might receive in a typical classroom, Langer (2007) looked at the interpretations provided by educational interpreters. Using videotaped samples collected during an EIPA evaluation, the teachers' classroom communication and interpretations were analyzed to determine how much information was correctly represented. Five classroom lessons were selected from the EIPA, including first-grade math and calendar lessons, fourth-grade art and English lessons, and a fifth-grade history lesson. Interpretations were stratified to evenly represent those who scored an average of a 2.5, 3.5, and 4.5 on the EIPA, which represents about plus or minus one standard deviation of skills as shown in Schick et al. (2006). In addition, three expert interpreters provided interpretation of the same materials; each were RID certified, had a deaf family member, had more than 25 years of experience, and were recommended by the Deaf community as "the best in Colorado." The expert interpreters were intended to provide a "gold standard" and not a true comparison group. Rather than score all of the teachers' communication, those elements of the interpretation were selected that seemed highly relevant to classroom learning (Table 13–2).

Results show that interpreters varied widely in their ability to convey essential classroom communication, as shown in Figure 13–3. It appears that even expert interpreters miss a great deal of classroom communication. The expert interpreters conveyed 67%–92% of the information (range 50%–100%). The educational interpreters conveyed less information (32%–69%; range 0%–100%); the types of errors and omissions were similar in both the expert and educational interpreters. All of the educational interpreters conveyed the teachers' communication about word definitions most of the time (about 70%), but most struggled with representing the teacher's beliefs or their talk about others' beliefs (about 30%) or teachers' communication intended to increase the relevance of new classroom information to the students' lives (about 30%). It thus seems that other major issues here may be as important as interpreting skills.

Although the EIPA provides lesson plan material to interpreters prior to their performance, they are interpreting for a new teacher with new information and without much information about what the teacher intends the students to learn. As importantly, teachers' classroom communication is often so fast that even highly skilled interpreters are forced to make decisions about what to represent and what to delete. The results reflect, in part, the interpreter's beliefs and understanding about what information is important to convey, rather than reflecting the teachers' goals. That is, we are seeing the teacher's communication filtered by three factors: the

Table 13–2.   Descriptions of Categories Coded in the Interpretation of the Teachers' Communication

Category	Description
Beliefs	Teacher's communication that conveys what people think or believe or how people may differ in their understandings and beliefs
Relevance	Teacher's communication connected classroom content to student's world knowledge and experience
Directing	Teacher's communication that directs attention, such as to a picture
Participation	Teacher's communication that solicits participation
Explicit directions	Teacher's directions such as, "Label the slave states and the free states. Make sure you make a key."
Semantic	Teacher's communication that provides explicit information about the definitions or categorization of words
Concepts	Major concepts of the lesson

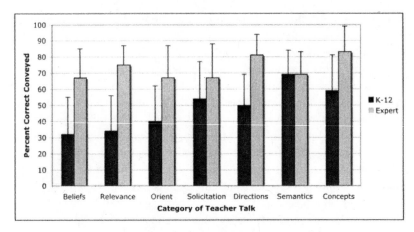

Figure 13–3. Percent of information in the teacher's talk conveyed in an interpretation, for selected categories of information (K–12 *n* = 40; Expert *n* = 3).

interpreter's skills, his cognitive understanding of the materials, and the teacher's goals.

Langer (2007) investigated how these inaccurate interpretations affect deaf adults' understanding of important elements in a fourth-grade art lesson. She showed a group of 19 deaf adults an interpretation produced by one of the K–12 interpreters, with a pre-test of knowledge and a post-test of learning. Most of the deaf adults had a college education, and 42% had deaf parents. Although a hearing control group understood 96% of the art teacher's communication, the deaf adults, watching through the interpreter, learned only 41% (SD = 21.1) of the targeted information. It is easy to predict that a DHH child or youth, with delays in language and reading and emerging comprehension monitoring (Markman, 1979), might be even more affected by a lack of interpreting quality than an adult. It is important to note that 80% of the deaf adults said in a post-test interview that the quality of the interpretation caused them to work hard to understand the information, and many used words such as "painful," "frustrating," and "battle."

A Model of Learning Within an Interpreted Education

Although we know that students can learn through an interpreted education, considerable variability exists among children (Kurz, 2004) and college students (Marschark et al., 2004, 2005). Much of the research and analysis regarding educational access with an interpreter has focused on the interpreter's *interpreting* skills, either directly (Schick et al., 1999,

2006) or indirectly (e.g., Jones et al., 1997) or the teacher's discourse (Jones, 2004; Winston, 2004). However, K–12 classrooms are complex learning environments, and to better understand how children might learn in an interpreted education, we need a framework or model for the constellation of factors that may impact the student's ability to learn and achieve academic success, particularly in domains that challenge conceptual thinking, such as science, social studies, and math. This model of learning through an interpreter is shown in Figure 13–4, which represents the broad factors that likely affect learning in DHH students. Interpreter factors, such as performance skills, cognitive and metacognitive skills, as well as knowledge of content, serve as a foundation to help implement a student's individualized educational program (IEP), which specifies annual goals and accommodations. Interpreter factors also include knowledge of the classroom content and teacher's objectives. Many student factors also come into play, such as cognitive, language, speech, vocabulary, and reading skills that allow access to the raw material of learning, including the communication, beliefs, and attitudes of teachers and peers, as well as print materials necessary for learning. The student's knowledge of interpreting and of their consumer rights may affect how the student manages an interpreted education. Teacher and classroom factors also affect learning, in that teacher discourse and teaching styles and how they manage the educational environment may affect how well the interpreter is able to represent the classroom communication. Educational policies and practices affect all three of these domains—interpreter skills, teacher practice, and educational team practices—and determine which students are placed with an interpreter. In this section, support for including these factors in a predictive model is provided.

It is important that this model is not derived from a starting point of an adult community interpreter; rather, it is developed around the concept

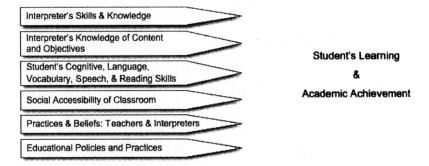

Figure 13–4. Model of factors that likely affect a student's learning in an interpreted education.

of the educational interpreter as a *related service provider*, the legal title provided by Individuals with Disabilities Education Improvement Act of 2004 (PL. 108–446, p. 118), typically termed IDEA 2004. The Final Regulations for IDEA 2004 declined to specify the skills and duties of educational interpreters and reads, "States are appropriately given the flexibility to determine the qualifications and responsibilities of personnel, based on the needs of children with disabilities in the State" (p. 46564; Federal Register, 2006). What follows is a discussion of each of the major factors of the model that may impact learning within an interpreted education.

Interpreter's Skills and Knowledge Related to Interpreting

The language, world knowledge, and cognitive skills that underlie the process of interpretation are complex, and there are models that focus on just this component (Cokely, 1992; Dean & Pollard, 2005; Napier, 2004; Roy, 2000; Seleskovitch, 1992; Setton, 1999; Witter-Merithew & Johnson, 2005). Many models of simultaneous interpreting incorporate components that are highly cognitive. For example, that proposed by Setton (1999) focuses on the dimensions of cognitive coordination involving the interpreter's resources and limitations in terms of their "competence and the flexibility of cognitive architecture" (p. 2). Other models are inspired by information processing theory and focus on the cognitive resources and requirements involved in interpretation (Gile, 1997; Massaro & Shlesinger, 1997). Although it seems obvious that an interpreter's skills and knowledge related to interpreting would affect student learning, no investigations have explored this relationship. Similarly, there is no research on the effect that the interpreter's knowledge about the interpreting process has on the quality of the interpretation in sign language, although there is research in spoken language interpretation that attempts to look at the factors that allow faithful interpretation (Ericsson, 2000; Shaw, Grbic, & Franklin, 2004). Witter-Merithew and Johnson (2005) developed a list of competencies for adult community interpreters, and *theory and knowledge* constituted one of the five domains essential for interpreter education. Information concerning the interpreting process is included in both the National Interpreter Certification Knowledge Exam, administered by the RID, and the EIPA Written Test, administered as part of the EIPA evaluation system. It should be emphasized that nearly all models of interpreting include significant aspects related to the interpreter's cognitive and metacognitive skills that impact critical analysis, language analysis, conceptualization, memory, pragmatic analysis, and other fundamental skills involved in interpretation.

We see some effects of the interpreter's metacognition at work in their omissions of information while interpreting text. Napier (2004) conducted a study to investigate interpreters' metacognitive awareness of their omissions in interpreting as a coping strategy in dealing with dense lecture text. Interpreters reviewed a videotape of their own interpretation immediately following its production, with the researcher, pausing the tape at omissions. They were asked whether they knew while they were interpreting when they had omitted something—that is, made a conscious omission— or whether they were unaware of the omission. Numerous unconscious omissions occurred (27%), but interpreters usually were aware of an omission while interpreting. Many were strategic omissions (26%), in which the interpreter reported making a conscious decision to omit something to enhance the effectiveness of the interpretation. There were also many omissions that the interpreter consciously made because his own lack of understanding or sign vocabulary knowledge. Another 14% were due to difficulties associated with lag time and translation issues. Interestingly, Napier found that the interpreter's educational level (no BA, BA, Graduate) did not influence the number or type of omissions, nor did their familiarity with the topic. Napier's research shows that an interpreter's metacognitive understanding clearly influences decision-making about how to cope with too much input to manage.

Interpreters' Knowledge of Educational Systems, Class Content, and Learning

Qualifications for interpreters involve more than fluency in two languages. A large amount of foundational knowledge underlies working as a related service provider in an educational setting with a developing student (La Bue, 1998; Roy, 2000; Schick, 2004; Seal, 2004; Shroyer & Compton, 1994; Stewart, Schein, & Cartwright, 2004; Witter-Merithew & Johnson, 2005). However, as previously described, interpreter education programs have mostly focused on the knowledge required to work with adults. Schick (2005, 2007), with input from experts in education and educational interpreting, developed an initial set of knowledge competencies specific to the K–12 setting and then used these to develop a basic written test for educational interpreters, the EIPA Written Test. The test assesses knowledge in 10 domains related to the K–12 setting including child development, professional practices, language and cognitive development, interpreting, educational practices, tutoring, and literacy. The test is currently required by two states as part of standards for educational interpreters (Colorado and Michigan), and it is required to obtain K–12 certification from RID. Figure 13–5 shows the results from a nationwide sample of educational interpreters ($n = 551$) on the EIPA written test. Clearly, interpreters vary in their knowledge of content related to interpreting as well as in basic English skills; the overall average was 83% correct ($SD = 10.15$). However, even

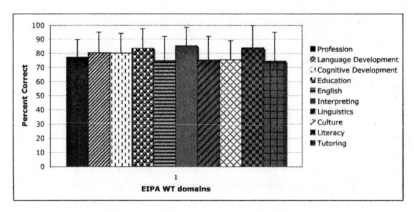

Figure 13–5. Results of the EIPA Written Test from educational interpreters (*n* = 551).

though the test was developed with expert input, we do not know how knowledge of educational interpreting relates to quality of interpretation in the classroom or to performance as a member of an educational team.

Because many DHH children are delayed in language and cognitive skills, an educational interpreter may need to scaffold the student's learning by modifying content, repeating key concepts, emphasizing new vocabulary, and the like. It seems essential that, like teachers and other paraeducators, the educational interpreter understand the child from a developmental and educational perspective, not just understand the process of interpretation. The educational interpreter is expected to help implement the student's IEP, by legal definition as a related service provider. The interpreter's understanding of how children learn and develop new skills seems essential to the process, if the interpreter is to do anything more than attempt to convey the teacher's and peer's communication verbatim. Given that the interpreter can never realistically convey all classroom communication, it is critical that the interpreter be able to make informed decisions about how essential a concept or communication is to the teacher's larger objectives.

As we know from Napier's work (2004), interpreters are altering the teacher's talk in conscious ways but, without understanding the educational needs and goals, these decisions will be based on some other metric of priority. When the interpreter does not understand the educational process, decisions will still be made, but they may not facilitate the teacher's educational outcomes, or they may not be in the child's best interests educationally. Although models of adult-to-adult interpreting include significant cognitive components, they are more about message analysis than thinking of the learning needs of the adult consumer. In fact, adult community interpreters typically do not alter content to make it more learnable; rather, the adult "listener" is viewed as in control. For the educational interpreter, the interpreting process would also include metacognitive thinking about the student, his skills, IEP goals, as well as thinking about how to best represent the information via translation. For interpreters who work with students with functional speech communication skills, interpreting may also involve thinking about when and what to interpret, in order to allow the student to independently manage as much of the communication as possible. For interpreters who work with children who have significant cognitive and language delays, effective interpreting means thinking about which aspects of the concept seem essential to convey and which seem like advanced details, which is really the type of thinking that teachers are required to do in daily practice. Given that most interpreters have little more than a single course related to interpreting in the K–12 setting, it is unlikely that interpreters are prepared for such professional obligations. Published program standards do not address these issues at all (Council of Interpreter Trainers, 2006; Witter-Merithew & Johnson, 2005).

We see the likely effect of this in research conducted by Langer (2007), previously described. She showed that both expert adult community interpreters and a wide range of educational interpreters were less likely to convey the teacher's talk about beliefs and attitudes, although they did convey the teacher's communication about word definitions and semantic categorization. This is probably not due to the skills of the interpreters; rather it is more likely a reflection of the interpreter's beliefs about the importance of this type of talk to student learning. For example, when the teacher said, "I've seen the movie once but I don't really remember" (p. 77), the teacher is essentially telling the children that her memory is faulty and they may have better recall than she does, basically an invitation to provide information and corrections. However, only 30% of the educational interpreters and 66% of the expert interpreters conveyed this notion. Many simply omitted it (32%), whereas others conveyed the erroneous fact that the teacher had never seen the movie. As Langer puts it, talk about beliefs and attitudes were communicated as facts or were simply omitted as if nonessential to the communication. However, the student's understanding of the beliefs and attitudes of teachers and peers is essential to the learning process, not extraneous communication (Astington & Pelletier, 1996, 2005; Sodian, Zaitchik, & Carey, 1991; Wellman & Lagattuta, 2005), and may also underlie important social skills (Lalonde & Chandler, 1995; Leekam, 1991; Yuill & Perner, 1987).

In summary, the interpreter's understanding of educational systems and practices, of the teacher's goals and objectives, and of the student's abilities and IEP goals would provide him with the context and information to guide how he manages classroom communication and how he omits and alters text due to task and skill reasons. We know that conscious decisions are being made that result in altered communication, but we have no idea whether the classroom teacher or the educational team would agree with the interpreter's decisions and the extent to which his decisions are driven by sound educational judgment.

Students' Skills: Cognition, Language, Vocabulary, Speech, and Reading Skills

It seems logical that the DHH student's skills may mediate or moderate learning in an interpreted education, but we actually know very little about how school-age children with hearing loss learn in real classrooms. We know DHH children with hearing parents typically enter school with significant language and vocabulary delays, compared with their hearing peers, even in recent studies with children with cochlear implants (Connor & Zwolan, 2004; Geers, 2003; Padden & Ramsey, 2000; Pisoni et al., this volume; Traxler, 2000). They often do not have the depth and breadth of conceptual knowledge, problem-solving skills, and cognitive organization that their hearing peers demonstrate (Marschark, 2003; Marschark, Lang, & Albertini, 2002). These delays in cognition, language, and vocabulary are typically implicated in the concomitant delays in academic achievement and reading (Lang, 2003; Marschark et al., 2002; Moores, 1996; Paul, 2003).

Some research looks at how individual differences (student factors) influence learning in an interpreted education in DHH college students. Marschark and his colleagues (2005) examined student learning of college lecture material in an interpreted condition and how it related to background variables. For their 105 DHH participants, the results showed that none of the student variables accounted for differences, including reading level, degree or age of onset of hearing loss, parental hearing status, use of assistive listening devices, or the age at which sign language was learned. Marschark and his colleagues have found similar results in other studies looking for factors that were predictive of comprehension (Marschark et al., 2004, 2006)—basically, the factors that we think are important are not. However, their participants were successfully matriculated at a university. It is impossible to generalize these results to K–12 students with a greater range of skills, given that high school graduation rates may be as low as 30% for students with hearing losses (Bowe, 2003).

Kurz's (2004) finding that DHH children with deaf families learned more through some interpreted lectures than their peers with hearing parents might be taken to imply that better language skills result in better learning. Numerous other differences exist between these two groups of children, however, including differences in their experiences and skills in using an interpreter. It is an important but unanswered question about how delayed a student can be in these skill domains and still have sufficient "horsepower" to learn in an interpreted educational setting, particularly in classes with abstract concept and vocabulary, such as science, social studies, and math (see Akamatsu, Mayer, & Hardy-Braz, this volume).

Delays in cognition, language, and vocabulary may moderate learning for any child in any classroom, but their effects might be amplified for deaf children in interpreted settings for several reasons. An interpreted education seems to place additional demands on cognitive processing (Schick, 2004). The student must coordinate visual attention between the interpreter and other visual information in the classroom (Hauser, Lukomski, & Hillman, this volume; Pelz, Marschark, & Convertino, this volume), which means that the DHH student likely receives less information than the hearing students (Winston, 2004). The DHH student also must figure out who is speaking in the classroom in order to make sense of the message (Schick, 2004), a requirement that is challenging to represent for many interpreters (Schick et al., 2006). For their part, educational interpreters are typically second-language learners, so the student must deal with a variety of accents and errors. As we know, the interpretation is likely to be a less rich and complex version of the teacher's communication in addition to being riddled with distortions, errors, and omissions (Langer, 2007), which make learning more challenging. We know from research with hearing students that even adolescents have difficulty identifying errors in communication, even when they are blatant (Markman, 1977, 1979). The student must contend with interpreted communication that is not in synchronization with what the hearing teacher and peers are doing, pointing to, and looking at (Winston, 2004). This short list of increased demands on cognitive resources is clearly incomplete; we really do not know all the factors that may be involved.

Marschark (2003), in a summary of what we know about cognitive skills in DHH students, concluded that they often have less efficient cognitive processing and retrieval strategies, and they are more variable in the content and organization of their cognitive system, all of which affect learning in the best of situations (also see Hauser et al., this volume). A less robust cognitive system, combined with the increased processing demands from learning through an interpreter, may predict large differences in learning between DHH students and their hearing peers within the same classroom environment. Delays in language and vocabulary may further moderate learning, especially because the teacher talk and learning objectives are scaffolded for students who are linguistically more mature.

Finally, the students' understanding of the interpreting process and their role in this process is likely to affect how effectively the student is able to learn in an interpreted classroom. For example, a student who understands that it is appropriate to ask the interpreter to slow down or clarify a concept, may be able to work with the interpreter and the classroom teacher to ensure better interpretation. However, this would require sophisticated metacognition, planning, and comprehension monitoring on the part of the student in order to manage communication and think about what would improve it. It also would require that schools teach students about their rights as a consumer, which is probably a questionable assumption.

Social Accessibility of the Classroom

Classrooms are complex social environments, and their social organization is quite different from that of family interaction (Cazden, 2001; Hertz-Lazarowitz, 1992; Rogoff, 1990; Sharan, 1990). One of the foundations of educational practice is the concept that the social milieu is pivotal to cognitive growth, knowledge construction, and social skills, grounded in the theories of both Piaget (1928) and Vygotsky (1978). Based on these theories, many classrooms are highly interactive, with the locus of learning in cooperative group activities in addition to teacher-centered instruction. This involves complex structures of organization, social groupings, and instruction that results in higher achievement and greater productivity than individually focused learning (Johnson & Johnson, 1991; Lew, Mesch, Johnson, & Johnson, 1986; Sharan, 1990; Sharan & Shaulov, 1990).

In addition to the positive effects of working with peers, there seems to be particular advantages for interaction and cooperative work with friends (Buklowski, Newcomb, & Hartup, 1996; Hartup, 1996a, 1996b; Ladd, 1990; Newcomb & Bagwell, 1996; Ryan, 2000). When children work with friends, they show more extensive exploration of a task and they retain more. Conversation is more vigorous and mutually oriented, with more negotiation rather than assertion, with more suggestions and elaborations. As Rogoff (1990, p. 174) maintains, "children may be freer to examine the logic of arguments with peers rather than adults." Hartup (1996a, 1996b) concluded that it is not just interaction with peers that is important, but there needs to be an emotional interdependence that constitutes closeness in relationships.

The issues of cooperative learning and developing friendships can be problematic within an interpreted education. First, DHH students may not have the maturity in social cognition skills that their hearing peers have. Research shows us that DHH children tend to be significantly delayed in fundamental aspects of social cognition, more specifically *theory of mind* (ToM) skills as measured with false-belief tasks (see Courtin et al., this volume). Theory of mind broadly refers to a person's understanding that others have beliefs, desires, and intentions that are different from one's own (for reviews see Astington, 1993; Bartsch & Wellman, 1995). Studies have shown that DHH children do not develop an understanding of false belief until around 8 years of age or later, a benchmark that hearing children achieve at about

age 4 (Peterson, 2004; Schick, de Villiers, de Villiers, & Hoffmeister, 2007).
Given these delays, it might be more difficult for some DHH students to interpret the intentions of others, regardless of whether an interpreter is used.

However, accessing the social culture of the classroom may be particularly different in an interpreted education, which is, by definition, a form
of secondhand communication. The DHH student may see all classroom
communication through a single individual, creating a social barrier between peers and the teacher. Both DHH children and adults report being left
out, feeling socially isolated, with significant difficulties connecting with
individuals other than the interpreter (Foster, 1988, 1989; Kurz & Langer,
2004; Mertens, 1991; Ramsey, 1997; Shaw & Jamieson, 1997). Teachers'
and students' communication contains a great deal of information about
their beliefs, expectations, and understanding that is not often contained
in their language or vocabulary but rather in aspects of speaking, such as
tone of voice and prosody (see Schick, 2004 for discussion). This type of
information seems to be particularly difficult for interpreters to convey
(Bülow-Møller, 1999; Chernov, 1996; Janzen & Shaffer, in press; Schick
et al., 2006). In the Langer (2007) study, for example, interpreters who
were highly skilled and those with less skills were both likely to omit the
teacher's talk that related to ToM, as if the facts of what the teacher said
were important, but how she thought or felt was not.

The reduced information about the intentions of teachers and peers
might also affect how the DHH student views the teacher's goals in terms
of learning (Astington & Pelletier, 2005; Frye & Ziv, 2005). As Richardson
(this volume) points out, DHH students often view learning in terms of the
memorization of facts, which may be in part due to being educated through
an interpreter who views his role as a conduit, reproducing in a literal way
what the teacher says. If the teacher's beliefs and attitudes are rendered
useless by the interpreting process or by the student's lack of expertise in
understanding the intentions of others, what the student sees is a collection of facts that might lead her to believe that her role is to memorize or
reproduce those facts, rather than put them into a broader context of thinking about what it all means.

There is evidence that the quality of interactions that DHH students
have with teachers and peers is affected by an interpreted education (Kurz &
Langer, 2004; Lang, Stinson, Kavanaugh, Liu, & Basile, 1998; Ramsey, 1997).
Ramsey (1997) conducted an ethnographic study that included extensive
classroom observations of deaf students who were in both a general education classroom and a self-contained classroom. One of the teachers in
Ramsey's study confessed that she had difficulty connecting with her deaf
students. She found the students' eye contact with the interpreter during
communication disconcerting and alienating. Kurz and Langer (2004)
interviewed 20 DHH K–12 students about their beliefs and understanding of an interpreted education. Many of the students commented about

issues related to social accessibility. For example, some students preferred a teacher's lecture to group discussions, because the difficulties related to interpreting made discussions difficult to understand and created a barrier to participation. Many students said that they participated less frequently in an interpreted class than in a class with direct communication. Some students expressed concerns about their confidence in the quality of the interpretation, which was an obstacle to participation.

From the limited research available regarding how well school-aged DHH students develop friendships with hearing peers, there is some indication that it is probably challenging. Research with preschool DHH children (ages 3–5 years) shows that the DHH students were just as likely as hearing students to have a temporary or long-term friend, but only 14% of their peer relationships were characterized as such; most were nonfriends (Lederberg, 1991). Despite the fact that the DHH children used very little language, they were able to develop relationships with hearing children. In a related study, Lederberg (1987) showed that for a group of deaf children, those with high language skills were more likely to engage in triadic interactions and to use language with hearing peers. However, it likely becomes increasingly difficult to develop friendships for school-aged DHH children. Ramsey (1997) reported that elementary-aged DHH students' interactions with hearing peers were mostly superficial and often the hearing peer assumed the role of teacher, not that of a peer.

Kurz, who is a deaf adult who received much of her K–12 education in an interpreted setting, reports, "I honestly do not think the interpreters were able to help me bond with hearing students naturally" (p. 42). Kurz also found that when she entered high school, "socializing with hearing kids got harder" (Kurz, p. 43). What Kurz wanted to communicate became more complex, but communication with hearing peers was "limiting and frustrating" (p. 43). She concluded that her DHH peers "were hungry for communication with other hearing students, and yet at the same time, we were not comfortable having the interpreters following us outside of class.... it was considered uncool" (p. 43). Kurz came to the realization that "even the best interpreter could not meet my social needs" (p. 43). The students in Kurz and Langer's interview study (2004) reported that the interpreters tended to interpret only official classroom business, and interestingly, they were unsure about whether this was school policy or teacher/interpreter preference, indicating that they were unclear about their rights to interpretation. Many individuals report that their educational interpreter was their main confidant and friend (Kurz & Langer, 2004), a parent figure (Zawolkow & DeFiore, 1986), or a caregiver (Stewart, Schein, & Cartwright, 2004).

Finally, it is important to note that interpreting a distributed conversation, such as in a classroom discussion, is more difficult than interpreting a monologue lecture (Winston, 2004). Research using the EIPA has shown that educational interpreters have difficulty representing who is speaking; that is, an interpreted discussion can often look like a single speaker is talking. Even when the interpreter is able to signal a speaker shift, the interpreter may not fully identify the individual, but just note that it was not the teacher. Given this, the student may not know that peers are making significant contributions and may not have access to which peer made which comment, which provides rich information about the personalities and skills of others.

Despite the fact that the social aspects of a classroom are essential to learning, development, and academic achievement, there are many significant barriers to having access to the social life of the classroom as an authentic member. The student may not have a rich understanding of social cognition, which may reduce how well she understands the social context and intentions. The DHH student may have particular difficulty becoming friends with peers, which can affect social development, quality of life, and academic achievement. The interpreting challenge posed by distributed discussion is significant, particularly because team interpreters are very rare in the K–12 setting.

Educational Practices and Beliefs of the Teachers and Interpreters

Several important factors must be consider relative to how teachers and interpreters view their roles and the nature of the teacher's educational practices and styles of discourse. A major aspect in how well a student can learn in an interpreted education relates to the professional practices of the members of the educational team, including the classroom teacher and the interpreter. Because educational interpreting is an emerging profession, standards of practice are not well-defined or established (Antia & Kreimeyer, 2001; Bolster, 2005; Seal, 1998, 2000; Witter-Merithew & Johnson, 2005). Many of the standards of practice that are established for interpreting for adults are problematic in a K–12 setting, which has many legal obligations to the student to fulfill. Some adult interpreting practices do not seem to be in the best interest of a developing child.

A great deal of controversy exists in the field about how engaged or involved the educational interpreter should be in the education of a DHH student, other than providing a faithful rendition of the classroom communication. Because codes of professional conduct have been developed for the adult community, and in many instances educational interpreters are expected to transfer principles such as confidentiality and right to autonomy into a K–12 setting, conflicts arise in roles and responsibilities (Scheibe & Hoza, 1986; Seal, 2004; Stedt, 1992; Witter-Merithew & Dirst, 1982; Zawolkow, & DeFiore, 1986).

Many interpreters and interpreter educators thus believe that an educational interpreter has no real role in the education of the student; that the interpreter should be a neutral communication mediator (see Antia & Kreimeyer, 2001; Stewart & Kluwin, 1996), although some researchers consider this neutrality to be impossible (Janzen & Shaffer, in press; Turner, 2005). For example, many interpreters believe that if the student appears to have difficulty understanding the interpreted message, it is not their responsibility to inform the teacher; rather it is the teacher's responsibility to find out. In their view, informing the teacher would be violating what they see as the child's right to confidentiality, which seems to trump the child's right to an accessible and fair education (Humphrey & Alcorn, 1994; Scheibe & Hoza, 1986).

Stewart and Kluwin (1996) examined guidelines relevant to this issue from 15 school districts and concluded that there are a wide range of expectations and practices within schools with little research to guide practice. In an ethnographic study of 65 educational interpreters who had completed a certificate program in educational interpreting, Bolster (2005) found that many educational interpreters viewed their responsibility as simply providing an interpretation, whereas others viewed themselves as an educational professional, working with the classroom teacher and the educational team to maximize student outcomes. Her recommendations included an open-minded dialogue about the interpreter's role, with attention to challenging traditional views about these roles as well as discussion about the appropriateness of using a code of ethics in the K–12 setting that was developed for adult consumers. This conflict regarding the role that interpreters have in a K–12 setting is reflected in a quote from Kurz (2004). She recalls an interpreter who spent time out of class reviewing class discussion of Greek mythology, a challenging subject in eighth grade. Kurz reflects, "Many faculty of interpreter training programs teach their interpreter students not to discuss homework assignments outside of their interpreting roles because this practice would violate their code of ethics for interpreting. Debate has been ongoing about this sticky role. I have always felt that educational interpreters many times serve as an assistant, tutor, and language model" (p. 43).

Confusions also exist among classroom teachers and educational teams about the role and responsibilities of the educational interpreter. One ethnographic interview study of three interpreters over a 3-year period showed that members of the educational team disagreed about the educational interpreter's roles and responsibilities (Antia & Kreimeyer, 2001). The classroom teachers reported that they worked with the interpreters to plan and facilitate instruction for the DHH student, and they preferred a full-participant role for the interpreter. In contrast, the special educators and administrator preferred a more restricted model of interpreting, one in which the interpreter provides a translation of the communication but all other responsibilities belong to the classroom teacher.

Bolster (2005) reported that of 65 educational interpreters who had completed an educational interpreting certificate program, only 57% were invited to the IEP meetings as a participant. A thorough understanding of the student's IEP goals may help the interpreter shift an emphasis on a particular form. We know that interpreters appear to be making decisions (perhaps unconsciously) about what to prioritize (Napier, 2004), but in some cases it may not be an informed decision. The interpreter is actually in the unique position to provide modifications, expansions, and clarifications for the DHH student. Given that the teacher's talk is targeted to scaffold typically developing students, the DHH student may need additional assistance because of delays in language, vocabulary, cognition, and the difficulty that most children have metacognitively monitoring their comprehension. However, without training and discussions with the educational team, it is also possible for the interpreter to take the content and language level to an inappropriately low level, based on incorrect assumptions regarding the student's skills. The interpreter may be able to provide the student with input that is better scaffolded but only if he is trained to do so.

Many classroom teachers do not seem to view the interpreter as a partner in serving a student. In a survey of 59 general education teachers who work with educational interpreters, only 54% reported that they discussed the issue of the roles and responsibilities of the educational interpreter (Beaver, Hayes, & Luetke-Stahlman, 1995). Many classroom teachers view the educational interpreter as "responsible" for the DHH student, without fully understanding the competencies, or lack thereof, that the individual brings to that task. Although educational interpreting is a widespread practice, it is clear that not a great deal of effort has been made to understand the dynamics of the educational team, which includes the classroom teacher, deaf educator, speech-language pathologist, parents, and educational interpreter.

Of course, much of this debate—about whether interpreters should or should not be active participants in the educational team—seems to miss the essential questions of what is in the best educational interest of the individual student and what will maximize learning. Rather, the debate seems to be an a priori discussion of what the interpreter should or should not do. Any a priori decision regarding interpreting practices in the classroom seems counter to IDEA regulations, which requires that the student's IEP drives the provision of services. Many decisions regarding practices can only be made within the context of the IEP team. It is important to note that there is little research to guide professionals in understanding the best practices for teachers and interpreters.

The teacher's discourse and teaching style can influence the quality of interpretation. The teacher's management of the classroom discourse also affects how accessible a classroom is when interpreted. Winston (2004) analyzed teachers' talk, predicting how accurately it could be interpreted. Her sample of classrooms consisted of teacher-led discussions and no samples of peer-to-peer group work. She identified elements of teacher's style of communication that would directly impact the quality of the interpretation:

- Teachers' pacing: Teachers who speak quickly and encourage rapid turn-taking and overlapping talk among students are predicted to be the most difficult to interpret. Other teachers talk more slowly, allow quiet space between their questions and students' responses, and regulate responses by calling on specific students by name, which Winston predicts is easier to interpret.
- Explicitness and redundancy of teachers' discourse: Some teachers repeated information and rephrased or reformulated important information to give it more weight. Other teachers were less explicit in their talk, such as using vague pronominal references, or assuming that students would recall elements from previous class discussion or lecture.
- Management of turn-taking in the classroom: Teachers who regulate the flow of discussion, identifying students by name and repeating key information, are predicted to be easier to interpret than teachers who have a more freewheeling management of discussion, allowing students to talk without being recognized or to talk while others are talking.
- Cooperative learning activities as opposed to mostly class lecture: Winston (2004, p. 142) predicts that lectures "are the most visually accessible and, therefore, the most interpretable environment." However, from what we know about learning, educators typically consider lecture as a less accessible form of pedagogy, a clear conflict. The student's learning may be affected by how successful the teacher and the interpreter are at providing access to classroom activities involving group interaction.

In summary, many aspects of educational practice and belief affect how the interpreter works, either as a member of the educational team or as a communication conduit, which in turn may affect student learning. Part of the role conflict for educational interpreters is grounded in trying to apply a model of interpreting that was developed for adult consumers, who are independent and autonomous, to an educational setting in which the educational team has a legal obligation to maximize education. The practices and beliefs of all the team members affect their daily practices in ways that are highly relevant for learning.

Policies and Regulations

As reported earlier, many state departments of education have established minimum standards for educational interpreters. However, the concept of standards, policies, and/or regulations is more complex than simply establishing a minimum skill level in interpreting skills. The quality of access in the classroom is also dependent on the interpreter's knowledge of the interpreting process, educational practices, the student's IEP, the teacher's goals and objectives, as well as many other aspects of education. Most states have focused mostly on the skills component and little on the knowledge component. The vast majority do not have degree requirements beyond the high school level.

Regardless of whether a state has regulations, a separate and important question is how easy is it to obtain emergency credentials. All states allow school districts to hire individuals on an emergency provision if they cannot find a more qualified person. Sometimes, emergency credentialing is not well regulated or so broadly defined that a highly unqualified person may be allowed to work for years without evidence of improving or with any serious threat to keeping a job.

It is highly likely that policies and regulations concerning interpreter's qualifications do affect a student's learning. It is essential that states have policies that credential and monitor personnel, have requirements in a constellation of skills and knowledge, and ensure that unqualified interpreters improve or move out of their jobs.

Summary and Implications

Gaining access to a regular education classroom through an educational interpreter is a complex cognitive process with many interrelated factors. This chapter attempts to provide an overview of the range of skills and factors that would influence how much and how well a child would learn within an interpreted education. There are good reasons why many people focus on the interpreter's skills in interpreting, because many individuals do not have what is considered minimum performance skills. A clear need exists to continue efforts and reforms in improving and requiring interpreter preparation. However, many other domains of practice and skill may mediate and moderate learning in an interpreted education. These include student factors, such as their speech, language, vocabulary, and reading skills, as well as their skills in metacognitive thinking and social cognition. In addition to the interpreter's language and interpreting skills, aspects of their understanding of the educational system, teaching objectives, and understanding of the classroom content likely affect their ability to convey not just the factual content of the classroom communication, but also their ability to communicate the teacher's and peers' intentions and beliefs. The teacher's beliefs about the interpreting process, pedagogical discourse, and how well the interpreter works as a team member with the teacher can also influence the quality of the interpretation. Educational policies and regulations underlie all of this, in that they provide legal definitions, right or wrong, of the skills that interpreters are required to have and practices that are to be followed regarding an interpreted education.

It is obvious from reviewing the research related to learning within an interpreted K–12 setting that little empirical evidence is available to guide us when making decisions about individual students and their needs. Although educational interpreting is a widespread practice, little data is available to help educational teams determine best practices. Most of what we do know focuses on college students and other adults, typically with interpreters who have been selected because of their high level of interpreting skills. We need research on K–12 students, with their broader range of skills and developmental needs, to ensure educational access, with information about how the interpreter's skills affect the quality of interpretation.

There are positive aspects to this complexity of factors, in that they provide multiple avenues that we can pursue in scaffolding information for students who have access challenges because of a placement in a regular education classroom. Providing the interpreters with access to educational team meetings, the student's IEP, and teacher manuals for textbooks may help the interpreter make better choices about how to prioritize competing needs. Similarly, an interpreter may provide the classroom teacher with information about what discourse and management styles facilitate interpretation. This model provides direction for a multipronged approach in improving our ability to ensure access within an interpreted education.

It is easy to view what we know about interpreted education and the challenges it brings to learning as a widespread indictment against the practice; however, that seems unfair and perhaps unrealistic. Evidence suggests that students *can* learn through an interpreted education. Furthermore, choosing a school placement for a student is complex, and families and educational programs must weigh a variety of factors, often concluding that no ideal option exists. The DHH students who were interviewed by Kurz and Langer (2004) seemed cognizant of the compromises inherent in choosing an interpreted education over one involving direct communication. Furthermore, much of what is written about the relative pros and cons often assumes that the DHH student cannot use spoken communication, and the student's skills are severely delayed. In reality, only about 9% of children have a severe or profound hearing loss (Blanchfield, Feldman, & Dunbar, 2001). It is highly likely that in the future many more students will have some degree of functional skills in spoken communication and that language and literacy outcomes might well improve (see Leigh, this volume). Even with amplification (both hearing aids and CIs), the noisy acoustic environments that are typical of K–12 classrooms pose serious listening challenges. We may likely see an increase in the number of families who choose to scaffold their child's learning environment with an educational interpreter, regardless of their ability to use spoken communication in some situations.

Acknowledgments

Preparation of this chapter was supported in part by a grant from the U.S. Department of Education, Office of Special Education Programs, Programs of National Significance (H325 N010013).

References

Antia, S., & Kreimeyer, K. (2001). The role of interpreters in inclusive classrooms. *American Annals of the Deaf, 146,* 355–365.

Antia, S., Reed S., & Kreimeyer, K. (2005). Written language of deaf and hard-of-hearing students in public schools. *Journal of Deaf Studies and Deaf Education, 10,* 244–255.

Astington, J. W. (1993). *The child's discovery of the mind.* Cambridge, MA: Harvard University Press.

Astington, J. W., & Pelletier, J. (1996). The language of the mind: Its role in teaching and learning. In D. Olson & N. Torrance (Eds.), *Handbook of education and human development: New models of learning, teaching, and schooling* (pp. 593–619). Cambridge, U.K.: Blackwell Press.

Astington, J. W., & Pelletier, J. (2005). Theory of mind, language, and learning in the early years: Developmental origins of school readiness. In B. D. Homer & C. Tamis-Lemonda (Eds.), *The development of social cognition and communication* (pp. 205–230). Hillsdale, NJ: Erlbaum.

Bartsch, K., & Wellman, H. (1995). *Children talk about the mind.* New York: Oxford University Press.

Beaver, D. L., Hayes, P. L., & Luetke-Stahlman, B. (1995). In-service trends: General education teachers working with educational interpreters. *American Annals of the Deaf, 140,* 38–46.

Blamey, P. J., Sarant, J. Z., Paatsch, L. E., Barry, J. G., Bow, C. P., Wales, R. J., Wright, M., Psarros, C., Rattigan, K., & Rooher, R. (2001). Relationships among speech perception, production, language, hearing loss, and age in children with impaired hearing. *Journal of Speech, Language, and Hearing Research 44,* 264–285.

Blanchfield, B., Feldman, J., & Dunbar, J. (2001). The severely to profoundly hearing-impaired population in the United States: Prevalence estimates and demographics. *Journal of the American Academy of Audiology, 12,* 183–189.

Bolster, L. A. (2005). *Time-compressed professionalization: The experience of public school sign language interpreters in mountain-plains states.* Unpublished doctoral dissertation, Virginia Polytechnic and State University, Blacksburg.

Bowe, F. (2003). Transition for deaf and hard-of-hearing students: A blueprint for change. *Journal of Deaf Studies and Deaf Education, 8,* 485–493.

Buklowski, W. M., Newcomb, A. F., & Hartup, W. W. (1996). *The company they keep: Friendships in childhood and adolescence.* Cambridge, U.K.: Cambridge University Press.

Bülow-Møller, A. M. (1999). Existential problems: On the processing of irrealis in simultaneous interpreting. *Interpreting, 4,* 145–168.

Burch, D. D. (2002). Essential education for sign language interpreters in pre-college educational settings. *Journal of Interpretation, 7,* 125–149.

Cazden, C. (2001). *Classroom discourse: The language of teaching and learning.* Portsmouth, NH: Heineman.

Chernov, G. (1996). Taking care of the sense in simultaneous interpreting. In C. Dollerup & V. Appel (Eds.), *Teaching translation and interpreting 3: New horizons.* Papers from the 3rd Language International Conference, Elsinore, 9–11 June 1995 (pp. 223–31). Amsterdam: John Benjamins.

Cokely, D. (1992). *Interpretation: A sociolinguistic model.* Burtonsville, MD: Linstok Press.

Commission of Education of the Deaf. (1988). *Toward equality: Education of the deaf.* Washington, DC: U.S. Government Printing Office.

Connor, C. M., & Zwolan, T. A. (2004). Examining multiple sources of influence on the reading comprehension skills of children who use cochlear implants. *Journal of Speech, Language, and Hearing Research, 47,* 509–526.

Council of Interpreter Trainers. (2006). National interpreter education standards. www.cit-asl.org/natl_stand.htm (Retrieved September 12, 2006).

Dahl, C., & Wilcox, S. (1990). Preparing the educational interpreter: A survey of sign language interpreter training programs. *American Annals of the Deaf, 135,* 275–279.

Davis, J. (2005). Code choices and consequences: Implications for educational interpreting. In M. Marschark, R. Peterson, & E. Winston (Eds.), *Sign language interpreting and interpreter education* (pp. 112–141). New York: Oxford University Press.

Dean, R. K., & Pollard, R. Q. (2005). Consumers and service effectiveness in interpreting work: A practice profession perspective. In M. Marschark, R. Peterson, & E. Winston (Eds.), *Sign language interpreting and interpreter education* (pp. 259–282). New York: Oxford University Press.

Ericsson, K. A. (2000). Expertise in interpreting: An expert-performance perspective. *Interpreting, 5,* 187–220.

Federal Register. (August 14, 2006). Vol. 71, No. 156.

Foster, S. (1988). Life in the mainstream: Reflections of deaf college freshmen on their experiences in the mainstreamed high school. *Journal of Rehabilitation of the Deaf, 22,* 27–35.

Foster, S. (1989). Educational programs for deaf students: An insider perspective on policy and practice. In L. Barton (Ed.), *Integration: Myth or reality?* (pp. 57–82). London: The Falmer Press.

Frishberg, N. (1990). *Interpreting: An introduction.* Silver Spring, MD: Registry of Interpreters for the Deaf Publications.

Frye, D., & Ziv, M. (2005). Teaching and learning as intentional activities. In B. D. Homer & C. S. Tamis-LeMonda (Eds.), *The development of social cognition and communication* (pp. 231–258). Mahwah, NJ: Lawrence Erlbaum.

Gallaudet Research Institute. (2006). Regional and national summary report of data from the annual survey of deaf and hard of hearing children and youth. http://gri.gallaudet.edu/Demographics/ (Retrieved 29 September 2006).

Geers, A. (2003). Predictors of reading skill development in children with early cochlear implantation. *Ear and Hearing, 24,* 59S–68S.

Gile, D. (1997). Conference interpreting as a cognitive management problem. In J. H. Danks, G. M. Shreve, S. B. Fountain, & M. K. McBeath (Eds.), *Cognitive processes in translation and interpreting* (pp. 196–214). Thousand Oaks, CA: Sage Publications.

Hartup, W. W. (1996a). Cooperation, close relationships, and cognitive development. In W. M. Buklowski, A. F. Newcomb, & W. W. Hartup (Eds.), *The company they keep: Friendships in childhood and adolescence* (pp. 213–237). Cambridge, U.K.: Cambridge University Press.

Hartup, W. W. (1996b). The company they keep: Friendships and their developmental significance. *Child Development, 67,* 1–13.

Hatfield, N., Caccamise, F., & Siple, P. (1978). Language competency: A bilingual perspective. *American Annals of the Deaf, 123,* 847–51.

Hayes, P. L. (1992). *Interpreters in educational settings responsibilities, concerns, and recommendations.* Paper presented at the Issues in Language and Deafness: The use of sign language in educational settings: Current concepts and controversies, Omaha, NE.

Hertz-Lazarowitz, R. (1992). Understanding interactive behaviors: Looking at six mirrors if the classroom. In Hertz-Lazarowitz, R. & Miller, N. (Eds.), *Interaction in cooperative groups: The theoretical anatomy of group learning* (pp. 71–101). New York: Cambridge University Press.

Humphrey, J. A., & Alcorn, B. J. (1994). *So you want to be an interpreter? An introduction to sign language interpreting.* Amarillo, TX: H and H Publishers.

Individuals with Disabilities Education Improvement Act of 2004 (PL 108–446).

Janzen, T., & Shaffer, B. (in press). Intersubjectivity in interpreted interactions. In J. Zlatev, T. Racine, C. Sinha, & E. Itkonen (Eds.), *The shared mind: Perspectives on intersubjectivity.* Philadelphia: John Benjamins.

Johnson, C. D. (2005). *Colorado Individual Performance Profile: Data trends.* Presented at the Colorado Symposium on Deafness, Colorado Springs, CO.

Johnson, D. W., & Johnson, R. T. (1991). *Learning together and alone: Cooperation, competition and individualization.* Englewood Cliffs, NJ: Prentice Hall.

Johnson, L. (2005). *Final Project Report.* Office of Special Education Programs.

Jones, B. (2004). Competencies of K–12 educational interpreters: What we need versus what we have. In E. Winston (Ed.), *Educational interpreting: How it can succeed.* (pp. 113–131). Washington, DC: Gallaudet University Press.

Jones, B. E., Clark, G. M., & Soltz, D. F. (1997). Characteristics and practices of sign language interpreters in inclusive education programs. *Exceptional Children, 63,* 257–268.

Kluwin, R. N., & Moores, D. F. (1985). The effects of integration on the mathematics achievement of hearing impaired adolescents. *Exceptional Children, 52,* 153–160.

Kurz, K. B. (2004). *A comparison of deaf children's comprehension in direct communication and interpreted education.* Unpublished doctoral dissertation, University of Kansas, Lawrence.

Kurz, K. B., & Langer, E. C. (2004). Student perspectives on educational interpreting: Twenty deaf and hard-of-hearing students offer insights and suggestions. In E.A. Winston (Ed.), *Educational interpreting: How it can succeed* (pp. 9–47). Washington, DC: Gallaudet University Press.

La Bue, M. A. (1998). *Interpreted education: A study of deaf students' access to the content and form of literacy instruction in a mainstreamed high school English class.* Unpublished dissertation, Harvard University, Cambridge.

Ladd, G. W. (1990). Having friends, keeping friends, making friends, and being liked by peers in the classroom: Predictors of children's early school adjustment? *Child Development, 61,* 1081–1100.

Lalonde, C. E., & Chandler, M. J. (1995). False belief understanding goes to school—on the social-emotional consequences of coming early or late to a first Theory of Mind. *Cognition and Emotion, 9,* 167–185.

Lang, H. G. (2002). Higher education for deaf students: Research priorities in the new millennium. *Journal of Deaf Studies and Deaf Education, 7,* 267–280.

Lang, H. G. (2003). Perspectives on the history of deaf education. In M. Marschark & P. E. Spencer (Eds.), *Oxford handbook of deaf studies, language, and education* (pp. 9–20). New York: Oxford University Press.

Lang, H. G., Stinson, M. S., Kavanagh, F., Liu, Y., & Basile, M. (1998). Learning styles of deaf college students and teaching behaviors of their instructors. *Journal of Deaf Studies and Deaf Education, 4,* 16–27.

Langer, E. C. (2007). *Classroom discourse and interpreted education: What is conveyed to deaf elementary school students.* Unpublished Doctoral Dissertation, University of Colorado, Boulder.

Lederberg, A. R. (1987). Temporary and long-term friendships in hearing and deaf preschoolers. *Merrill-Palmer Quarterly, 33,* 515–533.

Lederberg, A. R. (1991). Social interaction among deaf preschoolers: The effects of language ability and age. *American Annals of the Deaf, 136,* 53–59.

Leekam, S. (1991). Jokes and lies: Children's understanding of intentional falsehood. In A. Whiten (Ed.), *Natural theories of mind* (pp. 159–174). Oxford, England: Blackwell.

Lew, M., Mesch, D., Johnson, D. W., & Johnson, R. T. (1986). Positive interdependence, academic and collaborative skills and academic group contingencies on achievement and mainstreaming. *American Educational Research Journal, 23,* 476–488.

Lineham, P. (2000). *Educational interpreters for students who are deaf and hard of hearing.* Project Forum at National Association of State Directors of Special Education, Inc.

Livingston, S., Singer, B., & Abramson, T. (1994). Effectiveness compared: ASL interpretation versus transliteration. *Sign Language Studies, 82,* 1–54.

Markman, E. M. (1977). Realizing that you don't understand: A preliminary investigation. *Child Development, 48,* 986–992.

Markman, E. M. (1979). Realizing that you don't understand: Elementary school children's awareness of inconsistencies. *Child Development, 50,* 643–655.

Marschark, M. (2003). Cognitive functioning in deaf adults and children. In M. Marschark and P. E. Spencer (eds.), *Oxford handbook of deaf studies, language, and education* (pp. 464–477). New York: Oxford University Press.

Marschark, M. (2007). *Raising and educating a deaf child, 2nd edition.* New York: Oxford University Press.

Marschark, M., Lang, H. G., & Albertini, J. A. (2002). *Educating deaf students: From research to practice.* New York: Oxford University Press.

Marschark, M., Leigh, G., Sapere, P., Burnham, D., Convertino, C., Stinson, M., Knoors, H., Vervloed, M.P.J., & Noble, W. (2006). Benefits of sign language interpreting and text alternatives for deaf student's classroom learning. *Journal of Deaf Studies and Deaf Education, 11,* 421–437.

Marschark, M., Sapere, P., Convertino, C., Seewagen, R., & Maltzan, H. (2004). Comprehension of sign language interpreting: Deciphering a complex task situation. *Sign Language Studies, 4,* 345–368.

Marschark, M., Sapere, P., Convertino, C., & Seewagen, R. (2005). Access to postsecondary education through sign language interpreting. *Journal of Deaf Studies and Deaf Education, 10,* 38–50.

Marschark, M., & Sapere, P. (2005). Educational interpreting—Does it work as well as we think? In J. Mole (Ed.), *International perspectives on interpreting* (pp. 5–20). Brassington, U.K.: Direct Learned Services Ltd.

Massaro, D., & Shlesinger, M. (1997). Information processing and a computational approach to simultaneous interpreting. *Interpreting, 1,* 12–53.

Mertens, D. M. (1991). Teachers working with interpreters. *American Annals of the Deaf, 136,* 48–52.

Monikowski, C. (2004). Language myths in interpreted education: First language, second language, what language? In E. Winston (Ed.), *Educational interpreting: How it can succeed* (pp. 48–60). Washington, DC: Gallaudet University Press.

Moores, D. F. (1992). A historical perspective on school placement. In T. N. Kluwin, D. F. Moores, & M. G. Gaustad (Eds.), *Toward effective public school programs for deaf students: Context, process, and outcomes* (pp. 7–29). New York: Teachers College, Columbia University.

Moores, D. F. (1996). *Educating the deaf: Psychology, principles, and practices* (4th ed.). Boston: Houghton Mifflin.

Murphy, H. J., & Fleischer, L. R. (1977). The effects of Ameslan versus Siglish upon test scores. *Journal of Rehabilitation of the Deaf, 11,* 15–18.

Napier, J. (2004). Interpreting omissions: A new perspective. *Journal of Research and Practice in Interpreting, 6,* 117–142.

Newcomb, A. F., & Bagwell, C. (1996). The developmental significance of children's friendship relations. In W. M. Buklowski, A. F. Newcomb, & W. W. Hartup (Eds.), *The company they keep: Friendship in childhood and adolescence.* Cambridge, U.K.: Cambridge University Press.

Padden, C., & Ramsey, C. (2000). American Sign Language and reading ability in deaf children. In C. Chamberlain, J. Morford, & R. I. Mayberry (Eds.), *Language acquisition by eye* (pp. 165–189). Mahwah, NJ: Lawrence Erlbaum Associates.

Paul, P. V. (2003). Process and components of reading. In M. Marschark & P. E. Spencer (Eds.), *Oxford handbook of deaf studies, language, and education* (pp. 97–109). New York: Oxford University Press.

Peterson, C. (2004). Theory-of-mind development in oral deaf children with cochlear implants or conventional hearing aids. *Journal of Child Psychology and Psychiatry 45,* 1096–1106.

Piaget, J. (1928). *The child's conception of the world.* London: Routledge.

Portney, L. G., & Watkins, M. P. (2000). *Foundations of clinical research: Applications to practice.* Upper Saddle River, NJ: Prentice Hall Health.

Ramsey, C. L. (1997). *Deaf children in public schools: Placement, context, and consequences.* Washington, DC: Gallaudet University Press.

Ramsey, C. L. (2004). Theoretical tools for educational interpreters, or "The true confession of an ex-educational interpreter." In E. Winston (Ed.), *Educational interpreting: How it can succeed* (pp. 206–226). Washington, DC: Gallaudet University Press.

RID or Registry of Interpreters for the Deaf (2006a). Interpreting and ITP FAQ. http://rid.org/terpfaq.html (Retrieved 2 October 2006).

RID or Registry of Interpreters for the Deaf (2006b). National Interpreter Certification. http://rid.org/nicdescrip.pdf (Retrieved 15 October 2006).

Rogoff, B. (1990). *Apprenticeship in thinking.* Oxford, U.K.: Oxford University Press.

Roy, C. (2000). *Interpreting as a discourse process.* New York: Oxford University Press.

Ryan, A. M. (2000). Peer groups as a context for the socialization of adolescents' motivation, engagement, and achievement in school. *Educational Psychologist 35,* 101–111.

Scheibe, K., & Hoza, J. (1986). Throw it out the window! (The code of ethics? We don't use that here): Guidelines for educational interpreters. In M. L. McIntire (Ed.), *Interpreting: The art of cross-cultural medication: Proceedings of the Ninth National Convention of the Registry of Interpreters for the Deaf* (pp. 173–182). Silver Spring, MD: Registry of Interpreters for the Deaf.

Schick, B. (2004). Educational interpreting and cognitive development in children: Potential relationships. In E. A. Winston (Ed.), *Educational interpreting: How it can succeed* (pp. 73–87). Washington DC: Gallaudet Press.

Schick, B. (2005). Final report: A national program for evaluating educational interpreters (Office of Special Education H325N010013).

Schick, B. (2007). EIPA Written Test. http://www.classroominterpreting.org/EIPA/standards/index.asp (Retrieved 17 July 17 2007).

Schick, B., de Villiers, P., de Villiers, J., & Hoffmeister, R. (2007). Language and theory of mind: A study of deal children. *Child Development, 78,* 376–396.

Schick, B., & Williams, K. (2004). The Educational Interpreter Performance Assessment: Current structure and practices. In E. A. Winston (Ed.), *Educational interpreting: How it can succeed* (pp. 186–205). Washington, DC: Gallaudet Press.

Schick, B., Williams, K., & L. Bolster (1999). Skill levels of educational interpreters. *Journal of Deaf Studies and Deaf Education 4,* 144–155.

Schick, B., Williams, K., & Kupermintz, H. (2006). Look who's being left behind: Educational interpreters and access to education for deaf and hard-of-hearing students. *Journal of Deaf Studies and Deaf Education 11,* 3–20.

Seal, B. C. (1998). Guidelines for inservicing teachers who teach with educational interpreters. *RID Views, 15,* 34–36.

Seal, B. (2000). Working with educational interpreters. *Language, Speech, and Hearing Services in the Schools, 31,* 15–25.

Seal, B. C. (2004). *Best practices in educational interpreting.* Boston, MA: Allyn and Bacon.

Seleskovitch, D. (1992). Fundamentals of the interpretive theory of translation. In J. Plant-Moeller (Ed.), *Expanding horizons* (pp. 1–13). Silver
Spring, MD: Registry of Interpreters for the Deaf.

Setton, R. (1999). *Simultaneous interpreting: A cognitive-pragmatic analysis.*
Philadelphia, PA: John Benjamins Publishing.

Sharan, S. (1990). Cooperative learning: A perspective on research and
practice. In S. Sharan (Ed.), *Cooperative learning: Theory and research*
(pp. 285–300). New York: Praeger Publishers.

Sharan, S., & Shaulov, A. (1990). Cooperative learning, motivation to learn,
and academic achievement. In S. Sharan (Ed.), *Cooperative learning:
Theory and research* (pp. 173–202). New York: Praeger.

Shaw, S., Grbic, N., & Franklin, K. (2004). Applying language skills to interpretation: Student perspectives from signed and spoken language programs. *Interpreting 6,* 69–100.

Shaw, J. A., & Jamieson, J. R. (1997). Patterns of classroom discourse in an integrated elementary setting. *American Annals of the Deaf, 142,* 369–375.

Shroyer, E. H., & Compton, M. V. (1994). Educational interpreting and teacher
preparation: An interdisciplinary approach. *American Annals of the
Deaf, 139,* 472–479.

Sodian, B., Zaitchik, D., & Carey, S. (1991). Young children's differentiation of
hypothetical beliefs from evidence. *Children Development, 62,* 753–766.

Stedt, J. D. (1992). Issues of educational interpreting. In T. N. Kluwin, D. F.
Moores, & M. G. Gaustad (Eds.), *Toward effective public school programs
for deaf students: Context, process, and outcomes* (pp. 83–99). New York:
Teachers College, Columbia University.

Stewart, D., & Kluwin, T. N. (1996). The gap between guidelines, practice,
and knowledge in interpreting services for deaf students. *Journal of Deaf
Studies and Deaf Education, 1,* 29–39.

Stewart, D. A., Schein, J. D., & Cartwright, B. E. (2004). *Sign language interpreting: Exploring its art and science.* Boston, MA: Allyn and Bacon.

Stuckless, R., Avery, J., & Hurwitz, A. (1989). *Educational interpreting for deaf
students: Report of the national task force on educational interpreting.*
Rochester, NY: National Technical Institute for the Deaf/Rochester Institute of Technology.

Traxler, C. B. (2000). The Stanford Achievement Test, 9th edition: National
norming and performance standards for deaf and hard-of-hearing students. *Journal of Deaf Studies and Deaf Education, 5,* 337–348.

Turner, G. H. (2005). Toward real interpreting. In M. Marschark, R. Peterson, &
E. Winston (Eds.), *Sign language interpreting and interpreter education*
(pp. 29–56). New York: Oxford University Press.

Vygotsky, L. S. (1978). *Mind in society: The development of higher psychological processes.* Cambridge, MA: Harvard University Press.

Wellman, H. M., & Lagattuta, K. H. (2004). Theory of mind for learning and
teaching: The nature and role of explanation. *Cognitive Development, 19,*
479–497.

Winston, E. A. (1994). An interpreted education: Inclusion or exclusion? In
R.C. Johnson & O.P. Cohen (Eds.), *Implications and complications for
deaf students of the full inclusion movements* (Gallaudet Research Institute Occasional Paper 94–2). Washington, DC: Gallaudet University
Press.

Winston, E. (2004). Interpretability and accessibility of mainstream class-
    rooms. In E. Winston (Ed.), *Educational interpreting: How it can succeed*
    (pp. 132–167). Washington, DC: Gallaudet Press.
Witter-Merithew, A., & Dirst, R. (1982). Preparation and use of educational
    interpreters. In D. G. Sims, G. G. Walter, & R. L. Whitehead (Eds.), *Deaf
    and communication: Assessment training* (pp. 395–406). Baltimore:
    Williams and Wilkins.
Witter-Merithew, A., & Johnson, L. J. (2005). *Toward competent practice: Con-
    versations with stakeholders.* Alexandria, VA: The Registry of Interpreters
    for the Deaf.
Yuill, N., & Perner, J. (1987). Exceptions to mutual trust: Children's use of
    second-order beliefs in responsibility attribution. *International Journal of
    Behavioral Development, 10,* 207–223.
Zawolkow, E. G., & DeFiore, S. (1986). Educational interpreting for elementary
    and secondary level hearing-impaired students. *American Annals of the
    Deaf, 131,* 26–28.

Chapter 14

Approaches to Studying Among Deaf Students in Higher Education

John T. E. Richardson

There is an established research literature concerned with how students set about learning in higher education. I begin this chapter by briefly reviewing this literature, focusing on the extent to which students' approaches to learning are affected, on the one hand, by their perceptions of their academic context and, on the other hand, by their conceptions of learning and of themselves as learners. Next, I examine the approaches to studying adopted by deaf students being taught in mainstream contexts, in which I conclude that deaf students are more likely than are hearing students to hold a reproductive conception of learning that regards learning in higher education simply as a process of memorizing new information.

This finding could be explained by the kinds of teaching to which deaf students are exposed. There is indeed a parallel research literature concerned with how instructors set about teaching in higher education, and so I briefly review that literature, too. Nevertheless, in mainstream settings, the distinctive characteristic of deaf students who communicate using sign language is that their access to the curriculum is mediated by interpreters. I conclude this chapter by speculating that sign language interpreters adopt a reproductive conception of interpreting that can undermine instructors' attempts to adopt student-centered approaches to teaching and that promotes a reproductive conception of learning in their students.

Approaches to Studying in Higher Education

Interview-based research carried out in Britain and Sweden during the 1970s found that hearing students in higher education tend to adopt two different approaches to studying: an approach that is aimed at understanding the meaning of their course materials, or an approach that is aimed at being able to reproduce those materials for the purposes of assessment (Laurillard, 1979; Marton, 1976). A meaning orientation tends to be associated with good academic performance, whereas a reproducing orientation tends to be associated with poor performance. Nevertheless, the same student can exhibit different approaches to studying in different situations. In general, the choice of one approach over another seems to depend on the content, context, and demands of particular tasks (for a review, see Richardson, 2000, chap. 2).

Various questionnaires were developed to measure approaches to studying in larger numbers of students. Investigations using such instruments confirmed that the same students may adopt different approaches, depending on the demands of different course units (Eley, 1992), the quality of the teaching (Vermetten, Lodewijks, & Vermunt, 1999), and the nature of the assessment (Scouller, 1998). Once again, performance tends to be positively associated with the adoption of a meaning orientation but negatively associated with the adoption of a reproducing orientation, although students whose performance is so poor that they are at risk of failing their courses outright may simply not exhibit any coherent approaches at all (for a review, see Richardson, 2000, p. 183).

Eley (1992) found considerable variability in how different students perceived the demands of the same courses, and this suggests that the impact of contextual factors on students' approaches to studying is mediated by their perceptions of their environment. To measure variations in students' perceptions, Ramsden (1991) devised the Course Experience Questionnaire (CEQ). The original version consisted of 30 items in five scales that had been identified in previous research as reflecting different dimensions of effective instruction. The defining items of each of the five scales are shown in Table 14–1. In each case, the respondents indicate their level of agreement or disagreement with the relevant statement using a 5-point scale. Half of the items refer to positive aspects of courses, but the other half refer to negative aspects and are scored in reverse.

Since 1993, an adapted version of the CEQ has been administered each year to all new graduates from Australian universities. This version only contains 17 of the original 30 items, but it includes a sixth scale concerned with fostering "generic" skills (such as problem solving or teamwork). For research purposes, Wilson, Lizzio, and Ramsden (1997) suggested that the Generic Skills scale should be added to the original CEQ to yield a 36-item questionnaire. Lawless and Richardson (2002) adapted this for use in distance education, replacing the Good Teaching scale by scales relating to Good Materials and Good Tutoring.

Lawless and Richardson also adapted a short version of Ramsden and Entwistle's (1981) Approaches to Studying Inventory (ASI). This instrument contains 32 items in eight subscales measuring a Meaning Orientation and

Table 14–1. Defining Items of the Original Course Experience Questionnaire

Scale	Defining Item
Good Teaching	Teaching staff here normally give helpful feedback on how you are going.
Clear Goals and Standards	You usually have a clear idea of where you're going and what's expected of you in this course.
Appropriate Workload	The sheer volume of work to be got through in this course means you can't comprehend it all thoroughly.[a]
Appropriate Assessment	Staff here seem more interested in testing what we have memorized than what we have understood.[a]
Emphasis on Independence	Students here are given a lot of choice in the work they have to do.

Adapted from Ramsden (1991, p. 134).
[a] Items to be scored in reverse.

a Reproducing Orientation. Table 14–2 provides brief definitions of its constituent subscales. Once again, the respondents indicate their level of agreement or disagreement with each item using a 5-point scale. Lawless and Richardson administered both instruments to students taking three arts courses and three science courses by distance learning with the U.K. Open University and obtained data from roughly 1200 respondents.

They found that the respondents' scores on the CEQ and the ASI shared nearly half of their respective variation, implying a very close association between the two sets of scores. In general, the students' perceptions of the academic quality of their courses were positively correlated with their scores on Meaning Orientation, and they were negatively correlated with their scores on Reproducing Orientation. In other words, students' perceptions of the academic quality of their courses are directly related to their adoption of desirable forms of learning but are inversely related to their adoption of undesirable forms of learning.

These findings have since been replicated in a wide variety of educational contexts, including both campus-based programs (Sadlo & Richardson, 2003) and distance education (Richardson, 2005b), and in academic subjects as diverse as computer science (Richardson & Price, 2003), occupational therapy (Sadlo & Richardson, 2003), and engineering (Richardson, 2006). The results of these investigations are consistent with the idea mentioned earlier: that the effects of contextual factors on students' approaches to learning are mediated by their perceptions of their academic environment. Nevertheless, students still vary in their approaches to studying, even when variations in their perceptions of their courses have been taken into account (Sadlo & Richardson, 2003).

Table 14–2.   Subscales Contained in the 32-Item Approaches to Studying Inventory

Subscale	Definition
Meaning Orientation	
Deep Approach	Active questioning in learning
Interrelating Ideas	Relating to other parts of the course
Use of Evidence	Relating evidence to conclusions
Comprehension Learning	Readiness to map out subject area and think divergently
Reproducing Orientation	
Surface Approach	Preoccupation with memorization
Syllabus-Boundness	Relying on staff to define learning tasks
Improvidence	Overcautious reliance on details
Fear of Failure	Pessimism and anxiety about academic outcomes

Adapted from Ramsden and Entwistle (1981, p. 371).

Conceptions of Learning in Higher Education

One possible explanation for this last finding is that students adopt one approach over another, depending on their conceptions of learning and on their conceptions of themselves as learners. Säljö (1979) asked 90 students aged between 15 and 73 at institutions of postsecondary education in Sweden what "learning" meant to them. He found five different conceptions:

1. Learning as the increase of knowledge
2. Learning as memorising
3. Learning as the acquisition of facts, procedures, etc., which can be retained and/or utilised in practice
4. Learning as the abstraction of meaning
5. Learning as an interpretative process aimed at the understanding of reality (p. 19)

Säljö described Conceptions 1–3 as "reproductive" conceptions of learning, and he described Conceptions 4 and 5 as "reconstructive" conceptions of learning.

Van Rossum and Schenk (1984) carried out a study with 69 psychology students at a university in the Netherlands. They asked the students to read a short text and then to describe how they had approached the task of reading the text and how they approached their studies in general. Van Rossum and Schenk were able to classify the students into Säljö's five conceptions of learning. Most of the students who showed Conceptions

1–3 had adopted a reproducing orientation to read the text, but most of the students who showed Conceptions 4 and 5 had adopted a meaning orientation. In other words, the approaches to studying that students adopt in particular learning tasks are linked to their underlying conceptions of learning.

Van Rossum and Taylor (1987) interviewed 91 arts students at a Dutch university. They confirmed the existence of Säljö's five conceptions of learning, but they found a sixth conception that they characterized as

6. A conscious process, fuelled by personal interests and directed at obtaining harmony and happiness or changing society (p. 19)

Van Rossum and Taylor found that men and women were equally likely to hold these various conceptions of learning, but that older students were more likely than were younger students to hold the more sophisticated Conceptions 4–6.

Martin and Ramsden (1987) used Säljö's scheme to classify 60 first-year history students at two universities in the United Kingdom. Their conceptions of learning were distributed between Conceptions 2 and 5 but were concentrated in Conceptions 3 and 4. (No student exhibited Conception 1.) Nevertheless, there was a direct relationship between the students' conceptions of learning and their academic performance at the end of the year. Those students who achieved the lowest grades all exhibited Säljö's Conceptions 2 or 3, whereas those students who achieved the best grades all exhibited Säljö's Conceptions 4 or 5.

Morgan, Gibbs, and Taylor (1981) also confirmed the existence of Säljö's five conceptions of learning in 29 students who were taking courses by distance learning with the U.K. Open University. Marton, Dall'Alba, and Beaty (1993) followed 10 of these students through their studies over a period of 6 years. In their later years of studying, some showed the sixth conception of learning found by Van Rossum and Taylor, which Marton et al. called "Changing as a person." Marton et al. argued that the six conceptions constituted a hierarchy through which students proceeded during the course of their studies in higher education.

Figure 14–1 summarizes the various relationships that I have described thus far among students' approaches to studying, their conceptions of learning, and their perceptions of their academic environment. This captures the influences on study behavior in science as well as a wide range of other academic disciplines.

Approaches to Studying in Deaf Students

Richardson, MacLeod-Gallinger, McKee, and Long (2000) administered the 32-item version of the ASI to deaf and hearing students at the Rochester

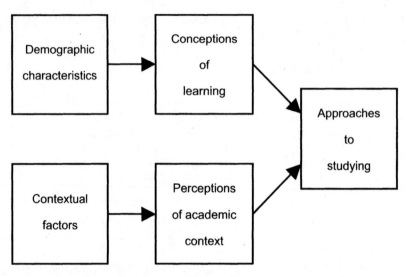

Figure 14–1. An integrated model of students' approaches to studying, conceptions of learning, and perceptions of their academic context (from Richardson, 2005a, p. 676).

Institute of Technology in the United States. They obtained responses from 149 deaf students who were being supported through the National Technical Institute for the Deaf and from 121 hearing students. As in earlier investigations in which the ASI had been used with American students, its subscale structure proved to be qualitatively different in this new context. Even so, the basic distinction between a meaning orientation and a reproducing orientation was preserved.

The deaf students obtained higher scores than did the hearing students on Meaning Orientation, especially in terms of the adoption of a critical approach in their studies and in seeking internal structure in the specific topics being studied. Nevertheless, they also obtained higher scores than did the hearing students on Reproducing Orientation, especially in their anxiety about their academic work and in their level of difficulty in relating together ideas on different topics. The trend for deaf students to obtain higher scores on Reproducing Orientation was more marked in those students who preferred to communicate using sign language (either in addition to speech or in preference to speech).

Although Richardson et al. (2000) identified differences between deaf and hearing students in their approaches to studying, they provided no evidence as to the origins of those differences. In terms of the model shown in Figure 14–1, deaf students might tend to adopt different approaches to studying *either* because they hold different conceptions of learning *or* because they have different perceptions of their courses (or, conceivably, for both these reasons). Research in mainstream higher education has yet to yield a reliable instrument to measure conceptions of learning in large groups of participants (although cf. Richardson, 2007). However, the CEQ provides a robust means of measuring students' perceptions.

Richardson, Barnes, and Fleming (2004) administered the CEQ and the 32-item ASI to 41 deaf students at two universities in the United Kingdom and to 31 hearing students who were taking the same degree programs. The deaf students were classified into those who preferred to communicate using speech, those who preferred to use sign language, those who preferred to use speech accompanied by sign, and those who had no preference between speech and sign, yielding five groups of students in all. Table 14–3 shows the mean scores obtained by these five groups on the eight subscales and the two major scales of the ASI.

Responses to the ASI are coded on a scale from 0 to 4 and then totaled to yield scores on each subscale. Of the eight subscales, five contain four items, and so the possible range of scores is from 0 to 16. However, the Surface Approach subscale contains six items, so that the possible range

Table 14–3.   Mean Scores of Deaf and Hearing Students on the Approaches to Studying Inventory

	Hearing Students	Deaf Students by Communication Preference				Effect Size
		Speech	Sign	Speech with Sign	Speech or Sign	
n	31	10	12	8	11	
Meaning Orientation						
Deep Approach	11.90	11.60	11.83	12.88	12.18	.03
Interrelating Ideas	11.32	12.30	12.17	12.38	11.82	.04
Use of Evidence	10.23	11.00	11.33	12.13	10.45	.05
Comprehension Learning	11.35	8.80*	9.58	11.25	11.36	.11
Total	44.81	43.70	44.92	48.63	45.82	.03
Reproducing Orientation						
Surface Approach	13.23	14.10	17.08**	15.00	16.18*	.17*
Syllabus-Boundness	8.26	9.30	9.92**	8.13	10.09**	.19**
Improvidence	9.10	10.00	10.25	10.88	11.36*	.11
Fear of Failure	6.71	4.60*	7.33	5.75	8.64*	.17*
Total	37.29	38.00	44.58**	39.75	46.27**	.23**

Adapted from Richardson et al. (2004, p. 111). The measure of effect size is eta squared, the proportion of variance in the dependent variable explained by membership of the different groups. Significant effect sizes and significant differences between the deaf students and the hearing students are marked by asterisks.
* $p < .05$; ** $p < .01$.

of scores is from 0 to 24; moreover, the Syllabus-Boundness and Fear of Failure subscales each contain three items, so the possible range of scores is from 0 to 12. Finally, 16 items contribute to each study orientation, and so the possible range of scores for Meaning Orientation and Reproducing Orientation is from 0 to 64.

Comparisons among the scores obtained by different groups of students on a questionnaire may be statistically significant but of little theoretical or practical importance. This can be addressed by computing a measure of the size of the relevant effect (see Richardson, 1996). For each of the scales and subscales, eta squared is provided as a measure of effect size. This expresses the proportion of variance in the scores that is explained by membership of the different groups. Cohen (1988, pp. 285–287) suggested that effect sizes of .0099, .0588, and .1379 should be described as "small," "medium," and "large," respectively.

There was no significant difference between the deaf and hearing students in their scores on Meaning Orientation, and this indicates that deaf students are just as likely as are hearing students to engage with the meaning of their course materials. However, the deaf students obtained significantly higher scores than those of the hearing students on Reproducing Orientation and on three of its constituent subscales. This was specifically a characteristic of those deaf students who preferred to use sign language, either in preference to speech or in addition to speech. In terms of Cohen's (1988) criteria, these effects would be described as large in size and hence of both theoretical and practical importance. In broad terms, these results were consistent with those found by Richardson et al. (2000).

Richardson et al. (2004) noted that the scores obtained by all 72 students on the CEQ shared 68.2% of their variance with their scores on the ASI. At the level of individual students, then, the results confirm the existence of a close relationship between perceptions of academic quality and approaches to studying. However, were the differences between the deaf and hearing students in their scores on the ASI reflected in differences in their scores on the CEQ? Table 14–4 shows the mean scores obtained by the five groups of students on the six scales of the CEQ. The responses are coded on a scale from 1 to 5 and then averaged to yield scores on each scale. Consequently, the possible range of scores is from 1 to 5. Once again, eta squared is provided as a measure of effect size.

The deaf students obtained significantly higher scores than those of the hearing students on the Generic Skills scale and the Emphasis on Independence scale. This was specifically a characteristic of those students who preferred to use sign language or speech accompanied by sign. In terms of Cohen's (1988) criteria, these effects would be described as large in size and thus again of both theoretical and practical importance. In other words, these deaf students were more likely to perceive themselves as gaining generic skills and personal autonomy. Richardson et al. suggested that this

Table 14–4.   Mean Scores of Deaf and Hearing Students on the Course Experience Questionnaire

| | Hearing Students | Deaf Students by Communication Preference | | | | |
		Speech	Sign	Speech with Sign	Speech or Sign	Effect Size
n	31	10	12	8	11	
Appropriate Assessment	3.66	3.55	3.11	3.56	3.50	.05
Appropriate Workload	3.18	2.79	2.83	3.40	2.69	.07
Clear Goals and Standards	3.35	3.48	3.28	3.80	3.38	.03
Generic Skills	3.45	3.82	3.93*	4.08*	3.68	.12
Good Teaching	3.56	3.58	3.76	4.03	3.88	.06
Emphasis on Independence	2.98	3.18	3.56*	3.85**	3.12	.17*

Adapted from Richardson et al. (2004, p. 111). The measure of effect size is eta squared, the proportion of variance in the dependent variable explained by membership of the different groups. Significant effect sizes and significant differences between the deaf students and the hearing students are marked by asterisks.
* $p < .05$; ** $p < .01$.

was a result of the additional learning support that they were receiving in their studies at both the participating universities. Barnes (2006) discussed how this support could enhance students' perceptions and performance.

As was explained earlier, one would expect higher ratings of the academic quality of degree programs to be associated with lower scores on Reproducing Orientation, and yet the deaf students obtained higher scores on the latter scale. This makes it rather implausible that the differences among the five groups in their CEQ scores could explain the differences among the five groups in their ASI scores. To test this notion, analyses of covariance were carried out to control for variations in the students' CEQ scores. Table 14–5 shows the scores obtained by the five groups on the ASI, adjusted for variations in their CEQ scores.

There was still no significant difference between the deaf students and the hearing students in their scores on Meaning Orientation. In addition, the deaf students still obtained significantly higher scores than did the hearing students on Reproducing Orientation and on two of its constituent scales. As before, this was specifically a characteristic of deaf students who preferred to use sign language, either in preference to speech or in addition to speech. In terms of Cohen's (1988) criteria, these effects would again be described as large in size and hence of both theoretical and practical importance.

These results show that deaf students are more likely than hearing students to adopt a reproducing orientation, even when variations in their perceptions have been statistically controlled. Referring to the model in Figure 14–1, this suggests that deaf students are more likely to adopt a

Table 14–5. Mean Scores of Deaf and Hearing Students on the Approaches to Studying Inventory, Adjusted for Variations in Scores on the Course Experience Questionnaire

| | Hearing Students | Deaf Students by Communication Preference | | | | Effect Size |
		Speech	Sign	Speech with Sign	Speech or Sign	
n	31	10	12	8	11	
Meaning Orientation						
Deep Approach	12.08	11.57	11.75	12.54	12.05	.02
Interrelating Ideas	11.57	12.33	11.93	12.08	11.57	.02
Use of Evidence	10.87	10.78	10.68	11.32	10.15	.01
Comprehension Learning	11.31	8.90*	9.79	11.59	10.91	.09
Total	45.83	43.57	44.15	47.52	44.67	.03
Reproducing Orientation						
Surface Approach	13.31	13.60	17.07**	15.88	15.79*	.16*
Syllabus-Boundness	8.44	9.27	9.44	7.73	10.41**	.19**
Improvidence	9.52	9.99	9.51	10.75	11.08	.07
Fear of Failure	6.89	4.45*	7.01	6.12	8.36	.16*
Total	36.16	37.32	43.02*	40.47	45.64**	.19*

Unpublished data from Richardson et al. (2004). Significant effect sizes and significant differences between the deaf students and the hearing students are marked by asterisks.
* $p < .05$; ** $p < .01$.

reproducing orientation, not because they rate their courses less positively than do hearing students, but because they are more likely than hearing students to hold reproductive conceptions of learning.

Approaches to Teaching in Higher Education

How do students acquire more sophisticated conceptions of learning? The fact that older students are more likely to exhibit reconstructive conceptions than are younger students (Van Rossum & Taylor, 1987) indicates that life experience itself is an important factor. However, Säljö (1979) suggested that reconstructive conceptions were more likely to be found in students who had had experience of higher education. Accordingly, if deaf students are more likely than are hearing students to hold reproductive conceptions of learning, perhaps this is a result of their experiences in the classroom and in particular of how they are taught.

Research into instructors' approaches to teaching in higher education was directly modeled on the concepts, methods, and findings of research on students' approaches to learning. Trigwell and Prosser (1993) interviewed 24 instructors on first-year courses in chemistry and physics at Australian universities. They found five approaches to teaching among the instructors that were differentiated in terms of their intentions and teaching strategies. Some approaches were teacher-focused and were aimed at the transmission of knowledge to the students, but others were student-focused and aimed at bringing about conceptual change in the students.

Prosser and Trigwell (1993) then developed the Approaches to Teaching Inventory (ATI) to measure the teaching behavior of large numbers of instructors. Trigwell, Prosser, and Waterhouse (1999) showed that students whose instructors adopted a student-focused approach judged by their scores on the ATI were more likely to adopt a meaning orientation and were less likely to adopt a reproducing orientation than were those whose instructors adopted a teacher-focused approach. In other words, a student-focused approach to teaching engenders more desirable forms of learning in the students than does a teacher-focused approach.

Prosser and Trigwell (1997) also devised the Perceptions of the Teaching Environment Inventory to measure various aspects of the perceived teaching context. They found a close relationship between instructors' perceptions of their teaching context and their approaches to teaching according to their scores on the ATI. In particular, the instructors who adopted a student-focused approach were more likely than the instructors who adopted a teacher-focused approach to report that their departments valued teaching, that their class sizes were not too large, and that they had control over what was taught and how it was taught.

Lindblom-Ylänne, Trigwell, Nevgi, and Ashwin (2006) devised a Finnish translation of the ATI, using back-translation into English to ensure the accuracy of the translation. They asked university instructors in Finland to complete the Finnish version of the ATI with regard to their regular teaching context and then a second time with regard to a less usual context of their own choosing. They found that the instructors tended to adopt a more student-focused approach in the less usual teaching context than they did in their regular context. The difference in question was relatively modest, which might be due to the fact that the researchers had no control over the instructors' choice of alternative contexts.

Even so, the results obtained by Lindblom-Ylänne et al. (2006) are consistent with the idea that the same instructors may adopt different approaches to teaching in different teaching contexts. Further evidence on this matter was obtained in an unpublished survey of instructors of sign language and sign language interpreting in the United States (Winston, 2005). Among other things, the participants were asked to describe their favorite or most effective teaching activity and discuss why it had been successful, and they were similarly asked to describe their least favorite or effective teaching activity and discuss why it had not been successful.

The favorite activities were often examples of student-focused teaching that was intended to develop skills of critical thinking, decision making, or self-assessment in the students. Sometimes these were activities that were not directly linked to any formal assessment. The least favorite activities were often examples of teacher-focused teaching or of a teacher-focused evaluation of the students' performance. Typically, these were activities that the instructors felt had to be carried out in a specific way to comply with institutional or other external requirements. These results tend to support the notion that instructors' approaches to teaching are influenced by their perceptions of their teaching environment.

Conceptions of Teaching in Higher Education

Even when they are confronted with the same teaching context, however, different instructors may still adopt different approaches to teaching. Researchers have argued that approaches to teaching reflect different underlying conceptions of teaching (for a review, see Norton, Richardson, Hartley, Newstead, & Mayes, 2005). Indeed, interview-based investigations have identified several different conceptions. Kember (1997) reviewed these studies and suggested that most of them converged on five different conceptions of teaching:

1. Teaching as imparting information
2. Teaching as transmitting structured knowledge
3. Teaching as an interaction between the instructor and the student
4. Teaching as facilitating understanding on the part of the student
5. Teaching as bringing about conceptual change and intellectual development in the student.

Surveys of instructors in the United States have found that beliefs about teaching vary markedly across different disciplines and that these variations are related to the instructors' beliefs about the nature of the discipline that they are teaching (Braxton & Hargens, 1996; Stark, Lowther, Bentley, & Martens, 1990; Stark, Lowther, Ryan, & Genthon, 1988). In a questionnaire-based study carried out in the United Kingdom, Norton et al. (2005) found that instructors teaching the same discipline at different institutions had relatively similar conceptions of teaching, but that conceptions of teaching varied across different disciplines. In particular, science teachers attached more importance than arts or social science teachers to training students for jobs but less importance to interactive teaching.

The previous section referred to an interview-based study by Trigwell and Prosser (1993), who identified different approaches to teaching in 24 instructors of first-year chemistry and physics. They also asked the instructors about their conceptions of teaching and their students' conceptions of learning. Exploring these data further, Trigwell and Prosser (1996) found that instructors who held a particular conception of teaching tended to adopt a commensurate approach to teaching and to ascribe an analogous conception of learning to their own students. Thus, instructors who held a student-centered and learning-oriented *conception* of teaching were more likely to adopt a student-focused *approach* to teaching and more likely to ascribe reconstructive conceptions of learning to their students.

Nevertheless, more than half of the instructors in this study described approaches to teaching that were less learner-focused and more teacher-focused than would have been expected from their reported conceptions of teaching. This drift toward more teacher-focused approaches to teaching and away from more learner-focused approaches to teaching was confirmed in the study by Norton et al. (2005). It suggests that contextual factors tend to frustrate instructors' attempts to adopt student-centered approaches to teaching. For example, senior professors who hold traditional, teacher-focused conceptions of teaching might raise issues about standards and coverage of the curriculum (e.g., Estes, 1999), or the students themselves might induce their instructors to adopt a more didactic approach to teaching (e.g., Newman, 2004).

Figure 14–2 summarizes the various relationships that I have described thus far among instructors' approaches to teaching, their conceptions of teaching, and their perceptions of their teaching environment. This captures

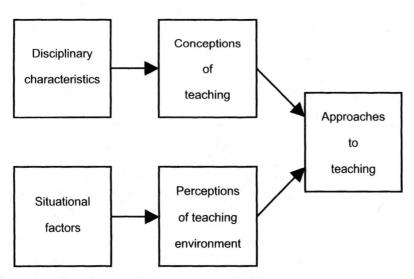

Figure 14–2. An integrated model of instructors' approaches to teaching, conceptions of teaching, and perceptions of the teaching environment (from Richardson 2005a, p. 679).

the influences on teaching behavior in science as well as a range of other academic disciplines. All the research on these topics has been concerned with hearing instructors teaching hearing students in mainstream educational settings. There is no research into whether deaf or hearing instructors have different approaches, conceptions, or perceptions when working with deaf students in mainstream or separated settings.

In Chapter 11 of this volume, Hauser, Lukomski, and Hillman refer to analogous studies of deaf and hearing teachers teaching deaf and hearing children in K–12 settings. In Chapter 13, Schick also mentions a study by Ramsey (1997) in which a K–12 teacher reported having difficulty in connecting with deaf students because they paid attention to the sign language interpreter rather than to her. This raises the possibility that, in higher education, hearing instructors adopt teacher-focused approaches to teaching when teaching deaf students and that this in turn causes deaf students to hold reproductive conceptions of learning. At present, however, we simply have no evidence on this matter one way or the other.

Approaches to Sign Language Interpreting in Higher Education

When deaf students take classes in mainstream educational settings, they are often taught by hearing instructors supported by sign language interpreters. In Chapter 13, Schick cites a study by Kurz and Langer (2004) involving deaf and hard-of-hearing students at all levels from elementary school to graduate school. Some reported a preference for teacher-focused activities such as lectures simply because of the practical problems inherent in learning through interpreters from group discussion. A more fundamental possibility, however, is that deaf students adopt particular approaches to studying and particular conceptions of learning because of the different ways in which educational interpreters construe their role.

The interpreter's task is to translate the instructor's message (the source information) into its sign language equivalent (the target information) and also to facilitate communications between the deaf students and the instructor. Linguists distinguish two approaches to interpretation: In *literal* translation, "the linguistic structure of the source text is followed, but is normalized according to the rules of the target language"; in *free* translation, "the linguistic structure of the source language is ignored and an equivalent is found based on the meaning it conveys" (Crystal, 1987, p. 344).

Pollitt (2000) argued that effective interpreting required the judicious use of both approaches:

> The student studying . . . English Literature will not benefit from a free, discourse (interactive) type interpretation of a Shakespearean text if the purpose is to memorise it verbatim for the forthcoming exam.

> Of course, many . . . English Literature classroom discussions focus on understanding the purpose and meaning of whole chunks of Shakespeare, and here the interpreter will be required to tread carefully, choosing interactive or literal interpreting strategies as appropriate. (p. 62)

This assumes that approaches to interpreting are under the instructor's strategic control and can be adapted to meet the demands of different teaching contexts.

But what do interpreters actually do in higher education contexts? Napier (2002) video recorded a lecture on sign language acquisition in deaf children and asked 10 interpreters with experience of university interpreting to translate it into Australian Sign Language, as if to support a deaf university student. She video recorded their output and randomly chose three interpreted sentences from each interpreter for analysis. Each of the sentences was classified as exhibiting a literal interpretation style or a free interpretation style, and the interpreters were classified as having a literal approach or a free approach depending on whether their sentences exhibited a literal interpretation style or a free interpretation style.

Five of the 10 interpreters showed both approaches, and this is consistent with the idea that approaches to interpretation can be adapted to the demands of different contexts. More specifically, the interpreters tended to switch from a free approach to a literal approach if the lexical density of the source text increased. However, the other five interpreters consistently used one approach over the other (at least, within the three interpreted sentences that were sampled). This shows that different interpreters adopt different approaches to interpreting even when they are interpreting the same source text in the same teaching context.

Napier concluded that "there did not seem to be any major relationships between the translation style and level of education of each interpreter" (p. 289). In fact, her data are at least indicative of such an association. On the one hand, two interpreters had no postsecondary qualifications, and both exclusively used a literal approach. On the other hand, the other eight interpreters had qualifications of an undergraduate or postgraduate nature, and six of these interpreters used a free approach (in two cases, exclusively). It would thus appear that interpreters who themselves have experience of higher education are more likely to adopt a free approach when interpreting in the context of higher education.

Conceptions of Sign Language Interpreting in Higher Education

The observation that different interpreters adopt different approaches to interpreting even when they are interpreting the same lecture suggests that their approaches reflect different underlying conceptions of sign language interpreting. One would therefore like to know more about interpreters' conceptions of sign language interpreting and about their conceptions of themselves as sign language interpreters. As Marschark, Sapere, Convertino, and Seewagen (2005) remarked, "Study of educational interpreters' beliefs about what they are doing and why would be most informative" (p. 78).

Unfortunately, as Cokely (2005) complained: "To date there continues to be a lack of coordinated, basic research that can inform the practice of interpreting and transliterating and the preparation of interpreters and transliterators" (p. 16). A literature search by Seal (2004, pp. 195–196) of refereed publications between 1988 and 2002 yielded only 18 articles concerned with sign language interpreting in postsecondary educational settings, and most were purely descriptive accounts. Salevsky (1993) suggested that interpreters themselves were reluctant to allow their work to be investigated and denied the very need for such research. It might be noted that the single study by Napier (2002) on approaches to interpreting was based on behavioral analyses of interpreting rather than on self-reports collected through interviews or questionnaires administered to interpreters themselves.

Roy (1993) considered the ways in which sign language interpreters talked about interpreting. She remarked that professional interpreters often talked about themselves as some kind of neutral communication link, as "a kind of channel or bridge through which communication between two people can happen" (p. 133). Roy maintained that this notion assumed "extreme personal non-involvement by the interpreter" (p. 137), and she captured this idea by the metaphor of a conduit. This can arguably be characterized as a "reproductive" conception of interpreting.

Roy suggested that this conception was particularly prevalent among sign language interpreters because their expectations were "built on monologic, public situations where the flow of the message is basically one-way and the receiver is seen as passive," such as formal conference presentations. These situations were "the most visible, most publicized, and most accessible to public notice, scrutiny, and research studies" (p. 149). In these situations, it is perhaps quite reasonable to expect an interpreter to be impartial and detached and to concentrate on delivering an accurate translation of the presenter's message.

Roy argued that the conduit model persisted, especially in the context of interpreter education:

> The assumption at work here is that, if the only requirement for doing interpreting is to transform the surface tokens of one language to the surface tokens of the other language, then speed and the tokens are the only things to be mastered. The focus of training also rests on the superficial physical aspects of the communication event which reinforce the notion that the interpreter's task is largely mechanical and that the interpreter's role in the event is passive. (p. 146)

Cokely (2005), too, argued that interpreter training programs adopted quantitative notions of accuracy, emphasizing the maintenance of temporal synchrony with the original message, regardless of the level of comprehension in the audience.

A specific implication of the conduit model is that educational interpreters have no real contribution to make to the process of teaching and learning in higher education. This is a notion that Schick discusses in the context of K–12 education in Chapter 13 of this volume. In addition, any sign language interpreter who takes monologic public situations as the model for educational interpreting is effectively endorsing a teacher-focused conception of teaching. Thus, educational interpreters may seek to be neutral in their role as interpreters, but they cannot be neutral in their role as mediators of teaching and learning. Schick argues that, in practice, interpreters make implicit assumptions about the relevance of different kinds of classroom communication, leading them to distort or omit utterances on the part of the teacher that they consider to be extraneous to the learning process.

Roy (1993) went on to argue that most interpreters worked, not in large monologic settings, but in smaller settings that involved face-to-face interaction between the various participants. She characterized these events as "intercultural and interpersonal rather than simply mechanical and technical" (p. 151). As a consequence, interpreters would need to take an active role that required extreme personal involvement as opposed to extreme noninvolvement. This can arguably be characterized as a "reconstructive" conception of interpreting. Indeed, Roy suggested that "most interpreters now recognize different interpretations of roles and functions that grow from smaller, 'real-life' situations in which the interpreter must take an active, participatory stance" (p. 149; see also Roy, 2000).

In these situations, Metzger (1999, pp. 157–160) pointed out that sign language interpreters who confine themselves to giving literal translations of spoken messages will omit the paralinguistic information normally accessible in interactive discourse (such as a speaker's tone of voice or direction of gaze). This undermines the notion that they are simply neutral conduits, because they may fail to communicate key aspects of the speaker's meaning. Interpreters who provide free translations will convey this information by generating their own additional utterances. Thus, by taking an active role that anticipates the participants' needs, they render interactions much more similar to regular monolingual discourse.

Turner and Harrington (2001), too, argued that the interpreter could not be a conduit:

> Interpreting isn't like this—if you're honest, goes the message to practitioners, then however much you cling to the *idea,* you know that you don't *actually* operate in accordance with it in your own practice (and physically, nor could you) and anyway you wouldn't be able to do a very effective job if interpreting *were* like this. (p. xi)

Dean and Pollard (2005) adopted a similar stance in opposition "to those who hold perceptions of interpreting work as a near literal process of transposition between languages" (p. 265).

However, saying "interpreting isn't like this" leaves it wholly mysterious why many sign language interpreters should articulate the conduit model and why many interpreting educators still seek to inculcate that model into their students. Roy pointed out that it might be disguised behind the language of communication theory as a model about human information processing. For instance, Marschark, Sapere, and Seewagen (2005) stated that in educational interpreting "interpreters are supposed to facilitate the effective flow of classroom communication" (p. vi). This still assumes that there is something neutral called "information" that can be passed from the instructor to the student. My own impression is that the conduit model is indeed alive and well, even if it sometimes wears different clothes.

Figure 14–3 summarizes the various relationships that I have proposed to exist among interpreters' approaches to interpreting, their conceptions of interpreting, and their perceptions of the interpreting context.

Summary and Implications

Hearing students in higher education adopt different approaches to their studies: Some adopt an approach oriented toward the meaning of their course materials; others adopt an approach oriented toward being able to

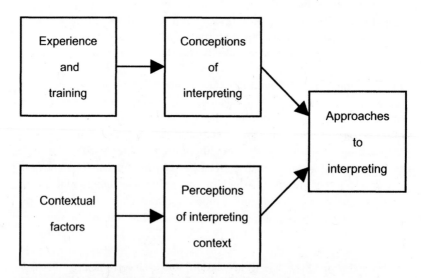

Figure 14–3. An integrated model of sign language interpreters' approaches to interpreting, conceptions of interpreting, and perceptions of the interpreting context.

reproduce the course materials for the purposes of academic assessment. These approaches to studying are influenced by their perceptions of their academic context, such that students who have more positive perceptions of the quality of their courses are more likely to adopt desirable approaches to studying. However, they are also influenced by their underlying conceptions of learning (see Figure 14–1).

There are very few studies concerned with the approaches, conceptions, and perceptions of deaf students. Nevertheless, investigations in both the United States and the United Kingdom have found that deaf students exhibit a meaning orientation and a reproducing orientation to their studies, but that, in comparison with hearing students, they are more likely to exhibit a reproducing orientation. This is not because they perceive their courses as lower in academic quality: On the contrary, they may rate their courses more highly because of the additional forms of learning support that they receive in their studies.

When variations in the students' perceptions of their academic context are statistically controlled, deaf students still tend to be more likely than are hearing students to adopt a reproducing orientation. This was reflected in an effect that would be regarded as being of both theoretical and practical importance, but it was obtained in a single study with relatively modest samples of students, and it is therefore in urgent need of replication. However, it suggests that deaf students are more likely to hold a reproductive conception of learning and less likely to hold a reconstructive conception of learning than are hearing students.

Equally, hearing instructors in higher education adopt different approaches to teaching. Some adopt a teacher-focused approach based on the transmission of information, but others adopt a student-focused approach based on bringing about conceptual change in their students. These approaches to teaching are influenced by their perceptions of their teaching context, such that instructors who feel that their departments value teaching, that their class sizes are not too large, and that they have control over their teaching are more likely to adopt a student-focused approach and are less likely to adopt a teacher-focused approach. Nevertheless, instructors' approaches to teaching are also influenced by their underlying conceptions of teaching (see Figure 14–2).

No research evidence exists on whether deaf or hearing instructors have different approaches, conceptions, or perceptions when instructing deaf or hearing students in mainstream or separated settings. One can easily envisage a host of worthwhile studies using both quantitative and qualitative methods to investigate such issues. Nevertheless, my purpose in describing the research on approaches, conceptions, and perceptions of teaching was to encourage readers to envisage the possibility of investigations into the approaches and conceptions of sign language interpreting that are held by sign language interpreters.

When supporting hearing instructors who are teaching deaf students in a mainstream setting, interpreters adopt different approaches to interpreting: Some adopt a literal approach, but others adopt a free approach. These approaches are influenced by at least certain characteristics of the interpreting context, in that some interpreters adapt their approach to the linguistic properties of the source text. Some writers have argued that sign language interpreters should also be able to adapt their approach in order to achieve different learning outcomes, but there is no research evidence that this actually occurs in real-life interpreting situations. Nevertheless, interpreters' approaches to interpreting also seem to be influenced by their underlying conceptions of interpreting (see Figure 14–3).

The literature on sign language interpreting describes two conceptions of interpreting: a reproductive conception based on the idea that the interpreter is a passive, neutral communication link or conduit, and a reconstructive conception based on the idea that the interpreter is an active, engaged participant. It has been argued that the training and assessment of interpreters have traditionally promoted the reproductive conception, but that the demands of real-life interpreting contexts are accommodated better by the reconstructive conception. Clearly, all these ideas stand in need of validation through empirical investigations.

Even so, these ideas have important pedagogical implications, especially when one considers the relationship between an instructor's approach to teaching and an interpreter's approach to interpreting. Earlier, it was noted that instructors with a reproductive conception of teaching are likely to adopt a teacher-centered approach to teaching that promotes a reproducing orientation in the students. Equally, an interpreter with a reproductive conception of interpreting is likely to adopt a literal approach to interpreting that in turn promotes a reproducing orientation among deaf students who prefer to communicate using sign language.

Instructors who have a reconstructive conception of teaching may adopt a student-focused approach to teaching that promotes a meaning orientation and aims at bringing about conceptual change in the students. They may succeed in the case of hearing students and deaf students who communicate using speech. However, their attempts may well be undermined in the case of deaf students who communicate using sign, if their interpreters adopt a literal approach to their task. If these students are repeatedly exposed to a literal approach to interpreting, it is also likely that they will persist in holding a reproductive conception of learning.

The silver lining behind this cloud is that the converse can also be argued. An interpreter who holds a reconstructive conception of interpreting is likely to adopt a free approach to interpreting, to be an active participant in the classroom, and to take into account the students' needs and expectations. This may promote a meaning orientation among deaf students who prefer to communicate using sign language and encourage them to acquire a reconstructive conception of learning. (It might even compensate for instructors who adopt a teacher-centered approach to teaching.) However, this can only be achieved if interpreter education not only promotes a reconstructive conception of interpreting but also provides interpreters with an appreciation of the processes of teaching and learning in higher education.

Acknowledgments

Parts of this chapter are based on the article cited as Richardson (2005a). I am most grateful to Peter Ashworth, Marc Marschark, and Christine Monikowski for discussions that led to the ideas expressed here. I am also grateful to Lynne Barnes and Joan Fleming for their comments on a previous draft of this chapter.

References

Barnes, L. (2006). Formal qualifications for language tutors in higher education: A case for discussion. *Deafness and Education International, 8,* 106–124.

Braxton, J. M. & Hargens, L. L. (1996). Variations among academic disciplines: Analytical frameworks and research. In J. C. Smart (Ed.), *Higher education: Handbook of theory and research* (Vol. 11, pp. 1–46). New York: Agathon Press.

Cohen, J. (1988). *Statistical power analysis for the behavioral sciences* (2nd ed.). Hillsdale, NJ: Erlbaum.

Cokely, D. (2005). Shifting positionality: A critical examination of the turning point in the relationship of interpreters and the Deaf Community. In M. Marschark, R. Peterson, & E. A. Winston (Eds.), *Sign language interpreting and interpreter education: Directions for research and practice* (pp. 3–28). New York: Oxford University Press.

Crystal, D. (1987). *The Cambridge encyclopedia of language.* Cambridge, U.K.: Cambridge University Press.

Dean, R. K., & Pollard, R. Q., Jr. (2005). Consumers and service effectiveness in interpreting work: A practice profession perspective. In M. Marschark, R. Peterson, & E. A. Winston (Eds.), *Sign language interpreting and interpreter education: Directions for research and practice* (pp. 259–282). New York: Oxford University Press.

Eley, M. G. (1992). Differential adoption of study approaches within individual students. *Higher Education, 23,* 231–254.

Estes, D. M. (1999, August). *Issues in problem-based learning.* Paper presented at the annual meeting of the National Council of Professors of Educational Administration, Jackson Hole, WY. (ERIC Document Reproduction Service No. ED450469.)

Kember, D. (1997). A reconceptualisation of the research into university academics' conceptions of teaching. *Learning and Instruction, 7,* 255–275.

Kurz, K. B., & Langer, E. C. (2004). Student perspectives on educational interpreting: Twenty deaf and hard of hearing students offer insights and suggestions. In E. A. Winston (Ed.), *Educational interpreting: How it can succeed* (pp. 9–47). Washington, DC: Gallaudet University Press.

Laurillard, D. (1979). The processes of student learning. *Higher Education, 8,* 395–409.

Lawless, C. J., & Richardson, J. T. E. (2002). Approaches to studying and perceptions of academic quality in distance education. *Higher Education, 44,* 257–282.

Lindblom-Ylänne, S., Trigwell, K., Nevgi, A., & Ashwin, P. (2006). How approaches to teaching are affected by discipline and teaching context. *Studies in Higher Education, 31,* 285–298.

Marschark, M., Sapere, P., Convertino, C., & Seewagen, R. (2005). Educational interpreting: Access and outcomes. In M. Marschark, R. Peterson, & E. A. Winston (Eds.), *Sign language interpreting and interpreter education: Directions for research and practice* (pp. 57–83). New York: Oxford University Press.

Marschark, M., Sapere, P., & Seewagen, R. (2005). Preface. In M. Marschark, R. Peterson, & E. A. Winston (Eds.), *Sign language interpreting and interpreter education: Directions for research and practice* (pp. v–x). New York: Oxford University Press.

Martin, E., & Ramsden, P. (1987). Learning skills, or skill in learning? In J. T. E. Richardson, M. W. Eysenck, & D. Warren Piper (Eds.), *Student learning: Research in education and cognitive psychology* (pp. 155–167). Milton Keynes, U.K.: Society for Research into Higher Education & Open University Press.

Marton, F. (1976). What does it take to learn? Some implications of an alternative view of learning. In N. Entwistle (Ed.), *Strategies for research and development in higher education* (pp. 32–42). Amsterdam: Swets & Zeitlinger.

Marton, F., Dall'Alba, G., & Beaty, E. (1993). Conceptions of learning. *International Journal of Educational Research, 19,* 277–300.

Metzger, M. (1999). *Sign language interpreting: Deconstructing the myth of neutrality.* Washington, DC: Gallaudet University Press.

Morgan, A., Gibbs, G., & Taylor, E. (1981). *What do Open University students initially understand about learning?* (Study Methods Group Report No. 8). Milton Keynes: The Open University, Institute of Educational Technology. (ERIC Document Reproduction Service No. ED 203 748.)

Napier, J. (2002). University interpreting: Linguistic issues for consideration. *Journal of Deaf Studies and Deaf Education, 7,* 281–301.

Newman, M. (2004). *Problem-based learning: An exploration of the method and evaluation of its effectiveness in a continuing nursing education programme.* London: Middlesex University.

Norton, L., Richardson, J. T. E., Hartley, J., Newstead, S., & Mayes, J. (2005). Teachers' beliefs and intentions concerning teaching in higher education. *Higher Education, 50,* 537–571.

Pollitt, K. (2000). On babies, bathwater and approaches to interpreting. *Deaf Worlds, 16,* 60–64.

Prosser, M., & Trigwell, K. (1993). Development of an Approaches to Teaching questionnaire. *Research and Development in Higher Education, 15,* 468–473.

Prosser, M., & Trigwell, K. (1997). Relations between perceptions of the teaching environment and approaches to teaching. *British Journal of Educational Psychology, 67,* 25–35.

Ramsden, P. (1991). A performance indicator of teaching quality in higher education: The Course Experience Questionnaire. *Studies in Higher Education, 16,* 129–150.

Ramsden, P., & Entwistle, N. J. (1981). Effects of academic departments on students' approaches to studying. *British Journal of Educational Psychology, 51,* 368–383.

Ramsey, C. L. (1997). *Deaf children in public schools: Placement, context, and consequences.* Washington, DC: Gallaudet University Press.

Richardson, J. T. E. (1996). Measures of effect size. *Behavior Research Methods, Instruments, and Computers, 28,* 12–22.

Richardson, J. T. E. (2000). *Researching student learning: Approaches to studying in campus-based and distance education.* Buckingham, U.K.: Society for Research into Higher Education and Open University Press.

Richardson, J. T. E. (2005a). Students' approaches to learning and teachers' approaches to teaching in higher education. *Educational Psychology, 25,* 673–680.

Richardson, J. T. E. (2005b). Students' perceptions of academic quality and approaches to studying in distance education. *British Educational Research Journal, 31,* 7–27.

Richardson, J. T. E. (2006). Perceptions of academic quality and approaches to studying among technology students in distance education. *European Journal of Engineering Education, 31,* 421–433.

Richardson, J. T. E. (2007). Mental models of learning in distance education. *British Journal of Educational Psychology, 77,* 253–270.

Richardson, J. T. E., Barnes, L., & Fleming, J. (2004). Approaches to studying and perceptions of academic quality in deaf and hearing students in higher education. *Deafness and Education International, 6,* 100–122.

Richardson, J. T. E., MacLeod-Gallinger, J., McKee, B. G., & Long, G. L. (2000). Approaches to studying in deaf and hearing students in higher education. *Journal of Deaf Studies and Deaf Education, 5,* 156–173.

Richardson, J. T. E., & Price, L. (2003). Approaches to studying and perceptions of academic quality in electronically delivered courses. *British Journal of Educational Technology, 34,* 45–56.

Roy, C. B. (1993). The problem with definitions, descriptions, and the role metaphors of interpreters. *Journal of Interpretation, 6,* 127–154.

Roy, C. B. (2000). *Interpreting as a discourse process.* New York: Oxford University Press.

Sadlo, G., & Richardson, J. T. E. (2003). Approaches to studying and perceptions of the academic environment in students following problem-based and subject-based curricula. *Higher Education Research and Development, 22,* 253–274.

Salevsky, H. (1993). The distinctive nature of interpreting studies. *Target, 5,* 149–167.

Säljö, R. (1979). *Learning in the learner's perspective: I. Some common-sense assumptions* (Report No. 76). Göteborg, Sweden: University of Göteborg, Institute of Education.

Scouller, K. (1998). The influence of assessment method on students' learning approaches: Multiple choice question examination versus assignment essay. *Higher Education, 35,* 453–472.

Seal, B. C. (2004). *Best practices in educational interpreting* (2nd ed.). Boston: Allyn & Bacon.

Stark, J. S., Lowther, M. A., Bentley, R. J., & Martens, G. G. (1990). Disciplinary differences in course planning. *Review of Higher Education, 13,* 141–165.

Stark, J. S., Lowther, M. A., Ryan, M. P., & Genthon, M. (1988). Faculty reflect on course planning. *Research in Higher Education, 29,* 219–240.

Trigwell, K., & Prosser, M. (1993). Approaches adopted by teachers of first year university science courses. *Research and Development in Higher Education, 14,* 223–228.

Trigwell, K., & Prosser, M. (1996). Changing approaches to teaching: A relational perspective. *Studies in Higher Education, 21,* 275–284.

Trigwell, K., Prosser, M., & Waterhouse, F. (1999). Relations between teachers' approaches to teaching and students' approaches to learning. *Higher Education, 37,* 57–70.

Turner, G. H., & Harrington, F. J. (2001). The campaign for real interpreting. In F. J. Harrington & G. H. Turner (Eds.), *Interpreting interpreting* (pp. vi–xiv). Coleford, U.K.: Douglas McLean.

Van Rossum, E. J., & Schenk, S. M. (1984). The relationship between learning conception, study strategy and learning outcome. *British Journal of Educational Psychology, 54,* 73–83.

Van Rossum, E. J., & Taylor, I. P. (1987, April). *The relationship between conceptions of learning and good teaching: A scheme of cognitive development.* Paper presented at the annual meeting of the American Educational Research Association, Washington DC.

Vermetten, Y. J., Lodewijks, H. G., & Vermunt, J. D. (1999). Consistency and variability of learning strategies in different university courses. *Higher Education, 37,* 1–21.

Wilson, K. L., Lizzio, A., & Ramsden, P. (1997). The development, validation and application of the Course Experience Questionnaire. *Studies in Higher Education, 22,* 33–53.

Winston, E. A. (2005). Designing a curriculum for American Sign Language/English interpreting educators. In M. Marschark, R. Peterson, & E. A. Winston (Eds.), *Sign language interpreting and interpreter education: Directions for research and practice* (pp. 208–234). New York: Oxford University Press.

Chapter 15

A New Research Agenda
for Writing-to-Learn

Embedding Cognition in Discipline

Lisa M. Hermsen and Scott V. Franklin

At the turn of the twentieth century, when open admissions and professional curricula increased, the rhetorical training in a "gentleman's education" was replaced by "basic writing," compartmentalized in English departments (Russell, 1991). In nineteenth-century education, classical rhetorical training had been embedded as disputation throughout a curriculum according to the tradition of Hugh Blair, Chair of Rhetoric and *Belles Lettres* at the University of Edinburgh and one of the first great theorists of written (as opposed to oral) discourse. Prior to the advent of mass education in the modern American university, no first-year classes and no research field were available in "composition."

Early in the twentieth century, for the first time, systematized writing instruction was delivered in first-year composition classes that emphasized "plain style" for a "general reader." Despite this directed attention to writing instruction, by the latter half of the twentieth century, educators, administrators, and politicians alike bemoaned a so-called crisis in literacy, complaining that students were not, in fact, learning to write by the time they graduated from college. Special writing instruction for emerging writers (writers using a nonstandard form of written English), "basic writers," and English as a-Second-Language (ESL) students was supported by new Writing Labs offering "tutoring" for grammatical correctness and attempting to provide necessary remediation. Nevertheless, writing instruction, particularly for deaf students, was limited to instruction in grammatical and lexical usage. This "current-traditional" model focused nearly all attention on handbook exercises and sentence-modeling, leaving behind the rhetorical skills associated with written tasks. Eventually, writing instruction for emerging, basic, ESL, and deaf students would emphasize a broader level of literacy, assuming that attention to lower-level skills would emerge through greater attention to critical literacy. Emphasis then shifted to writing tasks that are meaningful and purposeful for the students in a curriculum, tasks in which content, form, and use are integrated (Marschark, et al 2002, p. 176).

To this point, despite the radical changes in delivery of education and literacy arts in the college curriculum, there had been no examination of the nature of writing, how it is learned, or how it can be taught. Not until the 1960s did the study of writing become professionalized as Composition Studies, with empirical research into writers' thinking during the composing process. Research produced throughout the 1970s and early 1980s used methods like Think-Aloud or Read-Aloud Protocol Analysis to identify the cognitive processes that writers use during text production (Flower & Hayes, 1981). Using these research methods, Hayes and Flower (1980) built a model of the writing process, based on three-parts, including (a) planning, (b) translating, and (c) reviewing. Planning includes determining a purpose and audience, generating ideas, and selecting effective rhetorical strategies. Translating involves turning plans into written text. Reviewing involves the process of evaluating and revising the produced text. Perhaps the most important implications of this research are the claims made for what the model tells us about what expert writers and novice writers do differently when they engage in writing activities. What is now referred to as the "cognitive process movement" radically altered writing instruction, with implications for deaf education.

Process movement research influenced writing instruction for both hearing and deaf writers by teaching writing process techniques to boost writers' confidence (Meath-Lang & Albertini, 1984). Composition courses began to teach students how to use each piece of the writing model in all writing tasks, and a frequently used mantra—"process over product"—is still voiced in many composition classrooms. For instructional purposes, the most important observation in this research is that expert writers manage all three parts of the model in a hierarchical but nonlinear complex, cognitive act. That is, expert writers perceive writing as goal-directed, generate ideas while planning strategies, and are able to translate and review ideas simultaneously. Novice writers, conversely, tend not to engage, or do not engage as successfully in this three-part process (Berthoff, 1981; Kaufer, Hayes, and Flower, 1986), tending to get "stuck" in translation. Expert student writers, in contrast to novice student writers, spend more time with the revision of their writing.

Although the process movement increased our understanding of how successful writers manage writing and learning activities, the research was criticized because it occurred within simulated writing contexts (Smago-rinsky, 1994). Evidence was gathered in "laboratory" settings, in which students talked out loud in the presence of researchers as they wrote in response to a given prompt. Claims about the cognitive processes of student writers were based on narrowly defined samples of students in a decontextualized settings. Researchers still interested in addressing the cognitive processes underlying writing have broadened their scope and adjusted their methods, attempting to account for the context in which writers are composing and for the social and cultural backgrounds of individual writers (Brandt, 1992; Flower, 1993). In newer attempts to account for the writing process, researchers in composition studies and in deaf education have emphasized both cognition and context, arguing that students should learn to write as they would in the context of real-world communication.

Socio-cognitive approaches to writing research attempt to accomplish two important goals. First, research about cognition is taken out of the laboratory and placed in more naturalistic settings (Dyson, 1984). Methods like think-aloud protocols are replaced or triangulated by student interviews and written drafts (Brandt, 1992; Geisler, 1994). This approach has been particularly popular recently with regard to supporting and extending the writing skills of deaf students (see Albertini & Schley, 2003; Marschark et al., 2002, Chapter 8). Second, socio-cognitive research includes more diverse samples of writers and materials, attempting to address a variety of cognitive styles and recognizing the social experiences and literacy practices that student writers bring to the process (Delpit, 1988). Researchers outside of composition studies, in educational research like deaf education, also have influenced writing instruction. Nontraditional students—that is, those who are not hearing Eurocentric male students of the class most familiar with acceptable models of writing in mainstream United States—are now encouraged to produce writing according to their own prior knowledge, experience, and composing processes (Mayer, 1999).

The most recent emerging theories and research designs reflect the influence of studies in genre analysis (Bazerman, 1988; Berkenkotter & Huckin, 1995). A *genre* is a standard form of textual discourse, for example, a memo, policy recommendation, literature review, or lab report. According to current theory, one key difference between novice and expert writers is the ability to move from one genre to another and thus adapt to different contextual situations, including different academic settings. Socio-cognitive approaches to instruction that take a genre approach assume that students will write more effectively if they understand the goals and features of a target genre. Deaf education also argues that genre analysis can affect success in writing by making publication or formal evaluation a final act of the process. When students link writing to action, they engage in "dynamic literacy" that provides the motivation and content for writing (Mayer, 1999).

When writers are made aware of the fact that they are not writing simply to write, but are writing to accomplish different goals in different contexts that require different strategic language usage, they are more successful at launching their own projects. Socio-cognitive theories of process informed by genre become all the more salient when we witness students struggling with particular disciplinary practices and specialized academic discourses. In these terms, novice student writers assume no other purpose for writing than recitation and examination, whereas expert student writers are able to provide a meta-analysis as they write—to reflect upon the writing activity as a communicative strategy located within an epistemological situation.

The communicative strategies of particular genres in disciplinary writing present obvious obstacles even to expert writers (Kelly & Bazerman, 2003). For example, humanistic writing calls for research from sources and requires an ability to pose an interesting question and marshal evidence from relevant primary and secondary sources to address the question. The specialized form of scientific writing, on the other hand, calls for empirical inquiry by posing a hypothesis, using deliberate observation and experimentation to collect data, and then drawing conclusions based on the data. Students who have learned to write in the humanities and are unfamiliar with the new academic setting in science will likely struggle with specialized demands of scientific writing; students must become experts all over again, now at the specific, goal-directed activity required by scientific writing (Kelly & Bazerman, 2003).

This view of writing as context- and discipline-dependent has changed the research focus in Composition Studies from modeling the cognitive processes underlying general writing tasks to documenting the socio-cognitive processes underlying context-specific writing. If, as it is suspected, different students use different writing processes in different situations, research is required to unpack the complex dynamics of cognition, writing, and genre. Students arriving in college courses who are less able to move from one academic setting to another and fail to adapt to the communicative strategies of each are clearly disadvantaged. Research seeks to illuminate interventionist instruction that may help both novice and expert writers identify key features of "strange" or specific writing assignments and direct writers' attention to differences in expectations from one situation to another. Within this research philosophy, Selfe (1997) insisted that writing assessment treat participants and programs as existing primarily within specific contexts. Such investigation still requires careful study of writing and writers, while demanding more careful study of the writing activity in social context (Albertini, Bochner, Dowaliby, & Henderson, 1997).

This chapter proposes a research agenda that would gather methodologies from cognitive development process research, socio-cognitive research, and genre-analysis research to provide a coherent and comprehensive understanding of writing in the university curriculum. The essential argument is for the application of these methodologies to writing instruction in deaf education. This approach would require studying the cognitive underpinnings of deaf writers and accounting for different process models. Writing instruction would target writing processes with special emphasis on planning and revising so that deaf writers acquire the meta-rhetorical awareness (understanding how writing gets written; Mayer, 2007) to negotiate genre constraints from discipline to discipline.

Writing to Learn and Learning to Write

Recent methods for teaching, assessing, and evaluating the literacy skills of hearing and deaf students have focused on understanding students' competencies—and having students integrate the processes of writing—in *writing across the curriculum (WAC)*. Theories of WAC and the related *writing in the disciplines (WID)* accept the post-process premise that the writing process is not formulaic and emphasize the constraints upon process given the specialized contexts writers must negotiate. Opinions expressed by leaders in WAC and WID have provided support for the idea that there are not only specialized ways of writing but specialized ways of knowing. Thus, if writing and learning are connected to the acquisition of knowledge in the discipline, writing may effectively facilitate content learning.

Since the early 1980s, WAC initiatives have theorized a link between language and learning, positing writing as a higher-order tool for content learning ("write-to-learn," e.g., Applebee, 1985; Emig, 1977; Fulwiler & Young, 1982; Knoblauch & Brannon, 1983; McLeod, 1989; Odell, 1980). Models of writing in WAC remain closely tied to cognitive processes, assuming that learning takes place in a cognitive space between "telling" and "transforming." As the writer writes and rewrites, it is assumed that "to the extent that changing text changes thought, writing will influence the development of knowledge" (Albertini & Schley, 2003, p. 124). WAC models focus on the process of writing as a rhetorical action. Instruction in writing for deaf students, in particular, has reflected this widespread, internationally accepted writing model.

Other initiatives promoting WID theorize that the activity of writing within a specific discipline introduces students to that discipline's epistemology (Herrington, 1981; Kaufer & Young, 1993; Kiefer, 1990; Russell, 1991), thus facilitating both content and procedural learning. Students who learn to write in disciplinary strategic ways are also learning what questions can be asked, what counts as evidence, what the rules of method are, and what lexical features must be adapted (Monroe, 2002, 2003). Put simply, WID proponents argue that "a specialized concept of disciplinary knowledge is integrated with a specialized conception of writing" (Carter, 2007). WAC and WID models have achieved institutional endorsement and academic acceptance because they promote intuitively accurate practices that persist as theoretically sound.

The theory and practice of WAC and WID have burgeoned as the major strategies in teaching academic writing, often resulting in writing-intensive courses even in the hard sciences. Nevertheless, research into WAC and WID models' specific claims has yet to develop enough to provide conclusive supporting evidence. Assessment of WAC and WID programs did not occur until the 1980s, and even recent research into the theory and practice of WAC and WID initiatives has been limited to local, classroom-based student writing assessments and/or program-specific assessments (Bazerman et al., 2005; Bazerman & Russell, 1994; McLeod, 1988; Walvoord, 1992; Young & Fulwiler, 1986). Only recently have leaders such as Anson (2004) called for rigorous evaluation of the relationship between writing-to-learn and (a) content knowledge, (b) intellectual development, and (c) better disciplinary writing.

Ackerman (1993) provided an early review of the research regarding WAC and the "writing-to-learn claims." In this review, he argued: "writing specialists tend to ignore the second half of the write-to-learn equation 'learning and knowledge' and believe that the process and attributes of writing will inevitably lead to learning" (p. 352). Ackerman reported finding 35 studies in which researchers attempted to give "empirical scrutiny" to the relation between writing tasks and the promotion of learning but also noted that such studies "excluded the writing of multiple drafts or writing in more complex, social relations" that modeled actual academic writing behavior in the discipline (p. 346). He thus urged researchers to study the act of writing as evaluation of and participation in disciplinary knowledge and to use text quality to analyze the cognitive processes associated with writing (see Akamatsu, Mayer, & Hardy-Braz, this volume; Mayer, 1999).

After reviewing studies conducted in both the sciences and humanities, Ackerman concluded that writing likely does "complicate and thus enrich the thinking process" but "only when writing is situationally supported and valued" (p. 359). That is, writing works as an aid to learning only when integral to disciplinary instruction. For example, student performance on multiple-choice tests did not appear to benefit from writing assignments (Joyner, Kelly & Larkin-Hein, 2002). Supporting Ackerman's conclusions, Klein (1999) also noted the lack of empirical measures that demonstrate writing's value to the learning process. Specifically, Klein argued that it is the cognitive processes assumed in models of writing to learn that "have long gone without direct empirical examination" (p. 207). Without making such assumptions, Klein asks *how* writing can lead to learning and *how* its effects can be strengthened.

WAC and WID initiatives make explicit the striking claim that writing assignments facilitate learning of disciplinary content and mandate a role for writing in higher education with implications—perhaps different implications—for every discipline. Given these claims, it is neither surprising nor out of place for educational research from across domains to investigate the relationship of writing to content learning. Some of the most interesting educational research recently has come from the fields of mathematics and science (Ediger, 2006; Ellis 2004; Florence & Yore, 2004; Patterson, 2001; Sandoval & Millwood, 2005; Yore, Hand, & Florence, 2004). A meta-analysis of 48 school-based writing-to-learn programs by Bangert-Drowns, Hurley, and Wilkinson (2004), for example, cited previous claims for writing as a strategy for enhancing learning but concluded that the whole body of research offered ambiguous conclusions. At best, this thorough review of research indicated only that "writing does appear to facilitate learning to some degree under some conditions" (p. 32). Although conclusions show some positive effects of writing to learn activities, confirmation from additional primary research is still needed. In early research design "the nature of beneficial writing tasks, the pedagogical contexts in which they should be embedded, and the ways that learning should be assessed were unidentified" (p. 31). More controlled research environments and multiple research designs that consider how writing-to-learn operates on student cognition in real classrooms are necessary (Mayer, 2007).

Recent discipline-specific education research has enriched our understanding of the situational aspects of learning, allowing us to more readily interpret composition that is embedded within a disciplinary class. Physics education research, for example, has revealed common misconceptions, epistemologies, and affect-issues (e.g., gender bias or learning style preferences) that interfere with the learning process (Elby, 1999). Although the student is still seen as an individual learner, the frequency with which these issues appear in statistical studies suggests that it is possible to make some generalizations about the learning process within an introductory physics classroom. It is the knowledge of these situational idiosyncrasies that allows us to address Anson's (2004) call for research, understanding the cognitive process of learning with a proper respect for the disciplinary situation.

Given the potential significance of content teaching within a WAC or WID model, the various assumptions about writing and learning require investigation to evaluate the cognitive processes that influence writing to learn and measure the role of disciplinary context. Our goal now is to lay out the details of how such a research agenda might proceed, for deaf as well as hearing students. Our recommendation is coherent with the best research practices in deaf education, which emphasize the connections among reading, writing, and learning. In the reading-to-write approach, students use reading as a tool for writing. In this practice, reading is identified as a strategy leading to informal writing strategies, including records of personal experiences, reflection on observations, and predications based upon analysis and interpretations. This approach is very similar to writing-to-learn strategies emphasized by WAC models of writing in academic settings, including emphases on within-discipline writing. Another approach to writing instruction in deaf education targets reading in disciplinary content areas. This approach is based on the recognition that different skills are required to read well in specific disciplines. Because reading skills differ from the humanities to the social sciences to the sciences, students must be taught to read somewhat differently and to apply metacognitive strategies to interpret the texts (see Marschark & Wauters, this volume). Evidence shows that deaf students who read science texts at a higher level are also better at comprehending the material and composing as skilled writers.

Lang (2001) and Marschark et al. (2002) argued that, although reading research in deaf education has traditionally focused on lexical and grammatical fluency, evidence from reading-to-learn and reading-across-the-curriculum efforts, as well as from specific content areas, points to a need for investigations concerning *writing* within disciplines. We therefore are advocating an empirical educational research design that treats writing as a socio-cognitive phenomenon within a complex dynamic of genre activity from discipline to discipline. This design would examine the cognitive processes of students with varying academic and demographic backgrounds during discipline-specific composition. Writing within designated genres thus would reflect both recognition of domain-specific writing requirements and "apprenticeship" with particular content knowledge. This approach is unique in testing the fundamental assumptions of WAC and WID in the context of discipline-specific ways of knowing.

The case study we describe here showcases the multimodal research design and recommends that more work be done to research the important assumptions for helping students engage with the local writing goals they might encounter across the curriculum. Our research agenda, treating writing-to-learn as both a cognitive and a disciplinary activity, will need to be directed into educational practices—will need to be translatable as teaching strategies that can develop a writer's agility at directing writing goals in disciplinary fields and professions.

Explorations in Physics

The classroom context for this model and the subsequent case study is *Explorations in Physics (EiP)*, an introductory course designed for nonscience. Explorations in Physics is a concept-oriented physics course that is based upon physics education research and incorporates guided-inquiry techniques with small group projects in a collaborative learning environment. Explorations in Physics centers on common themes that run through the different sciences with an emphasis on physical science. At Rochester Institute of Technology (RIT), EiP draws its students from a variety of majors such as information technology, computer science, and economics, and includes a significant number of deaf students. Explorations in Physics seeks to instill in students a level of scientific literacy that would include conceptual knowledge of physics, as well as the rhetorical conventions of particular texts, including lab reports and poster presentations. Our underlying assumption is that students' careers will require the ability to learn and evaluate new information and to communicate this information to varied audiences, and thus the course has physics-specific goals but more general aspirations.

To account for complex socio-cognitive processes of writing in physics, we are blending three related activities: (a) primary trait scoring, (b) revision-based analysis, and (c) key stroke analysis. These assessment strategies represent both traditional and contemporary strategies used in composition research and can effectively be applied in a multimodal research design to analyze students' socio-cognitive engagement with practices of writing in various disciplines.

Primary Trait Analysis

As a research and/or a pedagogical instrument, primary trait analysis (PTA) establishes learning outcomes as criteria for assignment-based assessment. That is, PTA identifies the assignment-specific traits that are observable criteria for specific written assignments. In its initial formulations (Lloyd-Jones, 1977), PTA focused on the specific approach that a writer might take to be successful on a specific writing task. For example, a lab report would include an "observation" as part of its logical structure. Primary trait analysis scales remain an important and effective approach to assessment of student mastery over rhetorical purposes.

The analysis begins by identifying the major aspect(s) or criteria that readers consider when assessing the written product or behavior. The primary traits to be analyzed in this case are the particular rhetorical *moves* in a lab report. These include common features or expectations for introductory paragraphs, concepts to be covered, organizational options, conventions for sentence structure, rules of evidence, and methods for analysis or interpretation, all of which can be discerned in the features of a text. For example, a single rhetorical move in a physics lab report would be to provide detailed accounts of procedures (e.g., Swales & Najjar, 1987). The traditional physics lab report is rhetorically quite complex (Bazerman, 1984). Students are expected (and instructed) to provide background, a detailed yet succinct description of the activities, and place their findings within a larger framework. It is not surprising that, when faced with such a far-reaching project, students often struggle to develop a coherent document.

Based upon these primary traits, we identified rhetorical moves conventional for lab reports. We then devised criteria to code five rhetorical moves: *Motivation*, *Procedure*, *Observation*, *Inference*, or *Speculation* (MPOIS). This trait analysis, although extremely simplistic, captures many elements of scientific writing including (a) the importance of carefully describing one's procedure, (b) the primacy of observation, and (c) the difference between inference and speculation. A sample piece of coded writing is shown in Figure 15–1.

The MPOIS rubric then links it rhetorical moves to specific criteria for writing in a physics lab. The inclusion of criteria and the sequencing of criteria in lab reports guide students through the epistemological assumptions that support study of physical phenomena. This particular rubric is designed to fit the EiP course and assigned reports; other courses and disciplines might use a radically different rubric. The combined approach garnered immediate endorsement as an instructional tool from physics faculty at RIT untrained in generic composition, indicating its value within the physics discipline. Future use of this rubric (and similar rubrics in

This being found, we began to experiment more with buoyant force and its relation to

M

water displaced by an object when it's dropped in water. **P** By performing several

experiments with an overflow can and measuring the amount of water displaced, we

I

were able to conclude that buoyant force on an **P** object and the amount of water

displaced by the same object are related to each other, and seemed to be equal to each

P

other. Thus, we began to experiment with the possibility of calculating buoyant force

on object simply by measuring its volume and predicting the amount of water it will

displace. We created a set standard based on the amount of water displaced by an

object of a certain volume, and then used that standard to predict the buoyant force

on objects of different volumes.

Figure 15–1. Writing sample that has been coded with the MPOIS (Motivation, Procedure, Observation, Inference, or Speculation) rubric. It is possible to identify gross features of student writing, such as the number of procedural or inference statements.

different disciplines) can add to our understanding about the connection between writing activities and discipline-based epistemologies and content understanding.

Another tool that can be helpful in research on writing processes is *cohesion analysis*. Coding for cohesion analysis sorts devices like repetition, conjunction, or parallelism, and focuses on how sentences are linked to form reference chains throughout a document. Because cohesive elements make meaning, coding for cohesion can document whether writers are struggling to make meaning within the bounds of the text, and whether they are extending reference chains to preceding text or to something that has yet to be introduced. In addition, because the types and extension of reference chains will vary across genres and disciplines, cohesion analysis can study whether students apply rhetorical strategies when composing texts in particular content domains.

Revision-Based Assessment

Revision has long been commonly regarded as a central part of the writing process, in part because it enhances the final written document and also because it requires students to rework ideas, thus potentially enhancing learning (Flower & Hayes, 1981). Faigley and Witte (1981) recognized that for revision to work as an effective learning activity, a distinction needed to be made between text-based revisions that affect meaning and surface changes that do not. Faigley and Witte were mainly concerned with elements related to linguistic operations, as students revise for small corrections at the surface level (spelling) or extensive revision like sequence of ideas and idea-based cohesive strategies (rather than adding a quick "however"). Schwartz (1983) added to these observations by identifying three major revision patterns: (a) language regeneration, in which a student deletes text and begins again from scratch; (b) structural reformulation, in which students simply cut and paste text; and (c) content reassessment, in which students engage in deep revision to accommodate audience and purpose. Schwartz's model is largely concerned with the writer's approach to content as applied to context, attention to language as matching aesthetic constraints and expectations, and consideration of mechanics as delivering precise and readable prose. Berkenkotter (1983) has since advocated writing instruction that emphasizes professional awareness of genre in disciplines, workplace, and community. The now commonly held belief, based on experimental approaches to revision and held throughout Composition Studies, is that guided revision, in which writers wrestle with text at the deep level of purpose and context, can be a way to facilitate discovery and create new knowledge (Horning & Becker, 2006).

Key-stroke Analysis

The moments of revisionary writing demonstrate the extent to which knowledge is also transformed/developed through writing. Capturing the process of revision in writing within naturalistic writing settings has been all but impossible, requiring intrusive think-aloud protocols or relying upon memory and post-drafting interviews alone. Software that traces a composing process can display stages of a complete written draft, including the first and last draft. However, the most recent technologies in key-capture software allow researchers to trace every keystroke within a drafting session. Such software records the composing process in real time during any writing task in nearly any context. Keystroke capture software products are available, for example, that reveal all the typological differences not only between first and second drafts, but within a single writing episode or session.

A format, referred to as S-notation (Kollberg, 1998), has been developed to facilitate the reconstruction of a writing episode. In S-notation, interruptions in writing are noted by | | i where i represents the order of interruptions. Insertions and deletions are marked with {inserted text}i and (deleted text)i. An example of this notation (taken directly from Kollberg) is

I am writing a {short}1 text.| |1. It will (probably)2 | |3 be revised (somewhat)3 later.| |2. Now (I am | |4)4 it is finished.

The interpretation of this is as follows: First the author wrote "I am writing a text." Then she went back and inserted the word "short." Next she wrote "It will probably be revised somewhat later," after which she deleted the words "probably" and "somewhat." Finally, she wrote "Now I am," changed her mind and deleted the words "I am" and inserted "it is finished" to produce:

I am writing a short text. It will be revised later. Now it is finished.

A more substantial example of S-notation will be discussed later to illustrate the type of significant revision event that we believe indicates the potential pedagogical value of writing assignments. S-notation is a very promising technique because the method gives us a fairly accurate record of a writers' process while writing. The method gives both writer-specific and context-specific knowledge of length of compositing time; type of changes made at the word, sentence, or paragraph level; deletions and insertions; and pauses or interruptions. In sum, S-notation, supported by participant interviews, allows us to see all the actions that occur during a writing session and then make observations about working memory, planning abilities, cognitive processes, and writing methods.

Multimodal Research Agenda: A Case Study

Our goal in presenting the following case study is to demonstrate both the possibility and promise of probing the socio-cognitive writing process within a disciplinary context using the methods just identified (Mayer, 1999). As the case study strongly suggests an evolution in the student's understanding within a single writing episode, we come closer to connecting the writing process to explicitly discipline-specific content understanding within physics. It would be foolhardy to draw general conclusions about learning from a single case study. Nevertheless, we believe that the following approach, which combines PTA with revision-based assignments and key-stroke analysis, presents a significant, new, and viable research method to track both writing and content understanding within the disciplinary situation. Research shows clearly that in novice writers, ESL writers, basic writers, and even expert writers, a socio-cognitive approach to post-process genre-based pedagogy can develop a metarhetorical—"understanding how writing gets written"—(Bertoff, 1981) awareness that leads to more successful text production.

Analyses of Primary Traits in Lab Report Drafts

A PTA was used to analyze approximately 600 (hearing) student writing samples during a full academic year. Students were required to submit weekly reports that documented the week's activities while placing them within a larger context. To allow students to incorporate faculty feedback, as well as to encourage the connectedness of all the activities, labs were cumulative. Students were told to revise their initial entry and integrate the new weeks' activities into one seamless lab entry. During the quarter, students wrote three separate lab reports (two topical + one project), each of which was revised three to four times. Feedback included an assessment of the student's writing ability, including comments on the extent of the student's revisions. Students were given a description of the assessment scheme, with examples of Motivation, Procedure, Observation, Speculation, and Inference statements. They were also provided with numerous writing samples demonstrating both positive and negative elements of scientific writing, according to the scheme.

We should emphasize that this categorization, especially the difference between inference and speculation, is fluid. Over the course of the quarter, as a result of ongoing discussions with students, we gradually settled into a reliable articulation. Although students had little trouble with identifying statements as motivating (anything providing background or motivation for research, e.g., "It is interesting that boats float while rocks sink") or procedural (e.g., "We placed the block in the water"), the remaining three criteria required some discussion. To our surprise, it became apparent that many students did not know what was meant by an observation. This was illustrated in a classroom discussion about the following sentence on buoyancy:

> *While dropping the wooden blocks into water, the buoyant force proved to be a rather important factor pushing against the object.*

Although some students claimed that this was an observation of the buoyant force, others argued that this was an inference, the observation being that the block floated. The class finally agreed (with subtle urging from the instructor) that the observation was that the block floated at the surface of the water. Based on other observations, an appropriate inference was that the forces on the block were in balance. The existence of the buoyant force in balance with gravity was then a reasonable speculation.

Figure 15–2 shows the frequency of occurrence from two different reports, A and B. (*A1/B1* is the first draft of journal *A/B*, *A2/B2* the second.) Several features are noteworthy. Speculative sentences, which initially made up 35% of all student writing, dropped after feedback to about 25% and remained at that level for the rest of the quarter. Motivating statements, a catch-all category that includes both necessary introductory sentences

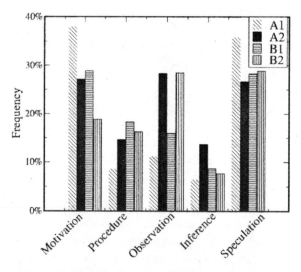

Figure 15–2. Frequency of occurrence of sentences designated as Motivation, Procedure, Observation, Inference and Speculation in student essays. A1/A2 refer to the first and last versions of the first student essay, B1/B2 to the first and last versions of the second student essay. Significant shifts are seen in student style, away from unnecessary motivation and speculation and toward a more complete description of procedure and observations. Salient inferences, unfortunately, do not show a significant increase frequency.

but also unnecessary "filler" sentences that students often include, also fell by about 10%. Inference plays a critical role in physics; it is what allows the experimentalist to generalize from a series of observations to a physical "law" of nature. Nevertheless, despite repeated attempts to define an inference and give examples, students never understood this well enough to consistently generalize their observations.

One would expect that the experience of writing report *A* (with its four revisions) would have some impact on the second journal. One can see in Figure 15–2 how the first draft of the second journal (*B1*) has fewer motivation and speculation sentences than *A1*. The emphasis on procedure also remains, and so we believe it is justified to claim that some shift in style has occurred. Students are much more precise in describing both their procedure and the actual observations, key characteristics of writing in physics. The low frequency of observation-type sentences in both journals *A1* and *B1* is due, we believe, to the fact that the first week's activities involved few direct observations rather than a regression on the part of the students.

Coding the primary trait criteria allows us to look at complex performances and to identify precise outcomes. The coding makes possible a graphical display of student writing; the *writing graph* for the full journal from which Figure 15–1 was taken is shown in Figure 15–3. Note the

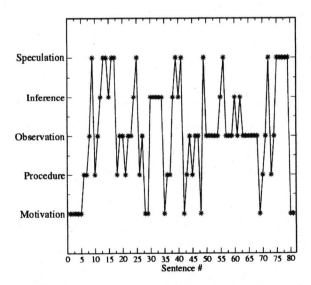

Figure 15–3. Writing graph of a student writer's paper. Note the preponderance of statements that describe an observation and that, with few exceptions, inferences and speculations are preceded by an observation or description of procedure. This may indicate a favorable epistemology, the student recognizing that physics ideas must be supported by the observations.

large number of statements classified as observations and how frequently an observation is followed by an inference (this student was atypical in his ability to make inferences). Twenty-two of the 25 inference and speculative statements (88%) are immediately preceded by an observation or description of procedure. This could indicate a favorable epistemology that recognizes that the foundations of physics principles lie in the observations, as opposed to common belief that observations exist to support ideas. It is impossible, however, to determine the truthfulness of this claim without interviewing the student.

The writing graph for a second student writer is shown in Figure 15–4; the differences are immediately apparent. There is a lack of inference and speculative sentences, a dearth particularly noteworthy from the concluding sentences, where one might expect more summative types of sentences. Also apparent is a "procedure-observation" cycle (sentences 21–26). This is a common finding in science writing, in which students write "We did this and saw this" without making any broader conclusions.

Analysis of Student Revisions

If learning is an evolution of understanding, then it should be reflected not only in what is written, but what is changed. It is generally accepted that for writing to be pedagogically effective, the student must spend a significant amount of time revising, either explicitly on paper or implicitly in her

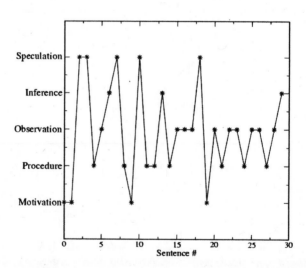

Figure 15–4. Writing graph of a second student writer's paper. Note the dearth of speculative or inferential statements, an absence particularly significant at the end of the essay. The "Procedure–Observation" cycle is one quite common in introductory science writing.

head (Flower & Hayes, 1981; Mayer, 1999). Revision analysis is a tool that allows us to quickly identify the key changes in a document that might indicate learning has occurred.

If a student sees the purpose of a writing assignment as an opportunity to display knowledge to the instructor, proceeds to write down what she knows, and then stops, there is no need for revision. In fact, many students appear incapable of revising even when explicitly instructed to do so, tending to "revise" by excising anything the instructor has indicated does not belong without replacing it with necessary text to hold the document together. Or, if the instructor notes that a particular turn of phrase or idea is valuable, the student then tries to repeat it as often as possible. Either way, the student is not seeing revision as an opportunity to reorganize his thoughts. And yet, this mental reorganization can lead to real content learning.

We now know that expert writers will spend more time developing plans for the text and making revisions to the text than will novice writers (Flower & Hayes, 1981; Horning & Becker, 2006). Here, too, however, time spent on revision depends on the specific writing task. When the goals of a text present problems for the writer, revision is difficult, and selecting alternate strategies may simply be guesswork. We have found that draconian shortening of revision assignments is necessary to impress upon students the need to reorganize their reports. Simply asking students to revise or slightly shorten a report results in "revision by excision," as students cut extraneous words but do not significantly revise the content. This avoids the very process we desire students to perform: the development of a coherent framework that structures the report.

To lead students into a reflective writing mode that encourages revision, we implemented two-part *revision-based writing assignments* in the EiP classroom. In the first part of the assignment, students were asked to write a report with a well-defined length. When this was submitted, students were immediately and without any feedback, asked to revise their report to half its original length. This drastic change ensured that simply cutting extraneous words could not reach the word limit. A total of 60 students completed four assignment pairs. A sample pair prompt is:

Write a 250-word report on the connection between net force and how objects act when placed in a liquid (or released within the fluid). Include class observations to support your reasoning.

which was followed by:

Take the previous report and rewrite it, shortening it to 125 words.

Students submitted these assignments in electronic form using a word processor with the Track Changes feature enabled. This allowed us to see immediately the differences between versions. On a computer screen, the inserted and deleted text was colored differently; in Figure 15–5, text inserted in the second version is italicized whereas excised text is crossed out. The figure illustrates the difficulty a novice writer has satisfying the draconian reduction in word count merely by cutting text.

Note the complete absence of any inserted text in Figure 15–5. The student cut as many words as he felt he could but then became frustrated at being unable to reach the desired length of 125 words. This prompted instruction on the *coherence* of his paragraph. For example, it was pointed out that his introductory and concluding sentences were unrelated, and that the first two sentences could be, but were not, thematically related to his last five. Rather than a single coherent report, the student seemed to have written two separate theses, joined only by spatial proximity. With this explicit guidance

---

~~Yes there is a connection because the forces determine how it moves through the liquid~~

With a small ball of clay tested in a jar of water to see if it would float. It ~~immediately~~ sunk to the bottom showing that the net downward force had to be stronger coming down than going up. ~~The next object that we experimented on was a large bouncy ball that just floated on the top of the water. This showed us that the net force was zero because it was just floating on the water causing equilibrium between upward and downward forces.~~ The last object that we used ~~in our experiment~~ was a ping pong ball. We took the ping pong ball and submerged it under water and it ~~immediately rose straight up~~ rose to the top. This showed that the upward ~~net~~ forces were much stronger than the downward net forces. There were two forces acting up on the ping pong ball which were buoyant force and the forces of the water pushing up from below. ~~One force was acting down on the ping pong ball and that was the force of the water acting down from above.~~ Because the ping pong ball was going up we know that the forces acting upward had to be greater than the forces acting downward.

Figure 15–5. Student essay on the relationship between net force and buoyancy, as prompted by the assignment described in the text. The student initially wrote a 250-word essay and then revised it to 125 words. Because the Track Changes feature of Microsoft Word was enabled, we can clearly see where the student made changes. Italicized text has been inserted during the revision process whereas ~~smaller crossed out~~ text has been deleted.

toward writing a coherent report, the student was finally able to reach the desired length with a report that indicated a much improved understanding of the physical phenomena of net force and buoyancy despite the fact that no explicit content instruction had occurred. The evidence presented here is not intended as definitive proof of learning. Rather, it highlights the possibilities of a research agenda that focuses on revision both from a rhetorical and content perspective. The explicit connection between the two is highly suggestive and provides a clear path for future research.

A sample of a more sophisticated student writer's work is shown in Figure 15–6. One can see significant changes between versions. Rhetorically, the writing has become more active ("gravity pushes something down" and "We call this a zero net force") and transitions are more sophisticated ("There must also be" and "By subtracting these two weights"). From a physics perspective, the student was now focusing on the underlying concept of net force rather than the apparent differences between floating and sinking. Although it has often been posited that improved writing is indicative of greater content understanding, this is a strong instance in which a shift in writing style has been demonstrated to be directly connected with an evolution in understanding. This type of revision, seen in many students in the case study presented next, is powerful evidence that the *writing process itself* can bring about a change in understanding that is, actual learning. The act of revising thus becomes an important mechanism for cognitive change.

Analyzing the Composition Process with Key-capturing Software

The process of planning and revision as goal-directed, disciplinary writing is evident in analysis of a student's attempt to respond to disciplinary concepts and epistemic knowledge specific to physics. Figure 15–7 shows the S-notated output of a student responding to the following prompt:

> *60 mL of a mystery substance weighs 90 oz. Write a 250-word report explaining, in detail, how you can use this information to predict the weight of 90 mL of the substance in two ways: through the ideas of proportionality and density.*

Our focus is with the first words the student wrote: "I don't know anything about density; however, there are at least a couple of ways of determining in [sic], or at least I'm told." He then spent 2.5 minutes writing about how to solve the problem by setting up a simple proportionality. Then, realizing that he then needed to describe a second solution involving density, he paused and thought without writing for 30 seconds. His next action was incredibly suggestive: he erased the opening clause "I don't know anything about density" and inserted a placeholder introductory

Sinking and floating usually seems like a simple idea. ~~The activity that involved using force meters is the one that really opened my eyes to the world of sinkers and floaters. Even though this activity had nothing to do with water, the concepts finally fit together in my mind.~~ Obviously, gravity ~~is present in pushing~~ *pushes* something down ~~towards the earth~~ when it is dropped. ~~in water. It was also obvious that there was another force pushing up on the floaters to keep them at the surface,~~ *There must also be another force from the water pushing on the object,* ~~but~~ *yet this force* ~~must be~~ *is* in equilibrium with gravity or the object would *always move.* ~~simply fly up out of the water.~~ We ~~would~~ call this a ~~net force of zero~~ *zero net force, since the forces* ~~were~~ *are* ~~in~~ balanced. The ~~upward~~ force from the water ~~that I mentioned was really the one that we had not understood previously to the activity~~ *is called buoyancy.* ~~However, using the force meters and lifting weights slightly with our hands, but leaving enough hanging that the force did not drop to zero, I finally understood the idea of this ``buoyant force'' that is present in the water.~~ While the water does not ~~not fully~~ support the object *entirely, it presses up on it* ~~just~~ enough to create an ~~sort of~~ ``apparent weight'', though ~~Of course,~~ *the object's true weight* ~~still does not change~~ *never changes.* ~~Yet, we have all noticed that some things feel lighter in water than they do out of water.~~ *By* ~~taking this apparent weight and subtracting it from its real weight~~ *subtracting these two weights, we* ~~should be able to see~~ *can find* ~~how much force the water is using to push up on the object we drop into it~~ *the buoyant force.* ~~Once these forces eventually balance out, we end up with a net force of zero, causing the object to settle somewhere in the water.~~ What decides if the object sinks or floats is where ~~these forces balance out~~ *in the water the zero net force occurs.*

Figure 15–6. Student essay buoyancy that shows significant excision but little thoughtful revision. The student was, in fact, unable to reduce the length to the requested 125 words, in part due to the fact that the first two sentences are unrelated to the next five.

{Density is an important part of modern science, finding its way into many fields including chemistry, optics, and physics. Typically, if given a total amount of substance and a weight, one can find the weight of a different amount of the same substance. One may also be able to use formulas to calculate a density PAUSE by plugging numbers into it, but what it all boils down to, in this case, is the total amount of "stuff" within a specific volume.}4‖5

(I don't know anything about density; however,)3 ‖4 There are at least a couple ways of determining {it}7 {the weight of a substance} (, or at least I'm told)5‖6 {when its mass and volume are known}6 ‖7. PAUSE The simplest way of determining it would be through the use of proportionality. In the example, a sample of 60 ml of substance weighed 90 ounces. The question asks to determine how much 90 ml of the same substance would weigh. To set this (this up‖1)1 proportionality one must PAUSE set up a ratio. So, 60 ml over 90 ounces is equal to 90 ml over x ounces. By cross-multiplying and (dividing‖2)2 solving for x, one can find the value of x, which is the PAUSE weight of the 90 ml of substance. (Another way of determining the total amount of mass)9‖3, PAUSE Another way of determining the total weight of the system would be to simply divide PAUSE 90 ounces by 60 ml. Density is defined as mass over volume, so by doing this, one has found the density. Once the density has been found, a person simply must multiply this number by a new given amount to find the new mass. This is the same procedure as before, but practiced in a different way.

Figure 15–7. Writing sample rendered using S-notation. The enclosure of the introductory paragraph in braces { } indicates it was added after much of the following text was written. Similarly, the phrase in parentheses (I don't know anything about density) was the first text written and removed just before the new introductory paragraph was written.

paragraph about density's importance, including a definition of density as "the total amount of stuff in a volume." Having thus concluded that he did know something about density, he returned to the end of his report, described how one could use density to answer the question, redefined density as mass per volume, and, remarkably, related this to his previous use of proportionality, writing that "this is the same procedure as before, but practiced in a different way."

How can one interpret this writing process? The explicit statement "I don't know anything about density" was a candid self-reporting of the student's initial state of ignorance. As the student wrote, he appeared to reach a series of increasingly sophisticated conceptions of density. He begins with the standard, oft-memorized formula of "mass over volume." The relative crudeness of his understanding is seen in his use of the term "over" for the mathematical operation of division and by his earlier statement that one "may also be able to use formulas to calculate a density by plugging numbers into it." Clearly, he is seeing density as a relation between given numbers (an object's weight and volume) and not as an abstract characteristic of a substance. In between writing these two sentences, however, he gives a clue to a more sophisticated view when he writes that "it all boils down to, in this case, is the total amount of 'stuff' within a specific volume." It is in his concluding sentence, however, that he appears to make the most significant leap of understanding. By relating density to his previous method of proportionality, he unifies two concepts that, when he sat down to write, were completely separate in his mind. It is this synthesis that is at the heart of writing coherently, and it is particularly impressive that the student accomplished this without *any* instruction. The writing task, it seems, forced him to teach himself about density.

Summary and Implications

We are arguing for a research agenda based upon a multimodal approach within a disciplinary context. Our agenda is consistent with recent theory that learning-to-write, and thus writing-to-learn, is not a general activity but one thoroughly embedded in disciplinarity. Our general claims are that direct tests of the fundamental assumption of WAC and WID programs might be translated into teachable strategies for both novice and expert writers. If writing tasks associated with course content can and do improve the quality of students' overall learning of subject matter, educational practices ought to identify key features of writing in various disciplines.

Our case study outlines an approach that would move deaf education in the direction suggested by Lang (2001) and others (e.g., Marschark et al., 2002). Our predictions—that writing and learning are cognitively connected and that instruction in discipline-specific writing also leads to discipline-specific knowing—if investigated carefully and thoroughly, could lead to pedagogies that would teach deaf students how to write in the genre of specific disciplines, accommodating the expectations of an audience and the constraints of the purpose (Mayer, 2007). By explicitly teaching deaf students how to use their individualistic writing process, with emphasis on deep revision and how to think metacognitively about the writing task, students will also begin to think in the process of the discipline: describing or reasoning, observing or analyzing, hypothesizing or interpreting (see Hauser, Lukomski, & Hillman, this volume; Marschark & Wauters, this volume).

The research agenda we are proposing is particularly advantageous because it is naturalistic and designed to capture the writing process of students, with attention to literacy backgrounds and social contexts under which they compose texts. The agenda is also situated within a particular discipline within science—a physics classroom—with a specialized means of inquiry (see Marschark & Hauser, this volume). Finally, the agenda targets a specific genre-type: scientific inquiry in a science report. Similar to research already completed in reading and content areas, but with focus on the cognitive processes of writing, especially revision, and with a naturalistic but situation-specific setting, we hope to articulate a pedagogy designed to move all students from novice to expert writers, with the metacognitive skills necessary to adapt their writing and thinking processes as they travel from their history class to their physics class. In the case of deaf writers, we hope to provide them with sufficient support to allow them to function in such settings at a level comparable to their hearing peers.

Our approach is a radical departure from prior assessments of writing-to-learn, which have traditionally used general writing tasks (e.g., short-answer summaries, note-taking, and journaling) with uncertain results. The ability to record a writing episode has become increasingly more sophisticated and, importantly, less intrusive. Methods to capture each keystroke as a text is created (on a computer) have been developed, as have associated techniques to analyze this data (Kolberg, 1998). These tools, most prominently S-notation, highlight the order in which revisions occur within a single document and represent the order, range, and internal structure of writing and revising activities. Of fundamental importance is the noninvasive nature of this method. Students can compose a document wherever they choose in a variety of editors on their own computers (although we have also developed an on-line version). It is therefore possible to conduct empirical studies of revision strategies without intruding on the writing process.

Although these methods are not new, the methods have not been used together within a disciplinary context to assess the relationship of writing to learning for deaf education (Albertini et al., 1997). Each method accomplishes a separate task. Primary trait analysis captures the lexical structures and rhetorical moves of the final written document as a sample of disciplinary discourse. Version-control captures revisions made between writing sessions, allowing us to note general changes in a written document and potential shifts in content knowledge. Key-stroke analysis captures revisions made during a single writing session, thus emphasizing learning as it might occur during the actual writing process. By applying these three methods in a multimodal engagement and to a disciplinary set of writing practices, this study presents alternatives to student assessments or program evaluations as research into claims of WAC and WID. In so doing, this study works as a unique model for sustained, empirical, and rigorous inquiry of socio-cognitive approaches to writing instruction. By examining differences between novice and expert writers as well as deaf and hearing writers (at different levels of expertise), we hope to further both pedagogy and understanding of the cognitive foundations of writing by students at various educational levels

In addition to establishing the viability of embedding these research methods in the classroom, we have also shown the methods' enormous potential at establishing a connection between writing and learning. The multimodality of the agenda is critical to this point. This type of triangulation (Creswell, 1998; Yin, 2003) is a well-established technique in qualitative and case-study research. Although the particulars of each assessment are discipline-based, this broad research agenda is not necessarily tied to our chosen context. Rather, it is immediately ready for adaptation in almost any disciplinary course with a significant writing component. The groundwork is therefore prepared for large-scale research in a variety of academic situations.

The model research methods and the case study from the discipline of physics do not offer definitive conclusions about the socio-cognitive underpinnings of writing processes in disciplinary contexts. General points of discussion speak to pedagogy that would engage all students as expert writers, introducing them to the rhetorical norms posed by various academic, disciplinary fields. When instructors identify the ways of writing—using rubrics to set criteria and provide evaluation, and using revision-based assignments to prompt problem solving and strategic writing—students come to understand what "counts" as good writing within a discipline. For students, and for deaf students in particular, writing should become less strange and more transparent. Further, as students develop the writing process within a content area, they are learning about disciplinary ways of knowing: conceptual knowledge, mode of reasoning, and lexical features. When writing is emphasized as a procedural and goal-directed activity within a discipline/curriculum, approaches to grammar and mechanics are not ignored, but they are relegated to the final editing and proofreading stages. We believe that a multimodal research agenda that embeds the process of writing within local disciplinary sites will tell us how successful deaf and hearing students manifest the ability to write in an educational setting, and that writing instruction inside the disciplines would direct students as both writers and learners.

References

Ackerman, J. (1993). The promise of writing to learn. *Written Communication, 10*, 334–370.

Albertini, J. A., & Schley, S. (2003). Writing: Characteristics, instruction, assessment. In M. Marschark & P. E. Spencer (Eds.) *Oxford handbook of deaf studies, language, and education.* New York: Oxford University Press.

Albertini, J. A., Bochner, J. H., Dowaliby, F., & Henderson, J. B. (1997). Valid assessment of writing and access to academic discourse. *Journal of Deaf Studies and Deaf Education, 2*, 71–77.

Anson, C. (2004, May). *Writing to learn versus learning to write.* Paper presented at the Seventh National WAC Conference, St. Louis, MO.

Applebee, A. N. (1985). Writing and reasoning. *Review of Educational Research, 54*(4), 577–596.

Bangert-Drowns, R. L., Hurley, M. M., & Wilkinson, B. (2004). The effects of school-based writing-to-learn interventions on academic achievement: A meta-analysis. *Review of Educational Research, 74*(1), 29–58.

Bazerman, C. (1984). Modern evolution of the experimental report in physics. *Social Studies of Science, 14*, 163–196.

Bazerman, C. (1988). *Shaping written knowledge: The genre and activity of the experimental article in science.* Madison: University of Wisconsin Press.

Bazerman, C., Little, J., Bethel, L., Chavkin, T., Fouquette, D., & Garufis, J. (Eds.). (2005). *Reference guide to writing across the curriculum.* West Lafayette, IN: Parlor Press and the WAC Clearinghouse.

Bazerman, C., & Russell, D. (Eds.). (1994). *Landmark essays in writing across the curriculum.* Davis, CA: Hermagoras Press.

Berkenkotter, C., & Huckin, T. N. (1995). *Genre knowledge in disciplinary communication: Cognition, culture, power.* Hillsdale, NJ: Erlbaum.

Berkenkotter, C. (1983). Decisions and revisions: The planning strategies of a publishing writer. *College Composition and Communication, 34*, 156–169.

Bertoff, A. (1981). Recognition, representation, and revision. *Journal of Basic Writing, 3*, 19–32.

Brandt, D. (1992). The cognitive as the social: An ethnomethodological approach to writing process research. *Written Communication, 9*, 315–355.

Carter, M. (2007). Ways of knowing, doing, and writing in the disciplines. *College Composition and Communication 58*(3): 385–418.

Creswell, J. W. (1998). *Qualitative inquiry and research design: Choosing among five traditions.* Thousand Oaks, CA: Sage Publications.

Delpit, L. D. (1988). The silenced dialogue: Power and pedagogy in educating other people's children. *Harvard Educational Review, 58*, 280–298.

Dyson, A. H. (1984). Learning to write/Learning to do school: Emergent writers' interpretations of school literacy tasks. *Research in the Teaching of English,* 18, 233–264.

Ediger, M. (2006). Writing in the mathematics curriculum. *Journal of Instructional Psychology, 33*(2), 120–123.

Elby, A. (1999). Another reason that physics students learn by rote. *American Journal of Physics, 67,* S52.

Ellis, R. (2004). University student approaches to learning science through writing. *International Journal of Science Education 26*(15), 1835–1853.

Emig, J. (1977). Writing as a mode of learning. *College Composition and Communication, 28,* 122–28.

Faigley, L., & Witte, S. (1981). Analyzing revision. *College Composition and Communication, 32,* 400–408.

Florence, M. K., & Yore, L. D. (2004). Learning to write like a scientist: Coauthoring as an enculturation task. *Journal of Research in Science Teaching* 41(6), 637–668.

Flower, L. (1993). Cognitive rhetoric: An inquiry into the art of inquiry. In T. Enos & S. C. Brown (Eds.), *Defining the new rhetorics* (pp 171–190). Newbury Park, CA: Sage.

Flower, L., & Hayes, J. (1981). A cognitive process of writing. *College Composition and Communication, 32,* 365–387.

Fulwiler, T., & Young, A. (1982). Introduction. In T. Fulwiler & A. Young (Eds.), *Language connections: Writing and reading across the curriculum* (pp. ix–xiii). Urbana, IL: National Council of Teachers of English.

Geisler, C. (1994). *Academic literacy and the nature of expertise.* Hillsdale, NJ: Erlbaum.

Graves, H. B. (2005). *Rhetoric in(to) science: Style as invention in inquiry.* Hampton Press.

Hayes, J. R., & Flower L. (1980). Identifying the organization of writing processes. In L. Gregg & E. Steinberg (Eds.), *Cognitive process in writing: An interdisciplinary approach* (pp 3–30). Hillsdale, NJ: Erlbaum.

Herrington, A. (1981). Writing to learn: Writing across the disciplines. *College English, 43,* 379–387.

Horning, A. S., & Becker A. (Eds.) (2006). *Revision: History, theory, and practice.* West Lafayette, IN: Parlor Press.

Joyner, P. Kelly, & Larkin-Hein, T. (2002). Writing and Physics: An Interdisciplinary Approach. Presented at the IEEE/ASEE Frontiers in Education Conference, Boston, MA.

Kaufer, D., Hayes, J., & Fower, L. (1986). Composing written sentences. *Research in the Teaching of English, 20,* 121–140.

Kaufer, D., & Young, R. (1993). Writing in the content areas: Some theoretical complexities. In L. Odell (Ed.), *Theory and practice in the teaching of writing: Rethinking the discipline.* Carbondale: Southern Illinois University Press.

Kelly, G. J., & Bazerman, C. (2003). How students argue scientific claims: A rhetorical semiotic analysis. *Applied Linguistics, 24,* 28–55.

Kiefer, K. (1990). An alternative to curricular reform: Writing in the natural science/engineering curriculum. In *Proceedings of the core across the curriculum conference,* October 6–8. Keystone, CO: The American Association for the Advancement of Core Curriculum.

Klein, P. D. (1999). Reopening inquiry into cognitive processes in writing-to-learn. *Educationa Psychology Review, 11*(3), 203–270.

Knoblauch, C., & Brannon, L. (1983). Writing as learning through the curriculum. *College English, 45,* 465–474.

Kollberg, P. (1998). S-notation: A computer-based method for studying and representing text composition (Licentiate thesis) TRITA-NA-P9808, IPLab–145. Department of Numerical Analysis and Computer Science, KTH.

Lang, H. (2001). Construction of meaning in the authentic science writing of deaf students. *Journal of Deaf Studies and Deaf Education 6,* 258–284.

Lloyd-Jones, R. (1977). Primary trait scoring. In C. R. Cooper & L. Odell (Eds.), *Evaluating writing.* (pp. 33–66). Urbana, IL: National Council of Teachers of English.

Marchark, M., Lang, H. G., & Albertini, J. A. (2002). *Educating deaf students: Research into practice.* New York: Oxford University Press.

Mayer, C. (1999). Shaping at the point of utterance: An investigation of the composing processes of the deaf student writer. *Journal of Deaf Studies and Deaf Education, 4,* 37–49.

Mayer, C. (2007). What really matters in the early literacy development of deaf children. *Journal of Deaf Studies and Deaf Education, 12.*

McLeod, S. H. (ed.). (1988). *Strengthening programs for writing across the curriculum.* San Francisco: Jossey-Bass.

McLeod, S. H. (1989). Writing across the curriculum: The second stage, and beyond. *College Composition and Communication 40*(3), 337–343.

Meath-Lang, B., & Albertini, J. (1984). Keeping the purpose before the learner: A notional-functional curriculum framework for deaf students. *Teaching English to Deaf and Second-Language Students, 2,* 4–11.

Monroe, J. (Ed.). (2002). *Writing and revising the disciplines.* Cornell, NY: Cornell University Press.

Monroe, J. (Ed.). (2003). *Local practices, local knowledges.* Cornell, NY: Cornell University Press.

Odell, L. (1980). The process of writing and the process of learning. *College Composition and Communication, 36,* 42–50.

Patterson, E. W. (2001). Structuring the composition process in scientific writing. *International Journal of Science Education 23,* 1–16.

Russell, D. R. (1991). *Writing in the academic disciplines, 1870–1990: A curricular history.* Carbondale: Southern Illinois University Press.

Russell, D. R. (1997). Rethinking genre in school and society: An activity theory analysis. *Written Communication, 14,* 504–554.

Sandoval, W. A., & Millwood, K. A. (2005). The quality of students' use of evidence in written scientific explanations. *Cognition and Instruction 23*(1), 23–55.

Schwartz, M. (1983). Two journeys through the writing process. *College Composition and Communication, 34,* 188–201.

Selfe, C. (1997). Contextual evaluation in WAC programs. In K. B. Yancey & B. Huot (Eds.), *Assessing writing across the curriculum: Diverse approaches and practices* (pp. 51–68). Greenwich, CT: Ablex.

Swales, J., & Najjar, H. (1987). The writing of research article introductions. *Written Communication, 4* (2), 175–191.

Walvoord, B. E. (1992). Getting started. In S. H. McLeod & M. Soven (Eds.). *Writing across the curriculum: A guide to developing programs.* Newbury Park, CA: Sage.

Yin, R. K. (2003). *Case study research: Third edition.* Thousand Oaks, CA: Sage Publications.

Young, A., & Fulwiler, T. (1986). *Writing across the disciplines: Research into practice.* Upper Montclair, NJ: Boynton/Cook.

Yore, L. D., Hand, B. M., & Florence, M.K. (2004). Scientists' views of science, models of writing, and science writing practices. *Journal of Research in Science Teaching 41*(4), 338–369.

Chapter 16

What We Know and What We Don't Know About Cognition and Deaf Learners

Peter C. Hauser and Marc Marschark

This chapter has two goals. The first is to put the idea of *deaf cognition* into a larger historical and theoretical context. The second is to consider specific *foundations and outcomes* of growing up deaf that reflect real differences between deaf and hearing individuals in today's world (versus ideal or theoretically possible worlds) as well as differences among deaf individuals. Together, we believe that these discussions can point the way toward a more comprehensive scientific understanding of human cognition and development, as well as better ways to optimize the educational and personal success of deaf learners of all ages. Recognizing that other investigators and commentators coming from several orientations have made efforts to understand learning by deaf individuals, we propose to take a somewhat unique tack. Building on other chapters in this volume and many works that have preceded them, we hope to identify issues in need of attention from investigators, rather than to propose solutions.

Despite the significant progress being made in research and practice relating to the development and education of deaf children, there is not enough of it. Misunderstandings and misconceptions still exist concerning what it means to be deaf,[1] and well-meaning people in social, academic, and administrative spheres all too often create as many hurdles to success as those they seek to remove. We may not have all the answers, but some of the questions have become quite clear.

---

1. We leave questions surrounding what it means to be Deaf to other investigators in more appropriate venues.

Those Who Ignore History...

It was not so long ago that arguments raged in the literature concerning whether there was a "psychology of deafness" (Hoffmeister & Harvey, 1996; Paul & Jackson, 1993). In large measure, this debate centered on philosophical and cultural issues rather than issues of psychology per se. Perhaps the initiating event in the literary jousting, however, was this introduction to Myklebust's (1960, p. 1) *Psychology of Deafness*:

> A sensory deprivation limits the world of experience. It deprives the organism of some of the material resources from which the mind develops. Because total experience is reduced, there is an imposition on the balance and equilibrium of all psychological processes. When one type of sensation is lacking, it alters the integration and function of all of the others. Experience is now constituted differently; the world of perception, conception, imagination, and thought has an altered foundation, a new configuration. Such alteration occurs naturally and unknowingly, because unless the individual is organized and attuned differently, survival itself may be in jeopardy.

While intuitively obvious at some level, Myklebust's notions about the lack of hearing altering the way one goes about interacting with the world was tainted by his rather pessimistic views concerning the potential of deaf individuals. His view was consistent with a zeitgeist in which deaf people who could not speak were deemed to be lacking language and in which poor academic achievement (and academic opportunities) resulted in deaf adults' often being illiterate and underemployed. Consistent with North American psychology at the time—when it was still a decidedly behavioristic one—Myklebust sought the specific variable(s) that might be identified as the locus of underachievement by deaf adults and children. A more European-type approach—viewing the child as an organismic whole in interaction with the environment and those in it—was not yet even on the horizon with regard to deaf children in America (but see Conrad, 1979; Tervoort, 1975). Still, some investigators saw utility in seeking to better understand the psychological foundations of development in deaf children, an effort later pioneered by investigators like Meadow (1968, 1976, 1980) and Schlesinger (1978; Schlesinger & Meadow, 1972).

In commenting on the underlying assumption of Myklebust's efforts to understand the psychological consequences of hearing loss, Marschark (1993) noted:

> The implications of [Myklebust's statement] are broad and numerous, but precisely which ones are drawn depend on the theoretical orientation that one brings to its reading. Perhaps a first impulse will be to dismiss it as an outmoded and decidedly negative approach to deafness, intended to focus attention on audiological and rehabilitation issues and ignoring of the resilience of deaf children. On closer examination, however, Myklebust presents what are some self-evident truths: That most deaf children will experience a more limited world than hearing children, that their interactions with the

world will involve somewhat different rules and constraints, and that these differences will have a variety of significant implications for the psychological development of deaf children.

Yet, with the emerging recognition of Deaf culture and greater empowerment among deaf individuals and the parents of deaf children, the distinction between cultural sensitivity and political correctness was often blurred. As a result, politics and philosophy frequently trumped science (including psychology), much as it had for the previous 100 years. Even in the 1990s, then, suggestions that deaf children might think differently from hearing children, that the lack of effective communication in their early social environments might lead to less than optimal outcomes, and that deaf children differ from hearing children in more ways than just hearing thresholds and dependence of vision were greeted with considerable ambivalence if not outright indignation. Some commentators argued that any attempt to describe deaf children as different from hearing children was a sign of oppression (Lane, 1992, 2005) or indicative of a pathological view of deaf children (Hoffmeister & Harvey, 1996). In an effort to demonstrate that sign language was fully comparable to spoken language and that deaf children from deaf families were as developmentally advantaged as hearing children from hearing families, consideration of differences between deaf and hearing children and even explanations of the considerable diversity among deaf children relative to hearing age-matched peers were largely banished from the research agenda. Where did this self-imposed research censorship get us?

While investigators were documenting the characteristics of natural signed languages and the important role of sign language in development, scarce attention was given to the variability of language abilities among deaf children—even among those of deaf parents (Kuntze, 1990). No consideration was given to the fact that, because roughly 95% of deaf children have hearing parents, most deaf parents of deaf children, themselves, often were raised in homes with impoverished parent–child communication and, as a result, were not native users of the language they taught their children. Various studies examined the socialization (e.g., attachment, mother–child interactions) of deaf children of deaf parents relative to deaf children of hearing parents and hearing children of hearing parents, but variability as a function of socioeconomic status, language orientation, and multigenerational deaf families versus "first-generation" deaf families received no attention. Indeed, these issues are all still missing from the research agenda, even if they have become more theoretically interesting and practically important with changes in educational placement for deaf children in recent years.

More to the point of the present chapter, in responding to decades if not centuries of deaf individuals being relegated to the ranks of the linguistically and mentally deficient, the climate of the 1990s led to an end of studies into cognitive and educational implications of being raised in an environment lacking in full access to communication in the family, to social interactions with diverse adults and children outside the home, and to quality educational opportunities. Instead, investigators turned to studies of deaf children of deaf parents to describe what is possible in optimal environments. Yet, those children comprise less than 5% of the population of deaf children. Thus we were led, for example, to studies on the larger population of deaf children focusing on the use of cochlear implants (CIs) and subsequent speech development rather than testing whether the cognitive, linguistic, and social advantages observed in the 5% of deaf individuals with deaf parents could be extended to the remaining 95%.

Studies such as Vernon's (1968/2005), demonstrating that deaf and hearing individuals have the same range of IQ scores, were prominently quoted, while demonstrations of consistent quantitative and qualitative differences in scores even on nonverbal (performance) IQ tests were uncritically ignored (see Braden, 1994; Marschark, 1993, chapter 7 for reviews). Findings indicating that hearing parents tended to be over-controlling and directive with their deaf children (e.g., Henggeler, Watson, & Cooper, 1984) were used to castigate hearing parents, even though it was obvious that this pattern of behavior was the result of poor communication skills (Greenberg & Marvin, 1979) and could be ameliorated with proper training (Mohay, Milton, Hindmarsh, & Ganley, 1998). Further, in some contexts, such over-control appears to be necessary—at least in the minds of some mothers—in order to keep children safe (Lederberg & Mobley, 1990). In short, although scientific advances were being made in language development, social processes, sign language linguistics, and other domains, many areas of significant challenge for deaf youngsters were set aside.

Perhaps most salient for parents and educators has been the stagnation in long-term academic achievement by deaf students. Most indicators have failed to show any significant change as a function of their mass entrée into local public schools or the availability of sign language in early intervention programming (Qi & Mitchell, 2007; Traxler, 2000), even if the latter advance has been shown to have significant benefits during the early school years (Calderon & Greenberg, 1997). More recent efforts to demand greater accountability among schools and programs for the deaf as well as general education classrooms and to require demonstrations of adequate yearly progress by deaf students, appear to be languishing as an unfunded mandate. Many, if not most deaf children still enter school lagging in language fluencies (in any modality) relative to hearing children, and lack of social maturity still interferes with peer interactions and school success.

Deaf children raised by deaf parents, in contrast, often have age-appropriate language, social skills, and school readiness. These children are often placed in classrooms with other deaf children who might not have fluent expressive or receptive language skills or the ability to visually attend to language discourse in the classroom. Teachers then often need to attend to children coming from the "majority" (those with hearing parents) who are unable to respond to the teacher's prompts or understand what is going on in the classroom. More skilled deaf children likely will not be able to flourish in such environments, while teachers may develop negative assumptions about the abilities of deaf children at-large. Perhaps then, rather than presuming that language in one modality or another or schooling in one kind of program or another is a panacea, it is time to fully understand the cognitive, social, and linguistic functioning of deaf children and adjust our educational placements and practices so as to accommodate their strengths and needs. Instead, some of the most notable advances in offering opportunity to deaf children have blocked the very doorways they sought to open.

A Brave New World

Leigh (this volume) has well described the potential of recent advances in early newborn hearing screening and technology that offer deaf individuals and their families new alternatives with regard to communication and early intervention programming. Although such developments offer promise for very young children, the changing nature of the population they aim to support creates a moving target for those who provide support services and educational programming for older children. As Abbate (2007, p. 2) noted, "The expanded heterogeneity of the population is also demonstrating the increasing limitations of a singular approach to instruction and communication... [We] continue to be challenged to ensure that varied interventions are available in order to maximize progress at different developmental periods."

Instead of educational settings being accountable and monitoring deaf children's progress so as to be able to alter communication and instructional programming, there is a continuing tendency to seek a "one-size-fits-all" point of view and place blame on the child. This situation is evidenced in the common reference to "implant failures"—children who have received CIs but have not developed spoken language—rather than recognizing that the underlying variability in etiologies, prior language experience, and cognitive flexibility makes cochlear implantation an unpredictable business for any child (see Pisoni et al., this volume). Without flexibility and ongoing assessment, many deaf children are being "tracked" into placements and learning systems not much more appropriate than the segregated vocational training they might have faced a century ago. Certainly, some educational programs and school districts are more aware and supportive, and many parents of deaf children serve as effective advocates, often with the support of regional and national organizations created for that purpose. What we are seeking, however, is evidence-based practices, informed by rigorous and reliable quantitative and qualitative research. Because of their heterogeneity, it is unlikely that many educational methods provide a "best fit" for all or even most deaf learners.

Communication and instructional methods, as well as educational placements, have to serve the needs of individual students. To the extent that they do not, it is the system that fails, not the child. Our goal, therefore, is to push for an integrated and objective research agenda intended to bring together the previously disparate domains of investigation relevant to the cognitive foundations of learning by deaf children and adults.[2] The chapters of this volume are a step in the right direction, but much more is needed.

"Hardware" and "Software" Differences

It is a truism to suggest that, aside from the auditory system, most deaf and hearing children are born with the same physical and neurological potential.[3] It is equally evident, however, that differences in early environments affect both behavior and brain development. Not only do individuals in more experientially rich environments show different brain activation, but qualitatively different perceptual and social experience—whether due to differences in hearing status or socioeconomic status—can result in differences in brain organization and behavior (see Bavelier, Dye, & Hauser, 2006; Bavelier, Newman, Mukherjee, Hauser, Kemeny, Braun, & Boutla, in press; Hauser, Lukomski, & Hillman, this volume; Noble, Norman, & Farah, 2005, for discussion). Similarly, differences in hearing and socioeconomic status are seen to be related to children's language development (Anderson & Reilly, 2002; Hart & Risley, 1995). Most such relationships are best described as reflecting "differences" between individuals or groups. A few might offer intellectual or behavioral advantages (Akamatsu, Musselman, & Zweibel, 2000). Others put individuals at a disadvantage, whether in schooling, socialization, or eventual employment.

Findings offered by Dye, Hauser, and Bavelier (this volume) and Pelz, Marschark, and Convertino (this volume) are an interesting case in point. A variety of studies have demonstrated enhanced visual attention to peripheral stimuli by deaf individuals (e.g., Dye, et al., this volume; Neville & Lawson, 1987; Proksch & Bavelier, 2002; Swisher, 1993). This ability is

---

2. This is not to discount the importance of social–emotional foundations of learning, an area particularly in need of investigation, but those issues are better addressed by others more knowledgeable in that domain

3. Secondary disabilities actually are more common among deaf than hearing children for reasons relating to the etiologies of their hearing losses, but children with multiple challenges are not at issue here.

most likely adaptive, as it helps deaf individuals attend to, for example, possible sources of danger, other individuals who seek their attention, and environmental stimuli that lead to incidental learning. This line of research thus suggests that the less one hears, the more one relies on vision to navigate through the world, an accommodation consistent with *compensation theory* (Bavelier & Neville, 2002), which proposes that when one sense is deprived, the remaining senses are enhanced, rather than deficiency theory. Such findings also are in accord with anecdotal claims that hearing children of deaf parents "turn off their ears" so that they can visually attend better and that hearing drivers turning down music when reading street signs.

Although the enhancements found in deaf individuals' peripheral visual attention can be described as advantageous, deaf children are particularly vulnerable to visual distraction from activities going on around them. Recognition of such differences in visual cognition between deaf and hearing individuals is helpful both practically—in the design and arrangement of educational settings—and theoretically, and potentially elucidates persistent gaps in academic achievement relative to hearing peers. Meanwhile, Pelz et al. report convergent findings in an in situ classroom experiment, indicating that, regardless of the potential effects of distracting stimuli in the environment, native-signing deaf adults, "oral" deaf adults, and hearing adults do not differ significantly in their abilities to utilize information presented in the periphery. Such findings do not make earlier results any less interesting, but help to sharpen the understanding of psychological causes and effects (Myklebust, 1960) and call for more educational research on the visual learning experiences of deaf students.

A similar psychological unfolding can be found in research relating to memory. Early studies described apparent deficiencies in memory functioning of deaf adults and children (see Marschark, 1993, chapters 9 & 10). Findings were variously attributed to generic language difficulties (Mott, 1899), educational disadvantage (Pintner & Patterson, 1917), and lack of real-world experience (Furth &Youniss, 1964). Later studies more precisely demonstrated that deaf children were inconsistent in their intentional utilization of prior knowledge during recall (Liben, 1979) and frequently failed to recognize the multidimensional nature of to-be-remembered stimuli (Ottem, 1980). Potential differences in memory between hearing and deaf children as a function of verbal versus nonverbal memory coding had been hypothesized early on (e.g., Furth, 1966; Furth &Youniss, 1964), and later studies provided convergent evidence in memory for both verbal and nonverbal stimuli (Lichtenstein, 1998; see Marschark & Wauters, this volume).

Meanwhile, explanations for longer memory spans in hearing than deaf individuals and in deaf individuals who use spoken language relative to those who use sign language (Pintner & Patterson, 1917) have shown a similar evolution. With a greater understanding of the nature of memory, and of working memory in particular, assumptions concerning general intellectual and educational delays offered by Pintner and Patterson were replaced by evidence that deaf and hearing individuals have comparable memory capacities, but that coding via sign language takes up more "space" than spoken language in limited-capacity temporary stores (Lichtenstein, 1998; Marschark & Mayer, 1998). Boutla, Supalla, Newport, and Bavelier (2004) argued further that the observed differences, as a function of using spoken or sign language, reflect modality-specific differences in short-term memory, a system particularly suited to sequential, phonological coding thanks to our evolutionary history as primarily oral–aural communicators. Bavelier (2007) extended this discussion, describing the results observed in various short-term and working memory tasks as "tendencies" rather than "differences," a position supported by evidence obtained by investigators who made similar claims decades earlier (e.g., Belmont, Karchmer, & Bourg, 1983). Such studies have elucidated differences in relatively linguistic/verbal short-term memory between deaf and hearing individuals; they do not deny that those differences exist. Meanwhile studies on the other "half" of short-term memory, which involves storing visual information, have shown a greater spatial short-term memory span among deaf and hearing sign languages users (Capirci, Cattani, Rossini, & Volterra, 1998; Wilson, Bettger, Niculae, & Klima, 1997) and similar visual working memory and short-term memory for geometric figures among deaf and hearing individuals (Hauser, Cohen, Dye, & Bavelier, 2007).

Unfortunately, acceptance of the reality of such cognitive differences has not led to any obvious changes in educational practice. Recognition that memory for sequences may be problematic (viz., worse) for many deaf children relative to hearing age-matched peers, and perhaps for deaf children who sign relative to deaf peers who use spoken language, clearly should affect some of the day-to-day activities occurring in classrooms. Additionally, recognition that signers have an advantage in processing, and presumably learning, visual–spatial information could be helpful when deciding instructional strategies for courses with high visual demands, such as mathematics or science. It may be that skilled and experienced teachers of the deaf implicitly take account of such issues during instruction (see Marschark & Wauters, this volume) as deaf teachers and parents appear to do (see Hauser et al., this volume). Hypotheses of this sort have not been examined, however and, with few exceptions, potential implications for problem solving and learning in domains such as mathematics have not been considered (but see Bull, this volume). It would not stretch the imagination to suggest that short-term memory differences also affect reading comprehension and writing (see Hermsen & Franklin, this volume), but although such relationships have been described (see Marschark & Wauters, this volume), transfer of that knowledge to pedagogical practice appears to be lacking. Research described by Pisoni et al. (this volume) clearly demonstrates that these issues remain for deaf children who receive CIs, and it thus appears that this is one empirical domain that will be with us for some time to come.

A number of other demonstrable cognitive differences between deaf and hearing learners also have direct relevance for the classroom. Various studies have provided evidence of both qualitative and quantitative differences in deaf and hearing students' world knowledge (Marschark & Wauters, this volume) and their approaches to studying (Richardson, this volume) and problem solving (Kelly, this volume; Nunes et al., this volume). Both lower-level cognitive processes (Bebko & Metcalfe-Haggert, 1997; Dye et al., this volume) and higher-level executive functioning and metacognition (Courtin, Melot, & Corroyer, this volume; Hauser et al., this volume; Marschark & Wauters, this volume) have been implicated in performance differences observed between deaf and hearing students and, in some cases, among deaf students varying on some dimension or other. Yet the fact that courses in developmental psychology are relatively rare in teacher training programs—and essentially nonexistent in interpreter training programs—is but one indicator that deaf children are not receiving optimal levels of educational support. Perhaps more importantly, until such information is provided in some usable form to parents of young deaf children and providers of early intervention services, many deaf children likely will arrive at school with somewhat different learning strategies than most of their (hearing) classmates. They also will continue to be taught by teachers who are not fully cognizant of differences in knowledge, language fluency, and learning styles, having been raised with and taught a teaching style different from that needed by deaf students. Information about deaf learners and how best to educate them, gleaned by experienced and successful educators, must be passed along to those who can utilize it in research, the training of future teachers, and in their own classrooms.

Issues, Questions, and Answers

The development and education of deaf children are domains that cannot be considered separately (Akamatsu, Mayer, & Hardy-Braz, this volume). As such, the search for a full understanding of foundations and outcomes of cognition and learning among deaf individuals must simultaneously consider interactions among experience, language, and learning—all of these in both formal and informal settings. Marschark, Lang, and Albertini (2002) suggested that deaf children may not need anything different from hearing peers by way of support from parents and significant others in development and education. Rather, they may need more of what they do receive in order to ensure that their knowledge and skills are functionally equivalent to those acquired, perhaps more easily, by hearing children. That is, although cognitive organization differences exist between deaf and hearing individuals, many of the processes and abilities of the two populations are the same even within the visual domain (Hauser et al., 2007).

If this discussion and findings from other chapters in this volume are to be taken at face value, however, differences in the experience, language, and learning of deaf and hearing children are as likely to be qualitative as quantitative, and hence the Marschark et al. proposal may be quite wrong. In view of the considerable heterogeneity of the population of deaf children, their statement may be an overgeneralization and, for various children, "more," "different," and "the same" may be sufficient. In the discussion that follows, therefore, our references to deaf individuals refer to the population as a whole, with all of its diversity. Assumptions that particular subgroups (e.g., deaf children of deaf parents or those with CIs) are exempt from the points made below will be dangerous and probably wrong. Further, focusing on any particular group that, lacking rigorous investigation, is believed to be immune from the cumulative and interactive implications of being deaf will fail to capture the true nature of the deaf population and the issues in need of attention.

Language

In almost any treatment of the development of deaf children, language emerges as the first and primary factor considered. It usually does not have such primacy in treatments of education, however, where matters of placement, literacy, and sometimes communication modality come to the fore. That situation is regrettable for a variety of reasons (see Abbate, 2007; Akamatsu et al., this volume; Marschark & Wauters, this volume). Because of their hearing losses and the early environments in which they are reared, most deaf children enter school lacking fluency in either spoken or signed language. Universal hearing screening, early intervention, and CIs are relatively recent advances that have had significant impact on this situation, but even those deaf children who have had access to these opportunities still tend to lag behind hearing peers in language development (see Leigh, this volume) as well as cognitive skills (Pisoni, this volume). Effective communication with parents and others, fluent language that can be utilized in the acquisition of literacy and other academic skills, and the internal language frequently involved in reasoning and problem solving are essential for learning (Hauser et al., this volume; Marschark & Wauters, this volume). They also have been implicated in many of the developmental challenges previously ascribed to hearing loss per se. Are there any deaf children for whom language is not an issue?

Deaf children who are relatively fluent in spoken language, regardless of whether they have CIs or not, are not in the same situation as hearing children. Functioning in an environment with degraded (analog or digital) auditory input, such children will miss some proportion of information, misunderstand another proportion, and have to depend on vision to a greater extent than their hearing peers. Lacking full simultaneous access to both visual and auditory stimulation, they not only will be at a disadvantage with regard to incidental learning, they also will miss exposure to a variety of cause–effect relationships involving multiple agents, objects, and actions. A variety of educational and psychological studies have demonstrated that information presented in visual and auditory modalities together leads to better comprehension, learning, and memory than information in either modality alone, even if all of the information is included (e.g., a diagram and text rather than speech). Significant hearing losses, even if aided, result in reduced fidelity of incoming auditory information. As a result, aspects of cognitive development that are tied to effective communication, such as development of theory of mind, frequently are seen to be delayed in deaf children who rely on spoken language, even if they utilize CIs (Courtin et al., this volume; Peterson, 2004; Remmel, Peters & Sawyer, 2004).

With numerous demonstrations that deaf children of deaf parents reach language milestones in much the same order and at much the same rate as their hearing peers, most investigators consider their language development to be "normal." That does not mean, however, that growing up with a signed language is equivalent to growing up with a spoken language. As mentioned earlier, deaf children of deaf parents are often taught beside children with delayed language development and by teachers who are not familiar with the learning strategies used by visual learners. Aside from cognitive and language issues relating to the diversity of conversational partners (e.g., more informal interactions with adults lead to larger vocabularies, Hart & Risley, 1995; Nelson, 1973), research described earlier in this chapter also indicates that growing up using primarily a signed language has some specific (and perhaps some as yet unidentified) neurological and behavioral/cognitive implications (Hauser et al., this volume). With the exception, perhaps, of the acuity of peripheral vision, it remains unclear to what extent most of these observed differences are truly a function of using a visual and spatial language, rather than being tied more to specific linguistic aspects of sign language (e.g., relative reliance on lexicalized signs versus inflections); the quality and quantity of language exposure rather than modality; or other factors. At the very least, being educated through sign language carries its own practical challenges including teachers' sign skills (Lang, McKee, & Conner, 1993; Marmor & Petitto, 1979) and interpreters' skills (Schick, this volume), as does being educated either by teachers of the deaf who often lack educational backgrounds in the content areas they teach or mainstream teachers unfamiliar with the strengths, needs, and cognitive styles of deaf learners (Marschark & Wauters, this volume). Only by understanding these differences can we take advantage of the strengths that deaf students bring to various learning contexts (Akamatsu et al., 2000) and accommodate their needs.

It is perhaps an understatement to argue for more research concerning the potential interactions of language modality, cognitive development, and learning. At the same time, with growing awareness that the foundations of learning by deaf students are not identical to those of hearing students, there are greater opportunities for distinguishing the effects of language—modality, fluency, and linguistic characteristics—than ever before. The need no longer exists to argue about whether deaf children can be appropriately educated in sign (at least within educated circles), and the questions now concern the subtle and not-so-subtle implications of varying degrees of sign language fluency. Similarly, as long as technologies such as digital hearing aids and CIs remain less than 100% effective, it has to be recognized that even when a deaf child has intelligible or even excellent speech, they will not be hearing everything that their hearing classmates are. And, regardless of the degree of residual hearing, those with any hearing loss most likely place a greater reliance on vision.

Parents may be drawn to spoken language because it makes a child seem similar to their siblings and seems to allow for fluent parent–child communication or because, perhaps unconsciously, they think their beliefs, thoughts, and values can be passed to their child only through their home language. Other parents fear they will not be able to effectively interact with or develop an appropriate attachment with their child if they have to use a new language. Some simply may believe that their child would have a greater success in acquiring their home language than would they in learning a new one. Regardless of a deaf child's ability to assimilate in the hearing world and function smoothly there, deaf individuals still are not the same as hearing individuals socially, adaptively, or cognitively. Instead they are living and functioning in a world that is different from their own. Rather than ignoring implications of their limited auditory perception and assuming that "all is well," it is essential that with these children, too, investigators consider the relationship of language and cognition without a priori assumptions.

Before leaving language, it is probably necessary to state what appears to us to be obvious: our convenient division between individuals who use spoken language and those who use sign language is largely a fiction. Regardless of the hearing status of their parents, their hearing thresholds, and their educational placements, most deaf students are exposed to both language modalities. Hard-of-hearing students are in a similar situation.

Although most hard-of-haring students tend to rely more on spoken language than sign language, progressive hearing losses and various social and contextual factors frequently result in significant familiarity with, if not fluency in sign language. The visual skills involved in speechreading are interesting in their own right, and there is some evidence of subtle cognitive consequences of being a long-time speechreader (Campbell & Dodd, 1998; Dodd, Hobson, Brasher, & Campbell, 1983).

In the face of widely varying fluencies in sign and spoken language, coupled with variability in the degree and frequencies of hearing losses, investigations of the sort proposed here usually will yield only approximate results. Group data will mask individual characteristics, just as surely as consideration only of individuals or small samples will lead to erroneous overgeneralizations. It is precisely in the balancing of individual differences and consistency across individuals that we believe most fruitful information will be found.

Medical and Psychological Challenges Facing Deaf Learners

Whether one likes it or not, abundant evidence now suggests that a significant proportion of deaf children are affected by learning disabilities and other neurological, physical, or psychological issues (see Hauser et al., this volume; Hauser, Wills, & Isquith, 2005). Estimates of the prevalence of learning disabilities vary widely, from 5% to near 25%, but it appears generally accepted that medically related factors affect 30%–40% of deaf children (see King, Hauser, & Isquith, 2006). Beyond the obvious challenges for parents of those children and potential implications for social development, it is difficult to ascertain the extent to which research data are affected by such factors. Some investigators seek to avoid such issues by conducting research only with deaf children of deaf parents.

As we noted earlier, excluding such individuals from research studies and increasing the study's internal validity might reduce variability in data sets and offer clearer theoretical insights, but it also detracts from external validity and the practical utility of the research. Just as important from our perspective, if research involving deaf adults and children is intended to improve their opportunities and quality of life, rather than or in addition to contributing to basic science, research of the sort described in this volume must include the full range of individual differences. Basic research is certainly needed to sort out the factors contributing to the variability found among deaf students. Yet more applied educational research bridging basic science to the classroom also is urgently required, as the education of deaf children has not improved significantly for almost a century (Pintner & Patterson, 1917; Traxler, 2000). In short, we need it all. As the characteristics of this population change (Leigh, this volume), this will not be easy, but it will be all the more important.

Social Influences, Siblings, and Peers

We began this chapter urging that research concerning deaf children consider the whole child, using an integrative, holistic perspective. Aside from investigators specifically interested in social cognition and related areas (e.g., Courtin et al., this volume; Hauser et al, this volume), the influence of social factors is rarely included in research into cognitive processes among deaf or hearing individuals. In the case of deaf children, social and emotional factors may have greater significance for development, learning, and cognition (broadly defined) than is the case for hearing children. We have already noted the importance of diverse experience to language development (Hart & Risley, 1995; Nelson, 1973). Decades of research have documented the importance of hearing children's learning from their siblings and peers. To the extent that a deaf child's effective social circle is smaller than that of the hearing child, and insofar as opportunities for incidental learning are fewer, we would expect that the influence of any given individual in the child's environment would be somewhat greater. Studies involving hearing children also have shown specific effects on intelligence and language as a function of birth order and number of siblings, and we suspect that such factors would have equal or greater effects on the development of deaf children. Alternatively, communication barriers in any other of these issues may serve to reduce the impact of those variables, in a sense further attenuating opportunities for informal learning.

As was the case in the previous section, we do not claim here that consideration of social and emotional factors in the cognitive functioning and academic achievement of deaf students will be easy. Nor do we expect that our urging will lead a significant number of investigators to undertake such studies. Nevertheless, it is essential that researchers and practitioners take such issues into account in conducting research, interpreting results, and deciding on the applicability of experimental findings in any particular context.

Looking Ahead While Glancing Back

Kathryn Meadow-Orlans has always emphasized the importance of understanding the past successes and errors in our field if we are to make progress—indeed, we took the title of this section from her. As a pioneer in exploring the relationships among language, social–emotional functioning, and learning by deaf children, Meadow-Orlans recognized that only through a holistic view of children within their families, schools, and society, could we optimize their educational opportunities. Looking back, investigators' seeming obsessions with particular aspects of deaf children's development are reflected in educational interventions that came into (and went out of) vogue every few years. In that sense, clearly, research and practice have not truly lost touch with each other. Much more rarely, however, have practitioners had opportunities to help establish the research agenda in this field.

If it is now evident that some cognitive (and neuropsychological and social) differences exist between deaf and hearing learners, it is far less evident how important these are and what we should do about them. In large measure, we assume that most of the variability among deaf individuals will be irrelevant or only minimally related to the primary elements of educational progress. Such differences may be of theoretical utility and some might even be useful as we develop a better understanding of how the specific strengths of deaf children (e.g., mental manipulation, visual attention) might be used to offset specific educational challenges.

Many more areas in which deaf individuals may be advantaged have not been explored. Deaf adults and children who sign, for example, have been shown to have better face discrimination abilities than deaf and hearing nonsigners, at least for components of facial expressions that have linguistic significance (Bettger, Emmorey, McCullough, & Bellugi, 1997). We thus might expect that such individuals are better at reading subtle, interpersonal social–emotional cues. That skill would necessarily be related to theory of mind skills and, following Courtin et al. (this volume), we would expect variation as a function of parental hearing status or early language fluency (Hauser et al., this volume). Similarly, evidence indicating advantages in memory for spatial locations by signers (Capirci et al., 1998; O'Connor & Hermelin, 1973; Wilson et al., 1997) might prove useful in fostering learning strategies that offset challenges inherent in the multimedia nature of mainstream classrooms, which demand deaf students' divided attention to visual materials and language (either signed or spoken; see Pelz, et al., this volume; Pisoni et al., this volume; Schick, this volume).

In specific areas of instruction, similarities and differences between deaf and hearing students are offering insights of theoretical and practical significance. We now know, for example, that the mental representation of number in deaf children is fully comparable to that in hearing children (Bull, this volume; Hauser et al., 2007). Although particular kinds of problems can be shown to pose consistent difficulties for deaf learners (Kelly, this volume), investigators like Nunes et al. (this volume) have demonstrated that alternative teaching skills can be fully effective if we use what we already know to look for them (Richardson, this volume).

In short, it is now evident that subtle and not-so-subtle differences exist in the cognitive foundations of learning among deaf learners and between deaf and hearing learners. The time has passed for us to be satisfied with such demonstrations. It is incumbent on those who are curious about such variation to investigate, or at least provide hypotheses, about how such findings might inform practice. Similarly, teachers, deaf individuals, and parents—as well as providers of interpreting, audiological services, and early interventionists—must be involved in establishing the research agenda. Otherwise, valuable insights into real-world functioning of deaf students will be lost to generalizations or sample limitations of laboratory research. One has only to look at the remarkable progress over the past two decades in studies of natural signed languages, language development, and neuropsychology to see the potential for significant advances in the educational sphere as well. A "neuropsychology of deafness" may not exist, but what we have learned about executive function, brain organization, and cognitive functioning must be more than the basis for research publications and intellectual discussion. Hearing loss might "deprive the organism of some of the material resources from which the mind develops," but our inherent resilience ensures that we will take advantage of other resources. The result thus is not a state of deficiency, but one of difference—a difference that has not received much attention in educational research and practice.

References

Abbate, L. (2007). *A report on early intervention.* Longmeadow, MA: Willie Ross School for the Deaf.

Akamatsu, C. T., Musselman, C., & Zweibel, A. (2000). Nature vs. Nurture in the development of cognition in deaf people. In P. Spencer, C. Erting, & M. Marschark (Eds.), *Development in context: The deaf children in the family and at school* (pp. 255–274). Mahwah, NJ: Lawrence Erlbaum Associates.

Anderson, D., & Reilly, J. (2002). The MacArthur Communicative Development Inventory: Normative data for American Sign Language. *Journal of Deaf Studies and Deaf Education, 7,* 83–119.

Bavelier, D. (2007, June). Similar working memory capacity but different serial short-term memory span in signers and speakers: Theoretical and practical implications. Presentation at Cognitive Underpinnings of Learning by Deaf and Hard-of-Hearing Students conference. Rochester, NY.

Bavelier, D., Dye, M.W.G., & Hauser, P. C. (2006). Do deaf individuals see better? *Trends in Cognitive Science, 10,* 512–518.

Bavelier, D., & Neville, H. (2002). Cross-modal plasticity: Where and how? *Nature Reviews Neuroscience, 3,* 443–452.

Bavelier, D., Newman, A., Mukherjee, M., Hauser, P., Kemeny, S., Braun, A., & Boutla, M. (in press). Encoding, rehearsal, and recall in signers and speakers: Shared network but different engagement. *Cerebral Cortex.*

Bebko, J. M., & Metcalfe-Haggert, A. (1997). Deafness, language skills, and rehearsal: A model for the development of a memory strategy. *Journal of Deaf Studies and Deaf Education, 2,* 131–139.

Belmont, J. M., Karchmer, M. A., & Bourg, J. W. (1983). Structural influences on deaf and hearing children's recall of temporal/spatial incongruent letter strings. *Educational Psychology, 3,* 259–274.

Bettger, J. G., Emmorey, K., McCullough, S. H., & Bellugi, U. (1997). Enhanced facial discrimination: Effects of experience with American Sign Language. *Journal of Deaf Studies and Deaf Education, 2,* 223–233.

Boutla, M., Supalla, T., Newport, E., & Bavelier, D. (2004). Short-term memory span: Insights from sign language. *Nature Neuroscience, 7,* 991–1002.

Braden, J. P. (1994). *Deafness, deprivation, and IQ.* New York: Plenum.

Calderon, R., & Greenberg, M. (1997). The effectiveness of early intervention for deaf children and hard of hearing children. In M. J. Guralnik (Ed.), *The effectiveness of early intervention: Directions for second generation research* (pp. 455–482). Baltimore: Paul H. Brookes.

Campbell, R., & Dodd, B. (Eds.). (1998). *Hearing by eye II: The psychology of speechreading and auditory-visual speech.* London: Taylor and Francis.

Capirci, O., Cattani, A., Rossini, P., & Volterra, V. (1998). Teaching sign language to hearing children as a possible factor in cognitive enhancement. *Journal of Deaf Studies and Deaf Education, 3,* 135–142.

Conrad, R. (1979). *The deaf school child: Language and cognition.* London: Harper and Row.

Dodd, B., Hobson, P., Brasher, J., & Campbell, R. (1983). Deaf children's short-term memory for lip-read, graphic and signed stimuli. *British Journal of Developmental Psychology, 1,* 353–364.

Furth, H. G. (1966). *Thinking without language.* New York: The Free Press.

Furth, H. G., & Youniss, J. (1964). Color-object paired associates in deaf and hearing children with and without response condition. *Journal of Consulting Psychology, 28, 3,* 224–227.

Greenberg, M. T., & Marvin, R. S. (1979). Attachment patterns in profoundly deaf preschool children. *Merrill-Palmer Quarterly, 25,* 265–279.

Hart, B., & Risley, T. R. (1995). *Meaningful differences in the everyday experience of young American children.* Baltimore: Paul H. Brookes Publishing Co.

Hauser, P. C., Cohen, J., Dye, M.W.G., & Bavelier, D. (2007). Visual constructive and visual-motor skills in Deaf native signers. *Journal of Deaf Studies and Deaf Education, 12,* 148–157.

Hauser, P. C., Dye, M.W.G., Boutla, M., Green, C. S., & Bavelier, D. (2007). Deafness and visual enumeration: Not all aspects of attention are modified by deafness. *Brain Research, 1153,* 178–187.

Hauser, P. C., Wills, K., & Isquith, P.K. (2005). Hard of hearing, deafness, and being deaf. In J. E. Farmer, J. Donders, & S. Warschausky (Eds.), *Neurodevelopmental disabilities: Clinical research and practice* (pp. 119–131). New York: Guilford Publications, Inc.

Henggeler, S. W., Watson, S. M., & Cooper, P. F. (1984). Verbal and nonverbal maternal controls in hearing mother-deaf child interaction. *Journal of Applied Developmental Psychology, 5,* 319–329.

Hoffmeister, R., & Harvey, M. A. (1996). Is there a psychology of the hearing? In N. S. Glickman & M. A. Harvey (Eds.), *Culturally affirmative psychotherapy with deaf persons* (pp. 73–98). Mahwah, NJ: LEA.

King, B. H., Hauser, P. C., & Isquith, P. K. (2006). Psychiatric aspects of blind-
    ness and severe visual impairment, and deafness and severe hearing loss
    in children. In C. E. Coffey & R. A. Brumback (Eds.), *Textbook of pediatric
    neuropsychiatry* (pp. 397–423). Washington, DC: American Psychiatric
    Association.

Kuntze, M. (1990). ASL: Unity and power: Communication issues among deaf
    people. *The Deaf American Monograph, 40,* 75–77.

Lane, H. (2005). Ethnicity, ethics, and the Deaf-world. *Journal of Deaf Studies
    and Deaf Education, 10,* 291–310.

Lane, H. L. (1992). *The mask of benevolence: Disabling the Deaf community.*
    New York: Knopf.

Lang, H. G., McKee, B. G., & Conner, K. N. (1993). Characteristics of effective
    teachers: A descriptive study of perceptions of faculty and deaf college
    students. *American Annals of the Deaf, 138,* 252–259.

Lederberg, A., & Mobley, C. (1990). The effect of hearing impairment on the
    quality of attachment and mother-toddler interaction. *Child Develop-
    ment, 61,* 1596–1604.

Liben, L. S. (1979). Free recall by deaf and hearing children: Semantic cluster-
    ing and recall in trained and untrained groups. *Journal of Experimental
    Child Psychology, 27,* 105–119.

Lichtenstein, E. H. (1998). The relationships between reading processes and
    English skills of deaf college students. *Journal of Deaf Studies and Deaf
    Education, 3,* 80–134.

Marmor, G. S., & Petitto, L. A. (1979). Simultaneous communication in the
    classroom: How well is English grammar represented? *Sign Language
    Studies, 8,* 99–136.

Marschark, M. (1993). *Psychological development of deaf children.* New York:
    Oxford University Press.

Marschark, M., Lang, H. G., & Albertini, J. A. (2002). *Educating deaf students:
    From research to practice.* New York: Oxford University Press.

Marschark, M., & Mayer, T. (1998). Mental representation and memory in deaf
    adults and children. In M. Marschark & M. D. Clark (Eds.), *Psychological
    perspectives on deafness* Vol. 2. (pp. 53–77). Hillsdale, NJ: LEA.

Meadow, K. (1968). Early manual communication in relation to the deaf
    child's intellectual, social and communicative functioning. *American An-
    nals of the Deaf, 113,* 29–41.

Meadow, K. P. (1976). Personality and social development of deaf people.
    Journal of Rehabilitation of the Deaf, 9, 1–12.

Meadow, K. P. (1980). *Deafness and child development.* Berkeley, CA: Univer-
    sity of California Press

Mohay, H., Milton, L., Hindmarsh, G., & Ganley, K. (1998). Deaf mothers
    as communication models for hearing families with deaf children. In
    A. Weisel, (Ed.), *Issues unresolved: New perspectives on language and
    deaf education* (pp. 76–87). Washington, DC: Gallaudet University Press.

Mott, A. (1899). A comparison of deaf and hearing children in their ninth
    year. *American Annals of the Deaf, 44,* 401–412.

Myklebust, H. E. (1960). *The psychology of deafness.* New York: Grune and
    Stratton.

Nelson, K. (1973). Structure and strategy in learning to talk. *Monograph of the
    Society for Research and Child Development, 38,* (149), No. 1–2.

Neville, H. J., & Lawson, D. S. (1987). Attention to central and peripheral visual space in a movement detection task: An event related potential and behavioral study: II. Congenitally deaf adults. *Brain Research*, 405, 268–283.

Noble, K. G., Norman, M. F., & Farah, M.J. (2005). Neurocognitive correlates of socioeconomic status in kindergarten children. *Developmental Science, 8*, 74–87.

O'Connor, N., & Hermelin, B. M. (1973). The spatial or temporal organization of short-term memory. *Quarterly Journal of Experimental Psychology, 25*, 335–343.

Ottem, E. (1980). An analysis of cognitive studies with deaf subjects. *American Annals of the Deaf, 125*, 564–575.

Paul, P., & Jackson, D. (1993). *Toward a psychology of deafness: Theoretical and empirical perspectives.* Boston: Allyn and Bacon.

Peterson, C. (2004). Theory-of-mind development in oral deaf children with cochlear implants or conventional hearing aids. *Journal of Child Psychology and Psychiatry, 46*, 1096–1106

Pintner, R., & Patterson, D. G. (1917). A comparison of deaf and hearing children in visual memory for digits. *Journal of Experimental Psychology, 2*, 76–88.

Proksch, J., & Bavelier, D. (2002). Changes in the spatial distribution of visual attention after early deafness. *Journal of Cognitive Neuroscience, 14*, 687–701.

Qi, S., & Mitchell, R. E. (April, 2007). *Large-scaled academic achievement testing of deaf and hard-of-hearing students: Past, present, and future.* Paper presented at the annual meeting of the Research on the Education of Deaf Persons SIG of the American Education Research Association, April 10, 2007, Chicago, IL.

Remmel, E., Peters, K., & Sawyer, A. (2004, May). *Theory of mind and language development in children with cochlear implants.* Poster presented at the annual convention of the American Psychological Society, Chicago, IL.

Schlesinger, H. S. (1978). The effects of deafness on childhood development: An Eriksonian perspective (pp. 157–172). In L. S. Liben (Ed.), *Deaf children: Developmental perspectives.* New York: Academic Press.

Schlesinger, H. S. & Meadow, K. P. (1972). *Sound and sign: Childhood deafness and mental health.* Berkeley, CA: University of California Press.

Swisher, M. V. (1993). Perceptual and cognitive aspects of recognition of signs in peripheral vision. In M. Marschark & M. D. Clark (Eds.), *Psychological perspectives on deafness* (pp. 229–265). Hillsdale, NJ: Lawrence Erlbaum Associates.

Tervoort, B. (1975). *Developmental features of visual communication.* Amsterdam: North-Holland Press.

Traxler, C. B. (2000). The Stanford Achievement Test, 9th Edition: National norming and performance standards for deaf and hard of hearing students. *Journal of Deaf Studies and Deaf Education, 5*, 337–348.

Vernon, M. (1968/2005). Fifty years of research on the intelligence of deaf and hard of hearing children: A review of literature and discussion of implications. *Journal of Rehabilitation of the Deaf, 1*, 1–12. Reprinted in the *Journal of Deaf Studies and Deaf Education, 10*, 225–231.

Wilson, M., Bettger, J., Niculae, I., & Klima, E. (1997). Modality of language shapes working memory: Evidence from digit span and spatial span in ASL signers. *Journal of Deaf Studies and Deaf Education, 2*, 150–160.

Author Index

Subject Index

Note: Figures, tables, or footnotes are indicated by *f, t,* or n. after the page number, respectively.